The Broad Church

A Biography of a Movement

Tod E. Jones

LEXINGTON BOOKS
Lanham • Boulder • New York • Oxford

LEXINGTON BOOKS

Published in the United States of America
by Lexington Books
A Member of the Rowman & Littlefield Publishing Group
4501 Forbes Boulevard, Suite 200, Lanham, Maryland 20706

PO Box 317
Oxford
OX2 9RU, UK

British Library Cataloguing in Publication Information Available

Library of Congress Cataloging-in-Publication Data

Jones, Tod E., 1961-
    The Broad Church : a biography of a movement / Tod E. Jones.
      p. cm.
    Includes bibliographical references and index.
    ISBN 0-7391-0611-2 (cloth : alk. Paper)
      1. English literature—19th century—History and criticism. 2. Broad Church
Movement. 3. Christianity and literature—England—History—19th century. 4. Christian
literature, English—History and criticism. 5. Coleridge, Samuel Taylor, 1772-1834—
Religion. 6. England—Intellectual life—19th century. 7. Carlyle, Thomas, 1795-1881—
Religion. 8. Arnold, Matthew, 1822-1888—Religion. 9. England—Church history—19th
century. 10. Cambridge (England)—Church history. 11. Oxford (England)—Church
history. I. Title.

PR468.R44J66 2003
820.9'3823—dc21
                                                                        2003040145

Printed in the United States of America

The Broad Church

He that will finde Truth,
must seek it with a *free judgment*, and a *sanctified minde*:
he that thus seeks, shall finde;
he shall live in Truth, and that shall live in him;
it shall be like a stream of living waters issuing out of his own Soule;
he shall drink of the waters of his own cistern, and be satisfied;
he shall every morning finde this Heavenly *Manna*
lying upon the top of his own Soule, and be fed with it to eternal life;
he will finde satisfaction within, feeling himself in conjunction with Truth,
though all the World should dispute against him.

John Smith
(1618-1652)

Contents

Preface

Quid Athenis et Hierosolymis? Quid Academiæ et Ecclesiæ? What has Athens to do with Jerusalem, the Academy with the Church? The question is Tertullian's, but is not as foreign or ancient as the Latin may lead us to suspect. Indeed, I seem to hear Tertullian's voice behind the quizzical smiles of colleagues and the skeptical frowns of theologians, who wonder, each in their own way, why a professor of English has written a book on Church history. It is the same sentiment that provoked H. P. Liddon to complain that the dean of Westminster, A. P. Stanley, was attempting to transform the Church of England into "a mere Literary Society" and which led J. H. Blunt to suppose that the Broad Church movement had its origin in "the instinctive opposition" that amateurs and generalists are inclined to have toward the positive conclusions of "exact theological learning." To answer Tertullian, I need only borrow from Origen, who recognized that we may find, even in the writings of pagans, the *logos spermaticos* or "seeds of the Word." Through exposure to every art form, from every source, our minds and hearts are trained to discern the shades of beauty and truth, and it is not through "sacred" literature alone that God is revealed to us.

The book that you now have in your hands has been a work of passion. Whether it is also a work of scholarship, I must leave to the judgment of others. According to Thomas Carlyle, "No nobler feeling than this, of admiration for one higher than himself, dwells in the breast of man." For most of my life, my heroes have been preachers and clergy, and I too pursued a vocation in Christian ministry. After being trained in the Church of Christ (American Campbellite) tradition, I preached for a small congregation in rural Sulphur Rock, Arkansas, before relentless doubts regarding plenary inspiration and the miraculous aspect of revelation compelled me to abandon the pulpit. Desiring nothing so much as to return to the security of that community in which my identity had been shaped and from which I was now alienated, I sought argument and debate, but my brethren could only misunderstand my predicament and motive. Moreover, my mind, having been stretched, would never return to its former dimensions.

In the divine order of things, I met with an Episcopal priest, Reverend Dr. Gary McConnell, in whom I first discerned Christ's love for poetry and young poets. He introduced me to a new community of faith *and* doubt in which I have found a profound tolerance, a loving acceptance, and a tradition both meaningful and beautiful. In this context, years after leaving the ministry, I learned from Broad Churchmen to embrace doubt as an essential quality of a living and, therefore, changing faith. I relate this part of my experience only because, in some measure, it may make up for what I lack in "exact theological learning." With one foot in Jerusalem and another in Athens, my stance may not appear secure, but my view is much broader.

Acknowledgments

Never has a scholar been more blessed than I in the choice of his companion. Without the support of my wife, Karen, this book could not have been written. She was at my side throughout the research and composition of my doctoral dissertation, *Christianity and Culture: Matthew Arnold, Charles Kingsley, and the Broad Church Movement* (1997), and she has listened patiently and responsively to every part of this larger and more comprehensive work. She has been the first to read the chapters and the first to suggest revisions, and from the beginning, she has been to me a source of constant encouragement and strength.

My mentor and colleague at the University of Maryland, Professor William S. Peterson, added to his unceasing labors the review of my chapters. His suggestions regarding content and style, in addition to our many little talks about things Victorian and Anglican, contributed in incalculable ways toward the production of the final manuscript.

With heartfelt gratitude, I acknowledge the contribution of the late Reverend Dr. Charles P. Price, Professor Emeritus of Virginia Theological Seminary, who was first to suggest that I might write a cultural study of the Broad Church movement. Without his encouragement, it is improbable that I should ever have accepted the task. During my first two years of preparatory study, he suggested readings and challenged me with questions. His death in 1999 came before the first chapter could be written, and I cannot but regard it as an inestimable loss, both to myself and to the quality of my completed manuscript.

Finally, I must acknowledge my indebtedness to retired Episcopal Bishop John Shelby Spong, who took the time to correspond with me on the subject of the Broad Church movement, and to the many university libraries which have generously made their resources and assistance freely accessible.

Introduction

What Is the Broad Church?

Whenever I mention the title of this book, almost invariably, the first question that I am asked is "What is the Broad Church?" I anticipate the question, and yet, even after years of familiarity with the persons and works that constitute the Broad Church movement, I still feel, in company with one of its critics, that nothing else is "so difficult to describe and so easy to misinterpret."[1] This difficulty cannot, however, be ascribed to a sparsity of information. On the contrary, so abundant are the resources that, as soon as one sets about to define the movement, one is overwhelmed by multiple strategies of definition and varied viewpoints.

"Broad Church" can be defined by etymology as a term of Saxon derivation,[2] by history as a term that had its origin in a joke told by Arthur Hugh Clough in the company of W. C. Lake and A. P. Stanley at Oxford in the late 1840s,[3] by synonym as the nineteenth-century equivalent of "Latitudinarian" and "Modernist,"[4] by comparison as a term like Latitudinarian, but different in that it indicates a broader range of liberalism,[5] by contrast as emphasizing reason, as opposed to the imagination of the High Church and the affections of the Low Church,[6] by negation as "not a party," "not a group," "not a faction," and "not an organised alliance,"[7] by social usage as "a party,"[8] by genus as one of "the three parties which divide the Church of England,"[9] by classification as being comprised of Aristotelian and Platonist, Theoretical and Anti-theoretical individuals,[10] by parts as consisting of rational and emotional elements,[11] by description as comprehensive, radical, and conservative,[12] by process as that which begins by asking first what the Reason and Conscience can teach,[13] *by cause* as a reaction against the Evidentiary school of Paley or the Tractarian school of Newman and Pusey,[14] or by consequence as either a school promoting Truth and Justice or a tree the fruits of which "must be the apples of Sodom and the clusters of Gomorrha."[15]

Any of these tactics of definition might be pursued with profit. Each has been employed, at one time or another, as a rhetorical device by which the critic argues

1

from his or her perspective, and the definitions arrived at generally reveal the author's bias. I have made no effort in this book to conceal my own sympathy with the leaders of the Broad Church movement or my substantial agreement with their conclusions. Even so, the records by which the movements of the Broad Church can be traced are matter of historical and public record, and since the most promising means of knowing what Matthew Arnold and Benjamin Jowett were pleased to call "the thing as in itself it really is" is to study the thing itself rather than a definition of the thing, I have made it my constant effort to reveal the leaders of the Broad Church and their thought in sufficient detail to allow my readers to construct their own definition of the movement.

One critic, arguing that "the Broad Church movement has consisted . . . in the unconscious and unforeseen development of a principle," has concluded that it would be impossible to write "anything like a history" of the movement. "All that is possible," he concludes, is "to endeavour, as it were, by a succession of landmarks, to trace roughly its rise and progress."[16] My endeavor has not been to write a history of a principle. Even if such a thing *were* possible, it would not have been possible for *me* to do it. Were it possible for me to do it, it would not have been possible for you to *read* it; for—as Charles Merivale once remarked, in reference to the books of James Mozley—"It is no use being instructive if you are so dull one can't read your books."[17] Instead, I have attempted to clothe principles in flesh and blood and write a *biography* of the Broad Church movement. After all, biography is not only the form by which the Christian Church has traditionally received its instruction; it is also the form by which the Victorians preferred to know the minds and hearts of those who had passed through their midst and disappeared. People engage with, but do not identify with, safely disembodied ideas, and Shelley was not the only other-worldly soul who fell upon the thorns of life and *bled*.

The four chapters into which this book is divided represent the four major conduits through which the vital intellectual and liberty-loving impulses of the Broad Church movement spread. Julia Wedgwood describes the poet-philosopher S. T. Coleridge as "the father of the Broad Church,"[18] and truly, if any one person can be identified as the founder or chief instigator of the movement, that person must be Coleridge. James Martineau, the Unitarian theologian, in "Personal Influences on Present Theology" (1856), identifies "three movements, distinguished by the names of Newman, Coleridge, and Carlyle" to which he ascribes "the altered spirit, in regard to religion, pervading the young intellect of England."[19] Although Martineau insists that the Coleridgean school is not synonymous with the Broad Church, he recognizes that the Coleridgeans may be considered as a part of this larger whole, if by Broad Church we signify a "resistance to unchristian narrowness and unworthy fears."[20] James H. Rigg, writing in 1857 from an Evangelical perspective, elaborates on Martineau's thesis of a Cambridge Coleridgean school and also identifies affinities between Cambridge and Oxford liberal movements.[21] Thus, even though the Broad Church movement as a whole cannot be attributed to the influence of

Coleridge, the impact of his thought is sufficiently pervasive within the movement to warrant the attention and position given to him in the opening chapter of this book. A number of critics have pointed not to Highgate, but to Oriel College as the location from which the Broad Church first developed. One critic suggests, "If we are to look anywhere for its fountain-head, it would probably be in the Common Room of Oriel College; yet neither Whately, nor Copleston, nor Arnold can be held responsible for the existence of the movement in any further sense than that they first in Oxford taught men to look things in the face, and to inquire and to think for themselves."[22] Dennis Wigmore-Beddoes ventures a little further, stating that "in the group of Anglicans known as Noetics, . . . who, in their critical and liberal attitude, exhibited something of the spirit of the Latitudinarians, the Broad Church, before it received its name, has its existence."[23] F. D. Maurice, writing in 1860, thought it probable that, if such a "party" could exist, it may have had its origin "in that creed which is contained in Whately's books."[24] Another critic supposes that Dr. Arnold was "the first Broad Churchman."[25] More than one author has distinguished this group as the Aristotelian leg of the Broad Church, as opposed to the Platonist or Coleridgean leg.[26] As with all generalizations, exceptions can be identified, but this simplification may be trusted as a useful heuristic from which to begin a study of the movement.

The Coleridgean element was strongest at Cambridge. When William Palmer, in 1849, wrote his article "On Tendencies toward the Subversion of Faith," he identified John Sterling as the central figure around which a host of friends and associates of similar liberal views and philosophical tendencies gathered.[27] While undergraduates at Cambridge, F. D. Maurice and Sterling reshaped the "Apostles" club, turning it into what has been called "the cradle of the Broad Church movement."[28] Sterling had been the pupil of J. C. Hare, the Coleridgean tutor at Cambridge who delivered, in 1828, the sermon which one author has identified as the inaugural speech of the Broad Church movement.[29] Moreover, Archdeacon Hare's 1847 Charge, *Means of Unity*, was recognized by a sympathetic critic as representative of the Broad Church.[30] Hare's colleague and friend at Cambridge, Connop Thirlwall, the translator of Schleiermacher's *Luke*, is largely known as the bishop who, when called a Broad Churchman, declared, "To hold a prominent place in such a brotherhood as answers to my conception of the Broad Church, would to me appear a most enviable distinction."[31] Other associates of Hare were Daniel Macmillan and his younger brother Alexander, whom Hare helped to establish as booksellers in Cambridge. Alexander, following the footsteps of his brother, subsequently became "the most enthusiastic admirer and exponent" of Maurice, and during the 1860s and '70s, Macmillan and Co. could be said to be "the intellectual centre" of the Broad Church.[32] Although the relation of Maurice to the movement will be considered in detail in the third chapter, it is, perhaps, sufficient to note here that he is generally regarded as the most influential theologian within the Broad Church.

Finally, there is a later movement in Oxford, beginning at about the time of the condemnation of W. G. Ward by Convocation in February 1845 and culminating in the publication of *Essays and Reviews* in March 1860, that is often identified as representative of the Broad Church. In fact, immediately prior to Convocation's meeting, A. C. Tait—the later archbishop of Canterbury—published an open Letter to the Vice-Chancellor in which he distinguishes four separate theological schools in the Church of England: (1) the school which "claims for itself the title of Anglo-Catholics," (2) "the small compact body of the decided followers of Mr. Newman," (3) the Evangelicals, and (4) "a large and growing body of young men, who are, for the most part, what is called Low Church in matters of discipline, and whose doctrinal theology is in a great measure modified, if not formed, by the study of the great Protestant writers of the Continent." This fourth school, which "contains by far the greatest amount of the talent of the rising generation," is characterized by comprehensive "theological sympathies," embracing Carlyle and Schleiermacher on the one hand, and Newman and Möhler on the other.[33] It is to this fourth school that Maurice refers when he suggests that, if "Broad Church" does not refer to Whately's creed, it may signify "that which has arisen at Oxford out of the reaction against Tractarianism." The theologian's grandson tells us that, of this movement, "Dean Stanley had been for all practical purposes for many years the leader."[34] A. P. Stanley had been, together with Benjamin Jowett, Frederick Temple, Arthur Clough, Matthew Arnold, and a number of other socially prominent persons, members of an Oxford debating club called the "Decade." The closing chapter of this book examines Decade members' relationships and the formative influences of the Broad Church upon this school, as well as their own contributions to the movement.

Many of the ideas propagated by Broad Churchmen, if not actually representative of modern Anglican liberalism, anticipate it. In some ways, their writings might even be regarded as superior to those composed in a more secular age. Their works generally combine "a diffusive and expansive spirit," "a disposition to recognize and appreciate that which is true and good under all varieties of forms, and in persons separated from one another by the most conflicting opinions,"[35] with a genuine regard for the sentiment attached to traditional forms and respect for the Establishment. Then, as now, this reverence for Tradition and earnest seeking of Truth, or the "juggling of these two factors, the emotional, located in the truth of the human heart, and the rational, located in the critical faculties of the mind," resulted in what is called "the Broad Church compromise."[36] In an age that makes a virtue of plain-speaking, the moral integrity of Broad Churchmen tends to be suspect. Thus, Leslie Stephen attacks at length this facet of the movement:

> The great merit of Broad Churchmen is that they try to meet arguments fairly, and admit in theory the importance of searching, fair, and unfettered inquiry. If they admitted it in practice as well as in theory, there would be no more to be said. . . . But I am now speaking of those members of the Broad Church who, feeling that their sentiments fit with a certain awkwardness into the phraseology officially provided for them, substantially argue that they are justified in using strained versions of ordinary

language, because the law has sanctioned very wide methods of interpretation. . . . Now I cannot conceive any doctrine more fatal to genuine veracity of mind than one which exalts into a duty what seems to me the most dangerous habit of forcing our genuine convictions into the moulds of ancient thought.[37]

Stephen is one among a small number of prominent clergymen, including Charles Wodehouse and Stopford Brooke, whose consciences protested against compromise and who, as a result, resigned their orders. This moral protest calls to mind a much earlier debate between Erasmus and Luther.

Wedgwood suggests, "In some sense, indeed, the Broad Church is older than the Anglican Church," and that "the Church of England would have been a peculiarly appropriate home for such a mind as Erasmus."[38] It is my contention that something of the spirit of Erasmus was sewn into the very fabric of Anglicanism, a spirit that was never more evident in the Church of England as it was in the Broad Church movement of the nineteenth century. This is especially true in that the Broad Churchmen are representative of Anglicanism as a system—which is not to say that they are to any degree more Anglican than High Churchmen or Evangelicals, but only that the Broad Churchmen's tolerance and attitude toward comprehension is more fully in line with that Erasmian policy adopted by the framers of the polity of the national church. As A. P. Stanley states, the English Church "is, by the very condition of its being, not High, or Low, but Broad."[39] Moreover, the Broad Churchmen's moderation and method of slow advance, their carefulness not to become a stone of stumbling or a rock of offense, their capacity for intellectual subtlety, and their loyalty to the ideal of an established church—these were their Erasmian virtues. But, to reformers of a Lutheran stamp, they were vices to be despised.

In Mrs. Humphry (Mary Augusta) Ward's best-selling novel, *Robert Elsmere* (1888), the eponymous character, after finding that he can no longer believe in miracle, gives up his orders in the Church of England. Wanting to remain active in a Christian ministry, he attempts to work alongside a reformer of similar opinions:

> But Mr. Vernon was a Broad Churchman, belonged to the Church Reform movement, and thought it absolutely necessary to "keep things going," and by a policy of prudent silence and gradual expansion from within, to save the great "plant" of the Establishment from falling wholesale into the hands of the High Churchmen. In consequence he was involved, as Robert held, in endless contradictions and practical falsities of speech and action.[40]

Elsmere, although a religious hero of the modern age, is nevertheless a hero of the Lutheran stamp, and his decision to separate from Vernon is a contemporary illustration of Luther's separation from Erasmus. Both men stand firmly on moral ground, but whereas Vernon considers foremost his relationship to God *as a member of the body of Christ*, Elsmere emphasizes his relationship to God *as an individual*.

Although "the men who pass before us" in Mrs. Ward's novel no doubt are, as Walter Pater observed, "composite of many different men we seem to have known,"[41] the character of Elsmere is surely modeled, however loosely, after John Sterling.[42] Sterling, after working for a short period as J. C. Hare's curate, came to the conclusion that even the broadest philosophical minds of the Anglican Church had compromised with the issues of biblical inspiration and doctrinal authority. He abandoned his clerical position in the church and died shortly thereafter, still a young man and an honest doubter. Before the youthful Robert Elsmere dies, in his final letter to a Broad Churchman, he argues, "We must come out of it. The ground must be cleared; then may come the re-building. Religion itself, the peace of generations to come, is at stake. If we could wait indefinitely while the Church widened, well and good. But we have but the one life, the one chance of saying the word or playing the part assigned us."[43]

There is an apocalyptic urgency in Elsmere's position that repudiates the philosophic historicism and the meditation *sub specie æternitatas* that calmly acknowledges the revelation to each generation as a link in a great chain that stretches out or spirals into the grey mist of centuries and millennia to come. Elsmere is Lessing's "enthusiast": "He wants this future to come quickly, and to be made to come quickly through him. A thing over which nature takes thousands of years is to come to maturity just at the moment of his experience. For what part has he in it, if that which he recognizes as the best does not become the best in his lifetime?"[44] The Broad Churchman, on the other hand, realizes that, though there is an immediacy in God's revelation of himself to the rational and moral sense, he nevertheless reveals himself progressively to the understanding. Humanity is, thus, always potentially evolving. It is this faith of the Christian Humanist that recognizes in the progressive truths of today the commonplaces of tomorrow, and it is this hope of the Christian Humanist, illuminated by divine love, that recognizes in our neighbors of today "the herald of a higher race."[45] Ward herself appears, eventually, to have adopted something like this position, and her later novel *The Case of Richard Meynell* (1911) "expressed her conversion to the principle of reform from within."[46]

As Hugh R. Haweis argues, in *The Broad Church, or What is Coming* (1891), the Broad Churchism of *Robert Elsmere* is "completely sterile and impossible":

> Not to throw up our "Holy orders" in a panic, but to justify them by patient reconstruction, prayer, and meditation—not to break up the Church of England, but to enlarge, vitalise, and reform it—not to denounce or flout its theological standards, but to understand and rehabilitate them. Such are the chief functions of the Broad Church clergy, and in their exercise, they are prepared to give the lie direct to every characteristic of the Broad Church vicar (as he is sketched) according to Robert Elsmere.[47]

The Broad Churchman, properly identified—that is, the Churchman who is such only *because* he is first a Christian, and whose tolerance springs up not as a weed of indifference, but as a flower of knowledge, and which is at once the expression of wisdom, love, and humility—is the Christian Humanist of the Anglican Church in the nineteenth century. It is his faith that God *will* reveal himself: truth will supplant falsehood, light will overcome darkness, and the crooked paths will be made straight. He concludes that there is neither good sense nor love in splitting a church today over a realization that, if true, will be added to the unwritten creed of tomorrow. Because he is passionate for truth, his heart warms toward the Luthers and Robert Elsmeres, all of the martyred lovers of truth and so-called heretics of yesterday; but, through reason and faith in God, he knows that the praise of all partisanship and triumphs of division is, after all, merely a praise of folly.

Notes

1. Julia Wedgwood, "The Life of Charles Kingsley," *Spectator* (13 and 20 January 1877), in *Nineteenth Century Teachers, and Other Essays* by Julia Wedgwood (London: Hodder and Stoughton, 1909), 79-95, 88.

2. Evelyn Abbott and Lewis Campbell, *The Life and Letters of Benjamin Jowett, M.A.*, 2 vols. (London: John Murray, 1897), 1:209 n.

3. Katherine Lake, ed., *Memorials of William Charles Lake* (London: Edward Arnold, 1901), 35. Arthur Penrhyn Stanley, *Essays Chiefly on Questions of Church and State, from 1850 to 1870* (London: John Murray, 1870), 8 n. Charles R. Sanders observes, "Benjamin Jowett, according to the *New English Dictionary*, said that the term was first proposed, in his hearing, by Arthur Hugh Clough" (*Coleridge and the Broad Church Movement* [Durham: Duke University Press, 1942], 7). Although it is not at all improbable that Clough used the term in the presence of Jowett, either when Stanley and Lake were present, or on some other occasion, Jowett's biographers appear to have been unfamiliar with any statement by their subject to this effect.

4. Dennis G. Wigmore-Beddoes, *Yesterday's Radicals: A Study of the Affinity between Unitarianism and Broad Church Anglicanism in the Nineteenth Century* (Cambridge: James Clarke and Co., 1971), 15.

5. Hastings Rashdall, "Clerical Liberalism," in *Anglican Liberalism*, by Twelve Churchmen (London: Williams and Norgate, 1908), 77-134, 82-83.

6. R. E. B., "The Broad Church Movement," *Fraser's Magazine* 17 (March 1878): 353-64, 355.

7. Owen Chadwick, *The Victorian Church: Part I* (New York: Oxford University Press, 1966), 545. Margaret A. Crowther, *Church Embattled: Religious Controversy in Mid-Victorian England* (Hamden, Conn.: Archon Books, 1970), 29-30. William John Conybeare, "Church Parties," *Edinburgh Review* 98, no. 200 (October 1853), 273-342, 334.

8. Wedgwood, 87-88; R. E. B., 354.

9. Conybeare, 273.

10. Frederick Denison Maurice, "Essay on Archdeacon Hare's Position in the Church with Reference to the Parties that Divide It," Introduction to *Charges* by Julius Charles Hare (1856), in *The Victory of Faith*, ed. E. H. Plumptre, 3rd ed. (London: Macmillan and Co., 1874), xvii-lxxxix, xix. Charles Richard Sanders, "Was Frederick Denison Maurice a Broad-Churchman?," *Church History* 3, no. 3 (1934); reprint, Chicago: University of Chicago Libraries, 1934), 10-11. Conybeare, 333.

11. Victor Shea and William Whitla, "The Broad Church Compromise," in *Essays and Reviews: The 1860 Text and Its Readings* (Charlottesville: University Press of Virginia, 2000), 123-26, 124.

12. Hugh R. Haweis, "The Broad Church: Or, What's Coming?," *The Contemporary Review* 57 (June 1890): 900-10, 902.

13. J. E. Symes, *Broad Church* (London: Methuen and Co., 1913), vii.

14. James Martineau, "Personal Influences on Present Theology," *National Review* (October 1856), in *Essays, Reviews, and Addresses*, 4 vols. (London: Longmans, Green, and Co., 1890), 1:219-81, 224; Baden Powell, "On the Study of the Evidences of Christianity," in Shea and Whitla, 233-61, 248; A Layman of the Established Church, *Puseyism: The School of the Infidels, or "Broad Church" the Offspring of "High Church"* (London: Arthur Miall, 1865), 35-36.

15. Julius Charles Hare, *Thou Shalt Not Bear False Witness against Thy Neighbour: A Letter to the Editor of the English Review* (London: John W. Parker, 1849), 13; "The New Oxford School, or Broad Church Liberalism," *The Biblical Repertory and Princeton Review* 33 (January 1861): 59-84, 83.

16. R. E. B., 355.

17. Charles Merivale to W. C. Lake, 12 December 1884, in Lake, 269.

18. Julia Wedgwood, "Samuel Taylor Coleridge," *Contemporary Review* (April 1895), in *Nineteenth Century Teachers*, 1-28, 21.

19. Martineau, 1:226-27. Alfred W. Benn says of this article by Martineau, "Here we find a signal exemplification of the close contract existing between Unitarianism and the Broad Church party within the Church of England" (*The History of English Rationalism in the Nineteenth Century*, 2 vols. [1906; reprint, New York: Russell & Russell, 1962], 2:71).

20. Martineau, 1:225.

21. James H. Rigg, *Modern Anglican Theology: Chapters on Coleridge, Hare, Maurice, Kingsley, and Jowett, and on the Doctrine of Sacrifice and Atonement* (London: Alexander Heylin, 1857).

22. R. E. B., 355.

23. Wigmore-Beddoes, 26.

24. F. D. Maurice to Isaac Taylor, 10 April 1860, in Frederick Maurice, ed., *The Life of Frederick Denison Maurice, Chiefly Told in His Own Letters*, 2 vols. (New York: Charles Scribner's Sons, 1884), 2:359.

25. Julia Wedgwood, "Arthur Penrhyn Stanley," *Contemporary Review* (September 1881), in *Nineteenth Century Teachers*, 96-118, 100. J. H. Blunt's *Dictionary of Sects, Heresies, Ecclesiastical Parties, and Schools of Religious Thought* notes that the Broad Church "is generally traced back to Dr. Arnold" (London: Rivingtons, 1874), 85.

26. For example, Maurice and Sanders (*vide* note 10, above).

27. Hare, 11.

28. John Connop Thirlwall, *Connop Thirlwall: Historian and Theologian* (London: S.P.C.K., 1936), 56.

29. N. Merrill Distad, *Guessing at Truth: The Life of Julius Charles Hare* (Shepherdstown, W.Va.: The Patmos Press, 1979), 48.

30. Conybeare, 333.

31. Connop Thirlwall, "Dr. Littlefield's Article on 'Church Parties,'" *Contemporary Review* 26 (October 1875): 703-5.

32. Thomas Hughes, *Memoir of Daniel Macmillan* (London: Macmillan and Co, 1883), esp. 145-65; Charles L. Graves, *Life and Letters of Alexander Macmillan* (London: Macmillan and Co., 1910), 102-3.

33. Archibald Campbell Tait, *A Letter to the Rev. the Vice-Chancellor of the University of Oxford* (London: Blackwood and Sons, 1845), 11-17; excerpts reprinted, *Correspondence of John Henry Newman with John Keble and Others, 1839-1845*, ed. Birmingham Oratory (London: Longmans, Green, and Co., 1917), 94-97.

34. Maurice, 2:359-60.

35. Abbott and Campbell, 1:299; Thirlwall, "Dr. Littlefield's Article," 703.

36. Shea and Whitla, 124.

37. Leslie Stephen, "The Broad Church," *Fraser's Magazine* 81 (March 1870), in *Essays on Freethinking and Plainspeaking* (London: Longmans, Green, and Co., 1873), 1-40, 14, 22, 33.

38. Wedgwood, "Arthur Penrhyn Stanley," 102.

39. A. P. Stanley, "The Gorham Controversy," *Edinburgh Review* (July 1850), in *Essays*, 3-45, 8.

40. Mrs. Humphrey [Mary Augusta] Ward, *Robert Elsmere* (London: Smith, Elder and Co., 1888), 414-15.

41. Walter Pater, "Robert Elsmere," *The Guardian* (28 March 1888), in *Essays on Literature and Art*, ed. Jennifer Uglow (London: J. M. Dent and Sons, Ltd., 1973), 153-60, 154. Oscar Wilde admired the "clever caricatures" of *Robert Elsmere* ("The Decay of Lying," in *The Complete Works of Oscar Wilde* [New York: Harper and Row, 1989], 970-92, 975).

42. William S. Peterson observes that Elsmere's "physiognomy and temperament are close to those of John Sterling, whose biography by Carlyle Mrs. Ward had undoubtedly read"; however, Peterson agrees with Pater that Elsmere is indeed "a composite figure" (*Victorian Heretic: Mrs. Humphrey Ward's Robert Elsmere* [Leicester: Leicester University Press, 1976], 134-35). In leaving the Church of England to erect a new religious society, "The New Brotherhood of Christ," Elsmere is, in fact, suggestive of Charles Voysey (1828-1912), who, after being deprived of his orders, founded the Theistic Church in London in 1871.

43. Ward, 603.

44. Gotthold Lessing, "The Education of the Human Race" §90, trans. F. W. Robertson and Henry Chadwick, in *Lessing's Theological Writings*, ed. Henry Chadwick (Stanford: Stanford University Press, 1957), 97.

45. Alfred, Lord Tennyson, *In Memoriam*, CXVIII.14. Cf. Frederick Temple: "We may expect to find, in the history of the human race, each successive age incorporating into itself the substance of the preceding" ("The Education of the World," in Shea and Whitla, 137-64, 138).

46. Basil Willey, "How 'Robert Elsmere' Struck Some Contemporaries," *Essays and Studies, 1957*, ed. Margaret Willy (London: John Murray, 1957), 53-68, 56.

47. H. R. Haweis, *The Broad Church, or What is Coming* (London: Sampson Low, Marston, Searle, and Rivington, 1891), 13-15.

1

Samuel Taylor Coleridge

The Reverend John Coleridge, vicar in the market town of Ottery St. Mary in Devon and headmaster of King's Grammar School, was fifty-three years old in the year 1772. His wife, Ann, was forty-five. Their marriage had been fruitful, and the Coleridge clan had multiplied. When Francis was born, two years earlier, he was thought by all to be the last. He was their ninth child, and as Ann's youngest and most handsome son, Francis was, perhaps, heir to a disproportionate effusion of maternal fondness. But now, on 21 October—even though Ann had her hands more than full and, no doubt, felt herself well beyond satisfaction in the contemplation of her brood—there was the shrill cry of infant demands coming once again from the nursery. This child had come trailing a little too far behind the clouds of glory, and he wasn't nearly so beautiful as Francis; he rather took after father John.

First Domestic Loves

Their only daughter, Anne, affectionately known by all her brothers as Nancy, was only five years old at the time of Sam's birth. Yet, she was to occupy a special position in the emotional development of her youngest brother. In March 1791, after receiving the news of her death, Coleridge concluded in a sonnet, "Better to die, than live and not be lov'd!"[1] Throughout most of his life, he would envy the close filial bonds enjoyed by his friends Charles Lamb and William Wordsworth with their sisters, respectively Mary and Dorothy.[2] Three years after Anne's death, he included these lines in a poem to Charles:

> I too a Sister had, an only Sister –
> She lov'd me dearly, and I doted on her!

11

> To her I pour'd forth all my puny sorrows
> (As a sick Patient in a Nurse's arms)
> And of the heart those hidden maladies
> That e'en from Friendship's eye will shrink asham'd.
> O! I have wak'd at midnight, and have wept,
> Because she was not![3]

Anne appears to have made up, as best she could, for the love that Coleridge *felt* that he did not receive from his mother. Significantly, however, there remained a void in Coleridge's earliest emotional experience that left him questioning his worthiness to be loved.

Tragically, that question seemed to young Coleridge to have been answered by the events of late 1781 and early 1782. His violent sibling rivalry with Francis pushed both parents toward sending the older brother away. Francis was then twelve, and it was determined that he would enter the navy. The Reverend Coleridge, after setting his son aboard a convoy to Bengal, returned from Plymouth on the night of 4 October, went to bed tired and upset, and within hours was dead, the result of a heart attack. From young Coleridge's perspective, he himself had been the cause of separation between Francis and his parents, and, thus, the cause of his father's death as well. If ever there had been a need for tender reassurances from his mother, Coleridge deeply felt that need now. However, Mrs. Coleridge, with distresses of her own, and soon under the burden of financially straitened circumstances, made the difficult decision to send both Anne and Samuel away. Anne would learn to be a shop assistant at Exeter, and little Coleridge would attend a boarding school in London.

At the end of March 1782, Coleridge was made the ward of Christ's Hospital, and thus was he—as he reflected in 1797—"from the spot where first I sprang to light / Too soon transplanted, ere my soul had fix'd / Its first domestic loves."[4] He would ever after identify himself as an "orphan."[5] Throughout his years of formal education, both at Christ's Hospital and at Cambridge, he would return to Ottery St. Mary no more than three or four times,[6] and when he received a letter in November 1809 informing him, as he related to Robert Southey, "that my poor Mother is near her end, and dying in great torture, . . . & she wishes to see me before her death," yet he refused to go, stating as his pretense, lack of funds.[7] The truth, rather, appears to be that by the time he was ten years old Coleridge felt himself irrevocably detached from his mother, resented her for the failure of their relationship, and subsequently pronounced as a fact that which he felt already to be true—that she had died to him as a mother.

This early experience of Coleridge is important to us in that it provides the most probable explanation for our subject's habitual inwardness, his constant escape into the life of the mind, and—along with his opium addiction—it may account for his life-long struggle to accept himself as one deserving of love and to realize a personal Other that would love him unconditionally. At the very least, this information should serve to blunt the edges of our criticism as we concern ourselves with the mistakes of his life and to sharpen our admiration as we reflect upon his successes.

Christ Hospital

Within the Grammar School at Christ Hospital it was inevitable that Coleridge would ultimately fall under the scrutiny of James Bowyer, the headmaster who supervised the Classical Sixth Form, the Deputy Grecians. What is surprising is only that it took so long. Coleridge was an obsessive reader with an astounding gift of memory. Encouraged by his father, he began reading the Bible at the age of three. Before his fifteenth year, as he would relate in the *Biographia Literaria*, "I had bewildered myself in metaphysicks, and in theological controversy. Nothing else pleased me. History, and particular facts, lost all interest in my mind."[8] It must have been this relative disregard for the objects of the understanding, "particular facts," that resulted in his being overlooked by Bowyer until about 1785. He was brought to the headmaster's attention by Thomas Middleton, who, to his great amazement, had found Coleridge reading Virgil "for pleasure." Thereafter, Bowyer took the young scholar under his rod. Coleridge, after reading Voltaire's *Philosophical Dictionary*, declared himself an "infidel," and Bowyer responded, "So, sirrah, you are an infidel, are you? then I'll flog your infidelity out of you."[9] As late as 1815, Bowyer's "severities" furnished material for the plot of Coleridge's nightmares.[10]

As De Quincey observed of the dreams of an opium-eater, "The minutest incidents of childhood, or forgotten scenes of later years, were often revived," and these scenes were such as to shape terror out of gloom and anxiety.[11] Just as it was at Christ Hospital that Coleridge acquired the material for his nightmares, so too was it there that he was first given the substance for their production. During the winter of 1790-1791 Coleridge was periodically ill with rheumatic fever, and for protracted periods the nurses kept him dosed with opium to ease his pain and help him sleep. When Coleridge left Christ Hospital, he did not leave as an addict, but he had soaked in unawares "venom with the rain from Heaven,"[12] and there was no antidote to be had.

On the lighter side, it is worth noting that Middleton, afterwards first Bishop of Calcutta, became and remained one of Coleridge's closest friends during his school years. It was at Christ Hospital that Coleridge met and began his lifelong friendship with Charles Lamb, "my gentle-hearted Charles" of later verse. It was there that he took up the study of prosody and first became seriously active as a creative writer. Moreover, it was there that he discovered his natural predilection for Platonic philosophy and, by it, established an intellectual foundation that served him well after his move to Jesus College, Cambridge, in the autumn of 1791.

Cambridge and Platonism

One of the many similarities between Coleridge and Schleiermacher was their early and continuous interest in Plato; however, even though Coleridge never wrote the commentaries or delivered the university lectures that Schleiermacher did, it can safely be asserted that what Coleridge called the "dear *gorgeous* Nonsense" of Plato remained more central to his philosophy.[13] Basically, this is because, despite the attractions of pantheism, Coleridge would never allow himself to accept a monistic perspective, not even the dual monism posited by Spinoza. Thus, for A. R. Vidler, "the first thing to notice" in any study of Coleridge "is that he was convinced of the reality of an invisible world upon which the visible world, the world of nature, is dependent, and to which it is secondary."[14] To Coleridge's understanding, the material world was created by a Spirit Being *ex nihilo*. Although ultimate reality, that which is eternal and infinite, is spirit, matter has an existence, albeit temporal and finite, other than as spirit phenomena. This epistemological realism grounded in the dualism of Plato and the Bible would not only serve as the underlying premise to much of Coleridge's poetry but would become a cornerstone in the construction of his mature philosophy and theology.

John Muirhead observes that, during the very years that Coleridge was a student at Jesus College, the halls of Cambridge were witnessing, once again, a revival of interest in Platonism, this time through the translations of Plotinus by Thomas Taylor, "which Coleridge could hardly have failed to notice."[15] It was in these years that he began to read the Cambridge Platonists. William Hazlitt tells us that, while at Cambridge, Coleridge "was deep-read in . . . Cudworth's Intellectual System (a huge pile of learning, unwieldy, enormous)."[16] The influence of *The True Intellectual System of the Universe* (1678) is, perhaps, evident in these lines from "The Eolian Harp," written by Coleridge in 1795, just after leaving Cambridge:

> And what if all of animated nature
> Be but organic Harps diversely fram'd,
> That tremble into thought, as o'er them sweeps
> Plastic and vast, one intellectual breeze,
> At once the Soul of each, and God of all?[17]

Just as Cudworth's *Plastick Nature* hypothesized "*Reason Immersed and Plunged* into Matter and, as it were, *Fuddled* in it and *Confounded* with it," acting upon nature as an "inward principle,"[18] so too does Coleridge imagine an "intellectual breeze" that shapes and animates nature from within. Thus, for Coleridge, God as Creator is both transcendent to matter, *natura naturata*, and is immanent in nature as *natura naturans*, endowing it with form and ensuring its reality. This is, in fact, a form of "panentheism," although the term itself had not yet been coined.[19] Coleridge resisted, as the "worst superstition," pantheism, the idea of "God / Diffused through all, that doth make all one whole,"[21] but insisted on the actual presence of God in nature.[22]

According to Coleridge, "the early study of Plato and Plotinus," along with Proclus, Ficino, and Bruno, paved the way for his reception of the *Cogito quia sum* (I think because I am).[23] The premise "I am," not the Cartesian "I think," is the beginning point of all philosophy. There is, thus, the existence of both the physical being, the *natura naturata*, and the "intellectual breeze" operative within, the *natura naturans*, before there is self-consciousness. Then, "the moment, when the soul begins to be sufficiently self-conscious, to ask concerning itself, & its relations, is the first moment of its *intellectual* arrival into the World."[24] From existence, the soul arrives at a state of "being," in which it is aware of its spiritual center and enters into a sacred sympathy with the spirit that, while *infusing* all of nature, is not *diffused* throughout it. Once the individual attains to a state of being, he or she begins to recognize creation as an interwoven system of signs that bears witness to the attributes of the Creator. This recognition, in its effect, closely resembles the Platonic experience of anamnesis or recollection, and Ronald Wendling is not amiss in describing the process of awakening from existence to being as "the beginning of a Platonic ascent"—specifically, an ascent "from sense perception to knowledge of the transcendental realities imaged in the temporal world."[25]

At the end of 1794, after leaving Cambridge without his degree, Coleridge wrote the first draft of "Religious Musings." His belief in the soul's ascent in a process of deification is given clear expression:

> And blest are they,
> Who in this fleshly World, the elect of Heaven,
> Their strong eye darting through the deeds of men,
> Adore with steadfast unpresuming gaze
> Him Nature's essence, mind, and energy!
> And gazing, trembling, patiently ascend
> Treading beneath their feet all visible things
> As steps, that upward to their Father's throne
> Lead gradual—else nor glorified nor loved.
> . . . .
> Tis the sublime of man,
> Our noontide Majesty, to know ourselves
> Parts and proportions of one wondrous whole!
> This fraternises man, this constitutes
> Our charities and bearings.[26]

"Religious Musings" went through several revisions before its publication in *Poems on Various Subjects* (1796), and an archaeological reading of the poem might note the varied strata of influence—of Plato, Plotinus, David Hartley, Joseph Priestley, and George Berkeley. Coleridge's fellow conspirator in the Susquehanna scheme, Robert Southey, wrote in 1808 of his old friend's shifting intellectual preoccupations since the Cambridge years: "Hartley was ousted by Berkeley, Berkeley by Spinoza, Spinoza by Plato."[27]

Other thinkers would, indeed, engage Coleridge's mind, arouse his enthusiasm, and leave their marks in his poetry and philosophy as they passed like welcome but transient guests through his mental life, but with Plato Coleridge had entered into a lifelong dialogue and would never cease to listen to his *gorgeous* Nonsense." Plato's voice would never be more distant than the Chorus in an Æschylian drama. Joined with Plato's voice in this Chorus were other "mystic" philosophers who, Coleridge gratefully acknowledged, "acted in no slight degree to prevent my mind from being imprisoned within the outlines of any single dogmatic system. They contributed to keep alive the *heart* in the *head*; gave me an indistinct, yet stirring and working presentiment, that all the products of the mere *reflective* faculty partook of DEATH."[28]

Marriage and Friendship

When Coleridge left Cambridge and, at least, until 1802, he was a Unitarian in religion—or, as he prefers, "a *psilanthropist*, one of those who believe our Lord to have been the real son of Joseph, and who lay the main stress on the resurrection rather than on the crucifixion." Christ was uniquely the Son of God by adoption, and although his followers do not have the guilt of their sins eliminated through vicarious expiation, they are, nevertheless, raised by the powerful love of God to walk in newness of life. By his own account, he was a Trinitarian *ad norman Platonis* (that is, after the manner of Plato) as early as 1795. Although willing to consider "the *idea* of the Trinity a fair scholastic inference from the being of God, as a creative intelligence, . . . seeing in the same no practical or moral bearing, [he] confined it to the schools of philosophy."[29]

Unitarianism was not then as it is now. It was, basically, an Arian or Socinian sect of Christianity, and the guiding light was Joseph Priestley (1733-1804). Priestley, the author of the *Institutes of Natural and Revealed Religion*, a *History of the Corruptions of Christianity*, and a *History of the Early Opinions concerning Jesus Christ*, was one of the founding members of the Unitarian Society in Birmingham. His views succeeded in arousing violent protest, forcing him, in 1791, to flee to London. Three years later, just as Coleridge was planning to leave Cambridge, Priestley journeyed to Northumberland, Pennsylvania, where he was to spend the last decade of his life. Roughly 2,000 hardy souls followed Priestley with the intent of setting up communistic societies on the banks of the Susquehanna,[30] but Southey and Coleridge were not to be among them.

It was as a *psilanthropist*, or believer in Christ's mere humanity, that Coleridge delivered the Bristol Lectures on Revealed Religion (May-June 1795) and—after abandoning Pantisocracy and marrying Sara Fricker—produced the nine issues of *The Watchman* (March-May 1796). Financially, the periodical was a failure and the subsequent bankruptcy of its editor would have landed him in jail had not the philanthropic Unitarian Thomas Poole paid the printer's fees. At the beginning of 1797, Coleridge—now with a newborn son, Hartley—bought a cottage adjacent to Poole's mansion in Nether Stowey, and there retired to write verses for the *Morning Post* and study ethics and psychology.[31]

The brief period that Coleridge lived at Nether Stowey was one of his happiest, and as it concerns his labors as a poet, the most remarkably productive period of his life. Even though his marriage with Sara had been arranged, largely by Southey, in connection with the Pantisocracy scheme, and even though Coleridge had in fact loved Mary Evans "almost to madness,"[32] he managed surprisingly well to adapt himself to circumstances. Three days after the marriage Mrs. Coleridge was "the woman whom I love best of all created Beings."[33] "Perhaps," as Robert Barth suggests, "he could make love happen by sheer dedication and force of will."[34] At any event, and despite the fact that the pair were temperamentally ill-suited for one another, their cottage life together appears to have been, for the most part, congenial. Sara was an intelligent woman, but she had little sympathy with the abstract philosophizing and imaginative life of her husband, as is evident by her pious rebuke in the last stanza of "The Eolian Harp." What Coleridge truly required to stimulate his thought and creativity was "the society and neighborhood of one, to whom [he] could look up with equal reverence, whether [he] regarded him as a poet, a philosopher, or a man."[35]

A year had passed by since William Wordsworth had read through Coleridge's *Poems on Various Subjects.* That had been in April of 1796, immediately after its publication. Subsequently, he had been in correspondence with the author. They had, of course, discussed and shared their poetry, and Coleridge's early appreciation of Wordsworth as a poet "unrivalled among the writers of the present day in manly sentiment, novel imagery, and vivid colouring,"[36] no doubt fueled the first spark of friendship. Now, Wordsworth showed up unannounced for a brief visit at Stowey, and the two poets, both at work in composing verse dramas, discussed their prospects for publication. Coleridge was also putting the finishing touches on *Poems*, and no sooner was it in the publisher's hands, in June 1797, than he walked the distance to Racedown to return a visit to Wordsworth and his sister, Dorothy. This was the beginning of a series of exchanges that was to comprise their friendship. Richard Holmes writes, "Wordsworth wanted above all else to be a great poet, and Coleridge told him he was; Coleridge wanted above all else to be poetically wonderful and intellectually inspiring, and the Wordsworths showed him this was true. Each gave the other his ideal self; it was the essence of Romantic friendship."[37]

With the assistance of Poole, the Wordsworths were, within a month, able to relocate to the country house of Alfoxden, four miles outside of Stowey. During their move, Charles Lamb came from London on a visit, and suddenly the cottage at Stowey was overflowing with new voices and activity. In all the commotion, Sara accidentally spilled boiling milk on her husband's foot, disabling him from joining his friends on a scenic tour of the countryside. Perhaps, there was the intervention of a

jealous and mischievous Muse, attracted to Stowey by the assemblage of her devotees and eager to have Coleridge all to herself. After all, even if we take the accident
itself as a sign of ill-omen, betokening domestic chaos, the result of the accident, the
writing of the charming and brilliant conversational poem "This Lime-Tree Bower
My Prison," is equally auspicious of a year of inspired genius. It was a year that
would witness the creation of "The Rime of the Ancient Mariner," "Frost at
Midnight," "Fears in Solitude," "The Nightingale," and "Kubla Khan," and would
end in the publication of *Lyrical Ballads* (1798), Coleridge and Wordsworth's
collaborative "experiment."

Supernatural Love

In planning *Lyrical Ballads*, "it was agreed," says Coleridge, "that my endeavours
should be directed to persons and characters supernatural, or at least romantic; yet
so as to transfer from our inward nature a human interest and a semblance of truth
sufficient to procure for these shadows of imagination that willing suspension of
disbelief for the moment, which constitutes poetic faith."[38] Of the four poems by
Coleridge that were included in the first edition—"The Rime of the Ancient
Mariner," "The Nightingale," and two extracts from the Spanish drama *Osorio*—
only "The Ancient Mariner" truly satisfies this agreement.

The "semblance of truth" that we find in the experience of the Mariner is
essentially religious. Coleridge has presented us with a mythical and pre-scientific
narrative through which he has interwoven a pattern of sin, repentance, grace, and
expiation. The "hellish" shooting of the albatross manifests the Mariner's state of
sin, his inherent depravity, just as the subsequent cursing of nature amplifies his
bondage to sin, memorably symbolized in the hanging of the albatross around the
Mariner's neck. From this condition of "Life-in-Death" and spiritual drought the
sinner is released when, in silent communion with nature, he finds his heart opened
to its beauty. From this appreciation springs forth love, and from love an unconscious blessing of nature that frees the Mariner to pray and releases him from the
state of bondage. His release is, however, contingent upon his continuing in a peni-
tential mission of evangelism, spreading the good news that God remains benevo-
lently active in his creation. His closing words to the wedding guest neatly
summarize Coleridge's own message as a Unitarian preacher:

> He prayeth best, who loveth best
> All things both great and small;
> For the dear God who loveth us,
> He made and loveth all.[39]

Central to the poem is "the psychological and existential aspects of sin emphasized by Augustine,"[40] and, in fact, Coleridge's letter of 10 March 1798 to his bro-

ther George, written two weeks before the completion of the poem, declares the author's steadfast belief in original sin:

> I believe . . . that from our mothers' wombs our understandings are darkened; and even where our understandings are in the Light, that our organization is depraved, & our volitions imperfect; and we sometimes see the good without *wishing* to attain it, and oftener *wish* it without the energy that wills & performs—And for this inherent depravity, I believe, that the *Spirit* of the Gospel is the sole cure.[41]

The Mariner is, then, representative of Everyman, not only in the incapacity of his will and the deficiencies of his understanding, but also in his need of redeeming grace. Alfred Benn, responding directly to this passage from Coleridge's letter, and thinking perhaps of the author's opium addiction, makes this observation:

> One can understand . . . that the sense of sin, conceived as an overwhelming fatality, should have been particularly active with Coleridge. It is less intelligible that he should have generalised this deep and well-founded consciousness of his own delinquencies into a comprehensive indictment of human nature as such; and that he should have regarded the spirit of the Gospel as a cure for the world at large when it was proving so totally inoperative in his own particular instance.[42]

If, however, we dismiss so readily Coleridge's existential experience as peculiar to himself or to those in a state of addiction, then we would have to conclude that St. Paul, Augustine, Luther, and millions of other Christians have made the same error of generalizing their experience. On the other hand, the spiritual condition described by St. Paul in the seventh chapter of the Letter to the Romans (or by Coleridge in the sixth stanza of Part IV of "The Ancient Mariner") does, in fact, appear similar to the experience of addiction, and Coleridge's description of the human predicament apart from grace is not unlike that described by De Quincey as being peculiar to the opium-eater: "The opium-eater loses none of his moral sensibilities, or aspirations: he wishes and longs, as earnestly as ever, to realize what he believes possible, and feels to be exacted by duty; but his intellectual apprehension of what is possible infinitely outruns his power, not of execution only, but even of power to attempt."[43] The truth, then, appears to be that the common experience of depravity, of generally not being able to perform the good that one knows one ought, is merely augmented and emphasized by the concomitant state of addiction, or of generally not being able to stop doing the evil that one knows one ought to stop.

Thus, it seems reasonable to conclude that, even if it was the problem of addiction that engendered in Coleridge a more acute awareness of original sin—as inherent depravity, not as inherited guilt[44]—the addiction itself, in addition to its physical dimension and effects, merely acted as a stimulant to the symptoms of the greater ailment. Coleridge's personal condition, then, resulted in making him more profoundly aware of what is, presumably, true of everyone's condition. Moreover, *if* Coleridge found that the spirit of the Gospel was operative in his particular instance, then he would have had good reason to believe that it would, at the very least, be no less operative in the case of one not addicted. Now, Benn would, ostensibly, have us believe that, because the Gospel effected no miraculous cure, setting Coleridge free from the physiological demands and consequences of chemical addiction, that it was ineffectual in delivering him from the bondage of sin and death. I can think of no better response than that provided by Coleridge himself in his later years:

> When . . . Satan, the tempter, becomes Satan the accuser, saying in thy heart:—"This sickness is the consequence of sin, or sinful infirmity, and thou hast brought thyself into a fearful dilemma; thou canst not hope for salvation as long as thou continuest in any sinful practice, and yet thou canst not abandon thy daily dose of this or that poison without suicide. For the sin of thy soul has become the necessity of thy body, daily tormenting thee, without yielding thee any the least pleasurable sensation, but goading thee on by terror without hope. Under such evidence of God's wrath how canst thou expect to be saved?" Well may the heart cry out, "Who shall deliver me from the *body of this death*,—from this death that lives and tyranizes in my body?" But the Gospel answers—"There is a redemption from the body promised; only cling to Christ. . . . It may be better for thee to be kept humble and in self-abasement. The thorn in the flesh may remain and yet the grace of God through Christ prove sufficient for thee. Only cling to Christ, and do thy best."[45]

Although it was evident, both to his friends and enemies, that Coleridge lacked moral strength of will, yet he possessed a tender conscience and the responsive heart of a child. While always his own worst accuser, he was yet quick to praise others, and while towering above his critics as a mental giant, he yet remained remarkably free from intellectual pride. In circumstances that would have crippled worldly men with dark despair, he leant upon the staff of Christian hope and continued on the way of his pilgrimage.

Patronage

While writing "The Ancient Mariner" Coleridge frequently preached at Unitarian chapels, and on Christmas Day, 1797, he received an offer of a position as minister for a congregation at Shrewsbury. This came fast on the heels of another offer, made by the editor of the *Morning Post*, to work full time as a journalist. In a letter to Josiah Wedgwood—the maternal grandfather of Charles Darwin and patron of the literati, who had made his fortune in the pottery business—Coleridge weighed the two options carefully, as though he must decide between two evils, one of which was absolutely necessary to free him from pecuniary anxieties.[46] He decided upon the ministerial position, and set out on 13 January 1798 in order to deliver his inaugural sermon. That same morning the nineteen-year-old William Hazlitt rose before daybreak to walk the ten muddy miles that separated Wem from Shrewsbury. As he explained, "A poet and a philosopher getting up into a Unitarian pulpit to preach the Gospel, was a romance in these degenerate days, a sort of revival of the primitive spirit of Christianity, which was not to be resisted."[47]

Two days later, Coleridge paid the customary courtesy visit to the neighboring Unitarian minister. This was Hazlitt's father at Wem, and as the two conversed, young Hazlitt sat silently by, listening, admiring, hardly feeling then what he was later to call "the pleasure of hating." On the next morning, Hazlitt came down to breakfast to find that Coleridge had just received a letter from Thomas Wedgwood, the son of Josiah, "making him an offer of £150 a-year if he chose to waive his present pursuit, and devote himself entirely to the study of poetry and philosophy. Coleridge," Hazlitt mused, "seemed to make up his mind to close with this proposal in the act of tying on one of his shoes."[48] The implication behind this statement is worse than false. If the expression of his gratitude was ever hampered, it was because Coleridge accepted benevolence as an undeserving debtor. It motivated him to *prove* himself worthy. In this case, the generous patronage of the Wedg-wood's delivered Coleridge from entering into a position that he feared would have tempted him towards intellectual dishonesty, and instead gave him leisure for traveling and the reading of old folios.

Germany

As early as March, he and Wordsworth were planning their trip to Germany. During the following month, Hazlitt spent a three-weeks' visit with them, while they walked the countryside and converted their experience into verse. In mid-May, Sara had her second child, the ill-fated Berkeley, and by the end of June *Lyrical Ballads* was in the publisher's hands. Finally, on 16 September 1798, Coleridge, along with the Wordsworths and the conspicuously silent John Chester, sailed off from the harbor of Yarmouth, arriving at the port of Hamburg three days later. Within the week, Coleridge and Wordsworth visited with the poet Klopstock and, then, they split apart to follow their very different agendas. Coleridge and Chester escaped from the "Huddle and Ugliness, Stink and Stagnation" of Hamburg and made their way to the island-town of Ratzburg for the early winter. There Coleridge acquired "a tolerable sufficiency in the German language," so that by 4 January he was able to report, "I now read German as English—that is, without any *mental* translation." Already he was reading Lessing's controversial tracts, including the Reimarus "Fragments," and was planning on writing a Life of Lessing. Feeling adequately prepared in the language, Coleridge made the dangerously cold stagecoach journey in early February through Hanover to the university town of Göttingen.[49] Coleridge had no way of knowing that, as he crossed the Hartz mountains, his son Berkeley passed away.

During the month of February 1799, while Schleiermacher was in Potsdam writing the *Speeches on Religion*, Coleridge attended morning and evening classes at the university and studied transcriptions of Johann Gottfried Eichhorn's lectures on the New Testament.[50] Eichhorn (1752-1827) argued that the synoptic Gospels did not arrive at their final form until the second century, and he accounted for their similarities, particularly in the sayings of Jesus, by suggesting that these *logia* were recorded in an earlier Aramaic document, an *Ur-Evangelium*. Despite the evidence of Charles Parry's letter from Göttingen, which suggests that an intellectual antagonism was formed between Coleridge and Eichhorn,[51] there can be no doubt, in the light of *Confessions of an Inquiring Spirit*, that Eichhorn had a profound effect on the development of Coleridge's ideas regarding the doctrine of inspiration and the practice of biblical exegesis. If William Paley (1743-1805) and the English rationalist tradition in theology yet exercised any residual influence on Coleridge's thought, the impact of Lessing and Eichhorn now dissolved that influence irrevocably. Following the Wolfenbüttel librarian's famous maxim—a maxim which, by the way, Lessing himself had formulated based upon a principle first enunciated by Spinoza[52]—Coleridge would no longer regard the accidental truths of history, such as recorded in the Scriptures, as proof for the necessary truths of reason. The effect of the lectures of the Göttingen theologian was to solidly reinforce this maxim, so that twenty years later, in 1819, shortly before Coleridge began work upon the *Confessions*, he advised his youngest son, Derwent, to read Eichhorn's introductions in order that he might learn "to attach no more than the supportable weight" to the "outward evidences of our holy and spiritual Religion."[53]

Spinoza

While in Germany, Coleridge also acquired a copy of the 1789 enlarged edition of Jacobi's "On Spinoza's Doctrine," a veritable anthology of letters and lengthy quotations, not only from Spinoza, but from Bruno, Leibniz, and Kant as well. The first edition of this book had propelled Schleiermacher into a long critical engagement with the works of Spinoza and Kant, and now the second edition was to have the same effect upon Coleridge. Both Schleiermacher and Coleridge were intellectually attracted to the coherent system of Spinoza, but Schleiermacher, with his healthy, strong, and vibrant will, was not threatened by the philosophical implications of pantheism. The "freedom" that both Spinoza and Schleiermacher celebrate is not the sort of freedom from which Coleridge could derive the sustenance of hope. Only those who experience themselves as *already free* can embrace their participation in the ever-flowing will of God or Nature, whereas those who, like Coleridge, are acutely sensitive to a mind-body conflict will, in general, find it more difficult to accept that the redemptive freedom that God offers through Christ can, in any sense, be identical to the law of Nature. Still, Coleridge could not bring himself to deny that there was significant truth in Spinoza. Jacobi, having first followed his reason and having been led by it into Spinozism, extricated himself "from the affair," as he says, "by a *salto mortale*," an intellectual somersault, which alone allowed him to maintain his belief "in an intelligent personal first cause of the world."[54] It was a retreat to Christian Platonism, and as a retreat it cost Jacobi his reputation as a systematic philosopher. There is a legitimate comparison to be made between Coleridge and Jacobi, yet the poet in Coleridge would not permit a simple renunciation of what he deeply experienced as a communicative involvement with Nature. Thomas McFarland observes, Coleridge "never rejected the external world, and, in fact, ultimately found neither Kant nor Plato sufficiently orientated towards nature to satisfy him—ultimately only Christianity satisfied him."[55]

If we can accept as credible and chronologically accurate the anecdote of "Spy Nozy" in the *Biographia Literaria*—and there is reason to question its historical accuracy[56]—then Spinoza had been a topic of conversation at Stowey as early as the summer of 1797. A local constable, suspecting French democratic sympathies in Coleridge and Wordsworth, had petitioned the government to send down an agent, a spy, "*pour surveillance* of myself and friend." Later, Coleridge, probably through hearsay, learned of the details of the investigation and represented them rather comically:

> He had repeatedly hid himself, he said, for hours together behind a bank at the sea-side (our favorite seat) and overheard our conversation. At first he fancied, that we were aware of our danger; for he often heard me talk of one *Spy Nozy*, which he was inclined to interpret of himself, and of a remarkable feature belonging to him; but he was speedily convinced that it was the name of a man who had made a book and lived long ago.[57]

There is no reason for us to doubt that, twelve years after the publication of the Jacobi-Mendelssohn debate, two intellectually curious and inquiring Englishmen would be sensing the aftershocks of the controversy. Perhaps, the significance of Coleridge's account lies in the fact that, besides attesting to his sense of humor, it is indicative of the intellectual stimulus that made Europe so appealing to both poets. In fact, if we bear in mind that before the 1802-1803 publication of Paulus's two-volume edition, any edition of Spinoza's work was hardly accessible, we might fairly conclude that the mere possibility of acquiring Jacobi's work was incentive enough for Coleridge to have decided upon the trip to Germany.

Coleridge was among the first Englishmen to read through Paulus's Spinoza,[58] decades before any English translation became available. This more careful study did not, however, result in any essential change in Coleridge's position. Throughout the years of transition, while he moved toward the Christian orthodoxy of the 1816 "Confessio Fidei," there remained constant his high regard for Spinoza—but only as a philosopher, not as a theologian. For Coleridge, religion was the meeting ground of philosophy and poetry, the place where the head and the heart united.[59] He reflects in the *Biographia Literaria*, "For a very long time indeed I could not reconcile personality with infinity; and my head was with Spinoza, though my whole heart remained with Paul and John."[60] It was not until he had fully accepted Trinitarianism that Coleridge identified Spinozism, which had appeared largely consistent with religion, as ultimately antagonistic to Christian theism.

It is worthwhile to depart from the chronological progression of this study in order to broadly trace the development of Coleridge's attitude toward Spinozism. In 1803, the Unitarian Coleridge mused, "If Spinoza had left the doctrine of Miracles untouched . . . his Ethics would never, could never, have brought on him the charge of *Atheism*."[61] By 1809 the extent to which Spinoza was to be excluded from religious considerations was considerably clarified. In *The Friend*, Coleridge observes, "This is indeed the dread punishment attached by nature to habitual vice, that its impulses wax as its motives wane. . . . What then is or can be the preventive, the remedy, the counteraction, but the habituation of the intellect to clear, distinct, and adequate conceptions concerning all things . . . ." If Coleridge had ended his comment here, no disagreement with the *Ethics* would have been apparent. On the contrary, the sentiment thus given would be Spinozan. As he continues his sentence, however, Coleridge significantly limits the value of clear conceptions to "all things that are the possible object of conception" and reserves the rightful place of "deep feelings . . . for objects, which their very sublimity renders indefinite, no less than their indefiniteness renders them sublime: namely, to the Ideas of Being, Form, Life, the Reason, the Law of Conscience, Freedom, Immortality, God!"[62] Coleridge here parts company with Spinoza at the same place that Schleiermacher does, moving onward in the direction of religion on the path of "deep feelings." Like Schleiermacher, Coleridge also moves beyond Kant, recognizing that these feelings concur with and legitimize the indefinite ideas of the Reason.

If, in 1809, the *Ethics* is still heralded as a work not contrary to religion, three years later Spinozism is renounced as a "false" philosophy—because, no doubt, insofar as it is a complete system, it excludes the possibility of God as Person and Creator. Henry Crabb Robinson, who, in 1800, had followed Coleridge to Germany and had met Goethe, Schiller, and Herder, and had studied under Fichte and Schelling, made the following record in his diary for 8 November 1812, the day that Coleridge borrowed his copy of Spinoza:

> In the course of a few minutes while standing in the room, Coleridge kissed Spinoza's face at the title page, said his book was his gospel, &, in less than a minute, added that his philosophy was after all false. Spinoza's system has been demonstrated to be false, but only by that philosophy of all other philosophies. Did philosophy commence in an *It is* instead of an *I am*, Spinoza would be altogether true. And without allowing a breathing space he parenthetically asserted:—"I however believe in the doctrines of Christianity, even of the Trinity."[63]

This inconsistency in Coleridge's attitude toward Spinoza becomes glaringly obvious when, in 1815, he declares, "At no time could I believe, that *in itself* and *essentially* [the *Ethics*] is incompatible with religion, natural, or revealed: and now I am most thoroughly persuaded of the contrary."[64] *Not incompatible with natural or revealed religion!* Surely, this is the sentiment of the *psilanthropist*, not of the Augustinian who believes that the very process of human reasoning is itself a revelation of the Trinity. Neither is it his final word, for ultimately he would emerge on the side of Jacobi and declare, "Pantheism is equivalent to Atheism, and . . . there is no other Atheism actually existing, or speculatively conceivable, but Pantheism."[65] Even if Coleridge had adopted the position of Herder, noting what I believe to be a legitimate distinction between pantheism and Spinozism, the unequivocal equation of pantheism and atheism, without any parenthetical hesitations or exceptions, would appear to many critics, as it has to McFarland, as a definitive rejection of Spinoza.

Inconsistency in an author may lead his interpreters into uncertainties, but Coleridge's inconsistencies led Alfred Benn to passionate contempt. With the above passage from Robinson's diary before him, Benn remarks on Coleridge's protestation of orthodoxy, "He who comes across such declarations from lips which have kissed the lips of Spinoza, must be always asking himself how much they signify."[66] A few pages later, Benn reminds his readers, "We must bear in mind the sort of writer with whom we have to deal, a master of the most impalpable distinctions and the subtlest equivocations, a slothful, pusillanimous dreamer, in whom sincerity, if it ever existed, had been destroyed by the use of laudanum."[67] These comments, besides being hateful and generally unworthy of their author, have now gone the way of all bad criticism, and they are here resurrected not solely as a historical curiosity, but because they provide a poignant contrast to the more sympathetic and critically sensible perspective of McFarland:

> This inability either really to accept or wholeheartedly to reject pantheism is the central truth of Coleridge's philosophical activity. . . . As with the dilemma of Hamlet, who not indecisive *in himself*, is confronted with alternatives that *in themselves* admit of no right solution, so with the dilemma of Coleridge: he could not resolve the ambivalences of the *Pantheismusstreit* without diminishing one whole side of his awareness and vital commitment. And so he bore the pain of conflicting interests rather than choose the anodyne of a solution that did violence to the claims of either side in the conflict.[68]

This interpretation of Coleridge's inconsistency actually receives support from an eyewitness, for Robinson, in his entry of 8 November, goes on to note that his brother Anthony "afterwards observed C. has a comprehensive faith & love—but contrary to my expectation, he was pleased with these strange bursts in C. rather than offended with them—at least they seemed to impress him with a better opinion of his sincerity."[69]

Indecision and insincerity are enemies by nature, although they do sometimes don the same uniform. Is not this why we are advised, "Judge not by appearance, but judge with righteous judgment"?[70] Whereas Tartuffe does not cease to practice his piety before men, St. Peter publicly denies his Lord three times in a single night. St. Peter's indecision was the result of momentary moral weakness, but Coleridge's was intellectual, betraying nothing more than a respectable hesitation to decide *with finality* whether Spinozism is antagonistic to Christianity.

Samuel Agonistes

Coleridge delayed his return perhaps longer than he conscientiously could, knowing of his wife's sorrow, but the subsequent history of his relationship with Sara suggests that he had already become emotionally estranged from her. In June 1799 he departed from Göttingen with thirty pounds of books, and after an unsuccessful attempt to retrieve Lessing's manuscripts from the library at Wolfenbüttel, he slowly and reluctantly made his way back to his cottage in Stowey. The Wordsworths had now settled at Grasmere, and within a few months Coleridge had made the acquaintance of their close friends, the Hutchinsons—including Sara, the "Asra" of heartfelt verse.

But this was verse that would be written during his darkest years, years of intellectual uncertainty, vocational ambiguity, mortifying addiction, betrayed confidences, abusive editorial reviews, and—alas!—unrequited love. Between the second edition of *Lyrical Ballads* (1800) and the "Confessio Fidei" (1816), Coleridge traveled a path that has been meaningfully compared with the pilgrim's descent through the winding, ever-narrowing Inferno. It was a journey that promised no exit, even as the walls of Hell appeared to close in, and Sirenic echoes of "Abandon all hope" reproduced themselves, echoes creating echoes, creating madness, inviting destruction. Although it is beyond the scope of this chapter to provide the Malebolgian details of the journey and, moreover, beyond the capacity of this writer to imagine, let alone communicate, the Cocytian anguish of the pilgrim, no interpreter will ever sense the depth of conviction that lies beneath Coleridge's statements of Christian faith without first acquiring some sense of the existential crises that made vitally necessary a Divine Redeemer.

During these years we find in Coleridge a steady shift in the weight of his intellectual concerns. Initially, the transition is from poetry toward philosophy and literary criticism. Philosophy came to Coleridge much in the same way as she had come to Boethius, that other Christian Platonist poet-philosopher in bondage—that is, she came as a nurse:

> When she [Philosophy] saw that the Muses of poetry were present by my couch giving words to my lamenting, she was stirred a while; her eyes flashed fiercely, and said she, "Who has suffered these seducing mummers to approach this sick man? Never do they support those in

sorrow by any healing remedies, but rather do ever foster the sorrow by poisonous sweets. These are they who stifle the fruit-bearing harvest of reason with the barren briars of the passions: they free not the minds of men from disease, but accustom them thereto."[71]

Turning his mind to Kant and Schelling, Coleridge found a "medicine to ease his pains," but the medicinal value was largely anaesthetic rather than curative. This he expresses in the transcendental "Dejection: An Ode" (1802):

> For not to think of what I needs must feel,
>   But to be still and patient, all I can;
> And happy by abstruse research to steal
> From my own nature all the natural man—
> This was my sole resource, my only plan.[72]

"Dejection" is itself a witness to the fact that, although verse was still satisfying the poet's need to reflect upon and express his feelings, it was also nourishing his depression. Coleridge would never completely separate himself from his great artistic talent, yet from 1798 onwards—as he notes in a letter of 1818—his most "genial hours" were those given to abstract thought:

> Lecturing is the only means by which I can enable myself to go on at all with the great philosophical work to which the best and most genial hours of the last twenty years of my life have been devoted. Poetry is out of the question. The attempt would only hurry me into that sphere of acute feelings, from which abstruse research, the mother of self-oblivion, presents an asylum.[73]

Thus Coleridge, with his remarkable memory and conversational ability, when he wasn't writing editorials, divided his time between reading and talking.

As Schleiermacher rightly observes, in "the Scholastic mode of treatment" there is no clear divide separating philosophy from theology,[74] and Coleridge, whose theology owes much to the speculative reason, makes no effort to distinguish the two. Whereas religion itself is dependent on the practical reason, its handmaiden is, nevertheless, philosophy. Coleridge's great philosophical work, which J. C. Hare styled "the forwarding the great atonement of philosophy with religion,"[75] stretches from studies in Lessing to meditations in Leighton, that most catholic of Scottish saints,[76] and is all of one piece. This is implicitly acknowledged by every critic who puts to use a passage from *The Friend* in order to elucidate a passage from *Aids to Reflection*. However, there can be no mistaking the fact that, beginning with *The Statesman's Manual* of 1816—or even with sections of the *Biographia* penned the year before—the author turned his attention to concerns from which he increasingly made application to religion, Christianity, and the Church of England.

Carlyle noted, in his *Life of John Sterling* (1851), "Coleridge sat on the brow of Highgate Hill, in those years, looking down on London and its smoke-tumult, like a sage escaped from the inanity of life's battle."[77] With the intervention of the physician James Gillman in 1816, if Coleridge did not in fact escape life's battle, he was at least escorted off the front lines. It was under the direct supervision and rehabilitative influence of Dr. Gillman and his wife that Coleridge managed to put some order into his life and collect and publish his widely scattered thoughts. All the while, the sage of Highgate attracted a steady flow of Thursday visitors, many of which came with the sole intent to listen to the meandering meditations of this unrivaled monologuist. John Sterling made repeated visits to Coleridge at Highgate, and in 1828 wrote the following panegyric to Richard Trench, the future archbishop:

> Coleridge's monologue is perhaps better even than his writing: for it is as profound, as nobly and precisely expressed; while it exhibits more of the union of poetry and philosophy than any of his books either in verse or prose, and is perhaps more fresh and flowing, and a little more adapted to ordinary comprehension than *the Friend* or *the Biographia*; not because it deals with less important subjects, or treats them less thoroughly, but because it abounds rather more in illustration, displays more variety of style, and is helped by the most expressive voice in the world, by the most speaking face, and an eye the very organ of benevolent wisdom.[78]

Not all of Coleridge's visitors were as capable of forgetting themselves in thoughtful receptivity and silent admiration. To Carlyle, an avid talker himself, prolonged *listening* was akin to repression, and he seems never to have quite recovered from the trauma of being silenced by the rival oracle. We would do well, then, to compare his reminiscence of Coleridge with Charles Darwin's recollection: "Carlyle . . . silenced every one by haranguing during the whole dinner on the advantage of silence."[79]

Coleridge's posthumously assembled and published *Table Talk* does justice to his conversation in that it is presented in the format of seemingly disconnected fragments. And it was not his conversation only that occasionally offended on account of its abrupt transitions. His published writings too, from *The Friend* to the *Aids*, are sometimes condescendingly defined as "fragments," but none—despite the vicious thrusts of Hazlitt's reviews[80]—are devoid of penetrating analysis and profound insight. In fact, the fragment itself is an intentional literary form, expressive of a post-Kantian Romantic ideal, and so "the Romantic fragment is a *philosophical* conception."[81] With this apology made, to a few of the more imminently ponderable reflections or "fragments" of Coleridge's later years we now direct our attention.

Reason and Religion

Robinson defined Coleridge's mature philosophy, particularly as revealed in *Aids to Reflection* (1825), "as an attempt to express Kantian principles in the English language & adapt it to popular religious sentiment."[82] No doubt, Robinson had in mind Coleridge's distinction between *Reason* and *Understanding*, which receives its fullest treatment in the *Aids to Reflection*. It is a distinction that Coleridge had made as early as 1806, when he defined the former as "all such notices, as are characterized by UNIVERSALITY and NECESSITY . . . and which are evidently not the effect of any Experience, but the condition of all Experience." Reason, therefore, is "most eminently the Revelation of an immortal soul, and it's [*sic*] best Synonime—it is the forma formans, which contains in itself the law of it's [*sic*] own conceptions," whereas the Understanding is "that Faculty of the Soul which apprehends and retains the mere notices of Experience."[83]

Here we see that, although Coleridge preserves the Kantian distinction between *Vernunft* and *Verstand*, recognizing that the latter, which entails data processed through abstract categories, can never provide us with the truth of the thing-in-itself, he nevertheless moves beyond Kant's Practical Reason by endowing it with Platonic consubstantiality in its relation to the Eternal Absolute, making it "the Revelation of an immortal soul." Thus, Robert Barth warns, "One should not overestimate Kant's importance in Coleridge's thinking."[84] For Kant, the very existence of a conscience that places demands on human behavior suggests the postulates of God, freedom, and immortality. These are, then, the inferences of Practical Reason, the belief in which itself provides moral assistance. What Kant's Practical Reason does not provide, however, is knowledge. As Muirhead notes, "There is a level of thought beyond the transcendental analysis, to which the genius of Plato had penetrated, but which all the talent of Kant had failed to reach."[85]

Robinson's observation is, then, essentially incorrect. Although Kant undoubtedly did more for Coleridge than merely help him to sort through and clarify his ideas, nevertheless the basic distinction between Reason and Understanding he had already absorbed largely through his readings in Plato, the Cambridge Platonists, Shakespeare, Milton, and Bacon. Moreover, Coleridge's principal mission as a religious writer was certainly not to popularize Kant. Other English writers and lecturers had been doing this as early as 1794.[86] Nor were his efforts, like those of Fichte, motivated by a desire to complete the Critical Philosophy. On the contrary, as Spinoza is to Descartes, so is Coleridge to Kant—that is, his work is essentially in reaction against him. "His great aim," writes Charles Sanders, "was to convince the public that the truth upon which the universe rested was *not* something which men made with their minds, but that it was an invisible, immutable, infinite, and eternal force revealing a living God."[87] The Reason is vitally connected with this eternal force, so that "At the annunciation of *principles*, of *ideas*, the soul of man awakes, and starts up, as an exile in a far distant land at the unexpected sounds of his native language."[88] The Reason does not postulate Truth; it recognizes it. It is "the Power of universal and necessary Convictions, the Source and Substance of Truths above Sense, . . . having their evidence in themselves."[89]

Both Coleridge and Schleiermacher found the Kantian distinction useful in their arguments against Enlightenment rationalism. Schleiermacher had asked his cultured readers to "turn from everything usually reckoned religion" and to "fix your regard on the inward emotions and dispositions," for the outward forms that religion acquires is always determined by something other than religion itself.[90] Likewise, Coleridge prefaced his *Aids to Reflection* by stating his intent "to establish the position, that whoever transfers to the understanding the primacy due to the Reason, loses the one and spoils the other."[91] Both recognized that, to the extent that religion is dependent on Reason, it does not concern itself with quantities, qualities, and the relation of particulars in time and space. Moreover, Schleiermacher would have agreed with Coleridge's remark, "The Reason first manifests itself in man by the *tendency* to the comprehension of all as one."[92] For Schleiermacher, however, religion develops in the realm of the feelings as a response to Reason. It consists in the sense and taste for the Infinite and the feeling of absolute dependence. Although the Reason informs both the feelings and the conscience—and, ideally, they should develop at a similar pace—these two are not intrinsically united, so that religion itself does not necessitate the involvement of the moral will. For Coleridge, on the other hand, "Religion, as both the corner-stone and the key-stone of morality, must have a *moral* origin," and any pretense of the former without the latter is a bold mockery.[93] Although he recognizes the connection between the feelings and the Reason, so that "The feelings will set up their standard against the understanding whenever the understanding has renounced its allegiance to the reason,"[94] religion, nevertheless, manifests itself through the Practical Reason—that is, by means of a will that is determined in its operation by the dictates of the conscience.

The following passage from *The Friend*, in which the Reason is defined in contradistinction to the Understanding, might best be described as Kantian Platonism with Coleridge's peculiarly British emphasis on the moral ought:

> In addition to sensation, perception, and practical judgment . . . concerning the notices furnished by the organs of perception, . . . God gave us REASON, and with reason he gave us reflective SELF-CONSCIOUSNESS; gave us PRINCIPLES, distinguished from the maxims and generalizations of outward experience by their absolute and essential universality and necessity; and above all, by superadding to reason the mysterious faculty of free-will and consequent amenability, he gave us CONSCIENCE—that law of conscience, which in the power, and as the indwelling WORD, of an holy and omnipotent legislator . . . unconditionally *commands* us attribute *reality*, and actual *existence*, to those ideas and to those only, without which the conscience itself would be baseless and contradictory, to the ideas of Soul, of Free-will, of Immortality, and of God![95]

Like Kant, Coleridge makes the demands of the conscience the foundation of his belief in freedom, immortality, and God; however, unlike Kant and more in the tradition of the Cambridge Platonists and other seventeenth-century divines, such as Archbishop Leighton, Coleridge believes that the conscience itself, apart from responding to the Moral Law discerned by the Reason, dictates that we attribute reality to that which the Moral Law presupposes. The conscience is, then, as Barth notes, "the faculty which provides the element of 'ought' in the acceptance of truth."[96]

Religion consists of more than Reason and conscience. If these two, operating in conjunction, are not productive of responsive acts of obedience, then the Reason remains speculative merely. It is, then, the operation of the will or the internal predisposition that determines the action of the moral subject and, in turn, decides whether the subject is, in fact, religious or spiritual. In the Christian experience, the conscience consists "of the coincidence of the human will with reason and religion. It might, perhaps, be called a *spiritual sensation*."[97] When the will is obedient to the Reason-informed conscience, the moral subject has attained *faith*. In other words, "Faith subsists in the *synthesis* of the reason and the individual will."[98]

Redemption

Given Coleridge's experience, it is not surprising that, in the debate between Erasmus and Luther over the freedom of the will, Coleridge tended to side with Luther, but he did so without compromising his belief in free will. He was able to perform this juggling act by redefining Luther's conception of will as power. Since "Luther confounds free-will with efficient power," his actual position cannot be equated with that of modern Calvinism, which denies the existence of human will. Rather, Luther believed in a captive will, a will that is set free through the process of spiritual regeneration.[99] This is, in fact, what Coleridge argued:

> Whenever by self-subjection to this universal Light [of the Conscience], the Will of the Individual, the *particular* Will, has become a Will of Reason, the man is regenerate: and Reason is then the *Spirit* of the regenerated man, whereby the Person is capable of a quickening intercommunion with the Divine Spirit. And herein consists the mystery of Redemption, that this has been rendered possible for us.[100]

Although Coleridge clearly felt that Luther's *Bondage of the Will* describes redemption in terms more consistent with the actual experience, it is also clear from this passage that, while struggling to balance self-determination with grace, he raises his standard—unwillingly perhaps—in the camp of Erasmus, and there, with his doctrine of "self-subjection," he is as vulnerable as Erasmus to the charge of Pelagianism. Thus, he makes no contribution to the classic theological debate, except perhaps by adding one further demonstration of its unresolvable aspect.

Where Luther and Erasmus are agreed is where Coleridge takes his stand against Deism: *Transmentation* or self-change is not only beyond human power, but it is at variance with common sense.[101] Redemption is possible only through outside influence, through the intervention of a Redeemer. Furthermore, since "Whoever needs not a Redeemer is more than human," it logically follows that "the Sinless One that redeemed Mankind from Sin, must have been more than Man."[102] Therefore, argues Coleridge, "On the doctrine of Redemption depends the *Faith*, the *Duty*, of believing in the Divinity of our Lord."[103] In other words, "Christianity and Redemption are equivalent terms," for belief in the possibility of Redemption implies belief in a Divine Savior.[104]

Although Coleridge is willing to argue this point, he is fully aware that, as an argument merely, it is unfruitful unless acted upon in faith. "Believe," Coleridge advises, "and if thy belief be right, that insight which gradually transmutes faith into knowledge will be the reward of that belief."[105] How is belief transmuted into knowledge? First, belief must become faith; that is, it must be acted upon in obedience to the Reason—in this case, the Speculative Reason. Then, obedience results in experience, and experience issues in insight: "Belief is the seed, received into the will, of which the Understanding or Knowledge is the Flower, and the thing believed is the fruit. Unless ye believe (saith the Prophet) ye cannot understand."[106] Redemption is not an after-life reward contingent upon our right belief, but is rather the gift of God consequent upon our faith. "Christianity is not a Theory, or a Speculation; but a *Life*. . . . Try It." What is there to prevent the experiment that results in the experience and insight that are their own proof? "Not the strong free Mind, but the enslaved will, is the true original Infidel in this instance."[107] Thus, the answer to Original Sin is Regeneration, but the evil that prevents Regeneration is Original Sin—for what is evil if not the failure of the will to subject itself to the Reason, the failure of the individual to pursue full existence or beingness in the presence of Being, the I AM.

The Understanding and Imagination

Without doubt, the extracts from Carlyle's writings *about* Coleridge are more entertaining than the actual prose writings *of* Coleridge, and so Carlyle has played no small part in perpetuating a critical error. The Sage of Chelsea provides us with this account of Coleridge's Thursday evening conversations:

> The constant gist of his discourse was lamentation over the sunk condition of the world; which he recognised to be given-up to Atheism and Materialism. . . . The remedy, though Coleridge himself professed to see it as in sunbeams, could not, except by processes unspeakably difficult, be described to you at all. . . . But how, but how! By attending to the "reason" of man, said Coleridge, and duly chaining-up the "understanding" of man: the *Vernunft* (Reason) and the *Verstand* (Understan-

ding) of the Germans, it all turned upon these, if you could well
understand them,—which you couldn't.[108]

All that is quite clear from this passage is that Carlyle himself did not or *would not*
understand Coleridge because of his own deep intellectual prejudice against Kant.
To Carlyle, Coleridge's religious philosophy would never be anything more than a
"thrice-refined pabulum of transcendental moonshine."[109] However, it is one thing to
say, with J. S. Mill, that "The nature and laws of Things in themselves, or of the hidden causes of the phenomena which are the objects of experience, appear to us
radically inaccessible to the human faculties," and to take issue with Coleridge and
"the peculiar technical terminology" that he employs in order to argue the opposite;[110] it is quite another thing to say that the terminology itself is inaccessible to the
human faculties. Certainly, there is some merit to Baron Bunsen's address to the
Englishman who says he does not understand German speculative philosophers:
"You say you do not understand them; which I find to be a polite English expression
implying that you will not listen to them, because you think them mad, or, at least,
because you do not care to know anything about the subject itself."[111] But, what is
most misleading in Carlyle's statement is the suggestion that, for Coleridge, the
Understanding has no part in religion.

Coleridge had argued the contrary as early as *The Statesman's Manual*: "I
consider it as the contra-distinguishing principle of Christianity that in it alone . . . the
Understanding in its utmost power and opulence *culminates* in Faith, as in its crown
of Glory, at once its light and its remuneration."[112] Although this is stated with
sufficient clarity, one would think, even for Carlyle, it must be admitted that *how* the
Understanding culminates in faith is not quite so clear. Let us begin, then, by recal-
ling the function of the Understanding: "The Judgments of the Understanding are
binding only in relation to the objects of our Senses, which we *reflect* under the
forms of the Understanding,"[113] and the forms of the Understanding have to do with
"quantities, qualities, and relations of *particulars* in time and space."[114] What
separates us from animals and makes our Understanding a peculiarly *human* Understanding is the capacity of reflection and generalization, a capacity dependent
upon language. Understanding is, therefore, discursive.[115] The man who is know-
ledgeable in the sciences and well versed in language is a man of Understanding, and
"as the powers of the understanding and the intellectual graces are precious gifts of
God, . . . every Christian, according to the opportunities vouchsafed to him, is bound
to cultivate the one and acquire the other."[116]

Although the Christian is to cultivate the Understanding, it is not to be used as
the principal means of faith—despite Archdeacon Paley's *Evidences* (1794) to the
contrary. Instead, "the man of healthful and undivided intellect" uses the Understanding as a tool, "as the means not the end of knowledge,"[117] and this is because,
"from Reason alone can we derive principles which our Understandings are to
apply."[118] Now, in unison with Carlyle, we ask, "But how, but how!" Unless there
is mediation between the Reason and the Understanding, how is the Understanding

to apply the principles of the Reason and so culminate in faith? Coleridge's answer to this question presents us with his most direct departure from Spinoza and the Cambridge Platonists—as well as from the prejudices of the Enlightenment—and is, perhaps, his most brilliant contribution to the philology, if not the philosophy, of religion. It is, says Coleridge, through "the living *educts* of the Imagination"; for

> that reconciling and mediatory power, which incorporating the Reason in Images of the Sense, and organizing (as it were) the flux of the Senses by the permanence and self-circling energies of the Reason, gives birth to a system of symbols, harmonious in themselves, and consubstantial with the truths, of which they are the *conductors*.[119]

It is the power of the Imagination that bridges the gap between the Reason and the Understanding, and it does so by means of *symbols*.

Coleridge observes in the *Biographia* that the operations of the Imagination differ in degree, and he recognizes this difference by distinguishing its *primary* and *secondary* operations. The primary Imagination, as "the living Power and Agent of all human Perception," is that which makes the Understanding possible. It is the synthetic power that sustains the subjective and involuntary process by which we create the world in order to know it, "a repetition in the finite mind of the eternal act of creation in the infinite I AM." More vital to art and religion is the secondary Imagination, which is "first put in action by the will and understanding." It is, thus, a voluntary process, of which neither all are capable nor capable in the same degree. This is that "magical power" that "dissolves, diffuses, dissipates, in order to re-create," that "reveals itself in the balance or reconciliation of opposite or discordant qualities," blending and harmonizing the natural and the artificial.[120]

This secondary Imagination is that which can create and interpret what Coleridge calls the *symbol*. "By a symbol I mean, not a metaphor or allegory or any other figure of speech or form of fancy, but an actual and essential part of that, the whole of which it represents." The symbol is characterized, above all, "by the translucence of the Eternal through and in the Temporal. It always partakes of the Reality which it renders intelligible; and while it enunciates the whole, abides itself as a living part in the Unity, of which it is the representative."[121]

This is all very abstract, and an illustration may assist the comprehension. Leslie Stephen correctly notes that, in "The Ancient Mariner," "the veil of the senses is nothing but a symbolism everywhere telling of unseen and supernatural forces."[122] Let us, then, look to the role that the secondary Imagination plays in the interpretation of this epic poem. Now, the Understanding recognizes a pattern in the administration of penalties that follow upon convictions of crime and perceives that each punishment is measured according to the conviction. Therefore, when the man of mere Understanding reads of the hanging of the albatross around the mariner's neck, he recognizes the administration of a penalty for an act of crime. He may also recognize irony, in that the victim of the crime becomes the instrument of punishment. The Reason, however, comprehends the universal aspect of sin, recognizes that sin originates out of no motive other than itself, and results in a bondage of the will and separation from God. When, therefore, the man in whom the Understanding is "effectually exerted in *subordination* to and in a dependent *alliance* with . . . Reason"[123] reads of the hanging of the albatross about the mariner's neck, his Imagination interprets the event as a symbol of spiritual condemnation for sin. On the other hand, when our effectual reader, unable to put down his volume of Coleridge, hears his wife murmuring something about "an albatross around her neck," he knows immediately that *this* albatross is not a symbol, but merely a metaphor signifying an unwanted and inescapable burden.

For Coleridge, Christ is more importantly a sign than a historical figure. When asked the question, "Do you believe our Lord to have been the Son of Mary by Joseph?," Coleridge replies, "It is a point of religion with me to have no belief one way or the other. I am in this way like St. Paul, more than content not to know Christ himself according to the flesh."[124] Rather than serving the purpose of an exemplar, Christ is, as Barth suggests, "an efficacious sign which is capable of bringing about in men what it signifies for them. What Christ is, through Redemption man must become."[125] What is the Idea of which Christ is the symbol, if not Humanity as it exists in the mind of God? Christ, then, is fully God, which, once enfleshed, is necessarily fully Human, the very perfection of Humanity. The religious imagination facilitates the union of subjective and objective, and Christianity is found in the meeting of the spiritual and the historical.[126] Thus, the religious or philosophic imagination is a prerequisite to any comprehension of the hypostatic union, and "They and they only can acquire the philosophic imagination, the sacred power of self-intuition, who within them-selves can interpret and understand the symbol."[127]

Scripture

Religious communication necessarily takes place largely by means of symbols, for "An IDEA, in the *highest* sense of the word, cannot be conveyed but by a *symbol*."[128] The symbolism in the *Ancient Mariner*, to the mind of the spiritually discerning, better conveys the Idea of Sin and Redemption than would a learned disquisition on the subject, although the latter may be necessary to prepare the Understanding. Religion, says Coleridge, "consists of ideas . . . that can only be spiritually discerned, and to the expression of which words are necessarily inadequate, and must be used by accommodation."[129] Surely, this is at least one reason why the visual arts, particularly icons, have occupied so prominent a place in the Christian Church. The Protestant fear of iconolatry would have no basis if icons had not an actual and even strong appeal to the Imagination.

In their flight from the religious imagination, the iconoclasts did not, however, escape from idolatry, says Coleridge. In substituting Scripture for Reason, the Letter for the Spirit, the Printed Image for the Living God, Protestants have been guilty of *Bibliolatry*. Francis Newman, a quarter of a century later, called *Bibliolatry* "the greatest religious evil of England."[130] This term, which appears to have been coined by Lessing but first used in English by Coleridge himself, signifies an idolatry "the main error of which consists in the confounding of two distinct conceptions, Revelation by the Eternal Word, and Actuation by the Holy Spirit."[131] What is necessary is not only a distinction between the concepts of *revelation* and *inspiration*, but also a clear idea of the nature of inspiration itself.

It is Coleridge's constant premise that all religion is, necessarily, revealed, for revelation is the communication of God through the agency of Reason. Because Reason is for humans a universal witness of consubstantiality with the Divine *Logos*, that which is genuinely revealed should find a direct appeal to the Reason of any person who is sensitively receptive. Coleridge's own experience is "that in the Bible there is more *that finds me* than I have experienced in all other books put together; that the words of the Bible *find me* at greater depths of my Being; and that whatever finds me brings with it an irresistible evidence of its having proceeded from the Holy Spirit."[132] Anticipating the objection that this "irresistible evidence" is too arbitrary and would limit the concept of Biblical revelation to that which is authenticated by the reader's own experience, Coleridge proceeds to offer a concession to conservative thought. Wherever the Biblical author plainly asserts "that not only the words were given but the recording of the same enforced by the special command of God," he takes the author at his word, "with the degree of confidence proportioned to the confidence required of me by the Writer himself."[133]

All revelation, as such, is necessarily and, therefore, infallibly true. Moreover, Coleridge is willing to accept, as a matter of faith, that all Scripture is written through inspiration. He posits, then, the following two premises:

(1) All revelation is inspired and infallibly true.
(2) All Scripture is inspired.

What Coleridge insists upon is that no deduction can be drawn from these premises. Without changing the second premise to read, "All Scripture is revelation," one cannot arrive at the conclusion, "All Scripture is inspired *and* infallibly true." The question may, then, be raised, "Does not *inspiration* itself suggest infallibility or inerrancy?" To this question, Coleridge confidently answers in the negative. Inspiration implies no more than "actuation by the Holy Spirit." Since there is no reason to doubt that this may take place during the communication of matters of the Understanding, it is theoretically possible that, when such communication occurs, not only may the content of an inspired and saintly theist appreciably resemble the content of an unregenerated materialist, but—God forbid!—the work of inspiration may actually contain more numerous or consequential errors in detail. Thus, it is we ourselves who err when we read Scripture with the expectation that the inspired saint is also an infallible historian and scientist.

A hermeneutics peculiar to the Scriptures receives no more warrant from Coleridge than it had from Spinoza. The idea that "we must not interpret St. Paul as we may and should interpret any other honest and intelligent Writer and Speaker" is handled with brusque contempt. The difference between St. Paul and Shakespeare is one of degree, not of kind. Although the Bible contains more revelation than any other collection of books and is fully inspired, it is nevertheless true that all literature may contain revelation, and any author who is led by Reason to faith may be actuated by the Spirit. Furthermore, the inspiration of a writer makes no claim upon the reader until his words are *received* under the actuation of the Spirit. A preacher may argue till doomsday that the Scriptures are inspired—"yet, *for* you they are not unless the truth, they contain, enter your understanding & marry with your desires and impulses."[134] Faith is requisite to the acknowledgment of inspiration, just as it is to the recognition of miracle. God's presence in the world is invisible except to the eye of faith, but the very purpose of interpretation is to appeal to the Understanding.

Coleridge was years ahead of his English contemporaries in his knowledge of the higher biblical criticism, and it is clear that he recognized that, unless his countrymen's expectations of Scripture and their understanding of the claims that Scripture made of itself were to change, their faith stood in jeopardy. His own experience was that the doctrine of biblical infallibility "plants the Vineyard of the Word with Thorns . . . and places snares in its pathways,"[135] and he had no reason not to suppose that those same snares would become deathtraps for unprepared pilgrims.

Confessions and Schleiermacher

With the spiritual welfare of young divinity students, like his son Derwent, in mind, Coleridge placed the completed manuscript of *Confessions of an Inquiring Spirit* in his publisher's hands in 1824, intending originally to have these Letters published as an appendix to *Aids to Reflection*. However, before the completed volume was ready for publication in the following year, he decided to withdraw the Letters as potentially damaging to the reception of the *Aids*.[136] If one considers the fate of Connop Thirlwall's introduction to and translation of Schleiermacher's *Critical Essay on St. Luke's Gospel*, also published in 1825, Coleridge's caution appears to have been well founded. Coleridge's publisher set the Letters aside and lost them. When they were recovered, a year later, the author had decided to include them in a series of six disquisitions. This anthology was, however, never finished, and so, although the Letters were circulated among friends, including Julius Charles Hare and Thomas Arnold, the *Confessions* was not published until 1840, years after Coleridge's death.

The *Confessions* reveals the abiding influence that Lessing and Eichhorn had upon Coleridge's critical thought, but it does not reflect Coleridge's meditations on Schleiermacher. This is simply because Coleridge did not begin to read Schleiermacher's work with any serious interest until 1826, when his publisher, who had been converted to Christianity through the influence of the *Aids*, sent him a copy of Thirlwall's translation.[137] By this time, of course, Coleridge had completed almost all of his own work. When we consider that both Coleridge and Schleiermacher had studied deeply in Spinoza, the Critical Philosophy, and transcendentalism in general, and that, consequently, many of their ideas are notably similar, the fact that Coleridge did not even read the *Speeches* until after the *Critical Essay* may appear to us as somewhat puzzling, but it is not a fact that we should overlook. One may place Coleridge among "the first Englishmen to read Schleiermacher," but one may not suggest that Coleridge's "ability to express what he found there in *our* ways of thinking . . . is one of the chief sources of his continuing value for us today."[138] Coleridge was not a popularizer of the thought of Schleiermacher; if he were, he would not rightly be regarded as the Father of the Broad Church movement.[139] Moreover, because Schleiermacher's influence was initially restricted to the handful of scholars who could read German, Coleridge was the principal intellectual stimulus in the early years of the movement. It was not until his star began to fade in the late 1850s that the more distant but brighter star of Schleiermacher became a clear and guiding light. One might, therefore, argue that Coleridge prepared certain minds for a more ready acceptance of Schleiermacher. Even then, however, the moral Reason of Coleridge—and of the Cambridge Platonists before him—maintained its hold in English theology, at least to the extent that theology remained the science of the Church and allied with pastoral care and homiletics.

The National Church

The Church and its relation to the State were the subjects of Coleridge's final book, *On the Constitution of Church and State, according to the Idea of Each*, published in 1830. In this work Coleridge expresses the "Idea" of a State by, first, borrowing the notion of "three estates" from the polity of the Three Estates of the sixteenth-century Franche-Comté. Although this is not the place for a detailed comparison, we might note that both represent the clergy as an estate, and whereas the Estates of the Comté include the nobility and the towns' high office-holders, Coleridge recognizes the "possessors of land" and the "mercantile, manufacturing, distributive, and professional bodies" as the powers, respectively, of permanence and progression.[140] "The object of the national Church," says Coleridge, is "to secure and improve that civilization, without which the nation could be neither permanent nor progressive." The national church is not, then, essential to the initial establishment of a State, but it is necessary to ensure "the harmonious development of those qualities and faculties that characterize our humanity."[141]

Crucial to an understanding of Coleridge's conception of the national or established church is its differentiation from the catholic or invisible church. The latter is the *ecclesia*, "the communion of such as are called out of the world." All true Christians are, by virtue of their salvation, members of this one body of Christ, whereas the national church, the *enclesia*, is no more than "an order of men chosen in and of the realm, . . . constituting an estate of that realm."As such, it is not a sect or a division, but rather a civilizing structure. Another name for the national church is the Clerisy, which, "in its primary acceptation and original intention, comprehended the learned of all denominations"—that is, *professional* denominations—"in short, all the so-called liberal arts and sciences, the possession and application of which constitute the civilization of a country, as well as the theological."[142]

Coleridge's Clerisy is not unlike the French Academy admired by Matthew Arnold, an authority established by the State for the purpose of imposing a high standard in matters of intellect, taste, and professional performance. Moreover, the Clerisy is not necessarily even Christian. If the citizens of the State are members of the *ecclesia*, then it stands to reason that the *enclesia* will be constituted of Christians, but the Clerisy is not absolutely dependent on any particular religion: "Christianity . . . [is] no essential part of the being of the national Church, however conducive or even indispensable it may be to its well being."[143] But, this is not to say that it could, theoretically, include Catholics. There are, says Coleridge, "only two absolute disqualifications." Practically, there is only one. The first disqualification is "allegiance to a foreign power, or the acknowledgement of any other visible head of the Church, but our sovereign lord the King." The second disqualifying mark is subordinate to the first: "compulsory celibacy in connection with, and in dependence on, a foreign and extra-national head."[144] Coleridge had read Joseph Blanco White's *Practical and Internal Evidence against Catholicism* (1825) with approval,[145] and concluded, apparently, that Henry VIII had been right in his determination that Thomas More and John Fisher were no longer to be trusted as loyal servants of the State.

If Coleridge had completed *On the Constitution* a year earlier, he may not have felt a need to preach on the necessary disqualifications of Catholics. Southey, Blanco White, and many others, had already fulfilled, and with admirable depth and fervor, what they conceived to be their Protestant duty in this regard. Nevertheless, in April 1829 George IV, despite his personal inclinations, signed the Catholic Emancipation Bill that days earlier had been approved by the House of Lords. The majority of Englishmen were opposed to it, but the real threat of civil war in Ireland ultimately persuaded the government to recognize the claims of Roman Catholics. Although it was not an enlightened conscience that supplied the principal motivation behind the bill, the British government was, nevertheless, more trusting than Coleridge, for when Parliament reassembled, three Catholic peers were allowed to take their seats—after taking an oath of allegiance. Coleridge's remarks may, then, be interpreted as a refusal to recognize the constitutionality of Parliament's reform.

Toleration

The basis of Coleridge's distrust of Roman Catholics was, of course, political. Although he passionately disagreed with the doctrine of transubstantiation and thought the virginity of Mary a superfluous tradition, it was not because of any strictly *religious* difference that he begrudged Catholics political equality. In fact, Coleridge's pronouncements concerning doctrinal differences in religious matters contributed toward creating a climate of opinion that became characteristic of the Broad Church movement.

Coleridge adhered to Benjamin Whichcote's belief that "it is better for us, that there shou'd be *Difference* of Judgement; if we keep *Charity*."[146] Disagreement should not be sought out, but neither should it be avoided, as it indicates a need for discussion and clarification of the truth. Therefore, says Coleridge in *The Friend*, "As much as I love my fellow-men, so much and no more will I be *intolerant* of their Heresies and Unbelief—and I will hold forth the right hand of fellowship to every individual who is equally intolerant of that which he conceives such in me." In the same essay he follows Jacobi in defining "the only true spirit of Toleration" as a "conscientious toleration of each other's intolerance."[147] No doubt, Coleridge, with his natural talent at oratory, welcomed a good debate, but the genuineness of his love for truth and for truth seekers in general can hardly be doubted. As he notes in his *Lay Sermon*, an absence of quarrels in a marriage "would excite a strong suspicion of a comparative *indifference* in the feelings of the parties towards each other, who can love so coolly where they profess to love so well."[148]

His later approach to Unitarians (*psilanthropists*) may shed light as well on his attitude toward Spinozists. Coleridge here responds indignantly to the assertion that he had denied Unitarians to be members of the *ecclesia*:

> God forbid! For how should I know, what the piety of the Heart may be, or what Quantum of Error in the Understanding may consist with a saving Faith in the intentions and actual dispositions of the whole moral Being in one Individual? Never will God reject a soul that sincerely loves him: be his speculative opinions what they may: and whether in any given instance certain opinions, be they Unbelief, or Misbelief, are compatible with a sincere Love of God, God only can know.—But this I have said, and shall continue to say: that if the Doctrines, the sum of which I *believe* to constitute the Truth in Christ, *be* Christianity, then Unitarian*ism* is not, and vice versa.[149]

If Trinitarian*ism* is Christianity, then Unitarian*ism* is a heresy, but whereas "man may perchance determine, *what* is a heresy; . . . God only can know, *who* is a heretic."[150] The difference is cause for argument, but not for division. All that is strictly essential in Christianity is "that the same spirit should be growing in us which was in the fulness of all perfection in Christ Jesus."[151] Only that which impedes this development might rightly be made a cause of separation. Division in the church is justified only when unity would inevitably result in a direct affront to the moral conscience.

The Heart *and* the Head

Coleridge also bequeathed to the Broad Church movement his stance on the legitimate place of the intellect in a life of faith. His antagonism toward Paley was not, as we have seen, an attack on the role of the Understanding in religion, but was rather an attack on the Understanding's usurpation of the role of the Reason. When the Understanding is not subservient to the Reason, it attempts to erect faith on the fragile foundation of "evidences." In *Natural Theology or Evidences of the Existence and Attributes of the Deity Collected from the Appearances of Nature* (1802), Paley—possibly borrowing from Culverwell's rich store of metaphor or from Glanvill's analogies—made the famous teleological argument that, just as we must infer from an observation of the mechanism of a watch that "there must have existed, at some time, and at some place or other, an artificer or artificers who formed it for the purpose which we find it actually to answer: who comprehended its construction, and designed its use," so too must we infer from "the contrivances of nature," which "surpass the contrivances of art," the existence of an intelligent Creator.[152] Paley's "evidences" for the existence of God are objects of sensation, perception, and practical judgment; as such, they appeal to the Understanding and attempt to build a house of faith on sand.

Although Coleridge did not go nearly as far as Søren Kierkegaard (1813-1855) in denying place of importance to the Understanding in matters of religion, their attitude toward Christian "evidences" is, nevertheless, significantly similar. Anti-Climacus, in *The Sickness unto Death*, aims, paradoxically, to defend Christianity by rescuing it from all defenses:

> One can see now how extraordinarily stupid it is to defend Christianity, how little knowledge of humanity it betrays, how it connives if only unconsciously with offense by making Christianity out to be some miserable object that in the end must be rescued by a defence. It is therefore certain and true that the person who first thought of defending Christianity in Christendom is *de facto* a Judas No. 2: he too betrays with a kiss, except his treason is that of stupidity. To defend something is always to discredit it.[153]

Kierkegaard is less polite than Coleridge, less in need of sympathy and, thus, less concerned about giving offense. Still, the frustration that Coleridge felt in reaction to the popularity of Paley is patent: "*Evidences* of Christianity! I am weary of the Word. Make a man feel the *want* of it; rouse him, if you can, to the self-knowledge of his *need* of it; and you may safely trust it to its own Evidence."[154] Coleridge places the evidences of Christianity where the Gospels place them, in the experience that is itself both the cause and the effect of faith. This is not to discredit philosophy or theology, for "all effective faith pre-supposes knowledge and individual conviction."[155] Moreover, "the energies of the intellect . . . are necessary to keep alive the substantial faith in the heart."[156] An un-thinking or anti-intellectual Christian is, for Coleridge, an oxymoron. The Under-standing, if it is not informed, cannot effectively serve the Reason, and to the extent that it is uninformed, it will be ineffectual both as an interpreter of the symbolic and as a guide in the application of the dictates of the Reason. As long as the Under-standing is subordinate to the Reason, there can be no risk involved in doubt. Coleridge counsels, "Never be afraid to doubt, if only you have the disposition to believe, and doubt in order that you may end in believing the Truth." The real danger to every Christian—and to Christianity itself—is not honest doubt, but uninformed belief, for "he, who begins by loving Christianity better than Truth, will proceed by loving his own Sect or Church better than Christianity, and end in loving himself better than all."[157]

Prefatory Conclusion

Dogmatic theologians now give little attention to Coleridge, and the practicality and even viability of the philosophical basis of natural theology is too often doubted both by secular philosophers and theologians to recommend Coleridge's work as a fertile source of religious truth. Four decades ago, Howard E. Root, fellow and dean of Emmanuel College, lamented that "what we have to face today is a divorce of natural theology from the mind and imagination of the most sensitive segment of our society." That observation is certainly no less true today, and if Root's message to his colleagues at Cambridge could be heard today, it would sound forth a vindication of all that Coleridge represented as a Christian thinker:

> Natural theology must begin with the natural world, the external world in which we live and the internal world which gives our life and experience its impetus and shape. . . . The best text-books for contemporary natural theologians are not the second-hand theological treatises but the living works of artists who are in touch with the springs of creative imagination.[158]

The Sage of Highgate was uniquely qualified, appointed by heaven and earth, to fulfill the office of natural theologian. Whether he succeeding in bridging the gulf between natural and dogmatic theology may be safely left open to disputation without at all jeopardizing his stature as Nature's Priest.

When Coleridge died on the morning of 25 July 1834, his seminal influence had so promiscuously impregnated England that F. D. Maurice, writing in 1860, could say, "His words, little as they might be understood or heeded at the time, wrought so secretly and so effectually upon the minds of his younger contemporaries, that there is perhaps no Conservative speech or pamphlet of our day which is not different from what it would have been if the Essays in the 'Friend' had not been written."[159] As Vidler has noted, "It was characteristic of Coleridge to scatter seed-thoughts that fertilized in other minds."[160] Coleridge might have protested in Pauline fashion, demurely pointing out the fact that whereas he scattered seed and others watered, God gave the increase. Even so, since those fertilized minds include Thomas Arnold, Julius and Augustus Hare, Frederick Denison Maurice, Charles Kingsley, and Matthew Arnold, the Broad Church movement may, as a generalization, be called "the Coleridgean movement,"[161] and Coleridge is justly given the paternal status of "Father of the Broad Church movement."

Frederick W. Farrar, in his Bampton Lectures of 1885, remarked, "Fifty years ago the Shibboleth of popular orthodoxy was the indiscriminate anathema of 'German theology.' If in these later days the Church of England has made an immense advance, the progress is perhaps more due to Samuel Taylor Coleridge than to any ordained or professional theologian."[162] To relate in this chapter, even briefly, the history of Coleridge's influence upon the Broad Church would be redundant, since the outlines of that history will become increasingly evident in the chapters that follow. Instead, the words of Thomas Arnold, in a letter of 1839 to John Taylor Coleridge, followed by a few words from Dr. Arnold's worshipful pupil, may serve as a fitting conclusion to this chapter and a transition to the next:

> I have just got the fourth volume of your Uncle's Literary Remains, which makes me regard him with greater admiration than ever. He seems to hold that point which I have never yet been able to find in any of our English Divines, and the want of which so mars my pleasure in reading them. His mind is at once rich and vigorous, and comprehensive and critical; while the [ethos] is so pure and so lively all the while. He seems to have loved Truth really, and therefore . . . she filled him, as it were, heart and mind, embuing him with her very self, so that all his being comprehended her fully and loved her ardently; and that seems to me to be true wisdom.[163]

"Beauty and wisdom" were the two qualities of Coleridge's writings that most impressed themselves on the mind of Arthur Penrhyn Stanley. In these Coleridge's writings seemed to surpass all others; but, there was one quality lacking—clarity: "If he had but been able to write like Arnold, what a man he would have been!"[164]

Notes

1. S. T. Coleridge, "On Receiving an Account That His Sister's Death Was Inevitable" line 14, in *Poetical Works*, ed. Ernest Hartley Coleridge (New York: Oxford University Press, 1912), 20.

2. See, for example, H. Crabb Robinson's note of 24 Mar. 1811: "I recollect too . . . his saying that he envied Wordsworth his having had a sister & that his own character had suffered from the want of a sister" (*Blake, Coleridge, Wordsworth, Lamb, Etc.: Selections from the Remains of Henry Crabb Robinson*, ed. Edith J. Morley [New York: AMS Press, 1967], 38).

3. Coleridge, "To a Friend" lines 12-19a, in *Poetical Works*, 78-79; first published in *Poems on Various Subjects* (1796). Cf. Letter to Edith Fricker, 17 Sept. 1794: "I *had* a Sister—an only Sister. Most tenderly did I love her! Yea, I have woke at midnight, and wept—because *she was not*" (*Collected Letters of Samuel Taylor Coleridge*, ed. Earl Leslie Griggs, 6 vols. [Oxford: Clarendon Press, 1956-1959], 1:102).

4. Coleridge, "To the Rev. George Coleridge" lines 17-19a, in *Poetical Works*, 174.

5. See, for example, *Biographia Literaria: Or Biographical Sketches of My Literary Life and Opinions*, 2 vols., ed. James Engell and W. Jackson Bate, vol. 7 of *The Collected Works of Samuel Taylor Coleridge* (Princeton: Princeton University Press, 1983), 1:16.

6. Richard Holmes, *Coleridge: Early Visions, 1772-1804* (New York: Pantheon, 1989), 24.

7. *Collected Letters*, 3:261.

8. Coleridge, *Biographia Literaria*, 1:15-16.

9. James Gillman, *The Life of Samuel Taylor Coleridge* (London: William Pickering, 1838), 20-24; Holmes, *Coleridge: Early Visions*, 28-30.

10. Coleridge, *Biographia Literaria*, 1:11.

11. Thomas De Quincey, *Confessions of an English Opium-Eater and Other Writings* (New York: Oxford University Press, 1996), 68.

12. "To the Rev. George Coleridge" line 29, in *Poetical Works*, 174.

13. *Collected Letters*, 1:295.

14. Alec R. Vidler, *F. D. Maurice and Company: Nineteenth-Century Studies* (London: SCM, 1966), 209.

15. John H. Muirhead, *Coleridge as Philosopher* (1930; reprint, New York: Humanities Press, 1970), 38. Thomas Taylor (1758-1835), a London bank clerk who believed in the historic personality of Orpheus and defended neo-Pythagorean mathematics as scientifically valid, devoted himself to translating works by Plato, Aristotle, Plotinus, Proclus, Porphyry, and other Greek authors (*Concise DNB, Complete to 1930* [Oxford: Oxford University Press, 1930], 1280). His publications include *Concerning the Beautiful; or, A Paraphrased Translation from the Greek of Plotinus, Ennead I, Book VI* (London: T. Payne and Son, B. White and Son, and G. Nicol, 1787) and *Five Books of Plotinus* (London: Printed for E. Jeffrey, 1794).

16. William Hazlitt, "Mr. Coleridge," *The Spirit of the Age, or Contemporary Portraits* (1825), in *Selected Writings*, ed. Ronald Blythe (New York: Penguin Classics, 1982), 232-44, 237.

17. Coleridge, "The Eolian Harp" lines 44-48, in *Poetical Works*, 102.

18. Ralph Cudworth, *The True Intellectual System of the Universe*, I.iii.37, 2 vols. (London: Printed for Richard Royston, Bookseller, 1678; facsimile reprint, New York: Garland Publishing, 1978), 1:155, 155b (after 156).

19. One compromise between traditional theism and pantheism is *panentheism*, the belief that all things exist in God. This term was first coined by K. C. F. Krause to describe his own position, which can be summarized by two propositions: (1) All things are God; (2) God is not equal to all things (Thomas McFarland, *Coleridge and the Pantheist Tradition* [New York: Oxford University Press, 1969], 268).

20. McFarland, 268.

21. Coleridge, "Religious Musings" lines 130b-32, in *Poetical Works*, 114.

22. See, for example, "Fears in Solitude" line 188, in *Poetical Works*, 262.

23. Coleridge, *Biographia Literaria*, 1:144-46.

24. *The Notebooks of Samuel Taylor Coleridge*, ed. Kathleen Coburn and Merton Christensen, 4 vols. (Princeton: Princeton University Press, 1990), 3:3593.

25. Ronald C. Wendling, *Coleridge's Progress to Christianity: Experience and Authority in Religious Faith* (London: Associated University Presses, 1995), 161.

26. Coleridge, "Religious Musings" lines 45b-53, 126b-30a, in *Poetical Works*, 111, 113-14.

27. Muirhead, 46.

28. Coleridge, *Biographia Literaria*, 1:152.

29. Coleridge, *Biographia Literaria*, 1:179-80, 204.

30. Holmes, *Coleridge: Early Visions,* 89.

31. Coleridge, *Biographia Literaria*, 1:187.

32. *Collected Letters*, 1:113; cf. 1:170.

33. *Collected Letters*, 1:160; cf. "My Sara—best beloved of human beings" ("To the Nightingale" line 24, in *Poetical Works*, 94).

34. Robert J. Barth, S.J., *Coleridge and the Power of Love* (Columbia: University of Missouri Press, 1988), 32.

35. Coleridge, *Biographia Literaria*, 1:188.

36. "Lines Written at Shurton Bars" line 5 n., in *Poetical Works*, 97.

37. Holmes, *Coleridge: Early Visions*, 150.

38. Coleridge, *Biographia Literaria*, 2:6.

39. Coleridge, "The Rime of the Ancient Mariner" lines 614-17, in *Poetical Works*, 209.

40. J. A. Stuart, "The Augustinian 'Cause of Action' in Coleridge's *Rime of the Ancient Mariner,*" *Harvard Theological Review* 60, no. 2 (1967): 177-211, 179.

41. *Collected Letters*, 1:396.

42. Alfred William Benn, *The History of English Rationalism in the Nineteenth Century*, 2 vols. (New York: Russell and Russell, 1962), 1:239. Philip C. Rule, S.J., refers to this *History* as "an incredibly bigoted book" ("Coleridge's Reputation as a Religious Thinker: 1816-1972," *Harvard Theological Review* 67 [1974], 289-320, 300). Benn is anticipated by Moncure D. Conway: "When I say that the evil intellectual influence of that period was represented by Coleridge, I do not wish to say anything to the personal discredit of that eminent man" (*The Parting of the Ways* [Finsbury: Printed for the Author, 1872], 8).

43. De Quincey, 67.

44. Coleridge insists that original sin "stands in no relation whatever to Time, can neither be called *in* time nor *out of* time" (*Aids to Reflection*, ed. John Beer, vol. 9 of *The Collected Works of Samuel Taylor Coleridge* [Princeton: Princeton University Press, 1993], Aph Sp Rel B Xb, Comment, 287). He is, furthermore, in agreement with Schleiermacher's observation: "The idea of a change in human nature entailed by the first sin of the first pair has no place among the propositions which rank as utterances of our Christian consciousness" (*The Christian Faith*, 2nd ed., ed. H. R. Mackintosh and J. S. Stewart [Edinburgh: T. & T. Clark; New York: Charles Scribner's, 1928; reprint, New York: Harper and Row, 1963], 72.3; 298).

45. Henry Nelson Coleridge, ed., *The Literary Remains of Samuel Taylor Coleridge*, 4 vols. (London: Pickering, 1839), 4:29-30.

46. *Collected Letters*, 1:366. Samuel Smiles has a brief biographical section on Josiah Wedgwood in *Self-Help; with Illustrations on Conduct and Perseverance* (1859).

47. William Hazlitt, "My First Acquaintance with Poets," *The Liberal* (1823). Reprint, *Selected Writings*, 44-45. In identifying Coleridge as both a poet and a philosopher, Hazlitt was extending what he knew the author of the *Biographia* would recognize as high praise, for Coleridge, in reference to Shakespeare and Milton, had observed, "No man was ever yet a great poet, without being at the same time a profound philosopher" (*Biographia Literaria* 2:25-26). However, later, in *The Spirit of the Age, or Contemporary Portraits* (1825), Hazlitt suggests that, "in trying to subject the Muse to *transcendental* theories," Coleridge failed as both poet and philosopher (*Selected Writings*, 234).

48. Hazlitt, "My First Acquaintance," 46-51.

49. *Collected Letters*, 1:432-55; Coleridge, *Biographia Literaria*, 2:191-92, 1:205-06.

50. Eichhorn's lectures on the New Testament were published in the three-volume *Introduction to the New Testament* (1804-1815). The equally long *Introduction to the Old Testament* had been published in 1787, followed by introductions to the Apocalypse (2 vols., 1791) and to the inter-testamental Apocrypha (4 vols., 1795).

51. Holmes, *Coleridge: Early Visions*, 229; reference to Clement Carlyon, *Early Years and Late Reflections*, 2 vols. (1836), 1:100-01.

52. Gotthold Lessing, "On the Proof of the Spirit and of Power," in *Lessing's Theological Writings*, trans. Henry Chadwick (Stanford: Stanford University Press, 1956), 53. Spinoza, in the *Theological-Political Treatise* (chap. 4), argues that the knowledge of God is "a knowledge deriving from general axioms that are certain and self-evident, and so belief in historical narratives is by no means essential to the attainment of our supreme good" (trans. Samuel Shirley [Indianapolis: Hackett Publishing Co., 1998], 52).

53. *Collected Letters*, 4:929.

54. Friedrich H. Jacobi, *Letters to Herr Mendelssohn on the Doctrine of Spinoza* (Breslau, 1785; reprinted in H. Scholtz, ed., *The Main Writings Relative to the Pantheism Debate between Jacobi and Mendelssohn*, Berlin, 1916; reprinted in *The Spinoza Conversations between Lessing and Jacobi*, trans. and ed. G. Vallee, J. B. Lawson, and C. G. Chapple (New York: University Press of America, 1988), 78-125, 88.

55. McFarland, 129.

56. *Vide* Holmes, *Coleridge: Early Visions*, 159.

57. Coleridge, *Biographia Literaria*, 1:193-94.

58. Coleridge borrowed the two volumes from Henry Crabb Robinson and kept them for one year, between November 1812 and November 1813 (Cf. *Blake, Coleridge, Wordsworth, Lamb, Etc.: Selections from the Remains of Henry Crabb Robinson*, 134, and *Collected Letters*, 3:461).

59. In the *Lay Sermon* of 1817, Coleridge wrote, "Religion is the Poetry and Philosophy of all mankind; unites in itself whatever is most excellent in either" (*Lay Sermons*, ed. R. J. White, vol. 6 of *The Collected Works of Samuel Taylor Coleridge* [Princeton: Princeton University Press, 1972], 197).

60. Coleridge, *Biographia Literaria*, 1:201.

61. *Notebooks*, 1:1379.

62. Coleridge, *The Friend: A Series of Essays in Three Volumes to Aid in the Formation of Fixed Principles in Politics, Morals, and Religion with Literary Amusements Interspersed* (1818; reprint, *The Friend*, 2 vols., ed. Barbara Rooke, vol. 4 of *The Collected Works of Samuel Taylor Coleridge* (Princeton: Princeton University Press, 1969), 1:105-06.

63. Morley, *Blake*, 134. From Göttingen, in 1801, Robinson wrote, "Coleridge I heard became a convert to [Spinoza] in Germany" (*Crabb Robinson in Germany, 1800-1805*, ed. Edith J. Morley [London: Oxford University Press, 1929], 74).

64. Coleridge, *Biographia Literaria*, 1:152-53.

65. *Literary Remains*, 4:223-24.

66. Benn, 1:245.

67. Benn, 1:262-63.

68. McFarland, 107.

69. Robinson, 134.

70. Gospel of St. John 7:24.

71. Boethius, *The Consolation of Philosophy* I.i., trans. W. V. Cooper (New York: The Modern Library, 1943), 4.

72. Coleridge, "Dejection: An Ode" lines 87-91, in *Poetical Works*, 367.

73. *Collected Letters*, 4:893.

74. Friedrich Schleiermacher, *The Christian Faith* 28.3, 1:122.

75. Julius Charles Hare, "Samuel Taylor Coleridge and the English Opium-Eater," *The British Magazine and Monthly Register* 7 (1835), 15-27, 23.

76. *Vide* John Tulloch's St. Giles' lecture on Archbishop Leighton in *Scottish Divines* (Edinburgh: Macniven and Wallace, 1883), 109-48.

77. Thomas Carlyle, *The Life of John Sterling*, pt. 1, chap. 7 (1851; reprint, New York: P. F. Collier and Son, 1901), 54.

78. Sterling to Trench, 16 May 1828, in Mary Trench, ed., *Richard Chenevix Trench, Archbishop: Letters and Memorials*, 2 vols. (London: Kegan Paul, Trench and Co, 1888), 1:8. Julius Charles Hare, "Sketch of the Author's Life," in *Essays and Tales, by John Sterling*, 2 vols. (London: John W. Parker, 1848), 1:1-232, 27-28.

79. Charles Darwin, *Autobiography*, ed. Nora Barlow (New York: W. W. Norton, 1958), 113. This observation was, by no means, uncommon. Anna Maurice, the wife of the Victorian theologian, is noted to have said, "Mr. Carlyle has been here talking for hours in praise of silence" (*The Life of Frederick Denison Maurice*, ed. Frederick Maurice, 2 vols. [New York: Charles Scribner's Sons, 1884], 1:229), and Principal Shairp, in his biographical sketch of Thomas Erskine, refers to Carlyle as "the sage who has praised silence so well, but fortunately does not practice it" (John Campbell Shairp, *Portraits of Friends* [Boston: Houghton, Mifflin and Co., 1889], 104).

80. See, for example, William Hazlitt's pre-emptive strike against *The Statesman's Manual* in the *Examiner* (December 1816): "Of all the cants that ever were canting in this canting world, this is the worst!"; "What wretched stuff is all this!"; "Greater nonsense the author could not write, even though he were inspired expressly for the purpose" (J. R. De J. Jackson, ed., *Samuel Taylor Coleridge: The Critical Heritage*, 2nd ed., 2 vols. [New York: Routledge, 1995], 1:253-62).

81. Rodolphe Gasché, "Ideality in Fragmentation," Forward to *Philosophical Fragments* by Friedrich Schlegel, trans. Peter Firchow (Minneapolis: University of Minnesota Press, 1991), vii-xxxii, ix-x.

82. Morley, *Blake*, 88.

83. *Collected Letters*, 2:1198.

84. Robert J. Barth, S.J., *Coleridge and Christian Doctrine* (New York: Fordham University Press, 1987), 25.

85. Muirhead, 83.

86. Ann Loades mentions F. A. Nitsch, A. F. M. Willich, and John Richardson as English translators and popularizers of Kant in the last decade of the eighteenth century ("Coleridge as Theologian: Some Comments on His Reading of Kant," *The Journal of Theological Studies* 29 [1978], 410-26, 412-14.

87. Charles Richard Sanders, *Coleridge and the Broad Church Movement* (Durham, N.C.: Duke University Press, 1942), 27.

88. Coleridge, *The Statesman's Manual*, ed. R. J. White, vol. 6 of *The Collected Works of Samuel Taylor Coleridge* (Princeton: Princeton University Press, 1972), 24.

89. Coleridge, *Aids*, Aph Sp Rel B VIIIb, 216.

90. Schleiermacher, *On Religion: Speeches to Its Cultured Despisers*, trans. John Oman (Louisville: Westminster/John Knox Press, 1994), 18, 33.

91. Coleridge, *Aids*, Preface, 8.

92. Coleridge, *Statesman's Manual*, 60.

93. Coleridge, *Biographia Literaria*, 1:202; *The Friend*, 1:409.

94. Coleridge, *Friend*, 1:432.

95. Coleridge, *Friend*, 1:112.

96. Barth, *Coleridge and Christian Doctrine*, 28.

97. Coleridge, *Statesman's Manual*, Appendix C, 66-67.

98. Coleridge, "Essay on Faith," in *Literary Remains*, 4:437-38.

99. See Coleridge's notes on Luther's *Table Talk* (*Literary Remains*, 4:20) and *Aids*, 159-60.

100. Coleridge, *Aids*, Aph Sp Rel B VIIIb, 217.

101. Coleridge, *Aids*, M & R Aph L, Comment, 132; Preliminary Aph Sp Rel, 141.

102. Coleridge, *Aids*, Aph Sp Rel B Xa, 256.

103. Coleridge, *Aids*, Aph Sp Rel B II, Comment, 184.

104. Coleridge, *Aids*, Aph Sp Rel B XVII, Comment, 307.

105. Coleridge, "Evidences of Christianity," in *Literary Remains*, 1:387.

106. Coleridge, *Aids*, Aph Sp Rel B V, Comment, 194.

107. Coleridge, *Aids*, Aph Sp Rel B VII, Comment, 202-03.

108. Carlyle, *Life of John Sterling*, pt. 1, chap. 7, 58.

109. Carlyle, *Life*, pt. 1, chap. 8, 61.

110. John Stuart Mill, "Coleridge," *London and Westminster Review* (March 1840), in *Mill on Bentham and Coleridge*, ed. F. R. Leavis (London: Chatto and Windus, 1950), 99-168, 114.

111. Christian Karl Josias Bunsen, *Hippolytus and His Age, or, The Beginnings and Prospects of Christianity*, 2 vols. (London: Longman, Brown, Green, and Longmans, 1854), 2:327.

112. Coleridge, *Statesman's Manual*, 46.

113. Coleridge, *Aids*, Aph Sp Rel B VIIIb, 218.

114. Coleridge, *Statesman's Manual*, Appendix C, 59.

115. Coleridge, *Aids*, Aph Sp Rel B VIIIb, 218-24.

116. Coleridge, *Aids*, Introduction Aph XII, Comment, 17-18.

117. Coleridge, *Statesman's Manual*, Appendix C, 68.

118. Coleridge, *Friend*, 1:199.

119. Coleridge, *Statesman's Manual*, 29.

120. Coleridge, *Biographia Literaria*, 1:304, 2:16-17.

121. Coleridge, *Statesman's Manual*, 30; Appendix C, 79.

122. Leslie Stephen, "Coleridge," in *Hours in a Library*, 3 vols. (1874; reprint, London: Folio Society, 1991), 3:317-43, 335.

123. Coleridge, *Aids*, Preliminary Aph Sp Rel, p. 141.

124. *Literary Remains*, 3:102.

125. Barth, *Coleridge and Christian Doctrine*, 148.

126. Coleridge, *Confessions of an Inquiring Spirit*, ed. H. J. Jackson and J. R. de J. Jackson, vol. 2 of *The Collected Works of Samuel Taylor Coleridge* (Princeton: Princeton University Press, 1995), 1116-70, 1119, 1168.

127. Coleridge, *Biographia Literaria*, 1:241-42.

128. Coleridge, *Biographia Literaria*, 1:156.

129. *Literary Remains*, 4:63.

130. Francis William Newman, *Phases of Faith* (1850; reprint, New York: Humanities Press, 1970), 137.

131. Coleridge, *Confessions*, 1165-66. Adam S. Farrar states, "Henke, 1752-1809, Professor at Helmstädt, is said to have been the first who made use of the term 'Bibliolatry' in the preface to his *Lineamenta Instit. Fidei Christianae*. He probably however only brought it into use" (*A Critical History of Free Thought in Reference to the Christian Religion* [London: John Murray, 1862], 329 n.).

132. Coleridge, *Confessions*, 1123.

133. Coleridge, *Confessions*, 1124.

134. *Notebooks*, 3440.

135. Coleridge, *Confessions*, 1124.

136. Jackson, H. J., and J. R. de Jackson, Introduction to *Confessions*, 1111-16, 1113 n.

137. *Collected Letters*, 6:543.

138. John Coulson, Forward to *The Religious Thought of Samuel Taylor Coleridge* by David Pym (New York: Barnes and Noble, 1979), 7.

139. The appellation "Father of the Broad Church movement" was given to Coleridge as early as 1895 (Julia Wedgwood, "Samuel Taylor Coleridge," *Contemporary Review* [April 1895], in *Nineteenth Century Teachers, and Other Essays* by Julia Wedgwood [London: Hodder and Stoughton, 1909], 1-28, 21). Josiah Wedgwood is Julia's great-grandfather.

140. Coleridge, *On the Constitution of the Church and State*, ed. Henry Nelson Coleridge (London: William Pickering, 1839), 25-26.

141. Coleridge, *On the Constitution*, 46-47.

142. Coleridge, *On the Constitution*, 48-49.

143. Coleridge, *On the Constitution*, 60.

144. Coleridge, *On the Constitution*, 85-86.

145. *Collected Letters*, 5:528.

146. Benjamin Whichcote, "Moral and Religious Aphorisms," no. 569, from *Moral and Religious Aphorisms*, ed. John Jeffrey (1703), revised by Samuel Salter (1753); excerpts reprinted in *The Cambridge Platonists*, ed. C. A. Patrides, the Stratford-upon-Avon Library, vol. 5 (London: Edward Arnold, 1969), 326-36, 331.

147. Coleridge, *Friend*, 1:98, 96.

148. Coleridge, *Lay Sermon*, 199.

149. Coleridge, *Biographia Literaria*, 2:245-46.

150. Coleridge, *Biographia Literaria*, 1:122.

151. Coleridge, *Aids*, Aph Sp Rel B [XXIV] On Baptism, 367.

152. William Paley, *Natural Theology*, 13th ed. (London: Faulder, 1810; excerpts reprinted in *Classical Readings in Christian Apologetics*, ed. L. Russ Bush [Grand Rapids: Academie Books, 1983], 352-65). Cf. Nathaniel Culverwell's *Discourse of the Light of Nature* (1652): "Thus God set up the world as a fair and goodly clock, to strike in time, and to move in an orderly manner" (ed. Robert A Greene and Hugh MacCallum [Toronto: University of Toronto Press, 1971], 26) and Joseph Glanvill, who, in considering the theory that the human body developed by means of "a *fortuitous range of Atoms*," remarks, "To

suppose a *Watch*, or any other the most curious *Automaton* by the blind hits of *Chance*, to perform diversity of orderly *motions* . . . with an unparallel'd exactness, and all without the regulation of Art; this were the more pardonable absurdity" (*Scepsis Scientifica* [London: E. Cotes, 1665], 32).

153. Søren Kierkegaard, *The Sickness Unto Death*, trans. Alastair Hannay (New York: Penguin Classics, 1989), 119.

154. Coleridge, *Aids*, Conclusion, 405-06.

155. Coleridge, *Friend*, 1:104.

156. Coleridge, *Lay Sermon*, 180.

157. Coleridge, *Aids*, M & R Aph XXV, 107. Cf. J. S. Mill, "Coleridge," 113.

158. Howard Eugene Root, "Beginning All Over Again," in *Soundings: Essays Concerning Christian Understanding*, ed. A. R. Vidler (Cambridge: Cambridge University Press, 1962), 3-19, 17-18.

159. Frederick Denison Maurice, *Sequel to the Inquiry, What Is Revelation?* (Cambridge: Macmillan and Co, 1860), 178.

160. Vidler, 206.

161. John Tulloch, *Movements of Religious Thought in Britain during the Nineteenth Century* (New York: Charles Scribner's Sons, 1885), 11.

162. Frederick W. Farrar, *The History of Interpretation* (1885, reprinted, Grand Rapids: Baker Book House, 1961), 422.

163. Arthur Penrhyn Stanley, *The Life and Correspondence of Thomas Arnold, D.D.*, 2 vols., 12th ed. (London: John Murray, 1881), 2:140.

164. Rowland E. Prothero, *The Life and Correspondence of Arthur Penrhyn Stanley, Late Dean of Westminster*, 2 vols. (New York: Charles Scribner's Sons, 1894), 1:114.

2

Thomas Arnold
and the Oxford Noetics

Historically, Oxford has always represented the English Church in its didactic aspect. In the twelfth and thirteenth centuries, Oxford's priories and abbeys were Augustinian and Cistercian properties. In 1542, Henry VIII created the See of Oxford, appointing Robert King as its first bishop. To the colleges of Oxford, England sent her sons to be developed into ministering deacons and priests. Therefore, to those who held the Church of England dear, the teaching of Oxford dons, as well as the loyalty of its scholars, was of paramount concern. During Elizabeth's reign, in 1571, in order to ensure the development of the Church along Protestant lines, the colleges were incorporated by Act of Parliament into a university and Robert Dudley, earl of Leicester, introduced into the university the requirement of subscription to the Articles of Faith by each student at the time of matriculation.

Alma Mater of Anglican Orthodoxy

Oxford's inherent resistance to change is almost proverbial. Although the seed of Renaissance humanism, the Platonism of the Florentine Academy, was planted in England first at Oxford, principally through the evangelical work of John Colet, the pervasive and deep roots of Aristotelian scholasticism had deprived Oxford of all but a deceptively promising topsoil. Upon this soil Colet sowed the seed, "and anon it sprang up, because it had no depth of earth: and when the sun was up, it caught heat, and for lack of rooting withered away."[1] Fortunately, some of that seed was taken up by John Fisher, the professor of divinity at Cambridge who, in 1504, was appointed chancellor of the university. Through Fisher's encouragement, Erasmus labored at Cambridge, and their cooperative endeavors infused into this young and developing community a spirit of intellectual progressivism or liberalism.

As Cambridge attracted a different set of scholars, the difference between the two universities tended to perpetuate itself. In contradistinction to its younger sister, Oxford came to represent *conservative* Anglican theology. After all, Oxford was, as a matter of historical fact, the old school. Even the reactionary counter-movements that sprang up within Cambridge tended to be, by Oxford standards, progressive. Puritanism, as a reaction rising up from within the ranks of the humanists, was not so much against humanism as against what it perceived as its tendency to develop an inordinate faith in the capacities of human reason. Puritanism found its more natural enemy in scholasticism and effectually increased the intellectual distance between the reforming and High Church parties, straining relations to the breaking point.

In order to filter out Puritan reformers from clerical service, James I, through the Canons of 1603, imposed upon all clergy and graduates from Oxford a requirement of subscription to the Liturgy.[2] While Puritanism at Cambridge would provoke, ultimately, a response in the highly moral and latitudinarian theology of the Platonist School, at Oxford it aroused the fury of William Laud, for whom schism was tantamount to sedition. His appointment in 1628 to chancellor of the university signified King Charles's unwillingness to allow for any separation from established formularies and polity. Laud insisted upon decency and order, and by systematically and thoroughly investigating every avenue and corner of Oxford academic life, punishing with a too-heavy hand and expelling in haste, he largely succeeded in purifying the fount of orthodoxy from what he regarded as corrupting influences. Finally, after the Restoration, as Dean Stanley noted, "Subscription to the Articles was extended, and the force of the subscription to the Liturgy immensely increased, by the Act of Uniformity passed under Charles II, with the express purpose of driving from their places in the Church as many of the Puritan clergy as could be conveniently displaced."[3]

At Oxford the requirement for undergraduates to subscribe to the Articles and Liturgy of the Church of England remained in force until it was abolished by Act of Parliament in 1854. Under this requirement of subscription virtually no progress could be made in the discipline of theology without raising fierce opposition. Indeed, at the beginning of the nineteenth century it was generally assumed that construing from the Greek New Testament was all of the formal "theological" training required for effective service in the Church. J. T. Coleridge recalled that, at Oxford in 1811, "the earnest ones amongst us were diligent readers of Barrow, Hooker, and Taylor,"[4] but none of this reading was requisite for a baccalaureate. In 1833 Edward B. Pusey could complain, "One fortnight comprises the beginning and end of all the public instruction which any candidate for holy orders is required to attend previously to entering upon his profession."[5] At about this time, half of the undergraduates at Oxford aimed to become parsons, and two-thirds of those who actually graduated put their college degree to use as a ticket towards ordination.[6] It was the intention of Oxford to train none of these prospective churchmen to perceive differences in religious belief or interpretation as natural, let alone necessary, to the life of a community. Religious truth was, as far as the English Church was concerned, handed down linearly, not acquired dialectically. As an unavoidable result, intellectual differences within the Church resulted in party strife fueled by attitudes of intolerance and self-righteousness.

Although Cambridge must figure largely in any study of the precursors to the Broad Church movement, Oxford has the first claim to our attention as we examine the rise of the movement. If the Broad Church was ever to progress beyond seedtime to harvest, if it was ever to succeed as a movement within the Church, it had to acquire leaders among the clergy. In order to achieve this end, something in addition was required to the handful of clergymen who, in 1830, read Coleridge with more than curiosity. Tutors first, and then students, would have to acquire reading skills in modern languages, particularly in German. New ideas and modern books would have to be introduced into tuition for consideration and discussion. The natural sciences would have to attain to positions of respect aside the humanities. In regard to the Scriptures, the Protestant ideal of private interpretation would have to receive more than lip-service, for as Jeremy Bentham observed in 1817, the traditional Oxford system implied—despite protestations to the contrary—an infallible church.[7] In short, essential to the full development of the Broad Church movement was educational reform, both at the universities and at the public schools that prepared their students for higher learning.

This chapter will focus primarily on the contribution of persons associated with two educational institutions, Oriel College of Oxford and the public school of Rugby. A number of significant personalities are common to both, but the towering figure of Thomas Arnold, referred to by the historian of Oriel as "the founder of the Broad Church school,"[8] demands the first place in our attention. Charles R. Sanders notes, Arnold "lived to promote the movement for eight years after the death of Coleridge; but like Coleridge he lived in the seedtime, not in the harvest, which began about 1848 and which in a sense has continued ever since."[9] This chapter, like the previous, begins in seedtime, but it will take us to the first gleanings of a ripe and abundant harvest.

The Reform of Oriel and the Rise of the Noetic School

As far as Oxford is concerned, the early eighteenth century was—before the sobering influence of William Law's *Serious Call to a Devout and Holy Life* (1729) and the Wesleys' Holy Club—"the darkest age in the University history." G. R. Balleine states the matter in a satirically academical manner: "Three subjects, and three subjects alone, were able to stir the interests of the senior men—the virtue of the college port, the progress of the college lawsuit, and the latest fashion in dilettante treason."[10] As Evangelicalism was essentially a domestic movement, with its center in the home, and as its intrusion into Oxford was largely prevented, its effect there was gradual and never thorough. Arthur Hugh Clough, the Victorian poet, had a more blunt explanation for the failure of Evangelicalism to establish a foothold in Oxford. For him, as for other proud Oxonians, Oxford is simply the sort of place "where anything so 'ungentlemanly' and 'coarse' and in such bad taste as Evangelicalism would never be able to make very much way."[11]

So conservative of its ways was Oxford that, at the end of the eighteenth century, a gentleman could still get a degree there without having to work for it. If he was selective in his choice of examiners, and could get his hands on a decent preparation manual, a sort of Cliff's Notes put together by entrepreneurial graduates, then he might spend one week in concentrated study for every year he spent at Oxford. After John Eveleigh (1748-1814) became provost of Oriel in 1781, he worked closely with Cyril Jackson, dean of Christ Church, to create and pass a University Examination Statute that would stipulate, for all of the colleges, a consistent standard for undergraduate academic achievement. After Convocation—that is, the governing assembly of Masters and Doctors at Oxford—passed the statute in 1800, it was no longer possible for even the most genteel of men to qualify for a bachelor's degree without having, as a minimum requirement, a facility of expression in Latin, along with a knowledge of the Gospels in Greek, the fundamentals of Aristotelian philosophy, and the 1562 Articles of the Church.[12]

Eveleigh also worked together with John Parsons, a fellow of Balliol, to create the Honors Examination. Those students whose academic ambitions rose above the minimum requirement were, for the first time, distinguished from "pass degree" candidates through a second competition, success in which was, in 1807, divided into first and second class honors. The honors exam was divided into two sections, humanities and mathematics. Thus, Eveleigh and Jackson introduced a system of academic competition that made it possible for a student to graduate from Oxford not only with honors, but with that highest honor, a "double first." As William Tuckwell states, "The dry bones were stirred: bold invasion of venerable torpidity generated a new temper in the University."[13]

Eveleigh's legacy to Oriel is not merely that he raised the level of education among the applicants to fellowships at Oxford, but that, having done so, he began the process of removing the restrictions that applied to six of the eighteen fellowships offered at Oriel.[14] Founders of fellowships often restricted them to graduates from either a particular college or geographical region. Although the statutes of the founders were, presumably, created with the intent of encouraging academic excellence from their alma mater or hometown, the restrictions often had the opposite effect because an applicant would have little or no competition for the award. By removing the restrictions, Eveleigh sought to increase competition and provide the college with a wider pool of applicants from which to draw. An early example of Eveleigh's method can be seen in the election of 1795, when the provost and fellows of Oriel, after rejecting as incompetent the candidates for a restricted fellowship, set aside the governing statutes and invited Edward Copleston, a distinguished scholar of Corpus Christi, to apply. He did so and, of course, won the election.[15]

Removing the restrictions on Oriel fellowships would, alone, have eventually raised the intellectual caliber of its fellows. But Eveleigh further reformed the election process in such a way that made it unique in Oxford and, understandably, controversial. The social connections and academic honors that a candidate possessed were "wholly disregarded by the electors, who looked at his papers unbiased by opinion outside."[16] Although part of the exam was viva-voce, the papers carried the greatest weight. The examination process was both mentally and physically demanding. The period of examination lasted four consecutive days, Monday through Thursday following Easter, from 10 a.m. until dusk, in a candle-lit hall that was exceptionally cold.[17] The exam itself consisted of Latin and Greek translations, Latin and English essays upon literary and philosophical themes, and answers to mathematical questions. The papers were read and discussed by the whole body of fellows together. *Multum, non Multa* was Copleston's maxim, "quality rather than quantity; to exercise the mind rather than to pour in knowledge." Instead of looking for indications of wide reading, he and the other fellows looked for originality and skill in prose composition. The strongest candidates were, finally, invited to dine with the provost and fellows in order to have their character and compatibility assessed.[18] The result was that, by the time of Eveleigh's death in 1814, Oriel College "contained some of the most distinguished personages, the most vigorous minds, and the most attractive characters in Oxford."[19]

The new set that gathered in the Oriel Common Room around the teapot or under the stately portraits of past provosts were called *Noetics*—that is, "Intellectuals." Details regarding the coinage of the name appear to be lost. According to John Tulloch, "The new Oriel men . . . seem to have rejoiced in the reputation of superior mental penetration and independence."[20] Although this might suggest that the name originated from within the group itself, Tulloch's statement is based on a prior remark made by Thomas Mozley: "The new Oriel sect was declared to be Noetic, whatever that may mean, and when a Fellow of the College presented himself in the social gathering of another society, he was sure to be reminded of his pretence to intellectual superiority."[21] Judging from this anterior statement, it would seem at least equally probable that the term "Noetic" originated as an ironic gesture of reproach for pretentiousness, imagined or real.[22] This would also explain why attempts to define the Noetics as a School of Thought have been more often misleading than revelatory. It is important to keep in mind that the fellows of Oriel were first called Noetic because of a *common attitude*, a "spirit of questioning,"[23] which—while stimulating "liberality of thought"[24]—did not, as a rule, result in *common thought*. "Old institutions, accepted principles and beliefs, were rudely and fearlessly investigated, and called upon to justify themselves at the bar of utility and reason."[25] And yet, it must be noted that the questions of the Noetics did not begin in skepticism, nor—as a general rule—did they end in doubt; unlike the intellectuals of the next generation, they questioned in full assurance that Christianity is reasonable and satisfying to the logical mind.

Having said this, I must also add that the Noetics can be divided into two groups, which can be identified as first- and second-generation Noetics. The direct influence of the original Noetics, consisting of fellows elected under Provost Eveleigh, gave rise to a second group that, in the 1830s, espoused viewpoints decidedly more sophisticated and liberal. As one historian recently noted, "During the 1820s Noeticism was not tantamount to doctrinal liberalism; no one could reasonably have disputed the orthodoxy of Copleston, Hawkins, and Davison. After 1829, however, Noeticism moved in the direction of a more self-conscious liberalism."[26] This was the liberalism that evoked the Oriel reaction led by Richard Hurrell Froude and John Henry Newman, which ultimately developed into the Oxford Movement.

The First-Generation Noetics

Among the noteworthy crew who obtained their fellowships under Eveleigh were EDWARD COPLESTON (1776-1849), who, two years after his election in 1795, became tutor to the college and captain in the University Corps, which had formed in expectation of a French invasion. John Hughes, an Oriel man himself (and the father of Oriel men George and Thomas Hughes), served under Copleston's command and remembered him as an exceedingly vigorous and able leader.[27] A fellowship in those days came with a horse, and Copleston was, moreover, a skilled equestrian. Like his horse, Copleston needed to be spurred, for beneath the heavy load of his mental gifts, "he languidly pursued the tenor of his ways."[28] In the years 1808 to 1810, when the *Edinburgh Review* launched a series of anonymous strikes against the Aristotelian and classical education of Oxford, Copleston went into battle, retaliating with a series of brilliant and satiric "Replies." From 1802 to 1814 he occupied the chair of professor of poetry and gave lectures in Latin that were, years later, much admired by J. H. Newman.[29] His tutorial lectures on logic were pulled together out of his own studies in classical sources and were noted for their originality. He was worldly, a stylish dresser, socially polished, and the guest of numerous literary and political elites. By unanimous vote among the fellows, in 1814 Copleston succeeded Eveleigh as provost. He is praised by Tuckwell as "monarch in his day alike of Oriel and of Oxford, dethroner of uncreating Chaos, supreme for twenty years over the new *sæclorum ordo*," and by Tulloch as "the original master-mind of the movement."[30]

JOHN DAVISON (1777-1834) was a student under Copleston and, afterwards, a fellow of Oriel and a prominent figure in the Common Room for nearly two decades. In Tuckwell's influential study, Davison is excluded from the circle of Noetics on the ground that he "stood aloof" from the movement, having a "mental constitution" that parted him from Copleston and Whately.[31] Nevertheless, Davison was "one of the most astute religious liberals of the day,"[32] and Arnold looked up to him "with exceeding reverence," generally overrating him as "intellectually eminent and capable of guiding others to truth."[33] At a time when the exploits of Napoleon were exciting the imagination of pseudo-expositors of apocalyptic prophecy,[34] Davison, in his Warburtonian Lectures on *The Nature and History of Prophecy* (1819-1820), emphasized the role of the Hebrew prophet as a religious and moral teacher to his contemporary countrymen, and asserted that "what is merely ingenious or subtle in the exposition of Prophecy has little chance of being true."[35] According to Davison, "To foretell future events was scarcely so much the office of the Prophets, as to be Preachers of Righteousness."[36] Davison's lectures, particularly his concept of the historical development of prophecy, made a significant impression on Francis Newman, who afterwards "read as with fresh eyes" the Epistles of St. Paul.[37]

RICHARD WHATELY (1787-1863) and JOHN KEBLE (1792-1866) both gained their fellowships at Oriel in 1811. Keble had graduated from Corpus Christi in 1810 with a double first, the second person to attain this honor—the first having been Robert Peel in 1808. Keble's father, a former fellow of Corpus Christi, was an old friend of Provost Eveleigh.[38] With these qualifications and connections Keble could have secured an election in almost any college of Oxford, but a fellowship at Oriel— where such distinctions were disregarded—was at this time the greatest prize of intellectual merit that a graduate could win. Whately, on the other hand, although for years an admiring pupil and friend of Copleston, lacked the academic awards and self-esteem of Keble. He was, however, remarkably ambitious and refused to allow a double second to be the measure of his academic success. Following his graduation from Oriel in 1808, he remained at Oxford and imposed upon himself a three-year discipline of rigorous study. His reading was selective, but he mastered the books he read—the major treatises of Aristotle, Bacon's *Essays* and *Novum Organon*, Butler's *Analogy of Religion*, and Locke's essays. If the attempt shows deliberation, it also suggests a certain desperation. Forever after, despite the preferment that was later granted him, Whately looked back upon the winning of his Oriel fellowship as the greatest triumph of his life.[39]

Whately and Keble make an interesting study in contrasts. Whately is, without exception, recognized as the prototypical Noetic, for "no one exemplified better than he the ideal of the Oriel Fellow as a man whose mind was an instrument rather than a receptacle."[40] As the disciple of Copleston, Whately's expertise was in logic and rhetoric. Like Thomas Arnold, he was a Whig, and Whigs at Oxford were, in these years, never without opportunity to sharpen their tools of controversy. Eventually—in 1826 and 1828 respectively—he would publish standard college texts in *Logic* and *Rhetoric*. He and Davison habitually prepared themselves in advance for postprandial argument in the Oriel dining room. This made for what Mark Pattison refers to as "wholesome intellectual ferment"[41]; however, "these animated dialectics" were often rendered more colorful by Whately's habit of eating and talking simultaneously, and they left many dinner guests complaining "that Oriel Common Room *stunk* of Logic."[42] Keble, on the other hand, was temperamentally incapable of civilized debate. He could not be contradicted without losing his cool. "It is true," concedes Mozley, "there were one or two in our college who might have tried the temper of an angel, but there really was no getting on with Keble without entire agreement, that is submission."[43] If Keble was touchy, he was also sensitive and expressive of religious feelings in ways that defied reduction to a syllogism. He was a gifted poet, and between the publication of Whately's *Logic* and *Rhetoric*, Keble came out with a collection of verse for the Sundays and holy days of the year. The Christian sentiment and devotional quality of Keble's *Christian Year* (1827) met with praise across party lines.[44]

In short, Whately and Keble were sufficiently different in values and character to allow for a mutual offering of begrudging respect from a distance. Thomas Arnold's first impression of Whately is telling in this regard: "Whately is a very singular man—a hard dry logician, with one of the clearest, soundest heads I ever knew, . . . but he wants poetry terribly, and has nothing of the richness of John Keble or Coleridge about him."[45]

"Keble," says James Anthony Froude, "was a representative of the devout mind of England."[46] He was a son of a country churchman, a Tory through-and-through, the heir of old-fashioned values and an unworldly but dogmatic piety. He combined steadfast loyalty to the Anglican Church, its bishops and traditions, with a righteous contempt for popery and dissent. He had, adds Dean Church, "strict and severe principles of duty,"[47] and by these principles he determined his own conduct and measured the conduct of others. The firmness of his Anglican faith was obvious to those about him and made him the natural counselor to those whose confidence in the Articles was less secure.[48] Although he took his place among the fellows in the Common Rooms of Oriel, his unquestioning faith endowed him with a distinctly anti-Noetic charisma, by which he would soon become the subversive nucleus of a reactionary party.

Whately may have been "entirely lacking in any Christian mystical sense,"[49] but he had rich gifts to offer the kingdom of Christ that Keble knew not how to value. As J. H. Newman testified of Whately, "He, emphatically, opened my mind, and taught me to think and to use my reason."[50] In 1819, Whately published his first major work, *Historic Doubts relative to Napoleon Buonaparte*. This is a satire written in the tradition of Swift and carefully aimed to let the hot air out of Hume's widely puffed essay, "On Miracles." Whately applies Hume's principles of philosophic inquiry toward an investigation of the foundations of our belief in the existence and exploits of Napoleon and concludes "that those on whose testimony the existence and actions of Buonaparte are generally believed, fail in ALL the most essential points on which the credibility of witnesses depends."[51] W. J. Fitzpatrick is undoubtedly correct when he says, "The object of the Napoleon pamphlet was to show the fallacy of sceptical criticism in general."[52] Yet, as an analogical argument, Whately's satire can be read in more ways than one, and it is amusing to find Baden Powell observing that "the *real* conclusion" of the *Historic Doubts* is "simply this—*there is a rational solution*, a *real* conformity to *analogy and experience*, . . . that the Bible narrative is no more properly *miraculous* than the marvellous exploits of Napoleon I."[53] Although extremely popular in the nineteenth century,[54] this short volume is sadly neglected today. It remains, nevertheless, an excellent text by which to awaken inquiry into the weaknesses—as well as the real strengths—of Hume's essay.

In 1822 Whately delivered his Bampton Lectures on *The Evils and Dangers of Party Spirit*. While defining *party*-feeling as no other than *social*-feeling and allowing for its necessity, Whately urged against its abuses. According to Whately, although compartmentalization is advantageous to a large unit, it is susceptible to degeneration and becomes a danger as the compartments cease to work for the good of the whole and to subordinate themselves to a common authority.[55] This united-and-segregated vision of the Church is hardly, it should be observed, a Broad Church ideal; however, it is considerably more liberal than the attitudes of exclusion that had continued to separate those very parties that the Anglican compromise had physically joined. Moreover, as we shall see, Whately's lectures left an impression upon Arnold that contributed to the formation of his *Principles of Church Reform* (1833).

In the same year in which he presented the Bampton Lectures, Whately published his *Essays on Some of the Peculiarities of the Christian Religion*. Differentiating historical from practical revelation, Whately boldly postulated that what is historical is neither essentially religious nor "properly a point of miraculous revelation."[56] The divine intent of inspiration is not to provide historical or scientific details that are speculatively suggestive or gratifying to the curiosity; rather, its purpose is to influence and direct conduct. Therefore, "We must not expect to learn any thing from revelation, except what is in a *religious* point of view practically important for us to know."[57] Davison's lectures had not taken Whately this far, but they had undoubtedly pointed him in this direction. Now, Whately suggests the hermeneutic application of his argument and, in doing so, shows the forward path to Arnold and Hampden: "With respect to the right understanding of what *is* revealed, it is evident . . . that the most *practical* interpretation of each doctrine that can fairly be adopted is ever likely to be the *truest*."[58]

Whately is, very likely, the anonymous author of *Letters on the Church by an Episcopalian* (1826). At the time of its appearance, it was widely ascribed to Whately, although it appears that he neither admitted nor repudiated his authorship. Certainly, he would have dissociated himself with the Letters had he found therein anything with which he disagreed, and it seems safe to say that his hand was in their production. In agreement with Richard Hooker's *Polity*, the anonymous Episcopalian takes the position that, *in a Christian nation*, Church and State are a coextensive society, over which there can be but one Sovereign ruler; however, when Hooker concludes, that "There is not any man of the Church of England but the same man is also a member of the commonwealth; nor any man a member of the commonwealth, which is not also of the Church of England,"[59] the Episcopalian takes exception. Because the commonwealth is a worldly kingdom and the Church a spiritual kingdom, it is possible, he reasons, for the same man to be included within the former while, at the same time, excluded from the latter. Even so, it is not Hooker, but William Warburton's elaboration upon Hooker, *The Alliance between Church and State* (1736), that the Episcopalian attacks for its logical inconsistencies.

In opposition to Warburton, he draws a line of demarcation between the legislative and ecclesiastic functions and properties of the State and Church. The fact that the Church and the State have in common one ruler is accidental, not necessary, and does not imply an alliance between the two institutions. As the Sovereign delegates his authority in civil affairs to the ministers of Parliament, so too, in ecclesiastical affairs should he delegate his authority to the ministers of the Church.[60] The practical result toward which this argument leads is an established Church independent of parliamentary interference. It was to this work that Newman expressed indebtedness in his *Apologia*, declaring that it taught him "the existence of the Church, as a substantive body or corporation" and fixed in him "those anti-Erastian views of Church polity, which were one of the most prominent features of the Tractarian movement."[61]

With the publication of Whately's *Essays on Some of the Difficulties in the Writings of the Apostle Paul* (1828)[62] and *Errors of Romanism Traced to their Origin in Human Nature* (1830), the Noetic day reached high noon. Whately contends, in the first of these two books, against the errors of Calvinism; in the second, against the errors of Roman Catholicism. The first addresses problems associated with hermeneutics; the second, problems associated with human proclivity. The first book is rightly acclaimed for its genius. It will be discussed in the final chapter of this work in connection with Matthew Arnold. The second book, however, is flawed. Not only are the alleged errors "as applicable to Anglicanism as to 'Romanism,'"[63] but—as Mozley notes in reference to a work by Convers Middleton that allegedly "proved beyond a doubt the identity of all that we in England call Roman Catholicism with Paganism"—to the thoughtful reader the question then arises, "whether these Pagan faiths and customs are utterly wrong, without foundation, without benefit."[64] In other words, one cannot assume divine disapproval of a religion by accounting for its ideas, sentiments, and ceremonies through their appeal to human nature, *unless* one can first establish that human nature is always and necessarily contrary to the divine will. Without having proved this underlying presumption, Whately's book—although certainly not devoid of merit—failed to persuade anyone who was not already prejudicially anti-Catholic.

EDWARD HAWKINS, after securing a double first from St. John's in 1811 and serving his college as tutor for a year, was elected to fellowship in 1813, the last full year of Eveleigh's leadership. For some time following his election, he appeared to be in complete concord with Whately, and he was, with Arnold, an admirer of Davison. Hawkins, Whately, and Davison all preached against the Evangelical imposition of Sabbatarian restrictions upon the Christian observance of Sunday. This doctrine of freedom from the Fourth Commandment of the Decalogue was the "Oriel heresy" that Francis Newman says he embraced sometime shortly after his matriculation in 1822.[65] Hawkins parted company from the Noetics, however, within five years, when he developed a theory of the relationship between Tradition and Scripture that he would espouse throughout his life. His 1818 oral dissertation *On Unauthoritative Tradition*—published in the following year—asserted that the rightful use of the Scriptures is to enforce and establish the preliminary and cate-chetical instruction of the Church. According to this view—a view that Charles Gore would espouse in *Lux Mundi* (1889)[66]—Christian doctrine is to be taught by the Church and supported by, not deduced from, Scripture. It was this "unhappy sermon on Tradition" that, as we shall see and as Thomas Arnold observed, "contributed to the mischief"[67] that quickly developed in Oriel College after Arnold had left it. Second-generation Noetics R. D. Hampden and Baden Powell would, in 1839, provide excellent treatises on Tradition as countermeasures to that mischief, then fully developed.[68]

Hawkins further developed his dissertation in the Bampton Lectures of 1840, *An Inquiry into the Connected Uses of the Principle Means of Attaining Christian Truth*. In this series of lectures, he asserted that the greater part of Christian Revela-tion, "that is to say, every thing, *or nearly every thing*, which it is necessary for us to know and believe in order to salvation, is contained, either expressly or by implication, in the Canonical Books of the Old and New Testament."[69] Three truths of Revelation that are, according to Hawkins, learned through the combined use of the Church and Scripture are Trinity in Unity, the legitimacy of infant baptism, and the divine origin of Episcopacy.[70] The "Indefectibility" of the Church, says Hawkins, must allow for a certain weight of authority in Tradition, which, although not infallible, rightly claims "respect and deference."[71] When Hawkins asserted that his argument is directed "against the Theory of the exclusive independent study of the Scriptures,"[72] Arnold was quick to recognize a straw man and protested that the real issue is not whether aids, scholarly or traditional, can be used to assist biblical interpretation, but whether Scripture is *alone* necessary to salvation and authori-tative in matters of faith.[73]

Whately, who admired the logical consistency of Hawkins's theory, was slower to protest. Throughout the 1820s he praised Hawkins's "excellent little work on Tradition" for clearly establishing that the New Testament does not contain an intro-duction to or compendium of Christian doctrine. Nevertheless, Whately always insisted—on the basis of the principle of analogy between natural and revealed truth—on applying the Baconian inductive method to Scripture as a means of ascertaining the truth of any Christian doctrine, so that, "by a diligent comparison of one passage with another," one might attain "sufficient knowledge of all necessary truth."[74] Hawkins, on the other hand, denied that the comparative study of the Scriptures could ever be sufficient for the attainment of Christian doctrine as a whole and that, moreover, "it is almost impossible that the Christian should have first discovered for himself in the Scriptures *any one* of the great leading doctrines of Christianity."[75] Ultimately, Whately would more directly oppose Hawkins's theory—after the mischief had already been done—with a counterargument that he might have gleaned from Jeremy Taylor, that Scripture was written as a substitute rather than a supplement of Tradition, specifically "to guard against the dangers of Tradition."[76]

The Second-Generation Noetics

With the death of Eveleigh, Copleston became provost, and it is during his period of office, from 1814 to 1828, that the Noetics attained fame and prominence at Oxford. Added to the Noetics under the provostship of Copleston were RENN DICKSON HAMPDEN (1793-1868), THOMAS ARNOLD (1795-1842), BADEN POWELL (1796-1860), and JOSEPH BLANCO WHITE (1775-1841). Hampden, after graduating from Oriel with a double first, was elected as fellow in 1814, but he remained in Oxford for only one year beyond his probationary year, and then, in 1816, accepted a curacy and surrendered his fellowship. Arnold's election to fellowship took place in 1815. Baden Powell, although never a fellow, obtained a first class in mathematics from Oriel in 1817 and is traditionally regarded as a Noetic, as is Blanco White, who was made an honorary fellow of Oriel in 1826.

In addition, and also distinguishing the ranks of fellows under Copleston, were Richard William Jelf (1798-1871), elected in 1821, John Henry Newman (1801-1890), elected in 1822, Edward Bouverie Pusey (1800-1882), elected in 1823, and Richard Hurrell Froude (1803-1836) and Robert Wilberforce (1802-1857), both elected in 1826. This group of scholars, while brilliant and independent in thought, were greatly influenced by the lectures of Charles Lloyd, then Regius Professor of Divinity and, from 1827 until his death in 1829, bishop of Oxford. Lloyd's lectures on the Prayer Book demonstrated that it "was but the reflexion of medieval and primitive devotion, still embodied in its Latin forms in the Roman-Service books," thus instilling in his pupils' hearts a sympathy with the pre-Reformation Church.[77] It was Lloyd who first taught Newman to distinguish between the decrees of the Council of Trent and popular concepts associated with Roman Catholicism. Another coadjutor was William Palmer, "a man of exact and scholastic mind, well equipped in all points of controversial theology." This associate of Lloyd published, in 1832, "by far the best book in the English language on the history and significance of the offices of the English Church—the *Origines Liturgicæ*."[78] Ultimately, after Copleston's departure, this later group of Oriel fellows, under these external sources of influence, brought a voice of dissent into their college and, for two decades, succeeded in obstructing the light of the Noetic torch.

Of all the Noetics, Thomas Arnold made the greatest contribution to the development of the Broad Church movement. The remainder of this chapter will, therefore, focus largely upon his life and work, while taking into consideration the ideas and achievements of the other fellows of Oriel, both Noetics and counter-Noetics, primarily in their relation to Arnold.

Arnold at Oxford

The mature mind of both S. T. Coleridge and Thomas Arnold was fundamentally religious; but whereas Coleridge's candle burnt brightest over politics and poetics,

Arnold's spent itself over politics and history. As might be expected, the two men had much in common, but they were also as different as poetry and history could be. Both used the imagination, but—to use Coleridgean terms—whereas the poet depended on the eyes and ears of the Secondary Imagination, Arnold nurtured and relied upon the workings of the Primary Imagination. His childhood games were often the sportive recreations of battles from the *Iliad*, and as he grew and his historical education embraced Priestley, Russell, Gibbon, Mitford, and Smollett, his education in geography kept pace, and the places of the world gradually came to be associated with historical personages and events, chiefly battles. And while his curiosity fueled his eagerness to master the classical languages and the works of Thucydides, Herodotus, and Livy, his enthusiasm for the heroes of history implanted deep within his psyche high ideals of social and patriotic conduct.

Arnold was elected from Winchester as scholar of Corpus Christi in 1811. Here he occupied the old rooms of Bishop Jewel and first became acquainted with Keble and John Taylor Coleridge—although within a year both would transfer to other colleges as they obtained fellowships at Oriel and Exeter respectively. According to Coleridge, it was during this time that he introduced Arnold to the Lake Poets, after his uncle sent him a volume of *Lyrical Ballads*.[79] Had Arnold not been a Whig, and thus necessarily an able debater, his familiarity with the poet-philosopher Coleridge might have extended no further. But Arnold had a talent for controversy and, with Ulyssean courage, wit, and love of engagement, could defend himself against all the leaders of the Common Room at once with scarcely ever so much as a momentary loss of temper.[80] After Keble and Coleridge had both left Corpus, Arnold sought to put his rhetorical talents to the test in the social arena of the Attic Society, recently founded by James Randall and Augustus Hare.

> Yes! sure 'tis he! 'tis Hare whose *gamut* voice
> Bids treason flourish, Jacobins rejoice;
> Who tells in *alt* what ills our State disgrace,
> And mumbles out corruption's fall in *base*.[81]

In the company of this body of debaters "political Tommy" acquired several lifelong friends, but none so close as Augustus, through whom he would soon come to know and admire the Cambridge brother, Julius.[82] J. C. Hare, a great admirer of S. T. Coleridge, was to become the principle link between Arnold and the Cambridge group of the developing Broad Church movement. Perhaps it would be useful to note at this point that, although it is sometimes stated that the Noetics disliked Coleridge "as a misty thinker" and "knew nothing of the philosophical movement which was taking place on the continent,"[83] these assessments are fully accurate only in regard to the first-generation Noetics.

In 1814 Arnold graduated from Corpus Christi with a first class in the humanities, and in the following year he competed for a fellowship at Oriel. His English essay failed to receive a favorable reception by the examining fellows; yet, Whately astutely recognized evidence of potential and pressed this evidence upon the other examiners.[84] Subsequently, Arnold developed a bond with Whately that, despite the physical distance that often kept them apart for protracted periods, only grew stronger with the passage of time. Arnold remained a resident fellow during the probationary first year, as required by Oriel statutes, and then removed to Kensington, where his mother, aunt, and crippled sister, Susannah, had taken up residence. For four years he earned a decent living through private tuition, and since almost all undergraduates hired private tutors before examinations, this was steady employment. Possibly, if Oriel had appointed Arnold as a college tutor, he would have kept his fellowship longer than he did, although this would have necessitated taking up residence again at Oxford; but, although Keble was called upon to fill a vacancy as tutor in early 1818—an appointment that he kept until 1823—there was no opening for Arnold.

At the end of the year, James Hearn requested assistance at his curacy in pastoral Laleham. Here Arnold could teach Sunday School and make visitations while tutoring a younger set of boys in preparation for their university entrance exams. First, however, Arnold would have to be ordained deacon, and as there was the hurdle of subscription obstructing the path to ordination—a hurdle that, for the first time in Arnold's life, seemed too high to safely get over, he appealed to his friends Keble and J. T. Coleridge for counsel. Lacking Hawkins's presumptive trust in Tradition, and placing all of his faith on the certain revelation of Scripture, Arnold was troubled—as Keble later related in a letter to Coleridge—about "the doctrine of the blessed trinity," for "it is a defect of his mind that he cannot get rid of a certain feeling of objections."[85] Keble advised Arnold to stop inquiring and to busy himself with prayer and practical duties. Coleridge thought this "the wisest advice," and perhaps, for a while, Arnold followed it.[86] At any rate, he was ordained on December 20 and left Oxford at the beginning of 1819.

Blanco White

If Arnold did not, during the first two years of his fellowship, actually meet Joseph Blanco—now going by the awkward Anglicization "Blanco White"—certainly he must have heard, in the Oriel Common Room, considerable talk about this fascinating man. He was the second-generation descendant of an Irishman whose fortune had allowed him to emigrate to Seville and there marry and prosper as a merchant. Superior academic abilities soon distinguished Blanco, and after election as fellow at the College of St. Mary, he obtained a Licentiate of Divinity and was further honored by preferment to the post of *Magistral* or preacher in the chapter of King's Chaplains. While in orders, the irrepressible conviction came upon him that his religious faith revolved upon a circular argument. He explains, "I believed the infallibility of the church because the Scripture said she was infallible; while I had no better proof that the Scripture said so, than the assertion of the church." For ten years, he felt himself bound by familial ties of affection to his country and church, until, as he states, "the approach of Buonaparte's troops to Seville enabled me to quit Spain, without exciting suspicion as to the real motive which tore me for ever from every thing I loved."[87]

After his arrival in England, the influence of Archdeacon Paley's apologetics and the sincere Christianity of a few who befriended him, including Robert Southey, convinced him that he could find satisfaction in the Church of England. He signed the Thirty-nine Articles on 20 August 1814, thereby transferring his ecclesiastic orders from Rome to England and, at the same time, becoming a citizen of England. He immediately committed himself to two years of study at New College, Oxford, in order to learn Greek and better familiarize himself with Anglican theology.[88] During these two years—before he relocated to Holland House as tutor of the son of Lord Holland—he established an acquaintance with Hampden and William Bishop—both fellows of Oriel—and it seems likely that, on some occasion, he would have been casually introduced to Arnold.

O Absalom!

Into Arnold's resigned fellowship was elected from Merton College the first-born son of S. T. Coleridge and a cousin of J. T. Coleridge.[89] Hartley Coleridge's fellowship was warmly supported by James Tyler, who thought he discerned some latent greatness in the young man. Tyler's judgment was completely trusted by Copleston. When in April 1819 the Sage of Highgate learned of his son's election as probationary fellow of Oriel, he was ecstatic. The son whose childhood innocence had added its own purity and joy to those magical years at Nether Stowey, and in whose first wayward steps the poet was loath to trace the broader outline of his own footprints—this son would now attain the stability and contentment that had been so elusive in the father's life. Yet, it was not to be. As one popular account has it, when other fellows complained of Hartley's dress and manners, Tyler zipped his lips. When rumors reached him of more serious misconduct, he plugged his ears. But when, while riding home one Sunday from his parish, he came across a man drunk in the gutter of Oriel Lane, he refused to cover his eyes.

Keble wrote up the charges against Hartley, Hawkins informed him that his continued fellowship would be "an indulgence not at all consistent with the spirit of our Foundation," and Whately advised him to seek spiritual renewal in the wilderness of Canada.[90] Tyler shrugged his shoulders. When the news reached Highgate in June 1820 that Hartley's fellowship was, on account of public drunkenness, not to be renewed, the father was convulsed in agony. For the next three months he sought by every possible diplomatic means to have Hartley reinstated, and finally, in October, he made the journey to Oxford to expostulate and plead with Copleston in person. There was a slight chance that Hartley might retain his fellowship as a permanent nonresident, and Copleston suggested to the father that they meet again a month later in London. But, in the meantime, additional incriminating evidence was produced, and the appeal was lost. It was a sad event in the life of Hartley, "that beautiful fallen spirit, overcome by one accursed habit,"[91] but a tragic chapter in the life of the elder poet, who would feel this loss of paternal hope throughout his few remaining years.[92]

Two years after Hartley's dismissal, Tyler would campaign successfully for the election of John Henry Newman.

The Laleham Decade

It is not the purpose of this chapter to retell Arnold's history, told already so well by Stanley and others, but the period between 1819 and 1828 must not be skipped over. In this decade, which bore the fruits of Whately's Noetic genius, Arnold's character, opinions, and talents ripened to full maturity in the context of . . . what shall I call it— a quiet and studious life? Well, not exactly. Shortly after relocating his family to a cottage in Laleham, Arnold met Mary Penrose, the sister of an old school friend, and in August 1820 the couple married. Soon, the tutor became the patriarch of a growing and noisy clan. In 1821 Jane was born; 1822 ended with the arrival of Matthew; in the following year Thomas (the younger) was added, and four more children, three surviving, were born before the family uprooted itself from Laleham. Ultimately, there were to be nine "dogs"—as the paterfamilias referred affectionately to his children—in the Arnold litter. Somehow, the father managed, beginning in 1821, to work on a *Lexicon of Thucydides* (the first volume of which was published in May 1830) and, at the same time, to labor at a *History of Greece* (never completed) and articles on Roman history (published in the *Encyclopedia Metropolitana*). "The fundamental principle of Arnold's conception of history," notes G. P. Gooch, "was that it was a divine process, and that man was a moral being accountable for his actions."[93] Arnold's literary aspiration was to "complete plain and popular histories of Greece and Rome, of a moderate size, cleared of nonsense and unchristian principles."[94]

During this period Whately, who had married in 1821 and had begun to build his own family, made periodic visits to the Arnold home. He loved children, and Mary seems to have enjoyed his company. Whately was always to be a close friend of the family. But, after presenting the Bampton Lectures in 1822, Whately left Oxford for three years of parochial work in Suffolk, and by the time he returned in 1825, Arnold had already broadened the basis of his ideas and had set himself apart from the older school of Noetics.

Francis Newman, in reference to the 1820s, reflected, "If at this period a German divinity professor had been lecturing at Oxford, or German books had been accessible to me, it might have saved me long peregrinations of body and mind." Similarly, A. P. Stanley once remarked to Mark Pattison, "How different the fortunes of the Church of England might have been if Newman had been able to read

German."[95] The Germans had already struggled beyond the conflicts of rationalism and anti-intellectual dogmatism into a mediating theology, which recognized the claims of reason without abandoning the essential truths of Christianity.

There was no person in England at this time better situated to put Arnold in contact with German theology and the contemporary work of Coleridge than the brother of his friend Augustus. However, it was not for religious advice that Arnold contacted J. C. Hare. Arnold's principle concerns were not those of Francis Newman; that is, his questions were, in the main, historical rather than theological. Arnold describes his labors and interests in a letter of 1824:

> I am now working at German in good earnest, and have got a master who comes down here to me once a week. I have read a good deal of Julius Hare's friend [Barthold] Niebuhr, and have found it abundantly overpay the labour of learning a new language, to say nothing of some other very valuable German books with which I am becoming acquainted, all preparatory to my Roman History.[96]

J. C. Hare must have been particularly eager to place a volume of Schleiermacher into the hands of Arnold, but until Arnold acquired greater facility with the language, he was unwilling to labor over any German not directly related to his historical researches.[97] Thus, Hare had to be patient, but Niebuhr's rationalist approach to history—so destructive to cherished myths made virtually sacred in the volumes of Livy, Polybius, and Plutarch—was eminently attractive to Arnold, who saw in the German historian's critical method an ideal type of scholarship. And when Hugh James Rose, the appointed Christian Advocate at Cambridge, attacked Arnold's article on Niebuhr in the *Quarterly Review* of June 1825, Arnold identified the error in Rose's stance on German divines—"as if ignorance and blind following the opinions of others were the habits that best become Christians."[98]

At about the time that Arnold's article on Niebuhr was published, Whately returned triumphantly to Oxford as doctor of divinity and principal of St. Alban's Hall. He appointed J. H. Newman as his vice-principal. Shortly afterward, Keble moved into the curacy of Hursley, in the vicinity of Winchester Cathedral. A circle of admiring pupils, R. H. Froude, Robert Wilberforce, and Isaac Williams, followed Keble to his new home. Newman would soon be added to their number. Arnold, "like a good neighbour," came down to see Keble just after Christmas, 1825. "How very unaltered he is," Keble remarked, "and how very comfortable and contented; he is one of the persons whom it does one good to think of when I am in a grumbling vein."[99] It is pleasant to think of Arnold as still equally the friend of Keble and Whately. But there were, even at this time, political tensions mounting and alliances being formed that would, for Keble, soon make the thought of Arnold anything but a curative for a grumbling vein.

The Catholic Emancipation Debate

In 1793 the elective franchise was extended to the pauper tenantry of Ireland, its "forty-shilling freeholders." It was supposed that this extension of democracy in Ireland was little more than an impractical gesture; after all, the paupers were Catholics and the only representation that Ireland had in Parliament was by Anglicans, who were, until the Act of Union (1800-1801), only responsible for the English interests of Ireland. In 1800 the British government became politically responsible for the Catholics of Ireland, above 80 percent of the population. If the only people in Ireland who had the vote were still the gentry and the "fifty-pound freeholders," then the notion of opening up a seat for a Catholic member of Parliament would not have been so pressing an issue. The gentry and large property holders had never sought, by anything close to a majority, Catholic representation. However, now that a significantly large portion of Ireland had a vote and a voice by which they demanded direct representation, the situation was considerably changed.

In 1824 Robert Southey had published his *Book of the Church*, which hailed the virtues of English Protestantism and warned the nation of the danger of admitting into Parliament Roman Catholics, whose loyalties would demand that they subvert the established Church. Charles Butler responded in the same year with the *Book of the Roman Catholic Church*, vindicating the patriotism of Catholics and denying that there could be any conflict of interests between their loyalties to the Pope and to the English Constitution.[100] Blanco White, who saw the providence of God at work in sending him to England for such a time as this, took up arms on the side of Southey and wrote his *Practical and Internal Evidence against Catholicism, with Occasional Strictures on Mr. Butler's Book of the Roman Catholic Church* (1825). This book, or series of six Letters, was dedicated to Copleston, with whom Blanco White had been in correspondence on the subject, the two men taking different positions. Blanco White argues that it is the Roman Catholic's "unquestionable duty to undermine a system of which the direct tendency is, in his opinion, the *spiritual and final* ruin of men," and that, therefore, no *authentic* Roman Catholic can be expected to support the interests of the English Church.[101] J. T. Coleridge requested from Blanco White a shorter and simplified version of his argument, and the author obliged by writing *The Poor Man's Preservative against Popery*, in which the argument is presented in dialogue form.

Copleston proposed to Convocation on 24 April 1826 that the degree of Master of Arts be conferred on Blanco White "in consideration of his eminent talents and learning, and of his exemplary conduct during his residence at Oxford, but more especially on account of those able and well-timed publications by which he has powerfully exposed the errors and corruptions of the Church of Rome."[102] The degree was quickly granted, and Blanco White returned to Oxford in October 1826 as an honorary fellow of Oriel.

These were strange times, and it is amusing—if not somewhat disorienting—to think of the two sides forming up against each other for debate in the Oriel Common Room. Newman and Blanco White, with violins in hand, coming in together in high spirits after playing Beethoven in a string quartet, would be immediately piqued by the pro-emancipationist dialogue of Hawkins and the infuriatingly logical Whately. To say that a lively debate would ensue is to understate the case. The Catholic Emancipation issue touched upon the most fervently held political and religious convictions and not infrequently struck unguarded nerves. Keble and Arnold, though neighbors, were safely apart from the fray of the Common Room, and as long as Arnold could hold his tongue, Keble could check his temper. But "political Tommy" loved a good debate.

Rugby

In October 1819 Arnold was approached with the offer of a position as one of the masters at Winchester. In response, he stated that he had come to regard his home in Laleham "as my settled and permanent home in this world. My present way of life I have tried, and am perfectly contented with it; and I know pretty well what the life of a master of Winchester would be, and feel equally certain that it would be to me excessively disagreeable."[103] There was nothing about teaching *per se* that Arnold found disagreeable; what he objected to was teaching in a public school, where the combination of boys so influences their individual attitudes and behaviors as to virtually emasculate the masters' moral presence among them. This was, for Arnold, "the great curse of public schools."[104] As a private tutor, Arnold could spend time with each boy, not only in instruction, but in walking, running, and swimming, and he could impress upon every pupil "that there was a work for him to do—that his happiness as well as his duty lay in doing that work well." Bonamy Price, one of these pupils from Laleham—who would later work under Arnold as a master at Rugby and would, ultimately, occupy the chair of professor of political economy at Oxford—recalled Arnold's "wonderful power of making all his pupils respect themselves, and of awakening in them a consciousness of the duties that God assigned to them personally."[105] Arnold knew that he could not hope to continue to exercise this influence as a master at a public school, and so he declined the offer when it was presented.

It is not likely that even the prospect of a headmastership would have interested Arnold in October 1819, but his circumstances had changed dramatically between then and October 1827. Now, his concerns for the education of his children, exasperated by an escalating financial debt and the rejection of his application for the professorship of history at London University, pushed him toward contemplating the vacancy at Rugby. Dr. John Wooll had resigned his position as headmaster, the trustees had published their request for applications, and the deadline was quickly approaching. Arnold discussed the possibility with Whately and Hawkins, he went on long walks—and still, he hesitated. Finally, he compressed his concerns into two questions, and brought them to Hawkins: (1) Would he have full discretion, without interference from the trustees, to exercise authority in matters concerning discipline? (2) Could he be assured, before having to subscribe to the Thirty-nine Articles, that they are Articles of Peace only, and that subscription implies acquiescence rather than complete agreement?[106] Quickly, Whately and Hawkins made the necessary inquiries, provided Arnold with the assurances he needed, and sent in their testimonials on his behalf. Whately urged that the trustees, like the fellows of Oriel, disregard the social positions and connections of the candidates and look to proven ability alone, and Hawkins predicted that Arnold, if given the opportunity, would reform public school education throughout England.[107]

Hawkins understood something about the character of Arnold; he knew that Arnold was an irrepressible reformer. Truly, Arnold was neither an Erasmus nor a Luther, but in him were combined something of the best of each. Furthermore, his mind was saturated with Thucydides, and he had the social consciousness of the patriotic hero. He made a most revealing remark when, at Laleham, he said of his garden, "There is always something to interest me even in the very sight of the weeds and litter, for then I think how much improved the place will be when they are removed."[108] Arnold did not need Dr. Pangloss to teach him that his duty in life consisted in cultivating his garden, but he did need success at Rugby to persuade him that his garden was the State and Church of England.

It should not be supposed that the trustees had no other candidates of proven ability. Benjamin Hall Kennedy, Dr. Butler's prize pupil from Shrewsbury, who had gone on to become president of the Cambridge Union debating club and had just graduated as Senior Classic, also applied for the position. What Kennedy lacked, however, was Arnold's years of experience as a tutor. In 1828, he would, nevertheless, win a fellowship at St. John's, and after two years of tutoring undergraduates, take a post as master at Harrow, and finally, in 1836, succeed Butler as headmaster at Shrewsbury. Kennedy would hold his distinguished position there for thirty-three years before returning to Cambridge as Regius Professor of Greek. We might safely presume that more than one trustee carefully weighed Hawkins' recommendation against Butler's. No doubt, more than one trustee would later have moments of deep regret for the favor he extended to the former.

Early in the morning of 18 December 1827, while the Arnold family was still in bed, the postman arrived with a letter from Sir Henry Halford, a trustee of Rugby and an uncle of the precocious H. Halford Vaughan, then a sixth form student at Rugby. Halford congratulated him on his appointment. Copleston, grateful that the dignity of Oriel was upheld, conferred upon Arnold the degree of Doctor of Divinity—an act that Mrs. Arnold deemed "almost ludicrous."[109] In these days, there were no Honorary Doctorate degrees, for all Doctorate degrees were, by definition, honorary. As Mozley notes, "For all the degrees in theology and law there was then no more examination than there is for a bogus degree at Philadelphia. In point of fact they were bogus degrees and nothing more." Oxford could then "make Doctors of Divinity as easily as Birmingham can make brass tokens."[110] Or, as another fellow of Oxford expressed it, the doctor's degree "may pass for a rhetorical flourish to round a sentence."[111] At best, the degree was a token of earned confidence, and its practical purpose in this instance was to intimate to the parents of young boys, "You may place your trust in this man's wisdom and ability."

It is beyond the scope of this chapter to adequately represent the condition of the public schools, either their discipline or curriculum, in early nineteenth-century England; but it is safe to say that their condition was such that they required a doctor's attention. Since Lytton Strachey would have us believe that "the public schools of those days were still virgin forests," uncorrupted by the introduction of morals and religion, which Arnold almost single-handedly flogged into little boys,[112] I must at least note what many others have already observed—that the little truth in Strachey's work is sufficient only to give potency to its errors and blatant falsifications. Evidently, Strachey did not even bother to read Arnold's 1835 essay "On the Discipline of Public Schools," and his description of the discipline at Rugby is without foundation—unless we can assume that he is describing, out of memory and an imagination fueled by deep-seated resentment, the situation at Abbotsholme under its headmaster and founder, Dr. Cecil Reddie. There, at Abbotsholme, the sixth form students were empowered to corporally punish the younger boys, and "Lytton must certainly have witnessed, if not actually been the subject of, one of the occasional floggings" that were administered by the headmaster himself and witnessed by the assembled school.[113] Clearly, the verbal flogging that Strachey has given to Arnold betrays all the anger and resentment that, while not indicative of childhood abuse, is nevertheless typically engendered by it.

Flogging was, virtually, a necessary evil to enforce order in institutions that were, almost unavoidably, factories of chaos. Prussia had recognized the need to replace boarding schools with day schools, but England was too fond of its traditions. And, as long as parents had the notion that a public school was the place to send incorrigible boys—where they would be sure to form themselves into packs and, lacking adult supervision for most hours of the day, compete with one another in all manner of naughtiness—then the power to flog would remain the masters' and headmaster's means of maintaining some semblance of authority. In 1832, a year of national stress and for Arnold, family loss, the headmaster once lost his temper and, on the mistaken testimony of an assistant master, flogged a boy in the classroom. It was a case that, because of the headmaster's outspoken views, received national attention and made his name odious to many parents, especially of the Tory persuasion.[114] Even so, what Arnold nearly accomplished at Rugby was to eliminate the need for corporal punishment by fearlessly expelling every pupil whose moral influence upon the school was less than desirable, even if the boy had not been convicted of flagrant violations.

In addition, Arnold restricted his own personal influence to the young men of the sixth form, in whom he would place his complete trust to work in association with the masters in maintaining order in the school. However, unlike Dr. Reddie and numerous headmasters before him, Arnold did not grant to any of his students the right to beat another student. On the other hand, he upheld "the power of fagging"—that is, the "power given by the supreme authorities of a school to the boys of the highest class or classes in it, to be exercised by them over the lower boys for the sake of securing the advantages of regular government amongst the boys themselves, and avoiding the evils of anarchy."[115] Boys below the fifth form were subject to being fagged; they could be ordered to carry messages, collect stray balls at games, and perform other menial duties. Arnold argued that, without the fag system, in which authority to command was lawfully placed in the most mature students, there would instead prevail, by the power of the strongest and meanest, the unlawful bully system. James Mozley, the brother of the author of the *Reminiscences*, judiciously observes of Arnold, "The fact that the Sixth Form was an instrument ready made for him . . . does not at all interfere with the credit due to him for converting it into such an instrument of government as he did."[116]

No boy at Rugby made it into the sixth form without proving himself capable of maintaining a standard of moral and academic excellence, and few young men made it through the sixth without developing into Christian gentlemen. This was Arnold's aim, by which he measured the degree of his success. According to W. C. Lake, the headmaster impressed upon his boys "above everything the *blessing of high ideals and of decided convictions*."[117] Arnold would have agreed with Schleiermacher, that "an invaluable advantage afforded by schools is, that there the sense of right is developed, and the boy acquires a sense of self-dependence. It is these two qualities that make the man."[118] But Arnold would have added that no man is ever fully a man unless he is also a Christian, and no male Christian is ever truly a Christian unless he is also a man.[119] Nothing was more essential to being a Christian than learning to be a gentleman, and thus Arnold's sermons in Rugby Chapel emphasized the moral character of Christianity almost to the exclusion of its dogmatic aspect.

Out of Rugby, during Arnold's headmastership, would come some of England's great educational, ecclesiastical, and social reformers, including H. Halford Vaughan, Charles Vaughan, A. P. Stanley, W. C. Lake, Arthur Clough, Thomas Hughes, and F. J. A. Hort. Hughes memorialized Rugby, from his own perspective as an athlete, in the unabashedly didactic *Tom Brown's Schooldays* (1857), and Stanley memorialized the school's headmaster in *The Life and Correspondence of Thomas Arnold, D.D.* (1844), a work that Tuckwell praises as "one of the seven great bio-graphies in the English language."[120] During Arnold's life, perhaps his greatest contribution to the Broad Church movement was his religious influence on the boys of Rugby, many of which gradually formed themselves into a circle of liberal thought at Oxford. Indeed, as headmaster of Rugby, his influence upon Oriel was arguably greater than it could have been had he obtained position there as a tutor, and it is largely to his credit that, in the 1840s, the Oriel Common-Room "was falling a good deal under the control of the Broad Church influences of the time."[121]

Catholics Emancipated, Oxford Divided

Reform was now in the air, and so was conflict. In view of the approaching warfare of ideas, it might appear that all of Oriel was, in 1828, assuming battle positions. While Arnold was busy in August packing his books and family for the two-day trip to Rugby, Copleston was getting situated as bishop of Llandaff, Hawkins was assuming the position of provost of Oriel, Newman was moving into the pulpit as vicar of St. Mary's, just vacated by Hawkins, and Samuel Hinds, an old friend of Whately's, was taking up Newman's former post as vice-principal of St. Albans. Not even the pen of Strachey could exaggerate the results that these changes would make possible.

The catalyst for conflict was not, however, this shuffling of chairs; rather, it was the brilliant and bold revolutionary gesture of the Irish Catholic demagogue Daniel O'Connor. In June 1828 he ran for office as representative of Clare County, Ireland. As a Roman Catholic, the law of England forbade that he sit in the House of Commons; however, there was no law that could forestall his running for office, and the contagious sympathies of the Irish "forty-shilling freeholders" were such that not only they, but all classes of Roman Catholics, were now ready to challenge the laws of England and demand fair representation by one of their own. Suddenly, Parliament found itself facing the threat of a bloody uprising, with the possible consequence of the loss of Ireland to Britain. The failure of Parliament to grant fair representation to its colonies had resulted, only half a century earlier, in an extremely costly war with the Americans. Now, the same threat was facing England once again.

Sir Robert Peel, whom Oxford had elected twelve years earlier as M.P. on an anti-emancipationist platform, recognized that the issue was no longer to be decided by the Protestant feelings of the English aristocracy. "A prudent Minister," he wrote in his *Memoirs*, "before he determines against all concession, against any yielding or compromise of former opinions, must well consider what it is that he has to resist, and what are his powers of resistance."[122] Having recognized that resistance was hopeless, Peel changed his stance. Then, he did the honorable thing and resigned his position, and immediately ran again for office.

Much of Oxford—including tutors J. H. Newman, R. H. Froude, and R. Wilberforce—was outraged, feeling that Peel's duty was to represent those who elected him, regardless of his personal thoughts. Moreover, this was—according to Keble and the three tutors—an issue that could rightly be determined only by the Church, as it was the Anglican Church that stood most in jeopardy by having Catholics in the House. It was becoming increasingly clear to Keble and his friends that a Parliament that failed to give adequate deference to the voice of the bishops was a Parliament that endangered the interests of an Established Church. Teacups shook in the hands of stoic Oxonians, and after Whately convinced Blanco White of the political necessity of Catholic Emancipation, an indignant Newman would walk no further with either Whately or Hawkins. G. A. Denison and Charles Neate, newly elected fellows, were disappointed to find the Oriel Common Room extraordinarily dull. "We found the reason to lie in this," Denison explained, "—that the men were afraid of one another: were living together under the restraint which attaches naturally to a sense of incipient—to become pronounced—divergence."[123]

Arnold, now situated in his office at Rugby, entered the public debate with his pamphlet "The Christian Duty of Conceding the Roman Catholic Claims" (1829). Proposing to consider the issue strictly from a religious point of view, ignoring expedience and temporal advantages, Arnold proceeds to make his argument on the basis of what is "the Christian duty" of the English toward the Irish Catholics. It is a historical fact, Arnold notes, that the English forcibly brought the Irish "into our national society"; therefore, he adds, "we must not shrink from the just consequences of our own act. . . . If Protestants urge that they cannot allow Catholics to have any voice in the government, why did they bring a Catholic people into political connexion with themselves?" Moreover, if England had left Ireland alone, the Irish would probably have experienced a Protestant Reformation, just as the other countries of Northern Europe, but "because Protestantism was associated in her eyes with subjugation and oppression, she clung the more fondly to her superstitions." If Protestants could only learn to treat their Roman Catholic neighbors with Christian kindness, they would ultimately find that, as the number of Catholics diminish with conversions, so too would any threat to Protestantism disappear. And, what if the very worse should befall England as the result of Catholic Emancipation? Arnold acknowledges, "No national evil that did not involve national sin could be greater in my judgment than the destruction of our Protestant Church Establishment"; yet, he is quick to add that "even the existence of our Establishment would be too dearly purchased, if it could only be upheld by injustice."[124]

Oxford, however, expressed itself in a judgment that was neither politically practical nor, by Arnold's telling, Christian. They rejected Peel and elected an anti-emancipationist as its representative in the House of Commons. "The worse part of the whole business," reflected Arnold from Rugby, "is the effectual manner in which the clergy generally, and of Oxford especially, have cut their own throats in the judgment of all enlightened public men—an evil more dangerous to their interests than twenty Catholic Emancipation bills."[125] If the demands of justice did not persuade Parliament to concede to the Roman Catholics, fear for the security of the State did, and on April 13 the Duke of Wellington, as prime minister, signed the bill and passed it along to King George IV, who, three days later, "hating the bill and sobbing as his gouty hand signed, . . . returned it approved." When Parliament reconvened at the end of the month, three Catholic peers and one commoner took the obligatory oath not to subvert the Established Church in England or Ireland and took their seats.[126]

The Decline of Oriel

H. Halford Vaughan left Rugby in the summer of 1829, having won all of the prizes that the school had to offer, including an Exhibition Award of £60 a year for up to seven years, as long as he maintained residence at Oxford. Matthew Arnold allegedly once told an Oxford friend that his father had considered Vaughan "the most able boy he had had under him at Rugby."[127] This seems improbable, in view of the brevity of the period in which Vaughan studied under Arnold and the later Rugby successes of Clough and Stanley, both of whom enjoyed friendly relations with the Arnold family. Even so, Vaughan was remarkably intelligent, and in 1835 he would obtain a fellowship at Oriel.

Vaughan matriculated at Christ Church just before the implementation of the 1830 Examination Statute. Due to the increase in the number of degree candidates, Oxford examinations now ceased to be conducted viva-voce, and as a result, greater emphasis was placed on English composition, philosophy, and familiarity with modern books and secondary literature.[128] The result of the Examination Statute was that a greater burden was placed on the college tutors, upon whom the principal education of undergraduates depended. Upon each tutor fell the responsibility of preparing for examinations the students assigned to him by the provost. One of the practical difficulties inherent in this system was that the tutor could proceed in his lessons only at the pace of the slower students, leaving many students to rely upon either private tuition or instructional books. The 1830 reform was one more push in the direction of much-needed specialization.

Another problem in the system was that there was no statute making tutoring compulsory for fellows. Since residency was only required during the probationary year, many of the older and more experienced fellows did not live at Oxford, and of this number many had assumed responsibilities in connection with a curacy or journal. For them, even if they could relocate to Oxford without forfeiting their positions, taking on the additional duties of providing college tuition would have been excessive. Thus, the provost's task of hiring tutors that would advance the reputation of the college was not by any means an easy one.[129]

In 1830 Hawkins had four college tutors, three of which were bound together by close friendship. As already noted, these three were Newman, Froude, and Wilberforce. They worked together to initiate such reforms that would allow them to meet the new demands of the university without sacrificing the quality of their lectures. First, they came to the same conclusion that Arnold had reached, that they needed the authority to expel unruly students. Hawkins granted it. Next, they decided to pool their students and divide them according to ability, so that the brightest or most advanced students would be in the same class. Finally, in compliance with the spirit of the new Examination Statute, Newman wanted to integrate new texts into the lectures. With these additional plans, the tutors approached Hawkins. Thomas Mozley gives his perspective on Hawkins's reaction: "The Provost received it with a suspicion amounting to dismay. He felt that the tutors would thereby have the tuition entirely in their own hands, and that he might find himself left out of the actual course of studies and out of the current of college thought and feeling."[130] Tuckwell pitched his voice with Mozley's, declaring that, as provost, Hawkins was, from the first, "despotic in the College, and in his intercourse with the Fellows watchfully jealous of his authority."[131] Only Pattison rushed to Hawkins's defense: "In the hands of the three tutors, all of them priests, narrow and desperate devotees of the clerical interest, the college must have become a seminary in which the pupils should be trained for church ends."[132]

There is no doubt that the three tutors conceived of their work as a "species of pastoral care." In this regard, they did not differ from Keble, who once told J. T. Coleridge that, were it not so, he could never conscientiously take up its duties.[133] However, Hawkins also regarded college tuition in this fashion, and we have already seen Arnold's thoughts on this matter. Thomas Turton, the Regius Professor of Divinity at Cambridge (1827-1842), thought the unique relation between a tutor and his pupils "a powerful instrument of religious education."[134] On the other hand, Connop Thirlwall, a tutor at Trinity College, Cambridge, thought that "it would be a somewhat exaggerated idea of the intimacy of this relation, to suppose that [a tutor] commonly thinks it a part of his duty, to inquire into the state of his pupil's religious feelings or habits," and J. C. Hare, who in 1830 was still classical lecturer at Trinity, agreed with him.[135] Even so, the fact appears to be that Pattison's defense of Hawkins is expressive of anachronistic sentiment; nobody at the time would have thought a tutor peculiar for bringing clerical notions into his tuition, although those tutors who actually did so were in the minority. Still, the clerical notions of the three tutors under consideration were not representative of the Noetics, and there can be little doubt that the provost keenly felt that the enthusiastic labors of his tutors were only widening the gulf between himself and "the current of college thought and feeling." As Hawkins sat brooding in his study, he described his dilemma in a letter to Copleston. The bishop, in turn, suggested that a provost might interfere "by way of counsel and advice," and—if this produced no effect—that all further assignment of pupils might be "to those tutors who agreed with him."[136] Pallas Athena stirred up the fool's heart within him, and rising to the occasion, the provost launched his crooked shaft.

When Hawkins decided to assign no further students to his innovative tutors, his decision would have, at least, four relatively immediate and certain consequences. *First*, he had to find new tutors, and failing to find them from among the current fellows of the college, Hawkins applied to Hampden, who had returned to Oxford in 1829 as a public examiner. Hampden's acceptance of the position in 1831 marked the beginning of cool relations between himself and Newman. *Second*, Hawkins's failure to obtain additional tutors of the caliber equivalent to the ones that he dismissed resulted in the decline of Oriel. "From this date," says Pattison, "the college began to go downhill." Balliol College, already running a close second to Oriel, now began to win the greater number of university honors and "rapidly shot ahead."[137] Thomas Hughes's harsh verdict is that, by 1840, "with the exception of

Christ Church, there was . . . probably no college in Oxford less addicted [than Oriel] to reading for the schools, or indeed to intellectual work of any kind."[138] *Third*, Hawkins's decision resulted in making Newman the master of his schedule. If Newman had been both vicar of St. Mary's *and* tutor of Oriel in 1833, it is doubtful that he would have had sufficient leisure to begin the publication of *Tracts for the Times*. *Fourth*, Hawkins initiated a competition between himself and Newman over the hearts and minds of the fellows of Oriel, which within a few years left the college all but shattered. If Hawkins had no cause to be suspicious and controlling in 1830, he had cause enough by 1836, and by all accounts he subsequently became a bitter and unpleasant man. Still, Hawkins was the man most responsible for preventing Oriel from falling entirely into the hands of the Tractarians. His irreplaceable service in this matter was well known, and it was his "capacity for taking trouble" that kept his name out of consideration for ecclesiastical preferment.[139] Years later, Newman, in his novel *Loss and Gain* (1848), would depict Hawkins as the character Joshua Jennings, the vice-principal who, by means of a "system of espionage," ferrets out "papistically inclined" undergraduates.

The Establishment

The Catholic Emancipation debate had been divisive not only in Oxford, but also within Parliament. The Tory party was split into two factions, and when the death of George IV in June 1830 necessitated a general election, the Tories lost thirty seats in Parliament. Within five months Wellington was ousted, and a Whig cabinet under Earl Grey came into power. The Whigs, responding to popular demand, promised England reforms, and they were quick to deliver. The first reform bill passed through the House of Commons in just over three weeks in March 1831. This Reform Act sought to reapportion the seats in Parliament so as to more accurately represent the nation and to extend the suffrage to ten-pound freeholders[140]—men only, of course. Voting rights were not extended to British women until 1918. The result of the first Reform Act would be middle-class political representation. However, on 8 October 1831, the House of Lords rejected the bill by forty-one votes, for which votes the bishops were, in the main, responsible.

The lower classes of England were outraged at the Church. The bishops were pilloried in the press as enemies of liberty living off the profits of corruption. *The Extraordinary Black Book* heralded the bishops' opposition to reform as "the climax of their legislative turpitude," and based it chiefly on their fears that reform "might involve a sacrifice of their inordinate emoluments."[141] They were terrorized by mobs, who burned effigies of them in public. But these symbolical expressions were not satisfying to all, and one bishop had his carriage stoned, while another was physically pulled out of a coach and assaulted. A popular cry was raised for the disestablishment of the Church, and the bishops—as the feast day for St. Thomas Becket approached—grew wiser in their meditations. The king and prime minister assailed them individually, coaxed them with the sharp edge of reason, and softened them with assurances of security. Strangely, Lord Howley, the mild archbishop of Canterbury, was unmoved in his opposition. Even so, on 13 April 1832 the bill passed in the House of Lords.

In the meantime, the Whig administration had not been slow to reward its friends and to place sympathizers into the seats of Parliament. In September 1831 "the high wranglers of Oxford were struck dumb" when Whately was appointed not bishop, but *arch*bishop of Dublin.[142] Arnold was offered a stall in Bristol Cathedral, but he declined: "I have always strenuously maintained that the clergy engaged in education should have nothing to do with church benefices."[143] Only a few months before, he had assured Whately, "One thing you may depend on, that nothing shall ever interfere with my attention to the school."[144] Whately too was committed to education and, particularly, to Oxford. Of course, a handsome living was attached to the mitre and crosier, but *archbishop* never could be to Whately more than a title and a position, whereas *professor* is what Whately was and ever would be. Those who knew him knew also that it was duty, not riches and glory, that called Whately away from his happiness.[145] In October, after appointing his old friend and associate Samuel Hinds as his secretary, the champion of first-generation Noeticism crossed St. George's Channel. Thomas Mozley is amused by the thought of Whately entering Dublin with "an armoury of pistols," for he had "a strange idea that his acceptance of the see was a service of danger."[146] Truly, though, the post was not without danger, and Whately—seen by both Irish Catholics and Protestants as a foreigner, a hireling, and a liberal in religion—was, quite possibly, the most hated man in Ireland.

What Whately had going most against him at this juncture in English history was simply that he now represented the Established Church—a Church that had not only failed to keep pace with the feelings of the people it claimed to serve, but that exacted taxes from the people, three quarters of which were either Catholics or dissenters, without any pretense of providing them service. Moreover, Whately's predecessor at Dublin, Archbishop Magee, had done everything in his power to make the Established Church more hateful to the Catholics of Ireland.[147] If Whately was in danger, it was because the Church itself was in danger. In January 1833 Arnold—who was now at Rydal with William Wordsworth making plans for the building of Fox How, his beloved home away from Rugby—wrote, "Nothing, as it seems to me, can save the Church, but an union with the Dissenters." Arnold's fear was occasioned by the passage of the Reform Bill, which made the dissenters "strong enough to turn the scale either for an establishment or against one." Moreover, Arnold observes, "at present they are leagued with the antichristian party against one, and will destroy it utterly if they are not taken into the camp in the defence of it."[148]

Arnold of Rugby had a plan to come to the rescue of the imperilled Church of England. The anonymous Episcopalian, as we have seen, also had a plan. His *Letters* suggested a policy of laissez-faire, that the legislative body of the government should simply leave the Church alone. Arnold now boldly replies, in the *Principles of*

Church Reform (1833), that it has been this very policy that has resulted in the turning of Parliament and the Church into "two hostile parties, each careless of union, and looking only to victory."[149] Moreover, such a policy implies "that the State's only object is the conservation of bodies and goods."[150] The difference between the two authors is not that one followed Hooker and the other did not. Both (and, we might add, S. T. Coleridge[151]) accepted the principle of identification of Church and State and followed Hooker in recognizing the reigning monarch as titular head of both;[152] but whereas the author of the *Letters* wished to separate the government civil from the government ecclesiastical, Arnold wished to see them fully united. This could be possible only by placing the civil government in the Church and the ecclesiastical government in the State. Arnold's opponents cried "Erastianism." As Baden Powell notes, Erastian theories "all tacitly if not explicitly assume the principle . . . that the *Legislature is a judge of religious truth*."[153] In defense of Arnold's views, we should note that, if the legislative branch of government is not distinguished from the ecclesiastic, and in matters religious *the State is the Church*, then one cannot reasonably conclude that the State exercises authority over the Church any more than that the Church exercises authority over the State. In Arnold's proposal, the Church as *enclesia*, united in its diversity, and not the Legislature, is the judge of religious truth.

As Arnold's letter (quoted above) suggests, his plan involved bringing the dissenters into the Church, and because he could not hope to convert the dissenters, he would instead convert the establishment. If the Church could be made to accommodate dissenters, they would cease to dissent, and the State would then come to recognize its unity with the Church. Arnold argued, "There seems to be no reason why the National Church should not enjoy a sufficient variety in its ritual, to satisfy the opinions and feelings of all." He suggested that "the church might be kept open nearly the whole of the Sunday, and we may hope, during some part at least of every week day;—the different services being fixed at different hours, and performed by different ministers." Arnold supposed that this arrangement would be productive of Christian unity, "And instead of an unseemly scene of one minister preaching against another, we should probably have an earnest union in great matters, and a manly and delicate forbearance as to points of controversy."[154] Although the largest part of Arnold's pamphlet is concerned with the practical aspects of bringing unity about, his intent was only to demonstrate that the unity itself—if one excepts Quakers and Roman Catholics[155]—is not an impossible dream.

Arnold had before complained of Hawkins's lectures on tradition, and now Hawkins took the opportunity to express his own complaints. He dispatched an angry letter to Arnold, chastising him for having written his pamphlet "with haste and without consideration" on subjects which he had not studied, did not understand, and which were beyond his proper province.[156] If Hawkins's letter proves nothing else, it at least betrays the level of confidence that the Oriel provost had in the Doctor of Divinity degree. But I think that it is also indicative of a growing coldness between Hawkins and Arnold, and reveals the limitations in the capacity of

Hawkins to entertain new ideas—such as we have already seen in his interaction with the three tutors. Arnold's pamphlet impressed Connop Thirlwall "with a great respect for the author," although it seemed to him "deficient in a practical point of view" and betrayed "great want of information as to the views and feelings of the Dissenters."[157] F. D. Maurice was moved by Arnold's "willingness to sacrifice reputation" for the sake of promoting unity, and he did not think "the extravagance of the scheme" a sufficient reason to reject it; however, against Arnold's plan Maurice protested "that the Church, as it now stands, is more really comprehensive than that alteration would make it."[158]

Arnold's Essay on Interpretation

In December 1831 Arnold had published a volume of Rugby sermons, to which he appended *An Essay on the Right Interpretation and Understanding of the Scriptures*. This *Essay*, now conjoined with his *Principles*, placed Arnold on the front lines of liberalism. In January 1833 A. P. Stanley, who had just matriculated at Balliol, reported the "painful" remarks made of Arnold by Newman and R. H. Froude. Froude, said Stanley, "really does consider him 'as a sort of special agent of the devil to deceive men by his apparent goodness.'"[159] The statement by Newman is probably that which is referred to in his *Apologia*. When someone had asked, in conversation, "whether a certain interpretation of Scripture was Christian? it was answered that Dr. Arnold took it; I interposed, 'But is *he* a Christian?'" Newman is anxious to make his remark appear innocent, and he explains, "I must have meant, 'Arnold answers for the interpretation, but who is to answer for Arnold?'"[160] However, it was reported to Arnold that what Newman had actually said was, "Yes, but first Dr. Arnold has to prove himself a Christian."[161] This latter retort seems more plausible, given Newman's feelings and the openness with which he was accustomed to express himself when in the company of Froude. Of course, this is not the sort of remark that the man who would one day be cardinal-deacon of St. George, Velabro, would have wished to have repeated, and the fact of its circulation must have pained him egregiously more than it did Arnold.

We must look now to the *Essay* if we would see what irritated Newman. Arnold's first rule of interpretation is "that a command given to one man, or to one generation of men, is, and can be, binding upon other men, and other generations, only so far forth as the circumstances in which both are placed are similar." Interpretation, thus, begins with historical exegesis, the separation of the essentials from the accidents of any given revelation, and an accurate knowledge of one's own situation. The second rule is that the "indirect use" of transitory commandments "may be universal, even although their direct use be limited. That is, from knowing what was God's will under such and such circumstances, we may gather, by parity of reasoning, what it will be in all other circumstances." If our circumstances are not the same as those to whom the commandment was given, yet they may be analogous, in which case an analogous application is to be sought in the Scripture. "It is these two rules," says Arnold, "taken together, which will enable us to use . . . every part of God's revelation to man, at once fully and rightly."[162]

From T. H. Horne's *Introduction to the Critical Study and Knowledge of the Holy Scriptures* (1818), Arnold had learned of the principle of accommodation, which urges that certain Old Testament passages referred to or quoted in the New are, in fact, applied or accommodated to the illustration of subjects foreign to their original scope and intent. This principle, in other words, recognizes that, occasionally, Scripture itself will take Scripture out of its original context in order to apply it in such a manner that it attains an entirely new sense. J. J. Conybeare, in his Bampton Lectures of 1824, was critical of the frequency with which the principle of accommodation was being applied as an interpretive tool. Conybeare perceived it as a popular device of rationalizing theologians.[163]

Arnold, however, extends the principle in order to suggest—as Lessing had suggested in "The Education of the Human Race"—a process of gradual revelation and *moral* accommodation. According to Arnold, God's commandments are adapted to human beings' intellectual and moral state of development, and so we find, in the Old Testament, commands given that could not have been given in the New Testament. For example, "The principle of accommodation is expressly allowed by Christ himself, when he declares the liberty of divorce to have been given to the Jews, 'on account of the hardness of their hearts.'"[164] By applying this principle to the Old Testament and Homer, Arnold is able to arrive at several brilliant, if not quite convincing, explications. When considering Samuel's command to Saul to utterly destroy the Amalekites and Agamemnon's similar command to Menelaus not to spare a single Trojan, Arnold explains, "In such a state of feeling, when lives were spared, it was not from humanity, but from avarice or lust; and, therefore, the command . . . was in fact a trial of their self-denial; it called upon them to renounce the ordinary fruits of victory."[165] When looking at the command of Moses to spare only the virgins among the women of Midian, Arnold declares, "God would never give such a command to any one whose moral feelings would be shocked by it; but they to whom it was addressed felt it only as a restraint on their self-indulgence." He then illustrates the point by noting Odysseus's pitiless slaughter of the disloyal female slaves of his household.[166]

At first sight, Arnold's interpretations may appear as the sort of disingenuous efforts so typical of those who are motivated by an anxious care to preserve some time-worn doctrine unable any longer to care for itself. But, if we keep firmly in mind Arnold's presupposition of the gradual moral development of the human race—of which history itself was supposed to testify—then the explications do begin to sound forth with, at least, a modest jingle of plausibility, if not quite the resounding ring of truth. Moreover, Arnold's method of interpretation might have prevented Charles Kingsley from taking a callous view toward the loss of lives. "Do you believe in the Old Testament?," he asked a friend in 1855. "Surely, then, say, what does that destruction of the Canaanites mean? If *it* was right, Rajah Brooke was right. If he be

wrong, then Moses, Joshua, David, were wrong."[167] Kingsley does not appear to
have considered that, if Arnold's doctrine of moral development is right, then Rajah
Brooke may be accountable to a different moral standard than that by which God
judged Moses, Joshua, and David.

Arnold also fully endorses Semler's concept of accommodation, which suggests that God's revelations are accommodated to our finite faculties: "The very
means by which we receive all our knowledge, that is, language, and the observations of our senses, are themselves so imperfect, that they could not probably
convey to the mind other than imperfect notions of truth."[168] In Coleridgean terms,
the tools of the *Understanding* are incapable of establishing anything beyond that
which is notional. Belief and unbelief in the reality to which revelation would direct
our faculties is, therefore, to Arnold, primarily a matter of morality rather than of
intellect. Redemption depends not upon belief itself, but on the will to believe, which
is determinative of our moral development and, at the same time, of our ability to
believe. Unbelief in miracles, for example, "can never be innocent, unless it were
inevitable; every difficulty in the Scriptures may be an excuse for it, if we are seeking
for excuses; but he who loves God and virtue will cling to them, not till he can find
an excuse for quitting them, but till he finds it impossible to abide with them."[169]

It is very clear from the *Essay* that Arnold has no difficulty in believing in the
miracles of Scripture. However, by 1840, his belief in miracle had become hardly
anything more than the vestige of a childhood faith. In a letter to Hawkins, he writes,
"The character of any supernatural power can be only judged of by the moral
character of the statement which it sanctions: thus only can we tell whether it be a
revelation from God, or from the Devil."[170] Miracle adds nothing and decides
nothing; it merely directs our attention to a statement the character of which must be
ascertained by our moral judgment, and, as Rowland Williams observes, "Those
cases in which we accept the miracle for the sake of the moral lesson prove the
ethical element to be the more fundamental."[171] Carlyle once remarked to J. A.
Froude that Arnold was happy in having died early, before he had to decide between
a life in the Church and fidelity to his understanding and conscience.[172] Arnold's
Christian faith, however, had already obtained a maturity that was beyond Carlyle's
comprehension, one that would have easily survived the inevitable shocks of intellectual life in the approaching decades.

When A. P. Stanley left Rugby in 1834, he spent much of the long vacation at
Herstmonceux with his "uncle"[173] J. C. Hare. While there, John Sterling brought out
S. T. Coleridge's "Letters on Inspiration." The author was recently deceased, and
the Letters were to be sent to Arnold before their publication as *Confessions of an
Inquiring Spirit*. Stanley thought the Letters written with a "beautiful spirit"—a
remark that probably brought to mind Goethe's "Confessions of a Beautiful Spirit"
in *Wilhelm Meister's Apprenticeship* (1795-1796), translated into English by
Carlyle in 1824; thus, Stanley may very well have had a hand in determining the title
for Coleridge's manuscript. Even so, Stanley preferred Arnold's *Essay*: "It struck
me, on thinking over the letters, what a thoroughly *Catholic* essay Arnold's is, its

only objects being to get as much good out of the Bible as possible, and remove stumbling-blocks without making any new ones."[174] Sterling ultimately came to share Stanley's enthusiasm for Arnold's pamphlet, and in a letter to Hare suggests that it is "worth, I suspect, all else on the subject in the English language, pointing out a principle, and leading on to more truth than it declares."[175]

Before leaving Arnold's *Essay*, we should note that this work, like his *Principles*, owes something to Whately. Mozley tells us that one of the topics on which Whately discoursed in the Oriel Common Room was "that the prohibition of idolatrous likenesses and emblems in the second commandment pointed beforehand to the true Image of God in the Son." Arnold also directs attention to the Socinian application of the second commandment as "an instance of the great mischief of applying to ourselves, directly, what was commanded of men under different circumstances."[176] A more significant point of comparison between the two Noetics can be found in their common belief that the greater part of Scripture is merely historical, and that the truth of Revelation or Inspiration is in no way threatened by bringing "critical, scientific, historical, and chronological" criticism to bear upon the historical books of Scripture.[177] It was this latter argument that led Francis Newman, upon his return from Persia, to seek out Arnold. Charles Lyell's *Principles of Geology* (1830-1833) was evoking serious doubts as to the historical and chronological truthfulness of the early chapters of Genesis, and "It was a novelty to me," says F. Newman, "that Arnold treated these questions as matters of indifference to religion." His visit to Arnold did not leave him convinced; nevertheless, "to see a vigorous mind, deeply imbued with Christian devoutness, so convinced, both reassured me that I need not fear moral mischiefs from free inquiry, and indeed laid that inquiry upon me as a duty."[178]

If, by the assessment of J. H. Newman, Whately and Arnold allowed too much liberty for interpretation and disputation concerning the truths of Christianity, Hampden erred in allowing too little. Whereas Whately and Arnold took away from Tradition its authority and invested it in the reason of the individual, Hampden insisted that religious authority could never belong either to Tradition or to the individual, since it is inherent only in divine inspiration and communicated in its effects. Newman identified these positions as alternative errors of Rationalism. In both positions, "The Rationalist makes himself his own centre, not his Maker, he does not go to God, but he implies that God must come to him."[179]

Hampden's Bampton Lectures

When Whately departed from Oxford in 1831, the Noetic torch was passed into the hands of R. D. Hampden, who, while philosophically more astute, had neither the spirit nor power of Whately and was completely indisposed to argument and self-defense in the political arena. He was the descendant of John Hampden, the leader of the Commons who defied Charles I in court in the famous Ship Moneys' Case of

Rex vs. Hampden (1637-1638), and who later, in 1643, only a few miles from Oxford, perished in battle against Royalist troops. Only Whig blood ran in the veins of R. D. Hampden, and this fact, in conjunction with his corresponding role as a Noetic, made him into a figurehead for the principles of liberalism at Oxford. Thus, when the religious dogmatists led by Newman measured Hampden's mettle and assumed that they could frighten him off the field, his Noetic peers, who identified him with their own cause, refused to allow a retreat.

After returning to Oxford in 1829 as public examiner, Hampden wrote a number of articles, including one on Thomas Aquinas for the *Encyclopedia Britannica.* Although the Reformation in England had done nothing to demote Aristotle's status in Oxford as "master of the sapient throng," the inevitable effect of the Enlightenment, particularly the influences of Bacon, Butler, Locke, and Paley, was to gradually reform theology so that it was no longer scholastic. And yet, Hampden's study of Thomism convinced him that Christian theology never made a clean break from Scholasticism, and that much of contemporary dogma still rested upon terms and presuppositions that had their origin in medieval philosophy. Therefore, when the heads of colleges nominated Hampden, in accordance with the Last Will and Testament of John Bampton, Canon of Salisbury (d. 1751), to deliver for the year 1832 a series of "eight Divinity Lecture Sermons" at St. Mary's, Hampden chose for his theme *The Scholastic Philosophy Considered in Its Relation to Christian Theology.*

The lectures were presented entirely in the spirit of the Protestant reformers, and no one attending could have anticipated the reaction that they would eventually provoke. In light of their significance to that approaching controversy, but not solely on account of it, they deserve our consideration. In fact, to quote Tuckwell in reference to Hampden's *Scholastic Philosophy,* "It may be said—and without fear of contradiction, since no one now reads or will read the book—that it exhibits wide, well-focused learning, and that it filled a gap in English theological literature."[180]

Lecture I, discussing the origin of Scholasticism, notes how the philosophy of Aristotle was initially taken up by apologists merely to defend Christianity against attacks. Although the Church had a more natural connection with Platonism and the Greek mind, in the process of using the rhetorical weapons of its enemies, "the Church became unawares Aristotelic."[181] By the eleventh century, the Church had endorsed the speculations of human reason in its efforts to counteract heterodoxical speculations: "The force of reason evidently began to be acknowledged and felt, as a powerful antagonist which the Church had fostered in its own system, and against which the Church therefore had need to fortify itself with weapons of the same temper."[182] The theologian of the middle ages could employ his reason in making logical deductions, as long as he did not propose anything new or contrary to received opinion.

In Lecture II Hampden waxes polemical. He declares his thesis, "that speculative logical Christianity, which survives among us at this day, . . . has been in all ages, the principal obstacle, as I conceive, to the union and peace of the Church of Christ."

Unlike the language of Scholasticism, the language of Scripture appeals not to our rational faculty, but rather to our emotions and moral sensibility or sense of duty—that is, Scripture teaches us "both how to feel, and how to act, towards God" and is "altogether inadequate in point of Science."[183] With the ascent of Scholasticism in the Church came the triumph of Realism or the assigning of an objective reality to mere ideas. "Nominalism, on the contrary, by denying any objective reality to general notions, led the way directly to the testimony of the sense and the conclusions of experience."[184] Hampden, thus, endorses nominalism as a philosophy of linguistics agreeable to the interpretation of Scripture and to the true relation between interpretive conclusions and the facts of religion. On the other hand, the Scholastic method can do no more than "frame a science of exact definitions." When it is employed to ascertain the truth of a thing, it merely gives "a more exact notion of the term by which it is signified."[185] Furthermore, by failing to regard "the Rhetorical nature of the Scriptures" or to appreciate them as essentially "a divine history of man," Scholasticism nullified the use of Scripture. "Scripture-arguments," Hampden insists, "are arguments of inducement, addressed to the whole nature of man—not merely to intellectual man, but to thinking and feeling man living among his fellow men;—and to be appreciated therefore in their *effect* on our whole nature."[186]

Lecture III, on Trinitarian Controversies, must have raised the hair on the back of Newman's stiff neck. After recounting the history of the debates concerning Arian and Sabellian doctrine, Hampden declares his own convictions in such a way as to evoke doubt whether, in fact, he has any convictions at all—or, at least, any that could be verbally expressed:

> The truth itself of the Trinitarian doctrine emerges from these mists of human speculation, like the bold, naked land, on which an atmosphere of fog has for a while rested, and then been dispersed. No one can be more convinced than I am, that there is a real mystery of God revealed in the Christian dispensation; and that no scheme of Unitarianism can solve the whole of the phenomena which Scripture records. But I am also as fully sensible, that there is a mystery attached to the subject, which is not a mystery of God.[187]

No inquisitor could hear such a confession without wondering whether Hampden truly believes the Trinitarian expressions in the catholic Creeds. Hampden himself answers evasively, "The only ancient, only catholic, truth is the Scriptural fact. Let us hold that fast in its depth and breadth—in nothing extenuating, in nothing abridging it—in simplicity and sincerity."[188]

In the following two Lectures, on Pelagian Controversies, Hampden again distances himself from the formulaic expressions of the Church. In regard to "our doctrinal statements on Predestination and Grace," he concludes, "I am not prepared . . . to vindicate those statements in their theoretic points, as the proper way in which the Divine Predestination and Grace should be apprehended by the Christian." Once more, the inquisitor in the pew asks whether the preacher can state specifically in what points the Articles of the Church are in error and in what ways they might be improved. But Hampden is again evasive: Predestination and Grace "are truths, it cannot be too often repeated, which concern more the heart than the intellect; and, in defining which accordingly, every attempt, however exactly and piously worded, must fail."[189] The proper response to the Revelation of Divine Agency is not to treat it "as a matter pregnant with consequences or inferences," but rather to respond in "simple, moral acquiescence and obedience"; and the proper response to the Revelation of Human Agency, as revealed in the fact of atonement, is to simply believe it and act upon it, "without the gloss of commentators, or the refinement of theorists."[190]

In Lecture VI, on the Moral Philosophy of the Schools, Hampden insists upon the separation of Ethics and Theology. Religion, according to Hampden, can only make us more fully aware of the ends toward which our moral nature directs, but it does not in the process in any way change our nature. The first object of the science of Ethics is, therefore, to ascertain our moral nature, and it is to this nature that Religion appeals. The science of Ethics is, in fact, so independent from Religion "that it would be nothing strange, or objectionable, in a Revelation, were we to find embodied in its language, much of the false Ethical Philosophy, which systems may have established." Where Scripture prescribes or commends certain activities, it is as subject to error as in any other point of mere science. Revelation, on the other hand, has to do with "the means of Religion," which consist not in activities, but rather in "holiness, separation from the world, devotion, stillness of the thoughts and the affections."[191]

In Lecture VII, we are given to understand that Sacramental Theology is derivative of "the general belief in Magic, in the early ages of the Church"—of the belief in "mystical unions of words with sensible things."[192] Hampden, looking out into his audience and seeing Newman and his friends, reminds them of the debt owed to the "Christian resolution of our Reformers," who "broke that charm which the mystical number of the Sacraments carried with it, and dispelled the theurgic system which it supported." Then, with a nod in the direction of Blanco White, he suggests, "We must ask of those, who have experienced the false comfort of that officious intercession of the sacramental system of the Latin Church. They will tell us, that, under that system, they knew not the liberty of the Gospel."[193]

Hampden brings his Bampton Lectures to a close with a sermon on the Nature and Use of Dogmatic Theology. He dismisses any distinction between Faith and Reason that would suggest that the two operate "as *distinct principles*" or that Faith demands a "pious submission" of the intellect.[194] Reason demonstrates that, whereas the Apostolic Fathers are valuable from both an historical and devotional perspective, "as authorities decisive of what is *true* or what is *false* in theological statement, they are in reality less valuable than the writings of a subsequent age."[195] Christian faith rests exclusively on the Scriptures, in which logical incoherence matters not.

Moreover, objections against the facts, as revealed in Scripture, cannot be met by logical argumentation, as to do so would be to concur with the presupposition upon which the objection is based—that is, that religious truths are directed to the rational faculty as opposed to the whole person. "Doctrinal statements of religious truth," declares Hampden, "have their origin in the principles of the human intellect. Strictly to speak, in the Scripture itself there are no *doctrines*." It is here that Hampden clearly parts ways with Whately's inductive approach to biblical hermeneutics. Revelation communicates and has its religious effect only through the words of Scripture *as they are given*. It is only the speculative theologian who, "by adducing text after text from an Epistle, . . . will contend that some dogmatic truth, some theory, or system, or peculiar view of divine truth, is asserted."[196]

In arriving at this conclusion, Hampden is resolving the "doubt" posited by Hooker in regard to doctrines deduced out of Scriptures, "how far we are to proceed by collection, before the full and complete measure of things necessary be made up. For let us not think," admonishes this worthy divine, "that as long as the world doth endure the wit of man shall be able to sound the bottom of that which may be concluded out of the Scripture."[197] Although unwilling to cast doubt on orthodox conclusions arrived at by adducing text after text, Hooker was clearly troubled by an inductive hermeneutics, and Hampden was either extraordinarily rash or remarkably courageous in cutting this Gordian knot.

The implication of Hampden's Lectures appears to be that the most that any Christian can rightly expect of another Christian—as a Christian merely, without respect to denomination—is sincere submission to the authority of the Scriptures in all points of faith. Any difference in understanding cannot be presumed as evidence of exclusion from the catholic and invisible Church of Christ. Newman was, for the moment, stunned beyond words, but he now knew, beyond any rational doubt, that Hampden was the *prodomos Antichristou* or "forerunner of Antichrist."[198]

In June 1832, shortly after the presentation of the Bampton Lectures, Blanco White left Oxford in order to join the Whatelys in their quiet home at Redesdale, outside of Dublin, where he could work on his *Observations on Heresy and Orthodoxy* (1835). Life at Oxford had become unbearable for him. In March, Augustus and Maria Hare had made an unannounced visit to his rooms, only to find him sickly and dejected, complaining of being "unable to do anything" other than work on his history of the Inquisition, a subject that had become "very painful and irritating to his feelings."[199] Within six months of his arrival in Ireland, he arrived at the conviction "that I am a decided anti-Trinitarian,"[200] and in early 1833 he resettled in Liverpool, where a large Unitarian community was developing under the ministries of J. H. Thom and James Martineau. Newman, who was at this time completing *The Arians of the Fourth Century* (1833), immediately recognized in Blanco White's defection the substance for propaganda against the theological liberals, particularly against Hampden. Basically, the argument is that, since the purple blossoms of Blanco White's liberalism exude the deadly perfume of Socinianism, we must beware that whosoever has come into contact with the tiniest petals or ripening buds of those blossoms, carries also the noxious and oppressive odors of the fatal malady.[201]

The fact that this ad hominem attack, though well known in the 1830s, is preserved nowhere so well as in Mozley's *Reminiscences* (1882) suggests that, after Newman's conversion to Roman Catholicism in 1845, it became an embarrassment. Mozley, undeterred by both Whately's and J. C. Hare's remonstrances against the old slander,[202] brushed the dust of debate aside and declared once more, "At the time the Lectures were written, there was only one man in Oxford who knew anything about the scholastic philosophy, and that was Blanco White. Hampden, an intimate friend of that gentleman from his first appearance in Oxford, was now thrown a good deal into his society." He continues, "My statement is that, in the latter part of 1831 and the early part of 1832, these two gentlemen saw a good deal of one another, and that one of them derived from the other material assistance in the way of information . . . in view of the lectures he was about to deliver."[203] The insidious imputation hardly disguised in Mozley's remarks evoked a furious reaction from Principal John Tulloch: "A writer who still virtually asserts that the Bampton Lectures were inspired, if not composed, in great part by Blanco White, notwithstanding the testimony of Dr. Hampden's family to the contrary . . . , and the absolute discrepancy between such a style as that of the Lectures and Blanco White's writings, is really unworthy of credence."[204] However, there is some truth to Mozley's remark that Hampden received "material assistance" from his friend if, by that phrase, we may understand that Blanco White enthusiastically recommended to Hampden Coleridge's *Aids to Reflection* (1825).

Hampden's Lectures express concurrence with Coleridge in a number of points, most of which can be found in *Aids to Reflection*. For example, a synopsis of Lectures I and II might be had in this single statement by Coleridge:

> Too soon did the Doctors of the Church forget that the *Heart*, the *Moral* Nature, was the beginning and the end; and that Truth, Knowledge, and Insight were comprehended in its expansion. This was the true and first apostasy—when in Council and Synod the divine Humanities of the Gospel gave way to speculative Systems, and Religion became a Science of Shadows under the name of Theology.[205]

The Nominalism that Hampden endorses in Lecture II also finds a corresponding expression by Coleridge: "Where the evidences of the Senses fails us, and beyond the precincts of sensible experience, there is no *Reality* attributable to any Notion, but what is given to it by Revelation, or the Law of Conscience, or the necessary interests of Morality."[206] In Lecture V, Hampden reached a conclusion in regard to Original Sin that Coleridge had also reached—that is, a belief in the fact itself, "the *tendency* to sin existing in human nature," without the explanation of the fact.[207] Both Hampden and Coleridge express serious disagreement with Paley's *Principles of Moral and Political Philosophy* (1785). Hampden argues against Paley's endeavor "to combine the separate principles of Ethics and Theology." In this point, Hampden is in concord with Schleiermacher, opposed to Coleridge.[208] However, he also, with Coleridge, argues against Paley's treatment of general consequences "as the chief and best criterion of the right or wrong of particular actions."[209] For Coleridge, morality is grounded upon Reason; for Hampden, morality is nature; for neither of them is it subject to anything external to our very being.

Coleridge certainly, and Hampden probably, is directly indebted to Jeremy Taylor, for whom "the act of believing propositions, is not for it selfe, but in order to certaine ends," which ends are to "encourage our services, or oblige them." In other words, there is no virtue in mere belief, but only in the obedience of faith. Moreover, it is impossible to eliminate variety of opinion, "yet the inconveniences arising from it might possibly be cured, not by uniting their beliefes, . . . but by curing that which caused these mischiefes," which are the mistaken notions that unity in opinions is possible, that there is inherent virtue in the belief of propositions, and that propositions other than St. Peter's Creed—that Jesus Christ is the Son of God—and those of the Apostle's Creed are necessary to salvation. In addition, "those Creeds are best which keep the very words of Scripture; and that Faith is best which hath greatest simplicity."[210] All of this Taylor had urged nearly two hundred years before Hampden's lectures in order to curb the violence of too-knowing and overzealous Christians.

Hampden's Lectures were published in 1833 and were admired by many, including Mark Pattison, future contributor to *Essays and Reviews* (1860), who found "the dissolving power of nominalist logic . . . wholly to my mind."[211] Thomas Arnold thought them "a great work, entirely true in their main points and I think most useful."[212] In fact, Arnold's letters clearly demonstrate that the influence of the Lectures was strongest upon him just after he had written his *Principles of Church Reform*. In one letter he expresses his "fervent hope, that if we could get rid of the Athanasian Creed, and of some other instances of what I would call the technical language of Trinitarianism, many good Unitarians would have a stumbling-block removed out of their path, and would join their fellow Christians." To his friend Baron Bunsen, the Prussian diplomat at the Vatican, he writes, "I dislike Articles, because they represent truth untruly, that is, in an unedifying manner, and thus robbed of its living truth."[213] Arnold, apparently—as we shall see—found Hampden's Lectures abundantly edifying and the lecturer himself altogether worthy of Noetic *esprit de corps*.

The Oxford Apostolicals

In December 1832 Newman had set out with R. H. Froude to the Mediterranean. After several months, the two parted ways, and Newman ventured back to Sicily alone, while Froude returned to Oxford. During the early summer of 1833, both men were gravely ill, but only Newman was to recover. When Froude was not isolated in his apartment, he sauntered into the Common Rooms, where he was occasionally met by William Palmer, the author of the recently published *Origines Liturgicæ*. They discussed the plight of the Church in England and decided to form an association to defend it against the encroachments of the State. Froude immediately set out to enlist Keble—who had now been professor of poetry at Oxford for over a year— while Palmer contacted Hugh James Rose, the editor of the conservatively orthodox *British Magazine*. Rose, then, invited Palmer and Froude to a conference at Hadleigh, scheduled for the end of July.

Meanwhile, John Newman returned to Oxford—coincidentally, on the same day that his brother, Francis, returned from his journeys in Persia—and five days later, Sunday, July 14, Keble preached his Assize Sermon on "National Apostasy." Keble insisted on the supernatural origin of the authority invested in the Church, an authority passed down from the apostles to the first bishops of the Church, and by means of an uninterrupted Apostolic Succession, currently possessed in full by the bishops of the Church of England. On this basis, he condemned the Irish Church Act, a legislative bill to suppress ten bishoprics in Ireland. Keble's viewpoint, and the perspective of many churchmen at the time, was that, although Parliament may prefer certain men for ordination as bishops, once the Archbishop has ordained them, they can no more be un-ordained than any Christian can be un-baptized. Thus, the idea of Parliament debating, on purely economical and political grounds, whether to eliminate certain bishoprics struck Keble as not merely an intolerable interference, but as a veritable Apostasy. It was a message to touch the heart of Newman, who says of July 14, "I have ever considered and kept the day, as the start of the religious movement of 1833."[214]

The Hadleigh Conference lasted four days, July 25-29. Froude and Palmer attended; Newman and Keble were both absent. Palmer's idea of an Association was debated, but the conference divided into two camps over the issue of Church establishment, and the conference ended with nothing decided. Initially, these two groups were distinguished as the "Conservatives" and the "Apostolicals," the former group believing, with Whately, that what the Church needed was separation from the legislative body of the State, not disestablishment and disendowment, the latter group caring only to restore the Apostolical authority and simplicity of the primitive Church, whatever the cost. Froude and Newman were to stand at the forefront of the radical "Apostolicals." Upon Froude's return from the conference, these two, along with a few others, met with Keble to chart a course of action. It was Newman who decided that what was needed was plain-speaking manifestoes, in which each contributor could write as he felt, without the revision of politically correct editors.

On 26 August Keble asked a friend, "What think you of a kind of association (as quiet and unpretending as may be, if possible even without a name) for the promotion of these two objects? first, the circulation of primitive notions regarding the Apostolical Succession, &c.; and secondly the protection of the Prayer-book against profane innovation." The work of this association, Keble goes on to explain, would be primarily educational, and would involve the circulation of Tracts.[215] Two weeks after this letter was written, the first three *Tracts for the Times* were published.

In Tract No. 1 Newman addresses his "Fellow Labourers" with all the rhetorical skill and evangelical embellishments of an experienced Tract writer. He commences with an apology for what might appear as presumption in taking upon himself the role of educator. "Yet speak I must," he insists, "for the times are very evil, yet no one speaks against them." He then quickly progresses to his argument: "Christ has not left His Church without claim of its own upon the attention of men. Surely not. Hard Master He cannot be, to bid us oppose the world, yet give us no credentials for so doing. . . . I fear we have neglected the real ground on which our authority is built—OUR APOSTOLICAL DESCENT."[216]

Arnold received his copy and was exceedingly vexed. How was it possible, he wondered, that the Oxford clergy could choose this time, with the Church in danger for having fallen out of sympathy with the nation, to boast their own egos by claiming supernatural authority and turning the Church itself into an object of veneration?[217] It was beyond all rational explanation: "It is like that phantom which Minerva sent to Hector to tempt him to his fate."[218] When Hawkins expressed the opinion that Arnold was overreacting, the headmaster responded to the provost so as to clearly state his position:

> You do not seem to me to apprehend the drift of these Tracts. . . . They are not defending the lawfulness or expediency of Episcopacy, which certainly I am very far from doubting, but its *necessity*; a doctrine in ordinary times gratuitous, and at the same time harmless, save as folly. But now the object is to provoke the clergy to resist the Government Church Reforms, and if, for so resisting, they get turned out of their livings, to maintain that they are the true clergy, and their successors schismatics. . . . All this is essentially schismatical and anarchical: in Elizabeth's time it would have been reckoned treasonable; and in answering it, I am not attacking Episcopacy, or the present constitution of the English Church, but simply defending the common peace and order of the Church against a new outbreak of Puritanism, which will endure nothing but its own platform.[219]

Unlike Hawkins, Whately fully understood and concurred with Arnold's position. He further recognized that what Newman was claiming on behalf of the English bishops was not, in fact, Apostolical Succession, but *Apostolical Descent*. He explains the difference. In the latter doctrine, "We are told that the divine Grace of the Christian Sacraments, and the efficacy of all a Clergyman's ministrations, depend on his having been ordained by a Bishop, who was himself ordained and consecrated by a person, who, in turn, derived his Orders from one who had again derived his, through a vast number of intermediate links, from the Apostles."[220] In other words, not only was a church not a true Church unless it was Episcopal, but a good man could not be safe unless he belonged to a Church with an *unbroken* succession of bishops. This doctrine of Apostolical Descent must have grated on the nerves of Archibald Campbell Tait, future archbishop of Canterbury, who had been brought up as a Presbyterian and was, in September 1833, only months away from graduating with honors from Balliol. Moreover, Arnold's plan to bring dissenters into the Church was, in view of this doctrine, nothing less than a blasphemy against the Holy Spirit, for Arnold was implying that even second-generation dissenters, who had not been baptized by an Episcopal priest, were already Christians.

Subscription and Dissent

In March 1834 sixty-three residents of Cambridge—including Connop Thirlwall, the translator of Schleiermacher—filed a petition to allow dissenters into the university. Lord Grey, who was sympathetic to the grievances of dissenters, introduced the petition into the House of Lords. Cambridge did not actually disallow dissenters from *entering* the university. There was no requirement at Cambridge to subscribe the Articles either upon matriculation or, since 1772, upon graduation, although a student would have to declare himself a member of the Church of England in order to obtain his degree. At Oxford, however, the situation was different. As previously noted, no person was enrolled into any of the colleges of Oxford without subscription to both the Articles and the Liturgy. In June, the House of Commons passed a bill that abolished subscription altogether, while allowing each college the right to exclude prospective students who refused to attend chapel.[221]

The bill was cast out of the House of Lords; however, the very fact that Parliament had considered it at all was enough to cause an uproar at both universities. Thirlwall, whose public protest—in the form of his *Letter to the Rev. Thomas Turton, D.D.*—had infuriated Christopher Wordsworth, the master of Trinity, was "invited" to resign his position as tutor. At Oxford the petitioners, humbled but undeterred in their object, proposed to Convocation that the declaration of assent "so far as my knowledge extends" be substituted for subscription. The advantage of the declaration is that its meaning is relatively obvious, whereas the significance of subscription is, to say the least, ambiguous. Perhaps, the obvious interpretation is that the subscriber agrees with every word of the Articles, but this implies that the matriculating student *understands* the Articles—that is, it implies an absurdity. As a result, everyone involved in subscription attached a different significance to the act. The official explanation of the university was that the student subscribed "by the mind and intention, not of him by whom the oath is taken, but of him by whom it is exacted."[222] This eliminated the need for the student to understand anything that he was subscribing to, other than the fact that he was agreeing to abide by the understanding of the administrator. Of course, this implied not only that the administrator understood the Articles, but that the student could (and would) have, at the least, a sufficient understanding of what the administrator understood to keep himself from violating his oath. Clearly, the "Explanation" failed to resolve the difficulties associated with subscription.

Hampden, who had only four months previous been preferred above Newman as professor of moral philosophy, now came out with his controversial pamphlet *Observations on Religious Dissent* (1834). Hampden's theological maxim is that "No conclusions of human reasoning, however correctly deduced, however logically sound, are properly religious truths—are such as strictly and necessarily belong to the scheme of human salvation through Christ."[223] For Hampden—as we have seen—because *religious* truth is nonempirical, it can be revealed only through language, and since the language of revelation is always necessarily contextual, the truth that the language reveals is embodied in the context itself and cannot be divorced from it. To the extent that any interpretation seperates the language of revelation from its context, it ceases to have the properties of revelation—that is, it ceases to convey religious truth. Although it is impossible not to reason *as* we read, when we reason *from* what we read *to* conclusions that are not directly revealed, we must question whether such conclusions are, in fact, Revelation and whether they are not, instead, "pious opinions." Moreover, "if all opinion, as such, is involuntary in its nature, it is only a fallacy, to invest dissent in religion with the awe of the objects about which it is conversant."[224]

In general agreement with Spinoza, Hampden separates religion from theology, which is a branch of philosophy: "Religion consists of those truths which are simply contained in divine revelation, with the affections, dispositions, and actions, suggested by them. Theological opinion is the various result of the necessary action of our minds on the great truths made known to us by the divine word." The type of differences between Christians that the requirement of subscription assumes as a basis for segregation and exclusion are merely theological opinions; "In religion, properly so called, few Christians, if any, really differ."[225] Whereas Spinoza had argued that the State is properly concerned with the maintenance and protection of religion, as opposed to philosophical opinion, Hampden now argues that the university should concern itself with exclusion on the grounds of religion, as opposed to theological opinion. Both reason that conduct, not ideas, is the legitimate concern of law. Prohibitive statutes and punitive measures are misused when they are intended to regulate opinion. "I do not scruple therefore to avow myself favourable to a removal of all tests," concludes Hampden, "so far as they are employed as securities of orthodoxy among our members at large."[226]

Hampden anticipates that his views will lead others to identify him as a *latitudinarian*. To this he objects, because the term "sounds to the ear like licentiousness in morals. . . . Were it not commonly understood in such a sense as this, I should not be concerned to remove the charge." Yet, he insists that, although the opinions of any communion of Christians may necessarily oppose the opinions of another communion, "I do not see that we are entitled to exclude any communion, merely as a distinct communion, from the name of the one Church of Christ." The reason for this inclusiveness is simple: religion is concerned with emotions and conduct, not with the intellect. Therefore, "It is no culpable latitudinarianism which includes within the limits of the Church, a dissent that the heart practically disowns."[227]

In case it were not already obvious, Hampden tells his readers that the present pamphlet has for its foundation the grounds already established in the Bampton Lectures of 1832. It was there that he demonstrated "the futility of an argumentative speculative theology" and pointed out "its tendency to corrupt and debase the truth revealed."[228] Among Hampden's readers were Thomas Arnold and Hugh J. Rose. Arnold immediately responded with a letter that deserves to be noted, although it is one that Stanley—understandably, given his own views respecting Hampden—thought it best not to publish:

> I had not anticipated, much as I admired your "Bampton Lectures," that your sentiments on so many points should be so much in agreement with my own. . . . Your view of the difference between Christian Truth and Theological Opinion is one which I have long cherished, and which I fondly look to as the means, under God, of bringing the Church of Christ to the only unity that is at once practicable and desirable,—that only unity which Christ and Christ's Apostles ever designed for it.[229]

Rose also took note of the connection between the Lectures and the author's current views and, in a frightful alarm, wrote to Newman, "You must notice Hampden's Lectures, and if possible move the university to condemn them, for they say he is to be made a bishop, and then what shall we do?"[230]

But, for the moment, Newman had to restrict himself to less public measures. After all, Hampden had once displaced him as Oriel tutor, and more recently he had snatched the professorship of moral philosophy out of his hands. Were he to publicly vilify Hampden now, people would attribute the attack to sour grapes. So, instead, Newman wrote the professor a candid letter: "While I respect the tone of piety which the pamphlet displays, I dare not trust myself to put on paper my feelings about the principles contained in it, tending as they do in my opinion altogether to make shipwreck of Christian faith." Hampden replied with courtesy, so Newman tried again. As the anonymous editor to a collection of pamphlets on the subscription issue, Newman wrote in the Preface that the author of the *Observations* was a Socinian. Hampden discerned the pen of Newman and responded with warmth and a trembling hand: "I charge you with malignity, because you have no other ground for your assault on me but a fanatical persecuting spirit."[231] Hampden was only beginning to know the malignant spirit that delighted in making sport of him.

When Convocation assembled in the Sheldonian Theatre on 20 May 1835 to vote on the proposal to substitute the declaration of assent in place of subscription, A. P. Stanley was present in the gallery with W. G. Ward. In a letter to his mother, Stanley records the event:

The place below was filled with M.A.'s. The doctors of divinity sat clothed in scarlet. . . . Then came the twenty-four heads—Hawkins and Hampden were hissed by the undergraduates. The Declaration was read, received with a scornful laugh, and proposed, '*Placetne vobis, domine doctores?*' '*Non placet*' ejaculated the bishop and various others. '*Placetne vobis, magistri?*' '*Non placet*' roared the Masters, and thereupon they waved their hats and caps, and gesticulated and yelled, the undergraduates responding from above.[232]

Thus was the proposal thrown out of Convocation by a majority of 459 against 57. In every age Socrates must quaff the antidote to reason. Philosophy appeared, for the time being, nearly extinct at Oxford, and all of Whately's swans suddenly found themselves dinosaurs endangered by the fresh tar pits of an unthinking orthodoxy and loyalty to tradition and party. A new song echoed from the narrow lanes of Oxford:

> This vile Declaration, we'll never embrace it,
> We'll die ere we yield—die shouting *Non placet*!

The Oxford Movement had its origin in the heat of passion and was now virtually progressing under its own momentum. Yet, it was during this time that E. B. Pusey, the Regius Professor of Hebrew and canon of Christ Church, gave to the Tractarians "a position and a name."[233] During the latter part of 1835, as R. H. Froude succumbed to illness, Pusey fully associated himself with the band that had gathered around Newman and Keble. Hitherto, this band had been called Apostolicals, Tractarians, Tractites, and Newmanites; henceforth, they would also be known as Puseyites. Pusey turned the *Tracts* into tomes, and commenced the *Library of the Fathers*. He also kept his violin in tune, and—unlike Blanco White—he was not averse to playing second fiddle to Newman.

The Oxford Malignants

On 19 January 1836 Edward Burton, the forty-two-year-old Regius Professor of Divinity, suddenly died. Archbishop Howley recommended to Lord Melbourne, the Whig prime minister, that the position be filled with either Pusey, Newman, or Keble (in that order). Melbourne smiled, then turned and conferred with Archbishop Whately and Provost Hawkins. Three weeks later, A. P. Stanley received a letter from his uncle, the secretary of the treasury, inquiring into Oxford opinion in regard to the competitors for the vacancy and, specifically, of Hampden's standing as a scholar and a divine. Stanley thought Hampden predominantly orthodox, but consistent in maintaining heterodox opinions, and that his *Moral Philosophy* reveals "a very inadequate sense of the superiority of Christian to Deistical and heathen morality."[234] Even so, there was no time for uncertainty on Downing Street, and the reply of Stanley's would not be read. All was decided: Hampden was to be appointed Regius Professor of Divinity.

Two months later, if you were to have stepped into a bookstore along the Strand, you would have found much interest given to two April publications. One of these was the first number of a serial novel by the *Morning Chronicle* journalist Charles Dickens. It was his first novel, and he called it *The Pickwick Papers*. The other item, not as amusing, but none the less entertaining, was an anonymous article in the *Edinburgh Review*, which had been dubbed by the editor "The Oxford Malignants."[235] Although it was not Arnold who gave this title to his article, he does follow Hampden in charging the Newmanites with malignancy, and so the title, however sensational, does reflect the tone of the work it introduces. Moreover, the title was entirely appropriate, since it was Oliver Cromwell who identified as "the Malignant Party" the loyalists to the fugitive king, Charles I.[236] The first Malignants at Oxford were, therefore, the Laudian renegades, who refused to acknowledge Cromwell as lord protector—and, as Mark Pattison observes, "of all malignants the Oxford malignants had been the mainstay of the royalist cause."[237] Arnold actually compares the Newmanites and their work to "the spirit and the proceedings of the High Church party under the Liberal Government that followed the Revolution"—that is, the Non-Jurors.[238]

Arnold's article follows the course of events subsequent to the appointment of Hampden as Regius Professor of Divinity. Thomas Mozley refers to this history as "a mythical account"[239] (a statement which, coming from Mozley, seems rather ludicrous), but nearly all of the details of Arnold's article have been substantiated by writers closely involved in the proceedings. On 10 February, upon hearing of Melbourne's decision, the Newman party immediately congregated in the Common Room of Corpus Christi and formed a committee for resistance. They put together a petition with seventy-three signatures and sent it off to King William IV—who, incidentally, had never heard of Hampden and supposed the petition to be typical of university politics. After this first meeting adjourned, Newman spent the entire night compiling his *Elucidations of Dr. Hampden's Theological Statements*, "consisting of a number of quotations from his work, classed in such an order, and separated in such a manner from the context, as might best serve the compiler's purposes." The *Elucidations* was an ingenious move on Newman's part, as it proposed to make accessible, in fifty short pages, Hampden's theological position and errors, thus removing the obstacle of having to actually read Hampden's works.[240] This was followed by a more elaborate work, prefaced by Pusey, in which Hampden's theological propositions are contrasted with the Thirty-nine Articles—"a selection made precisely in the same spirit, and conducted with the same honesty, as the famous selection of articles from Wycliff's works, which had the honour of being condemned by the Council of Constance."[241]

On 17 February Hampden's appointment was announced officially in the *London Gazette*. A week later, the resistance movement again assembled in Corpus, this time to sign a letter to the Heads of Houses, the executive committee of the university, petitioning the Heads to bring forward two measures against Hampden. The first would be in the form of a request to the bishops, asking them to substitute, as a prerequisite for ordination, attendance at the lectures of the Margaret Professor of Divinity in place of the customary attendance at the lectures of the Regius Professor of Divinity. The second would take the form of a proposal to Convocation to deprive the Regius Professor of his voice in the nomination of select preachers and in the recognition of heretical preaching. At first, the Heads of Houses refused to comply; however, "the unionists, by dint of sheer importunity and agitation, prevailed upon the Board to depart from their former resolution, and to propose the second of the two measures to Convocation."[242]

Convocation was scheduled for 22 March. This gave the Newmanites all the time they needed to alert Oxonian clergy and request their attendance. Meanwhile, Hampden wrote to Melbourne. The Regius Professor suggested that he could resign, lest his continuance in office result in any embarrassment. Melbourne refused any act of concession to the unreasonable agitation of a mob.[243] There was no retreat. On the 17th, as scheduled, Hampden presented his Inaugural Lecture. He entreated his persecutors:

> In the simple conviction . . . of my own sincerity of purpose, and not in the vanity of a fanatical confidence, do I solemnly profess in the face of the University, that it is my heart's desire to serve God faithfully and devotedly in that station in his Church in which He has placed me. And I ask only to be regarded with the kind and candid feelings which such a profession honestly made, naturally invites.[244]

Stanley, who was seated among the packed audience, describes the scene as "one of the most pathetic and impressive sights I ever saw—the Regius Professor defending himself before the whole University against the charge of heresy in the old magnificent school of divinity."[245] Hampden, exhausted, went home to a wife and children who greeted him with tears. Pusey went home to write another pamphlet, *Dr. Hampden's Past and Present Statements Compared.*

Convocation assembled. Again, the Sheldonian Theatre was packed with 450 excited students, country clergymen, and faculty. But, as Arnold explains, "By the Constitution of Oxford, if two Proctors are agreed, they can interpose a *veto* upon any measure brought forward by the Heads of Houses; and thus prevent it from being submitted at all to the votes of the Convocation."[246] These two proctors, elected annually, now exercised their right of veto. They rose from their seats, and as the crowd applauded and moaned, their lips could be seen to utter *Nobis Procuratoribus non placet.* As Nassau Senior observed in the London *Globe*, the assembly then broke up "amidst shouts, groans, and shrieks from galleries and area such as no deliberative assembly probably ever heard."[247] The Newmanites were not, however, defeated, for the proctors' term of office was to expire in April. A new Convocation was called for and scheduled for 5 May .

In the meantime, Arnold published his article, an attempt to bring into disrepute "the fanaticism of the English High Churchman." He found their "only exact resemblance" in the Hophni and Phineas school and in the Judaizers of the New Testament: "In the zealots of circumcision and the ceremonies of the law,—in the slanderers and persecutors of St. Paul; . . . in these, and in these alone, can the party which has headed the late Oxford conspiracy find their perfect prototype." But the Newmanites were not to be charged with mere *intellectual error*. If it were only that, it would stand to be confuted with tenderness; "But the attack on Dr. Hampden bears upon it the character, not of error, but of *moral wickedness*. . . . We see nothing of Christian zeal, but much of the mingled fraud, and baseness, and cruelty, of fanatical persecution."[248] Elsewhere Arnold had referred to the Oxford Movement as a new outbreak of Puritanism, and indeed the advantageous position that he takes from which to discharge his rounds is strikingly reminiscent of the position of Jeremy Taylor:

> Nothing [is] more furious than a mistaken zeal, and the actions of a scrupulous and abused conscience. When men think every thing to be their Faith and their Religion, commonly they are so busie in trifles and such impertinencies in which the scene of their mistake lies, that they neglect the greater things of the Law, charity, and compliances, and the gentlenesse of Christian Communion; for this is the great principle of mischiefe, and yet is not more pernicious then unreasonable.[249]

Yet, what is clearly present in Taylor's *Discourse* that is as conspicuously absent in Arnold's article is a tone of humble appeal and gentle persuasion.

Stanley had worshiped his former headmaster—nay, he had loved and admired him "to the very verge of all love and admiration that can be paid to man." Like A. H. Clough, he had experienced fully "the blessing of being under Arnold."[250] Upon first hearing Newman preach at St. Mary's, Stanley thought "the general tone, the manner, the simple language" very much like the sermons in Rugby Chapel. And Newman's ethos was no different than Arnold's: "There was the same overpowering conviction conveyed that he was a thorough Christian." Indeed, "they are of the very same essence, so to speak."[251] But the *Edinburgh* article had shown the headmaster as incapable not only of understanding the mind of Newman, but also of judging with moderation motives not understood. "It is a most sad thing," he mused, "and will, I fear, make the breach . . . irreparable."[252] Stanley regretted Newman's High Church notions, but supposed it insignificant whether Newman opened his eggs on the big end or the little end. The Church, he reasoned, should be broad enough to include him. Arnold, on the other hand, saw in Newman an antagonist spirit who would not rest until the Church was as narrow and dogmatic as himself.

Arnold's primary source of information for his article was a public *Letter to His Grace the Archbishop of Canterbury*, published the month before, and probably written either by Bonamy Price, an Arnoldite Evangelical vehemently opposed to the Tractarians,[253] or by Charles Dickinson, who had replaced Hinds in 1833 as Whately's private secretary. Dickinson is also believed to be the anonymous author of *The Pope's Pastoral*, a satirical letter written in the same year, pretending to be an expression of gratitude from the Pope to the Tractarians.[254] The evidence that Arnold followed the *Letter* closely, both in substance and in tone, is all circumstantial, but nevertheless convincing. There are, of course, some differences, and Arnold's style is more exuberant with indignation, but the similarities are overwhelming and not restricted to purely factual details. For example, whereas the author of the *Letter* observes, "Censure from some men may, in reality, be praise," Arnold states that the charges against Hampden are "known to proceed from authors whose censure was to be coveted by every good Christian minister."[255] The author of the *Letter* praises the provost of Oriel for "the manly and energetic part which he has taken throughout the whole business," and Arnold praises "the exemplary firmness of the Proctors."[256] Both authors note the high improbability that Hampden would have been appointed to the professorship of moral philosophy had there been any question whatsoever as to the orthodoxy and sincerity of his beliefs. Both emphasize that the "calumniators" or "conspirators," in denying the orthodoxy of Hampden, have implicitly denied the rectitude of the favorable judgment of the authorities responsible for his appointment. Moreover, both observe that, in requiring those same authorities to retract their favorable judgment, the conspirators are, thereby, requiring the authorities to confess their own error in judgment. Both authors note the inconsistency in the conduct of the conspirators in delaying so long before making their charge against Hampden. Both also emphasize the impropriety and partisan character of the proceedings against Hampden. There is no mistaking the fact that the two accounts are considerably similar, and not merely in their reporting of details. Clearly, Arnold's article, in order to be fully appreciated both as an historical document and as a polemical masterpiece, needs first to be fitted into its social context. Arnold belongs to a distinct circle of writers, who shared their ideas and drafts with one another and profited from this experience.

To complete the story of the Hampden controversy of 1836, we should note that, when Convocation reassembled on 5 May, the new proctors did not intervene, and the vote of "no confidence" in Hampden passed by a majority of 474 to 94. On this day Blanco White wrote in his journal, "For the first time since my arrival in 1810 I have this morning felt an impulse to quit this country."[257] For Blanco White, who had witnessed as a child the last *auto-da-fé* of the Spanish Inquisition, the scene at Oxford was painful beyond words. He saw in Newman a Protestant Pope "who, as surely as he lives, would persecute to the death if he had the direction of the civil power for a dozen years."[258] John Sterling saw in the treatment of Hampden a poignant contrast to the national appreciation shown to Schleiermacher: "It is not very difficult to perceive which plan is the more likely to make profound philosophical inquirers."[259] Even so, the Newmanite victory over Hampden was more symbolic than real, a flexing of ideological muscle. The legality of the second vote of Convocation was doubted, and although the statute of deprivation was allowed to stand, the Heads of Houses created a new Board of Examiners in Theology and put Hampden in the chief seat.

The talk of finding a suitable bishopric for Hampden was still in the air, but while the ashes of the controversy smouldered, Melbourne thought it impolitic to be caught again playing with matches. So, the talk came to nothing until 1847, when Prime Minister John Russell appointed Hampden to the See of Hereford. Nevertheless, in May 1836, Arnold found the idea of Hampden's preferment fraught with possibilities:

> I confess, if Hampden is to be made a bishop, I wish that they would put me in his place at Oxford.... And though the Judaizers hate me, I believe, worse than they hate Hampden, yet they could not get up the same clamour against me, for the bugbear of Apostolical Succession would not do, and it would puzzle even Newman to get up a charge of Socinianism against me out of my Sermons. Furthermore, my spirit of pugnaciousness would rejoice in fighting out the battle with the Judaizers, as it were in a sawpit; and, as my skin is tough, my wife's tougher, and the children's toughest of all, I am satisfied that we should live in Oxford amidst any quantity of abuse unhurt in health or spirits.[260]

Arnold longed to be on the front lines of battle, where he could be most useful, but he accepted the fact that no soldier chooses the field on which he is deployed. In September 1835, the government invited him to a seat in the Senate of London University. As he desired to be useful to the State as a reformer of education, and as he could do so without giving up Rugby, he gladly accepted the offer.

Achilles Ponders in His Tent

As the winter of 1836 approached, Arnold looked forward to a restful vacation at Fox How, his home in Westmoreland. This was precious time he would spend with family and friends, and in the quiet morning hours concentrate on writing the first volume of his Roman history. After the holidays, before the new year lost its frost, Clough and the Whately family arrived at Fox How as Arnold's guests. During the first week of February, when the whole bunch marched over Loughrigg to Rydal to visit the Wordsworths, even Arnold had a difficult time keeping up with the athletic and long-legged Clough. Arnold's daughter, Frances (Fan), just over three years old, struggled to make her way through the fern-stalks, the sight of which suggested, probably to Whately, Gulliver in the Brobdingnag cornfield—a scene created by his favorite satirist, a former dean of St. Patrick's.[261] Several years later, during a walk up Loughrigg, Whately was dismayed to come upon a young girl carrying a burden of milk from Rydal, her daily chore. Gregariously affectionate with children, Whately picked her up, placed her on his shoulders, and carried her to Fox How, from which location Matt and Tom walked her home.[262]

The vacation, although enjoyable and well spent, was not, for Arnold, carefree. His membership in the Senate of London University had required virtually nothing of him for a full year, while charters were pending. Then, on 28 November 1836, two charters of incorporation came into effect, by which University College, London— formerly, London University—and its establishment rival, King's College, London, were incorporated into the new London University, which alone was licensed to examine candidates for degrees. London University was, thus, set up in the fashion of Oxford and Cambridge—that is, as an incorporation of colleges. Unlike the aged sisters, however, London University was not a Church of England institution. The original London University, from the moment it opened its doors in 1829, excluded religion from the curriculum, and thus was sometimes referred to as "the godless institution of Gower Street." It was established as a college for dissenters, and its founding council reasoned that, although "religious discipline" is "the great and primary object of education," the diversity of the college necessitated that the religious education of its pupils remain the province of parents, guardians, and ministers. King's College also opened its door in 1829, with the intent of providing a "liberal and enlarged course of education" that included religious and moral instruction consistent with the doctrine of the United Church of England and Ireland.[263]

At the beginning of 1837 Arnold found himself on a Senate that had to determine requirements for degrees and the general content of examinations for a university that had merged a college of the Establishment with a college for dissenters. Both colleges were now incorporated into the Establishment, and the decisions reached by the Senate would set a precedent and suggest the direction into which all English institutions of higher learning would eventually follow.

Crabb Robinson was also on the Senate, and upon hearing that Arnold wanted to integrate religion into the examinations, he wrote his colleague a letter, urging caution. Arnold assured Robinson that he wanted the new university neither to bestow degrees of divinity nor to set up a theological faculty: "I am quite content with Degrees in Art. But then, let us understand what Arts are." It was Arnold's conviction that one could not have instruction in poetry, history, or moral philosophy without encroaching into the domain of religious education. This, as we shall see in the next chapter, was precisely Maurice's argument in his 1835 pamphlet, *Subscription No Bondage*. If, then—Arnold argued—the instructor fails to take into account "the authority and influences of Christianity," he unavoidably presents an irreligious and false view of the subjects he aims to teach.[264] The B.A. degree must imply a knowledge of the Scriptures. Perhaps, suggested Arnold, the exam could cover, in their original language, one Gospel and one Epistle of the candidate's own choosing. Moreover, the candidate could even be tested by an examiner of his own denomination, either a member of the Senate or a minister.[265]

The Senate scowled, sat mute, and shook their heads. None of the three bishops on the Senate thought it necessary or prudent to integrate religion into the examinations, yet this renegade headmaster insisted on his way as a matter of principle. They objected that Arnold gave no regard to Jews, Muslims, and unbelievers. In reply,

Arnold argued, London University is a State institution, and since the State and the Church are identical and the privileges of citizenship do not extend to infidels, the Senate must not think to accommodate them at such awful cost. Finally, on 2 December, Arnold succeeded by a vote of one in carrying a resolution that all degree candidates, as a general rule, shall pass an examination in one of the Gospels or Acts of the Apostles and in Scripture history.[266] The measure created a division in the Senate, and the opposing party determined to seek the attorney-general's opinion. At this time, Arnold complains of "the Antichrist of Utilitarian unbelief, against which I am fighting at the London University."[267] It was a fierce battle, and on 7 February 1838, the measure was overruled, and a new resolution was passed in regard to examinations in Scripture: "that all candidates for Degrees in Arts may, if they think proper, undergo such Examination."[268] Arnold was incensed and wanted to have nothing further to do with the university, but the fact that a Scripture examination was to be set up as an option left him feeling obligated to do the work.

A few days after this resolution was passed, while Arnold was still in London, he spent some hours in the studio of Thomas Phillips, where he sat for his portrait. Crabb Robinson and Bunsen kept him company, and—while Arnold had to remain perfectly still—they discussed Niebuhr's *History of Rome*. Strachey purports to detect "a slightly puzzled look on the face of Dr. Arnold." If the portrait does, in fact, capture the headmaster bemused, then—as Whitridge suggests—it may be due to the conversation of Arnold's companions;[269] but, it may also be accounted for by the bewildering direction taken by the London University Senate and by the awkward position in which Arnold suddenly found himself.

To the London Utilitarians, Arnold was a bigot; to the Oxford Tractarians, he was a heretic. In the summer of 1838 Arnold wrote a letter to Stanley that is wonderfully expressive of his feelings:

> When the faults of the London University revive all my tenderness for Oxford, then the faults of Oxford repel me again, and make it impossible to sympathise with a spirit so uncongenial. Wherefore I wish the wish of Achilles, when he looked out upon the battle of the ships, and desired that the Greeks and the Trojans might destroy one another, and leave the field open for better men.[270]

As the Myrmidon commander was to the king of Argos, so Arnold was to the chancellor of London University. Arnold resigned on 7 November 1838—and yet, he could not bring himself to leave the battlefield.

Subscription and Catholicism

Without the restrictions of religious tests and examinations, London University quickly became a popular institution in the nation, not only for dissenters, but for all who were disinclined to profess full agreement with the Articles and Liturgy of the

Church of England. Oxford and Cambridge now had to compete for students with "Stinkomalee." Of course, market considerations alone would never have been, for Oxford, a sufficient motivation towards secularization. In Henry Mansel's "Phrontisterion," the model Manchester man complains,

> At Oxford
> There's nought but bigotry and priestcraft. Tell them
> Of Institutions free to all religions,
> Where Jew, Turk, Infidel and Heretic
> May sit like brothers, studying modern science:
> They say the experiment's too dangerous
> For old, time-honoured bulwarks of the Church,
> And bid us try Stinkomalee. The bigots![271]

Convocation at Oxford was not particularly concerned about where Manchester men acquired their education. However, steadily increasing pressure from Parliament, as well as from within the university itself, was making it clear to the Heads of Houses that the issues relative to subscription required more energetic consideration.

During the long vacation of 1839, Stanley—who had just completed his probationary year as fellow of University College—received an invitation from A. C. Tait to join him at Bonn. Tait and W. G. Ward, fellows of Balliol, had been close friends of Stanley's almost from the beginning of his undergraduate years. Tait was now spending three months in residence at the University of Bonn, studying German literature and the Prussian system of education, while also preaching every Sunday and fulfilling the duties of English chaplain. Stanley eagerly set off to Bonn, where, for several weeks, he argued with Tait and the university professors over the practice and merits of subscription. "Tait takes the line," Stanley explained, "that you bind yourself to the living authorities, and that, if they do not put on the clauses the offensive interpretations, you need not."[272] Apparently, Tait accepted the Explanation of the Oath appended to the university laws. It was not an explanation very satisfactory to the conscience of Stanley, who was expected, in a few months, to take the oath for ordination. However, after returning to England and consulting Archdeacon Clarke, he had his doubts sufficiently removed. Arnold also offered Stanley some advice:

> Ordination was never meant to be closed against those who . . . cannot yield an active belief to the words of every part of the Articles and Liturgy as true, without qualification or explanation. . . . This consideration seems to me also decisive on à priori grounds. For otherwise the Church could by necessity receive into the ministry only men of dull minds or dull consciences; of dull, nay, almost of dishonest minds, if they can persuade themselves that they actually agree in every minute particular with any great number of human propositions.[273]

Stanley was to use this same argument when, as professor of ecclesiastical history at Oxford (just before his appointment as dean of Westminster), he wrote his public "Letter on the State of Subscription" (1863) addressed to Archbishop Tait, a letter in which he notes that his interest in the subject "dates as far back as when five-and-twenty years ago we discussed these questions together."[274]

Stanley's father, the reforming bishop of Norwich, was at this time involved in a petition to the House of Lords on the issue of subscription. The petition, which was drafted by Edward Stanley's chaplain, Canon Wodehouse, called attention to the discrepancy between the actual terms of subscription and the practice and feelings of the majority who subscribe. As A. P. Stanley states the case, "The subscription required is probably not construed literally by any single person who makes or receives it. A large number of those who make it look upon it as an act of humiliation, only to be justified by what they regard as sophistical casuistry."[275] Both of the Stanleys, father and son, understood that, if the petition did not stay clear from the terms of the Articles, then the argument regarding subscription would quickly become entangled in controversy and would be thrown out of Parliament. The petition, ultimately signed by sixty churchmen, including Arnold, was presented to the House of Lords by Whately on 26 May 1840. A. P. Stanley, who was in attendance, described the chilling effect as Blomfield, bishop of London, responded indignantly, "For myself, I should believe that *I was eating the bread of the Church unworthily* by subscribing to any Article which I did not implicitly believe!"[276] The terms of clerical subscription would not be relaxed until 1865, a quarter of a century later, and subscription at matriculation would not be abolished at Oxford until 1854.

For the most part, the bishops of the Church of England would soon be pushed into a more conservative posture on the issue. For that push, England had one man to thank: -John Henry Newman. Before Tract XC, it was presumed by both clergy and laity alike that not by the most sophistical casuistry could any Roman Catholic subscribe to the Thirty-nine Articles. The Articles, as a document of the Reformation, was regarded as a wall of separation between Protestant England and Papal Rome. Not all—not even most—Anglican clergymen agreed with the Articles in the strictest literal sense, and some certainly toyed with their consciences by slightly casuistical interpretations, whereas others, such as Arnold and Stanley, subscribed to the Articles as "Articles of Peace" merely. Surely, the English Church was not established upon sand, but neither was it set up upon a rock; rather, it rested on tough but malleable clay, which allowed for a certain degree of compromise. If, however, by some devilish sophistry, the Articles could be construed so loosely as to admit Catholics, and if the bishops would not withstand such devilry, then had not the foundation of the Church turned to sand? Moreover, would not the fall of it be great? So it seemed to many when, at the end of February 1841, Newman forced the question.

On Saturday morning, 27 February 1841, Tait was sitting at a table in his rooms enjoying a quiet period of reading, when Ward rushed in and, excitedly proclaiming "*Here* is something worth reading!," plopped down the latest edition of the *Tracts for the Times*. Tait was skeptical. He had reason to be. After all, Ward had converted over to Newmanism in 1838 and had been making a pest of himself ever since. Ward was a logician who could perform on his instrument with consummate skill. He had succeeded in confusing Stanley for a fortnight, until that champion of Broad Church liberalism broke the spell by a closer reading of St. Paul. Ward had taken even greater delight in confusing Clough, his pupil at Balliol, who had come to him from Rugby filled with enthusiasm for Arnold. How often Tait too must have had cause to look with bemused wonder at Ward and ask, "In a short time you think to make *me* a Newmanite?"

Tait drowsily flipped through the first pages. Its thesis is, as Newman presents it in the *Apologia*, "The Articles do not oppose Catholic teaching; they but partially oppose Roman dogma; they for the most part oppose the dominant errors of Rome." Or, as he says in the Tract itself, "That there are real difficulties to a Catholic Christian in the Ecclesiastical position of our Church at this day, no one can deny; but the statements of the Articles are not in the number." Moreover, "It is a *duty* which we owe both to the Catholic Church and to our own, to take our reformed confessions in the most Catholic sense they will admit."[277] Accordingly, the object of Tract XC is to examine in detail those Articles of the Church of England which are thought to be inimical to Roman Catholicism and, if possible, to demonstrate not only that they need not be interpreted as anti-Catholic, but that *they ought to be interpreted as Catholic*. In Tract I Newman had directly opposed the use of "forms of speech which have not been weighed, and cannot be taken strictly," and consistent with that sentiment, he now professes to have carefully weighed the language of the Articles and to have found that their strict and literal meaning is congruent with the conclusions of the Council of Trent.

By the time he had worked his way through three-quarters of this voluminous Tract, Tait knew that the decisive moment had arrived for a public protest. His Scottish temper now fully aroused, Tait rushed over to Ward's rooms, inquired as to the meaning of the Tract, and—satisfied that he had rightly understood it—drafted a Letter to the Editor. Three other tutors of Oxford signed the letter, and it was published on March 8. The concerns of the four tutors are tersely presented in one paragraph:

> The Tract has, in our apprehension, a highly dangerous tendency, for its suggesting that certain very important errors of the Church of Rome are not condemned by the Articles of the Church of England—for instance, that those Articles do not contain any condemnation of the doctrines—
> 1. Of Purgatory,
> 2. Of Pardons,
> 3. Of the Worshiping and Adoration of Images and Relics,
> 4. Of the Invocation of Saints,
> 5. Of the Mass,
> as they are taught authoritatively by the Church of Rome, but only of certain absurd practices and opinions which intelligent Romanists

repudiate as much as we do. It is intimated, moreover, that the
Declaration prefixed to the Articles, so far as it has any weight at all,
sanctions this mode of interpreting them, as it is one which takes them in
their "literal and grammatical sense," and does not "affix any new sense"
to them. The Tract would thus appear to us to have a tendency to mitigate
beyond what charity requires, and to the prejudice of the pure truth of the
Gospel, the very serious differences which separate the Church of Rome
from our own, and to shake the confidence of the less learned members of
the Church of England in the Scriptural character of her formularies and
teaching.[278]

This single Letter did as much to mold Tait's public reputation as any other deed in
his long and controversial career. Even as archbishop of Canterbury, he would be
known as the man who "hounded Newman out of Oxford."[279]

At the time of the Tract's publication, Stanley was in Rome and J. A. Froude
was in Ireland. Both later expressed disagreement with Tait's assessment. On 27
May 1841, after returning to England, Stanley wrote, "I have read No. 90 and almost
all its consequences. The result clearly is, that Roman Catholics may become members of the Church and universities of England, which I for one cannot deplore."
Froude testified that he regarded Newman's arguments to be "legally sound." In
addition, he thought that "Newman was only claiming a position for himself and his
friends which had been purposely left open when the constitution of the Anglican
Church was formed."[280] The Heads of Houses, however, were in sympathy with the
four tutors led by Tait and, without waiting for Newman's response, passed a resolution that "modes of interpretation such as are suggested in the said Tract, *evading
rather than explaining* the sense of the Thirty-nine Articles, and *reconciling
subscription to them with the adoption of errors which they were designed to
counteract*, defeat the objects, and are inconsistent with the due observance, of the
statutes of the University."[281] Bishop Bagot, of the See of Oxford, intervened and
asked Newman to discontinue the *Tracts*. Newman, of course, conceded. Ward too
intervened, publishing a defense of the Tract and resigning his tutorship at Balliol.
Remarkably, Tait and Ward, respecting each other's position and integrity, managed
to continue their friendship.

Arnold was grateful to Tait for his quick, "manly" response, and he wrote the
Balliol tutor a letter to express his indignation toward "the utter perversity of
language shown in the Tract, according to which a man may subscribe to an article
when he holds the very opposite opinions,—believing what it denies, and denying
what it affirms."[282] Arnold appears naively unaware that he is begging the question.
He assumes that Newman's "rules of interpretation" are perverting the meaning of
the Articles, when in fact the meaning of the Articles is entirely determined by the
rules of interpretation. Both Tait and Stanley grasped that the error of Newman was
not that he embraced a certain license in interpretation, but rather that he insisted that
his interpretation was the "strict and literal" one. As an earnest dogmatist, Newman
was in agreement with Bishop Blomfield that the only honest subscription was one

that honored the genuine meaning of the language—whatever that might be. Newman had modestly proposed to provide all prospective clergymen with a definitive answer to what that "strict and literal" sense *ought* to mean. It was this gesture, and not Newman's freedom of interpretation, that was rightly offensive to the Broad Churchman. Even so, one of the consequences to the Tract XC controversy was that it engendered, in orthodox churchmen, a fear of liberal interpretations, and thus it had the effect of delaying all reform touching subscription.

For Newman and Ward the die was cast. They had crossed the Rubicon and would end in Rome. In 1836 Arnold foresaw that Newman's "heresy" would not take "the form that Newman wishes, but its far more natural and consistent form of pure Popery."[283] Francis Newman claims to have recognized his brother's views as "full-blown Popery" by 1826, at the latest.[284] Strangely, neither Newman himself nor his closest acquaintances and friends knew whither he was headed until he was already there. Arnold did not live to see Newman's conversion to Romanism in October 1845, but it would have left him sadly satisfied, for the Church of England was, neither for Arnold nor for Newman, broad enough for the two of them. Stanley had learned much from Arnold, but he had also learned from Newman, and he had come to understand that the Church is not narrow, only constricted by the intolerance of its members.

Arnold's Return to Oxford

Although Arnold had no intention of leaving Rugby until age and circumstance should permit a conscientious retirement to the tranquility and beauty of Westmoreland, he fervently desired to have a voice and a position at Oxford. For years he had not cared that his detractors maligned him, but he began to feel that their whisperings in high places were having a nauseous influence upon his career. To Hawkins, he wrote in 1839, "I think I have endured too quietly a suspicion affecting me more directly professionally; a suspicion of heterodoxy such as was raised against Hampden, and which would exclude me from preaching before the University."[285] Hawkins himself probably had certain reservations. As provost of Oriel, he had a responsibility not just for the good of his scholars, but for the peace and general well-being of the university. Was it not enough that Oxford had to endure the Newmanite opposition to Hampden? How much worse might it have been had Hampden been possessed with the combative spirit of Arnold.

Bunsen, now Prussian minister at Berne, had concerns for Arnold's health, and thinking that the headmaster's work at Rugby had become a strain upon his constitution, spoke with Bishop Stanley, who in turn caught the ear of Melbourne.[286] Shortly thereafter, in early June 1840, Arnold received an offer of the wardenship of Manchester College. Arnold, however, declined, as the position would necessitate his departure from Rugby, and—as he explained to Bunsen—"Rugby, while it goes on well, is not a burden, but the thing of all others which I believe to be most fitted for me while I am well and in the vigour of life."[287]

What Arnold desired was not different employment, but additional work—specifically, an Oxford professorship. Three months later, Arnold wrote again to Bunsen, "I have now reason to know that I should never be appointed to one of those new professorships in Oxford, which above all other things would have been acceptable to me."[288] Why was he so certain? Melbourne was still prime minister, and Peel was out of favor with the queen, so the answer must be found at Oxford itself. Arnold had just received from Hawkins the Bampton Lectures for the year 1840. A thorough study of these lectures persuaded him that Hawkins had not only failed to recognize the consequences of his stance on Tradition, but that he had adopted a conciliatory attitude toward the Newmanites.

Arnold now presumed that Hawkins was out of sympathy with him, and upon this presumption, he surrendered all hope of a professorship. Subsequently, he wrote to Stanley, "My own desire of going to Oxford . . . is quenched now; I could not go to a place where I once lived so happily and so peaceably, and gained so much—to feel either constant and active enmity to the prevailing party in it—or else, by use and personal humanities, to become first tolerant of such monstrous evil, and then perhaps learn to sympathize with it."[289] The irony of this letter is that it was written on 8 March 1841, on the very eve of the publication of the protest by the four tutors. With that protest and the ensuing censure of Newman and resignation of Ward, the liberal party at Oxford began to stretch itself and feel its strength. It was, as yet, the strength of Rip Van Winkle after the sound of nine-pins had vanished into air. Many liberals, like J. A. Froude and Mark Pattison, had not yet recovered from the intoxication. Nevertheless, the potency of the draught was on the wane.

By the summer of 1841, Arnold's feelings about Oxford had changed. Hawkins had drafted the condemnation of Tract XC that was passed by the Heads of Houses, and Arnold was reassured that there was yet a kindred spirit at Oriel. In 1838 Whately had written, "I very much doubt between Oxford and Cambridge for my boys. Oxford, which I should otherwise prefer, on many accounts, has at present two-thirds of the steady-reading men, Rabbinists, *i.e.* Puseyites."[290] Although only months earlier Arnold had been unwilling to place even himself in the midst of what he imagined as the all-pervasive corrupting influence of Newmanism, now he was confident that Oxford was sufficiently safe for his oldest sons, Matt and Tom.[291] How much more confident he must have felt when, in August 1841, while vacationing at Fox How, "one week before the Tories came into power,"[292] he received from Melbourne the offer of the Regius Professorship of Modern History. The twenty-eight year professorship of Edward Nares had come to a timely close with his death, and Arnold embraced the vacancy as a providential blessing. His presence at Oxford might contribute to make it a safe place for his boys. Matthew matriculated at Balliol in October (at the same time that Clough graduated from Balliol with a disappointing double second), and less than two months later the Reverend Dr. Thomas Arnold entered into his professorial duties.

Stanley was present at the Inaugural Lecture on 2 December 1841 and sent an account of the event home. Upon the opening of the theater doors, "there was a regular rush," and as Arnold ascended the stage, he found himself facing "such an audience as no professor ever lectured to before, larger even than to hear the famous inaugural lecture by Hampden." He continues in a strain of excited hero worship:

> It was most striking, and to all who had been at Rugby most affecting, to see him at last standing there in his proper place, receiving the homage of the assembled University, and hear him addressing them in that clear, manly voice which one has known and loved so well. It lasted for an hour, was listened to with the deepest attention, and closed, as it had begun, with universal applause.[293]

If we suppose that Stanley is too partial as a witness, we should hear the contemporary testimony of R. W. Church, then a tutor at Oriel:

> The great lion at present is Arnold, and his lectures . . . have created a great stir in the exalted, the literary, and the fashionable world of Oxford. . . . Almost every Head goes with his wife and daughters, if he has any; and so powerful is Arnold's eloquence, that the Master of Balliol was on one occasion quite overcome, and fairly went—not quite into hysterics, but into tears—upon which the Provost remarked, at a large party, that "he supposed it was the gout."[294]

This Inaugural Lecture was, as were the lectures following, introductory to a study of modern history. Thus, they are generally denominated as Arnold's "Introductory Lectures." Unfortunately, what they were to introduce we know of only by a general outline, beginning with the fourteenth century and including terminal lectures on "The Life and Times of Pope Gregory the First, or the Great." What a wealth of informative and enjoyable reading Arnold would have left behind, had only providence allowed.

Before the Introductory Lectures began in February 1842, Arnold—with Matthew graciously assisting—had moved his family into their rented house on Beaumont Street, allowing them three delicious weeks. It was a triumphal experience for Arnold, as he steadily drew crowds of three to four hundred, found himself the center of a growing body of admirers, and visited his old stomping grounds in the thickets of Bagley Wood. At a feast in Oriel Hall on 2 February, he sat next to Newman. "Hawkins," says Tuckwell, "was unnecessarily nervous: the talk—it could hardly be otherwise—was general and harmless."[295] During this time, Arnold also joined Bunsen—who was just beginning his residence in England—at the Carlton Terrace in London, where they dined in the company of the king of Prussia, F. D. Maurice, and Thomas Carlyle.[296]

Arnold had written Carlyle two years earlier, upon reading in the newspapers that the author of *The French Revolution* (1837) was now writing on Chartism. In fact, Carlyle's pamphlet on that subject had already, in 1839, been published. Arnold, anticipating by a decade Henry Mayhew's articles in the *Morning Chronicle*, wondered if Carlyle would be interested in forming a society "to collect information as to every point in the condition of the poor throughout the kingdom, and to call attention to it by every possible means."[297] Carlyle had responded in as encouraging a manner as possible, without actually committing himself. Now, he was put at his ease by finding Arnold much too busy to think of involving himself *or others* in any grand schemes. In mid-May 1842, Carlyle even risked a visit to Rugby to see the great headmaster at his field of action. After spending the night, he journeyed with Arnold, Mary, and two of their sons to nearby Naseby field, where they "explored the scene of the great battle very satisfactorily."[298] Surveying the expansive pasture land, ten years later, Clough observed, "You may well imagine King Charles and his Cavaliers riding south-westward from Leicester, to run their heads against the wall of Cromwell's army."[299] The sagacious historian was, at this time, engaged in field work in connection with his edition of *Oliver Cromwell's Letters and Speeches* (1845). Just after his stop at Rugby, Carlyle made his fortuitous visits to the ruined abbey of Bury St. Edmunds and the workhouse of St. Ives—visits that stirred up the ruminations of *Past and Present* (1843).

Arnold's Death and *Life*

Perhaps, Carlyle had said something to stimulate the headmaster into taking up a diary of devotional meditations. Perhaps, he discussed the *Eikon Basilike* in some connection with his Cromwell. For whatever reason, Arnold now began intermittently to record his heavenward thoughts before retiring to bed.[300] On 31 May he wrote, "I would desire to remember my latter end to which I am approaching, going down the hill of life, and having done far more than half my work. May God keep me in the hour of death, through Jesus Christ; and preserve me from every fear, as well as from presumption." On the evening of 11 June, he added, "The day after tomorrow is my birthday, if I am permitted to see it—my forty-seventh birthday since my birth. How large a portion of my life on earth is already passed."[301] He died before seven o'clock the next morning of angina pectoris.

Matthew and some of the other Arnold children were already at Fox How, awaiting their father's arrival for the long vacation. W. C. Lake arrived from Rugby on Monday morning, the 13th, with the sad news. Stanley arrived shortly afterwards from Oxford, just in time to join the solemn pilgrimage to Rugby. There, he and Matthew and Thomas Hull selected the place for the burial, in the chapel itself and in the place of highest honor, in front of the communion table. After the funeral service, Stanley administered the communion to the Arnold family and friends. In August, he returned to preach the memorial sermon for the benefit of the reassembled boys. By that time Rugby had a new headmaster, Archibald Campbell Tait. After ascertaining that J. C. Hare had no interest in the position, Stanley, W. C.

Lake, and others "were very anxious for Tait's election to the post, believing him to be the one person who was most likely to continue the work in the spirit and with something of the power of his predecessor."[302]

At the end of July 1842 Stanley was at Herstmonceux with Archdeacon Hare and Baron Bunsen, providing assistance in the work of preparing the final volume of Arnold's *History of Rome* for the press. Bunsen, after attending Arnold's funeral, wrote to Hare, "O, what is the death of a great and good man! . . . I write *to you*, now *only* to you, all I think."[303] Hare too was overwhelmed with a sense of England's loss and wrote, "In an idolatrous age, one of the men we most need is an idoloclast. . . . Such an idoloclast we had in Dr. Arnold, a dauntless lover of truth, in the midst of an age when few seek or care for any truth, except such as seems to pamper their already bloated predilections and prepossessions."[304]

Before the summer had passed, Mrs. Arnold approached Stanley with her wish that he should create a complete memoir of her husband. Of course, Stanley threw himself into the work with all the enthusiasm and ardor of a knight errant. For the next two years, he spent every available day at Fox How, relying heavily upon the detailed records and letters carefully copied by Arnold's dutiful and loving wife. On one of these visits, Whately arrived to fetch his daughter and decided to remain for two days. The archbishop had suffered "two stunning blows" in the deaths of his closest friends, Arnold and Bishop Dickinson, and felt as though his props had been pulled out from under him.[305] Although both Whately and Stanley had enjoyed the closest of friendships with Arnold and had been introduced to one another in 1835, neither had ever entered into the other's company informally, and they knew not how much they had in common. Stanley was, almost despite himself, impressed with the archbishop, noting that "his kindness to Mrs. Arnold and the children was beautiful. The two youngest children jumped about him just as they used to do about their father."[306]

The biographer took advantage of the opportunity to read some of Arnold's letters that made direct references to his friend. In a letter of 1831, written soon after Whately's preferment, Arnold had written to George Cornish,

> Now I am sure that in point of real essential holiness, so far as man can judge of man, there does not live a truer Christian than Whately; and it does grieve me most deeply to hear people speak of him as of a dangerous and latitudinarian character, because in him the intellectual part of his nature keeps pace with the spiritual—instead of being left, as the Evangelicals leave it, a fallow field of all unsightly weeds to flourish in.[307]

Stanley, seeing the archbishop moved, was exceedingly uncomfortable, and yet everything had to be revealed. When the readings were done, the biographer was relieved to find that Whately completely approved. Stanley confides, "I do not know when I have been more affected than by seeing that rough, unimaginative man . . .

gradually give way, and at last take off his spectacles, and take out his handkerchief, and cry like a child over it."[308]

Conclusion

Stanley's *Life and Correspondence of Thomas Arnold, D.D.* appeared in print at the end of May 1844. The biographer had fulfilled his obligation, and relieved of the joyful burden of it, he set off for Germany with Benjamin Jowett. An era had passed, an epoch-making memoir had been born, and a new Oxford was coming into being. Newman, now hid away at the "Monastery" of Littlemore, read through the *Life* of Arnold and wrote to Keble, "I do not think that the book will produce any great *effect* in a wrong direction. Of course there is a great deal in it to touch people—but there is so little *consistency* in his intellectual basis, that I cannot think he will affect readers permanently." Newman could not have been more mistaken. "And further," Newman continues, "there is something quite of comfort to be gathered from his removal from this scene of action, at the time it took place; as if so good a man should not be suffered to commit himself *cominus* against truths, which he so little understood."[309] Again, Newman was quite mistaken, if he thought that, with Arnold out of his way, he could once again claim Oxford as his own. In fact, very soon, in February 1845, Convocation would pass a censure against Ward's *Ideal of a Christian Church Considered* and deprive its author of his degrees, and before 1846, Newman would remove himself, not only from Oxford, but from the Church of England.

Oxford had wearied of endless citations of bishops long dead, and minds were waking up from deep slumber. Mark Pattison records the transition with the feeling that derives from having lived through it:

> The truth is that this moment, which swept the leader of the Tractarians, with most of his followers, out of the place, was an epoch in the history of the University. It was a deliverance from the nightmare which had oppressed Oxford for fifteen years. For so long we had been given over to discussions unprofitable in themselves, and which had entirely diverted our thoughts from the true business of the place. . . . More than this, the abject deference fostered by theological discussion for authority, whether of the Fathers, or the Church, or the Primitive Ages, was incompatible with the free play of the intellect which enlarges knowledge, creates science, and makes progress possible. In a word, the period of Tractarianism had been a period of obscurantism, which had cut us off from the general movement; an eclipse which had shut out the light of the sun in heaven.[310]

It was during this Oxford *renascence*, this rebirth of confidence in the creative powers and benevolent energies of human reason, the *candle of the Lord*, that the

Life of Dr. Arnold made its appearance. Quickly it became required reading for anyone whose thoughts wanted stimulation and who was not afraid to think. Oxford was a brave new world, and the light that Arnold had delighted in now shone brighter there than ever.

The Noetics were no more; Coleridge was no more—but the Broad Church movement was presently spreading its influence across England. And as the generations that knew Arnold in the flesh passed away, the spirit of Arnold—*St. Thomas*, if you will—took on new meaning for the Church of England, so that in 1889 Thomas Cheyne could effectually call upon that spirit in an Oriel commemoration address:

> Would that some one might be raised up "in the spirit and power," not of Elias, nor of Moses, but of that Christian apostle of the school and the lecture-room, Thomas Arnold, to expound to you in modern language that stirring command which reverberates through the centuries, "Speak unto the children of Israel, that they go forward."[311]

Truly, unless a seed falls to the ground and dies, it cannot bring forth life. Arnold's early death, though tragic, had made possible the first and most influential hagiography of the Broad Church movement, through which Arnold's "spirit and power" would have its vivifying and liberating effect.

Notes

1. *Tyndale's New Testament*, ed. David Daniell (New Haven: Yale University Press, 1989), 37.

2. Convocation had already, in 1562, passed a decree mandating subscription to the Articles of Religion at the time of matriculation; in 1580 the Oath of Supremacy was imposed (Charles Edward Mallet, *A History of the University of Oxford*, 2 vols. [New York: Longmans, Green, and Co., 1924], 2:121). The object of subscription was, initially, to filter Roman Catholic influences out of the university.

3. Arthur Penrhyn Stanley, "A Letter on the State of Subscription in the Church of England and in the University of Oxford" (1862; reprinted in *Essays Chiefly on Questions of Church and State, from 1850 to 1870*, London: John Murray, 1870), 148-98, 178.

4. Arthur Penrhyn Stanley, *The Life and Correspondence of Thomas Arnold, D.D.*, 2 vols., 12th ed. (London: John Murray, 1881), 1:18.

5. Brock, M. G., "The Oxford of Peel and Gladstone, 1800-1833," *The History of the University of Oxford, Volume VI: Nineteenth-Century Oxford, Part I*, ed. M. G. Brock and M. C. Curthoys (Oxford: Clarendon Press, 1997), 7-71, 40; reference to E. B. Pusey, *Remarks on the Prospective and Past Benefits of Cathedral Institutions* (1833), 16.

6. Brock, 9.

7. Jeremy Bentham, *"Swear not at all": Containing an Exposure of the Needlessness and Mischievousness, as well as Antichristianity, of the Ceremony of an Oath* (London: R. Hunter, 1817), 48-50.

8. David Watson Rannie, *Oriel College* (London: F. E. Robinson and Co., 1900), 180. R. E. B., while discounting the notion that any single person can be regarded as a founder of the Broad Church, writes, "If we are to look anywhere for its fountain-head, it would probably be in the Common Room of Oriel College" ("The Broad Church Movement," *Fraser's Magazine* 17 [March 1878]: 353-64, 355).

9. Charles Richard Sanders, *Coleridge and the Broad Church Movement* (Durham, N.C.: Duke University Press, 1942), 91.

10. G. R. Balleine, *A History of the Evangelical Party in the Church of England*, rev. ed. (London: Church Book Room Press, 1951), 2.

11. A. H. Clough to J. P. Gell, 15 January 1838, in Blanche Clough, ed., *The Poems and Prose Remains of Arthur Hugh Clough*, 2 vols. (London: Macmillan and Co., 1869), 1:76.

12. Charles Edward Mallet, *A History of the University of Oxford: Modern Oxford* (London: Methuen and Co., Ltd., 1927), 166-68. Brock includes Joseph Butler's *Analogy of Religion* as one of the required readings for the Examination Statute of 1800 (10); however, other sources suggest that the *Analogy* was not added until 1830 (*vide* note 128, below).

13. William Tuckwell, *Pre-Tractarian Oxford: A Reminiscence of the Oriel "Noetics"* (London: Smith, Elder, and Co., 1909), 15.

14. K. C. Turpin, "The Ascendancy of Oriel," in *The History of the University of Oxford, Volume VI: Nineteenth-Century Oxford, Part I*, ed. M. G. Brock and M. C. Curthoys (Oxford: Clarendon Press, 1997), 183-92, 183-84. The last restriction was not removed until 1821 (E. G. W. Bill, *University Reform in Nineteenth-Century Oxford: A Study of Henry Halford Vaughan, 1811-1885* [Oxford: Clarendon Press, 1973], 25; Rannie, 185).

15. Tuckwell, 20.

16. Mark Pattison, *Memoirs* (London: Macmillan and Co., 1885), 77.

17. "*Admission* to a fellowship at Oriel, down to 1819 inclusive, took place on S. Margaret's day (20th July),—though the *Election* has ever been in Easter week" (John William Burgon, *Lives of Twelve Good Men*, 2 vols. [London: John Murray, 1888], 1:383 n). James Fraser, who passed the fellowship examination in 1840, noted that the results were declared on the following day, Friday. Following the announcement, there was, in the chapel, an after-noon formal ceremony of admittance, followed by a dinner with the Provost and Fellows (Thomas Hughes, *James Fraser: Second Bishop of Manchester: A Memoir, 1818-1885* [London: Macmillan and Co., 1887], 21). For an in-depth treatment of the Oriel fellowship examinations, see the letter of R. W. Church to H. P. Liddon (Henry Parry Liddon, "Appendix to Chapter III," *Life of Edward Bouverie Pusey*, 4 vols., ed. J. O. Johnston and Robert J. Wilson [London: Longmans, Green, and Co., 1893], 1:66-69). Edward Hawkins related to a friend that, during his examination, the room was so cold that two candidates, in order to warm themselves, had a boxing match (Burgon, 1:385). C. S. Lewis recalled that, when, in 1916, he took his entrance exam in Oriel Hall, "we all wrote in greatcoats and mufflers and wearing at least our left-hand gloves" (*Surprised by Joy: The Shape of My Early Life* [New York: Harcourt Brace and Co., 1956], 185).

18. Pattison, 78; Tuckwell, 24; Turpin, 184-85.

19. Thomas Mozley, *Reminiscences Chiefly of Oriel College and the Oxford Movement*, 2 vols. (London: Longmans, Green, and Co., 1882), 1:18.

20. John Tulloch, *Movements of Religious Thought in Britain during the Nineteenth Century* (New York: Charles Scribner's Sons, 1885), 43.

21. T. Mozley, 1:19.

22. Francis Warre Cornish comes to the same conclusion. The title "Noetics," he writes, "was probably given by detractors, annoyed by a supposed assumption of superiority which they may have felt but would not acknowledge to be well founded" (*The English Church in the Nineteenth Century*, 2 vols. [London: Macmillan and Co., Ltd., 1933], 1:188).

23. Vernon F. Storr, *The Development of English Theology in the Nineteenth Century, 1800-1860* (London: Longmans, Green, and Co., 1913), 251.

24. John Henry Newman, *Apologia Pro Vita Sua*, 1864 (New York: W. W. Norton, 1968), 45.

25. Tuckwell, 15.

26. P. B. Nockles, "'Lost Causes and . . . Impossible Loyalties': The Oxford Movement and the University," in *The History of the University of Oxford, Volume VI: Nineteenth-Century Oxford, Part I*, ed. M. G. Brock and M. C. Curthoys (Oxford: Clarendon Press, 1997), 195-267, 229. Pietro Corsi also clearly delineates between the "early" and "late" Noetics, placing Copleston, Davison, and Whately in the former (*Science and Religion: Baden Powell and the Anglican Debate, 1800-1860* [New York: Cambridge University Press, 1988], 74).

27. Tuckwell, 22.

28. John William Fitzpatrick, *Memoirs of Richard Whately, Archbishop of Dublin: With a Glance at His Cotemporaries & Times*, 2 vols. (London: Richard Bentley, 1864), 1:11.

29. Fitzpatrick, 25-32.

30. Fitzpatrick, 17; Tulloch, 42.

31. Tuckwell, 18.

32. Eugene L. Williamson Jr., *The Liberalism of Thomas Arnold: A Study of His Religious and Political Writings* (University: University of Alabama Press, 1964), 36.

33. Arnold to Justice Coleridge, Fox How, 24 January 1840, in Stanley, *Life*, 2:166; Arnold to W. C. Lake, Rugby, 17 August 1840, in Katherine Lake, ed., *Memorials of William Charles Lake, Dean of Durham, 1869-1894* (London: Edward Arnold, 1901), 161-62.

34. For example, Lewis Mayer, *A Prophetic Mirror: or, a Hint to England: Containing an Explanation of Prophecy That Relates to the French Nation, and the Threatened Invasion, Proving Bonaparte To Be the Beast That Arose out of the Earth* (London, 1803). Cf. Stanley, *Life*, 1:67; Mrs. Hare-Naylor to Lady Jones, Hurstmonceux Place, 1 February 1800, in A. J. C. Hare, *Memorials of a Quiet Life*, 9th ed., 2 vols. (London: A. Strahan and Co., 1873), 1:138.

35. Davison, *The Nature and History of Prophecy*, 1819-1820; qtd. in Storr, 187.

36. Davison, qtd. in Edward Hawkins, *An Inquiry into the Connected Uses of the Principal Means of Attaining Christian Truth* (Oxford: John Henry Parker, 1841), 72.

37. Francis William Newman, *Phases of Faith; Or, Passages from the History of My Creed* (1850; reprint, New York: Humanities Press, 1970), 4.

38. John Taylor Coleridge, *A Memoir of the Rev. John Keble, M.A., Late Vicar of Hursley* (Oxford: James Parker and Co., 1870), 9, 13, 47.

39. Donald Harman Akenson, *A Protestant in Purgatory: Richard Whately, Archbishop of Dublin* (Hamden, Conn.: Archon Books, 1981), 11-14; Tuckwell, 57.

40. Rannie, 176.

41. Pattison, 79.

42. Tuckwell, 58-59.

43. T. Mozley, 1:220.

44. According to the biographer of F. W. Robertson, "There was no book which he studied more carefully or held in higher honor than the 'Christian Year.' It seemed to him that some of its poems were little short of inspiration" (Stopford A. Brooke, ed., *Life and Letters of Fredk. W. Robertson, M.A.* [1865; 4th ed., New York: Harper & Brothers, n.d.], 103-04).

45. Thomas Arnold to his sister Fan, Oxford, 7 December 1815; in Arnold Whitridge, *Dr. Arnold of Rugby* (London: Constable and Co., Ltd., 1928), 26.

46. James Anthony Froude, *The Oxford Counter-Reformation*, in *Short Studies on Great Subjects*, 4th Series (New York: Charles Scribner's Sons, 1883), 151-235, 173.

47. Richard William Church, *The Oxford Movement: Twelve Years, 1833-1845*, 3rd ed., 1892 (New York: Archon Books, 1966), 26-27.

48. J. T. Coleridge, 149.

49. Akenson, 24.

50. J. H. Newman, *Apologia*, 22.

51. Richard Whately, *Historic Doubts relative to Napoleon Buonaparte*, 6th ed. (London: B. Fellowes, 1837; reprinted in *Richard Whately: A Man for All Seasons*, ed. Craig Parton, Edmonton, Alberta: Canadian Institute for Law, 1997), 39-93, 64.

52. Fitzpatrick, 1:14-15.

53. Baden Powell, "On the Study of the Evidences of Christianity," in Victor Shea and William Whitla, eds., *Essays and Reviews: The 1860 Text and Its Reading* (Charlottesville: University Press of Virginia, 2000), 233-61, 258.

54. Donald Akenson notes, "The work went into fourteen London editions in Whately's own lifetime, plus American editions and foreign translations, and was anthologized . . . in Henry Morley's 1886 collection of the most distinguished English pamphlet literature" (25-26).

55. Fitzpatrick, 1:24.

56. Richard Whately, *Essays on Some of the Peculiarities of the Christian Religion*, 1822, 6th ed. (London, John W. Parker, 1850), 150-51.

57. Whately, *Essays on Some of the Peculiarities*, 160-61.

58. Whately, *Essays on Some of the Peculiarities*, 162.

59. Richard Hooker, *Of the Laws of Ecclesiastical Polity*, ed. A. S. McGrade and Brian Vickers (New York: St. Martin's Press, 1975), VIII.1.ii., 336.

60. *Letters on the Church, by an Episcopalian*. See especially Letter IV. Reprinted in America as *Christianity Independent of the Civil Government* (New York: Harper and Brothers, 1837); cf. Tuckwell, 67, 79. Of these *Letters*, John Hunt declares, "They are unlike anything which Whately ever wrote or was known to hold." In support of his position, he observes that Whately's daughter "assumes that as he never acknowledged them he did not

write them" (*Religious Thought in England in the Nineteenth Century* [London: Gibbings and Co., 1896], 57-58 n.). However, it should be noted that Elizabeth Jane Whately does not, in fact, state any such assumption. Rather, she declares that, as her father "never avowed the authorship, the editor has felt some scruple as to mentioning it in connexion with his name" (*The Life and Correspondence of Richard Whately, D.D., Late Archbishop of Dublin*, 3rd ed. [London: Longmans, Green, and Co., 1875], 45 n.). Such a remark appears to me as just the sort of thing a dutiful daughter would say who, proud that her father had written the *Letters*, yet felt that she ought not publicly declare that which her father had left undeclared.

61. J. H. Newman, *Apologia*, 23.

62. Whately's title has been often misrepresented by the substitution of the more traditionally Anglican "St. Paul" for Whately's "Apostle Paul" (e.g., Fitzgerald, 1:35; Akenson, 45; Williamson, 39). It should, however, be noted that, according to Whately, the use of the term "Saint" to distinguish Apostles and Sacred Writers from other Christians is indefensible from a Protestant viewpoint (*Essays on Some of the Difficulties in the Writings of the Apostle Paul and in Other Parts of the New Testament*, 1828, 6th ed. [London: John W. Parker, 1849], 211-12 n).

63. Fitzpatrick, 1:36.

64. T. Mozley, 2:405.

65. Francis Newman, 4.

66. According to Gore, the apostolic writings "presuppose membership" in the Church "and familiarity with its tradition." Thus, "They are secondary, not primary instructors; for edification, not for initiation" ("The Holy Spirit and Inspiration," in *Lux Mundi: A Series of Studies in The Religion of the Incarnation*, ed. Charles Gore, 14th ed. [London: John Murray, 1895], 248).

67. Stanley, *Life*, 2:29.

68. Renn Dickson Hampden, *A Lecture on Tradition, Read before the University, in the Divinity School, Oxford, on Thursday, March 7th, 1839* (London: B. Fellowes, 1839); Baden Powell, *Tradition Unveiled: Or, An Exposition of the Pretensions and Tendency of Authoritative Teaching in the Church* (London: B. Fellowes, 1839).

69. Edward Hawkins, *An Inquiry into the Connected Uses of the Principal Means of Attaining Christian Truth* (Oxford: John Henry Parker, 1841), 22; my italics.

70. Hawkins, 46-50, 167-68, 179-80.

71. Hawkins, 192-204.

72. Hawkins, 92.

73. See, for example, Arnold to Hawkins, Rugby, 4 November 1835, in Stanley, *Life*, 2:15.

74. Richard Whately, *Essays on Some of the Peculiarities of the Christian Religion*, 205-06; *Essays on Some of the Difficulties in the Writings of the Apostle Paul*, 50-51, 51n.

75. Hawkins, 111; my italics.

76. Richard Whately, *Cautions for the Times: Addressed to the Parishioners of a Parish in England, by Their Former Rector* (London: John W. Parker and Son, 1853), 20-21; cf. Jeremy Taylor, *A Discourse of the Liberty of Prophesying, 1647* (Menston, Yorkshire: Scolar Press, 1971), 5.8, 92.

77. Church, 47.

78. Church, 98-99.

79. Justice Coleridge, Heath's Court, September 1843, in Stanley, *Life*, 1:14-15.

80. Stanley, *Life*, 1:11.

81. Unidentified author, qtd. in A. J. C. Hare, *Memorials*, 1:328. An account of the founding and short life of the Attic Society was provided by Archdeacon Randall to A. J. C. Hare (*Memorials*, 1:168-71).

82. Arnold and J. C. Hare did not, however, become personally acquainted until 1824, when Arnold wrote to him requesting help with his researches in German literature (N. Merrill Distad, *Guessing at Truth: The Life of Julius Charles Hare* [Shepherdstown, W. Va.: Patmos Press, 1979], 102-03).

83. Church, 79; Pattison, 79.

84. Stanley, *Life*, 1:24; Tuckwell, 97.

85. Stanley, *Life*, 1:18-20.

86. In a letter of 23 February 1820, Arnold wrote to George Cornish, "I believe I am usefully employed, and I am sure I am employed more safely for myself than if I had more time for higher studies" (Stanley, *Life*, 1:58).

87. Joseph Blanco White, *Practical and Internal Evidence against Catholicism* (London: John Murray, 1826), Letter 1, esp. 2-24.

88. Martin Murphy, *Blanco White: Self-banished Spaniard* (New Haven: Yale University Press, 1989), 95-98.

89. Stanley claims that it was Newman who was elected into Arnold's resigned fellowship (*Life*, 1:23), but this calculation would leave the fellowship vacant for over three years.

90. T. Mozley, 86-88; Richard Holmes, *Coleridge: Darker Reflections, 1804-1834* (New York: Pantheon Books, 1998), 514.

91. F. D. Maurice to Miss G. Hare, 7 February 1849, in *The Life of Frederick Denison Maurice, Chiefly Told in His Own Letters*, ed. Frederick Maurice, 2 vols. (New York: Charles Scribner's Sons, 1884), 1:501-02.

92. Holmes, 512-18.

93. G. P. Gooch, *History and Historians in the Nineteenth Century*, 2nd ed. (London: Longmans, Green, and Co., 1952), 299.

94. Arnold to J. T. Coleridge, Laleham, 3 March 1823, in Stanley, *Life*, 1:63.

95. Francis Newman, 15; Mark Pattison, 210. Basil Willey's remark, "The Tractarians needed no Tübingen critics to teach them that the Bible, and the Bible alone, could not be the rule of faith" (*Nineteenth Century Studies* [New York: Columbia University Press, 1949], 77) is really quite beside the point. What Tübingen critics might have taught the Tractarians is that the traditions of the Church are no less susceptible to critical revaluation than the Scriptures and that faith must, therefore, rest on something other than submission to an exterior dogma.

96. Arnold to W. W. Hull, Laleham, 30 September 1824, in Stanley, *Life*, 1: 66. Barthold Niebuhr's *Romische Geschichte* (1811-1812) would be translated into English by J. C. Hare and Connop Thirlwall and published in 1828.

97. Merton A. Christenson suggests that Arnold "confined his reading of German to works of history" for two or three years because "he was not yet able to distinguish among German theologians" ("Thomas Arnold's Debt to German Theologians: A Prelude to Matthew Arnold's *Literature and Dogma*," *Modern Philology* 55 (1957), 14-20, 15.

98. Arnold to John Tucker, Laleham, 1826, in Stanley, *Life*, 1:71.

99. J. T. Coleridge, 132-33.

100. Murphy, 131.

101. Blanco White, 47-48.

102. Copleston's address to Convocation, qtd. in Murphy, 138.

103. Arnold to F. C. Blackstone, Laleham, 28 October 1819, in Stanley, *Life*, 1:52.

104. Stanley, *Life*, 1:103.

105. Bonamy Price to A. P. Stanley, 1844, in Stanley, *Life*, 1:37.

106. Arnold to E. Hawkins, Laleham, 21 October 1827, in Stanley, *Life*, 1:73; Whitridge, 48-51. As Whitridge notes, Stanley's abridgement of this letter suggests that Arnold's sole concern was in regard to the free exercise of his authority as headmaster (52). Elsewhere Stanley notes that Arnold doubted the canonicity of the Epistle to the Hebrews ("A Letter on the State of Subscription," in *Essays*, 168). The hypothesis that the Thirty-nine Articles are "Articles of Union and Peace" is defined by Bishop Gilbert Burnet as the idea "that the subscription binds only to a general compromise upon those Articles, that so there may be no disputing nor wrangling about them. By this means they reckon, that though a man should differ in his opinion from that which appears to be the clear sense of any of the Articles; yet he may with a good conscience subscribe them, if the Article appears to him to be of such a nature, that though he thinks it wrong, yet is seems not to be of that consequence but that it may be borne with, and not contradicted" (*An Exposition of the Thirty-nine Articles of the Church of England* [1699; London: William Tegg and Co., 1850], 7). Burnet's theory is not without foundation. According to the chaplain of Archbishop Richard Bancroft (1544-1610), the imposition of subscription by his predecessor, John Whitgift, in 1584 was "for the preservation of unity and purity in religion, the preventing of further schism, and the discovery of men's inclinations either unto peace or faction" (Thomas Rogers, *The Catholic Doctrine of The Church of England: An Exposition of the Thirty-nine Articles*, ed. J. J. S. Perowne [Cambridge: Cambridge University Press, 1854], 11).

107. Tuckwell, 102.

108. Arnold to J. T. Coleridge, Laleham, 29 November 1819, in Stanley, *Life*, 1:55.

109. Mary Arnold's Journals, vol. 1, December 1828; qtd. in Park Honan, *Matthew Arnold: A Life* (London: Weidenfeld and Nicolson, 1981), 17.

110. T. Mozley, 1:177, 341. John Keble, who was elected professor of poetry at Oxford in 1831 and whose critical scholarship was made public knowledge by the 1836 publication of the first modern edition of Richard Hooker's *Polity*, was never granted a Doctorate degree.

111. Edward Churton, *A Letter to an Edinburgh Reviewer* (London: J. G. and F. Rivington, 1836), 6.

112. Lytton Strachey, *Eminent Victorians*, (1918; reprint, New York: Penguin Books, 1986), 165, 170, 187.

113. Michael Holroyd, *Lytton Strachey: A Biography* (New York: Penguin Books, 1971), 88.

114. The "case of March" is discussed by John Chandos in *Boys Together: English Public Schools 1800-1864* (New Haven: Yale University Press, 1984), 257-58.

115. Thomas Arnold, "On the Discipline of Public Schools," *The Miscellaneous Works of Thomas Arnold, D. D.*, ed. A. P. Stanley (London: B. Fellowes, 1845), 361-79, 371.

116. James Mozley, "Dr. Arnold," review of *The Life and Correspondence of Thomas Arnold, D.D.*, by Stanley (October 1844), in *Essays Historical and Theological*, 2 vols. (Oxford: Rivingtons, 1878), 2:1-67, 14.

117. Lake, *Memorials*, 18.

118. Friedrich Schleiermacher to Charlotte von Kathen, n.d., in *The Life of Schleiermacher: As Unfolded in His Autobiography and Letters*, trans. Frederica Rowan, 2 vols. (London: Smith, Elder, and Co., 1860), 2:250-51.

119. See, for example, Arnold to John Tucker, Laleham, 2 March 1828, in Stanley, *Life*, 1:75.

120. Tuckwell, 95. The other six are James Boswell's *Life of Samuel Johnson* (1791), John Lockhart's *Memoirs of the Life of Sir Walter Scott* (1837-1838), Robert Southey's *Life of Nelson* (1813), G. H. Lewes's *Life of Goethe* (1855), Thomas Carlyle's *Life of John Sterling* (1851), and Sir George Trevelyan's *Life and Letters of Lord Macaulay* (1876).

121. Rannie, 209.

122. Charles Stuart Parker, ed., *Sir Robert Peel: From His Private Papers*, 3 vols. (London: John Murray, 1899), 2:48.

123. George Anthony Denison, *Notes of My Life, 1805-1878* (Oxford: James Parker, 1878), 50.

124. Thomas Arnold, "Christian Duty of Conceding the Roman Catholic Claims," *The Miscellaneous Works of Thomas Arnold, D. D.*, ed. A. P. Stanley (London: B. Fellowes, 1845), 5-66.

125. Arnold to J. Lowe, Rugby, 16 March 1829, in Stanley, *Life*, 1:221-22.

126. Owen Chadwick, *The Victorian Church*, 2 vols. (New York: Oxford University Press, 1966), 1:7, 19-20.

127. Ms. of H. G. Liddell in Christ Church, cited in Bill, 10. In a letter of 1866, Matthew Arnold refers to H. Halford Vaughan as "the most striking man, as I think, of all the men who have ever gone out of Rugby since Papa went there" (*The Letters of Matthew Arnold*, 5 vols., ed. Cecil Y. Lang [Charlottesville: University Press of Virginia, 1996-2001], 3:96). Possibly, Liddell had misunderstood a similar remark.

128. Archibald C. Tait, who was a tutor for Balliol in 1834, states that, among the books on which the new examination tested, was Aristotle's *Ethics* and *Rhetoric* and Butler's *Analogy* (Randall Thomas Davidson and William Benham, *Life of Archibald Campbell Tait, Archbishop of Canterbury*, 3rd ed., 2 vols. [London: Macmillan and Co., 1891], 1:53-54. R. D. Hampden had insisted upon adding Butler's book to the examination (Pattison, 134).

129. Bill, 15; Turpin, 189.

130. T. Mozley, 1:230.

131. Tuckwell, 155-56.

132. Pattison, 97.

133. Keble to J. T. Coleridge, 29 January 1818, in J. T. Coleridge, 73.

134. Connop Thirlwall, *A Letter to the Rev. Thomas Turton, D.D., on the Admission of Dissenters to Academical Degrees* (Cambridge: Pitt Press, 1834), 17.

135. Thirlwall, 17; Julius Charles Hare observes, "The intercourse between a tutor and pupil at our large colleges in Cambridge is very seldom close enough for the tutor to become

acquainted with the intellectual and spiritual state of his pupils" (*Thou Shalt Not Bear False Witness against Thy Neighbour* [London: John W. Parker, 1849], 9).

136. Copleston to Hawkins, qtd. in Rannie, 201.

137. Mark Pattison, 88.

138. Thomas Hughes, *James Fraser, Second Bishop of Manchester: A Memoir* (London: Macmillan and Co., 1887), 24.

139. Burgon, 1:424.

140. The Catholic Emancipation Act had already raised the minimum qualification of the franchise in Ireland from forty shillings to ten pounds.

141. *The Extraordinary Black Book: An Exposition of Abuses in Church and State, Courts of Law, Municipal Corporations, and Public Companies* (London: Effingham Wilson, 1835), 7.

142. Fitzpatrick, 1:72-3. Whately's appointment was suggested to Lord Grey, who had no previous knowledge of the Oxford professor, by Henry Peter, Lord Brougham, the founder of London University (1:86).

143. Arnold to W. Tooke, Rugby, 18 June 1831, in Stanley, *Life*, 1:262.

144. Arnold to Whately, Rugby, 7 March 1831, in Stanley, *Life*, 1:254.

145. Tuckwell, 69-72.

146. T. Mozley, 1:270.

147. Fitzpatrick, 1:118-33.

148. Arnold to William K. Hamilton and Whately; Rydal, 15 and 17 January 1833, in Stanley, *Life*, 1:297-98.

149. Thomas Arnold, *Principles of Church Reform*, in *Miscellaneous Works*, 257-338, 275.

150. Arnold to W. W. Hull, Rugby, 30 April 1834, in Stanley, *Life*, 1:328-29.

151. For example, in *Aids to Reflection*, Coleridge argues, "The national church is no mere State-Institute. It is the State itself in its intensest federal union" (S. T. Coleridge, *Aids to Reflection*, ed. John Beer, vol. 9 of *The Collected Works of Samuel Taylor Coleridge* [Princeton: Princeton University Press, 1993], Aph Sp Rel B XI, 292). *Vide* chap. 1, 38-39.

152. Two years after the coronation of Victoria on 28 June 1838, Arnold wrote to J. C. Hare, "A female reign is an unfavourable time, I know, for pressing strongly the doctrine of the Crown's Supremacy" (Stanley, *Life*, 2:197).

153. Baden Powell, *The State Church: A Sermon Preached before the University of Oxford at St. Mary's on the 5ᵗʰ of November, 1850* (Oxford: T. Combe, 1850), 15-16 n.

154. Arnold, *Principles*, 306-07.

155. Arnold, *Principles*, 313.

156. Arnold to Hawkins, Rugby, 5 March 1833, in Stanley, *Life*, 1:301.

157. Connop Thirlwall to Bunsen, Trinity College, 5 May 1833, in *Letters Literary and Theological of Connop Thirlwall*, ed. J. J. Stewart Perowne and Louis Stokes (London: Richard Bentley and Sons, 1881), 107.

158. Rusticus, *Subscription No Bondage; Or, the Practical Advantages Afforded by the Thirty-Nine Articles as Guides in All the Branches of Academical Education* (Oxford: J. H. Parker, 1835), 117.

159. Rowland E. Prothero, *The Life and Correspondence of Arthur Penrhyn Stanley, Late Dean of Westminster*, 2 vols. (New York: Charles Scribner's Sons, 1894), 1:98.

160. J. H. Newman, *Apologia*, 39.

161. See Whitridge, 170 n. The Newmanites were not alone in questioning the legitimacy of Arnold's faith. The Evangelical editor of the *Record* (3 February 1845) asks, "Did he, even in death, rest intelligently and clearly on that fundamental doctrine [justification by faith], on which Luther declared the Gospel, as on a hinge, turned, and whosoever denieth which 'is not to be accounted,' in the words of Cranmer, as adopted by our Church, 'for a Christian man?' We cannot say. It does not appear" (Reprinted as *Brief Observations on the Political and Religious Sentinments of the Late Rev. Dr. Arnold, As Contained in His "Life" by the Rev. Arthur Penrhyn Stanley* [London: Seeley, Burnside, and Seeley, and Nisbet and Co., 1845], 19; cf. W. J. Conybeare, "Church Parties," *Edinburgh Review* 98, no. 200 [October 1853]: 273-342, 284).

162. Thomas Arnold, *An Essay on the Right Interpretation and Understanding of the Scriptures*, in *Sermons*, 2nd ed., 2 vols. (London: B. Fellowes, 1834), 2:421-80, 427-28.

163. J[ohn]. J[osias]. Conybeare, *An Attempt to Trace the History and To Ascertain the Limits of the Secondary and Spiritual Interpretation of Scripture* (Oxford: Oxford University Press, 1824), 27-28.

164. Arnold, *Essay*, 431.

165. Arnold, *Essay*, 446-48.

166. Arnold, *Essay*, 449-50.

167. Kingsley to John Ludlow; *Charles Kingsley: Letters & Memories*, ed. F. Kingsley, Bideford ed., 2 vols. (London: The Co-operative Publication Society, 1899), 1:374-75.

168. Arnold, *Essay*, 432-33.

169. Arnold, *Essay*, 459.

170. Arnold to Hawkins, Rugby, 14 September 1840, in Stanley, *Life*, 2:193.

171. Rowland Williams, "Bunsen's Biblical Researches," in Shea and Whitla, 181-203, 182.

172. *Froude's Life of Carlyle*, ed. John Clubbe (London: John Murray, 1979), 407.

173. A. P. Stanley used the term "uncle" with affectionate reverence to J. C. Hare, but not without some foundation in fact. Stanley was the son of Edward Stanley and Catherine Leycester; Catherine was the sister of Maria Leycester, who married Augustus Hare, the brother of J. C. Hare. Another of the Hare brothers, Marcus, a naval officer, married Lucy Anne Stanley, the daughter of Lord Stanley of Alderley, the elder brother of Edward. Thus, the two well-established families had become intertwined.

174. Prothero, 1:111-12.

175. John Sterling to J. C. Hare, June 1840, in "Sketch of the Author," *Essays and Tales, by John Sterling*, ed. Julius Charles Hare, 2 vols. (London: John W. Parker, 1848), 1:i-ccxxxii, cliv.

176. Mozley, 1:24; Arnold, *Essay*, 441-42.

177. Whately, *Essays on Some of the Peculiarities of the Christian Religion*, 150; Arnold, *Essay*, 468-69.

178. Francis Newman, 67-68.

179. John Henry Newman, "The Rationalistic and the Catholic Tempers Contrasted," 1835, *Essays and Sketches*, 3 vols. (New York: Longmans, Green and Co., 1948), 1:181-98, 185.

180. Tuckwell, 135. Tuckwell notes that the volume of Hampden's Bampton Lectures "which I disinterred from a College Library, venerable in disuse, dust, and damp, came to pieces in defiance of my careful handling" (128). I confess a similar experience. One cannot but wonder how few the copies are that remain.

181. Renn Dickson Hampden, *The Scholastic Philosophy Considered in Its Relation to Christian Theology* (Oxford: J. H. Parker, 1833), 10-12.

182. Hampden, *Scholastic Philosophy*, 34-36.

183. Hampden, *Scholastic Philosophy*, 53-54.

184. Hampden, *Scholastic Philosophy*, 70-71.

185. Hampden, *Scholastic Philosophy*, 82.

186. Hampden, *Scholastic Philosophy*, 90-93.

187. Hampden, *Scholastic Philosophy*, 146.

188. Hampden, *Scholastic Philosophy*, 149.

189. Hampden, *Scholastic Philosophy*, 199.

190. Hampden, *Scholastic Philosophy*, 201, 254.

191. Hampden, *Scholastic Philosophy*, 301-02.

192. Hampden, *Scholastic Philosophy*, 311-16.

193. Hampden, *Scholastic Philosophy*, 342-43.

194. Hampden, *Scholastic Philosophy*, 350-51.

195. Hampden, *Scholastic Philosophy*, 359.

196. Hampden, *Scholastic Philosophy*, 366-67, 374-75.

197. Hooker, I.14.ii., 156-57.

198. *The Letters and Diaries of John Henry Newman*, ed. Charles Stephen Dessain, 31 vols. (Oxford: Oxford University Press, 1961-1984), 5:210; Robert Pattison, *The Great Dissent: John Henry Newman and the Liberal Heresy* (New York: Oxford University Press, 1991), 64 n.

199. Maria Hare to Luce Stanley, 19 March 1832; in Augustus J. C. Hare, *Memorials*, 1:419-20.

200. Blanco White to Whately, 2 January 1835, in John Hamilton Thom, ed., *The Life of the Rev. Joseph Blanco White*, 3 vols. (London: John Chapman, 1845), 2:71; Murphy, 169.

201. "They urge," said Arnold, "that Hampden has a tendency to Socinianism. Of course he may have an *element* of Socinianism. Every great mind must of necessity have the germ of that which, *carried to excess*, becomes Socinianism" (Stanley, *Life*, 2:27 n).

202. J. C. Hare, for example, in the *Postscript to the Second Edition of Archdeacon Hare's Letter to the Dean of Chichester*, observes that those "who are at all acquainted with the writing of what was then called the Oriel School, will easily perceive that the Bampton Lectures, in their whole tone of thought, both philosophical and theological, are a genuine birth of that school, and did not need a refugee from Seville to graft them into it" (Henrietta Hampden, ed., *Some Memorials of Renn Dickson Hampden, Bishop of Hereford* (London: Longmans, Green, and Co., 1871), 28-29.

203. T. Mozley, 1:352-54.

204. Tulloch, 70 n.

205. S. T. Coleridge, *Aids*, Aph Sp Rel B IV, 192.

206. S. T. Coleridge, *Aids*, Aph Sp Rel B II, Comment, 167-68.

207. Hampden, *Scholastic Philosophy*, 224-25; cf. S. T. Coleridge, *Aids*, Aph Sp Rel B Xb, Comment, 287.

208. Hampden, *Scholastic Philosophy*, 267-69. Cf. Friedrich D. E. Schleiermacher, *On Religion* (1799), trans. John Oman (Louisville: Westminster/John Knox, 1994), 57-59; S. T. Coleridge, *The Friend*, 2 vols., ed. Barbara Rooke, vol. 4 of *The Collected Works of Samuel Taylor Coleridge* (Princeton: Princeton University Press, 1969) 1:409-10.

209. S. T. Coleridge, *The Friend*, 1:313-14.

210. Taylor, Preface, I.3, I.5, I.11, II.27; 2, 6-7, 12, 47.

211. Mark Pattison, 170-71.

212. Arnold to W. C. Lake, Rugby, 9 March 1836, in Stanley, *Life*, 2: 25; Tuckwell, 135.

213. Arnold to William Smith and Chevalier Bunson, Rugby, 9 March and 6 May 1833, in Stanley, *Life*, 1:306, 308.

214. J. H. Newman, *Apologia*, 41.

215. Keble to Dyson, 26 August 1833, in J. T. Coleridge, 219-20.

216. *Tracts for the Times*, Tract I, by members of the University of Oxford, 9 September 1833; in G. M. Young and W. D. Handcock, eds., *English Historical Documents 1833-1874* (New York: Oxford University Press, 1956), 339-40; A. O. J. Cockhut, ed., *Religious Controversies of the Nineteenth Century: Selected Documents* (Lincoln: University of Nebraska Press, 1966), 63-65.

217. In "Tracts for the Times" (1841), Arnold protests, "Mr. Newman and his friends have preached as their peculiar doctrine, not Christ, but the Church; we must go even further and say, not the Church, but themselves" (*The Miscellaneous Works of Thomas Arnold, D.D.* 1st American ed. [New York: D. Appleton and Co., 1845], 236-89, 246).

218. Arnold to Charles Longley, Rugby, 25 June 1834, in Stanley, *Life*, 1:334.

219. Arnold to Hawkins, Rugby, 14 April 1834, in Stanley, *Life*, 1:327; cf. 2:35-37.

220. Whately, *Cautions*, 306.

221. Chadwick, 1:79-81, 89-93.

222. "Appendix to the Laws," in Bentham, Appendix 1, 85-90, 86-87.

223. Renn Dickson Hampden, *Observations on Religious Dissent* (Oxford: J. H. Parker, 1834), 8.

224. Hampden, *Observations*, 5, 17.

225. Hampden, *Observations*, 20.

226. Hampden, *Observations*, 39.

227. Hampden, *Observations*, 27-32.

228. Hampden, *Observations*, 13.

229. Arnold to Hampden, Rugby, 17 May 1835, in Hampden, *Some Memorials*, 37.

230. Thomas Mozley, 1:352. Rose also wrote to Palmer, urging action, but Palmer cautioned "that any such measure might be productive of harm, in drawing public attention to statements which . . . would probably attract but little notice" (William Palmer, *Narrative of Events connected with the Publication of the Tracts for the Times, with an Introduction and Supplement extending to the Present Time* [London: Rivingtons, 1883], 129).

231. *Letters and Diaries of John Henry Newman*, 4:371, 5:81; Robert Pattison, 65-66.

232. Prothero, 1:144-45. A more thorough eyewitness description of the event is provided by a nonresident M.A. in *The British Magazine and Monthly Register* 7 (1835): 717-19.

233. Newman, *Apologia*, 59.

234. Prothero, 1:161.

235. A. P. Stanley preached the funeral sermons of both Dr. Arnold and Charles Dickens. Dickens, in his last will, had written, "I exhort my dear children humbly to try and guide themselves by the teaching of the New Testament in its broad spirit, and to put no faith in any man's narrow construction of its letter here or there" (Prothero, 2:317).

236. Edward Churton, *A Letter to an Edinburgh Reviewer, on the Case of the Oxford Malignants and Dr. Hampden* (London: J. G. and F. Rivington, 1836), 39-40 n.

237. Mark Pattison, "A Chapter of University History," *Macmillan's Magazine* (1875), in *Essays by the Late Mark Pattison, Sometime Rector of Lincoln College*, ed. Henry Nettleship, 2 vols. (Oxford: Clarendon Press, 1889), 1:318.

238. Thomas Arnold, "The Oxford Malignants and Dr. Hampden," *Edinburgh Review* 63 (April 1836): 225-39; reprinted in *Miscellaneous Works*, 1st American ed., 131-45, 142.

239. T. Mozley, 1:363.

240. In the following year, Hampden published as an independent work a fifty-page *Introduction to the Second Edition of the Bampton Lectures of the Year 1832* (London: B. Fellowes, 1837), both as a summary of his views and as a response to the allegations made against him.

241. Arnold, "Oxford Malignants," 135.

242. Arnold, "Oxford Malignants," 134.

243. Tuckwell, 140; Prothero, 1:156-57; David Cecil states that Melbourne "was determined to do nothing which looked like a surrender to the spirit of intolerance" (*Melbourne: The Young Melbourne and Lord M in One Volume* (London: Reprint Society, 1955), 247.

244. Renn Dickson Hampden, *Inaugural Lecture, Read before the University of Oxford in the Divinity School on Thursday, March 17th, 1836*, 3rd ed. (London: B. Fellowes, 1836).

245. Prothero, 1:161.

246. Arnold, "Oxford Malignants," 139.

247. Prothero, 1:158.

248. Arnold, "Oxford Malignants," 140-42, 144.

249. Taylor, II.38; 56-57.

250. Stanley to C. J. Vaughan, May 1834, in Prothero, 1:102; Clough to J. P. Gell, November 1835, in Clough, 1:62-63.

251. Stanley to his sister Mary, Oxford, 24 November 1834, in Prothero, 1:135.

252. Stanley, Oxford, 5 May 1836, in Prothero, 1:162.

253. A. H. Clough, in a letter of 5 May 1836 to J. N. Simpkinson, writes, "I agree with you about the Edinburgh Review Article, nearly, if not quite. I am very sorry it was written . . . . I am ashamed to say I have not yet read Price's" (*The Correspondence of Arthur Hugh Clough*, ed. Frederick L. Mulhauser, 2 vols. [Oxford: Clarendon Press, 1957], 1:28). Based on Walter E. Houghton's surmise, Clough's reference may be to an article by Bonamy Price on "Newman's *History of the Arians*" (*Wellesley Index*, 1:481). Price's later article on

"The Anglo-Catholic Theory" also closely follows Arnold's line of thought (*Edinburgh Review*, no. 92 [October 1851], reprinted as a pamphlet [Longman, Brown, Green, and Longmans, 1852]).

254. "The Pope's Pastoral" was first republished in *The Remains of Bishop Dickinson*, ed. Archdeacon West (London: B. Fellowes, n.d.); subsequently, it was included entire by Whately in his *Cautions for the Times*, 252-74.

255. *A Letter to His Grace the Archbishop of Canterbury: Explanatory of the Proceedings at Oxford, on the Appointment of the Present Regius Professor of Divinity* (London: B. Fellowes, 1836), 19; Arnold, "Oxford Malignants," 137. *The British Magazine*, after having noted the "wretched" *Letter*, supposed to have been written by "some one who has abused the confidence of some member of the Board of Heads," continued, in the following issue, to speculate that both the *Letter* and the article in the *Edinburgh Review* might have "come from the same hand." The editor continues, "It is difficult to decide the prize between these two compositions; it would be yet harder to say whether the article in the 'Edinburgh Review' deserves most credit for its reckless suppression of the truth, or for the temper with which it imputes motives and utters the very worst charges against individuals" (9 [1836], 436 n., 567).

256. *Letter*, 16; Arnold, "Oxford Malignants," 139.

257. Murphy, 178.

258. Thom, 2:222-23.

259. John Sterling, "Characteristics of German Genius," *Foreign Quarterly Review* (1842), in *Essays and Tales, by John Sterlilng*, ed. Julius Charles Hare, 2 vols. (London: John W. Parker, 1848), 1:382-421, 403.

260. Arnold to Whately, Rugby, 16 May 1836, in Stanley, *Life*, 2:35-36.

261. Arnold to J. T. Coleridge and G. Cornish, Fox How, 5 February 1837, in Stanley, *Life*, 2:61-64.

262. E. Jane Whately, *Life and Correspondence of Richard Whately, D.D., Late Archbishop of Dublin*, 3rd ed. (London: Longmans, Green, and Co., 1875), 221.

263. John William Adamson, *English Education, 1789-1902* (Cambridge: Cambridge University Press, 1964), 90-92.

264. Arnold to H. Crabb Robinson, 15 March 1837, in Stanley, *Life*, 2:69-70.

265. Arnold to Bishop Otter, Rugby, 30 April 1837, in Stanley, *Life*, 2:76-78.

266. Stanley, *Life*, 2:10.

267. Arnold to T. J. Ormerod, Fox How, 18 December 1837, in Stanley, *Life*, 2:88.

268. Stanley, *Life*, 2:11.

269. Strachey, 165; Whitridge, 44.

270. Arnold to A. P. Stanley, Fox How, 22 June 1838, in Stanley, *Life*, 2:107.

271. Henry Longueville Mansel, "The Phrontisterion; or, Oxford in the 19th Century," *Letters, Lectures, and Reviews*, ed. Henry W. Chandler (London: John Murray, 1873), 395-408, 397-98.

272. Prothero, 1:218-23; Davidson, 1:69-70.

273. Arnold to A. P. Stanley, Fox How, 20 December 1839, in Stanley, *Life*, 2:151-52.

274. Stanley, "A Letter on the State of Subscription," 149.

275. Stanley, "A Letter on the State of Subscription," 169-70.

276. Prothero, 1:244-47; Stanley, *Life*, 2:185.

277. Newman, *Apologia*, 72; Young and Handcock, 346-47.

278. Davidson, 1:81-82.

279. Davidson, 1:83.

280. Prothero, 1:296 (For Arnold's response, see his letter of 30 October 1841 to Stanley [Stanley, *Life*, 2:242-43]); J. A. Froude, 200-01.

281. Whately, *Cautions*, 231.

282. Arnold to Tait, Rugby, 11 March 1841, in Davidson, 1:86-87.

283. Arnold to W. C. Lake, Rugby, 18 November 1836, in Stanley, *Life*, 2:53.

284. Francis Newman, *Phases*, 7.

285. Arnold to Hawkins, Rugby, 12 January 1839, in Stanley, *Life*, 2:125.

286. John Campbell Shairp, after a visit to Rugby in 1844, described the work of the headmaster as "such as only one man out of ten could stand" (William Knight, *Principal Shairp and His Friends* [London: John Murray, 1888], 85). The work nearly killed Arnold's successor, Tait.

287. Arnold to Chevalier Bunsen, Rugby, 25 May and 13 June 1840, in Stanley, *Life*, 2:184, 186.

288. Arnold to Chevalier Bunsen, Rugby, 4 September 1840, in Stanley, *Life*, 2:190.

289. Arnold to Stanley, Rugby, 8 March 1841, in Stanley, *Life*, 2:214.

290. Church, 181 n.

291. Stanley, *Life*, 2:224.

292. Arnold to J. T. Coleridge, Fox How, 1 September 1841, in Stanley, *Life*, 2:237. On 26 May 1841 Robert Peel introduced a resolution into the House of Commons declaring "want of confidence" in Melbourne's administration. The resolution passed by a vote of one, and Parliament was dissolved. The first session of the new Parliament, on 19 August, again passed a vote of "want of confidence." This led to a resignation of ministers, and on 3 September 1841 Peel took office as prime minister.

293. Prothero, 1:307. F. W. Robertson, who attended Arnold's inaugural lecture as an undergraduate of Brazenose College, refers to the professor's reception as an instance of dramatic transition or "revulsion" of public feeling (Brooke, 37-38).

294. Richard William Church to Frederic Rogers, Oriel, February 1842, in Mary C. Church, ed., *Life and Letters of Dean Church* (London: Macmillan and Co., 1895), 34-35. Richard Jenkyns, master of Balliol, did, in fact, have the gout at this time. Following the lecture, "Mary & I," wrote Dr. Arnold, "walked up to Balliol to see Matt's rooms, & to call on Jenkyns, who had the Gout" (Park Honan, *Matthew Arnold: A Life* [London: Weidenfeld and Nicolson, 1981], 55).

295. Tuckwell, 124; cf. Prothero, 1:308.

296. Arnold to Herbert Hill, Oxford, 9 February 1842, in Stanley, *Life*, 2:262.

297. Arnold to Carlyle, Rugby, January 1840, in Stanley, *Life*, 2:159-60.

298. Arnold to Hawkins; Rugby, 19 May 1842, in Stanley, *Life*, 2:267.

299. A. H. Clough, 13 April 1852, in Clough, 1:177.

300. In June 1842, after Arnold's death, Stanley wrote to Clough, "For the last 3 weeks he had for the first time in his life kept from time to time a Diary of prayers and meditations, having said to Mrs. A. that so many good men had done so that it was perhaps a want of

humility in h im never to have tried anything of the kind" (Appendix II, in Howard Foster Lowry, ed., *The Letters of Matthew Arnold to Arthur Hugh Clough* [Oxford: Clarendon Press, 1932], 165).

301. Stanley, *Life*, 2:273, 281.

302. W. C. Lake to R. T. Davidson, 23 March 1888, in Davidson, 1:102-03. Cf. Matthew Arnold's testimonial in 1857 on behalf of the appointment of Frederick Temple to the position of Headmaster of Rugby: "In the most important qualities of a schoolmaster, . . . Mr. Temple, more than any other man whom I have ever known, resembles, to the best of my observation and judgment, my late father" (E. G. Sandford, ed., *Memoirs of Archbishop Temple*, 2 vols. [London: Macmillan and Co., Ltd., 1906], 1:153).

303. Bunsen to J. C. Hare, London, 19 June 1842, in Bunsen, *Memoirs*, 2:18-19.

304. Augustus J. C. Hare, *Memorials*, 2:241.

305. E. J. Whately, 219-20.

306. Prothero, 1:320.

307. Arnold to G. Cornish, Rydal, 23 December 1831, in Stanley, *Life*, 1:270.

308. Prothero, 1:320-21.

309. J. H. Newman to J. Keble, Oriel College, 13 June 1844, in *Correspondence of John Henry Newman with John Keble and Others, 1839-1845* (London: Longmans, Green, and Co., 1917), 321-22.

310. Pattison, 236-38. For a dissenting perspective, see Dean Lake's reminiscences in Lake, 48-49.

311. T. K. Cheyne, "The Divine Call in the History of a College: A Commemoration Sermon, Preached in Oriel College Chapel, October 20, 1889" (Oxford: Horace Hart, 1889), 6.

3

Cambridge Apostles and Prophets

The seventeenth-century Cambridge Platonist movement is the most obvious of English precursors to the Broad Church movement. We might, then, suppose that from Emmanuel College—those Cambridge halls that, "with ceaseless turmoil seething," carried the ancestral voices of Whichcote, Cudworth, Smith, and Culverwell—might now burst forth the mighty Coleridgean fountain that is the subject of this study. Instead, we find that, in the early years of the nineteenth century, Emmanuel is a retreat for the idle—that is to say, a gentleman's resort. We must look, rather, toward Trinity, "the stateliest and most uniform college in Christendom,"[1] the college of Thomas Cartwright and Walter Travers, Hooker's Puritan antagonists, and the most illustrious college of Cambridge in the nineteenth century.

In the beginning of the century, the Evangelical party exercised considerable influence at Cambridge. Evangelicalism had never been allowed a foothold at Oxford; one hundred years before the *Tracts for the Times*, in the early 1730s, the Wesleys and their little "Holy Club" had been hooted and pelted out of town. A few years later John Wesley had his fateful encounter with Peter Böhler, the Moravian missionary, and by the end of that decade England was aflame with the Evangelical Revival. Methodism was, at first, entirely a Church of England movement, and the Evangelicals rejoiced to find that Hooker's "Sermon on Justification" proclaimed their distinctive doctrine "with as full an emphasis, and with as fearless an unreserve, as the German Reformer, and as the founders of Methodism."[2] Those Arminian followers of Wesley and Calvinist followers of Whitefield who did not secede from the Church of England were, nevertheless, looked upon with suspicion and, often, with hostility.

The drawbridges over the Isis, and for a long while, over the Cam, would not be lowered to the Evangelicals or their sons, and the college walls could not be scaled. The gates had to be opened from within. The first significant breakthrough came in 1783, when Charles Simeon (1759-1836) acquired the pulpit of Trinity Church, Cambridge. With student conversions to Evangelicalism on the increase, it was now only a matter of time before the party gained sufficient strength from within the university to compel the lowering of a bridge. That time came in 1788, when the incomparable Isaac Milner (1750-1820), was appointed president of Queen's College. At the time, Queen's was thin, pale, lethargic, and generally consumptive. Milner determined upon a bold maneuver, a move that would make him a hero to some and a traitorous villain to others. An Evangelical himself, he opened the college's entrance examinations to like-minded Christians, and transformed Queen's into "a sort of School of the Prophets, the stronghold of Evangelicalism in Cambridge."[3] Fellows were humbled, tutors were deposed, all opposition was crushed, and before long Queen's was revitalized into one of the largest and most prosperous of Cambridge colleges.

A measurement of the ensuing influence of the Evangelical party at Cambridge may be inferred from the establishment there of an auxiliary branch of the British and Foreign Bible Society in December 1811. Unlike the Society for the Promotion of Christian Knowledge, an institution of the Church of England that distributed prayer books and tracts along with Bibles, the Bible Society was an interdenominational organization that, operating on the assumption that the Bible required no commentary, existed for the sole purpose of disseminating Scripture into all parts of the world. The Bible Society received staunch opposition from Christopher Words-worth,[4] future master of Trinity (1820-1841), and Herbert Marsh, the Lady Margaret Professor of Divinity (1807-1816), but the league of Evangelicals, led by Simeon, Milner, and William Wilberforce could not be withstood.[5]

A few years later, in 1820, a small group of undergraduate Evangelicals, all Tory in politics, formed themselves into an exclusive discussion group, the Conversazione Society. Perhaps because their number was originally limited to twelve, or perhaps because they were disposed toward missionary activity, they were nicknamed the "Apostles." This society was, practically, an effort to define the college elite in the absence of organized debate, during the interregnum of 1817-1821, when the Cambridge Union was closed. As we shall note, that elitist status could not long subsist on the basis of a heart strangely warmed and sentiment lazily inherited, and with the reopening of the union, the Conversazione Society would be sifted and purified as if by tongues of fire, till in the upper room only the true Apostles remained.

The Cambridge Union

Cambridge life in these years—before railroads and wire communications—was, especially during the winter months, dull uniformity. The students attended compulsory lectures, described as "a fixed and lifeless round of Euclid, Demosthenes, and Latin Declamation, with an occasional perfunctory divinity lecture to maintain the semblance of the religious foundation."[6] Amusement was to be found in conversation, gossip, and debate, usually around the dinner table or in the Common Rooms. Adam Sedgwick (1785-1873), who was to have the honor of being simultaneously Cambridge's foremost geologist and fossil, had taken his Master's in 1811 and complained of society among the fellows of Trinity: "Many are gloomy and discontented, many impertinent and pedantic; and a still greater number are so eaten up with vanity that they are continually attempting some part which they cannot support."[7] Undergraduates could not rely upon their tutors to supply them with means of diversion.

In November 1812, Julius Charles Hare (1795-1855) matriculated as a pensioner at Trinity College, Cambridge, and was followed in two years by his friend and fellow "Carthusian," or Charterhouse classmate, Connop Thirlwall (1797-1875). William Whewell (1794-1866)—the son of a Lancashire carpenter who would, in 1841, replace Christopher Wordsworth as master of Trinity—entered the college at about the same time as Hare, and together with Thirlwall, they formed the nucleus of a debating club. In 1814 three Cambridge debating clubs merged their ranks, forming the Union Debating Society, with Whewell as its president and Thirlwall as the secretary. Its first meeting was in February 1815. It was a success, and from that date, on every Tuesday evening, for one to two hours, the best of Cambridge students, up to two hundred, would flock in their gowns to the smoky Red Lion Inn to hear or participate in a debate on politics, religion, or literature.[8]

The speeches at the union sometimes irreverently handled the conservative point of view and debunked the status quo. For example, just after the Waterloo Campaign, Hare gave a speech "On the Question of the Propriety of the War against France."[9] Not all of the authorities at Cambridge could sit idly by while undergraduates presumptuously cast doubt upon the policies of Church and State. But these were not the days of Laud, when students' private assemblies and secret conventicles could be raided and disbursed as unlawful threats to the peace of the government. It seemed to Vice-Chancellor James Wood, master of St. John's, there was little he could do, so he watched and waited for an opportunity. It arrived in the form of a letter from a disgruntled member of the union. The student alleged that the time and energy demanded of him from the society, and which he had unselfishly given, had detracted from his studies and, as a result, had blighted his prospects at the university. Anyone could have seen that the letter was but a lame excuse for a want of discipline and the maturity to take personal responsibility for its consequences, but Wood twisted the letter into the justifiable cause that he needed to take action. On 24 March 1817, Wood sent the proctors to Red Lion Inn to interrupt the proceedings and disband the assembly. The proctors were answered by Whewell: "Strangers will please to withdraw, and the House will take the message into consideration."[10] Wood, however, was adamant against all remonstrance, and the union was closed down for four years, until the vice-chancellorship passed into the hands of Dr. Wordsworth.

By this one act, for which he will always be remembered, Wood served the cause of culture at Cambridge much in the same way that the sons of Jacob served the Hebrews by selling Joseph to the Midianites. This statement, no doubt, requires some explanation. Cambridge had a valuable but largely unappreciated resource in its professor of divinity, for Herbert Marsh had studied in Germany under Johann David Michaelis of Göttingen, through whom he had become conversant with the critical study of the Gospels. Upon his return to Cambridge, Marsh translated into English the four volumes of Michaelis's *Introduction to the New Testament* (1793-1801).[11] Although both his translation and his lectures on biblical criticism (1809-1816) went some ways toward familiarizing his pupils with German ideas, Marsh was not given any opportunity to provide the knowledge that alone would give students direct access to German minds. Nevertheless, Hare had learned German while living with his parents at Weimar, and now—with the union closed and Tuesday evenings free—he formed a reading club for the purpose of providing instruction in the German language. Thus, Wood inadvertently served the cause of culture.

In Hare's German reading club were Thirlwall, Whewell, and the former treasurer of the union, Hugh James Rose (1795-1838). Eight years later, in 1825, Rose—after spending a few months in Germany to round off the corners of his expertise—went before the university with his discourses on *The State of Protestantism in Germany, Described*. Hare was not amused. "To me," he confessed in his typically long-winded fashion, "it has always seemed that a careful examination of the subject matter is an indispensable preliminary to pronouncing judgment upon it: but this notion give such offense in England, and is so abhorrent to the procedure of our writers on theology, that one might almost suspect it must be a German heresy."[12]

Law and Literature

In October 1818 Hare, Thirlwall, and Whewell all obtained fellowships at Trinity College. At the time, there was no residency requirement for the fellows; thus, "Men of ambition went out into the world and boldly courted fortune, as soon as they had obtained their fellowships. . . . Those who despaired of success, or had no energy to strive after it, remained behind."[13] Whewell remained behind, but not for lack of energy or ambition. He was immediately made assistant tutor and, in 1819, he supported Professor Sedgwick in his efforts to institute the Cambridge Philosophical Society for the purpose of scientific concourse.[14] Hare and Thirlwall went their separate ways, but both departed for the Continent.

Hare spent Christmas in Paris with his brother Francis; Thirlwall went to Rome, where he had the opportunity to practice his German in the company of the Bunsens, and perhaps also with Barthold Niebuhr. Thirlwall impressed the baroness with his knowledge: "that he had read Mr. Niebuhr's Roman History proved him to possess no trifling knowledge of German, and as he expressed a wish to improve himself in the language, Charles ventured to invite him to come to us on a Tuesday evening, whenever he was not otherwise engaged." Possibly, there is a hint of exasperation in her observation that "Mr. Thirlwall has never missed any Tuesday evening since. . . . He comes at eight o'clock, and never stirs to go away till everybody else has wished good-night, often at almost twelve o'clock." Even so, the baroness found "a great many reasons for our being *very much* pleased with Mr. Thirlwall, yet I rather suspect him of being very cold, and very dry."[15]

At this time in their lives, both Hare and Thirlwall had intellectual reservations that conscientiously prevented them from taking Holy Orders. Both men were highly speculative, and while Hare—whose religious certainties had been defined by Kant—was beginning to fall under the spell of Coleridge, Thirlwall—to whom any religious certainty at all seemed impossible—was being persuaded by Pascal. Neither man could, therefore, entertain the thought of applying for a teaching position at Cambridge, and both decided, instead, to pursue legal studies in London. In doing so, they took full advantage of that tradition which, as Anthony Trollope explains, "prevails at the greatest of all our colleges, Trinity, Cambridge, in accordance with which certain years of grace are allowed, and a fellow may remain a fellow for a period of years without taking orders."[16] In late 1819 Hare, encouraged by his brothers Francis and Augustus, entered the Middle Temple at the Inns of Court, and in February 1820 Thirlwall entered Lincoln's Inn.

Whatever leisure hours the two could spare from the law, they gave to German literature, often meeting together for readings. Hare applied himself to the task of translating Baron de la Motte Fouqué's gothic tale of *Sintram and His Companions*. His translation appeared anonymously in 1820, during the period when he was attending Coleridge's Thursday soirees in Highgate. Hare and Coleridge shared a deep and informed appreciation for modern German literature, and the poet-philosopher may have offered critical advice regarding the fine art of translation. Coleridge, while in Rome in 1805-1806, had befriended Johann Ludwig Tieck and had translated one of his poems and had, in turn, received a visit from the German poet in June 1817.[17] Hare, from his own library of German works, then introduced Thirl-wall to Tieck's grimly ironic *novellen*, and the two began the translations of Tieck that were to continue sporadically for several years.

After Thirlwall had sharpened his linguistic tools, and when he was anxious to apply his talents more ambitiously, Hare placed into his hands a new edition of Schleiermacher's *Saint Luke* (1821). Undoubtedly, the influence of Professor Marsh's lectures, along with the realization that English readers were, as yet, nearly wholly illiterate on the issues regarding the Synoptics, had much to do with Thirlwall's selection from among Schleiermacher's works, but his choice also reflects a personal distaste for talk of religious feeling, a subject so central to Schleiermacher's earlier works, particularly the *Soliloquies* and *Speeches*.[18] Thirlwall's translation and 150-page Introduction would occupy his leisure hours for the next three years, leading to the 1825 publication of *A Critical Essay on the Gospel of St. Luke*.

In the literary circles of London an interest in German literature was quickly developing. If one were to accept the impossible task of identifying the single flake that set the snowball rolling, one could at least make a plausible case by pointing to the English translation of Madame de Staël's *De l'Allemagne*, which appeared in 1813, at the time of her visit to England. At the end of the decade John Scott launched the *London Magazine* (1820-1829). Although its founder's intent was merely to provide a counterblast against *Blackwood's*, it soon resulted in the duel that ended his life,[19] and in 1821 the magazine passed into the hands of John Taylor and John Hessey, who transformed it into one of the principle vehicles for the dissemination of critical reviews and translations of German literature. Carlyle, De Quincey, and Hazlitt—all admirers of German literature—joined the club life of the *London Magazine*. Hare, who had met Taylor in 1820, also entered the ranks of the London literati.

Coleridge and Hare

Coleridge exercised an immense and timely influence upon the religious development of Hare, without which it is uncertain whether he would have ever returned to Cambridge and taken orders in the Church. By April of 1822, Hare, in letters to Whewell, was making it known that the prospect of the ministry held attractions quite other than and apart from the worldly advantages attached to it. Three months later, on 16 July, he sent off a letter to Whewell announcing that he had received from Dr. Wordsworth the offer of a lectureship: "To be sure it is a tremendous undertaking, and attended with an overwhelming responsibility, to have to teach the flower of England's youth to walk straight in these crooked-going days."[20] It was a responsibility that Hare, trained by Plato and Kant and now armed with Coleridgean insights, was eager to accept.

The religious philosophy of Coleridge has already been considered in some depth, but it may be worthwhile to quickly survey the expression that Hare, in his first volume of published sermons, gave to its predominant features. For Hare, as for Coleridge, Christian Faith can be reduced neither to intellectual assent nor to feeling. "Indeed," said Hare, "a Faith which was merely a belief founded on the calculations of the Understanding, would be no Faith at all," just as a Faith that did not naturally result in works would be no Faith.[21] What are called "Evidences" may offer some small support to Faith, but they are powerless in generating it, for "the main seat of Faith is not in the Understanding, but in the Will and the Affections. . . . God, when He demands our Faith, calls upon us to give Him our Hearts."[22] The formative principle of Faith is confidence, trust, and reliance, which spring from a personal relationship with a loving and forgiving God. Thus, Hare would warn students, "Do not imagine that your knowledge will produce Faith; scarcely will knowledge strengthen it. Faith, as a practical power, can only be strengthened practically." Thus, "a single act of Faith, a single prayer offered up from the bottom of the heart, a single exertion of self-denial, of self-control, for Christ's sake . . . will do more to strengthen and establish your Faith, than all the learning of all the theologians."[23]

In Hare, as in Coleridge, the Practical Reason is given the chief seat in the synagogue of Faith. To those who have confused the Reason with the Under-standing, Hare argues, "The true antithesis is not between Faith and Reason, but between Faith and Sight, or more generally between Faith and Sense." And to those who have confused Faith with mere intellectual acquiescence, he continues, "Nor is the office of Faith to deliver man from the bondage of Reason, but from the bondage of the Senses, by which his Reason has been deposed and enthralled, and hereby to enable him to become Reason's willing, dutiful, and active servant." Thus, Hare, true to Coleridge, establishes that the opposition that is sometimes conceived to exist between Faith and Reason is "utterly groundless."[24]

Maurice and Sterling at Trinity

The undergraduates of Trinity were partitioned into three "sides," over each of which were assigned a tutor, assistant tutor, and staff. When Hare returned to Cambridge as classical lecturer in the autumn of 1822, he was assigned to Whewell's "side," and so the two taught their different subjects to the same group of students. Into this group there came, in October 1823, after Hare had a year's experience, a quiet, reserved Unitarian named Frederick Denison Maurice (1805-1872). Although it took some time for Hare to gain the least acquaintance with this shy student, Hare made a lasting first impression upon Maurice. After the inaugural week of classes, he reported home his admiration for the "lively" classical scholar: "I am particularly pleased with his manner, especially that of recommending books bearing upon the subject in question, but out of the regular College routine. For instance, Schlegel's celebrated work on Dramatic Literature he advised us to study attentively."[25] Maurice's letter suggests that Rose was no false prophet when he anticipated, in a letter to Whewell, that "Plato illustrated by Coleridge with excursuses on Kant will be the least of Hare's feats."[26] Yet, what is most remarkable is that this manner of teaching, of recommending reading "out of the regular College routine," would be praised by an undergraduate. Evidently, Maurice not only recognized the university as an institution for the pursuit of knowledge, but actually attended for the very purpose of the pursuit. Odd, indeed!

Despite Maurice's shyness, his out-of-the-ordinary character attracted the notice of his peers. John Stock, Maurice's closest friend upon arriving at Cambridge, brought him to the attention of the Apostles. Stock, an Evangelical, had been an Apostle since 1821, the year that the union resumed its debates. The Apostles' participation and rivalry in those debates had quickly shattered the ideological uniformity of its members, while at the same time bringing forward the importance of intellectual agility and congeniality. Since a unanimous vote from the Apostles was necessary for the election of a new member, Maurice had to have more in his favor than his friendship with Stock, and there can be no doubt that Maurice's manners and brilliance secured him the election. Even so, his own Bristol background, and the fact that his elder sisters, Elizabeth, Mary, and Anne, had not only converted from Unitarianism to Calvinist Evangelicalism, but had also been instrumental in the conversion of the Bristol physician who was the father of John Stock, were factors that worked mightily to Maurice's advantage. Several of the founding members of the Apostles were Evangelicals from Bristol, and *their* approval of the candidate was probably sufficient endorsement.[27]

A year passed by before John Sterling entered Trinity College. In October 1824 he too became one of Hare's pupils. In the "Sketch" of Sterling's life that Hare, years later, would write, he recalls the "genial intellect and spirit" that gained his affection. Sterling was not what Hare could properly refer to as "a good scholar," but "he was something better, inasmuch as he soon shewed that he could relish and delight in the beauty of Greek poetry, and the practical and speculative wisdom of Greek history and philosophy."[28] Although the details surrounding the beginning of Sterling's relationship with Maurice are lost, we know that Sterling took the active role in forming the friendship, and that, after Sterling was elected an Apostle in November 1825, he pushed Maurice into prominence.[29]

Sterling was a natural debater, and with his election the period of Apostolic domination over the union began. Benjamin Hall Kennedy, the future headmaster of Shrewsbury, who was elected to the Apostles a year before Sterling, had already become the preeminent speaker of the Whig or liberal faction, and when to his talents were added those of Sterling and, in 1826, of Charles Buller, the Apostles acquired the fame and prestige in Cambridge that has since dissipated, but has never disappeared. Carlyle, although he may have overstated his point in making Sterling "the acknowledged chief" in the union, has nevertheless described his talent well: "In coruscating wit, in jocund drollery, in compact articulated clearness or high poignant emphasis, as the case required,—he was a match for any man in argument before a crowd of men."[30]

Coleridge and Maurice

It was impossible for a person of Maurice's intellectual curiosity to have grown up in the home of a Unitarian minister, within walking distance to Bristol, and not to have read something by S. T. Coleridge. The differences in belief represented within the Maurice home set the future theologian thinking upon many subjects that had also passed through the poet-philosopher's mind. Years later, in a public letter to Derwent Coleridge, Maurice explained that, in the *Biographia Literaria,* "I seemed to see a writer, who was feeling his way into the apprehension of many questions which had puzzled me. . . . I learned from him, by practical illustration, how one may

enter into the spirit of a living or departed author, without assuming to be his judge."
Maurice found all of Coleridge's works principally interesting as the biography of
an intellectual sojourner, who "was able, after great effort and much sorrow, to
discover a resting place." Thus, Maurice conceived the merit of *The Friend* to reside
in the fact "that it is an inquiry, that it shows us what we have to seek for, and that
it puts us into the way of seeking." Far from tempting Maurice to reverence its
author as *the* authority on the subjects it treats of, its pages had the effect of teaching
Maurice to honor the most diverse thinkers, "which I otherwise should not have
understood, and might, through ignorance and self-conceit, have undervalued."[31]
Which of Coleridge's books Maurice read *before* coming up to Cambridge is
unclear, but it is probably safe to assume that these works that pertain most directly
to the author's own Unitarian and transitional period would have carried the
strongest appeal to the young Maurice.

Coleridge's writings, often supported by Hare's lectures and sermons,
endeared the Sage of Highgate to the developing mind of the Apostle. As Maurice
states the case, Coleridge is the "philosopher whom we revere above all living
philosophers, on account of the good, we believe, we have received from his
writings"; or, as Alec Vidler states, "Maurice came nearer to treating Coleridge as
a master than he did anyone else."[32] Yet, this word "master" must not be thought
synonymous with "authority." As Maurice's own statements suggest, Coleridge did
not teach him *what* to think, but rather *how* to think. Coleridge taught Maurice not
to conflate the leadings of the Reason with the imperfect dictates of the Understanding, to listen for the truth that lay not *in*, but rather *beneath* language and sense.
Maurice revered Coleridge, not for having supplied a fund of knowledge, but for
having imparted the wisdom that prepares the mind for seeking and finding
knowledge.

In 1825 Maurice migrated from Trinity College to Trinity Hall in order to take
classes in civil law preparatory for the Bar. Sterling joined Maurice later in the year,
at about the time when he and his coeditor, Charles Whitmore, were preparing for
the press the first issues of the short-lived *Metropolitan Quarterly Magazine* (1825-
1826). The position of Maurice was aggressively hostile against Benthamite utilitarianism and defensive of the English Romantic poets, grounded in the belief that
the soul of England was to be regenerated not through political machinery, but
through the spiritual influence of the poets. Two critical essays, on Wordsworth and
Shelley, were contributed by Derwent Coleridge,[33] who had taken his B.A. from
Cambridge in 1824. Thomas Arnold (the younger) insists that Derwent had "not a
fiftieth part of the power" of his older brother Hartley[34]—an observation that may
have been true, but a smart man at the races will overlook the hare and put his money
on the tortoise. Regrettably, the letters between Maurice and Derwent Coleridge
appear not to have survived, yet it is at least probable that they discussed the just-
published *Aids to Reflection* (1825). S. T. Coleridge's arguments on behalf of a
Trinity in Unity must have been working upon Maurice at this juncture of his life, and
his sympathies, as his biographer tells us, were moving in the direction of the Church

of England. [35] Still, Maurice was not ready to convert to Anglicanism, and—unable to subscribe to the 36th Canon[36]—he left Cambridge in the summer of 1826 without taking the LL.B. degree.

The London Debating Society

Sterling also became a disciple of the Sage of Highgate, first, through the combined influence of Maurice and Hare, and then—after leaving Cambridge for London in 1827, through the direct influence of Coleridge himself. Before taking wings, Sterling had befriended Richard C. Trench (1807-1886), the advocate of the Spaniard exiles in Somers Town and the translator of their poetry. Trench, the future archbishop of York, was elected an Apostle in 1827. He and Sterling readily entered into one another's feelings and exchanged sympathies, so that through the suggestion of the one, the other would come to champion the cause of General Torrijos,[37] and because Sterling was able to translate with so much affection and zeal the message of Maurice and Coleridge, the torch of the "mystics" was kept aflame and passed from hand-to-hand within the society of the Apostles.

Sterling, unlike Maurice, was neither quiet nor shy of society, and he would never neglect an opportunity to make the acquaintance of an author or artist whose work he revered. Through Hare, he obtained an invitation to Coleridge's table talk, and although Sterling, on at least one occasion, brought Trench along with him, Maurice declined to join them.[38] Years later, Sterling confided to Hare, "To Coleridge I owe *education*. He taught me to believe that an empirical philosophy is none, that Faith is the highest Reason, that all criticism, whether of literature, laws, or manners, is blind, without the power of discerning the organic unity of the object."[39] Hare, fully appreciating Sterling's point of view and his powers of debate, may also have set his young friend in the direction of the London Debating Society. However, given Sterling's talents and his consistently pleasant and gregarious personality, he might just as easily have acquired his invitation by some other means.

In 1825 two clubs, the Co-operative Society (a group devoted to the principles of Robert Owen, the English Socialist) and the Utilitarian Society (a group devoted to the principles of Jeremy Bentham and James Mill), came together to form the London Debating Society. At its first meeting, the subject given for debate was "Population," and pitted against each other were two men who would, ever afterwards, entertain the greatest respect for one another, Connop Thirlwall, now a lawyer, and John Stuart Mill. The latter reflected in his *Autobiography*, "The speaker with whom I was most struck, though I dissented from nearly every word he said, was Thirlwall. . . . His speech was in answer to one of mine. Before he had uttered ten sentences, I set him down as the best speaker I had ever heard, and I have never since heard any one whom I placed above him."[40]

By the time that Sterling and Maurice entered the debates, Thirlwall was no longer participating. In fact, they had passed each other by in 1827, when Thirlwall hastened back to Trinity in order to take deacon's orders and prevent his fellowship from expiring.[41] Moreover, the Debating Society itself had undergone some change, being now comprised of two broad groups, Liberals and Tories, each with differences within their own ranks. Maurice and Sterling introduced, says Mill, a third group, "the Coleridgeans," which were thought of "as a second Liberal and even Radical party, on totally different grounds from Benthamism and vehemently opposed to it."[42] Mill's "friendly intercourse" with the Coleridgeans, and the considerable use that he made of this association upon his development, is told frankly in his *Autobiography*. It is of interest to us here to note how he describes these two friends: "Maurice was the thinker, Sterling the orator, and impassioned expositor of thoughts which, at this period, were almost entirely formed for him by Maurice." As a thinker, Maurice impressed Mill as being, in intellectual power, "decidedly superior" to Coleridge himself.[43]

What the Coleridgeans gained from their intercourse with the Benthamites is less obvious. In a letter to Trench, Sterling complains, "I have been present in body at several of the debates of the London Debating Society; I have spoken once or twice, but it won't do. 'Pearls before,' etc. . . . I was going to be stoned with stones at Cambridge for being an enemy to religion, and now I am ground to powder by a Mill in London for excessive piety."[44] Maurice's description is no less derogatory. In his novel, *Eustace Conway* (1834), he has the autobiographical Conway attend, with his Benthamite friend, a meeting of Utilitarians in which the discussion centered upon "the great fact, that religion is *done* cheaper in France and America, and the great principle that free competition lowers the price of every article." After the meeting, Conway begins the conversation:

> "Oh, my dear Morton," said he, when the fresh air had a little restored him, "these wits! these wits!—only preserve me from these wits!"
>
> "Then you must give up politics, Conway. How the deuce do you expect to reform the world, if you separate yourself from all your brethren?"
>
> "But such brethren!—Their vile, vulgar arguments have very nearly turned me into a dutiful son of Alma Mater, a stiff churchman, and even an aristocrat!"[45]

Maurice's experiences in the London Debating Society were, at least, instrumental in convincing him that the effects of partisan debate were almost wholly negative. "Though I heard the most vital questions discussed every night," Conway explains to his sister, Honoria, "so ridiculous seemed the mimic fighting, that I never could bring myself to believe that it had a relation to any real thing."[46] Maurice observed that the participants of competitive debates tended to dig themselves into partisan trenches, an occupation quite adverse to the upward pursuit toward light. Debate might sharpen the wits, but it also divorced ideas from the feelings and observations with which those ideas are always associated in individual persons. Maurice would have agreed with this scholium of Spinoza: "Most controversies arise from this, that men do not correctly express what is in their mind, or they misunderstand another's mind. For, in reality, while they are hotly contradicting one another, they are either in agreement or have different things in mind, so that the apparent errors and absurdities of their opponents are not really so."[47] Thus, organized debate not only had an essentially unreal quality about it, but it was also inimical to sympathetic communication.

Both Maurice and Sterling arrived at this conviction about the role of debates and the importance of honest inquiry and communication in the necessarily *social* pursuit of truth. This conviction was transmitted to the Cambridge Apostles. Subsequently, by the end of 1830, when the "mystics"—now led by Arthur Henry Hallam—had become the largest group within the society, the Apostles had nearly completely withdrawn from the union. Debating and factionalism had become characteristically "un-Apostolic," and the members were, once again, selected on the basis of potential congeniality.[48] John M. Kemble, elected in 1826, left behind this statement about the character of the Apostles:

> No society ever existed in which more freedom of thought was found consistent with the most perfect affection between the members, or in which a more complete tolerance of the most opposite opinions prevailed. . . . To my *education* given in that society I feel that I owe every power I possess, and the rescuing myself from a ridiculous state of prejudice and prepossessions with which I came armed to Cambridge. From "the Apostles" I, at least, learned to think as a *free man.*[49]

The Athenæum and the Trinity Classicists

In the latter years of the 1820s there were two major sources of influence upon the Apostles, and both sources were formative currents in the incipient Broad Church movement. These were the London literary and critical journal, *The Athenæum* (not coincidentally bearing the same title as August and Friedrich Schlegel's journal), edited by Maurice (1828-1829), and the dual force of progressive scholarship in Hare and Thirlwall, two of Trinity College's classicists. These two founts of Coleridgean inspiration perfectly complemented one another, and the Apostles, receptive to both, and electing into their number in 1829 Arthur Henry Hallam, Richard Monckton Milnes, and Alfred Tennyson, were molding themselves into a legendary society.[50]

From January to July of 1828 Maurice contributed to *The Athenæum* a series of "Sketches of Contemporary Authors," including a relatively lengthy denunciation of the philosophical and rhetorical value of the work of James Mill (18 June 1828). At the close of July, when the friends of Maurice purchased proprietorship, Maurice became the editor. On 13 August appeared a laudatory review of *Guesses at Truth, by Two Brothers* (1827), the work of J. C. and Augustus Hare. Robert Southey liked to refer to it as "the Hare-brain'd *Guesses*," but Maurice called it "the offspring of good thoughts and good feelings," a work that "inherits the excellence of its parents." Attempting to account for what he supposed to be the work's unpopularity, Maurice notes that the book "does not fall in with the views of any party or sect," and secondly, that it does not "profess to be a system. The fault," he explains, "is not that they *are* 'guesses,' but that they do not *profess* to be any thing else. . . . The authors do not chime in with the weary 'ding-dong-bell' of class doctrines; but they have strong convictions of their own. They do not put forward a system, but they think systematically."[51]

At the end of the year, Maurice wrote a review of J. C. Hare's sermon "The Children of Light," which had been delivered at Cambridge the month before, on Advent Sunday, 1828. Tradition has it that, as the preacher continued into the dinner hour, the assembly "manifested their impatience by the most unseemly and unequivocal signs," so that, of those who heard the exordium, not half heard the peroration.[52] Yet, this sermon has been compared to Keble's "On National Apostacy," in that whereas the latter inaugurated the Oxford Movement, "The Children of Light" marks the advent of the Broad Church movement.[53] Indeed, if we consider Coleridge as the one who planted the seed of the movement, and if we look for the first fruits of that seed in the preaching of a Churchman, then Hare's sermon deserves serious consideration as a candidate for the inaugural proclamation of the Broad Church. The problem with making any such nomination is that it nearly necessitates that we conceive of the Broad Church as a partisan movement. Indeed, this was and is the popular conception and, as we shall see, it was also the reason why Maurice denied his part in the movement.

Taking Ephesians 5:8 as the text, "Ye were sometimes darkness; but now are ye light in the Lord: walk as children of light," Hare criticizes the delusion common in young men, "not merely that we are wiser than our ancestors, but that while we are perfectly wise and clear-sighted, our ancestors were utterly ignorant and blind." Although the value we place on intellectual illumination is praiseworthy, "our error," says Hare, "lies in persisting to wait on the earthborn flame, after we are aware, or may and ought to be aware, that it is nothing better." The light of the Gospel is the only truth that will bring us out of spiritual darkness. In a Wordsworthian vein, Hare declares that it is this light, aided by "the creative faculty of the Imagination," that will purge your eyes to see "that glory is abiding upon the earth" and will lead you "to look at Nature as you ought to look, . . . to pierce through her body to her soul, or rather to behold the workings of her soul in all the movements of her body."[54]

Illuminating the Gospel with the language of Coleridge, Hare observes that the "prime object and appointed task of the Reason" is not to create new tenets and systems of philosophy and religion, but "to detect and to apprehend the laws by which the Almighty Law-giver upholds and rules the world. . . . Indeed the business of Reason is not so much to divine what is not shown, as to discern and exhibit the consistency of that which is shown." On this basis, Hare departs from Kant, disagreeing that the Reason *provides* evidence for immortality; rather, says Hare, it honors the evidence of the consistency of the "instinctive voice of human nature."[55] He then applies this principle to his own appointed task, as a teacher of the classics: "Whatsoever I could discover in the works and thoughts of man, anterior to the Gospel, yet in harmony with the spirit of the Gospel, I would welcome as a fresh assurance that the Gospel is in harmony with the immortal part of man's nature, with that portion of God's image, which has not been wholly effaced."[56]

In this sermon we find the principle that is central to the development of Maurice's theological method, and it would be difficult to state it with greater clarity than as given by Hare himself: "Wherever an error or a folly has exercised a wide influence, we may be sure that it must have been the parody or caricature of some truth: and its extensive influence has mainly been owing to the likeness of this truth, which, however unconsciously, was discerned in it, notwithstanding the disfigurement."[57] It is the function of Reason to ascertain the truth and disencumber it from the baggage that has disguised and disfigured it. Since what Reason discovers are not the logical deductions and inferences of the Understanding, Hare refers to them as "Guesses," Maurice—in *The Kingdom of Christ*—as "Hints."

This principle supports the conclusion that Maurice had already arrived at in regard to debates. The object for truth-seekers is not to confound their opponents, but to understand them, for "you can only combat any prevalent error by seeking for the divine principle of which it is the counterfeit."[58] Of course, this method was, by no means, a new discovery. If it were, it would not have been of the Reason. Leibniz, writing on the differences between the Cambridge Platonists and the Materialists, remarks, "I have found that most philosophical sects are in the main right in their positive assertions, but not in their denials." Henry More was wrong in arguing that there is no phenomena that can be accounted for on mechanical principles, just as Hobbes was wrong in rejecting all metaphysical explanations.[59] Both were in possession of light that, by looking at too directly, blinded them to peripheral light. J. S. Mill simply rephrased Leibniz's observation when considering the contrary arguments of the Coleridgeans and Benthamites.[60]

In his Review, after lamenting that, since "the appearance of Leighton, and Cudworth, and Henry More," no great man has been produced by the Church of England, Maurice announces, "The sermon before us is the most hopeful omen we have discovered of better things to come." In its pages, he finds "a specimen of a union of all the faculties in the service of religion, which needs only be more extensively applied, to create works worthy of the best age of the Church of England." Hare demonstrates "an abundant power of thought . . . accompanied by a child-like simplicity and kindliness." Moreover, his message is "clothed in a style of such fresh, various, and imaginative beauty, as we can scarcely find equaled since the sermons of the 17th century."[61] Such extravagant praise does, indeed, appear to betoken, if not the dawn of a new age, the advent of a new movement.

At the close of 1828, Hare set off for a walking tour in Germany, during which he stopped at Bonn and visited Niebuhr, Tieck, Schleiermacher, and A. W. Schlegel.[62] Upon returning to England in 1829, Hare submitted several contributions to the *The Athenæum*, chief of which are a series of critical essays on modern German authors, entitled "The Museum of Thoughts."

Thus far, we have considered only the relation between *The Athenæum* and Hare; there is also an important connection between Sterling's contributions, particularly his series of Letters to the Bishop of Chester (April-May 1828), and Thirlwall's controversial *Letter to the Rev. Thomas Turton, D.D.* (1834). In the previous chapter I suggested that the originality of Dr. Thomas Arnold's article on "The Oxford Malignants" cannot be fully appreciated until it is recognized as a rhetorical participation in a sort of debating society, as a revision of and enlargement upon arguments shared within a circle of literary friends. As we shall see, this is no less true of Thirlwall's *Letter*, and although we must reserve our discussion of that *Letter* until we can do so in connection with Maurice's *Subscription No Bondage* (1835), it is important that we direct our attention now to Sterling's influential contribution.

In *The Athenæum* Sterling takes issue with Bishop Charles Blomfield's principle objection to London University, that its pupils were not to be taught Christianity. Sterling insists, "Religious instructions not nourished and animated with religious feeling, are the dead dry husks, fit only for the swine to eat." His argument is not that theological lectures are useless, but that "they can only be subsidiary" in that their function is to "shape a material already prepared for them." Thus, a professor may teach theology, but he cannot teach religion; that is, he cannot enter within the sphere of his pupils' hearts.[63] Sterling is bitterly ironic in addressing Blomfield's conviction that the theological training conducted at the older universities should serve as a model for London University. As to the supposed training itself, he observes that the only education that could be regarded as theological consists merely in exercises in Greek philology and rote memorization from Paley. Although Cambridge had recently been experimenting with lessons in Butler's *Analogy*, "the objects of the experiment are supposed to be rather remarkably distinguished in after-life for narrowness, and stupidity of intellect, to say nothing of an insolent intolerance which might seem imitated from some society of Dervishes, or troop of Franciscans."

This observation on the moral influence of Butler brings Sterling to his more general criticisms of the Cambridge system. Sterling reasons, if the object of religion is spiritual regeneration, then the bishop must consider carefully the sort of character development produced by the educational means of the university. "Knowledge," notes Sterling, "will best fulfil its task of regeneration when it is made an end and object in itself; when it is connected with no outward, sordid, personal calculations."[64] At Cambridge, however, "Knowledge is set before us, not as a bride to be wooed and worshipped for her beauty, her talents, and her virtue, but as a withered beldam, whose service can only be made endurable by the wealth and rank to which she can elevate her lovers." If looked at closely, the Cambridge competitions for honors and prizes are seen to produce only feelings of "envy and jealousy, and all the most evil forms of malignant selfishness."[65]

Sterling was not alone in his contempt for the Cambridge system of education. It was Hare's conviction too that they "who are to attain to any eminence in knowledge, must have a strong Faith in the desirableness of knowledge for its own sake." In addition, any system that fails to cultivate this Faith must also fail to cultivate "this great principle, that Truth, of whatsoever kind, is to be desired and aimed at for its own sake." By teaching students to pursue truth as a means to ulterior ends, the university inadvertently taught its students to regard religion also as a means to the attainment of rewards. Hare warns his listeners, "Whatever tends to make knowledge valued as the means of personal distinction, debases it; while at the same time it debases the character which is stimulated by such a motive."[66]

Conway and *Coningsby*

As early as Christmas 1828 Maurice began having thoughts of returning to Cambridge and taking Holy Orders. While at home, on leave from the legal studies and editorial duties of his London life, he spent his leisure hours writing his novel and conversing with his mother and severely ill sister, Emma, upon whom he based the character of Conway's sister, Honoria.[67] It was they who now encouraged Maurice to consider a return to Cambridge, and that thought quickly led to another. By February 1829 he was able to admit to his father, the Unitarian minister Michael Maurice, that he had recently begun to entertain the "loose speculation" of becoming a clergyman.[68] Maurice has, perhaps, in describing the inner turmoil of his fictional hero, recorded his own psychological condition at this transitional period of his life:

> Some men think it an act of great moral daring, to proclaim their doubts, whether an Aristocracy is not mischievous, and a Church establishment abominable. Eustace Conway endured many a fierce conflict, before he could find courage to acknowledge that either was necessary. . . . But it grieved him still more to think, that if he did unfortunately adopt the popular conclusion, he would find himself rank-and-file with the comfortable pluralists, and grinding landlords.[69]

The most difficult challenge that Maurice faced in accepting the conclusions to which his conscience led him was that such acceptance would place him in the midst of the very persons from whom his conscience most revolted: "O these gowns! these gowns! what monstrous contradictions will they not cover!"[70] Ultimately, Maurice, disregarding appearances, personalities, parties, and all popular opinions and taste, determined to pursue truth with a clear conscience. And when this pursuit placed him in a gown, he seemed to those around him the strangest contradiction of all.

As Maurice, upon his departure from Cambridge in 1826, had removed his name from the books, thus cutting himself off from all possibility of applying for a fellowship, Sterling now advised him to go to Oxford. This was advice that Maurice was inclined to accept, mainly as a means of rounding off the development of his character. As he explained to Hare, "If I could hope to combine in myself something of that freedom and courage for which the young men whom I knew at Cambridge were remarkable, with something more of solidity and reverence for what is established, I should begin to fancy that I had some useful qualities for a member of the English Church."[71] Had William E. Gladstone, the future prime minister, been known to Maurice *before* his arrival at Oxford, these fanciful associations of "solidity and reverence" with Oxford tradition would likely have been dispelled. In March 1829 Gladstone, an undergraduate of Christ Church, wrote, "The state of religion in Oxford is the most painful spectacle it ever fell to my lot to behold. . . . Here irreligion is the rule, religion the exception."[72]

Gladstone—who was making an effort, albeit inadequate, to keep up his friendship with A. H. Hallam after they had left Eton for different universities— knew of the Cambridge Conversazione Society and used it as a model in fashioning an Essay Society, popularly known as the "Weg"—after the initials of its founder.[73] In fact, a deputation from the Apostles, which included Hallam, had come to Oxford in 1829 as missionaries to establish "the school of Shelley as against the Byronic school at Oxford."[74] When Maurice entered Exeter College in December of that year, he must have appeared to Gladstone as part of this "invasion of the barbarians," and Hallam quickly sent off to his friend an informal letter of recommendation on Maurice's behalf:

> I do not myself know Maurice, but I know well many whom he has known, and whom he has moulded like a second nature. . . . The effect which he has produced on the minds of many at Cambridge by the single creation of that Society of the Apostles (for the spirit, though not the form, was created by him) is far greater than I can dare to calculate, and will be felt, both directly and indirectly, in the age that is upon us.[75]

This was not the only letter filled with admiration for Maurice that Gladstone would receive from Cambridge. The result of these communications was that, before long, the Apostle was a member of the "Weg," and—even though Gladstone found Maurice "difficult to catch and still more difficult to hold"[76]—Maurice had made a new and valuable friend.

Upon matriculating at Oxford, Maurice had signed the Thirty-nine Articles. He had not yet arrived at that full trust in the truth of all the Articles, but he had attained to a conviction "that the subscription to Articles on entering Oxford was not intended as a test, but as a declaration of the terms on which the University proposed to teach its pupils, upon which terms they must agree to learn."[77] This explanation appealed to Maurice as sensible, not only on the face of it, but historically as well, and it had the additional advantage of representing subscription to his conscience as an honest contract between parties, a clear statement of the terms of agreement.

Maurice appears to have led a very quiet life at Oxford. When not attending to his studies, essays and sermons, club room philosophizing, or common room small talk, he was hard at work on his novel. Finally, in February 1830, he sent home the final chapter. This marks a turning point in Maurice's life, for at about this same time, through his acquaintance with James Bruce—the future Lord Elgin, governor-general of India—Maurice was introduced to the work of Thomas Erskine (1788-1870). What Coleridge had been to Maurice as a Unitarian, Erskine was to be to him as a Trinitarian.[78] 1831 was eventful. The year began with the publication of Erskine's *The Brazen Serpent*, and Maurice immediately recognized its profound influence upon his thought. To his sister Priscilla he writes, "The peculiarities of his system may be true or not, but I am certain a light has fallen through him on the Scriptures, which I hope I shall never lose, and the chief tendency I feel he has awaked in my mind is to search them more and more."[79] On 29 March Maurice was baptized into the Church of England, and then went home to spend the next three months with his dying sister, Emma.

Sterling and Maurice had both agreed at the same time, in the autumn of 1828, to write a novel. Before the death of Emma, Maurice received a letter from Sterling, announcing that *Eustace Conway* had been accepted for publication. It would not actually be published, however, until 1834.[80] Sterling's work, *Arthur Coningsby*, which was also completed in early 1831, would not be published until 1833. The popular Unitarian preacher from Virginia, Moncure D. Conway (1832-1907),[81] thought that he could discern in these two *bildungsroman* "the Coleridge or Carlyle principle in the universe":

> When Coleridge is the inspirer the young pilgrim having wandered in the wilderness of doubt, and through the deeps and bye-ways of speculation, is sure to end at last in the old church. . . . Where Carlyle inspires the story's end, the pilgrim's way leads to something more tragical, so far as worldly result is concerned, but something more heroic than a snug parsonage and a comfortable living.[82]

Conway's pamphlet, although it purports to be on Maurice and Sterling, is an attempt to vilify Coleridge and vindicate Carlyle, and unfortunately, the author relies upon sophomoric generalizations, exaggerations, and misrepresentations to accomplish his object. Even so, the value of Conway's polemic lies in the fact that he has noted what Carlyle failed to note—that a reader of *Eustace Conway* and *Arthur Coningsby*, knowing that the protagonists are autobiographical, might have foretold the authors' ultimate parting of the ways.[83] Such remarkable wisdom, however, is generally reserved for hindsight. Charles Kingsley, in speaking of his own experience, provides the only certain commentary on the life of Sterling:

Those who discover much truth—ay, who make perhaps only one truth really their own, a living integral law of their spirits—must, in developing it, pass through many changes of opinion. They must rise, and fall back, and rise higher again, and fall and rise again, till they reach the level table-land of truth. . . . I fancy it is a law, that the greater the mind, the stronger the heart, the larger will the oscillations be.[84]

The fact remains, that in 1833, the two authors, Maurice and Sterling, were both preparing to enter the ministry and were comparatively indifferent to their novels, as neither was any longer able to identify with the intellectual and spiritual crises of his fictional hero.

Subscription

At the beginning of 1834, Maurice took Holy Orders and settled down as the curate of Bubbenhall. At this time, much was transpiring in the lives of his Cantabrigian friends. Sterling, having accepted J. C. Hare's invitation to become his curate at Herstmonceux, was preparing, once again, to follow Maurice's cue. Hare himself had recently returned from a lengthy Roman vacation in the company of Bunsen, and was now in the process of renovating Herstmonceux, so that it might accommodate his ever-expanding stock of books.

Meanwhile, the Cambridge political circuit was alive with debate on Professor Pryme's proposal that a Syndicate be appointed to consider the abolition or modification of religious tests. Pryme's gesture was quickly vetoed, whereupon a similar proposition was made strictly on the behalf of medical students. This too was vetoed. Finally, on 12 March 1834, the Senate, with Sedgwick as chairman, having no other recourse, sent a petition to both Houses of Parliament. This petition suggested "the expediency of abrogating by legislative enactment every religious test exacted from members of the University before they proceed to degrees, whether of bachelor, master, or doctor, in Arts, Law, and Physic," and suggested, moreover, that the practice of subscription is "at variance with the present spirit of English Law, and with the true principles of Christian toleration."[85] This petition, which was privately canvassed and signed by sixty-two resident members of Cambridge, including Thirlwall, was respectfully received in Parliament, but it was soon followed by a *Declaration* which controverted the opinions of the Senate and carried the weight of 101 signatures. Whereupon, Cambridge was divided, and the two sides began to argue their positions in newspapers, journals, and pamphlets.

Among the number of pamphlets was one by Dr. Thomas Turton, the Regius Professor of Divinity (1827-1845) and future bishop of Ely. Turton's *Thoughts on the Admission of Persons, without regard to their Religious Opinions, to certain degrees in the Universities of England* was, perhaps, the ablest statement of the case against the Senate's petition. It was promptly responded to by Thirlwall's *Letter to the Rev. Thomas Turton, D.D.* (1834).

Thirlwall begins by noting that Turton, by conflating "religious opinion" with religion itself, has "been led to confound names with things, and wishes with realities." It is Thirlwall's stated purpose "to disentangle this confusion."[86] We may recall that Sterling, in the *Athenæum* of 1828, insisted on distinguishing religion from theology. Although Thirlwall does not mention Sterling in this *Letter*, he is evidently in agreement with him. According to Thirlwall, if matriculating students do not already possess religious impressions, "circumstances can scarcely be conceived in which they have a fainter prospect of acquiring any, than those in which they are placed at the University." Even if students find means at the university of "nourishing their religious feelings, as well as enlarging their religious views, and of enlightening their religious convictions," the truth, nevertheless, remains: "Religion, humanly speaking, cannot be instilled into men against or without their will: we cannot even prescribe exercises, or propose rewards for it, without killing the thing we mean to foster."[87] As Sterling had noted, competition inevitably arouses motives less than congenial to feelings of piety.

Indeed, Sterling's Letters perfectly set the tone for Thirlwall's *Letter* to the Regius Professor of Divinity. Thirlwall makes irreverent use of a quotation from Christopher Wordsworth, who, in defense of the Cambridge system of mandatory attendance at religious services, had observed, "The alternative is not here between compulsory religion and any other religion, but between compulsory religion and no religion at all: for a voluntary religion would I fear soon be changed into no religion at all." To this the assistant tutor replies, "I cannot indeed draw such delicate distinctions as my friend seems to make in this passage: for as the epithet compulsory applied to religion appears to me contradictory, the difference between a compulsory religion and no religion at all is too subtle for my grasp." The most that the cause of religion may hope to gain from compulsory services "would be to suffer no incurable wounds."[88] Therefore, were he to be asked what might be done at Cambridge in the cause of true religion, Thirlwall, with Socratic irony, says that he should reply, "that it would be a great benefit to religion, if our daily services were discontinued, and if in their stead there was established a weekly service," one that "ought to be purely voluntary. . . . I think there is no reason to fear that *such* a voluntary system of religion would be changed into no religion at all."[89]

Although Christopher Wordsworth, the master of Trinity, had already heard—perhaps first from Sterling's Letters—nearly all of Thirlwall's arguments, never had he heard his own name put to such public humiliation by one of his assistant tutors. Dr. Wordsworth looked to William Whewell for vindication, and from this quarter he received it in the form of a public "Reply" to Thirlwall, a response that was no true *reply* at all, but merely asserted that compulsory chapel attendance was, in fact, a proven means of instilling discipline in the students. Whewell's response was significant, but only from a political perspective, in that it served as a public announcement that Thirlwall would have to stand alone before Wordsworth. No sooner was the "Reply" published than the master of Trinity invited Thirlwall to resign. The invitation was accepted without hesitation. Sterling, who had just taken orders and was now serving as curate at Hurstmonceaux, received reports at the annual Apostles' dinner, and conveyed them to Trench:

> They give melancholy accounts of the coldness produced among the people at Trinity by the late controversy. I think Thirlwall quite right as to the compulsory chapel-going; but as long as the system lasts, he was bound, I think, either to conform to it or to resign his lectureship, and certainly the writing such a pamphlet was a queer kind of conformity.[90]

Conform or *Resign*: these were now understood by Sterling to be the two alternatives for a minister in the establishment, and his letter states the case exactly as it was brought against Thirlwall. As a subordinate functionary of the Cambridge system, he was expected to publicly conform, regardless of his private opinions. To the translator of Schleiermacher, the pursuit of truth appeared to have priority over conformity, and his dismissal by Whewell and Wordsworth left him momentarily stunned.

Sterling's and Thirlwall's thoughts on university reform were not, however, sewn on rocky ground. The fruit their seeds brought forth was, for awhile, green, but it was not so delicate as to wither and die under the heat of the day. Time passed: Wordsworth, in 1841, was succeeded by Whewell; then, Whewell, in 1866, was succeeded by W. H. Thompson, one of Thirlwall's students who had been elected to the Apostles in 1830. Thompson, in 1869, was to take an active part in the legislation of the University Tests Bill. The measure that Lord Chief Justice J. D. Coleridge had introduced in 1866 for the repeal of religious tests at the universities "disconnected both the degrees and the teaching offices of the University from the Church of England," but it did not extend to nonteaching fellows. Thompson's contribution was to carry a resolution to amend Coleridge's bill in order to compel the universities to abstain from requiring declarations of religious belief upon admission to all fellowships. The University Tests Bill finally, on 13 June 1871, passed through the House of Lords, with Connop of St. David's, the baron of Llawhadden, in attendance.[91] His biographer notes, "At the last meeting to determine the working of the new measure, Thirlwall's opinion was quoted with full approval. One can imagine the sardonic smile with which he observed himself quoted as high authority for a measure condemned as sacrilegious only forty years earlier. He made no comment, nor was one needed."[92]

To Maurice, who had struggled over the issues relating to subscription and had studied the subject with more than usual thoroughness, the participants in the debate appeared to be concerned with every stasis of argument except the most crucial stasis of definition. Although they had differentiated religion from theology, they had merely assumed the accuracy of the popular signification of subscription. Furthermore, there was a growing body of men at Oxford, mostly of Oriel College, who were anxious to enlist Maurice's help in opposing the liberal camp. Thus, when, in 1834, Thirlwall published his *Letter to the Rev. Thomas Turton, D.D.*, and R. D.

Hampden came out with his *Observations on Religious Dissent*, Maurice availed himself of the opportunity to make a comment, one that, in his opinion, was most definitely needed to remove the difficulties felt by many to have attached themselves to the subject.

In *Subscription No Bondage* (1835), Maurice (writing under the pseudonym of "Rusticus") observes that the Church of England has never insisted upon subscription to the Articles as a test of conformity. The only security that the Church has of its members' allegiance is their participation in its acts and ordinances. Never has it imposed Articles upon communicants. On the other hand, subscription is imposed upon all clergymen, and its purpose, says Maurice, is "that they will not be superstitious teachers"—an explanation with which Charles Hardwick, the author of *A History of the Articles of Religion* (1851), is in complete accord: "The subscription of the clergy to Formularies of Faith is exacted with the hope of securing a similarity of doctrine in those who have deliberately undertaken the office of public teachers."[93] Maurice does not overlook the fact that the first royal mandate imposing subscription to the Articles, in June 1553, enjoined subscription also upon university students, but he does insist that this imposition in no way contradicted or broadened its original intent. Rather, the mandate assumed that all university students were preparing to become clergymen. As that assumption is no longer valid, and the Thirty-nine Articles are not, for matriculating students, an ecclesiastical guide to conformity in religious teaching, what, then, is their significance? Maurice answers, they are "conditions of thought, primarily designed to assist education by warning students against superstitions, which have hindered, and are likely to hinder, the pursuit of knowledge, and the attainment of truth."[94] In other words, they provide the students with the premises underlying all orthodox instruction in the universities, and Oxford, in requiring subscription, merely requires the matriculating students' consent to receive instruction based upon these premises.

What distinguishes Oxford from other educational institutions "is, not that she imposes conditions of thought upon her students, and that they assent and consent to them; for so far all institutions are alike; but that *she states* what are her conditions of thought."[95] The Thirty-nine Articles are, however, *theological*, and—according to Thirlwall's *Letter*—Oxford and Cambridge do not, apart from some Greek parsing out of the New Testament and readings in Paley and Butler, offer theological instruction. Assuming, for the moment, that Thirlwall has proved his point—despite evidence that had surfaced to the contrary[96]—Maurice proceeds to a lengthy demonstration that *any* instruction in the *Literæ Humaniores* that aims to represents them "as means to a knowledge of ourselves and of man; as means to the formation of a manly character," can fulfil its intention only "by imposing the conditions of a science which manifestly concerns Humanity as such, and in which it discovers its own foundation and laws," which science is Theology.[97] Thus, theology is not a subject to be reserved for graduates; it is not, as the Scholastics represent it, "the climax of all studies, the Corinthian capital of a magnificent edifice, composed of physics, politics, economics, and connecting them as parts of a great system with each other—but it is the foundation upon which they all stand." To understand this point, explained Maurice to a friend, is to understand "what I meant by calling myself a digger merely," for the business of theology "is not to build, but to dig," to uncover the underlying principles in which every thought must find its root if it would be a thought that is true for humanity.[98]

Having considered the objections to his argument that are implicit in Thirlwall's *Letter*, Maurice proceeds to Hampden's *Observations*. As we observed in the previous chapter, Hampden argues in this pamphlet, "No conclusions of human reasoning,"—even conclusions arrived at through the study of Scripture—"however correctly deduced, however logically sound, are properly religious truths." A religious formulary, such as a Creed or the Thirty-nine Articles, is, then, nothing more than "a human exposition" and "an artificial construction" of the doctrine of Scripture, and as such, it has no religious authority but, on the contrary, becomes an agent of dissent.[99] In response to Hampden, Maurice argues three points. *First*, if the Scriptures are a Revelation, if it tells us anything, "I can set down what it tells me; the simplest form in which I set it down is the best, provided I do actually set down what has been revealed." The Church's use of a creed is an homage to the Bible as a Revelation, not an offence to it; and therefore, to dispense with it "would be to say, the Bible is indeed a stupendous book, a most perfect revelation, the only authority, but it imparts no knowledge, it does not contain a single truth which is apprehensible to man." *Second*, were the Church to dispense with its Articles of Faith, then would the necessity of our own minds compel us to look to the Bible as a collection of articles and logical propositions. Therefore, Maurice concludes, if we would honor and preserve the Bible "in its true and real character as the record of the ways of God to man, . . . let not Articles be abolished from a fancy that the Bible supplies their place, but let them remain as strong and hardy conditions of thought, to discipline men's minds to the worthy and humble exposition of it."[100]

Maurice's *third* and most important point in responding to Hampden is that the Thirty-nine Articles, "these seven-times purified words of wisdom and truth," are the greatest aid to unity and "one of the best fortresses against the powers of division and disunion and hatred which are abroad in the earth."[101] Although—as Maurice argues elsewhere—there may not be a single minister in the Church of England who feels that these articles state his own beliefs as clearly and as decisively as he would like to see them set forth, yet the truth remains, "that Evangelicals, Low Churchmen, High Churchmen, *may* all sign the Articles, and may sign them honestly."[102] Moreover, although there may always be partisan systematizers, such as the Evangelical John Overton and the Romanist J. H. Newman,[103] who will insist upon the propriety of only one interpretation of the Articles, each party within the Church of England is a witness to some truth that the Articles maintain. And, if we recognize "that it is not the *negative* parts of each opinion which have most tendency to coalesce, but that the *positive* parts of these opinions are always struggling towards each other,"[104] then we might also recognize how necessary it is, for the preservation of a Catholic Church in a Protestant State, that the Articles be maintained.

Maurice's *Subscription No Bondage* hardly satisfied anyone. It was especially a disappointment to the Tractarians, for although it upheld subscription, the basis on which it did so would not have prevented Dissenters from violating the sanctity of the Common Rooms. As long as they were amenable to being lectured under the conditions of thought represented in the Articles, they would be free to matriculate. It was a disappointment to the petitioners, as it upheld the obnoxious practice on the basis of what it *might*, even perhaps *should*, mean, without sufficient regard to what subscription *does* mean in the thoughts and consciences of the great majority of students and faculty. As Maurice states the case, "I may tell you at once that no pamphlet ever made less impression upon the English public generally, or upon the smaller University public, for which it was chiefly intended."[105] Although the author would never change his position on the intent of the Articles and their usefulness in serving the ends of education and of the Church, he did later, in 1853, acknowledge that, because the Articles are not "accepted practically or by any great number in the sense in which I urged that they ought to be accepted, but in a different sense, which is dangerous to honesty," he was, therefore, wrong to have deduced "that subscription ought to be enforced at the universities."[106]

Sterling, Maurice, and Kingsley in London

In 1836 both Sterling and Maurice were again in London. In February of the previous year Sterling, on the advice of his doctor, gave up his duties as Hare's curate. Although he continued to reside at Herstmonceux and make the most of his access to its library until autumn—at which time he moved to Bayswater—the respiratory disease that would eventually take his life had already begun to curtail his activities, making it necessary for him to restrict himself, as much as possible, to warm and dry climates. Just after Sterling moved to Bayswater, Maurice was hired as chaplain at Guy's Hospital. In January 1836 he too moved to London.

Baron Bunsen, in the company of Monckton Milnes, attended the Sunday morning service at Guy's on 3 March 1839, and on the following day wrote to his wife:

> Nothing could be more touching than all I saw and heard there: the preaching of Gospel-truth in simplicity, by one of the finest and deepest minds of the most learned men in England, to *Christ's own congregation*, viz. cripples, blind, lame, even insane, aged men and women, invalids, convalescent, half-dying. The sermon was admirable; the latter half extempore, as I heard afterwards, although seemingly read.[107]

Bunsen was especially impressed by the concurrent "simplicity" and depth of Maurice's message. Though speaking of spiritual things to spiritual people, Maurice would clothe his message in a language appropriate to the education of his hearers. By all accounts, he was possessed in large measure by the mind of Christ, able to comfort those in affliction and grief. "Almost every man who knew him," observes

Alec Vidler, "would have turned to him, if it had been possible, 'in the hour of death, and in the day of judgment.'"[108] Guy's Hospital had not appointed a chaplain; it had found one.

Sterling's mind was now filled with his reflections on Schleiermacher. This marks the beginning of his parting from Maurice. As Carlyle notes, "Their views and articulate opinions, I suppose, were now fast beginning to diverge."[109] Although they had both acquired fundamental principles from Coleridge—principles that they would always cherish—they had now become the disciples of two very different theologians. While Sterling had fallen completely under the spell of Schleiermacher, Maurice had transferred much of his devotion to that other "apostle of the 'Christian consciousness,'" Thomas Erskine.[110] Moncure Conway would have us think of Sterling and Maurice as two ships that, having set sail from different ports and traveling to different destinations, chanced to meet in mid-ocean for a brief spell. This is a metaphor that may appeal to the imagination, but it exaggerates the actual differences between the two friends.

There was, however, this critical disparity in their pursuits of knowledge: whereas Maurice had chiseled into Coleridge as a quarry from which to acquire a solid foundation for his *pyramid* of truth, Sterling had looked to Coleridge as a promising Dædalus, an architect who might construct a *labyrinth* of truth. Sterling was not a builder; he was a hero of the practical Reason, a Theseus whose greatest ambition was to comprehend the pathway to truth, and in so doing, attain a conquest over the dead ends of the speculative intellect and over the Minotaur of evil. With Sterling it was a foregone conclusion that, any labyrinthian system that left him, after years of effort, without hope of victory, would simply be cast aside and its architect blamed for the failure. After all, Theseus could not be a hero without a Dædalus.

Sterling's disaffection towards Coleridge began in the library at Herstmonceux. Thirlwall's Introduction to Schleiermacher's *Luke*, so thorough and critical, left the impression on Sterling that Coleridge, in his Letters on Inspiration, had compromised the truth and had demonstrated that "he had not courage to incur the consequences of claiming, with one stride, the right to stand upon his own faith, and not upon other men's traditions."[111] Therefore, Sterling now looked to Schleiermacher, not to ascertain whether or in what manner this eminent theologian might contribute to the truths that had already been established by Coleridge, but rather to determine whether or in what manner Schleiermacher's system might satisfy his longings for a comprehensive paradigm of truth. Without identifying "the essential difference between him and Coleridge," Sterling nevertheless leaped into the new labyrinth, proclaiming its architect "the greatest spiritual teacher I have ever fallen in with."[112]

It now appeared to Sterling, following what seemed the implications of Schleiermacher's system, that the double operation of feeling and knowledge pointed to "a self-consciousness which is its own evidence of the truth."[113] Such a conclusion, countered Maurice, is "directly in opposition" to the feelings and intentions of a Christian theologian. The truth, rather, appears to be (1) "that the doctrine of a personal manifestation of God cannot rest merely upon the individual experience or feeling of its necessity"; (2) "that it must be sustained by a still more awful truth"; (3) "that that truth must in some sense have been given to men in order that they might enter into it."[114] Maurice would further explain that the feelings and intuitions of human consciousness are often seemingly contradictory and the ideas that are deduced from them, if placed into a system, would result in a monstrosity against which the conscience itself would rebel. Therefore, "What we ask for, is— not a System that shall put these ideas into their proper places, and so make them the subjects of our partial intellects, but—a Revelation which shall show us what they are, why we have had these hints and intimations of them, what the eternal substances are which correspond to them."[115] Sterling was unpersuaded, and while he went further toward a position of confidence in human consciousness as the evidence of and guide to religious truth, Maurice went in the opposite direction, toward a confidence that human consciousness is but the shadows on the wall, the evidence that there is a greater truth, for which, if we would apprehend, a revelation is necessary. When Sterling said, I have a deep and abiding sense that Christ is and, therefore, he is, Maurice retorted, Christ is, and therefore your consciousness tells you that he is, and the Gospels are given that you might find guidance and confirmation for your knowledge of him.

Finding Maurice intractable, unwilling to enter into his difficulties, impatient of his devotion to German theology,[116] Sterling attempted to find a sympathetic audience in Carlyle. That the author of *Sartor Resartus* (1833-34) had not the least interest in any post-Kantian theologian and refused to acknowledge the genius of Schleiermacher was a bitter frustration for Sterling. Although Carlyle was pleased to find in Sterling an intelligent mind, what was much more essential to their budding friendship was his receptive ear.

The two arranged for a long and loquacious February walk to the home of Frank Edgeworth. Carlyle knew of the reason that Sterling had given for his resignation from the curacy of Herstmonceux, but it seemed to him—perhaps, not *merely*, but certainly *fundamentally*—a convenient excuse to escape from a noxious confinement. Indeed, there were grounds for the suspicion, but there were also signs, "strange gorgon-faces of earnest Destiny," about Sterling. Their walk ended in near-tragic consequences, in Sterling's first severe pulmonary attack.[117] In August 1836 Sterling, needing to escape to the warm climate of Madeira, paid Carlyle a farewell visit, upon which occasion he chanced to notice a slim volume, *Nature*, by Emerson. Kindly, before bidding *adieu*, the host let the book slip into his friend's pocket.[118] Thus began two new adventures for Sterling: a literary acquaintance with the American transcendentalist, which was to develop into a deep respect and friendship, and the nomadic existence that was to be essential for his life's preservation.

It may be of interest to observe that as Sterling exited London stage left, the seventeen-year-old Charles Kingsley (1819-1875)—who had been for several years a pupil at Helston Grammar School, under the headmastership of Derwent Coleridge —entered London stage right. Kingsley's father had accepted the duties of the Chelsea Rectory, and so his family exchanged the natural surroundings and aristocratic society of Helston and Clovelly for the comparatively dismal atmosphere of middle-class London. This forced migration brought out the teenage rebel in Kingsley, as is evident in this letter to a friend, R. Cowley Powles:

> As you may suppose, all this clerical conversation (to which I am obliged to listen) has had a slight effect in setting my opinions on these subjects, and I begin to hate these dapper young-ladies-preachers like the devil, for I am sickened and enraged to see "silly women blown about with every wind," falling in love with the preacher instead of his sermon, and with his sermon instead of the Bible. I could say volumes on this subject that should raise both your contempt and indignation. I am sickened with its day-by-day occurrence.[119]

Even here, we can see distinct traces of the controversial clergyman's mature personality. The utter disdain for hypocrisy, the preoccupation with relations between the sexes, and the forceful, righteous expression of his thought and feeling: these were to be characteristic of him throughout his life. For the next two years, on every weekday, Kingsley would walk to and from King's College, and—like Hardy's Jude—he would read as he walked. Soon, the poetry of Southey, Coleridge, and Shelley he knew by heart.[120]

Kingsley knew nothing, at this time, of Maurice, except that which he had overheard from the postprandial chatter in the smoking room. Their paths had often approached each other, but had never crossed. Between 1819 and 1823, the Maurice and Kingsley families had lived within walking distance to one another. They knew some of the same people in Bristol, Clifton, and Frenchay, and it is likely that, on more than one occasion, the two reverend gentlemen, Michael Maurice and Charles Kingsley Sr., passed by each other on the street. Many years would go by before their sons would walk together. Kingsley and the theologian he was to call "Master" were not to meet until 1844, shortly before Sterling's death. But, were we inclined to look for portents, we might be tempted to regard this rotation of Sterling and Kingsley in the physical proximity of Maurice as, at least, symbolic of the consecutive, even contiguous, roles they were to play in their social relations with the great theologian of the Broad Church movement.

The Brazen Serpent and the Kingdom

As soon as Maurice and his sister Priscilla were settled at Guy's Hospital, Maurice took in a pupil who was looking to prepare himself for the university entrance exam. This was Edward Strachey, the first translator of Malory into modern English, who is more often recognized simply as the paternal uncle of the future Cambridge Apostle and essayist Lytton Strachey. Maurice and his student benefitted from one another, as the one provided lessons and guidance, and the other began, in August 1836, to serve as his tutor's amanuensis, writing out the drafts of the first letters that were, eventually, to be revised and incorporated into *The Kingdom of Christ*.[121] They were written at the request of a Quaker gentleman by the name of Samuel Clark (not to be confused with Samuel Clarke, the eminent Methodist scholar), and they originally appeared in the form of a series of tracts entitled Letters to a Quaker (1836-1838).

In 1838, while working on putting these letters into book form, Maurice was introduced to Erskine, then in London on business. To a sister, Erskine relates that he had met Maurice, "who is a very metaphysical man; I have not got into him yet; I hope, when I return to London, to know him better."[122] With the appearance of *The Kingdom of Christ; Or, Hints to a Quaker Respecting the Principles, Constitution, & Ordinances of the Catholic Church*—first published in 1838, and then significantly revised and republished in 1842[123]—we begin to recognize the depth to which Erskine's *Brazen Serpent* had influenced Maurice's thought, an influence that was neither transient nor peripheral and is equally evident in the later *Theological Essays* (1853).

As the subtitle of Maurice's treatise suggests, the subject of it is not the English Church, but rather the Catholic Church of Christ, of which the former is "merely one branch."[124] For Maurice, the true Church is necessarily and perpetually Catholic, for it rests upon truths "which do not depend for their reality upon our consciousness of them, but are the grounds on which that consciousness must rest." Though the Protestant nations have rightly asserted their protest against the proposition that the Catholic Church is, in its institutions, extranational and under the government of a visible head, the Church itself is not Protestant. Maurice explains, "Protestants say that every truth is to be realized by each man for himself, and that when a certain number of individuals have been made conscious of the same truth, they are to meet together and have fellowship in the profession of it." In other words, the systems of Protestantism practically deny that the truths of Christianity "do not depend for their reality upon our consciousness of them."[125] It is Maurice's constant message that our fellowship in Christ does not rest upon our individual notions, but rather upon *facts* that are independent of our consciousness and which free us to have fellowship when we come to know them as facts.

For both Maurice and Erskine, these are the three primary and foundational truths of the Catholic Church: (1) Christ is the universal head of humanity; (2) Christ is the revelation of the personality of God; (3) God has, through Christ, forgiven humanity. First, *Christ is the universal head of humanity*. Just as, in Adam, all of humanity have fallen, so in Christ, all have been redeemed. Erskine states, "Christ died for every man, as the head of every man, not by any fiction of law, not in a conventional way, but in reality as the head of the whole mass of the human nature, which, although composed of many members, is *one thing—one body*—in every part of which the head is *truly* present."[126] The head has, for the entire body, suffered the awful cost of sin, and so all of humanity has, in the person of Christ, died. Moreover, in Christ's resurrection, all have been made alive. Erskine's teaching concerning our twofold participation in Christ had immediate implications in regard to the significance of baptism, which Maurice not only recognized but completely accepted. The Christian idea of baptism "assumes Christ to be the Lord of men; it assumes that men are created in him; that this is the constitution of our race; that therefore all attempts of men to reduce themselves into separate units are contradictory and abortive."[127] For St. Paul, baptism "denoted that he would no more be the member of any sect, of any partial society whatever—that he was claiming his relation to the Son of God, the Head of the whole human race."[128]

Second, *Christ is the revelation of the personality of God.* The acceptance of this proposition is, to both Erskine and Maurice, the deciding factor in whether one's religion acknowledges a living God or a metaphysical abstraction. Erskine declares, "Righteousness is the very character of God, as revealed in Christ, namely, *Holy Love* forgiving sin without clearing it."[129] The only way to know and love God is through the revelation of his character in Jesus Christ, for—as Maurice observes— "One who knows that he is a person requires a personal object—an abstraction cannot satisfy him." On the other hand, "A Being who shows that he cares for me, and in whom all love dwells, proposes himself to me as an object of my trust; I trust him, and so enter into a knowledge and participation of his love. And that love works in me to will and to do of his good pleasure."[130] These statements belong to Maurice's autobiography as much as to his theology, for it was largely through reflecting upon his own experiences and deepest spiritual needs that Maurice developed into the theologian he was. In a revealing letter to his father, Maurice entered into an account of the feelings and thoughts that led him to an acceptance of the divinity of Christ:

> Truth, real inward truth, is the rarest, I think, of all things. . . . To attain to this truth, this heart truth,—not to fancy that I have it, but to have it,— is my greatest wish. I know I was formed in the image of God. I believe if I could behold God I should reflect His image. But I cannot behold Him. God, I am told, is a Spirit, and I am of the earth, earthly. I cannot, and would not if I could, abandon my belief that He is a lofty Spiritual Being; I cannot throw aside my own earthliness. . . . I would beseech you to observe attentively whether nearly every verse in the Old Testament does not exhibit these two apparently opposite and contradictory feelings; an acknowledgment of God as incomprehensible and infinite; a desire to see, to understand, to comprehend that same God. Yes, and just so far as the heathen attained any light did they begin to make the same acknowledgment and feel this same want. Is there a difficulty, a mystery here? Most unquestionably: but whence? In the heart of man. . . . If the Infinite, Incomprehensible Jehovah is manifested in the person of a Man, a Man conversing with us, living among us, entering into all our infirmities and temptations, and passing into all our conditions, [the heart] is satisfied; if not, it remains unsatisfied.[131]

Christian faith, faith in God's self-disclosure of his righteousness and love, as manifested in the person of Jesus Christ, was the *heart truth* that Maurice had sought for elsewhere in vain, and it was this truth that made itself felt within Maurice's deepest sense of being as the central *fact* upon which his existence and relationship with other persons rested.

Third, *God's forgiveness of humanity is a fait accompli.* As Christ, the head of humanity, has already suffered the penalty of sin, humanity no longer stands under condemnation. According to Erskine, the Scriptures teach "that all men, during this dispensation, are treated as the members of the righteous head; that is, that from all men, during this dispensation, the condemnation, which their character deserves, is withdrawn, and that on all men the light of God's forgiving love is shining." Although this may seem to imply a universal salvation, Erskine observes, "Every one whose eye is opened to the light receives life, and becomes a living and abiding member of Jesus Christ; whilst those who continue blind to it shut out the life, and remain dead, and exposed to condemnation."[132] The gifts of God are received through faith, and so, "Until you *know* this gift of love, although Christ be in you, yet you are without Christ; and though the hope of glory be in you, yet you are without hope."[133] Having accepted this doctrine of a forgiveness extended to all of humanity, both Erskine and Maurice necessarily rejected the dogmas of Calvinism. The Calvinist, says Maurice, "requires that we should suppose there is no object present, unless there be something which perceives it; and having got into this contradiction, the next step is to suppose that faith is not a receptive, but a creative power; that it makes the thing which it believes."[134] Faith does not create our forgiveness; it recognizes that we are forgiven—and upon that recognition, the believer receives the Spirit of Christ. In the *Essays*, Maurice declares, "The broad simple Gospel, that God has set forth His Son as the propitiation for sin, that He has offered Himself for the sins of the world, meets all the desires of these heart-stricken sinners. . . . Here is indeed a brazen serpent to which one dying from the bite of the old serpent can look and be healed."[135]

There are numerous other similarities—in addition to the three given above—in the messages of Erskine and Maurice. Among the more significant are (4) that the Old Testament is to be interpreted by the light of the New, (5) that the Gospel of John has a *theological* priority over the Synoptics, (6) that a failure to identify Jesus as the revelation of the character of God has resulted in the prevalence of an "atheism" in modern religious thought, (7) that "eternal life" consists in knowing God, (8) that all punishment of sin is the loving discipline of God for the purpose of effecting our sanctification, and (9) that God will ultimately claim his total conquest over evil, including sin and all of its effects. Three months after having met each other in London, Maurice sent to Erskine a copy of his work, now nearly completed. To a friend, Erskine remarked, "I do not think I ever saw an example of so high an appreciation of objective and formal Christianity joined with such a true sense of the value of what is subjective."[136] In 1852, Maurice dedicated a volume of sermons, entitled *The Prophets and Kings of the Old Testament*, to Erskine. Along with a copy of this book, Maurice sent a letter to Erskine, in which he says, "You will see by a book which will reach you by this post that I have taken a great liberty with your name. . . . I wished to tell others how much I believe they as well as I owe to your books, how they seem to me to mark a crisis in the theological movements of this time."[137]

Carlyle in London

While Sterling was in Madeira, his pregnant wife remained in London, where she was cared for by her sister, Anna Barton. Sterling had made every effort to bring his sister-in-law and Maurice together, but Mrs. Barton thought one speculative son-in-law more than enough, and was anxious to protect her daughter. From Madeira Sterling drew up a scheme, and planning a brief visit to England in August 1837, he arranged to meet both Maurice and Anna at Herstmonceux, neither knowing of the other's invitation. The meeting ended in the couple's engagement, and when Sterling returned again in October, he had the pleasure of officiating at their wedding.

During Sterling's curacy at Herstmonceux, Maurice had frequently visited, and it was during these visits that his friendship with Hare really began. Maurice's shyness had prevented any intimacy developing out of their earlier acquaintance, but in the company of Sterling, and probably as the result of his prompting, Maurice opened up. Priscilla, Maurice's sister, often accompanied him on these trips to Herstmonceux, and she quickly established a friendship with Maria Hare, the widow of Julius's brother, Augustus. Subsequently, Priscilla spent every summer with Maria, and when, in the summer of 1837, Priscilla brought along her younger sister, Esther, Julius Hare met for the first time the woman he would marry in 1844.

The relational tie that united Hare, Maurice, and Sterling cannot be reduced to a Broad Church fellowship. That it included this, there can be no doubt, but it was also much more. Between the three were alliances that had formed through years of common sympathies and friendships and were finally strengthened by matrimonial bonds. This must be fully appreciated if we would comprehend Hare's and Maurice's attitude toward Carlyle. For Carlyle had entered Sterling's life at a critical moment, just as the new curate was beginning an intense study of German theology, and just as he was about to give up the practical duties of a clergyman. We might surmise that Sterling's cogitations would have ultimately led him away from the Church of England even if he had never met London's social prophet, but as Carlyle's *Life of Sterling* (1851) clearly reveals, the prophet's influence could only have encouraged this result. Carlyle's antagonism toward the memory of Coleridge, his impatient dismissal of all the efforts of rationalizing Christians, and his utter contempt for ninety-nine out of every one hundred clergymen, though based on undoubted sincerity and the noblest motives, was still an attack on that which Hare and Maurice very nearly represented. Neither mistook the animosities of Carlyle as directed against them personally; even so, they could not but resent the fact that he had brought a sword to set one Apostle at variance against another.

In 1837 Carlyle was lecturing on the Revolutions of Modern Europe and attending Monckton Milnes's fashionable London "breakfasts." The cheery, charming, and chubby Milnes, who had been a pupil of Thirlwall's at Cambridge before he was elected to the Apostles, attracted the society of Cambridge and London elite. Perhaps it was at such a breakfast that Maurice first met Carlyle. Maurice's elder son and biographer tells us, "They met in society not infrequently; always more and more antagonistically. Up to a point they agreed exceedingly well: Carlyle always anxious to avoid the points of difference, my father never able to leave them alone."[138] According to Edward Strachey, although Maurice had "the greatest reverence for Carlyle," he was convinced that the feeling was not mutual, "for he is sure Carlyle thinks him a '*sham.*'"[139] There was, of course, an element of truth in Maurice's perception, even though his self-consciousness was often colored by a disturbing sense of inadequacy. Nevertheless, Maurice was quite oblivious to the fact that Carlyle's irritation toward him was produced not by what *he* said, but rather by what Sterling said; for Carlyle tells us that Sterling, now in the early stages of recovery from Coleridgean moonshine, "would still assert his transcendental admiration, especially if Maurice were by to help."[140] What the Sage of Chelsea most disliked about Maurice and Hare was their stubborn refusal to surrender their hold upon a man who was evidently inclined to make him an idol.

A most pleasant conquest came for this sage in October of 1839, when Sterling's laudatory essay on Carlyle's *Miscellaneous Works* appeared in J. S. Mill's *London and Westminster Review*. The subject of the review later acknowledged "the deep silent joy, not of a weak or ignoble nature, which it gave to myself in my then mood and situation." From Sterling's article Carlyle received "the first generous human recognition, expressed with heroic emphasis, and clear conviction" that his "poor battle in this world is not quite a mad and futile, that it is perhaps a worthy and manful one, which will come to something yet."[141] To Maurice, Sterling's article signified something else. He complains, in a letter to Trench, of "how much pain it has caused me" and speaks of "the fear and strangeness of seeing a friend go back to a stage which he fancied that he had passed through long ago."[142] Before publishing the review, Sterling had written to Hare, "Though I expect to lose friends and gain enemies, I am glad of having spoken out what seems to me true." He had taken his stand on behalf of views that he believed important, regardless of how disturbing others found them.[143] Now, he was on the defensive, and a confrontation ensued in which Maurice lost his cool, wrung his hands, and shrieked. It was a plainly un-Apostolic episode for which the theologian never forgave himself.[144]

Maurice was not the only new acquaintance made by Carlyle in 1837, and his meeting that year with Connop Thirlwall had happier consequences. Thirlwall, for his *Letter* to Turton and subsequent dismissal by Wordsworth, had been rewarded with a rectory in Yorkshire and election to the Senate of the University of London. The duties of this latter assignment frequently brought him into the city, where he made it a point to attend the social breakfasts of his former pupil. In fact, he continued to attend them at least until 1867.[145] His first meeting with Carlyle, however, occurred not in Milnes's apartment, but rather at Lincoln's Inn, in the smoke-filled rooms of Milnes's Apostolic friend, James Spedding. Here, Carlyle "found the future bishop 'a most sarcastic, sceptical, but strong-headed, strong-hearted man,'" and immediately developed a friendship with him.[146]

In July 1840, Prime Minister Melbourne, who enjoyed elevating *liberal* but not *heterodox* theologians[147]—that is to say, theologians who were as liberal as they could be without their preferments causing too much of a public uproar—offered Thirlwall the See of St. David's. Thirlwall's initial decision was to decline, but his friends continued to urge his acceptance. Struggling with uncertainty and unable to sleep, he went up to London and called upon Carlyle, "who was amazed to find any Englishman unwilling to be made a bishop." Carlyle, who had once, after reading *Guesses at Truth*, suggested that Hare should be raised to the episcopate, could now think of no man more worthy of the office than his friend Thirlwall.[148]

Kingsley Seeks and Finds

In the autumn of 1838 Kingsley matriculated at Magdalene College, Cambridge. Half a year later he was able to write home, "You will be delighted to hear that I am *first* in classics and mathematics also, at the examinations, which has not happened in the College for several years."[149] His favorite subject was then, as always, science, and Sedgwick had no one more attentive to his lectures than his pupil from Clifton, for the professor was just completing a decade of research on the geology of Devonshire.[150] But what especially interested Kingsley was Sedgwick's geological field lectures, which were delivered on horseback.

During the long vacation of 1839, Kingsley joined his family at Ipsden, in Oxfordshire, where his father had taken a parsonage for two months. There, on 6 July, the undergraduate met his future wife, Fanny Grenfell. She tells us that Kingsley was, at this time, "full of religious doubts, . . . sad, shy, and serious habitually; in conversation at one moment brilliant and impassioned—the next reserved and unapproachable—by turns attracting and repelling."[151] The two months passed by too quickly for the young couple, although the aristocratic Grenfells were nonethe-less eager for the departure of the parson's stuttering and pipe-smoking son.

Kingsley had promised Fanny he would read his Bible and pray, but in her absence, the presence not only of faith, but of hope and love as well, seemed to disappear into the gloom of despair. The following year at Cambridge was the darkest period in Kingsley's life: "He became reckless, and nearly gave up all for lost: he read little, went in for excitement of every kind, . . . anything to deaden the remembrance of the happy past, which just then promised no future."[152] Sporting, boxing, gambling, and drinking took their places among the amusements by which

Kingsley sought to escape from the pain of incomplete existence and from the spiritual necessity of becoming whole.

When Hare returned as select preacher to Cambridge in early 1839, to deliver his protest against J. H. Newman's *Lectures on Justification* (1838), Kingsley may have been in attendance. Rowland Williams, the future vice-president of St. David's College, who was in 1839 a Cambridge undergraduate of King's, not only attended, but afterwards wrote home, thanking God that the preacher, despite the "weakness and monotony" of his voice, was "likely to revive the gospel doctrine of justification by faith in all its simplicity."[153] If Kingsley was present, he would have heard that Faith was a practical principle, an act primarily of the Will, and not subservient to the Understanding: "While our Conscience, our Understanding, our Affections, and our carnal appetites are dragging us in opposite directions, the Will is torn and mangled, and almost dismembered: and from this misery nothing can save us, except the atoning power of Faith."[154] Kingsley was not yet ready to confess his misery and embrace a Deliverer, but by the end of 1840, he confided to Fanny, "Man does want something more than his reason! . . . But I have no spiritual Guide. I am told that before I can avail myself of the benevolence of Him in whom you trust, I must believe in His Godhead and His Omnipotence. I do not do this. And it is a subject on which I cannot pray."[155]

Kingsley had asked for a guide, and since, as the young Daniel Macmillan expressed it, "It is our sad lot to have no spiritual guides but books,"[156] Fanny sent her admirer Carlyle's *French Revolution* (1837) and Coleridge's *Aids to Reflection* (1825). It was an inspired choice of literature, peculiarly suitable for Kingsley's mind. In *Alton Locke* Kingsley would write in reference to *The French Revolution*, "That book above all first recalled me to the overwhelming and yet ennobling knowledge that there was such a thing as Duty; first taught me to see in history . . . the dealings of a righteous Ruler of the universe."[157] Years later, he would speak at the Royal Institution on the behalf of "the justly revered Mr. Thomas Carlyle," testifying "that he has taught men moral and intellectual courage; to face facts boldly, while they confess the divineness of facts; not to be afraid of Nature, and not to worship Nature; to believe that man can know truth; and that only insofar as he knows truth can he live worthily on this earth."[158] The impression that the *Aids* made upon Kingsley is less obvious, unless we surmise a Coleridgean influence behind his sudden decision to enter the ministry. By May of 1841, Kingsley was writing Fanny, "I feel as if, once in the Church, I could cling so much closer to God. I feel more and more daily that a clergyman's life is the one for which both my *physique* and *morale* were intended." In the same letter, he states, "My views of theoretical religion are getting more clear daily, as I feel more completely the necessity of faith."[159]

Generally, Coleridge's influence upon Kingsley was indirect, through the work of Maurice, but it was not less strong for that reason. Upon determining to enter the ministry, Kingsley's first sympathies, however tentative and ill-defined, were toward the Oxford Tractarians; "My heart strangely yearned towards them," he later confided to Fanny.[160] But while, on the one hand, a contempt for hypocrisy rendered him especially susceptible to the message of Carlyle, on the other hand, it soon left him feeling at odds with Newman. In March 1841 the last of the *Tracts for the Times*, No. XC, was published, and by June Kingsley was convinced that, "whether wilful or self-deceived, these men are Jesuits."[161] During the last half of the year, his reading was determined by the curriculum and his tutor, as he crammed for his degree. In February 1842 Kingsley emerged from the university with a first in the classical tripos and a second in mathematics. He then proceeded to Chelsea for five months spent in reading for his ordination and in writing his *Life of St. Elizabeth*, and it was during this brief but intense period of intellectual exertion that his expressed beliefs first reveal that indebtedness to Maurice which, thereafter, became increasingly characteristic of his theology.

Fanny had her own sympathies with the High Church party, and she was urging Kingsley to read William Palmer's *Treatise on the Church of Christ* (1838). He was too busy; however, at the end of January 1842, Maurice published his *Three Letters to the Rev. W. Palmer*, and our young postulant somehow found the time to read them. Kingsley's Cambridge friendships certainly played no small part in steering him toward Maurice. Tom Taylor, the future Christian Socialist, playwright, and editor of *Punch*, was now one of Kingsley's closest friends and a leading figure among the Apostles;[162] moreover, the Coleridgean-Maurician school of thought was gathering momentum at the university. John William Colenso (1814-1883), the future bishop of Natal, who was now a fellow of St. John's, speaks of "drawing water" with Coleridge and Maurice "from the deep well of Truth," and Rowland Williams, at about the same time, speaks of Coleridge as "my great idol."[163] So, with Taylor directing Kingsley toward Maurice and Fanny recommending Palmer, it was not at all surprising that Maurice's *Three Letters* to Palmer would catch his eye.

In the first two of these letters, Maurice responds to Palmer's assertion that the English Church is essentially Catholic and "that if she be Protestant, she is merely negative, schismatical, and heretical." According to Maurice, the Catholicity of the Church rests not upon dogmas and institutions, but upon "a living Personal Centre," and it was to recover this center that the nations protested against "the usurpation of the Pope over Christendom." Therefore, although Protestantism itself cannot produce Catholicity, it is nevertheless possible for the Church "to be most Catholic when she is most Protestant."[164] Kingsley was greatly impressed with the argument and, apparently—if he had not already read Maurice's public letter to Archdeacon Samuel Wilberforce, *Reasons for Not Joining a Party in the Church*, published in April of 1841—he now read this earlier pamphlet too. Here Maurice argued his position, "that the words *Party* and *Church* are essentially hostile to each other; that he who says, 'I will be a Churchman,' says in effect, 'I will *not* be a Partyman.'"[165] Having read these two pamphlets, Kingsley sends this reply to Fanny:

> I have not begun Palmer's work on the church yet, and shall not till after my ordination. I am afraid it is not catholic enough to suit me. I hate party books. Men think wrongly when they suppose that in order to combat

> error, they must not allow their opponents to have the least right on their
> side; no opinion in the world is *utterly* wrong. . . . But *I* want, like such
> men as Leighton, Jewell, and Taylor, to combine both the dogmatic and
> the experimental. We must be catholic; we must hold the whole truth; we
> must have no partial or favorite views of Christianity, like the Dissenters
> and the Tractarians.[166]

Already—as is evident from this letter—Maurice was becoming to Kingsley what Coleridge had never been to Maurice, his "Master."

On 10 July 1842 Kingsley was ordained and situated as curate amid the agricultural laborers and fir trees of Eversley. Perhaps, it was as a congratulatory gift, as well as a token of love, that Fanny now placed into his hands the latest edition of Maurice's *Kingdom of Christ*. Subsequently, Kingsley took up the mission to spread and popularize Maurice's theology. Maurice was the prophet, Kingsley the priest and poet who "gloried in interpreting, expanding, applying him."[167] In 1856, Kingsley would tell Maurice, "I am trying to express in a new form the ideas which I have got from you, and which I have been trying to translate into all languages, from 'The Saint's Tragedy' to 'Glaucus.' I have no other work on earth, and want none."[168] Generally, if one wishes to understand Kingsley's theology, one must seek to understand Maurice's, but this is not to say that the disciple's work is merely redundant or inferior. In truth, it is often that, yet Kingsley applied his own emphasis to those aspects of Maurician theology that appealed most strongly to his scientific and practical mind. According to William Harrison, Kingsley's son-in-law and curate at Eversley, "the two most distinctive features" of Kingsley's religious teaching were "that the world is God's world, and not the devil's, and that manliness is entirely compatible with godliness."[169]

Kingsley's first year at Eversley was desperately lonely. The Grenfells had packed Fanny off to the Continent for the Grand Tour, hoping that a year abroad, fresh experiences, and new acquaintances would break the incomprehensible hold that the relatively poor and unstable young man seemed to have upon her heart. Meanwhile, Kingsley—now among illiterate laborers living in squalid conditions, with his own income as curate so dismal that he could do little to help, working for a lazy and licentious rector, and with no sympathizing correspondence from Fanny—was compelled to enter into spiritual battle and find comfort in the peace granted to a conquering faith.

When Fanny returned, she threatened to enter into a High Church convent; then, she appealed to the well-connected Rev. Sydney G. Osborne, an in-law of the Grenfells. Osborne, who loved Fanny and did not dislike the curate of Eversley, found a promising position for Kingsley at Pimperne, in Dorsetshire.[170] Opposition relented, and the two were married on 10 January 1844. As it turned out, Kingsley was to have both Fanny *and* Eversley, for during the honeymoon, an irate cuckold of Eversley alerted the authorities, and the frightened rector crossed the English Channel. The parishioners successfully petitioned for the installation of their former curate into the vacancy, and so, in May, the Kingsleys began the process of settling into the Eversley Rectory.

Gains and Losses

In April 1840 Hare was elevated to the archdeaconry of Lewes, in Chichester. The appointment endowed him with an influence that he was quick to use to the advantage of his friends. Two months afterwards Maurice was elected professor of English literature and modern history at King's College, and his first lecture on "The Growth of the English Nation and its Literature" was presented on 20 October. Maurice was to hold his professorship at King's for thirteen years, during which time many persons who later acquired eminence—including Leslie Stephen and Henry Kingsley (Charles's brother)—sat at his feet, but none have left so interesting a depiction of both the lectures and the lecturer than Frederick Farrar (1831-1903), the later Broad Church dean of Canterbury. Farrar, upon admittance into King's in 1847, immediately became one of the ninety to one hundred students attending Maurice's course. "His lectures," Farrar tells us, "were meant to deal rather with the meaning and the philosophy of history than with those details which he knew that we could derive from any ordinary handbook. Certainly, his lectures were a strong intellectual stimulus to those of us who were at all capable of rightly apprehending them."[171] Many were not at all capable, and unfortunately, the lecturer's manner gave opportunity for some "utterly disgraceful interruptions." Maurice, while lecturing, in order to more perfectly attend to the workings of his mind, would habitually close his eyes. But, while this method facilitated the utterance of "a stream of majestic language," it also allowed for gestures and noises from the audience, the sources of which could be known only by the audience itself.[172]

If the students at King's were, frequently, too immature to be appreciative of Maurice's genius, Daniel Macmillan, the future publisher, knew of an audience that would be receptive. Macmillan, who—under the combined influence of Hare and Maurice—had left a Dissenting chapel and become a member of the Established Church, in the summer of 1842 proposed that the two authors address the working class in a series of tracts or a periodical.[173] Maurice was intrigued and met with Macmillan, but in the end both Maurice and Hare thought it insufficient that they had a message for the workers, if at the same time their style of expression lacked appeal. Maurice wrote Hare, "I fear that having been once used to newspaper stimulants, everything else will seem dull and unsatisfactory."[174] Evidently, Hare and Maurice were in need of an interpreter, a talented writer in possession not only of the right message, but also of the rhetorical gifts needed to persuasively address the working class. Neither then knew of any such person, but Hare did suggest to Macmillan, "The best apostles are those who rise out of the class they are preaching to," and offered to give what aid he could to assist the young tradesman in his efforts.[175]

Ultimately, this would lead to the establishment of Macmillan as a publisher in Cambridge.

In the meanwhile, Hare wrote to Sterling about the fields white for harvest, perhaps hoping that his former curate, even at the eleventh hour, would feel a calling toward this mission, but Sterling, upon hearing of the death of Thomas Arnold, had entirely given up on the Church of England as a moral agent in meeting the needs of the poor. To Hare, he responded, "Arnold I believe to have been one of the very few, perhaps the only man in England, seeing the whole evil, and prepared to make such changes in the Church-system as might possibly have rendered it effectual for its nominal purpose among those who most need a moral reform."[176] By Sterling's estimation, the time had now passed when the Church might have reformed itself in order to reform the nation. To Emerson he wrote with evident frustration, "Every grown man of nobler spirit is either theoretical and lukewarm, or swathed up in obsolete sectarianism." Not Maurice, not Hare, but "Carlyle is our one Man, and he seems to feel it his function, not to build up and enjoy, . . . but to mourn, denounce, and tear in pieces."[177]

Sterling had other causes for despair. For him, 1843 had ushered in the spectral shadow of death. He burst a pulmonary blood vessel and nearly perished in extensive hemorrhage. His friends and family prepared themselves for the worst, but Sterling once again, somehow, recovered. Then, just as the awful spectre seemed to depart, on Easter Sunday, it gathered up his mother into its embrace. The news reached him two days later, while he was patiently tending to Susannah, his wife, weakened but supposedly recovering from her confinement, having on Friday given birth to a girl. Sterling had, however, no time to compose himself before Susannah too faded away, leaving him, two hours later, bereaved of both mother and wife. By virtue of strength, he had cheated death, but death, it now appeared, would not be cheated.

Sterling now moved to Ventnor, on the southern coast of the Isle of Wight, to be nearer friends and Anthony, his brother. Anna Maurice (*neé* Barton), the younger sister of Sterling's deceased wife, now spent most of her time tending to the needs of her brother-in-law and his six motherless children. In the face of such personal sacrifice, Sterling complained of Carlyle's condemnation of the age as void of faith and heroism: "There is more of the heroism of domestic life now," Sterling said, "than in any age of the world."[178]

Finally, in April 1844, another blood vessel broke, and Sterling was prostrated, confined, and sentenced to a six-months' dying. Anna was now with him constantly, and Maurice came as often as his duties would allow, but Carlyle Sterling refused to see. Instead, he often now thought of Emerson, that "man beyond the Atlantic whom I never saw, and who yet is to me a true and understanding friend."[179] Bearing up under such weight of heavy sorrow, Sterling had little use now for the stern voice of the prophet and "anti-poet." In fact, he was to be the first of many, including A. H. Clough, Matthew Arnold, and William Thomson (archbishop of York, 1863-1900), who were to make the conscious decision to turn from Carlyle to Emerson.

For comfort Sterling now read from his Bible, and—as Carlyle has represented the case—"for about six months he sat looking steadfastly, at all moments, into the eyes of Death; he too who had eyes to *see* Death and the Terrors and Eternities; and surely it was with perfect courage and piety, and valiant simplicity of heart, that he bore himself."[180] What *Terrors* were these? In his last days, Sterling wrote to Hare, "Farewell! . . . We shall meet again, be well assured. Christianity is a great comfort and blessing to me, although I am quite unable to believe all its original documents. I am thankful for all things, and hope much."[181] To J. S. Mill he wrote, "Let us hope to meet upon some other height with a still nobler prospect. Heaven keep you." Mill responded, "I have never so much wished for another life as I do for the sake of meeting you in it. . . . I shall never think of you but as one of the noblest, and quite the most lovable of all men I have known or ever look to know."[182] To Emerson Sterling wrote, "You and I will never meet in this world. . . . My struggle, I trust, is nigh over. At present it is a painful one. But I fear nothing, and hope much."[183] Not Terror, but *Hope* was the keynote of the final days of Sterling's mortal life, and on 18 September 1844 all of his doubts became certainties.

None of the Kingsley family was aware that Lieutenant Gerald Kingsley, Charles's younger brother (born in 1821), had preceded Sterling out of this world by one day. His ship, the H.M.S. Royalist, had floundered for months in the Torres Straits, and with water, water everywhere, Lt. Kingsley had never a drop to drink. Five additional months were to pass before the news arrived in London.[184]

Convergence

While his wife tended to Sterling on the Isle of Wight, Maurice—together with his two boys and Edward, the twelve-year-old eldest son of Sterling—took up for the summer the rectory of Charles Kingsley, Sr., at Chelsea. At this time, the younger Kingsley was, in all the happiness and heroism of incessant labor, draining and patching the flooded rectory at Eversley, establishing clubs for the poor and classes for the illiterate, visiting the sick, and writing sermons. Therefore, it is at least pleasant to suppose—in a vacuum of evidence—that the elder Kingsley was absent from Chelsea because he was making every effort to lighten the burden of his son's, the new parson's, duties.

Just how busy Kingsley was may be inferred from the fact that he allowed more than a month to pass before he addressed a letter to Chelsea. He asked Maurice for practical advise in responding to the Baptists in his parish and expressed indebtedness "for the foundation of any coherent view of the word of God, the meaning of the Church of England, and the spiritual phenomena of the present and past ages." Moreover, he requested the privilege of the author's acquaintance.[185] Maurice welcomed the occasion but felt overwhelmed by the high estimation in which he was regarded: "How it grieves me to think of the disappointment you will experience when you find in what degree I deserve the opinion you have formed of me."[186] They met in the last week of July 1844, and Kingsley was not disappointed.

The two preachers' paths had now crossed, but they would not converge for another three years. In the meantime, Maurice's life would change in many ways. In March of 1845 Anna, his devoted wife, died, leaving him and his sister Priscilla to care for the children.[187] During the summer he was appointed both Boyle Lecturer and Warburton Lecturer. The first of these appointments resulted in the production of *The Religions of the World and Their Relation to Christianity* (1846), and the second bore fruit as *The Epistle to the Hebrews* (1846), which included a lengthy reply to J. H. Newman's theory of doctrinal development. In February 1846 he received the chaplaincy of Lincoln's Inn, and in June the Council of King's College—for two years, now, under the presidency of Dr. Richard W. Jelf—asked him and Trench to be professors in the new Department of Theology.

Thomas Hughes (1822-96), of Rugby and Oriel, was in his second year of studying for the bar at Lincoln's Inn when Maurice became chaplain. Before Maurice's appointment, the congregation numbered anywhere between eight and fourteen, depending on the weather. The attendance now began to increase dramatically, and within ten years the chapel was filled to capacity.[188] In the autumn of 1846, Hughes wrote to his fiancé, "We had an excellent sermon from Morris [*sic*] the reader, on the character of Esau, from 12th Hebrews, the afternoon's lessons. His views nearly coincide with Arnold's in one of his sermons, . . . but he brought out a new point to me, viz. how impossible it was for Esau to obtain the blessing after he had sold his birthright."[189] Hughes, who had read *Past and Present* (1843) while at Oxford, and had subsequently become an admirer of Carlyle, was just now at fisticuffs with the Everlasting No, but as he had a good deal of Esau's blood flowing in his veins, the chaplain's message touched his heart. He renewed his determination not to sell his birthright—Christ in us, the hope of glory—and henceforth became a lifelong disciple of Maurice. Hughes's *Manliness of Christ* (1879) recognizes both the Esau and the Jacob in the person of Christ and defines "manliness" as including much more than courage, but also, "for instance, tenderness and thoughtfulness for others."[190] This same message of Maurice's was also to have a major impact upon Kingsley, leading to his own Esau ministry, especially among soldiers during the Crimean War. It is this ministry that is sometimes derogatorily referred to as "muscular Christianity."

Another student at Lincoln's Inn, Walter Bagehot—the future author of the eminently readable introduction to English politics, *The English Constitution* (1867)—brought his close friend Richard Holt Hutton (1826-97) to hear an afternoon sermon by Maurice. Hutton's recollection is worth reading in detail:

> I went, and it is hardly too much to say that the voice and manner of the
> preacher . . . have lived in my memory even since, as no other voice and
> manner have ever lived in it. . . . There was intensity—almost too thrilling
> —and something, too, of sad exultation in every tone, as if the reader

were rehearsing a story in which he had no part except his personal certainty of its truth, his gratitude that it should be true, and his humiliation that it had fallen to such lips as his to declare it. . . . He seemed to be the channel for a communication, not the source of it.[191]

Hutton—later coeditor, first of *The National Review* and then of *The Spectator*—was, at the time, under the guidance of James Martineau, preparing for the Unitarian ministry. During the 1850s, Maurice would play an instrumental role in persuading Hutton of the truth of the Incarnation.

Near the end of 1846 Maurice received a visitor who knew nothing of him, except that a book of his had been reviewed in *The Spectator*. This visitor, John Malcolm Ludlow (1821-1911), had recently come from Paris, where he had studied Socialism and worked in a Lutheran and Calvinist society for the relief of the poor. Now tutoring law students, he was attempting without success to organize his pupils into a volunteer society for charitable visitations in the filthy, vicious, poverty-stricken neighborhoods around the Inns of Court. He was hoping that the chaplain would provide some direction for his efforts, but went away disappointed. In a letter to his mother, Ludlow describes Maurice as "a good man but very impractical."[192]

Meanwhile, Kingsley was also broadening his circle of acquaintance. During his schooldays at Helston, he had become fast friends with Cowley Powles. After a brief period as fellow students at King's, they went separate ways, Kingsley to Cambridge and Powles to Oxford, where he was now a fellow of Exeter College. Kingsley was in the habit of musing rather openly with his old friend:

> "I am just now a sort of religious Shelley, an Ishmaelite of catholicity, a John the Baptist, minus his spirit and power, alas!"[193]
> "My whole heart is set, not on retrogression, outward or inward, but on progression—not on going back in the least matter to any ideal age or system, but on fairly taking the present as it is, not as I should like it to be. . . . The new element is democracy, in Church and State. Waiving the question of its evil or its good, we cannot stop it. Let us Christianize it instead."[194]

Naturally, Kingsley's name and thoughts were, on occasion, mentioned in the Exeter Common Room, where Powles often enjoyed the company of James Anthony Froude (1818-1894). In 1845, Froude was deep in a sea of disillusionment, for he had followed the "kindly light" of the Newmanites only to find that the captain had abandoned his storm-tossed ship. Naturally, Froude would take an interest in Kingsley. In December of this year the two men first corresponded, but their mutual regard had, for the time being, no opportunity to ripen into friendship. Although Powles invited Kingsley to Oxford in 1846, parish and home duties kept him bound to Eversley. Domestic happiness for the Kingsleys increased early in 1846, with the birth of Rose, their eldest daughter. The following year brought them Maurice, their eldest son, named after one of the two sponsors, the other being Powles.

During these years, Kingsley was fruitful in other ways as well, as he carefully revised his *Life of St. Elizabeth* into the form of a verse drama. The work juxtaposes the joys and virtues of the conjugal life with the celibate life of St. Elizabeth of Hungary, and suggests that the latter was merely a perversion of the former. The point is emphasized in the development of the sadistic Conrad of Morpung, Elizabeth's spiritual adviser. This work was finished in the summer of 1847, and Kingsley sent it to Maurice, who subsequently took it with him on his journey to Linlathen. There, in the home of Erskine, Maurice read the manuscript, and—in response to the author's request—hesitantly agreed to compose a preface. By December, all was ready. With the preface and a commendatory note from Hartley Coleridge in hand, the author, with no little anxiety, proceeded to Pickering's, where the publisher refused it. With hopes deferred but not dashed, Kingsley quickly wrote a progress report to Fanny, gathered up his courage, and went to pay a visit to the father of a Cambridge friend, John Parker. *The Saint's Tragedy* appeared in print at the beginning of 1848 and immediately attracted the partisan fury of the Oxford Puseyites.[195]

As if to taunt his opponents and fuel his notoriety, Kingsley quickly penned an article for *Fraser's Magazine*, "Why Should We Fear the Romish Priests?" Writing on the pretense of quelling a fear that the number of English converts to Rome would, in a few years, result in a popular majority on the side of the Pope, Kingsley asks, "What man of genius have they had among them since the sixteenth century? . . . Among its converts it cannot name a single first-rate man." The insult to J. H. Newman is palpable, and lest the reader thinks it unjust, Kingsley explains: "Has not he by his later writings given the very strongest proof, that to become a Romish priest is to lose, *ipso facto*, whatever moral or intellectual life he might previously have had?" Therefore, he suggests, "We have nothing to fear from them—but *we have everything to fear from our own fear of them*. . . . Teach your children to pity the Jesuit for a silly pedant, and there will be no fear of their hereafter accepting him as a mysterious philosopher."[196]

It was an article that would have made Fox How roar with laughter, had Dr. Arnold only lived to read it. Even so, Oxford itself was now undergoing a liberal reaction to the movement that had transfixed it, and the students were in the mood for this slayer of gargoyles, Charles Kingsley. Exeter welcomed him as the newest literary lion. He wrote home to Fanny, "They got up a meeting for me, and the club was crowded with men merely to see poor me. . . . It is very funny and new. I dine this afternoon with Conington; tomorrow with Palgrave; Monday with Stanley, and so on."[197] They talked of poetry, politics, and religion, and Froude recalls, "If we could not follow Kingsley's reasonings, we honoured his enthusiasm and admired his talents." Froude was particularly impressed with the parson's indebtedness to Carlyle and his firm conviction "that the existing order of things could not and ought not to last." There is, perhaps, a hint of disappointment in Froude's realization that Kingsley, "unlike Carlyle, believed that the impending revolution was to be brought about by the working force of Christianity."[198]

Workmen of England

Carlyle had sounded the warning of impending revolution in his 1839 pamphlet on *Chartism*. In the 1830s, numbers of workers, laboring under an insupportable feeling of injustice, organized and converged under the political six-point agenda of the People's Charter.[199] Failing to obtain parliamentary consideration for their charter, the General Convention of 1839 published a "Manifesto of Ulterior Measures," assuring the working classes that they would prevail, "peaceably if we may, forcibly if we must."[200] Carlyle acknowledged the righteousness of the workers' conviction "that they are unfairly dealt with, that their lot in this world is not founded on right, not even on necessity and might, and is neither what it should be, nor what it shall be."[201] Friedrich Engels, then in Manchester, praised Carlyle for his courage to speak the truth, and in *The Condition of the Working Classes in England* (1845) prophesied that England would be the stage for the beginning of a proletariat uprising. Following the publication of Engels's book, the Irish famine multiplied the numbers of hungry workers in the industrial cities. Finally, the Chartists scheduled for April 1848 another General Convention in London, and this time they were aiming for a record five million signatures on the charter.

Meanwhile, in February, revolution broke out in Paris and threatened to spread to England. As April drew nigh, agricultural laborers beat their ploughshares into swords, the London genteel loaded their pistols, and the queen was dispatched to the Isle of Wight. The *Times* anticipated a mob of 200,000 Chartists in the city. Ludlow, who had previously visited Maurice before returning to France, now wrote from Paris, expressing his conviction that socialism had taken hold upon the consciences of the workmen, and that, if socialism were not Christianized, "it would shake Christianity to its foundation." Maurice responded, "I see my way but dimly; this, however, I do see, that there is something to be done, that God Himself is speaking to us and that if we ask Him what He would have us do, we shall be shown."[202] Ludlow recognized that a door of opportunity had been opened, and he immediately crossed the English Channel to convene with Maurice. By the end of March, the two were respectful friends, but "Ludlow had neither the self-confidence nor the dramatic instinct. . . . Maurice had neither the pugnacity nor the incisiveness to make an effective protest."[203] It appeared that the union of Maurice & Ludlow would advance no further than the 1842 union of Maurice & Hare.

Actually, by the time that the General Convention began, on 4 April, the threat of socialism had already worked against the Chartists.[204] It not only alienated from them the sympathies of the middle class, but even among the "physical force" faction of the Chartists, many of the workers were reconsidering their position, since the purpose, as well as the potential result, of revolution had been thrown into ambiguity. Although the convention did commence with talk of revolution, and although there were, undoubtedly, secret insurrectionist meetings—such as envisioned by

Disraeli in Book V of *Sybil* (1845)—the majority of the Chartists were now practically, if not theoretically, allied with the "moral force" party.

The "People's Charter" was to be submitted to the House of Commons on 10 April, and—as rumor and innuendo would have it—upon its reception there depended the peace of England. Kingsley's adventurous spirit had not allowed him to keep a safe distance during the Bristol riots of 1831, and it would not now endure the quiet of Eversley. On the morning of the fateful day he ventured into London with John Parker. By noon he was well assured that all talk of revolution had been gross exaggeration, and he quickly sent off a note of comfort to Fanny: "Large crowds, but no one expects any row. . . . The only fear is marauding in the suburbs at night; but do not fear for me, I shall be safe at Chelsea at 5."[205] After determining that his father was in no danger, Kingsley decided to visit Maurice, then at home nursing a bad cold. Maurice was unable to venture out, but he placed a letter of introduction into Kingsley's hands and sent him to Ludlow. Had Maurice any thought as to what schemes might inspire two such men as these on such a day as this, he would have, like Moses before the burning bush, hesitated and faltered, for he was a reluctant prophet. But, out of the desert, as it were, the spokesman that had been wanting had now appeared, and there would be no further delay.

Ludlow and Kingsley proceeded together to Kennington Common, where Feargus O'Connor, the Chartist demagogue and chief instigator behind the "physical force" faction, attempted to rally the Chartists to march upon Westminster. Matthew Arnold, now working in London as a clerk, had also come to Kennington Common to witness the events, and he "was much struck with the ability of the speakers."[206] As it turned out, a small faction followed O'Connor's lead, but Wellington's troops had blocked the bridges, and after a momentary standoff in the pouring rain, O'Connor's followers dispersed to their homes. In parliament, the National Petition was found to contain such signatures as "Victoria Rex," "Sir Robert Peel," "the Duke of Wellington," and "Mr. Punch," and the Charter's demands were simply dismissed.[207] The pathetic contrast between the threat of revolution and the soggy retreat of O'Connor's followers resulted in the popular but viciously unfair representation of the convention as a humiliating fiasco for the Chartist movement as a whole.

Ludlow and Kingsley, however, recognized an opportunity. Ludlow had been wanting to get a paper started; Kingsley had been obsessed with the idea of writing tracts. They returned to confer with Maurice, who liked the idea of tracts, but thought they should be addressed to the clergy. Kingsley urged the present need to tell the workers that they were not alone, that there were Churchmen who sympathized with their plight and believed that their goals were right, even when their means were wrong. Maurice conceded, and Kingsley stayed up all night writing a placard:

> WORKMEN OF ENGLAND! You have more friends than you think . . . ; men
> who are drudging and sacrificing themselves to get you your rights; men

who know what your rights are, better than you know yourselves, who are
trying to get for you something nobler than charters and dozens of Acts
of Parliament.... You think the Charter would make you free—would to
God it would! The Charter is not bad; *if the men who use it are not bad*!
But will the Charter make you free?... That I guess is real slavery; to be
a slave to one's own stomach, one's own pocket, one's own temper. Will
the Charter cure *that*? Friends, you want more than Acts of Parliament
can give....

Workers of England, be wise, and then you *must* be free, for you will
be fit to be free.[208]

Canon Raven refers to this placard, signed by "A Working Parson," as an epoch-
making "first manifesto of the Church of England, her first public act of atonement
for a half-century of apostasy, of class-prejudice and political sycophancy."[209] It was
posted around London early on the morning of the 11th. That evening, Kingsley
wrote Fanny, "Maurice has given me the highest proof of confidence. He has taken
me into counsel, and we are to have meetings for prayer and study, when I come up
to London, and we are to bring out a new set of real 'Tracts for the Times,'
addressed to the higher orders."[210]

A clerical meeting was arranged for the 12th at Hurstmonceux. There, Maurice
and Kingsley met with A. J. Scott and J. C. Hare. Hare proposed a penny periodical,
after the manner of Cobbett's *Political Register*, which could be addressed to the
working classes. Although Maurice did not mention the fact, this was very much
what Ludlow had earlier proposed.[211] On the 13th Kingsley returned to Eversley,
still full of ideas but physically exhausted. In the days that followed, Maurice came
to the realization that resources were wanting to pursue both the tracts and the
penny paper simultaneously, and so he and Ludlow decided to move ahead with the
periodical, which they then titled *Politics for the People*.

Politics for the People

The first issue of *Politics for the People* appeared on 6 May 1848. The publication
lasted for just three months and seventeen issues, the last of them, a supplement,
appearing in July. Ludlow, as the editor, contributed more articles—all under the
name of "John Townsend" or "J. T."—than any other single writer. These included
several series: "The Suffrage," "The Ballot," and "Party Politics." In issue No. 2 (13
May 1848) Ludlow strongly attacks "Monster Meetings," arguing, "The only object
of a Monster Meeting is this—a display of numbers. And what is a display of
numbers, but the terror of brute force?—and what is the terror of brute force, but the
worst shape of tyranny?"[212] Maurice—under the anonymity of "A Clergyman"—
contributed a series of articles on the working classes and the educational system of
England, and—being most at home with the Platonic manner of discussion—
included a series of dialogues on "Fraternity," "Liberty," and "Equality." In the first
of these, Maurice proposes that there is a universal fraternity based on a common

brotherhood in Christ. Therefore, "Men cannot be merely joined together in the support of certain plans, or in opposing them. They must learn to act and feel together as men."[213] Kingsley adopted the pugnacious ethos of "Parson Lot" for his "Letters to the Chartists" and "Letters to Landlords."

Other distinguished contributors to *Politics for the People* include Richard Whately, Arthur P. Stanley, Richard C. Trench, James Spedding, John Conington, Arthur Helps, and S. G. Osborne.[214] One name is conspicuously absent from this list: J. C. Hare. Of this sad fact some account must be made, and the most apparent cause is none other than Kingsley's "Letters to the Chartists." In the second of these, printed in issue No. 4 (27 May 1848), Kingsley makes a lengthy confession:

> If you have followed a very different "Reformer's Guide" from mine, it is mainly the fault of us parsons: we have never told you that the true Reformer's Guide, the true poor man's book, the true "God's Voice against Tyrants, Idlers, and Humbugs," was the Bible. Ay, you sneer, but so it is; it is our fault, our great fault, that you should sneer—sneer at the very news which ought to be your glory and your strength. It is our fault. We have used the Bible as if it was a mere constable's handbook—an opium-dose for keeping beasts of burden patient while they were being overloaded—a mere book to keep the poor in order.... We have told you that the Bible preached the rights of property and the duties of labour, when (God knows!) for once that it does that, it preaches ten times over the *duties of property* and the *rights of labour*.... I have been as bad as any one, but I am sick of it.[215]

Archdeacon Hare thought the confession too full—even *fulsome*. He complained to Maurice that Kingsley had no right to implicate other parsons in his own sins, that his letter would only reinforce the already adamant anti-clericalism of many Chartists, and that it would take years to undo the damage that "Parson Lot" had done to the reputation and mission of the periodical. Moreover, he thought that both Kingsley and Ludlow were conceited firebrands and that, if Maurice continued to endorse their message, he would find that his own usefulness as a minister would suffer, perhaps irreparably. Maurice responded warmly, noting that "there are hundreds of young men at Oxford and Cambridge, and I believe a great many Chartists and working-men, who will have a faith in him and in the clergy which they never had before, when they find he does care to take the beam out of his own eye before he begins to take the mote out of theirs." As for their being conceited young men, Maurice thought Hare should know that "either of those two would be glad to sit at your feet and receive your instructions and admonitions. I never met with men of a more reverent spirit."[216]

During this time, Maurice was courting Georgiana Hare, the half-sister of the archdeacon. Soon, on 4 July 1849, they married. The families of Maurice and Hare were now bound together by a double knot, and in the years that followed—during the publication of *The Christian Socialist* (afterwards *The Journal of Association*) and the work with the Working Men's Cooperative Societies—Ludlow would often suspect that, behind Maurice's hesitations and refusals to act, the influence of Hare was to blame.[217] Conversely, Maurice would, on occasion, suspect Ludlow of taking advantage of Kingsley's impetuous nature and wasting his energy and talents.[218]

The story of the Christian Socialist movement is too involved and has been told too well by others to justify any attempt to retell it in this chapter.[219] While Maurice continued to have an active role in the cooperation movement until the passing, in 1852, of the Industrial and Provident Societies Act, Kingsley's direct involvement with the movement came to an end with *Politics for the People*. There were a number of reasons for this. Unlike Ludlow, he had no experience with the machinery of cooperative societies, and so, recognizing that his commitments were first to his family and parishioners in Eversley, he wisely left the practical aspects of the movement in other hands. Moreover, in the autumn of 1848, Kingsley's health broke down, the result of physical and mental exhaustion. He did, nevertheless, continue to make a substantial contribution to public awareness of workers' employment and living conditions, particularly by means of his novels *Yeast* (1848) and *Alton Locke* (1850) and by his tract attacking the slop-shops, *Cheap Clothes and Nasty* (1848). It is to Kingsley's everlasting credit that, as Raven expresses it, "He tore away the veil from the eyes of the prudish and pharisaical; he revealed to them the horror of competitive industrialism in all its nakedness: they might shudder and protest, but they could not wholly forget."[220] In 1851 W. F. Hook, vicar in the manufacturing town of Leeds, might complain that Maurice and Kingsley "are impracticable and impractical theorists," but he could not deny that "their works are universally read and approved in this part of the world."[221]

Revolutionary Professors

Maurice's method of approaching in argument those with whom he differed was so deferential and sincere that his adversaries could never afterwards be his enemies. Like Glaucus before Diomedes, he would rather first identify in his opponent all that was virtuous and true, even if the exchange left himself vulnerable, than merely attack at once all that appeared vicious and false. However, in 1828, in the pages of *The Athenæum*, Maurice had dared to establish with painstaking detail the total ignorance and "contempt of all decency" betrayed in the literary criticism of John Wilson Croker, one of the founding members of and most constant contributor to the *Quarterly Review*.[222] Croker seems never to have forgiven Maurice this injury, and with all the patience of malice, he awaited the occasion to strike.

The occasion came, as Hare had anticipated, through Maurice's association with Kingsley, particularly at Queen's College. Maurice, from the beginning of their friendship, had been impressed with Kingsley's intellectual vigor, and in April of 1848—when the two were just beginning their great social work—he brought

Kingsley to see Jelf, the principal of King's College, who had already agreed to grant Maurice an additional lecturer to assist in his theological classes.[223] Although Jelf may have "expressed himself very anxious" to give the lectureship to Kingsley, the college council "deliberately rejected" the upstart parson, "not preferring another to him, but simply saying they will not have him."[224] Before the council had made its determination, on 1 May Queen's College opened its doors. This college, an off-shoot from the Governesses' Benevolent Institution, was established by a committee, organized and chaired by Maurice and comprised for the most part of professors from King's College, for the purpose of providing an education for governesses and female teachers. As a critic of the college indignantly observes, the professors of Queen's were "a self-constituted and self-elected body,"[225] and into this body Kingsley was appointed to provide lectures on English composition and English literature. The position, however, was kept only until the late autumn of 1848, when illness compelled the rector to seek rest on the coast of Ilfracombe.

The first attack on Maurice came in February 1849 by way of William Palmer's article "On Tendencies toward the Subversion of Faith," published in the *English Review*. Palmer's primary target was Hare, whose recent publications—particularly a second volume of university sermons, *The Mission of the Comforter* (1846), and the edition of Sterling's *Essays and Tales* (1848), including a "Sketch of the Author's Life"—were supposed to have had the effect of undermining the faith of the English Church by encouraging the study of German theology. Maurice's guilt was by way of association, and Hare, in his irate *Thou Shalt Not Bear False Witness Against Thy Neighbour* (1849), points out the fact that his friend could hardly read German and had never cared much for any theology not English. Hare observes that Palmer "wanted to accuse me of infidelity, to hold me up to public abhorrence as a teacher whose covert purpose is to propagate infidelity; and he also wanted to bring in Mr. Maurice as in some way or other an accessory in this crime. Doubtless too, if he could drag us to the stake, he would seize the torch and kindle it."[226] Although Hare had succeeded in vindicating himself and his friends, Palmer's article had already caused some anxiety within the council at King's, and Maurice warned Georgiana that his position at the college "may not be very secure."[227]

Croker also read Palmer's article and realized that, if Maurice's friendships with Hare and Sterling left the theologian susceptible to attacks from behind, his current sponsorship of Kingsley made him all the more vulnerable to a direct, frontal assault. Whether Croker himself actually wrote the article "Queen's College, London" appears to remain a mystery,[228] but no one doubts his contribution. The venom is unmistakable. The writer prepared for attack by reminding his readers that Queen's College was a public institution, incorporated by royal charter, and therefore, "if error ever does come to be taught by [its professors], public opinion will have a perfect right to step in and insist, not on the teacher altering his belief, . . . but on the teacher himself being changed." Moreover, if ever a college needed to be protected by public opinion, it was Queen's, for in its classes sat young, impressionable women into whose protective and nurturing charge were to be placed England's children.

The editor then proceeds to examine the contents of the volume of *Introductory Lectures Delivered at Queen's College* (1849) and purports to have discovered "traces of a school of so-called *theology* which seems to be gaining ground among us—a sort of modified pantheism and latitudinarianism—a system not of bringing religion into everything, but of considering everything as more or less inherently religious, which is near akin . . . to abnegating the proper idea of religion."[229] Moreover, Maurice is found guilty of challenging the popular distinction between "natural" and "revealed" religion and of adopting "a vague mistiness of style for the purpose of adding an aweful dignity to matters which are very simple in themselves." The editor's style is, evidently, to throw a vague mistiness of suspicion over his victims, but he did provide King's administrators with one concrete clue: look, he advised, at "the mode in which *words* are adapted, accommodated, not to say perverted, by these lecturers."[230] This was counsel that, as we shall see, would not be forgotten.

Kingsley fares much worse. The rector of Eversley, says the editor, distinguishes himself above all the other professors "by the Germanisms embroidered on his *prose*—another indication of leanings that require to be watched." What is meant by "Germanisms" is left unexplained, but possibly there is a word or two that Kingsley had adopted from W. H. Riehl, the German social and cultural historian, whose method Kingsley was attempting to apply to the study of English literature. George Eliot would later adapt Riehl's approach when developing the religion of human sympathy that adds such philosophical beauty to her *Scenes of Clerical Life* (1857).[231] The *Quarterly Review* editor, however, neither recognizes nor cares about Riehl's method. What most concerns him is the moral influence of Kingsley's application: "How would our readers like to receive into their families as a governess, one who had been taught to feel such an interest in 'tales of village love,'—who is prepared to take a 'personal interest in the actors' of the domestic 'life-drama'?"[232] The reader is, thus, invited to conceive of Kingsley's classroom as a breeding chamber for gossips, temptresses, and home-wreckers, a veritable school for scandal.

As soon as this article appeared, one of Queen's professors, C. G. Nicolay, who was also a librarian at King's, released to the press the fact that Kingsley was no longer one of their professors. This act, which Maurice perceived as a cowardly genuflection before the idol of public opinion, so outraged him that he immediately resigned as the chairman of the committee. He then published a public *Letter to the Lord Bishop of London*, declaring that, if illness had not forced Kingsley to quit Queen's, his lectures "would have done more to elevate the minds and characters of our pupils than almost any which it is possible for them to receive." As it is, Maurice says that he can only hope that the writer is correct "in believing that some of the spirit which [Kingsley's] lectures embody is to be found among us."[233] Maurice explains, that as young women receive the cultivation provided by a college, their intellectual, imaginative, and spiritual powers are stirred to life:

> They find capacities in their souls of which they never dreamed: they read books which call forth those capacities.... We are to tell them that these powers are there, because God created man in his image, that they can be truly exercised only when man claims his position as a creature restored in the image of the Son. On this principle we have thought it our business to make literature, not a plaything for holiday afternoons, but a serious work, which those who enter upon it at all are to enter upon as persons who are studying in God's sight.[234]

Maurice insists that it is not the business of Queen's College to treat literature as though it were suitable for shallow souls, and he especially objects to the editor's pretense of writing to protect women, when in fact he speaks of them with patronizing condescension, as though they entered into the college without consciences of their own, without that candle of the Lord that teaches them to resist immorality, without the Spirit of Christ that enables them to resist. "The part of this article which refers to ourselves and our ill-doings," says Maurice, "I can easily tolerate; the part which refers to these poor women makes my blood boil."[235]

Croker was not quite satisfied with the thought of having made Maurice's blood boil. The professor's supervision of *The Christian Socialist*, along with his staunch endorsement of Kingsley, did offer Croker an encouraging prospect at malicious wounding. Thus, a second attack from the *Quarterly Review*, Croker's article on "Revolutionary Literature," was launched in September 1851. After a lengthy prelude, in which he surveys the communist literature of France, the reviewer considers the recent works of Maurice and Kingsley as illustrations of an especially detestable perversion of "Communism." We are told not to be fooled by the name "Socialist," which—although it has the advantage of "keeping in the background the immorality and violence suggested by the term *community*"—has the exact same principle as Communism and arrives at the same results.[236] What could be more dangerous to the English people and their Constitution, asks Croker, than that their own appointed ministers should be stirring up insurrection in the name of Christianity?

> Incredible as it may appear, there is, it seems, a clique of educated and clever but wayward-minded men—the most prominent of them two *clergymen of the Church of England*—who, from, as it seems, a morbid craving for notoriety or a crazy straining after paradox—have taken up the unnatural and unhallowed task of preaching, in the press and from the pulpit, not indeed such open, undisguised *Jacobinism* and *Jacquerie* as we have just been quoting, but—under the name of '*Christian Socialism*,'—the same doctrines in a form not the less dangerous for being less honest.... Mr. Maurice, we understand, is considered the head of the school, and it certainly adds to our surprise to find [him] ... occupying the Professorial Chair of Divinity in *King's College, London*.[237]

Croker, certain that, if only he threw enough dirt and if only his dirt was sufficiently dirty, some of it was bound to stick, did not rest here. He anticipates that both

Maurice and Kingsley will protest with all their energy and cunning that they are motivated by nothing other than social benevolence, love for the poor, and reverence for the Bible; "but we can say that, whatever they may intend, the *effect* of what they do is in every view deplorable—dangerous for the rich, still more dangerous for the poor, and a perversion of Christianity, *offensive* alike to good sense, piety, and truth."[238]

Croker emphasizes the close teamwork and mutual admiration of Maurice and Kingsley, and then proceeds to define *Alton Locke* as "a defence of Chartist Socialism"—that is to say, a defense of a workers' revolution by violence, if necessary. Even the title of Kingsley's first novel, *Yeast*, suggests that this work "is meant to *ferment* in the minds of the people and prepare them to *rise* under the heat of the Socialist oven."[239] What else could be expected from a movement that took its impetus from the February Revolution of 1848. Why, the very titles of Maurice's articles on "Fraternity," "Liberty," and "Equality" are derived from the three words that form the motto of the new French Republic.[240] Croker concludes by appealing to the decency and piety of his readers, noting, "It is a greater anomaly in our present state of society than any that these pretended reformers have as yet produced, that the religion and morals of the country should be in any degree committed to such teachers."[241]

When Carlyle finished reading this article, he wrote to his brother John, "No viler mortal calls himself man than old Croker at this time." The attack on his friend Kingsley was nothing else than "very beggarly Crokerism, all of copperas and gall and human *baseness*."[242] Kingsley, himself, was hardly phased. As Matthew Arnold observed, of all the literary men he knew, Kingsley was "the most incapable of being made ill-natured, or even indifferent, by having to support ill-natured attacks himself."[243] But, we might ask, was there not an element of truth in Croker's review? Was it not a fact that Maurice and Kingsley were revolutionaries?

The first issue of *The Christian Socialist* had made its appearance on 2 November 1850, and it was preceded by a short series of tracts that set out to explain the general idea and aims of "Christian Socialism." In the first of these, a "Dialogue between Somebody (a person of respectability) and Nobody (the writer)," Maurice asserts his beliefs that "Christianity is the only foundation of Socialism, and that a true Socialism is the necessary result of a sound Christianity," that "the watchword of the Socialist is CO-OPERATION; the watchword of the Anti-socialist is COMPETITION."[244] Whereas the State is conservative of property and individual rights, it is the purpose of the Church to serve the interests of the community—that is, it is Communist in principle.[245] Although the Church recognizes that the State ought not to be Communistic, the Church is itself a commune and functions on the principle of cooperation, opposed to laissez-faire. Through the combined means of a Christian education and the establishment of cooperative associations, Maurice and his colleagues were attempting to help the workers to help themselves. The enterprise was, of course, *revolutionary* only insofar as Christianity itself is revolutionary, and—in this sense—to a society that has ears to hear only the Gospels of

Mammonism and of Dilettantism, the literature of Christian Socialism is, in fact, "Revolutionary Literature."

Scandal

To the polytheistic and emperor-worshiping Romans, Christianity seemed a form of atheism; to the Jews, the cross was a stumbling-block; to the Greeks, it was foolishness. Christ had warned his disciples against courting human favor, knowing that to please God, one must sometimes scandalize men. Maurice had, at first, hesitated before adopting the name "Socialist," but early in the year 1850, he wrote to Ludlow, "I see it clearly. We must not beat around the bush. . . . 'Tracts on Christian Socialism' is, it seems to me, the only title which will define our object, and will commit us at once to the conflict we must engage in sooner or later with the unsocial Christians and the unchristian Socialists."[246] Maurice had counted the cost, and thus he was not to be taken unawares, as Thirlwall had been in 1834. If the professor lost his chair, so be it; he knew that there were things far more aweful to be lost.

In November of 1851, Dr. Jelf communicated to Maurice that the trustees had become uneasy, that they had requested that he, as the president of King's College, look diligently into the professor's writings. "I see nothing," he concludes, "in any writings avowedly your own, inconsistent *per se* with your position as a professor of divinity in this college." Nevertheless, Jelf did see much cause for regret, particularly in that Maurice had never publicly expressed his disapprobation of that "reckless and dangerous writer," that "indescribably irreverent" preacher, Charles Kingsley. "I need not," says Jelf, "enlarge upon the consequences which such presumed approbation, unless openly disavowed, is likely to bring, not only upon the theological department, but . . . by implication upon the whole college." The article in *The Guardian* had brought the issue to a head, the council had become agitated, and therefore, Jelf advises, either "allay their just apprehensions" or "resign your office without delay."[247] In response, Maurice notes that Croker's article had been denounced as vicious misrepresentation by both *The Morning Chronicle* and *The Spectator*. Furthermore, if such vindications as these are insufficient to acquit, Maurice protests, "I cannot resign my office while such insinuations are current respecting me. . . . I ask for a full examination of anything I have ever written or uttered in any way." Since the members of the council have seen fit to express their doubts and suspicions, they are obligated, says Maurice, either to deprive him of his position or to extend a full acquittal.[248]

A clerical committee of inquiry was established. This committee included—in addition to Jelf—Charles J. Blomfield, bishop of London, and H. H. Milman, dean of St. Paul's. Maurice wrote to Hare, "I expect all justice from them, but I do not expect that I shall retain my place in the college." The most that he could hope for was that, prior to his dismissal, he would be acquitted of all ill-doings.[249] A month passed, and then the committee met to discuss its findings. Maurice's theology was satisfactorily sound. His sense of philanthropy and social responsibility were admirable. *But* there was that awful word, "Socialism." Therefore, "the committee cannot refrain from expressing their deep regret at finding that Professor Maurice's name has been mixed up with publications on the same subject which they consider to be of very questionable tendency."[250] Would it be too unreasonable a request—asked Jelf—that the professor might say something to the effect that he would do his utmost "to bear in mind the duty and importance of not compromising the college?"[251] In answer, Maurice observed that he could not know what might "compromise the college," but that he recognized the authority of the committee to determine what had such an effect.[252]

The Council of King's College had fully expected that the committee would find Maurice unfit as professor of theology; however, having relinquished its role in the investigation, the council could not now ignore the committee's conclusions and refuse its recommendation. Therefore, on 23 January 1852, the council resolved—for the time being, at any rate—to retain their professor. As Maurice's son observes, the trustees "did not forget the lesson, and resolved that in the future they would incur no such risks of a judicial investigation of facts interfering with the carrying out of the righteous decrees of current popular religious periodicals."[253]

In 1852 the scandal abated. At the beginning of the year Maurice ceased to be editor of *The Christian Socialist,* and—as the editorship fell into the hands of Thomas Hughes, soon afterwards replaced by Ludlow—the title itself changed to *The Journal of Association.* By the end of June, the Industrial and Provident Partnerships Bill, "which gave the whole co-operative movement its status," had received legal sanction.[254] Maurice had done his work; he had brought public recognition to the plight of workers and he had showed workmen how, by the principles of association, they could best help themselves. What Maurice had most wanted to do, however, was to make manifest to all the Kingdom of Christ. Cooperative societies were but one practical application of Christian principles and one dramatic illustration of the reality of Christ's kingdom. As the Working Men's Associations grew stronger, the theological foundation was increasingly felt to be an embarrassment and a hindrance to membership, and so Maurice found fewer opportunities to teach. Consequently, his thoughts were redirected towards the education of the working classes, and with the help of volunteers, including Ludlow and Hughes, as 1852 came to a close, weekly lectures on various subject began to be provided for both men and women.

As far as the council of King's College was concerned, 1852 was only the eye of the hurricane. By February of 1853 Maurice was busy writing a series of sermons for Unitarians. "My plan," he wrote to his dying sister, Priscilla, "is to preach sermons, which I can with a little alteration make into essays, on the questions in which they are most interested."[255] From the moment the book was conceived, *Theological Essays* promised to be controversial. Hare—whose health was now steadily deteriorating—wrote of it to Thirlwall, describing it as "a most noble book, worthy of Luther in its dauntless bravery, and fitted to deliver the Church from divers notions, offensive to reason & conscience." Even so, Hare, thinking of its author, solemnly noted, "A good deal of trouble, I am afraid, awaits him."[256] Maurice knew what he was getting into, but he resolutely set his face toward Jerusalem. The collection of seventeen essays made its appearance only a few months later, and after receiving Kingsley's response to it, the author thanked him for his judgment:

> I suppose I should generally demur to any such sentence as that the book might make an era in our ecclesiastical history. But on this occasion I don't, though it would not surprise me if it fell flat on its back, and did not rise again. . . . I knew when I wrote the sentences about eternal death, that I was writing my own sentence at King's College. And so it will be. Jelf is behaving very fairly, even kindly; but the issue is quite certain. I hope to be shown how I may act, so that my tumble may involve no loss of liberty to any English clergyman, but rather a growth of boldness and conviction.[257]

Kingsley applauded the bold essay with which Maurice had concluded the volume, "On Eternal Life and Eternal Death." The author had structured an argument on the basis of a strikingly peculiar interpretation of the word "eternal." The interpretation was one that Maurice had believed to be correct for many years, but he had never before insisted upon it. Now, he was urging it, and although Kingsley did not inquire into the author's motive, Maurice nevertheless explained: "My reason for arguing the point to the extent I have argued it is this: I feel that if it is to be an open question, we must take a higher ground than merely saying it is one. It ought to be open because neither I nor anybody else has a right to force a definition of the word eternal or a theory of punishment on any man, the Articles being silent."[258] In other words, Maurice was attempting to force a judicial decision upon the issue of whether or not a minister of the Church of England has the freedom to interpret Scripture publicly in a manner contrary to the popular imagination when the Articles of the Church are silent on the subject or passage being interpreted. This was not, of course, Maurice's only motive for the essay; truth always carries its own rewards; but, as far as ecclesiastical polity is concerned, it is a motive of considerable importance and one that, unfortunately, is often lost sight of behind the controversial interpretation itself.

The "Eternity" Question

The believer's present possession of eternal life is a fact that Erskine never grows weary of repeating. In *The Brazen Serpent*, he argues, "We have another life in Jesus, . . . even that eternal life which is in the Father, and was manifested in the Son. Yes, *we have it*, reader; there is no doubt on this matter; for 'this is the record, that God *hath given to us eternal life*, and this life is in his Son.'"[259] The "eternal life" is, thus, that life that is in Christ, the fruits of which are made ours through faith and the power of the indwelling Spirit. By all indications, Maurice adopted this teaching before he wrote the first edition of *The Kingdom of Christ*. As an interpretation, its positive message is both theological (in its proper sense of having to do with the existence and nature of God) and soteriological (having to do with the saving work of Christ), and both Erskine and Maurice emphasize it as such, but its negative message—that is, its indirect implications, by virtue of what it does *not* say—is primarily eschatological (having to do with last things). It was this latter aspect of the message that most troubled Maurice's critics.

Maurice recognized that one of the supposedly orthodox Christian teachings that Unitarians found difficult, if not impossible, to accept was the doctrine of eternal punishment for unbelievers. It was also a troublesome doctrine for many Anglicans. In *The Nemesis of Faith* (1849)—J. A. Froude's autobiographical novel of honest doubt that cost him his Oxford fellowship—Markham Sutherland says, in objection to the popular idea of hell, "I believe that fallen creatures perish, perish for ever, for only good can live, and good has not been theirs; but how durst men forge our Saviour's words '*eternal* death' into so horrible a meaning." He continues, "I believe that we may find in the Bible the highest and purest religion . . . ; and, oh, how gladly would I spend my life, in season and out of season, in preaching this! But I must have no hell terrors, none of these fear doctrines; they were not in the early creeds, God knows whether they were ever in the early gospels, or ever passed his lips."[260] At Kingsley's bidding—for Froude had found shelter at Eversley—Maurice read the novel. It seemed to him a "very awful" book, but also one that may be "very profitable." It would be a book profitable to the Church if it would only lead people to seek for the "old faith" and "the root of things."[261] Maurice's essay has, then, as its audience not merely conscientious and devout Unitarians, but also the many Markham Sutherlands in the Established Church.

In the Bible, as Ewald, Bunsen, and Matthew Arnold were all to insist, God is *the Eternal*. The life of God is, by definition, eternal life. W. F. Hook's *Church Dictionary* (1842) defines *eternity* as "An attribute of God, by which is meant infinite duration or existence, without beginning and without end."[262] "Shall we say," asks Maurice, "that Eternal means, in reference to God, 'without beginning or end'? How then can we affix that meaning to Eternal, when we are speaking of man's bliss or misery? Is that without beginning as well as without end?" No, the error lies in our attempt to define God as a "miserable philosophical abstraction," as a mere negation of time—*without* beginning and *without* end. The Bible depicts God as a being of Righteousness, Truth, and Love. To know these divine qualities within oneself and, thus, to realize His spiritual and inward presence, is to partake of "eternal life."[263] Is not the punishment of sin to feel the loss of these qualities, which is the necessary consequence of separation from God's eternal life? "What is Perdition but a loss? What is eternal damnation, but the loss of a good which God had revealed to His creatures, or which He had put them in possession?"[264] It is not, therefore, a future possession or a future loss; it is not even anything that we can attribute to time. Any person "who knows what it is to have been in a state of sin . . . must say that Christ has brought him out of the bonds of *eternal* death."[265]

Jelf was deeply disturbed. He asked Bishop Blomfield for his thoughts. He too was disturbed. Blomfield asked Trench, Maurice's fellow professor of theology at King's, for his thoughts. Trench replied, "I think Maurice's righteous desire to meet antagonists as far as he may, to take their ground, to the end that in the end he may lead them to his, is sometimes pushed too far, leads him into dangerous concessions, and otherwise proves a snare."[266] It was a politic answer—in the common estimation, very safe, very wise. The bishop approved, the archbishop approved, and Trench was afterwards preferred for the bishopric of Gloucester and Bristol. Maurice, on the other hand, was in the habit of appearing neither safe nor wise, and so Blomfield informed Jelf that, as long as Maurice held his chair, no theological students of King's would be received as candidates for Holy Orders.[267]

Jelf then drew up a lengthy response to Maurice's essay. This was, essentially, a declaration of reasons why, he thought, Maurice was unfit as a professor of theology. First, Jelf appealed to the 8th Article of the Church of England, which stipulates that the Nicean, Apostles', and Athanasian creeds "ought thoroughly to be received and believed," and he contended that Maurice had controverted the "damnatory clauses" (vv. 2 and 42) of the Athanasian Creed. To this, Maurice replied, noting that "the Athanasian Creed contains no explanation of the words Everlasting and Eternal, and that whatever sense of them we deduce from Scripture must be applied to them there."[268] Furthermore, Maurice observed that the 42nd Article, drafted during the reign of Edward VI, had condemned the notion that a purgation of sins after this life might lead to ultimate salvation. The fact that such an article was removed during the reign of Elizabeth gives the strongest evidence "that the members of the Church of England have perfect freedom on this subject."[269] There-fore, Jelf's novel idea that the King's College Council has the right to demand an assent to sundry *et cæteras* not included in the Articles of Religion is quite troubling. "I do not see," says Maurice, "how it can fail to alarm every man who attaches any sacredness to his oaths or his subscriptions."[270]

Second, Jelf protested that the controversial essay introduced a new conclusion of its author, one either different from that which he possessed at the time he was hired as a professor or one that he had intentionally concealed from his employers. In response, Maurice observes that, in 1845, before the Department of Theology was even established at King's, he had published a pamphlet, *The New Statute and Mr. Ward*, and that in this pamphlet he had expressly written these words: "I take the words 'æterna vita,' not as they are explained by any Doctor of the Church, by any Council, provincial or œcumenical, but as they are explained by our Lord Himself in His last awful prayer, 'This is life eternal, that they may know Thee the only true God, and Jesus Christ.'" In this same article, he had clearly stated, "It would be an outrage upon my conscience to express assent or consent to any Article which did put 'future state' in the Article for 'eternal life.'"[271] When, in 1846, Jelf approached Maurice and asked him to be a professor of theology, was he to assume that his recent publications had not first been carefully read? Moreover, if Jelf had then expressed his own view of the word "Eternal," that it was synonymous with "Everlasting," and if he had conveyed his expectation that every professor concur in this view, then Maurice would have answered at once, "Sir, I can have nothing to do with your College."[272]

We should note here, more than as a passing point of interest, that Maurice's position stated in the above two paragraphs, relative to the articles, is practically identical with that given by Archbishop Whately in *The Kingdom of Christ Delineated* (1841). Whately explains, it being the case that the articles have been "deliberately and *jointly* drawn up for the very purpose of precisely determining what it was designed should be determined respecting the points they treat of, . . . it seems impossible that any man of ingenuous mind can appeal from the Articles . . . to any other writings, whether by the same or by other authors." In other words, one cannot judiciously appeal to any theologian, including the very framers of the articles, for an authoritative interpretation of the formularies of the Church. "On the contrary," continues Whately, "the very circumstance that opinions going far beyond what the Articles express, or in other respects considerably differing from them, did exist, and were *well known and current*, in the days of our reformers, gives even the *more* force to their *deliberate omissions* of these."[273] This Oxford Noetic clearly understood that clerical subscription was as much intended to restrict in points of doctrine as it was intended to liberate in matters of interpretation. The agreement of Whately and Maurice on this fundamental principle is what unites them as leaders in the Broad Church movement.

The third protest that Jelf leveled against Maurice's position is that his interpretation implied the dangerous notion of ultimate salvation for all. To this charge the professor returns, "I have deliberately rejected the theory of Universalism, knowing what it is; and . . . I should as much refuse an Article which dogmatised in favour of that theory as one that dogmatised in favour of the opposite."[274] It seemed to Maurice that God had placed a veil over the subject of the soul's future state, that although the subject allowed for some speculation, any dogmatizing upon it would be irreverent:

> What I dare not pronounce upon is the *fact* that every will in the universe must be brought into consent with the Divine will. . . . Dare you make it a positive article of faith that God's will, being what the Scripture says it is, shall *not* finally triumph? Nevertheless there is such a darkness over the whole question of the possible resistance of the human will, that I must be silent, and tremble and adore.[275]

As to going into hell, "into the fire that never shall be quenched, where their worm dieth not,"[276] Maurice contends that these are but metaphors to signify the sting of the conscience and the burning wrath of God, and the question is not "whether that fire will go on burning, but what it will or will not consume."[277] If we conclude that the fire consumes neither sin nor sinner, then we had best remove our sandals and tread softly, for the ground upon which we tread is holy, and we come dangerously close to blaspheming against the Spirit of Christ. Maurice follows Origen and Erskine in this matter, without adopting either's elaborate eschatology. For Origen, the Lord's refining fire is medicinal and destroys the evil within the soul as it ascends through the seven heavens toward consummation.[278] Erskine had proclaimed that, in the brazen serpent, "we see a promise that death should die, and that he who had the power of death should be overcome and cast out," and that, "whilst the serpent remains, death remains. . . . He is the first enemy, and he is last to be destroyed. For it is not until after the thousand years are finished, that he, along with death and hell, are to be cast into the lake of fire."[279] Maurice wrote to Jelf, "You can explain to your satisfaction the words that Death and Hell shall be cast into the lake of fire. I do not profess to understand them; but they certainly convey to me an impression of a victory over all moral evil, over all which is contrary to the nature of God."[280]

By the end of August, Maurice had already determined that his continuation at King's was out of the question. Jelf wanted him to resign and to spare the college the inconvenience of a formal tribunal, but Maurice resisted, perceiving that his resignation might suggest to others that he had either confessed his heterodoxy or acknowledged the right of a college president to proclaim *ex cathedra* on doctrinal points undecided by the Articles. To Hare, Maurice wrote, "I have drawn the sword and thrown away the scabbard."[281] Subsequently, on 14 October 1853, all the correspondence between Jelf and Maurice were laid before the council. Two weeks later, on the 27th, the Council of King's College, led by R. W. Penn, Lord Howe, and deferring to the authority of the attending bishop, Blomfield, came to its decisions: (1) Maurice's views "regarding the future punishment of the wicked and the final issues of the day of judgment, are of dangerous tendency, and calculated to unsettle the minds of the theological students of King's College"; (2) Maurice's continuation at the college "would be seriously detrimental to its usefulness"; (3) the Council is "bound in justice" to acknowledge the zeal and ability with which Maurice has discharged his duties.[282]

Gladstone was also present at the council's meeting and documented its proceedings. Not all of the councilmen had bothered to read Maurice's *Essays*, and yet they were unmistakably in a lynching mood. "Certainly," reflects Gladstone, "there is a blinding power in theological rage, which often induces honest men to act like scoundrels."[283] Gladstone proposed that, before acting, the council should recommend that Blomfield "appoint competent theologians," who with care and judicious scholarship might compare Maurice's statements with the formularies of the Church and submit its findings as to whether his doctrines are conformable to or at variance with the Church. Three members were in favor of Gladstone's amendment; seven were opposed.[284]

What Gladstone did not, at the time, realize was that the proceedings of the council were in fact far more devious than he could have imagined. Lonsdale, bishop of Lichfield, who had preceded Jelf as the president of King's and had sent a letter to the council's secretary expressing some degree of sympathy with Maurice's theology, was—by an alleged "oversight" of this same secretary—left uninformed of the council's intent to meet.[285] Samuel Wilberforce, the bishop of Oxford, had written to Jelf as early as August to express his beliefs (1) that there ought not to be "such scandal as to [Maurice's] opinions as should lead to his sacrifice being necessary either for orthodoxy or for King's College" and (2) that there ought not to be "any fear that he will be a false teacher of those committed to him."[286] Seeing that Jelf was adamant, Wilberforce drew up a statement of the charges against Maurice and compared these against the actual doctrine of his essay, and in the process of doing so revised Maurice's expressions in order to make them more palatable. Maurice found this *formula concordiæ* of his teaching a "most full and most satisfactory exposition of its meaning," and so the bishop of Oxford sent this document, along with Maurice's remarks upon it, to the bishop of London. In the accompanying letter, Wilberforce went so far as to express his own belief that "Professor Maurice is entirely orthodox."[287] These documents and letters were, however, entirely ignored by Blomfield.

When Maurice found that he had been dismissed, effective immediately, from King's on the basis of his theological teaching—that he had, basically, been declared a heretic—without benefit of a theological investigation, he was understandably indignant. He was fully prepared to be dismissed on the grounds of his theological disagreements with Jelf, but—if he did not force the issue of a clergyman's freedom of interpretation, and if it appeared to the public that he had been judged and found guilty as a heretic—he would have failed of his purpose. Therefore, he wrote to the council itself, demanding a clear declaration of his guilt: "I think it due, then, to my own character as a clergyman, to the interests of the college, and to the liberties of the English Church, that I should call upon the council, if they pronounce a theological sentence upon me at all, to declare what Article of our faith condemns my teaching."[288] The council, however, following the pious example of Blomfield, turned a deaf ear.

As unfair as the proceedings against Maurice were, our sense of injustice must not lead us to conclude that, had he been granted an ecclesiastical trial, he would have been judged orthodox. A decade later, in late 1862, in the Court of Arches, H. B. Wilson, one of the contributors to *Essays and Reviews*, would be found guilty of heresy and deprived of his clerical office for one year on the ground of this statement:

> The Roman Church has imagined a limbus infantium; we must rather entertain a hope that there shall be found, after the great adjudication, receptacles suitable for those who shall be infants, not as to years of terrestrial life, but as to spiritual development—nurseries as it were and seed-grounds, where the undeveloped may grow up under new conditions—the stunted may become strong, and the perverted be restored.[289]

Upon appeal to the Privy Council, Wilson was acquitted in February 1864, after which Maurice's views upon the "Eternity" question could no longer be argued as opposed to the formularies of the Church of England.

Ludlow published an account of the sticky mess at King's, a story that was honey to the newspapers, and soon all of England was abuzz. The committee of professors at Queen's were, for the most part, sympathetic to their colleague's position. Even so, in the absence of their unanimous support, Maurice resigned. The workers came out *en masse* in support of their advocate. On 27 December, at the Hall of Association, they presented him with testimonials and a speech expressing their wish "that he might not find it a fall to cease to be a professor at King's College and to become the 'Principal of a Working Man's College.'" It was a wish that harmonized perfectly with his own, and so, by 7 February 1854, Maurice had drawn up the scheme which, after debate and revision, "became the basis of the organisation of the Working Men's College."[290]

In the years that followed, numbers of university graduates would obtain their teaching experience by volunteering their services to this college, and they would leave its halls having *received* an education that they could never have obtained at Oxford or Cambridge, for they would have learned something of the mind and heart of the working men and women of England. The students themselves would benefit from the art instruction of John Ruskin, D. G. Rossetti, Burne Jones, Madox Brown, and many other lesser known artists and critics. But art was not the only subject taught. Newly ordained graduates and fellows lectured on Latin, Greek, logic, history, literature, theology, and various other subjects, according to the demand. Thomas Hughes even taught a course on boxing.

"The Broad Church Poet"

As already noted, Maurice's influence among the Cambridge Apostles reached its peak during the early 1830s, when the society was under the leadership of Arthur Henry Hallam. Alfred Tennyson was an Apostle for only a few months, but he had no closer friend than Hallam. And, though the friendship would appear to have ended in September 1833 with a massive cerebral hemorrhage, Tennyson's devotion would prove to be as enduring as his friend's death was sudden. Much of that devotion was expressed in the 130 separate poems of *In Memoriam* (1850), but some of it is also found in the poet's continued regard for Maurice. During Tennyson's honeymoon vacation, in lieu of church services, he read prayers and Maurice's sermons.[291] In 1852, as poet laureate, he asked Maurice to be a godfather to his son, Hallam, and the honor was, to some extent, returned in *Theological Essays*. There, Maurice reprinted several stanzas from Tennyson's Prologue, "Strong Son of God." With the fifth stanza Maurice expressed his hearty assent:

> Our little systems have their day;
>   They have their day and cease to be:

They are but broken lights of Thee,
And thou, O Lord, art more than they.

"Yes!," responds Maurice, "it is deeply and eternally true that 'Thou, O Lord, art more than they.' And therefore it becomes us more earnestly, for the sake of our fellow-men and of all the thoughts and doubts which are stirring in them so mightily at this time, not to let the faith in an actual Son of God be absorbed into any religious or philosophic theories or abstractions."[292]

John Connop Thirlwall, Jr., the great-grandson of the bishop's nephew, refers to *In Memoriam* as "a poetic statement of Broad Church principles."[293] Although Tennyson's masterpiece defies so narrow a definition, we can detect a common strain of thought that runs from Coleridge, through Hare and Maurice, into this work. Certain sentiments expressed by Maurice in his published *Letter* to Jelf regarding the final state seem to be anticipated in these two stanzas:

Oh yet we trust that somehow good
  Will be the final goal of ill,
  To pangs of nature, sins of will,
Defects of doubt, and taints of blood;
          . . . .
Behold we know not anything;
  I can but trust that good shall fall
  At last—far off—at last, to all,
And every winter change to spring.[294]

In these lines F. W. Robertson (1816-1853), preacher to the Brighton working classes, recognized the "vague cry" of the human heart in anticipation of "the final eduction of good from evil." In the two stanzas printed below he finds confirmation that "the Atheism of the Understanding is annihilated by the Heart." In other words, as Robertson clarifies, "We feel God—do not find Him out."[295]

If e'er when faith had fall'n asleep,
  I heard a voice "believe no more"
  And heard an ever-breaking shore
That tumbled in the Godless deep;
A warmth within the breast would melt
  The freezing reason's colder part,
  And like a man in wrath the heart
Stood up and answer'd "I have felt."[296]

Tennyson seems, in such verses, to understand exactly what Maurice means by "revelation," how God communicates *facts* to humanity, truths that do not depend on feelings and vague sensations for their reality, but such truths as are revealed in the social and practical conscience of humanity. R. H. Hutton, in his article on "Tennyson's Theology," concludes, "No theologian ever held more earnestly than

Tennyson that if we are to have a clear vision of God at all, we must have it under the conditions of human life and action."[297]

Moreover, the poet agreed entirely with Maurice that the clearest vision of God possible for humanity is anthropomorphic, yet he distrusted all dogmatic expressions, such as in Articles of Faith. Thus, he wrote of Hallam's struggles to find religious truth as though they were his own struggles:

> Perplext in faith, but pure in deeds,
>   At last he beat his music out,
>   There lives more faith in honest doubt,
>   Believe me, than in half the creeds.[298]

As Maurice listened, it was natural for him to think of Sterling. In that friend, beneath the figments of the Understanding, there was indeed faith—not in any shibboleth or platitude of religion—but in Christ himself, who is the center of every person.

To recover this buried treasure, this pearl of great price, Maurice was willing to dig, and for his efforts he was often misunderstood, sometimes vilified, but always loved by those who knew him. Tennyson, too, in 1833, had been a victim of Croker's spleen. Indeed, so savage was the *Quarterly Review* criticism of *Poems*, so sensitive the poet, that a decade passed before a third volume of verse dared to parade its beauties before the public eye. The harsh treatment endured by Maurice evoked a measure of empathy from Tennyson; thus, after the theologian's dismissal from King's, the laureate sent him a verse-invitation:

> Come, when no graver cares employ,
> God-father, come and see your boy:
>   Your presence will be sun in winter,
> Making the little one leap for joy.
> For, being of that honest few,
> Who give the Fiend himself his due,
>   Should eighty-thousand college-councils
> Thunder "Anathema," friend, at you;
> Should all our churchmen foam in spite
> At you, so careful of the right,
>   Yet one lay-hearth would give you welcome
> (Take it and come) to the Isle of Wight.[299]

With the Working Men's College just beginning, Maurice was, for the time being, much too busy to take advantage of the offer, but he would eventually go and lose his hat in the wind.

The Apostles had sought Tennyson's society and had claimed him as one of their own in 1829, but he failed to attend meetings, and his membership status was soon retracted. In the following two decades the Conversazione Society regarded him as one of their own in a unique sense, without ever receiving in return any reciprocal interest. Finally, in June of 1855, the newly elected secretary for the society, F. J. A. Hort (1828-1892)—one of a number of Rugbeians under Arnold, including C. J. Vaughan, J. P. Gell, Richard A. Cross, and William Bryans, who went on to matriculate at Trinity[300]—announced at the annual dinner that no rules would be violated if Tennyson were to be reelected as an "Honorary Member." Maurice immediately seconded the motion, and—as Tennyson was not present to veto the proposal—the poet laureate once again became an official Apostle.[301]

The Great Debate

1855 began with the death of Archdeacon Hare and ended with the publication of Kingsley's most popular volume of homilies, *Sermons for the Times*. All of the great and characteristic doctrines for which Maurice contended are interpreted and restated in Kingsley's sermons. In his 1854 Preface to the *Theologia Germanica*, Kingsley had defined "eternity" as "that ever-present moral world, governed by ever-living and absolutely necessary laws, in which we and all spirits are now."[302] Accordingly, in the sermon entitled "Salvation," he argues, "To know God and Jesus Christ; that is eternal life. That is all the eternal life which any of us will ever have, my friends. . . . It is a life of goodness, and righteousness, and love, which are eternal as the God from whom they spring; eternal as Christ."[303] Kingsley is as straightforward as Cudworth, according to whom "the substance of Heaven" is Holiness, and were we not such sinners, "neither should we wish for any other Heaven, besides this."[304] Insisting—alongside Maurice, the Cambridge Platonists, and all the truly great philosophers—that the rewards of virtue are inherent, the rector of Eversley observes, "Living faith and good works do not merely lead to heaven, but are heaven itself, that true, real eternal heaven wherein alone men really live. . . . Eternal death, then, is to love no one; to be shut up in the dark prison-house of our own wilful and wayward thoughts and passions, full of spite, suspicion, envy, fear; in fact, in one word, to be a devil."[305] Maurice's presence is in every line, but it is like the presence of the commander in the speech of a noncommissioned officer to his troops. The speech is not measured, the words are not weighed; rather, the message is taken whole, translated, and communicated as to those whose sole task is but to listen and obey.

Henry Longueville Mansel (1820-1871) was not one of Kingsley's parishioners. He was not one of Maurice's disciples. In fact, he did not understand Maurice. They spoke as though in tongues to one another, the one asking, "What meaneth this?," the other mocking, "This man is full of new wine."[306] Mansel, a fellow of St. John's, Oxford, responded to Maurice's position on the "Eternity" question with a published *Letter* to a former fellow of St. John's, L. J. Bernays. Mansel begins by noting that, in order to appropriately deal with all of the issues involved in the question, he would need "a preliminary criticism of the laws and limits of religious thought." Such a work, "even had I the abilities or the leisure to attempt it," he states, "would be out of place here." Instead, Mansel determines to confine himself to what appears to be the primary question regarding "the character of Time, con-sidered as a form of human consciousness."[307] In looking at the question as such, it is obvious that the word "Eternity," as the opposite of "Time," can denote nothing other than a form of consciousness not subject to the law of succession, which is "no human conception at all," and so expresses not a conception, but "the negation of a conception, the acknowledgment of the possible existence of a Being concerning whose consciousness we can only make the negative assertion that it is not like our consciousness."[308]

Now, it seems to me that Mansel, intending to demystify the theologian, has merely taken a point of practical religion and misrepresented it as a metaphysical problem. Maurice, neither in his *Essays* nor in his *Letter* to Jelf, suggests that we are to enter into a consciousness of an "Eternity" that is relative to Time—that is, as a negative concept. Rather, Maurice has argued, in accordance with Scripture,[309] (*a*) that, although all of God's dealings with us, both now and hereafter, including His contest against evil, are represented to us as taking place in a context of time, (*b*) the consciousness of God is not subject to time. Even so, (*c*) God has revealed his con-sciousness to us through the mind of Christ, by his righteousness and love, (*d*) that the life that God has provided for us through Christ is ours through the trans-formation of our minds, by which process Christ, our hope of glory, is formed in us, (*e*) that we can know God not by striving to enter into a condition of consciousness inconceivable to us—which is an absurdity—but by entering into the mind of Christ, (*f*) that we become partakers of the life of God, the life of the Eternal, by knowing God through Christ, and (*g*) that we can be confident that we possess this eternal life—even though we cannot comprehend it—when we, with gratitude and humility, become sharers in the life of the resurrected Christ.

If the truth is to be told, the most insightful statement that Mansel makes in this unfortunate review is to be found in his concluding remarks: "Perhaps, after all, I may have partly misunderstood the position which I have controverted, and may have been fighting with a shadow of my own creation."[310] Hort begged Maurice to write a reply; it would be titled "On the Oxford Logic and its Relation to Theology." But Maurice had too much work on his hands, and besides—as he expressed himself to Kingsley—"What a weary task it is to be explaining and justifying ourselves. God will explain and justify us, if it is necessary, in His good time."[311] What could Maurice now say that he had not already said? Was it possible that he could have expressed himself more clearly? Could he have asked Mansel, without insulting him, to reread the literature that he had reviewed? Was it not the case that "those who refuse to deduce Eternity from Time . . . are simply unintelligible to him."[312] Perhaps, Maurice was wise in deciding not to reply at length, although he did publicly note—in the preface to the second edition of *Patriarchs and Lawgivers of the Old Testament*— that he thought Mansel's opinions unsound and dangerous. Still, if Maurice could have had any notion of the influence that the Oxford tutor would soon exercise over

English thought, we can trust that the singular urgency of the *duty* of a full and public reply would have revealed itself, in no uncertain terms, to Maurice's conscience.

That duty did, finally, become crystal clear toward the end of 1858, as Mansel, then reader in moral and metaphysical philosophy, was delivering his Bampton Lectures, *The Limits of Religious Thought Examined*. Oxford logician and preacher of Lincoln's Inn, William Thomson, the later Archbishop of York, visited Maurice at the time of the Bampton Lectures and spoke of them as "the most unalloyed Atheism that had been heard in England for generations."[313] To Evangelicals, Anglo-Catholics, and doubters searching for an easy road to "belief," the lectures did not in the least come across as Atheism. On the contrary, they were immediately heralded as "the latest expression of Oxford learning and Oxford orthodoxy, which promises to become the *Ductor Dubitantium* [or *Doubter's Guide*] for the nine-teenth century."[314]

The popularity of Mansel's lectures among Oxford students can easily be accounted for on the principle of the pendulum. As noted in the previous chapter, the Tractarian movement was a reaction against Noeticism, which had reached its peak in R. D. Hampden's Bampton Lectures of 1832. Then, Tractarianism overstepped itself in Tract XC, and with the condemnation of W. G. Ward's *Ideal of a Christian Church* (1844) and the secession of J. H. Newman in the following year, there entered in a new period of liberalism and a heightened sense of religious doubt. Now, in 1858—on the eve, as it were, of the controversially rationalist *Essays and Reviews* (1860)—a treatise appears, which appeals to the common sense and establishes the necessity of an external authority for religious truth on the basis of the absurdities of philosophical rationalism and speculation. For every student wearied from having his childlike acquiescence attacked, Mansel appeared as a Gideon in arms. "He was," says his biographer, "single-handed, contunding a host of unbe-lievers,—some, with unpronounceable names and unintelligible theories; and sending them flying before him like dust before the wind." The lectures were heralded as "a triumph seldom equaled and never surpassed by a Bamptom Lecturer."[315] To Mansel's honor, he was immediately appointed, without election, first Waynflete Professor of Moral and Metaphysical Philosophy. Even so, to Maurice, he appeared as a preacher of a gospel other than that which had been received, a gospel that, paradoxically, invites people to "give up the faith which has sustained their souls, that they may not become infidels."[316]

In response to Mansel, Maurice published *What Is Revelation?: A Series of Sermons on the Epiphany; to which are added Lectures to a Student of Theology on the Bampton Lectures of Mr. Mansel* (1859). In this volume—to borrow a phrase from a student of the debate—Maurice strikes Mansel's "shield in no unknightly or unchristian spirit, yet with the sharp end of [his] lance."[317] Despite the rather fierce blow, Mansel was not unhorsed, and encouraged by the indignation of the spectators, he exchanged his lance for a battle-axe, and returned with *An Examin-ation of the Rev. F. D. Maurice's Strictures on the Bampton Lectures of 1858* (1859). The weapon Mansel chose was, however, too unwieldy for his use, and he retired from the field with as much dignity as he could muster, protesting, "I have now done with Mr. Maurice and his criticisms. . . . I hold myself absolved from the obligation to take further notice of him."[318] With the arena to himself, Maurice dismounted and, removing his helmet and politely addressing the audience, delivered his *Sequel to the Inquiry, What Is Revelation?, in a Series of Letters to a Friend* (1860), in which he responds to the attack made against him in the *Examination.* Truly, this exchange might best be appreciated as a sort of literary joust. The object is not attained with any economy of energy, and the blows are often misplaced, but when the field is cleared, we should hope that there is this difference—that what is just and true may be no longer so much in doubt.

The thesis of Mansel's metaphysical sermons is that true and undefiled religion is this—to rest content within the limits of human thought and keep one's mind unspotted by the defilements of speculation, for ye shall know but partial truth, and that partial truth, by its regulative merits, shall set you free:

> If human thought cannot be traced up to an absolutely first principle of all knowledge and all existence; if our highest attainable truths bear the marks of subordination to something higher and unattainable,—it follows, if we are to act or believe at all, that our practice and belief must be based on principles which do not satisfy all the requirements of the speculative reason.[319]

Rejecting the Practical Reason of Kant, denying that there is any human faculty capable of transcending the categories by which all phenomena is recreated according to the capacities of a finite, conditional, and temporal being, Mansel argues that we can have no knowledge of the Infinite, the Absolute, and the Eternal as such. These terms do not even represent actual conceptions, but are only "negative ideas"—that is, by "Infinite" we signify what we do not know, that which is *not* finite.

The human consciousness, Mansel acknowledges, "contains the idea of God," but this is only a negative idea: "The very consciousness of our own limitations of thought bears witness to the existence of the Unlimited, who is beyond thought." Therefore, though "we are compelled to believe" in the existence of God, His existence "cannot be positively apprehended in any mode of the human Consciousness."[320] If we dare aspire to comprehend God, we shall be inevitably led into pantheism, but if we accept the limits of religious thought and "represent the Deity under finite symbols," then our religion must be based "on a more or less refined Anthropomorphism." This is, in fact, the highest religion to which humankind can aspire, and though our religious conceptions will be speculatively false, they will be regulatively true, "designed, not to satisfy our reason, but to guide our practice." A *true* religion is, thus, an accommodation.[321] We may and ought to believe, says Mansel, "that the knowledge which our Creator has permitted us to attain" and "the conceptions which we are compelled to adopt . . . cannot be total falsehood," but in believing this, "we desert the evidence of Reason, to rest on that of Faith."[322]

Whatever internal "evidence" we may have of God's existence, its primary purpose is to lead us to exercise our Understanding to discern the external evidences. Knowing that our judgment in regard to divine things is fallible, "we are bound to bear in mind that *exactly in proportion to the strength of the remaining evidence for the divine origin of a religion, is the probability that we may be mistaken in supposing this or that portion of its contents to be unworthy of God.*"[323] In other words, the more that the external evidence suggests that a religion is divine, the more likely it is that our internal "evidence," measuring things divine by things human, will judge that religion to be unworthy of God. By this manner of reasoning, Mansel arrives at his fundamental maxim: "*The primary and proper object of criticism is not Religion, natural or revealed, but the human mind in its relation to Religion.*"[324] As Maurice observes, Mansel's moral is that which Alexander Pope, in his "Essay on Man," expressed "as perfectly as it can be expressed":[325]

> Know then thyself, presume not God to scan,
> The proper study of mankind is man.

The system against which Mansel contends, that system that presumes God to scan and "whose final test of truth is placed in the direct assent of the human consciousness, whether in the form of logical deduction, or moral judgment, or religious intuition," is Rationalism. Appealing to his own reason or the reason of his age, the Rationalist claims "the right of determining what is essential to religion and what is not" and exercises "the privilege of accepting or rejecting any given revelation, wholly or in part."[326] This is the same enemy that H. J. Rose identified in the Preface to his *State of Protestantism in Germany, Described*. Rose distinguished three classifications of Rationalists: (1) those who receive Christianity as a system *only* because their reason approves of it; (2) those who, while purporting to accept Christianity, reject those parts of it that appear contrary to their reason "and consider the object of Christianity to be that of introducing into the world such a religion as reason can comprehend"; and (3) those who presume to establish on internal proofs, rather than on miracles, the divine nature of Christianity. This latter group "allow in theory that revelation may contain what are technically called much above reason," but in practice reject those doctrines that are allegedly contrary to reason. Thus, whereas the first two groups of Rationalists "set no limits at all to the powers of reason in matters of faith," this third group "set such a limit in theory but not in practice."[327] These three classifications correspond to Mansel's (1) Dogmatists, (2) Vulgar Rationalists, and (3) Mystics. Maurice falls into this latter group, whose method is "the method of Mysticism, and of that Rationalism which agrees with Mysticism, in referring the knowledge of divine things to an extraordinary and abnormal process of intuition or thought," professing "a knowledge of God by direct apprehension."[328]

Rose directed his attack against German forms of religious rationalism. Mansel, writing over thirty years later, established the connection between the post-Kantian rationalists of Germany and England, particularly of Schleiermacher and Francis Newman, although very many theologians are exposed to his contempt. What both Mansel and Rose have in common is their insistence upon the necessity of a submission to an external form of religious authority, whether that be ecclesiastical formularies or Scripture.[329] For Mansel, external evidences have their value in demonstrating that the weight of evidence is in favor of Scripture *as a Revelation from God*. Once this is demonstrated, the doctrines of Scripture "must be unconditionally received, not as reasonable, nor as unreasonable, but as scriptural."[330] Of course, doubts will persist, for God "has permitted speculative difficulties to exist as the trial and the discipline of sharp and subtle intellects, as he has permitted moral temptations to form the trial and the discipline of strong and eager passions."[331] In other words, doubts are to be thought of as trials of faith which can be overcome through prayer and a humble acceptance of the limits of our religious thought.

A more direct assault, from within the Church, against the principles of the Broad Church movement is difficult to imagine, and yet a refutation was to issue from none of the Broad Churchmen more intimately connected with Oxford, such as Benjamin Jowett or A. P. Stanley. Jowett, professor of Greek, always a target of Mansel's criticism, seems to have gone out of his way to avoid contact with the logician and never even owned a copy of one of his works.[332] Lionel Tollemache recalled running into Jowett immediately after one of Mansel's lectures: "How much have you learnt about the unconditional?" Jowett asked and, laughing, passed on, not waiting for a reply.[333] Years later, in a Balliol sermon of 1876, Jowett declared in his no-nonsense, Johnsonian manner of cutting through metaphysical knots, "The highest and best that we can conceive, whether revealed to us in the person of Christ or in any other, *that* is God." He goes on to explain, "Because this is relative to our minds, and therefore necessarily imperfect, we must not cast it away from us, or seek for some other unknown truth which can be described only by negatives."[334]

Baden Powell, professor of geometry—one of the two remaining "Noetics" at Oxford, the other being Edward Hawkins—and Stanley, professor of ecclesiastical history, also steered clear from a confrontation. From among the contributors of *Essays and Reviews*, only Rowland Williams condescended to take notice of Mansel. He expressed his regret that the lecturer had not "added the rudiments of Biblical criticism" to his dialectical abilities, and recognized that, as a result of this want of knowledge, "the author is a mere gladiator hitting in the dark, and his blows fall heaviest on what it was his duty to defend."[335] When, in 1861, Goldwin Smith, the Regius Professor of Modern History, launched his assault against the Bampton Lecturer, Matthew Arnold found him looking miserable—"and no wonder, for he passes his life in the most acrimonious attacking and being attacked." Arnold goes on to explain that, "in so small a society as that of Oxford, this sort of thing creates much embarrassment and scandal."[336] This may, in part explain the lack of opposition that Mansel met with for so long at Oxford. Francis Newman, former professor of political economy, had been attacked repeatedly and at length in the Notes to Mansel's lectures, but—even though he was no longer part of Oxford society, the fact that he was now being assailed from every direction by Evangelicals may account for his easy dismissal of Mansel.[337]

Maurice too had other adversaries and would have been content to leave the professor of moral and metaphysical philosophy to his logical devices, were it not for his growing popularity and position of influence. In little over a year, *The Limits of Religious Thought Examined* had gone into its fourth edition and was as popular in the United States as in England. Maurice was deeply troubled: "I found him telling the students who listened to him that they were to receive the Bible as a whole or not at all; so leading many to place it on their shelves as a book which it was safe to accept without any careful study of its contents; so driving others who felt doubts about particular passages, to cast it aside altogether."[338] For Maurice, as a refutation became increasingly a demand of the conscience, it ceased to be regarded as an option. "This is the ground of my conflict with Mr. Mansel," he explains. "He seems to me to crush the search after Truth, all that is expressed in the word *Philosophy*, by crushing at the same time the discovery of Truth, all that is expressed in the word *Revelation*."[339]

Perhaps the key to Maurice's difference with Mansel can best be detected in the manner in which they approach what Bishop Butler calls the *analogy* between Nature and Religion, or between things temporal and things eternal. As Mansel states the case, "With [Butler], the constitution of nature is the better known and clearer member of the analogy, which is employed to throw light on the parallel difficulties of religion, natural or revealed. . . . Mr. Maurice reverses the analogy, making revelation the better known term, which is to throw light on the difficulties in nature."[340] In noting this fact, Mansel supposed he was demonstrating that his opponent had failed to understand Butler and that, consequently, his method was fundamentally flawed. In fact, Mansel was only pointing out that with Maurice—as with Platonists generally—the difference between the spiritual and physical worlds is the difference between substance and form. All reality has its origin in God. The truths of theology or principles of religion are, therefore—as we have seen in *Subscription No Bondage*—the foundation upon which the study of all other sciences can take place. Nothing can be genuinely known unless and until we know God.

The issue between Mansel and Maurice is whether, in fact, we *can* know God. It is an issue that Mansel confuses and obfuscates, but it is, nevertheless, the central point of dispute. Although the lecturer is well aware that terms are not things, his scholastic method of argument leads him into the realist fallacy of conflating the *concepts* "Infinite," "Absolute," and "Eternal," with *that which is* Infinite, Absolute, and Eternal—the "I AM" that is the object of Christian worship. As Maurice explains, Mansel's "whole argument turns not on my consciousness of finite *things*, and my incapacity for being conscious of infinite *things*; but upon my consciousness of the *term* finite, and the *term* infinite."[341] Of course, if God is merely a cosmic abstraction, The Infinite, then we can have no consciousness of It; but, if God is an Infinite Being (or Person), to whom we, as spiritual beings (or persons) made in His image, are consubstantially related, then we may apprehend Him as one person apprehends another, through relationship. Maurice believes that we do have "a faculty of knowing the Being in whom we live and move, as a child knows its father." But, on the other hand, if Mansel is disputing the existence of "a faculty by which the child *comprehends* the Father, the Finite the Infinite, most persons, of all schools, would *in terms* repel so monstrous a notion."[342] Thus, Maurice distinguishes between knowing God by spiritual *apprehension* and knowing God by cognitive *comprehension*, and he specifically dissociates himself from the latter theory, a sort of vulgar rationalism. R. H. Hutton nicely summarizes Maurice's position: "To know is not to have a notion which stands in the place of the true object, but to be in direct communion with the true object, and this is exactly most possible, where theory or complete knowledge is least possible."[343]

There is not a single doctrine of Christianity our understanding of which is not significantly affected by how we respond to this central issue of whether we have any faculty by which we may apprehend God. Accordingly, we will settle the question whether the Incarnation is an accommodation to our finite capacities, "not to tell us what God is in His absolute nature, but how He wills us to think of Him in our present finite state," or whether it is an unveiling of the nature of God, "the actual discovery of what the Eternal Being is in the Person of a Man."[344] We will then determine whether Inspiration is a divine departure from the nature of things in order to communicate regulative truths to a few persons in order to satisfy our spiritual wants, or whether—because we are all spirit beings with Christ as our head and capable, through faith, of being united to God by His Spirit—there is a Divine Word to enlighten us and a Divine Spirit to inspire us.[345] We will then decide whether Revelation is contained in a book, to be taken whole or not at all, or whether it is that unveiling whereof the book speaks.[346] And, when we have made this last decision, we shall also know whether God desires that we submit our reason to the dogmas of an external authority, or whether there is a candle of the Lord that teaches us "that truth has never thriven except in conflict; that men have never sought the true peace till they have rejected the false peace; that those who make the soul a solitude, and call it peace, must part with the peace which passeth understanding and dwells in the knowledge of God."[347]

On Mars Hill St. Paul addressed the Athenians in regard to an altar with this inscription: *Agnosto Theo* (To the Unknown God). Using this as his text, the Apostle continues, "Whom . . . ye ignorantly worship, him declare I unto you."[348] From this same inscription, T. H. Huxley coined the term "Agnostic." References to the Mars Hill address can be found in Hamilton and Mansel, and it was from these two philosophers that both Herbert Spencer and Huxley developed the theory of Agnosticism.[349] Leslie Stephen tells us, "The Agnostic is one who asserts—what no one denies—that there are limits to the sphere of human intelligence. He asserts, further, what many theologians have expressly maintained, that those limits are such as to exclude at least what [G. H.] Lewes called 'metempirical' knowledge." Stephen had once sat at the feet of Maurice, but he could not discern those mystical truths that Maurice seemed to see as though in sunbeams. Subsequently, he came under the influence of Mansel, who in 1868, as Regius Professor of Ecclesiastical History, delivered his *Lectures on the Gnostic Heresies*. Stephen tells us, "The whole substance of his argument was simply and solely the assertion of the first principles of Agnosticism."[350]

Now, here is a paradox worthy of contemplation: Maurice had been deposed from his professorship for teaching that this is *eternal life*, that we may *know* the only true God, whereas Mansel, for proclaiming from the rooftops that we *cannot know* God, was, at the end of 1868, elevated to the deanery of St. Paul's. Well might the events have given Maurice "a kind of staggering sensation as if everything was turned upside down, and as if we were approaching a day in which the most utter denial would take the shape of unquestioning acquiescence."[351]

Darwin and the Essayists

In the years 1859 and 1860 both Kingsley and Maurice received royal or government preferment. First, Kingsley, shortly after preaching before Victoria and Albert at Buckingham Palace, was made one of Her Majesty's chaplains. In the following year Prime Minister Palmerston appointed Maurice to the ministry of the Chapel of St. Peter's, on Vere Street. At about the same time, Palmerston offered Kingsley the Regius Professorship of Modern History at Cambridge. Whewell, master of Trinity, initially opposed the appointment. The Rector of Eversley was not anyone's first choice. One church historian, somewhat unkind to Kingsley, states the case bluntly: "They had wanted someone else. But they had not wanted him much."[352] In 1864, Kingsley recklessly entered into controversy with J. H. Newman, who drew blood and left his victim to the feeding frenzy of the popular press.[353] Eventually, in October 1866, Maurice was elected to the professorship of moral philosophy, and for over two years, until Kingsley's resignation in 1869, Cambridge undergraduates had the rare privilege of concurrently attending lectures by both the Master and his interpreter. Kingsley's successor was another Maurician, John R. Seeley, the author of *Ecce Homo* (1865).[354] Maurice remained at Cambridge until his death on 30 March 1872. Had he lived another two years, he would have seen the elevation of Kingsley as canon of Westminster Abbey, a position under Dean Stanley that he hardly had occasion to enjoy before his own death on 31 January 1875. There can be no doubt that these appointments gave the "revolutionary" duo both position and respectability and so worked upon the public imagination in a manner contrary to that of the popular religious press.

In September 1860 Maurice preached his inaugural chapel sermons, on "The Faith of the Liturgy" and "The Doctrine of the Thirty-Nine Articles." Meanwhile, Kingsley was in Ireland, preparing his lectures in the company of his brother-in-law,

J. A. Froude. In November Kingsley triumphantly re-entered Cambridge to present his inaugural lecture on "The Limits of Exact Science Applied to History," which was followed by his first course, "The Roman and the Teuton." William Stubbs, afterwards bishop of Oxford (1889-1901), thought he recognized mutual influence:

> Froude informs the Scottish youth
>   That parsons do not care for truth.
> The Reverend Canon Kingsley cries,
>   History is a pack of lies.
> What cause for judgments so malign?
>   A brief reflexion solves the mystery—
> Froude believes Kingsley a divine,
>   And Kingsley goes to Froude for History.[355]

If Kingsley's professorship was, at first, a subject of amusement among mature scholars, the popularity of his lectures tended to arouse other, less pleasant, feelings. Yet, student evaluations counted for something then, as now, and Cambridge undergraduates flocked to Kingsley for history. "We crowded him out of room after room," remembers one of his students, "till he had to have the largest of all the schools, and we crowded that—crammed it. For undergraduates are an affectionate race, and every one of us who wished to live as a man ought to live, felt that the Professor of Modern History was a friend indeed."[356]

Charles Darwin's great work *On the Origin of Species* had appeared in November 1859, and the zoological and geological sections of the Cambridge scientific community, to which Kingsley was irresistibly attracted, were alive with debate. Theories of ascent and descent had always been popular with Platonists and occupy a central position in the Neo-Platonist cosmogony. Moreover, Cambridge Platonists Cudworth and More appealed to Aristotle for their theory of a Plastic Nature, an early modern notion of evolution, and thus, it should not be surprising to anyone that Kingsley, a self-professed Platonist, eagerly welcomed Darwin's theory, finding that it facilitated a greater understanding of God's "special Providences."[357] In a letter to a like-minded fellow professor, he explains "that the soul of each living being down to the lowest, secretes the body thereof, as a snail secretes its shell, and that the body is nothing more than the expression, in terms of matter, of the stage of development to which the being has arrived."[358] In keeping with this hypothesis, Kingsley has a fairy instruct little Tom, in *The Water Babies* (1863), "There are two sides to every question; . . . if I can turn beasts into men, I can, by the same laws of circumstance, and selection, and competition, turn men into beasts."[359] In a letter to Maurice, Kingsley observes that the theologians who refuse to acknowledge the truth of evolution "are forced to try all sorts of subterfuges as to fact, or else by evoking the *odium theologicum*." On the other hand, those theologians who accept the new discoveries "find that now they have got rid of an interfering God—a master-magician, as I call it—they have to choose between the

absolute empire of accident, and a living, immanent, ever-working God."³⁶⁰ Maurice
was a theologian of this latter type, accepting every discovery of truth as a revelation
of God to man.³⁶¹

Darwin's ink hardly had time to dry before, in 1860, a book was released that
resulted in the greatest theological scandal of the English Church since the publication of Tract XC. Seven articles thought to represent the progressive theology of
the Church were collected and, on March 21, published as a single volume, *Essays
and Reviews*. Two of the seven authors, Benjamin Jowett and Baden Powell, were
Oxford dons, although Powell—the only of the essayists to mention Darwin's
"masterly volume"³⁶²—died just weeks after the publication. Another of the authors,
Frederick Temple, graduate of Balliol, had succeeded A. C. Tait at Rugby as
headmaster and would, in 1897, follow him to Canterbury as archbishop. H. B.
Wilson and Mark Pattison were also Oxonians, the former a long-time fellow of St.
John's and one of the four tutors, including Tait, who launched the protest against
Tract XC; the latter was a fellow of Lincoln and author of the posthumously
published anti-Tractarian *Memoirs*. Only two of the seven were from Cambridge.
These were C. W. Goodwin, graduate of St. Catharine's Hall, and Rowland
Williams, who served as a tutor in classics at King's before becoming vice-principal
and professor of Hebrew at St. David's College, in Wales. Despite the ecclesiastical
furor raised by Williams's essay on "Bunsen's Biblical Researches"—which led to a
conviction in the Court of Arches on the charge of heresy, for which he was
afterwards acquitted by the Privy Council—the volume of essays was, understandably, associated in the public mind with Oxford.³⁶³

Within two months, the first edition of 1,000 copies had sold out. A second
edition was released in June. In August of 1860, *Essays and Reviews* was reprinted
in the United States, under a Unitarian editor, F. H. Hedge, who praised in it the
promise of the Broad Church, "whose characteristics are breadth and freedom of
view, and earnest spirit of inquiry and resolute criticism, joined to a reverent regard
for ecclesiastical tradition and the common faith of mankind."³⁶⁴ Now, as a lexical
item, "Broad Church," although used as early as the late 1840s, had not, before
1860, entered into common parlance. (See the Introduction.) It was, as yet, a term
in search of its meaning. Before the end of 1860, *Essays and Reviews* was heralded
as *the* representation of Broad Church views on various subjects, and consequently,
"Broad-Churchism" became, in popular usage, synonymous with Oxford liberalism.
Furthermore, because Oxford liberalism was frequently represented as the exaggerated reaction against the Oxford Movement, we find the enemies of liberalism
and rationalism now depicting the Broad Church as the heretical antithesis of
Tractarianism. Thus, in a pamphlet entitled *Puseyism the School of the Infidels, or
"Broad Church" the Offspring of "High Church,"* the anonymous author presents
his case that "Rationalism is the necessary action and result of Puseyism."³⁶⁵

For a period, there was a common association of the Broad Church "party" with
whatever liberal thought could be extracted from *Essays and Reviews*. An anonymous article appearing in 1861 under the editorship of the Presbyterian professor

Charles Hodge takes this view to its extreme. The author, beginning with the assumption that each contributor to *Essays and Reviews* is representative of a single Broad Church party, takes all of the contributions as parts of one whole. Thus, he manipulates the book as he would the Bible, handling its contents as though by a single author and attempting to ascertain a single, coherent doctrine by means of a deductive hermeneutic. For example, in order to arrive at "the ecclesiology of this school," he produces a concatenation of passages (identified only by page reference, not by author) from which he arrives at his definitional summary.[366] Thirlwall, unfortunately, perpetuated the error by his Episcopal Charge of 1863, in which he marveled that anyone could fail to see that the volume is "the product of one school."[367]

That the volume made an important contribution to the history of the Broad Church cannot be denied. Its authors were Christian scholars of varying ability, all more or less independent thinkers, and—although not all were clergymen—all were distinguished members of what Coleridge had called the *Clerisy*. We might even argue that their practice, as with all Broad Churchmen, was guided by principles of charity and toleration. Nevertheless, no church historian now alleges that the collection or any one of its essays is representative of the movement. This must be appreciated before we can develop any adequate conception of the position of Maurice and Kingsley in relation to what was then called the "Broad Church." To this end, we should first note their perspective, along with its context, on the controversial essays.

The agitation over *Essays and Reviews* commenced in October 1860, when Positivist critic Frederic Harrison—the same critic who would later attack Matthew Arnold's "Culture and Its Enemies" and who seems to have been perpetually prepared to be indignant whenever professed Christians dared to be modern—published his *Westminster Review* article on "Neo-Christianity," provoking to reaction the "toothless watchdogs of orthodoxy."[368] Wilberforce, bishop of Oxford, responded in his Episcopal Charge of 7 November. After quoting various objectionable phrases, mostly from Williams's and Wilson's essays, he appeals to the clergy of his diocese: "When these things are spoken, is it not time for us . . . to combine together in prayer, and trust, and labour, and love, and watching, lest whilst we dispute endlessly about the lesser matters of the law, we be robbed unawares of the very foundations of the faith?"[369]

One month later, on 7 December, almost 1,500 Oxonian clergymen met in Convocation to elect a new professor of Sanskrit—or, more accurately, to prevent the election of F. Max Müller, the German philologist who had published on Sanskrit and was a friend of Bunsen, Jowett, and Stanley. "On that occasion," records Stanley, "when the University rejected the services of the most eminent scholar within her walls, there was arrayed against him a vast mass of the Conservative elements of the country, both theological and political." Pusey's organizational talents were not wanting for the occasion. Out of the fermentation arose "the first distinct conception of an organized attack on the volume with which Professor

Müller's friends or country had been connected in the public mind."[370] At this time began the canvassing for signatures supporting the "Protest of the Clergy" (or "Oxford Manifesto"). This document, after noting that certain opinions in the offending volume have the "tendency . . . to annihilate the authority of the Bible as the Inspired Word of God," entreated the archbishop of Canterbury "to devise such measures as may, with God's blessing, 'banish and drive away' from our Church all such 'erroneous and strange doctrines.'"[371] This document, along with seventy-six pages of signatures recording the protest of about 8,500 clergymen, was presented to Archbishop Sumner on 13 March 1861. In the meanwhile, Wilberforce contributed to the cause by publishing a scathing, but anonymous, denunciation of *Essays and Reviews* in the January issue of *The Quarterly*.

Of course, the archbishop knew of the "Protest" before he received it, and he anticipated it by holding an episcopal conference, with the two archbishops and seventeen bishops in attendance, at Lambeth Palace on February 1. Oxford "Noetic" R. D. Hamden, now bishop of Hereford, strongly urged a course of legal persecution against the heretics, it being "a question of Christianity or no Christianity."[372] Tait, now bishop of London, condemned the entire volume, despite having acquitted several of the authors in private conversation with Stanley.[373] Both Stanley and Temple were more than mildly disappointed by what appeared to them as Tait's duplicitous conduct. The cool, level-headed Thirlwall, paraphrasing a passage from Glanvill's *Vanity of Dogmatizing*, dismissed the number of signatures on the petition as of no significance: "I consider them in the light of a row of figures preceded by a decimal point, so that however far the series may be prolonged, it never can rise to the value of a single unit."[374] Nevertheless, he too was persuaded to join ranks with Wilberforce against the essayists. "We must conclude," says Thirlwall's biographer, "that Wilberforce wove an extraordinary charm and succeeded in convincing Thirlwall that the clerical authors were sheer sceptics."[375] Immediately following the conference, Wilberforce drafted the "Episcopal Manifesto," which was published in the *Times* on 16 February. Expressing the opinion of the episcopacy, the document pronounces grave doubts as to the orthodoxy of the essayists: "We cannot understand how their opinions can be held consistently with an honest subscription to the formularies of our Church." Moreover, it assures the public that the bishops are considering the most promising means by which to censure the heretics and condemn their views.

This is the historical context in which we are to consider the letters of Maurice and Kingsley to Stanley. The first letter, written on 12 February, is from Maurice:

> I am greatly distressed at the Episcopal movement about the "Essays and Reviews." As my only hope of resisting the devil worship of the religious world lies in preaching the full revelation of God in Christ set forth in the Bible, I cannot have much sympathy with the book generally. But I look upon the efforts to suppress it as mere struggles to keep off the question, "What dost thou believe? dost thou believe in anything?" which must be

> forced upon each of us, the bishops included. The orthodoxy which
> covers our Atheism must be broken through, and whether it is done by the
> "Essays and Reviews" or in any other way, seems to me a matter of in-
> difference, though it is not a matter of indifference whether the Church
> shall be committed to a new persecution which must make the new
> reformation, when it comes, more complicated and terrible.[376]

The shape of the controversy developing appeared to Maurice as symptomatic of a constitutional disorder in the body of Christ, a disease infecting the Church much more deeply than imagined by the bishops. When Maurice speaks of "the orthodoxy which covers our Atheism," he is speaking in the dialect of Erskine, who tells us, "Where the living personality of God is lost, there is atheism." There may be an honest subscription to the Articles, a perfect adherence to the formularies, and a resisting of every appearance of evil, "and therefore the age thinks itself a religious and God-fearing age, but it is not the *living God* that is worshiped."[377] Maurice had no interest in protecting a religion, and he knew that God needed no protection. To the bishop of Argyll, Maurice wrote, "I feel, as Mr. Erskine does, how hopeless it is to extract any theology or humanity from the 'Essays and Reviews.' But I cannot think that the fears which are expressed of them betoken much confidence in the Bible or in God."[378] Maurice's own confidence in the compelling evidence of truth is clear from this statement of his pedagogical method:

> I know that if [young men] think, they must pass, some more, some less,
> consciously through phases of Arianism, Sabellianism, Tritheism,
> through Pantheism in many shapes. I know that they will be often on the
> borders of Atheism. I deliberately stir up the thoughts which will be
> drawn in these directions; I give them the pledge and hope of a home and
> resting-place after their toil; I say it is nigh, not far off. . . . Spinozism,
> Hegelism, Comtism—all may offer themselves to you on your pil-
> grimage; you may turn in for a while and rest in any of them; and God, not
> we, must, if our faith is true, teach you that there is any larger and freer
> dwelling-place than that which they afford.[379]

Although Kingsley himself had passed through several phases of thought before returning to Christianity, he did not fully share his master's optimism in regard to the power of truth over human depravity and ignorance. When approached by a curate with the inquiry, whether he should read *Essays and Reviews*, Kingsley responded, "By no means. They will disturb your mind with questions which you are too young to solve."[380]

On 19 February, after the publication of the "Episcopal Manifesto," Kingsley assured Stanley that, as the prevailing spirit in Cambridge was "live and let live," the essayists had nothing to fear from Cambridge dons and scholars. The ideas expressed in *Essays and Reviews* appear revolutionary to the Church only because the Church has for so long resisted their expression. On the other hand, the essayists had not provided anything useful, and so they could not expect to receive any grand gestures in their defense:

> There is little or nothing, says Cambridge, in that book which we have not all of us been through already. Doubts, denials, destructions—we have faced them till we are tired of them. But we have faced them in silence, hoping to find a positive solution. Here comes a book which states all the old doubts and difficulties, and gives us nothing instead. Here are men still pulling down, with far weaker hands than the Germans, from whom they borrow, and building up *nothing* instead. So we will preserve a stoic calm. We wish them all well. We will see fair play for them, according to the forms of English law and public opinion. But they must fight their own battle.[381]

The older generation of Christian scholars had already passed through the valley of the shadow of doubts; they had already learned that shadows are no substances, but only phenomena associated with passing clouds, mere vapors obstructing the light of day. Surely, reasoned Kingsley, as seasoned pilgrims, these Oxford dons have something more to offer their students than studies demonstrating the reality of the clouds.

Maurice and the Broad Church

No churchman or politician, without devoting time and labor to the study of Maurice's writings, could anticipate where Maurice would stand relative to any controversial issue. His principles were not those of any party and could not easily be surmised. Nevertheless, they were principles that were being adopted by others and were making a difference in the Church. Thus, both churchmen and politicians were beginning to feel themselves obliged to know Maurice, and—as his biographer states—"It was provoking to be obliged to know about him." Most people, then as now, resolved their dilemma not by actually reading his works, but "by dubbing him a Broad-Churchman, not that they had the faintest notion what they meant by the phrase, but that at least it was an expression of common use, and so one might be supposed to know something about it."[382]

The existence of a distinct Coleridgean School or Cambridge Theology and its relation to the Broad Church was noted by James Martineau in an 1856 article on the "Personal Influences on Present Theology."[383] In the following year, the Evangelical theologian James Rigg elaborated on Martineau's observation, demonstrating not only that Maurice, Kingsley, and Hare belong to the Coleridgean School, but also that this unique movement has unmistakable affinities with Oxford liberal theology. Rigg's book,[384] which appears to endorse, with qualifications, William Palmer's recognition in 1849 of a larger "School"—as discussed earlier in this chapter— attained a very modest circulation, and his conception of the Broad Church could not compete with the scandalmongering and sensationalism offered for public consumption subsequent to the publication of *Essays and Reviews*. Thus, in the early 1860s, what "one might be supposed to know" about the Broad Church was that it is a liberal party with roots in the Oxford reaction of the 1840s against the Tractarians, and that it had, moreover, obtained its tools of destruction from handbooks of logic and German critics.

As unsatisfactory as this popular definition now appears, Maurice no doubt had something like this in mind when the term "Broad Church" was brought to his attention a few months before the publication of *Essays and Reviews*. His response is significant: "I do not know well what the Broad Church is. I always took it to be a fiction of Conybeare's. If it means anything, I suppose it is a representation, under different modifications, of that creed which is contained in Whately's books, or of that which has arisen at Oxford out of the reaction against Tractarianism."[385] W. J. Conybeare had, in 1853, described the Broad Church as one of the three parties of the Church of England that, along with the Low and High Church, "have always existed, under different phases, and with more or less of life."[386] What Maurice calls Conybeare's "fiction" is, in fact, a logical and moral contradiction—a *party* that inscribes "no party" on its banners.

Charles R. Sanders, in his doctoral dissertation of 1935, *The Relation of Frederick Denison Maurice to Coleridge*, accounts for Maurice's persistent denial that he should be called a Broad Churchman. As I cannot improve upon the reasons given by Sanders, my only attempt here will be to support them with illustrations of my own choosing. First, Maurice "feared either that Broad-Churchmen were already a party or that they showed a strong tendency to become one."[387] We have seen that Maurice held as a fundamental *fact* that Christ is the Head of the human race, regardless of whether or not one accepts the fact. Baptism implies an acknowledgment of this fact and is a "sign of admission into Christ's spiritual and universal kingdom." The Christian idea of baptism "assumes Christ to be the Lord of man; it assumes that men are created in him; that this is the constitution of our race; that therefore all attempts of men to reduce themselves into separate units are contradictory and abortive."[388] All true Christian fellowship is possible through faith in our common relationship to God through Christ. This was God's broad Church. To make mere opinions the basis for fellowship seemed, to Maurice, to constitute a denial of a fellowship that God had already established and an attempt to create one upon some other foundation.

Second, Maurice regarded Broad Churchmen as "the sort of liberals who cared little or nothing for the time-honored beliefs and practices of the Church of England, or for the study of theology."[389] Whereas Maurice had argued, in *Subscription No Bondage*, that the Articles provide a foundation for thought, the Liberals had contended that the act of subscription implies "the renunciation of a right to think, and, since none could renounce that right, it involved dishonesty." These Liberals, wrote Maurice in 1870, "have acquired a new name. They are called Broad Churchmen now, and delight to be called so. But their breadth seems to me narrowness."[390]

To Maurice, the Thirty-nine Articles were not a deterrent to a more comprehensive fellowship, but were rather the only means whereby it might be attained: "I look upon them," he explained to Hare, "as an invaluable charter, protecting us against a system which once enslaved and might enslave us again; protecting us also against the systems of the present day. . . . With the Articles, we can defy them."[391]The prayer book too Maurice defended as "the protection of the Church against Anglicanism and Evangelicalism and Liberalism and Romanism and Rationalism, and till these different devils cease to torment us, I will, with God's help, use this shield against them, whether other people prefer their party prayers to it or not."[392] The Catholicity of the English Church seemed to depend upon the preservation of those time-tested formularies painstakingly composed not by mere flesh and blood, but rather by men who were inspired by a holy and indwelling spirit to rise above themselves and to serve the needs of a Christian nation.

What Maurice contributed to the Broad Church was, above all else, his clear recognition that, once the movement degenerated into a party, the appellation of "Broad Church" would become a contradiction. In 1850 A. P. Stanley, in his article on "The Gorham Controversy," defined the Church of England as, "by the very condition of its being, neither High nor Low, but Broad." "Broad Church," in this sense, as John Tulloch observes, "would not have been repudiated, but would have been willingly accepted by Mr. Maurice."[393] Maurice reminds us that our opposition is not against High Church views or Low Church views, but against the seeds of sectarianism, which would make of our opinions a basis for exclusion, and against that amnesia-producing empiricism that is forever striving to forget that Christ is the center and ground of all human fellowship. More than any other Victorian clergyman, Maurice emphasizes these points, both in his doctrine and by means of his practice, and for this service he is rightly regarded as *the* theologian of the Broad Church movement.

Notes

1. Thomas Fuller, *The History of the University of Cambridge, from the Conquest to the Year 1634*, ed. Marmaduke Prickett and Thomas Wright (Cambridge: Cambridge University Press, 1840), 236.

2. James Stephen, "The Evangelical Succession," *Essays in Ecclesiastical Biography*, 2 vols. (London: Longman, Brown, Green, and Longmans, 1849), 2:65-202, 128.

3. G. R. Balleine, *A History of the Evangelical Party in the Church of England* (1908; London: Longmans, Green, and Co., 1933), 127-28.

4. This Christopher Wordsworth (1774-1846), who was appointed master of Trinity in 1820 on the recommendation of Archbishop Sutton, the father of one of his pupils, is the brother of the poet William and the father of Christopher Wordsworth (1807-1895), bishop

of Lincoln (Robert Robson, "Trinity College in the Age of Peel," *Ideas and Institutions of Victorian Britain*, ed. R. Robson [London: G. Bell and Sons, 1967], 312-35, 314-15). It is to this latter Wordsworth that Matthew Arnold refers, when he writes to Huxley (December 1875), "the Bp of Lincoln is an aggravating old woman" (Cecil Y. Lang, ed., *The Letters of Matthew Arnold*, 5 vols. [Charlottesville: University Press of Virginia, 1996-2000], 4:290).

5. D. A. Winstanley, *Early Victorian Cambridge* (Cambridge: Cambridge University Press, 1940), 19-24; Francis Warre Cornish, *The English Church in the Nineteenth Century, Part I* (London: Macmillan and Co., 1933), 42-44.

6. John Connop Thirlwall Jr., *Connop Thirlwall: Historian and Theologian* (London: SPCK, 1936), 14.

7. John Willis Clark and Thomas McKenny Hughes, *The Life and Letters of the Reverend Adam Sedgwick*, 2 vols. (Cambridge: Cambridge University Press, 1890), 1:105.

8. Winstanley, 25.

9. N. Merrill Distad, *Guessing at Truth: The Life of Julius Charles Hare* (Shepherdstown, W.Va.: Patmos Press, 1979), 28.

10. Winstanley, *Early Victorian Cambridge*, 26-27. There is a strangely similar episode told in relation to Oxford's United (later, "Union") Debating Society (W. R. W. Stephens, ed., *A Memoir of Richard Durnford, D.D.* [London: John Murray, 1899], 47).

11. Mark Pattison was able to say, as late as 1860, "Of an honest critical enquiry into the origin and composition of the canonical writings there is but one trace, Herbert Marsh's Lectures at Cambridge, and that was suggested from a foreign source, and died away without exciting imitators" ("Tendencies of Religious Thought in England, 1688-1750," in Victor Shea and William Whitla, eds., *Essays and Reviews: The 1860 Text and Its Reading* [Charlottesville: University Press of Virginia, 2000], 387-430, 391-92).

12. Julius Charles Hare, *Thou Shalt Not Bear False Witness against Thy Neighbour: A Letter to the Editor of the English Review, with a Letter from Professor Maurice to the Author* (London: John W. Parker, 1849), 31-34.

13. Clark and Hughes, 1:106-07.

14. Clark and Hughes, 1:206.

15. Madame Bunsen to Her Mother, 16 March 1819, in Augustus J. C. Hare, *The Life and Letters of Frances Baroness Bunsen*, 2 vols. (New York: George Routledge and Sons, 1879), 1:138-40.

16. Anthony Trollope, *Clergymen of the Church of England* (1886; London: The Trollope Society, n.d.), 79.

17. Richard Holmes, *Coleridge: Darker Reflections, 1804-1834* (New York: Pantheon Books, 1998), 53, 450.

18. Distad, 35-40, 86-89; J. C. Thirlwall, 24-28.

19. John Gross, *The Rise and Fall of the Man of Letters: English Literary Life since 1800* (1969; reprint, Chicago: Ivan R. Dee, 1991), 22.

20. Distad, 41-42.

21. Julius Charles Hare, *The Victory of Faith*, ed. E. H. Plumptre, 3rd ed., (London: Macmillan and Co., 1874), 22, 29, 84.

22. Hare, *Victory*, 34.

23. Hare, *Victory*, 62.

24. Hare, *Victory*, 93-94, 98-99.

25. Maurice to His Mother, Cambridge, 23 October 1823, in *The Life of Frederick Denison Maurice, Chiefly Told in His Own Letters*, ed. Frederick Maurice, 2 vols. (New York: Charles Scribner's Sons, 1884), 1:48.

26. Distad, 45.

27. Peter Allen, *The Cambridge Apostles: The Early Years* (New York: Cambridge University Press, 1978), 69; Maurice, *Life*, 1:20, 28, 51-52.

28. Julius Charles Hare, "Sketch of the Author's Life," in *Essays and Tales, by John Sterling*, ed. J. C. Hare, 2 vols. (London: John W. Parker, 1848), 1:i-ccxxxii, ix.

29. Maurice, *Life*, 1:52, 56.

30. Thomas Carlyle, *The Life of John Sterling* (1851; reprint, New York: P. F. Collier and Son, 1901), 36, 41; Allen, 27-28.

31. Frederick Denison Maurice, "Dedicatory Letter to the Rev. Derwent Coleridge," in *The Kingdom of Christ: Or, Hints to a Quaker Respecting the Principles, Constitution, & Ordinances of the Catholic Church*, ed. Alec R. Vidler, based on the 2nd ed. of 1842, 2 vols. (London: SCM Press, 1958), 2:348-64, 350-54.

32. F. D. Maurice, "Mr. De Quincey and the London University," *The Athenæum* 61 (24 December 1828): 969; Alec R. Vidler, *F. D. Maurice and Company: Nineteenth Century Studies* (London: SCM Press, 1966), 215.

33. Allen, 36.

34. Thomas Arnold, *Passages in a Wandering Life* (London: Edward Arnold, 1900), 47. Richard Trench, in a letter of 20 March 1840 to Archdeacon Wilberforce, described Derwent Coleridge as "a clever and amiable man, but without even a shadow of his father" (Maria Trench, ed., *Richard Chenevix Trench, Archbishop: Letters and Memorials*, 2 vols. [London: Kegan Paul, Trench, and Co., 1888], 1:243).

35. Maurice, *Life*, 1:64.

36. The 36th Canon required "of such as are to be made Ministers" subscription to three Articles: 1. That the King is supreme governor over both Church and State; 2. That the Book of Common Prayer "containeth in it nothing contrary to the word of God; 3. That the Thirty-nine Articles are "agreeable to the word of God" (*The Constitutions and Canons Ecclesiastical* [London: Prayer-Book and Homily Society, 1852], 23-24).

37. The narrative of Sterling's relation with General Torrijos, and the tragic fate of Torrijos and his small band of patriot soldiers, including Robert Boyd, Sterling's cousin, is given in detail by Thomas Carlyle in his *Life of John Sterling* (1851), Pt. 1, Chs. 8, 9, and 13.

38. Of this period in his life, Maurice states, "I was still under the influence of Coleridge's writings—himself I never saw" (Maurice, *Life*, 1:178). Frances M. Brookfield observes that "Maurice was never a *companionable* thinker," but suffered from a distressing "moral unsociability" that he was unable to overcome (*The Cambridge "Apostles"* [New York: Charles Scribner's Sons, 1907], 216-17).

39. Sterling to Hare, 1836; in Hare, "Sketch of the Author's Life," xv.

40. J. S. Mill, *Autobiography* (1873; New York: Columbia University Press, 1924), 87-88; J. C. Thirlwall, 25.

41. Thirlwall's entrance into the ministry of the Church was, as his biographer states, "determined, in cold-blooded fashion, simply by force of circumstances in order to obtain a decent leisure for his literary pursuits" (J. C. Thirlwall, 40-41).

42. Mill, 90.

43. Mill, 107-08.

44. Sterling to Trench, 6 March 1828, in Trench, 1:7.

45. F. D. Maurice, *Eustace Conway: Or, the Brother and Sister*, ed. Elmer Cleveland Want, 2 vols. (Ph.D. Diss., Vanderbilt University, 1968), vol. 1, chap. 14, 1:170-72.

46. Maurice, *Eustace Conway*, vol. 1, chap. 6, 1:78-79.

47. Baruch Spinoza, *Ethics*, trans. Samuel Shirley (Indianapolis: Hackett Publishing Co., 1992), Pt. 2, Prop. 47, Scholium, 95.

48. Allen, 38-9.

49. John William Adamson, *English Education: 1789-1902* (Cambridge: Cambridge University Press, 1930), 72-73.

50. The Conversazione Society, somewhat misleadingly referred to as "the cradle of the Broad Church movement" (J. C. Thirlwall, p. 56), was to have for its members numerous persons later prominent for artistic, philosophical, theological, scientific, and political accomplishments, such as—to name only a few—Fenton J. A. Hort (1851), Frederick Farrar (1852), Alfred North Whitehead (1884), Bertrand Russell (1892), G. E. Moore (1894), G. M. Trevelyan (1895), E. M. Forster (1901), Lytton Strachey (1902), Leonard Woolf (1902), John Maynard Keynes (1903), and Rupert Brooke (1908).

51. Review of *Guesses at Truth, by Two Brothers*, in *The Athenæum*, no. 42 (13 August 1828), 656.

52. Arthur Penrhyn Stanley, "Archdeacon Hare," *Quarterly Review*, July 1855; reprinted in *Essays, Chiefly on Questions of Church and State, from 1850 to 1870* (London: John Murray, 1870), 536-71, 553.

53. Distad, 48.

54. J. C. Hare, "The Children of Light," *The Victory of Faith and Other Sermons* (London: Griffith, Farran, Okeden, and Welsh, n.d.), 153-59.

55. "Children of Light," 159-61

56. "Children of Light," 162-63.

57. "Children of Light," 154.

58. Frederick Denison Maurice, *What Is Revelation?: A Series of Sermons on the Epiphany* (Cambridge: Macmillan and Co., 1859), 44.

59. Leibniz to Remond; qtd. in Ernst Cassirer, *The Platonic Renaissance in England*, trans. James P. Pettegrove (1953; New York: Gordian Press, 1970), 153.

60. J. S. Mill, "Coleridge," *London and Westminster Review* (March 1840); reprinted in *Utilitarianism and Other Essays*, by J. S. Mill and Jeremy Bentham, ed. Alan Ryan (New York: Penguin Books, 1987), 177-226, 181.

61. Review of "The Children of Light," *The Athenæum*, no. 62 (31 December 1828), 977.

62. Distad, 55-56.

63. "The Lord Bishop of Chester and the London University: Letter I," *The Athenæum*, no. 26 (23 April 1828), 412.

64. "The Lord Bishop of Chester and the London University: Letter II," *The Athenæum*, no. 27 (30 April 1828), 426-27.

65. "Letter to the Bishop of Chester: No. III," *The Athenæum*, no. 29 (14 May 1828), 460.

66. J. C. Hare, *Victory*, 131.

67. The description of Honoria in vol. 2, chap. 18 of *Eustace Conway* is clearly intended as a encomium of the dying Emma Maurice.

68. Maurice, *Life*, 1:93-94.

69. F. D. Maurice, *Eustace Conway*, vol. 3, chap. 18, 898.

70. Maurice, *Eustace Conway*, vol. 3, chap. 4, 680.

71. Maurice to J. C. Hare, Oxford, 3 December 1829, in Maurice, *Life*, 1:179, 103.

72. *Correspondence on Church and Religion of William Ewart Gladstone*, ed. D. C. Lathbury, 2 vols. (London: John Murray, 1910), 1:2-3.

73. Roy Jenkins, *Gladstone: A Biography* (New York: Random House, 1997), 21.

74. Edmund Sheridan Purcell, *The Life of Cardinal Manning, Archbishop of Westminster*, 2 vols. (London: Macmillan and Co., 1896), 1:32.

75. A. H. Hallam to W. E. Gladstone; 23 June 1830, in Maurice, *Life*, 1:110.

76. Gladstone, qtd. in Charles Edward Mallet, *A History of the University of Oxford: Modern Oxford* (London: Methuen and Co., Ltd., 1927), 226.

77. Maurice to His Son, F. Maurice, 1870, in Maurice, *Life*, 1:181.

78. According to Charles R. Sanders, "there was no sign of change" in Maurice's position relative to Coleridge, although Maurice's "loyalty to Coleridge became increasingly conspicuous as he became more active and better known to the public" (*Coleridge and the Broad Church Movement* [Durham, N.C.: Duke University Press, 1942], 191). A. R. Vidler is right to take exception to Sanders's position. Vidler states, and I concur, "It is important to draw a distinction between Maurice's relation to Coleridge before and after his becoming a member of the Church of England, which is also to say before and after his becoming a theologian" (*F. D. Maurice and Company: Nineteenth Century Studies* [London: SCM, 1966], 215). Maurice's indebtedness to Erskine is discussed in greater detail in Walter Merlin Davies, *An Introduction to F. D. Maurice's Theology* (London: S.P.C.K., 1964).

79. Maurice to His Sister Priscilla, ca. January/February 1831, in Maurice, *Life*, 1:121.

80. Maurice, *Life*, 1:123-24, 163.

81. There is a good discussion of M. D. Conway in Warren Sylvester Smith, *The London Heretics: 1870-1914* (London: Constable & Co., 1967), 104-24.

82. Moncure Daniel Conway, *The Parting of the Ways: A Study on the Lives of Sterling and Maurice* (Finsbury: Printed for the Author, 1872), 12-13.

83. Carlyle confused Sterling's novel with Maurice's (Conway, 14-15; cf. Carlyle, *Life of Sterling*, Pt. I, Ch. 15, 91).

84. Charles Kingsley to Fanny Grenfell, Eversley, October 1843, in *Letters and Memories*, ed. F. E. Kingsley, 2 vols., Bideford ed. (London: The Co-operative Publication Society, 1899), 1:81.

85. Clark and Hughes, 1:418-19.

86. Connop Thirlwall, *A Letter to the Rev. Thomas Turton, D.D., on the Admission of Dissenters to Academical Degrees* (Cambridge: The Pitt Press, 1834), 4.

87. Thirlwall, *Letter*, 16-19.

88. Thirlwall, *Letter*, 20-21.

89. Thirlwall, *Letter*, 33.

90. Sterling to Trench,12 June 1834, in *Richard Chenevix Trench, Archbishop*, 1:159.

91. D. A. Winstanley, *Later Victorian Cambridge* (Cambridge: Cambridge University Press, 1947), 53, 70, 89.

92. J. C. Thirlwall, 83.

93. Charles Hardwick, *A History of the Articles of Religion* (Cambridge: John Deighton, 1851), 214.

94. Rusticus, *Subscription No Bondage, Or the Practical Advantages Afforded by the Thirty-Nine Articles as Guides in All the Branches of Academical Education* (Oxford: J. H. Parker, 1835), 13.

95. Rusticus, 22.

96. According to John Willis Clark, "[Thirlwall's] statements under this head were . . . completely refuted by Mr. Robert Wilson Evans, then a resident Fellow of Trinity, who published a detailed account of the lectures on the New Testament which he had given during the past year in his own college" (*Old Friends at Cambridge and Elsewhere* [London: Macmillan and Co., 1900], 117).

97. Clark, 56.

98. Maurice to Ludlow, Shrewsbury, 24 September 1852, in Maurice, *Life*, 2:136-37.

99. Renn Dickson Hampden, *Observations on Religious Dissent* (Oxford: J. H. Parker, 1834), 8-10.

100. Rusticus, 84-87.

101. Rusticus, 87, 102-03.

102. F. D. Maurice, *Thoughts on the Rule of Conscientious Subscription, on the Purpose of the Thirty-nine Articles, and on Our Present Perils from the Romish System: in a Second Letter to a Non-Resident Member of Convocation* (Oxford: John Henry Parker, 1845), x.

103. John Overton's *True Churchman Ascertained* "tried to prove from a careful examination of the Articles and the history of the Prayer Book that Evangelicals were 'the true Churchmen' and their opponents 'in a very fundamental sense dissenters from the Church of England'" (Balleine, 79-80; cf. John Hunt, *Religious Thought in the Nineteenth Century* [London: Gibbings and Co., 1896], 19). J. H. Newman's Tract XC urged the necessity of interpreting the Articles in a Catholic sense. William George Ward's *The Ideal of a Christian Church* replied that the articles were contradictory, and in their "*natural* and *straightforward* sense" could be subscribed to by neither Catholic nor Protestant (2nd ed. [London: James Toovey, 1844], 481).

104. Rusticus, 104.

105. Maurice to His Son, F. Maurice, 1870, in Maurice, *Life* 1:174; Charles Kingsley completely concurred with the arguments of Maurice's pamphlet (*Letters and Memories*, 2:204-05).

106. Maurice to Daniel Macmillan, 27 January 1853, in Maurice, *Life*, 2:154-55.

107. Frances Baroness Bunsen, *A Memoir of Baron Bunsen*, 2 vols. (London: Longmans, Green, and Co., 1868), 1:512.

108. Alec R. Vidler, *Witness to the Light: F. D. Maurice's Message for Today* (New York: Charles Scribner's Sons, 1948), 226-27.

109. Carlyle, *Life of Sterling*, pt. 2, chap. 3, 123.

110. John Tulloch, *Movements of Religious Thought in Britain during the Nineteenth Century* (New York: Charles Scribner's Sons, 1885), 138.

111. J. C. Hare, "A Sketch of the Author's Life," cxlii; cf. J. S. Mill's assessment of Coleridge: "He has been the great awakener in this country of the spirit of philosophy, *within the bounds of traditional opinions*" ("Coleridge," *London and Westminster Review* [March 1840], reprinted in J. S. Mill and Jeremy Bentham, *Utilitarianism and Other Essays*, ed. Alan Ryan [New York: Penguin Books, 1987], 177).

112. Sterling to J. C. Hare, April 1837, in Hare, "A Sketch," xcviii.

113. Sterling to J. C. Hare; ca. 1836, in Hare, "A Sketch," lxviii.

114. F. D. Maurice, *The Kingdom of Christ*, I.IV.i.3, 1:149-50.

115. F. D. Maurice, "The Son of God," *Theological Essays*, 2nd ed. (1853; reprint, New York: Harper & Brothers, 1957), 76-77.

116. Maurice to J. C. Hare, in Hare, *Thou Shalt Not Bear False Witness*, 69-70.

117. Carlyle, *Life of Sterling*, pt. 2, chap. 3, 121, chap. 4, 125-27; pt. 3, chap. 4, 243

118. Carlyle, relating this incident to Emerson in a letter of 8 December 1837, says, "By God's blessing there shall one day be a trio of us" (Charles E. Norton, ed., *Correspondence of Thomas Carlyle and Ralph Waldo Emerson, 1834-1872*, 2 vols. [Boston: James R. Osgood and Co., 1883], 1:141; Edward Waldo Emerson, *A Correspondence between John Sterling and Ralph Waldo Emerson, with a Sketch of Sterling's Life* [Boston: Houghton, Mifflin, and Co., 1897], 21).

119. Kingsley to Richard Cowley Powles, Chelsea, 1836, in Kingsley, *Letters and Memories*, 1:21-22.

120. Kingsley, *Letters and Memories*, 1:22-23.

121. Maurice, *Life*, 1:202f.

122. T. Erskine to his sister, Mrs. Stirling, Shanklin, 19 January 1838, in William Hanna, ed., *Letters of Thomas Erskine of Linlathen* (Edinburgh: David Douglas, 1878), 198.

123. In regard to the second edition of *The Kingdom of Christ*, Maurice said, in a letter of September 1841 to Edward Strachey, "As it expresses more of what I really think and believe, it is better *quoad me*, and if the universe don't approve it, the universe must write a book for itself" (1:309).

124. Maurice to T. Erskine, London, 8 August 1841, in Maurice, *Life*, 1:306.

125. F. D. Maurice, *The Kingdom of Christ*, I.IV.ii.3, 1:175.

126. Thomas Erskine, *The Brazen Serpent: Or, Life Coming through Death*, 3rd ed. (Edinburgh: David Douglas, 1879), 42.

127. F. D. Maurice, *The Kingdom of Christ*, II.IV.i.4; 1:275.

128. F. D. Maurice, "On Justification by Faith," *Theological Essays*, 148.

129. Erskine, 152.

130. F. D. Maurice, *The Kingdom of Christ*, I.IV.i.1, I.II.ii.2, 1:140, 93.

131. F. D. Maurice to Rev. M. Maurice; ca. 12 February 1832; in *Life* 1:134-36.

132. Erskine, 98-99.

133. Erskine, 120.

134. F. D. Maurice, *The Kingdom of Christ*, II.IV.iv.3, 2:80.

135. F. D. Maurice, "On the Atonement," *Theological Essays*, 109.

136. T. Erskine to Rev. Alex. J. Scott, Cadder, 21 April 1837, in Hanna, 180.

137. F. D. Maurice to T. Erskine, 21 Queen's Square, 21 December 1852, in Maurice, *Life*, 2:150; also in Hanna, 101-02.

138. Maurice, *Life*, 1:250.

139. Edward Strachey to Lady Louis, 23 July 1838, in Maurice, *Life*, 1:250-51.

140. Carlyle, *Life of Sterling*, pt. 2, chap. 3, 124.

141. Carlyle, *Life of Sterling*, pt. 3, chap. 1, 184.

142. Maurice to R. C. Trench, 11 October 1839, in Maurice, *Life*, 1:276. Similarly, Trench complains to Archdeacon Wilberforce, on 30 December 1839, "Have you seen Sterling's article on Carlyle in the *Westminster*? It has given me very great grief, and since I saw it, which was only a few days ago, I have not failed to tell him what I felt about it. It has caused me also quite as much wonder as pain" (Trench, 1:243).

143. Sterling to Hare, in J. C. Hare, "A Sketch of the Author's Life," cxxxii-iii.

144. Maurice was evidently thinking of his relation with Sterling as he wrote these lines: "The remembrance of hard and proud words spoken against those who were crying out for Truth will be always the bitterest in his life, that which recurs to him with the keenest sense of having grieved the Holy Spirit of God, of having brought upon him the curse of a brother's blood" (Frederick Denison Maurice, *What is Revelation?* [Cambridge: Macmillan and Co., 1859], 143).

145. J. C. Thirlwall, 90; Thirlwall to Betha Johnes, St. David's Day, 1867, in Connop Thirlwall, *Letters to a Friend*, ed. Arthur Penrhyn Stanley (London: Richard Bentley and Son, 1882), 115, 118.

146. *Froude's Life of Carlyle*, ed. John Clubbe (London: John Murray, 1979), 382.

147. David Cecil, *Melbourne:* The Young Melbourne *and* Lord M *in One Volume* (London: The Reprint Society, 1955), 245.

148. Distad, 135; J. C. Thirlwall, 112-13.

149. Kingsley to his parents, Cambridge, 31 May 1839, in Kingsley, *Letters and Memories*, 1:25.

150. Clark and Hughes, 1:529-39.

151. Kingsley, *Letters and Memories*, 1:28-29.

152. Kingsley, *Letters and Memories*, 1:30.

153. Rowland Williams, Sunday, 3 February 1839, in Ellen Williams, ed., *The Life and Letters of Rowland Williams, D.D.*, 2 vols. (London: Henry S. King and Co., 1874), 1:49.

154. Hare, *Victory*, 46-47.

155. Kingsley to Fanny Grenfell, December 1840, in Kingsley, *Letters and Memories*, 1:32.

156. Daniel Macmillan to his brother Malcolm, 22 July 1833, in Thomas Hughes, *Memoir of Daniel Macmillan* (London: Macmillan and Co., 1883), 26.

157. Charles Kingsley, *Alton Locke*, in *The Works of Charles Kingsley*, 28 vols. (London: Macmillan, 1880-85), 3:104.

158. Charles Kingsley, "Science," *Scientific Lectures and Essays*, in *Works*, 19:248-49.

159. Kingsley to Fanny Grenfell, May 1841, in Kingsley, *Letters and Memories*, 1:37.

160. Kingsley, *Letters and Memories*, 1:48.

161. Kingsley to his mother, Cambridge, June 1841, in Kingsley, *Letters and Memories*, 1:38.

162. Allen, 177.

163. John Colenso to T. Pattinson Ferguson, 10 April 1843, in George W. Cox, *The Life of John William Colenso, D.D., Bishop of Natal*, 2 vols. (London: W. Ridgway, 1888), 1:21; Williams, 1:42-43.

164. F. D. Maurice, *Three Letters to the Rev. W. Palmer, Fellow and Tutor of Magdalen College, Oxford, On the Name "Protestant"; On the Seemingly Ambiguous Character of the English Church; and on the Bishopric at Jerusalem* (London: J. G. Rivington and Co., 1842), 2-19.

165. F. D. Maurice, *Reasons for Not Joining a Party in the Church: A Letter to the Ven. Samuel Wilberforce, Archdeacon of Surrey: Suggested by the Rev. Dr. Hook's Letter to the Bishop of Ripon, on the State of Parties in the Church of England* (London: J. G. and F. Rivington, 1841), 7-8.

166. Kingsley to Fanny Grenfell, Chelsea, 7 May 1842, in Kingsley, *Letters and Memories*, 1:51-52.

167. John Martineau to Mrs. Kingsley, n.d., in Kingsley, *Letters and Memories*, 1:269.

168. Kingsley to Maurice, 1856, in Kingsley, *Letters and Memories*, 2:23.

169. William Harrison to Mrs. Kingsley, n.d., in Kingsley, *Letters and Memories*, 2:247.

170. Brenda Colloms, *Charles Kingsley: The Lion of Eversley* (London: Constable, 1975), 68-69.

171. Frederick W. Farrar, *Men I Have Known* (New York: Thomas V. Crowell and Co., 1897), 99-103.

172. Maurice, *Life*, 1:315-16.

173. Maurice, *Life*, 1:329; Distad, 152-53; Hughes, *Memoir*, 124-26.

174. Maurice to Hare, Guy's Hospital, 12 November 1842, in *Life*, 1:331.

175. Hare to Macmillan, 16 August 1842, in Hughes, *Memoir*, 128.

176. Sterling to Hare, September 1842, in Hare, "Sketch of the Author's Life," cxcix.

177. Sterling to Emerson, 29 March and 7 October 1843, in Emerson, 62, 71.

178. Hare, "Sketch," cxcvii.

179. Sterling to Emerson, Falmouth, 28 December 1841, in Emerson, 45.

180. Carlyle, *Life of Sterling*, pt. 3, chap. 6, 247.

181. Sterling to Hare, Ventnor, April 1844, in Hare, "Sketch," ccxiv.

182. Michael St. John Packe, *The Life of John Stuart Mill* (New York: The Macmillan Company, 1954), 287.

183. Sterling to Emerson, Ventnor, 1 August 1844, in Emerson, 91.

184. Kingsley, *Letters and Memories*, 1:106.

185. Kingsley, *Letters and Memories*, 1:103.

186. Maurice to Kingsley, Chelsea Vicarage, 19 July 1844; in Maurice, *Life*, 1:371.

187. Edward, Sterling's eldest son, who had stayed with the Maurices during his father's protracted illness, was—to Maurice's great regret—by the last will of Sterling transferred to the care of Francis W. Newman.

188. Maurice, *Life*, 1:427-29.

189. Thomas Hughes to Fanny Ford, 6 November 1846, in Edward C. Mack and W. H. G. Armytage, *Thomas Hughes: The Life of the Author of* Tom Brown's Schooldays (London: Ernest Benn Ltd., 1952), 52.

190. Thomas Hughes, *The Manliness of Christ* (Boston: Houghton, Mifflin and Co., 1881), 16-17.

191. Richard Holt Hutton, *Essays on Some of the Modern Guides to English Thought in Matters of Faith* (1887; reprint, Freeport, N.Y.: Books for Libraries Press, 1972), 316-17. Frederick Harrison, also a student at Lincoln's Inn who attended Maurice's sermons, accredits Maurice with demolishing "what remains of orthodoxy I had" (*The Creed of a Layman: Apologia Pro Fide Mea* [London: Macmillan and Co., 1907], 18-19).

192. N. C. Masterman, *John Malcolm Ludlow: The Builder of Christian Socialism* (Cambridge: Cambridge University Press, 1963), 45-47; Maurice, *Life*, 1:430-31.

193. Kingsley to Powles, 11 December 1845, in Kingsley, *Letters and Memories*, 1:110.

194. Kingsley to Powles, December 1846, in Kingsley, *Letters and Memories*, 1:114.

195. Kingsley to his wife, London, ca. December 1847, Kingsley, in *Letters and Memories*, 1:117-18; Maurice, *Life*, 1:443, 447.

196. Charles Kingsley, "Why Should We Fear the Romish Priests?," *Fraser's Magazine for Town and Country* 37 (April 1848): 467-74.

197. Kingsley, *Letters and Memories*, 1:119-20.

198. Waldo Hilary Dunn, *James Anthony Froude: A Biography*, 2 vols. (Oxford: Clarendon Press, 1961), 1:96-97.

199. William Lovett, one of the founders, in 1836, of the London Working Men's Association, together with Francis Place, an honorary member, drew up the list of demands that became the basis for the "People's Charter," published in 1838. Although the demands fluctuated between six and five in number (Carlyle consistently represents the Charter as having five points), the full list is as follows: (1) universal suffrage, (2) vote by ballot, (3) annual parliaments, (4) salaried members of parliament, (5) abolition of the property qualification for members of parliament, and (6) equal electoral districts.

200. John K. Walton, *Chartism* (New York: Routledge, 1999), 9-13.

201. Thomas Carlyle, *Chartism*, in *Selected Writings*, ed. Alan Shelston (New York: Penguin Classics, 1971), 149-232, 181.

202. Maurice, *Life*, 1:458.

203. Charles E. Raven, *Christian Socialism: 1848-1854* (London: Macmillan and Co., 1920), 99.

204. Walton, 32-33. Shaftesbury, the evangelical reformer and philanthropist, had a different explanation for the relative quiet of April 10th: "You know how the day so much dreaded passed over, and how all was tranquil, not the breath of a threat was uttered and why? Because God's blessing was on the work of our City Missionaries" (L. E. O'Rorke, *The Life and Friendships of Catherine Marsh* [London: Longmans, Green, and Co., 1918], 65-66).

205. Kingsley to his wife, London, noon, 10 April 1848, in *Letters and Memories*, 1:124.

206. Letter of Matthew Arnold to his mother, Wednesday, April 1848, in *Letters of Matthew Arnold: 1848-1888*, 2 vols., ed. George W. E. Russell (New York: Macmillan and Co, 1895), 1:8.

207. Llewellyn Woodward, *The Age of Reform: 1815-1870*, 2nd ed. (Oxford: Oxford University Press, 1962), 145.

208. Kingsley, *Letters and Memories*, 1:126-27.

209. Raven, 107-08.

210. Kingsley to his wife, London, evening, 11 April 1848, in *Letters and Memories*, 1:125.

211. According to Raven, Ludlow was present at this meeting and proposed the penny periodical (108). Raven probably misread Kingsley's letter of 12 April 1848 to his wife (*Letters and Memories*, 1:125). Maurice's letter to Ludlow on the 13th suggests that Ludlow was not present and that Maurice allowed Hare to make his own recommendations without being at all influenced by anterior plans (Maurice, *Life*, 1:460-61).

212. "Monster Meetings," in *Politics for the People* (London: John W. Parker, 1848), 26-28, 27.

213. "Fraternity," in *Politics for the People*, 2-5, 3.

214. The full list of contributors was included in the copy of the publisher, John W. Parker. The list from this copy, now lost, was transcribed into an edition owned by Mr. G. J. Gray. See Raven, Appendix A, for the entire list (371-75).

215. "Letters to the Chartists.—No. II," in *Politics*, 58-59.

216. Maurice to Archdeacon Hare, 28 May 1848, in Maurice, *Life*, 1:476-77.

217. Masterman, 124-25.

218. Maurice, *Life*, 2:27, 29.

219. For detailed studies of the early nineteenth-century Christian Socialist movement in England, see Torben Christensen, *Origin and History of Christian Socialism: 1848-54*, Acta Theologica Danica, vol. 3 (Universitetsforlaget i Aarhus, 1962) and Charles E. Raven, *Christian Socialism: 1848-1854* (London: Macmillan and Co., 1920). For a broader study of Christian Socialism in England, see Gilbert Clive Binyon, *The Christian Socialist Movement in England: An Introduction to the Study of Its History* (London: SPCK, 1931). A more comprehensive look at the subject is given by John C. Cort, *Christian Socialism: An Informal History* (Maryknoll, N.Y.: Orbis Books, 1988).

220. Raven, 173.

221. W. F. Hook to W. P. Wood, 6 October 1851, in *The Life and Letters of Walter Farquhar Hook*, ed. W. R. W. Stephens, 2 vols. (London: Richard Bentley and Son, 1880), 2:350.

222. F. D. Maurice, "The French Stage and Mr. Croker of the Quarterly Review," *The Athenæum* 25 (18 April 1828): 391-92.

223. Maurice, *Life*, 1:460. According to *Letters and Memories*, Kingsley was proposed "for the professorship of Modern History" at Queen's (1:123), but I am inclined to believe that the biographer has confused times and places.

224. Kingsley, *Letters and Memories*, 1:126; Maurice, *Life*, 1:478.

225. "Queen's College—London," *Quarterly Review* 172 (March 1850): 364-83, 369.

226. Hare, *Thou Shalt Not Bear False Witness against Thy Neighbour*, 16-17.

227. Maurice to Georgiana Hare, 14 February 1849, in Maurice, *Life*, 1:503.

228. The manuscript diaries of John Gibson Lockhart, editor of the *Quarterly Review*, in the possession of the National Library of Scotland, have the initials "E. H." marked in connection with this article (*The Wellesley Index to Victorian Periodicals: 1824-1900*, Vol. 1, ed. Walter E. Houghton [London: Routledge and Kegan Paul, 1966], 733). The only other known contributor to the *QR* with those initials is the statesman and art critic Sir Edmund Walker Head, whose contributions were published in 1864-65.

229. "Queen's College—London," 370-71, 373.

230. "Queen's College—London," 374, 376-77.

231. See George Eliot's review of Riehl's *Natural History of German Life* (1856), reprinted in George Eliot, *Selected Critical Writings*, ed. Rosemary Ashton (New York: Oxford University Press, 1992), 260-95.

232. "Queen's College—London," 381.

233. F. D. Maurice, *A Letter to the Right Hon. & Right Rev., The Lord Bishop of London, in Reply to the Article in No. CLXXII of the Quarterly Review, Entitled Queen's College, London* (London: John W. Parker, 1850), 37.

234. Maurice, *Letter to the . . . Lord Bishop of London*, 17-18.

235. Maurice, *Letter to the . . . Lord Bishop of London*, 46.

236. John Wilson Croker, "Revolutionary Literature," *Quarterly Review* 178 (September 1851): 491-543, 495.

237. Croker, 524.

238. Croker, 527.

239. Croker, 527, 531.

240. Croker, 525.

241. Croker, 536.

242. Thomas Carlyle to Dr. John Carlyle, 7 October 1851, in Charles Richard Sanders, *Carlyle's Friendships and Other Studies* (Durham, N.C.: Duke University Press, 1977), 32; C. F. G. Masterman, *Frederick Denison Maurice* (London: A. R. Mowbray and Co., 1907), 97. Carlyle's estimate of Croker's character is fully endorsed by Harriet Martineau, who styles him "the wickedest of reviewers," whose "foul and false political articles in the *Quarterly Review* . . . stand out as the disgrace of the periodical literature of our time" (*Biographical Sketches* [New York: Hurst and Co., n.d.], 61).

243. Matthew Arnold to Miss Kingsley, January 1875, in *Letters of Matthew Arnold, 1848-1888*, ed. George W. E. Russell, 2 vols. (New York: Macmillan and Co., 1895), 2:141.

244. F. D. Maurice, *Tracts On Christian Socialism, No. 1* (London: G. Bell, 1850), 1.

245. Maurice to Ludlow, 25 August 1849, in Maurice, *Life*, 2:8-9.

246. Maurice to Ludlow, Hastings, 1850, in Maurice, *Life*, 2:34-35.

247. Jelf to Maurice, King's College, 7 November 1851, in Maurice, *Life*, 2:78-80.

248. Maurice to Jelf, 21 Queen's Square, 8 November 1851, in Maurice, *Life*, 2:80-82.

249. Maurice to Hare, 19 November 1851, in Maurice, *Life*, 2:86-87.

250. Jelf to Maurice, 20 December 1851, in Maurice, *Life*, 2:90-91.

251. Jelf to Maurice, 17 January 1852, in Maurice, *Life*, 2:98.

252. Maurice to Jelf, 21 January 1852, in Maurice, *Life*, 2:99.

253. Maurice, *Life*, 2:102.

254. Raven, 300.

255. Maurice to Priscilla Maurice, 12 February 1853, in Maurice, *Life*, 2:156.

256. Hare to Thirlwall, 22 August 1853, in Distad, 188.

257. Maurice to Kingsley, Clyro, South Wales, 19 July 1853, in Maurice, *Life*, 2:167-68.

258. Maurice to Kingsley, Clyro, 2 August 1853, in Maurice, *Life*, 2:170.

259. Erskine, 172-73.

260. James Anthony Froude, *The Nemesis of Faith* (1849; reprint, New York: Garland Press, 1975), 16, 18-9. See also Maria Hare's notebook entry for 7 July 1837, on the difficulties of conceiving a punishment for the wicked (A. J. C. Hare, *Memorials of a Quiet Life*, 2:188).

261. Maurice to Kingsley, 9 March 1849, in Maurice, *Life*, 1:517.

262. Walter Farquhar Hook, *A Church Dictionary* (London: Houlston and Stoneman, 1842), 282.

263. Maurice, *Theological Essays*, 305-06.

264. Maurice, *Theological Essays*, 309-10.

265. Maurice, *Theological Essays*, 323.

266. R. C. Trench to the Bishop of Oxford, 12 August 1853, in Trench, 1:303.

267. Reginald G. Wilberforce, *Life of the Right Reverend Samuel Wilberforce, D.D.*, 3 vols. (London: John Murray, 1881), 2:208.

268. F. D. Maurice, *The Word "Eternal," and the Punishment of the Wicked: A Letter to the Rev. Dr. Jelf, Canon of Christ Church, and Principal of King's College*, 2nd ed. (New York: C. S. Francis and Co., 1854), 12.

269. Maurice, *Theological Essays*, 312-14.

270. Maurice, *The Word "Eternal,"* 13.

271. Maurice, *The Word "Eternal,"* 43; cf. F. D. Maurice, *The New Statute and Mr. Ward* (Oxford: J. H. Parker, 1845), 19-25.

272. Maurice, *The Word "Eternal,"* 14.

273. Richard Whately, *The Kingdom of Christ Delineated, in Two Essays on Our Lord's Own Account of His Person and of the Nature of His Kingdom, and on the Constitution, Powers, and Ministry of a Christian Church, as Appointed by Himself* (New York: Wiley and Putnam, 1842), 156-58.

274. Maurice, *The Word "Eternal,"* 24.

275. Maurice, *The Word "Eternal,"* 26.

276. The Gospel of Mark, 9:43-44.

277. Maurice, *The Word "Eternal,"* 29-30.

278. Origen, *De Principiis*, I-II; Charles Bigg, *The Christian Platonists of Alexandria* (Oxford: Clarendon Press, 1886), 224-32.

279. Erskine, 131, 234, 238.

280. Maurice, *The Word "Eternal,"* 30.

281. Maurice to Hare, 8 September 1853, in Maurice, *Life*, 2:180.

282. Maurice, *Life*, 2:191-92.

283. W. E. Gladstone to G. Wellesley, Hawarden, 2 November 1853, in *Correspondence on Church and Religion*, 1:360-61.

284. W. E. Gladstone to Lord Lyttelton, 29 October 1853, in Maurice, *Life*, 2:195.

285. Maurice, *Life*, 2:196, 200.

286. S. Wilberforce to Jelf, Lavington, 27 August 1853, in Wilberforce, 2:209.

287. Wilberforce, 2:210-14; Maurice, *Life*, 2:201-02. Wilberforce's judgment on the orthodoxy of Maurice's *Essays* should be weighed against his later efforts to pursue the ecclesiastical prosecution of John Colenso and H. B. Wilson for having made similar statements regarding everlasting punishment.

288. Maurice to the Council of King's College, Bloomsbury, 7 November 1853, in Maurice, *Life*, 2: 206-09.

289. Henry Bristow Wilson, "Séances historiques de Genève—the National Church," in Shea and Whitla, 275-309, 309.

290. Maurice, *Life*, 2:221, 233.

291. Peter Levi, *Tennyson* (New York: Charles Scribner's Sons, 1993), 207.

292. Maurice, *Theological Essays*, 75-76. The 1854 English edition of the *Theologia Germanica* (translated by Susanna Winkworth, prefaced by Charles Kingsley and Chevalier Bunsen, published by Longman et al.) reprints five stanzas of "Strong Son of God" on the verso frontispiece.

293. J. C. Thirlwall, 188.

294. Alfred Tennyson, *In Memoriam*, §54, lines 1-4, 13-16.

295. F. W. Robertson, *Analysis of Mr. Tennyson's "In Memoriam,"* 15th ed. (London: Kegan Paul, Trench, Trubner, and Co., 1901), C3r, D6v.

296. Tennyson, *In Memoriam*, §124, lines 9-16.

297. R. H. Hutton, "Tennyson's Theology," *Aspects of Religious and Scientific Thought* (London: Macmillan and Co., 1899), 402-08.

298. Tennyson, *In Memoriam*, §96, lines 13-16.

299. Tennyson, "To the Rev. F. D. Maurice," lines 1-12, *Maud, and Other Poems* (London: Edward Moxon, 1855), 145-46.

300. Charles J. Vaughan, in November 1834, established a short-lived Rugby Debating Society at Cambridge (Katherine Lake, ed., *Memorials of William Charles Lake* [London: Edward Arnold, 1901], 155.)

301. Allen, 134.

302. Charles Kingsley, Preface to *Theologia Germanica*, ed. Dr. Pfeiffer, trans. Susanna Winkworth, 2nd ed. (London: Longman, Brown, Green and Longmans, 1854), xi.

303. Charles Kingsley, "Salvation," *Sermons for the Times*, in *The Works of Charles Kingsley*, 28 vols. (London: Macmillan and Co., 1880-85), 23:16.

304. Ralph Cudworth, "A Sermon Preached before the House of Commons," *The Cambridge Platonists*, ed. C. A. Patrides (Cambridge: Harvard University Press, 1970), 111.

305. Kingsley, *Sermons for the Times*, in *Works*, 23:22, 24.

306. Acts of the Apostles 2:12-13. James B. Mozley (1813-1878), future Regius Professor of Divinity at Oxford, in his review of "Professor Maurice's *Theological Essays*" (January 1854) took the same line of argument as Mansel against Maurice (*Essays Historical and Theological*, 2 vols. [London: Rivingtons, 1873], 2:255-309, 281ff).

307. Henry Longueville Mansel, "Man's Conception of Eternity: An Examination of Mr. Maurice's Theory of a Fixed State out of Time," *Letters, Lectures, and Reviews*, ed. Henry W. Chandler (London: John Murray, 1873), 107-21, 109.

308. Mansel, "Man's Conception of Eternity," 110-11.

309. For the New Testament assertion that God is not subject to time, see 2 Pet. 3:8; Heb. 13:8.

310. Mansel, "Man's Conception of Eternity," 121.

311. Maurice to D. Macmillan and Kingsley, 23 February and 19 October 1854, in Maurice, *Life*, 2:237-38, 249.

312. F. D. Maurice, *Sequel to the Inquiry, What is Revelation?* (Cambridge: Macmillan and Co., 1860), 19.

313. Maurice, *Life*, 2:333.

314. F. D. Maurice, *Letters to a Theological Student Preparing for Orders: On Mr. Mansel's Bampton Lectures*, in *What Is Revelation?*, Letter I, 132. The phrase "*Ductor Dubitantium*" should be understood in the sense in which it is used by Jeremy Taylor in his book by that title—that is, as a guide resolving doubts as to courses of action or thought.

315. John William Burgon, *Lives of Twelve Good Men* (London: John Murray, 1888), 184-85.

316. Maurice, *Letters to a Theological Student*, Letter VIII, 338.

317. Charles Peter Chretien, *A Letter to the Reverend F. D. Maurice, on Some Points Suggested by His Recent Criticism of Mr. Mansel's Bampton Lectures* (London: John W. Parker, 1859), 3-4. Although not all of Maurice's readers considered his response that of a gentleman, John Young, in his own very capable response to Mansel, calls Maurice's protest "fervent, eloquent, and noble" and such as "must deepen the already profound respect and love with which he is regarded" (*The Province of Reason: A Criticism of the Bampton Lecture on "The Limits of Religious Thought"* [New York: Robert Carter and Brothers, 1860], III.1, 127).

318. Henry Longueville Mansel, *An Examination of the Rev. F. D. Maurice's Strictures on the Bamptom Lectures of 1858* (London: John Murray, 1859), 96-97.

319. H. L. Mansel, *The Limits of Religious Thought Examined*, 1st American ed. (Boston: Gould and Lincoln, 1860), Preface, 27.

320. Mansel, *Limits*, 66, 128, 220-21.

321. Mansel, *Limits*, 113-14.

322. Mansel, *Limits*, 144.

323. Mansel, *Limits*, 208-09.

324. Mansel, *Limits*, 61.

325. Maurice, *What Is Revelation?*, 478-79.

326. Mansel, *Limits*, 47-48.

327. Hugh James Rose, *The State of Protestantism in Germany, Described*, 2nd ed. (London: C. J. G. and F. Rivington, 1829), xxiii-xxvi.

328. Mansel, *Limits*, 71-72.

329. Rose and Mansel both published critical responses to *Essays and Reviews* ("Bunsen, the Critical School, and Dr. Williams," by H. J. Rose, in *Replies to "Essays and Reviews"* [Oxford: John Henry and James Parker, 1861], 55-127; "On Miracles as Evidences of Christianity," by H. L. Mansel, in *Aids to Faith: A Series of Theological Essays*, ed. William Thomson [New York: D. Appleton and Co., 1862], 9-52).

330. Mansel, *Limits*, 168.

331. Mansel, *Limits*, 219.

332. Peter Hinchliff, *Benjamin Jowett and the Christian Religion* (Oxford: Clarendon Press, 1987), 91.

333. Lionel A. Tollemache, *Benjamin Jowett: Master of Balliol* (London: Edward Arnold, n.d.), 72.

334. Benjamin Jowett, "Christ's Revelation of God," *Sermons on Faith and Doctrine*, ed. W. H. Fremantle (New York: E. P. Dutton and Co., 1901), 77-94, 92.

335. Rowland Williams, "Bunsen's Biblical Researches," in Shea and Whitla, 181-232, 214.

336. Matthew Arnold to his mother, 6 November 1861, in Lang, 2:98.

337. F. Newman's most popular adversary was Henry Rogers, the author of the anonymous *Eclipse of Faith* (1854), which by 1860 was in its tenth edition (William Robbins, *The Newman Brothers* [London: Heinemann, 1966], 112).

338. Maurice, *Sequel to the Inquiry*, 279.

339. Maurice, *What Is Revelation?*, 163.

340. Mansel, *An Examination*, 30 n.

341. Maurice, *What Is Revelation?*, 301.

342. Maurice, *Sequel to the Inquiry*, 47.

343. R. H. Hutton, *Theological Essays* (1895), 89-90, qtd. in Walter Merlin Davies, *An Introduction to F. D. Maurice's Theology* (London: S.P.C.K., 1964), 14.

344. Mansel, *Limits*, 143; Maurice, *What Is Revelation?*, 381.

345. Maurice, *Theological Essays*, 236-37.

346. Maurice, *Sequel to the Inquiry*, 280.

347. Maurice, *What Is Revelation?*, 477.

348. Acts of the Apostles 17: 23.

349. Thomas Henry Huxley, "Agnosticism" (1889), in *Agnosticism and Christianity and Other Essays* (Buffalo: Prometheus Books, 1992), 161.

350. Leslie Stephen, "An Agnostic's Apology," in *An Agnostic's Apology and Other Essays* (London: Smith, Elder, and Co., 1893), 1-2, 9.

351. Maurice to Erskine, 10 February 1859, in Maurice, *Life*, 2:346.

352. Owen Chadwick, *The Spirit of the Oxford Movement: Tractarian Essays* (New York: Cambridge University Press, 1990), 107.

353. This is not to say that Kingsley's position was unsound. "Both Max Müller and T. H. Huxley maintained that the less adroit controversialist was in the right" (Kingsbury Badger, "Christianity and Victorian Religious Confessions," *Modern Language Quarterly* 25 (1964): 86-109. See also F. Meyrick, *But Isn't Kingsley Right After All?: A Letter to the Rev. Dr. Newman* (London: Rivingtons, 1864) and G. Egner, *Apologia pro Charles Kingsley* (London: Sheed and Ward, 1969).

354. Sheldon Rothblatt discusses Seeley's ideological relation to Maurice and Kingsley (*The Revolution of the Dons: Cambridge and Society in Victorian England* [New York: Basic Books, 1968], Ch. 4).

355. William Holden Hutton, *William Stubbs, Bishop of Oxford: 1825-1901* (London: Archibald Constable & Co., Ltd., 1906), 102-03.

356. A Professor in the University of Cape Town to Mrs. Kingsley, n.d., in Kingsley, *Letters and Memories*, 2:133.

357. Kingsley to Mr. Bates, n.d., in Kingsley, *Letters and Memories*, 2:174.

358. Kingsley to Professor Rolleston, Cambridge, 12 October 1862, in Kingsley, *Letters and Memories*, 2:150; cf. 1:283-84.

359. Charles Kingsley, *The Water Babies* (1863; New York: Oxford University Press, 1995), 131.

360. Kingsley to Maurice, n.d., in Kingsley, *Letters and Memories*, 2:175.

361. Maurice, *Life*, 2:452.

362. Baden Powell, "On the Study of the Evidences of Christianity," in Shea and Whitla, 233-61, 258.

363. The model upon which *Essays and Reviews* was based is arguably that of the *Oxford Essays*, first published in 1855 (Shea and Whitla, 10-12).

364. F. H. Hedge, Introduction to *Recent Inquiries in Theology, by Eminent English Churchmen: Being "Essays and Reviews,"* reprinted in Shea and Whitla, 630.

365. *Puseyism the School of the Infidels, or "Broad Church" the Offspring of "High Church": with a Few Words to The Evangelicals, by A Layman of the Established Church* (London: Arthur Miall, 1865), 36-37.

366. "The New Oxford School, or Broad Church Liberalism," *The Biblical Repertory and Princeton Review* 33 (January 1861): 59-84.

367. Connop Thirlwall, *A Charge Delivered to the Clergy of the Diocese of St. David's* (October 1863), abridged in Shea and Whitla, 643-47, 647.

368. Shea and Whitla, 637; Basil Willey, *More Nineteenth Century Studies: A Group of Honest Doubters* (New York: Columbia University Press, 1956), 160-67.

369. Samuel Wilberforce, *A Charge Delivered at the Triennial Visitation of the Diocese, November, 1860*, abridged in Shea and Whitla, 640.

370. Arthur Penrhyn Stanley, "Essays and Reviews," *Edinburgh Review* (April 1861), in *Essays Chiefly on Questions of Church and State, from 1850 to 1870* by A. P. Stanley (London: John Murray, 1870), 146-96, 151-52.

371. "The Protest of the Clergy," in Shea and Whitla, 655-56.

372. Shea and Whitla, 648.

373. A. P. Stanley to the Bishop of Oxford, 19 February 1861, in Randall Thomas Davidson and William Benham, *Life of Archibald Campbell Tait, Archbishop of Canterbury*, 3rd ed., 2 vols. (London: Macmillan and Co., 1891), 1:286.

374. Thirlwall, 235; cf. Joseph Glanvill: "*Authorities* alone with me make no *number*, unless Evidence of Reason stand before them: For all the *Cyphers* of *Arithmatick*, are no better then a single *nothing*" (*The Vanity of Dogmatizing: Or Confidence in Opinions* [London: B. C., 1661], chap. XV, 143-44; *Scepsis Scientifica: Or, Confest Ignorance the Way to Science* [London: E. Cotes, 1665], chap. XVII, 106).

375. Thirlwall, 228.

376. Maurice to Stanley, 12 February 1861, in Maurice, *Life*, 2:382-83.

377. Erskine, 226.

378. Maurice to Bishop Ewing, 28 February 1861, in Maurice, *Life*, 2:384.

379. Maurice to Kingsley, 26 October 1865, in Maurice, *Life*, 2:504-05.

380. Kingsley to Bishop Sumner; n.d., in Kingsley, *Letters and Memories*, 2:138.

381. Kingsley to Stanley, 19 February 1861, in Kingsley, *Letters and Memories*, 2:136-37.

382. Maurice, *Life*, 2:527.

383. James Martineau, "Personal Influences on Present Theology," *National Review* (October 1856), reprinted in *Essays, Reviews, and Addresses*, 4 vols. (London: Longmans, Green, and Co., 1890), 1:219-81, 224-25.

384. James H. Rigg, *Modern Anglican Theology: Chapters on Coleridge, Hare, Maurice, Kingsley, and Jowett, and on the Doctrine of Sacrifice and Atonement* (London: Alexander Heylin, 1857).

385. Maurice to Isaac Taylor, 10 April 1860, in Maurice, *Life*, 2:359.

386. William John Conybeare, "Church Parties," *The Edinburgh Review* 98, no. 200 (October 1853), 273-342, 273.

387. Charles R. Sanders, *Was Frederick Denison Maurice a Broad-Churchman?: A Part of a Dissertation Submitted to the Faculty of the Division of the Humanities in Candidacy for the Degree of Doctor of Philosophy* (Chicago: University of Chicago Libraries, 1934), 8.

388. Maurice, *The Kingdom of Christ*, II.iv.i., 1:261, 275.

389. Sanders, *Was Frederick Denison Maurice a Broad-Churchman?*, 9.

390. Maurice, *Life*, 1:183-84.

391. Maurice to Hare, 15 January 1845, in Maurice, *Life*, 1:399.

392. Maurice to Strachey, 2 March 1849, in Maurice, *Life*, 1:512.

393. A. P. Stanley, "The Gorham Controversy," *Edinburgh Review* (July 1850), in *Essays*, 3-45, 8; Tulloch, 261.

4

Matthew Arnold
and the Oxford Decade

Matthew Arnold came up to Balliol in what has been called "the Annus Mirabilis of Balliol scholars, the zenith of the golden prime."[1] Richard Jenkyns, who was responsible for opening the competitions for Balliol scholarships, had been master of his college since 1819, and in the autumn of 1841 the college boasted of a select body of scholars and commoners, eighty in number. The *Tracts for the Times* had already ceased publication. Number XC had been released in February 1841 and resulted in the protest of the four tutors, led by Balliol senior tutor A. C. Tait. This one tract had caused such an uproar that the bishop of Oxford requested that the entire series be discontinued. After the Hebdomadal Board acquiesced in the censure of Number XC, William G. Ward, in May, resigned his Balliol tutorship.[2]

The tension in the air had not time to dissipate before other issues came to the foreground. For instance, there was the heavily politicized contest over who should succeed Keble as professor of poetry, a contest which focused principally on the partisan affiliations of the contestants—Isaac Williams, author of the controversial Tracts LXXX and LXXXVII, "On Reserve in Communicating Religious Knowledge," and the rather innocuous James Garbett, whose chief offense came *after* his election to the chair in January 1842, when he called Wordsworth a pantheist.[3] Another contemporary source of debate was Baron Bunsen's pet project, the success of which J. H. Newman came to regard as "one of the greatest of mercies," as it forced him to recognize the Church of England as Protestant.[4] This project was the establishment in Jerusalem of an Anglo-Prussian episcopate that would exercise jurisdiction over English and German Protestants in Palestine. Finally, there was the erection, just down the street from St. Mary's, of the Martyrs' Memorial in honor to the three Protestant Prelates of the Church of England who, through martyrdom, bore "witness to the sacred truths which they had affirmed and maintained against the errors of the Church of Rome."[5] Although a proposal for the monument was first brought forward as early as 1838, the unabashedly Foxean sentiment of the project brought faggots to straw and raised the temperature in Oxford until long after the laying of the cornerstone on 19 May 1841.

In this year of controversy, young Arnold, upon arrival at Oxford in October, was quickly elected into the ranks of a small and private debating society, then only five years old, named the Decade. William C. Lake, who had become president of the Oxford Union just after the halcyon days of Gladstone and Manning, was dismayed at finding that the stirring public debate of years past had become overshadowed "by the rows of Private Business."[6] Recognizing that the union was, for whatever reason, failing to stimulate higher thoughts, Lake, together with Benjamin Brodie, founded the Decade.[7] J. D. Coleridge provides what is, despite its vague generalizations and clichés, the best description extant of the idea or essence of the club:

> There was a society called the Decade in those days (a Balliol scout, long since gone to his rest, persisted in embodying the external world's judgment on it by always calling it the Decayed) which I think did a good deal for the mental education of those of us who belonged to it. . . . We discussed all things human and divine—we thought we stripped things to the very bone—we believed we dragged recondite truths into the light of common day and subjected them to the scrutiny of what we were pleased to call our minds. We fought to the very stumps of our intellects, and I believe that many of us—I can speak for one—would gladly admit that many a fruitful seed of knowledge, of taste, of cultivation, was sown on those pleasant if somewhat pugnacious evenings.[8]

The reminiscences of several of the Decade members, when considered collectively, offer an imperfect outline of the society, and if the record books are ever brought to light, they may provide us with the details needed to complete the picture. Nevertheless, a short list of the society's members can be assembled. The more prominent of the members, at least for the purpose of this chapter, were—besides William Charles Lake (1817-1897) and Benjamin Collins Brodie (1817-1880)—Arthur Penrhyn Stanley (1815-1881), Richard William Church (1815-1890), Edward Meyrick Goulburn (1818-1897), John Campbell Shairp (1819-1885), Benjamin Jowett (1817-1893), John Duke Coleridge (1820-1894), Frederick Temple (1821-1902), Arthur Hugh Clough (1819-1861), Theodore Walrond (1824-1887), Thomas (or Tom) Arnold (1823-1900) and, of course, his brother Matthew (1822-1888). Other members appear to have included John F. B. Blackett, George Butler, John Conington, Chichester Fortes-cue, Richard Cowley Powles, Constantine Estlin Prichard, James Riddell, John Billingsley Seymour, and Samuel Waldegrave.[9] The elected members were voted into this select society without ever being aware that they were candidates. It was, therefore, as Lake admits, "open to the charge of being rather narrow and exclusive."[10] On the other hand, the advantage of this procedure is that it eliminates canvassing. The members met in each other's rooms in order to discuss a predetermined subject, and each member would, in turn, provide the topic that he would introduce by means of a prepared speech.[11] The society recognized no settled and sanctified "truth" that was not open to debate. J. H. Newman, upon hearing a reference to the Decade, said, "Ah! that is a Balliol Society in which they discuss whether Saint Charles was a Martyr or not."[12] We are told, "Strauss and Comte, Mill and Bentham, Coleridge, Carlyle, and Maurice appear as factors again and again in the discussions."[13] When we read in R. W. Church's journal, "There is something in Maurice, and his master Coleridge, which wakens thought in me more than any other writings almost," we know that he had not been forsaking the assembly of the elect.[14] Eventually, its members did begin to lose interest. Even so, the Decade survived longer than its name suggests; it was supplanted by the Oxford "Essay Club," founded in 1852 by George Butler's younger brother, Arthur, and his friend George Goschen.[15]

So significant were Arnold's relationships with his fellow Decade members, especially with the main group (as delineated above), not only during his initial years at Oxford in the 1840s, but throughout his life, that they require individual notice. Arnold, writing in 1866 to Shairp, provides the hint which this chapter aims to follow:

> *Multi multa loquuntur: ideo fides parum est adhibenda* [*There are many people who talk a lot, and for that reason little attention is paid to them*], says Thomas à Kempis: but the voices I do turn to are the voices of our old set, now so scattered, who, at the critical moment of opening life, were among the same influences and (more or less) sought the same things as I did myself. What influences those before and after us have been or may be among, or what things they have sought or may seek, God knows. Perhaps the same as we, but we cannot know, cannot, therefore, be sure of understanding them and their criticisms on what we do.[16]

The "old set"—those whose minds were shaped by the same movements of the Time-Spirit, had read the same books, had debated the same issues, and had quaffed together the cup of Oxford sentiment and been intoxicated thereby—they alone were Arnold's fellow countrymen whose opinions had meaning to him. In a letter to his mother, Arnold observes "how the space of ten years, coinciding very much with the appearance of Papa's Life and the beginning of his wide influence, makes the difference between men of the past and men who can in some degree understand the present."[17] For Arnold, the movement of thought in the years 1843-1853 divided past and present, and only those of his generation who had been engaged with that movement were truly his contemporaries.

The Elect

The founding members of the Decade were, as already stated, Lake and Brodie. Lᴀᴋᴇ had been a pupil at Rugby for two years when Dr. Arnold became headmaster. A confrontation in 1830 marked a turning point in his life: "Now, Lake, I know you can do well if you choose, and I shall expect you to do so." That firm, yet gentle, reprimand, spoken in the deep and rough accents of the headmaster, was sufficient to forever change Lake's character: "Whatever I was, I was never an idle boy again."[18] A few years later Lake was, along with C. J. Vaughan and Stanley, one of the sixth form's triumvirate, who "acted and reacted upon each other in an extraordinary way, stimulating each other's abilities and helping to form each other's characters, to their great mutual benefit."[19] As such, he was one of Dr. Arnold's favorites and was invited with the family to Fox How during vacations.

Lake entered Balliol in 1835, obtained a first in Classics in 1838, and was immediately elected fellow. By the end of the next year his "Newmanistic tendencies" were obvious to all of his old friends.[20] In 1842 he succeeded Robert Scott as tutor of ancient and modern history. William Tuckwell, the anecdotal chronicler of Victorian Oxford, was a Balliol undergraduate in '42. From him we learn that Lake "was not liked either as Tutor or as Proctor. His manner was cold, sarcastic, sneering, and a certain slyness earned him the nickname of 'Serpent.'"[21] Arnold only corroborates Tuckwell's report: "Lake is . . . a perfect child—if all does not go as he wishes it, he can neither keep his temper, nor conceal that he has lost it."[22] Still, one former pupil of Lake's recalls, "Those students with whom he took special pains almost invariably gained First Classes in the Final Schools," and with affectionate remembrance records that his tutor was on familiar terms with his pupils, "devoted almost his whole time to their instruction, and conciliated their affections in a marked way."[23] For good or ill Lake served his college until 1858, when he took the college living in the agricultural parish of Huntspill, Somersetshire, "then a very valuable incumbency, but a secluded, unhealthy, stagnant village in the Bristol Channel marshes." Apparently, by hiring a capable curate, Lake found that he could still reside comfortably in London.[24] A few months after the elevation of Tait to the archbishopric of Canterbury in November of 1868, Lake was offered the deanery of Durham, which post he happily accepted.

The cofounder of the Decade, Bʀᴏᴅɪᴇ, was the son of the surgeon Sir Benjamin Brodie, who served as J. C. Hare's physician prior to the archdeacon's death in 1855.[25] Although "a very constant companion" of Lake's, this younger Brodie left Oxford in 1838, after taking his degree, and lost contact with his college friends. Nevertheless, while in London during the 1840s, he developed friendships with later members of the Decade, such as J. D. Coleridge and Matthew Arnold. In 1854, after overcoming grave scruples against subscribing to the Articles, Brodie took his Master's degree, and in the next year was honored by Oxford with the chair of chemistry and, in 1872, with the honorary Doctorate in Civil Law.[26]

STANLEY had left Rugby and entered Balliol a year before Lake and quickly became friends with tutors Ward and Tait. The former, who confessed to Stanley his admiration for Whately and Arnold, soon became his most intimate friend. "What I do like very much in him," Stanley wrote to Vaughan, "is his great honesty, and fearless, and intense love of truth, and his deep interest in all that concerns the happiness of the human race. These I never saw so strongly developed in anybody."²⁷ In 1837 Stanley won both the Ireland Scholarship—for outstanding ability in Greek and Latin—and in competition against Brodie, the Newdigate Prize—for an English verse composition, "The Gipsies." Lake speaks of Stanley as "the most distinguished undergraduate in Oxford," and notes that, although the Decade "almost always had his company at our small gatherings after dinner, which were mostly in the rooms of Goulburn, Waldegrave, Stanley, and myself," Stanley's fellow members "were rather provoked by his being so entirely absorbed by Ward."²⁸

With Ward, Stanley attended St. Mary's, and in comparing Newman with Dr. Arnold, observed "two men differing to the last degree on points which one of them thinks of the greatest importance, and yet in all that is really valuable not only agreeing with, but like, each other." In fact, not only are they like each other, "they are of the very same essence, so to speak."²⁹ A greater compliment from Stanley could hardly be imagined, and yet Newman, writing to Lake in 1882, lamented "poor Stanley, who, up to his dying day, never, as far as I know, said a good word for me."³⁰ From Newman's perspective, Stanley's liberalism, whereby he could discover a common bond between the two men, was a far more dangerous enemy than outright contempt. By 1838, Stanley and Ward had divided over Tractarianism, and Stanley, fearing that the conservatism of some of the Balliol fellows would prejudice them against his election, stood for and won his fellowship at University College.

Before Stanley's appointment as tutor in April 1842, he spent much time abroad, finding traveling companions in Tait, Maurice, and Church. Afterwards, while Tait was pinned down at Rugby, Stanley spent most of his free time at Fox How, preparing Dr. Arnold's *Life*. As soon as the manuscript was finished, in 1844, he set off to Germany with Jowett. In October of the following year, Stanley was appointed select preacher at Oxford and, subsequently, delivered his Sermons on the Apostolical Age. Because Stanley exercised a significant influence upon Arnold's thought, these sermons, along with many of his later appointments and achievements, will be discussed at greater length in the course of this chapter.

CHURCH, largely remembered as the dean of St. Paul's who wrote *The Oxford Movement: Twelve Years, 1833-45* (posthumously published in 1891), entered Wadham College in 1833 and was elected into the Oxford Union in February of the following year. There, two years later, he entered into communication with Lake, and through their association was brought into the newly formed Decade toward the end of 1836, after graduating with a first in October. What is most interesting about his brief period of association with the Decade is that the members' mixed appreciation of Newman's sermons acted upon him as a deterrent. In the fragmented "Recollections" left unfinished at his death, Church states that he put off going to St.

Mary's "because I thought it rather a fashion of a set who talked a kind of religious philosophy—Evangelico-Coleridgean, and claimed at once to admire Newman, whom the common set decried, and to admire with reserve."[31] In April 1838 Church competed against Mark Pattison for an Oriel fellowship and won.[32] On Christmas Day, 1839, in company with Stanley, Church was ordained. Afterwards, he came into close fellowship with the Newman set. In 1853 he took the living of agricultural Whatley, in Somersetshire, which he held until Gladstone offered him, following the death of Dean Mansel in 1871, the vacancy of St. Paul's.

Like Church, GOULBURN came to Oxford as an Evangelical; Goulburn, however, remained an Evangelical. Arnold refers to him as "a very narrow-minded Evangelical."[33] Although his first years at Oxford were spent in Balliol, in 1839, upon graduating with a first in Classics, he was elected into fellowship at Merton and appointed tutor, in which capacity he served until 1841. Then, just as Arnold was entering Balliol, Goulburn left Oxford with his M.A. to take up the principal curacy of Holywell. There he remained until the end of 1849.

When Tait was transferred from Rugby to the deanery of Carlisle, Goulburn competed for the headmaster's position against Lake, George Cotton (then an assistant master at Rugby, and later bishop of Calcutta), and former Rugbeian John Philip Gell (who had just returned from several years of distinguished service in Van Diemen's Land or Tasmania). Nobody supposed that Goulburn stood a chance. Arnold and Clough, placing character above every other consideration, were in support of Gell and vehemently opposed to Lake. Yet, Lake could count among his supporters Tait, Stanley, Jowett, C. J. Vaughan, F. Temple, R. Lingen, and J. D. Coleridge. To use Stanley's expression, "the whole University of Oxford" wanted Lake's election. Goulburn contemplated standing aside, but was persuaded by relations not to withdraw. The Rugby Trustees—upon whose decision the appointment depended—were in a pickle, for they could not quite make out whether Lake was a "Puseyite" or an "Arnoldite." They resolved their difficulty by concluding that his opinions were in an unsettled state and that he was, therefore, unfit for the post.[34] Cotton and Gell were quickly passed over as liberals. As one Rugby historian observes, "It was undoubtedly Goulburn's known hostility to liberalism in religion which commended him to the Rugby Trustees."[35] During his first year at Rugby, Goulburn returned to Oxford to deliver his Bampton Lectures on *The Doctrine of the Resurrection of the Body, as Taught by Holy Scripture.*

SHAIRP came to Balliol from Glasgow University in October 1840, after having gained a Snell Exhibition. It was the Snell that brought a number of Scotsmen, including Tait, to Balliol. In early 1841 Shairp was attracted to the company of Clough, for whom he felt an "idealising hero-worship," and before the end of winter he attended a "wine" at Clough's unheated and ill-furnished lodgings near Holywell Church. There Shairp, with his thick Scottish brogue, joined a discussion, first on Wordsworth and, then, on Coleridge's *Aids to Reflection*.[36] He had brought with him from Scotland "a familiarity with philosophical writers and subjects which is not common among University students in England."[37] All of Shairp's friends remember his moist-eyed recitations of Burns and Scott, his colorful waistcoats, his hard-riding, and the thieving staghound, Gruim, that went wherever his master went and ate whatever his master ate. Clough and Shairp became fast friends, and during the 1840s, they accompanied each other during several long vacations.

In Shairp's attitude towards Newman's sermons or "high poems" we can detect that reserved admiration that Church found so distasteful. Even so, it is sincere and recognizes the religious element in what Arnold would identify as "morality touched by emotion":

> As [Newman] spoke, how the old truth became new! how it came home with a meaning never felt before! He laid his finger—how gently, yet how powerfully!—on some inner place in the hearer's heart, and told him things about himself he had never known till then. . . . After hearing these sermons, you might come away still not believing the tenets peculiar to the High Church system; but you would be harder than most men, if you did not feel more than ever ashamed of coarseness, selfishness, worldliness, if you did not feel the things of faith brought closer to the soul.[38]

In 1844, Shairp graduated with a second and spent the following year reading for the Oriel fellowship examination. As with most Scotsmen, he struggled with English composition, and the fellowships that year went to Matthew Arnold and Henry Coleridge, J. D.'s younger brother who would soon follow Newman Romeward. After escaping with Clough and Thomas Arnold to the Walronds' home in Calder Park, Scotland, Shairp returned in 1846 to accept Tait's offer of a position as assistant master at Rugby. In that year he gained the trust and made a lifelong impact upon one of his pupils, G. D. Boyle, who was, at the time, preoccupied with thoughts of Newman and his secession. "Shairp," Boyle recollects, "talked the whole matter over with me in the kindest and pleasantest way, and told me how much good he had received from men who had been hearty admirers of Arnold, and had caught something of his inspiring and enlivening power."[39] At Rugby, Shairp spent the next eleven years of his life, until, in 1857—again through Tait's assistance—he gained a post at St. Andrews to teach Latin.

JOWETT, who entered Balliol in 1836, became a fellow two years later, while still an undergraduate. Perhaps, the outcome of that election would have been different had Stanley chosen to compete at his own college, but his decision made it possible for both himself and Jowett to gain fellowships in the same year. Even so, their friendship would not ripen until 1845, the year of their travels in Germany. In the meantime, the two had opportunities to become acquainted with each other at the meetings of the Decade, and it is likely that it was through this acquaintance that Jowett came under the influence of Dr. Arnold.[40] George Butler, who was admitted into the society in 1842, describes Jowett as one "very quiet in manner," who "does not show off to advantage in a roomful of men."[41] This rather shy fellow of Balliol began to take part in the teaching of his college in October 1841 and was chosen to succeed Tait as tutor in the following year. As his biographer notes, "Jowett's power as a teacher did not at once fully assert itself." In fact, it was not until the autumn of 1844, when he began his Hegelian lectures on the history of philosophy, that "the larger scope of his thoughts" began to reveal itself. Scholars such as Clough and Matthew Arnold "were too conscious of their own powers to see what lay beneath their youthful teacher's quiet but rather peremptory manner," and thus neither Arnold nor Jowett took the other seriously during these early years.[42] Of all that Arnold owes to this Balliol tutor, there is little that did not, at first, come to him through Walrond and Stanley.

Even so, up until 1855, Jowett—with Lake by his side as friend and fellow tutor—had done extraordinary service for his college and had met with only honor and success. But then, after the death of Jenkyns, Jowett ran for the position of master of Balliol. In opposition, Robert Scott entered into the list. Scott was the former Balliol tutor who, in 1843, gained international distinction as the coauthor (with H. G. Liddell) of the Greek-English Lexicon. Moreover, for the past ten years he had gained the public's trust as the impeccably orthodox headmaster of Westminster. The election was evenly split, and Lake held the deciding vote. At the last moment, Lake was "talked over . . . on theological grounds" by his High Church friend H. P. Liddon.[43] Scott became master, a position that he held until 1870, when Jowett, then professor of Greek and more embittered by life's ironies, finally took the chair.

John Duke COLERIDGE, the son of Dr. Arnold's lifelong friend John Taylor, entered Balliol with a scholarship in April 1839. Having been given by nature a remarkable memory, Coleridge made use of it by "taking infinite pains to acquire a command of language and a certain peculiar refinement of utterance." By the end of his second term his silvern speech had earned him a position of respect in the union, and in 1840 he gained the added distinction of being the first undergraduate elected into the Decade.[44] By this time he was a reverent disciple of Newman: "The genius, the penetration, the sanctity, perhaps, too, the *eironeia* of Newman drew him by an irresistible spell, and never relaxed their hold."[45]

Coleridge, like Stanley, hid his inner life and, to most who knew him, seemed cold and distant. Matt, however, had known J. D. for years. In fact, Dr. Arnold had lent Fox How to the Coleridges while J. D. prepared for the Balliol scholarship exam. Coleridge now returned the favor by introducing Matt into the higher social circles of Oxford, including the meetings of the Decade and the services of St. Mary's. Later, Matt would send volumes of his father's sermons to Coleridge, saying, "I neither expect nor desire that they should change your admiration for Newman. I should be very unwilling to think they did so in my own case, but owing to my utter want of prejudice (you remember your slander) I find it perfectly possible to admire them both."[46]

In February 1842 Coleridge—on account of an intestinal disorder, his lifelong thorn in the flesh—was forced to leave Oxford with a "pass" degree. Yet, in the following year, he triumphantly returned to Oxford, not only as fellow of Exeter, where he joined the society of James Anthony Froude and R. Cowley Powles, but also as president of the union. Before making his final exit from Oxford in 1844 and beginning his meteoric career in law, the future lord chief justice of England privately printed a selection of his poetry in the form of a small book, *Memorials of Oxford*, which he distributed among friends.

TEMPLE was elected Blundell scholar in 1838 and came into residence at Balliol in the following year. The Blundell was the only closed scholarship that Jenkyns had been unable to eliminate, and so the Balliol master often feigned a contempt for its scholars as "inferior men."[47] Temple, however, was quick to reveal that he was in no way inferior, earning a double first in May 1842. After this exhibition of learning, Jenkyns was glad to extend to him the right hand of fellowship. Of course, his abilities had been known before these successes, and he was brought into the Decade in 1840, just after Coleridge's election. At this time, he and Coleridge differed from the other members of the Decade in that, not only were they the only undergraduates, they were also the only Tories. What the friends of Temple remember, however, is his open manner and hearty laugh, his studious and abstemious ways, and his exemplary virtue and conduct. He was another who admired Newman with reserve, "finding in the sermons, as Shairp did, something much greater than the system which they were supposed to advocate."[48] Temple accepted the apostolical succession of the Anglican episcopacy as "a part of God's truth," but recognized as implicit not that dignity of office that Newman insisted upon, but rather "the continuity of the spiritual life" and dignity of the Church as a whole.[49]

Temple was in close sympathy with Tait and, in 1842, succeeded Ward as tutor in mathematics. Working alongside Jowett, the two developed a lasting friendship and, for a brief period, conspired together to publish a translation of Hegel's Logic. Three years later Temple was elected junior dean of Balliol. Then, in 1848, he abandoned Oxford to spend the next ten years working for the Education Office, first as examiner, then as principal of Kneller Hall Training College, and finally as inspector of training schools. In 1857, when Goulburn submitted his resignation to the trustees of Rugby, Matthew Arnold sent that body a testimonial: "In the most important qualities of a schoolmaster, . . . Mr. Temple, more than any other man whom I have ever known, resembles, to the best of my observation and judgment, my late father."[50] Temple was elected and, at the beginning of the new year, startled the Trustees by making his entrance into the school on foot and carrying his own bags. He remained at this post for eleven years, until his nomination as bishop of Exeter in 1869. Subsequently, in '85, he was transferred to London, and finally, in '97 appointed archbishop of Canterbury.

The Inner Circle

Of the members of the Decade, the last four that concern us here, A. H. Clough, Walrond, and the Arnold brothers, enjoyed a particularly close friendship and form something of a subdivision, which is often referred to as the Clougho-Matthean set.

Tom Arnold provides his recollections:

> After I came up to University in October [1842], Clough, Theodore
> Walrond, my brother and I formed a little interior company, and saw a
> great deal of one another. We used often to go skiffing up the Cherwell,
> or else in the network of river channels that meander through the broad
> meadows facing Iffley and Sandford. After a time it was arranged that we
> four should always breakfast at Clough's rooms [at Oriel] on Sunday
> morning. Those were times of great enjoyment.[51]

CLOUGH was the senior member of this "interior company," nearly four years
older than Matthew. Born in Liverpool, Clough, as a child of three, had migrated
with his family to Charleston, Virginia, where his father prospered as a cotton
merchant. There he remained for over five years, nurtured by his affectionate and
earnestly Evangelical mother, until he was returned to England for formal education.
He entered Rugby in 1829 and, although he had numerous relatives in England and
Wales who opened their homes to him, he had no home of his own other than Rugby
until his parents returned to Liverpool in the summer of 1836. Upon entering into the
sixth form, Clough (or, as his schoolfellows called him, "Yankee Tom") took up
residence in the schoolhouse, where Matt and Tom noted his frequent presence
inside the Arnolds' private quarters. Tom Arnold would later recall that Mrs.
Arnold, "who marked his somewhat delicate health, conceived a great liking for him.
His gentleness, and that unwonted *humanity* of nature which made him unlike the
ordinary schoolboy, caused him to be a welcome guest in her drawing-room."[52]
    Clough entered Balliol with a scholarship in 1837. His entire undergraduate
experience was under the tutelage of Ward, Tait, and Scott, and with the first of
these three he was especially close. Within three months of taking residence at
Oxford, he writes to J. P. Gell, "I am great friends with Brodie, and still more so, I
think, with Ward, whom I like very much. I have seen more of him and of Lake than
of any one else."[53] A year later he adds this revealing admonition:

> If you were to come here (as I hope you will after your degree is done
> with), you would at once have Ward at you, asking you your opinions on
> every possible subject. . . . I don't quite like hearing so much of these
> matters as I do, but I suppose if one can only keep steadily to one's work
> (which I wish I did), and quite resolve to forget all the words one has
> heard, and to theorise only for amusement, there is no harm in it.[54]

Although Ward believed in objective truth, he was too skeptical to believe that there
was more to be hoped for than logical consistency. Knowing and Being appear to
have been, for him, sufficiently dissociated to permit theorizing "only for amusement" without in the least jeopardizing his feeling of relationship with God. Thus, he
could be persuaded by J. S. Mill on Monday, be converted to Dr. Arnold's point of
view on Wednesday, be thoroughly Newmanized on Friday, and still take Holy

Communion on Sunday. For Clough, Ward's theorizing and logic-crunching was intellectually, morally, and spiritually exhausting. As a child at his mother's knee, he had heard Christ's words, "Ye shall know the truth." Religious truth, the highest truth of all, was, evidently, not only objective, but within reach of discernment, and every man had a moral duty to seek it and to abide in it, if he would also abide in God.

For two years Clough was "like a straw drawn up the draught of a chimney,"[55] and when the draft dissipated, Clough found himself up in the air, with logical consistency as his only parachute, and with a fearful uncertainty, not *how* he might best make contact with the terra firma of Truth, but whether he *could* make contact at all. In August of 1840, after a three-weeks' vacation with Ward at Grasmere, Clough confides to a friend, "That I have been a good deal unsettled in mind at times at Oxford, and that I have done a number of foolish things, is true enough, and I dare say the change from Rugby life to its luxury and apparent irresponsibility has had a good deal of ill effect upon me."[56] A year later he stunned all of Balliol by failing to make the class list, and for awhile there was a real possibility that he might have to leave Oxford, but in the spring of '42 he secured his place by winning a fellowship at Oriel. During the next few years—beginning just after the sudden death of Dr. Arnold—Clough was, as H. F. Lowry observes, "falling back upon his own morality and character, wherein the intuitions of faith lay, and thinking less about positive proofs and the importance of them." Arnold too was, during these years, striving to secure his faith beyond the sphere of traditions and dogmas.[57]

Of Clough's participation in the Decade more information has been preserved than of anyone else's. It appears that he was not elected into the society until after he gained his fellowship. Shairp remembers hearing Clough speak twice at the Decade between 1843 and '45: "The first time was in Oriel Common-room; the subject proposed: 'That Tennyson was a greater poet than Wordsworth.' ... Clough spoke against the proposition, and stood up for Wordsworth's greatness with singular wisdom and moderation." On another occasion, when the argument was "That the character of a gentleman was, in the present day, made too much of," Clough, in his slow, deliberate manner, addressed the society for nearly two hours, speaking neither for nor against the proposition.[58] Tom Arnold recalls that, in 1844 or '45, Clough spoke in support of "a resolution that I had proposed in favour of Lord Ashley's Ten Hours' Bill" and against "the doctrines of *laissez-faire* and the omnipotence and sufficiency of the action of Supply and Demand."[59] John Conington, who in 1846 became a scholar of Magdalen College and was made secretary of the Decade, observes that he first met Clough at a meeting that year, on 14 February: "I can recall," says Conington, "his commanding manner, and the stately serene tones in which he delivered a kind of prophecy of the new era which in a few days was to be inaugurated, and told us that 'these men (the manufacturers) were the real rulers of England.'" Later in the year, on 9 June, Clough spoke partly in favor of the proposition "That any system of moral science, distinct from a consideration of Christianity, is essentially imperfect." Conington appears to have had the books of the Decade for the years of 1846 through the early part of '48, and notes that, during this time, Clough appeared at Decade meetings on five other occasions. During one evening, on 6 March 1847, he made five separate speeches, supporting "with qualifications" the proposition "That the study of philosophy is more important for the formation of opinion than that of history."[60] Two months later, Robert Morier attended a Decade meeting in which Clough addressed the topic of the advisability of a separation between Church and State. All of the speakers were agreed that the separation was inevitable. According to Morier, Clough, as a speaker, was second only to Conington.[61] Dean Boyle remembers attending a Decade meeting in which Clough spoke "for nearly an hour on the social questions so prominent at the time of the Revolution of 1848. It was a marvelous speech, and his words as to the duties of property sank into my soul." Clough concluded with an allusion to a passage in Carlyle's *Sartor Resartus*, "and when he had done speaking, some one who was present, said, 'These are words to think about, not to attempt to answer.'"[62]

WALROND, known to his friends as "Todo," entered Rugby in 1834, where, despite his small stature, he became captain of the football (soccer) team.[63] He was, evidently, athletic, and years later he would spar off against Matt for a game of tennis. He was in the sixth form at the same time as the two oldest of the Arnold brothers, and after being successfully tutored by Clough for the Balliol scholarship, entered Oxford in 1842. As a Scot, he was often with Shairp during vacations, on long walks and reading parties, which, on occasion, also included Clough and Tom. While hiking along the shore of Loch Ericht, this group shared the adventure that Clough's imagination later stretched into *The Bothie of Tober-na-Vuolich*.[64] Walrond also became part of an "inner circle" that gathered around Jowett, which included William Sellar, Alexander Grant, Francis Palgrave, and H. J. S. Smith: "They were on the best terms of good fellowship, and devotedly attached to Jowett as their teacher and friend, submitting to his insistent criticism only because of his evident good will towards them."[65]

Walrond took a first in 1846, and immediately accepted an invitation from Tait to become an assistant master at Rugby.[66] Afterwards, in 1848, he became a master, which position he held until '51, when, having gained a fellowship at Balliol in the year before, he was appointed tutor. He left Oxford in 1857 in order to work for the civil service, first as examiner and, subsequently, as commissioner. In 1869, after Temple's preferment to a bishopric, Walrond stood for the headmastership. Arnold, along with Temple, supported his election, but with reservations: "he is too old and *set*."[67] The Rugby Trustees, instead, created a national scandal and brought the school into disrepute by appointing—on the basis of outdated and readdressed letters of recommendation—the conservative Henry Hayman.[68] Throughout his life, Walrond remained a close friend of the Arnolds, was present at Matt's wedding, and, two years later, was godfather to his second son, Trevenen William ("Budge"). To him had fallen the task and honor of editing Stanley's letters, but his own death intervened, and so his chief contribution to literature is *The Letters and Journals of James, Eighth Earl of Elgin* (1871). When Walrond died, no one was found to edit his letters or write his life. Thus, he remains, as Cecil Lang observes, "the most obscure by far of what Tom Arnold called 'the little interior company.'"[69]

To Tom, Matt wrote in 1857,

> You alone of my brothers are associated with that life of Oxford, the *freest* and most delightful part, perhaps of my life—when with you and Clough and Walrond I shook off all the bonds and formalities of the place, and enjoyed the spring of life and that unforgotten Oxfordshire and Berkshire country.[70]

TOM ARNOLD, shortly after the death of his father in June of 1842, entered University College and took up rooms just opposite to Stanley, who insisted on looking out after him. Once or twice Tom went to hear Newman preach at St. Mary's, but, as he recalls, "the delicacy and refinement of his style were less cognisable by me than by my brother, and the multiplied quotations from Scripture . . . confused and bewildered me." Tom took a first in *Literæ Humaniores* in 1845, after which he was elected to a foundation scholarship at University. This scholarship would have, inevitably, led to fellowship, and—as Tom observes—"common prudence dictated that this opening to a life career should not be cast aside." However, the "hungry forties" were a time of social discontent, not of prudence, and Tom chose, instead, to remove to London, where he read law at Lincoln's Inn and offered unrequited love to Henrietta Whately. He also attended to the sermons of Maurice, but the preacher's strong sense of objectivity had an air of unreality to it. In describing his own state of mind at the time, Tom says, "There seemed to be nothing which was not matter of opinion."

At the beginning of 1847, he accepted a position as clerk in the Colonial Office, and in November, with Utopian dreams in his pocket, boarded a steamer, and set out to take possession of the 200 acres of New Zealand property that Dr. Arnold had purchased in the days before Fox How.[71] What was not in Tom's pocket was the land grant. That had been committed to the care of trustees in England. Even so, as it was clear to Tom, upon his arrival, that the acres his father had bought were not the best, and since the agent in control of the territory's colonization generously offered an exchange, Tom assumed that the trustees would defer to his judgment. Therefore, he traded and invested all of his money in the clearing of this new plot of ground and the building of a hut (which he called "Fox How"), and when he finally received word from the trustees that he was to make no exchange or sale of land, Tom was broke.[72] In October of 1848, through the intervention of Charles Stanley—the brother of Arthur who was, then, captain of the Royal Engineers at Hobart Town—Tom was offered the post of inspector of schools in the colony of Van Diemen's Land. He promptly accepted.[73] There he was to find "the answer to the questions which had never ceased to harass me since I grew to manhood—what, namely, is the ideal of human life, and what the discipline by which that life should be controlled." While working as school inspector he met and married Julia Sorrell, who shortly thereafter gave birth to Mary (later Mrs. Humphry Ward), and in 1856 he converted to Roman Catholicism, surrendered his inspectorship, and returned to England.[74]

MATTHEW ARNOLD's position relative to the Decade very nearly suffered the same fate as Tennyson's relationship to the Apostles—that is, it was almost terminated. On the occasion of the great debate regarding the comparative merits of Tennyson and Wordsworth, it was Arnold, not Clough, who was scheduled to defend the Lake poet. Arnold never showed. "Matt, you must make a speech," Coleridge remonstrated with him. "Why," answered Arnold, "I never did such a thing in my life."[75] There were members who thought his attitude too flippant for their society, but the truth is that the spirit of the Decade was often too contentious for Arnold. "I had rather live in a purer air than that of controversy," he would later confide to his mother.[76] The pursuit of truth and the creation of a poem alike required calm reflection and delicacy of tact and judgment. Undoubtedly, the society of the Apostles at Cambridge would have been more congenial for Matt. Even Clough had "become quite a convert to the Cambridge set's superiority," although, he added, only in Oxford—or, at least, "in the grandness of the idea of it"—could one find the full measure of "public and political and national feeling."[77]

Dr. Arnold had planted the seed of this "Oxford idea" in Matt, but not even Oxford itself could force the seed to germinate. Matt was resistant. He was, at this time of his life—if I may take a metaphor from St. Luke's Gospel—a Mary, not a Martha; he was willing to give to necessity and institutional systems what they demanded of him, and the fact that he was unwilling to give more did not mean that he was lazy or rejected his duty, but rather, that he saw a better way. There is, in fact, a good deal of the youthful Schleiermacher of the *Soliloquies* to be found in young Arnold: "Leisure is my dear divinity," wrote Schleiermacher; "by her favor man learns to understand and to determine himself. It is in leisure that ideas ripen unto power which easily governs all when the world calls for action." Though Arnold's "silent effort" appeared from without as mere idleness, it served the "inward task of self-development."[78]

Self-Development

In the critical years of 1843-1853 the Time-Spirit was not idle, but—acting through Spinoza and Schleiermacher, Hegel and Strauss, Coleridge and Maurice, Carlyle and Emerson—was vigorously at work upon the consciousness of the Decade. St. Paul had pleaded, "That we henceforth be no more children, tossed to and fro, and carried about with every wind of doctrine."[79] Arnold looked about him and saw caps and gowns blowing in every direction. In books he found the "Children of the Second Birth, / Whom the world could not tame."[80] There was, for example, Obermann, the romantic hero who, for the sake of self-knowledge, in an impulsive moment, delivers himself from bondage to society and seeks refuge for his soul in the Swiss Alps.[81] From this example, Arnold gleans, "He only lives with the world's life,

/ Who hath renounced his own."[82] In Glanvill's *Vanity of Dogmatizing* (1661), Arnold finds that "oft-read tale" of the Scholar-Gipsy,[83] an immortal figure, who, like Senancour, renounces all in order to attain a purer life and a freer thought. However, unlike the author of *Obermann*, Arnold's scholar-gipsy does not return to society, but keeps himself unspotted by the world, aloof from the "strange disease of modern life."

> But fly our paths, our feverish contact fly!
>   For strong the infection of our mental strife,
>   Which, though it gives no bliss, yet spoils for rest;
>   And we should win thee from thy own fair life,
>   Like us distracted, and like us unblest.
>   Soon, soon thy cheer would die.[84]

What Arnold's scholar-gipsy has most to lose through contact with modernity is his hope of "the spark from heaven," that living hope for which he leaves behind his Oxford friends in exchange for the vagabond life.[85]

For Arnold, however, there can be no renunciation. He realizes that neither Senancour nor even the Carthusian monks in the Swiss Alps can escape the modern world, the sights and sounds that "make their blood dance and chain their eyes."[86] The principle of renunciation attains its ultimate realization not in Obermann, but in that ardent soul, Empedocles, who, unwilling to make contact with a corrosive society and weary of solitude, chooses death, for "only death / Can cut his oscillations short, and so / Bring him to poise."[87] This recognition of the impossibility of the romantic principle of renunciation is, for Arnold, a significant step in his journey toward maturation and social responsibility, for it throws him back upon the classical principle of resignation.

Resignation, that Stoic virtue of accepting, without aversion or resistance, the things that are not within our power, came to Arnold as a necessity rather than a blessing. It lacked both the apparent heroism and the willful rebellion of renunciation, and it promised no paradise regained. The lost joy and innocence of Arnold's nostalgic verse is *forever* lost, and when "the world cries your faith is now / But a dead time's exploded dream," the principle of resignation offers "not joy, but peace" and a "sad lucidity of soul."[88]

If the letters of *Obermann* give us "the lamentations of the soul on a journey from the centre, while it knows well that its rest remains at the centre,"[89] the early verse of Arnold—and certainly his best verse—presents the lamentations of the soul restlessly seeking a true center, after the false has been displaced. Of course not all of the poet's verse represents the poet's voice, and in his letters Arnold more than once expresses his impatience with critics who "fix on the speeches of Empedocles and Obermann, and calmly say, dropping all mention of the real speakers, 'Mr. Arnold here professes his Pantheism,' or 'Mr. Arnold here disowns Christianity.'"[90]

Still, there is something of the pilgrim Dante in Arnold, as he calls upon the wisdom of past masters for spiritual guidance.

Recognizing that "a man is a just and fruitful object of contemplation much more by virtue of what spirit he is of than by virtue of what system of doctrine he elaborates,"[91] Arnold turned to the *Bhagavad Gita* and found the Quietist's ethic of "detachment." Afterwards, turning to Spinoza, he discovered the promise of a philosopher's freedom in apprehending all things *sub specie æternitatis*. But even before Arnold mined these sources of inspiration, he first found something of lasting value in what he heard and saw at St. Mary's. Arnold would later write to Newman, "We are all of us carried in ways not of our own making or choosing, but nothing can ever do away the effect you have produced upon me, for it consists in a general disposition of mind rather than in a particular set of ideas." From Newman, Goethe, Wordsworth, and Sainte-Beuve, Arnold learnt "habits, methods, and ruling ideas," fundamental principles and centering practices that preserved against fragmentation.[92]

Fellowship by Synthesis

Arnold had an awful habit of putting off work and relying, instead, upon his brilliance and charm. After procrastinating until the day before Responsions, he begged Temple to help him cram for logic. Temple obliged, and Arnold passed, answering every question.[93] In the summer of 1844, Arnold, Clough, and Walrond formed a reading-party at Fox How, but while Clough and Walrond studied, Arnold fished. That autumn Arnold came away from "Schools" (final exams) not so unscathed, having placed in the second class. Nevertheless, he redeemed himself on 28 March 1845, when he won, in competition against Shairp, a fellowship at Oriel.[94]

When Arnold returned to Oxford after the long vacation, he found that he had become a minor celebrity. In fact, all of England was becoming acquainted with "Matt" or "Crab"—as his father at times called him. Stanley's *Life and Correspondence of Thomas Arnold, D.D.* had been released at the end of May 1844, and by the beginning of '45 had reached its fourth edition. Sixteen years later, even after Matt's first three volumes of poetry had been published, he would still find himself "far oftener an object of interest" as the son of Dr. Arnold, than for anything he himself had achieved.[95] A somewhat bemused Arnold quickly learned to accept awkward queries and impolite fascination from Stanley's readers.

Arnold himself had become one of these readers. He was "delighted" by his father's letters. "I did not know," he writes to his mother, "that he had felt or entered upon many of the difficulties there discussed." The letters did not merely augment his understanding of his father, but provided him with deeper insight and appreciation. This was especially true in regard to Dr. Arnold's ecclesiastical views and religious beliefs: "I could not have believed I should find anything to enjoy so fully and so fully to go along with."[96] It was a revelation to Arnold to find out just how much there was within himself that he owed to his father, but through the intellectual influence of the letters themselves, Arnold would ultimately come to owe a substantial, if not equal, debt to Stanley's *Life and Correspondence*.

In October 1845, while Newman was preparing to secede from the Church of England, Stanley was appointed select preacher in the place of Samuel Wilberforce. Before the preacher delivered his first sermon to the congregation at St. Mary's in February, he met in daily converse with Jowett, and when the first draft was prepared, he circulated it to men of divergent views—not with the vain hope of pleasing all, but in order to give criticism its due regard. In "The Three Apostles," Stanley identifies the three (SS. Peter, Paul, and John) as each a representative of a part of the universal Church, as each a type of Churchman, and in doing so, he arrives as "the most practical and obvious" lesson, which is "the solemn, I might almost say the awful, sanction, thus given, to the union of the most various tempers, thoughts and views, within the pale of our Christian sympathy."[97] That Stanley had learned from the Tübingen school is clear, for he observes, "There was a time when the Churches of St. James knew nothing of the Churches of St. Paul—that nearly a whole generation passed away before either of them received the Gospel and Epistles of St. John—that the very highest truths concerning God and man are expressed by each of the Three in terms not merely dissimilar, but absolutely opposed, to the other."[98] It is, thus, not only the purpose of the Church of Christ to unite dissimilar elements, but it is by the very essence of Christianity that it has the power to do so.

Perhaps, this message would have been sufficient in itself to have branded Stanley a liberal and to have disqualified him as a candidate for the professorship of exegesis. But, Stanley had more to say. What, asks Stanley, is this precious Apostolical Succession so boasted of by the Newmanites? Is it not "the spirit" of the Apostles' example, "that new wonder which the world saw for the first time in their lives—and which alone is the imperishable part of an Apostle's office—the devotion of their whole energies for the love of Christ, to the moral and spiritual good of man"?[99] What, asks Stanley, are the Newmanites so fearful of in modern biblical criticism? "If criticism destroys much, it creates more. If it cuts away some grounds from our faith, it re-constructs out of the chasm others incomparably more secure. If the sea of doubt has advanced along one part of our coast, it has proportionably receded from another."[100]

When Stanley stepped back from the podium, Jowett was there to congratulate him on the success of his enterprise, assuring him that, on the whole, his "character for orthodoxy has rather gained than lost by it"; yet, later in the year, Stanley writes to a friend, "The odour of my heterodoxy has penetrated not only into the Board of Heads, but into the Cabinet of Whig Ministers."[101] On the one hand, Stanley's sermons barred him from immediate advancement and destroyed whatever chance he might have had of one day obtaining the professorship of divinity, but on the other hand, they demonstrated how biblical criticism could give support to the ideal of the Broad Church.

Arnold listened to Stanley's sermons attentively, and afterwards made use of what he heard in a letter to Jules Michelet, introducing Stanley to the French historian.[102] But, in his diary, Arnold noted his difficulty with Stanley's approach to religion: "The objection which really wounds and perplexes me from the religious side is that the service of reason is chilling to feeling, chilling to the religious mood, and feeling and the religious mood are eternally the deepest being of man, the ground of all joy and greatness for him."[103] It was the preponderance of the intellect over the emotion in Stanley that never ceased to disturb Arnold, who, in his letters, complains of the want of "deep religious power" in Stanley's sermons. And yet, the want of intellectual depth in a preacher was, to Arnold, equally as grievous. Of Temple, Arnold wrote home, "Perhaps he throws more emotion, and even passion, into his preaching than papa did, but, on the other hand, he does not give quite the same impression of depth and solidity."[104] The criticism, in this case, betrays the struggles of the critic, not to attain some meager balance of intellect and feeling in religion, but a method by which the most fully developed mind and heart might unite in a mutually beneficial and supportive faith.

The Forty Minus One

While Arnold turned inward to find the harmonizing principles that must be the basis of all true religion, and which would empower modern man to be at one with the Eternal, to pursue perfection, and attain happiness, Clough turned outward. He too sought a greater reality in religion than that which tradition seemed to offer, but Clough had neither Stanley's trust in the historical foundation of Scripture, nor Arnold's trust in the role of human subjectivity in religious inquiry. There was the ideal to which humanity aspired, that synthesis between Man and God, and *that* was Christ. And what did it mean to know Christ, if not to have and act upon the moral aspiration to do justice, love mercy, and walk humbly before God? This being the case, Clough truly felt that all mere dogmas—regardless of how high they were stacked and how many thousands bowed their knees to them—were but idols of the temple.

As early as 1843 Clough expressed his "repugnance" to signing the Thirty-nine Articles—something he had to do if he would work as a college tutor or take a degree. He says to J. P. Gell, with an obvious allusion to Maurice's pamphlet *Subscription No Bondage* (1835), "It is not so much from any definite objection to this or that point, as general dislike to subscription, and strong feeling of its being a bondage and a very heavy one, and one that may cramp and cripple one for life." Nevertheless, he did subscribe, all the while uncertain whether he did so "in a justifiable sense," and by the summer of 1844 was considering whether life would be more tolerable at London University.[105] During this same summer, after a stretch at Fox How, Clough spent some time in Liverpool with his family. George, his younger brother, had recently died in Charleston, and his father had returned home from the journey a broken and dying man.

In Liverpool the intellectual and moral tone was set by the Unitarian Church, particularly through the ministries of James Martineau and J. H. Thom. It was in Liverpool that Blanco White had settled in 1833 and died in '41. Clough was drawn by chords of sympathy to the religious struggles and doubts of this Spanish Catholic priest-turned-Anglican-turned-Unitarian. "He could not be otherwise than he was," Clough wrote to a friend; "he could not but fancy throughout his life that he was being bullied into a sham belief."[106] In September of 1845, while in Scotland with Tom, Walrond, and Shairp, Clough read through Thom's *Life of the Rev. Joseph Blanco White* and found it "strong meat." He confides to Gell, "almost it persuaded me to turn Unitarian, that is, for the moment; and even now I feel no common attraction towards the book and the party who have brought it out, viz. the high Unitarians."[107] After returning to Liverpool, Clough left for Rugby, spending the Christmas there with Matt and Shairp, as they all waited in hopes that "St. Francis" would soon be there.

Francis Newman—or Frank, as he was known by his friends—argues, in a pamphlet published in 1881 titled *What is Christianity without Christ?*, that "the goodness of the Christian, as of the Christ" consists not in a creed, but in "a substantive moral essence," and that the *imitatio Christi* is "identical with an aspiration after all human virtue—an aspiration to obey God."[108] This appears to have been Newman's thought at least as early as 1850, as indicated in *Phases of Faith*, and it is very much like the concept that Clough adopted shortly after his meeting with Frank. Writing in May 1847 to his sister, Clough reflects, "I cannot feel sure that a man may not have all that is important in Christianity even if he does not so much as know that Jesus of Nazareth existed." This being the case, biblical criticism has ceased to trouble him: "Trust in God's justice and love, and belief in His commands as written in our conscience, stand unshaken, though Matthew, Mark, Luke, and John, or even St. Paul, were to fall." Yet, Clough was not at all prepared to abandon Christianity. In all of his speculations, he continues, "Coleridge has been to me the antidotive power; he was a philosopher and a firm believer." For Coleridge, as for Dr. Arnold, the critical questions revolved around the inspiration and historicity of the Scriptures, but now, "the thing which men must work at" is the philosophical basis of Christianity, "problems of Grace, and Free Will, and of Redemption as an idea, not as a historical event."[109] Thus, as early as 1847, Clough had arrived at the phase of faith in which religious language becomes metaphor. He knew already the answer to his "Easter Day" doubts:

> Though He be dead, He is not dead,
> Nor gone, though fled,
> Not lost, though vanished;
> Though He return not, though
> He lies and moulders low;

> In the true creed
> He is yet risen indeed;
> Christ is yet risen.[110]

There is no mysticism in Clough's "Christ is yet risen." It is not a conviction borne of a deep and inward communion with a spiritual presence. Such experiences may be possible, and might even seem meaningful, but they were too subjective for Clough. Thus, in the autumn of 1847, Clough publicly lashed out against Frank: "The belief that religion is, or in any way requires, devotionality, is, if not the most noxious, at least the most obstinate form of *ir*religion."[111] Afterwards, Martineau wrote consolingly to a stunned Newman, expressing his disappointment in Clough: "I find it possible to sympathise more or less with almost *any* faith; but I cannot sympathise with *no*-faith."[112] Afterwards, when Newman released his *Phases of Faith*, Arnold tossed in his two cents, telling Clough that the book was enough to make one think "that enquiries into articles, biblical inspiration, etc., etc., were as much the natural functions of a man as to eat and copulate."[113] But Arnold and Clough, in attacking Frank, assaulted each another, for Arnold could not dispense with the mystical "inward spring"—of which "one must not talk, for it does not like being talked about, and threatens to depart if one will not leave it in mystery"[114]— and Clough could not dispense with "enquiries into articles, biblical inspiration, etc., etc."

By the end of 1847 the Clougho-Matthean set had broken apart. In the year before, Walrond had taken a permanent teaching position at Rugby. In the spring of '47 Matt, after returning from six weeks in Paris, cleaned out his rooms at Oriel and moved to London, taking a position as secretarial assistant to the fourth Marquis of Lansdowne, junior lord of the Treasury under Russell. In the autumn Tom, packing Spinoza, Hegel, and Walrond's rifle, migrated to New Zealand. Clough still felt that his tutorship at Oriel placed him in a false position, as it was his only by virtue of having subscribed to the Articles, and now that his friends had dispersed, he had to face his conscience alone. He confessed his difficulties candidly to Oriel's provost, Edward Hawkins. He, in turn, explained that it was impossible to suppose that subscription meant that the intellect would always give its assent, that difficulties would not come and go.[115] But, on the other hand, Carlyle was voicing his horror and stern condemnation against all insincerities, and Clough was listening. Finally, at the end of January 1848, he writes to Tom, "I have given our Provost notice of my intention to leave his service (as tutor) at Easter." This would be Easter, 1849. Five months later, Tom enthusiastically responds, trying to interest his friend in a scheme for a college in New Zealand to "be founded expressly on the principle that no particular religion was to be taught there. . . . Supposing, that I were elected Principal, do you think there would be any chance of your accepting a Professorship?"[116]

Not all of Clough's friends could be so optimistic and sympathetic. When, after returning from Paris with Emerson, Clough announced his intent to surrender his fellowship and take a position at University College in London, Shairp remonstrated with him, urging that he keep both feet on the ground. In reply, Clough reminded Shairp "that no man moves without having one leg always *off*, as well as one leg always *on*, the ground."[117] Arnold peevishly supposed that Clough had merely exchanged one bondage for another, becoming instead—as Clough himself willingly admitted—the "lacquey and flunkey" of the Time-Spirit. And when, after the fellowship—and with the fellowship, a steady income—was resigned, and the *Bothie* was the rave of Clough's old Oxford friends, Arnold was beyond irritation and half-seriously entertained the notion of breaking the friendship: "better that," he reasoned, "than be sucked for an hour even into the Time Stream in which they and he plunge and bellow."[118] A few months later, in a more dispassionate moment, Arnold pleaded with his friend:

> My dearest Clough, these are damned times—everything is against one—the height to which knowledge is come, the spread of luxury, our physical enervation, the absence of great *natures*, the unavoidable contact with millions of small ones, newspapers, cities, light profligate friends, moral desperadoes like Carlyle, our own selves, and the sickening consciousness of our difficulties: but for God's sake, let us neither be fanatics nor yet chaff blown by the wind.[119]

Resignation

In 1849 Arnold had other reasons to be on edge, for his intimacy with Mary Claude (one of the more probable candidates for the "Marguerite" of tortured infatuation[120]) had come to an abrupt end, and his first volume, *The Strayed Reveller, and Other Poems*, failed to elicit from his friends half the applause they had given so uncritically to Clough's verse. J. A. Froude, whose *Nemesis of Faith* was publicly burned at Oxford in February, and who was making immediate plans to follow the examples of Clough and Tom—that is, to resign his fellowship and emigrate to Van Diemen's Land—told Kingsley that *The Strayed Reveller* was, like Arnold himself, calm, elegant, and shallow. A week later Froude wrote to Clough, "I admire Matt—to a very great extent. Only I don't see what business he has to parade his calmness and lecture us on resignation when he has never known what a storm is and doesn't know what he has to resign himself to."[121] The poet tried to be Stoic ("as I feel rather as a reformer in poetical matters, I am glad of this opposition"[122]), but his pride left him vulnerable and defensive.

    J. D. Coleridge was, at first, a kinder critic. After reading Arnold's poems, he wrote to his father, "I think one or two better than any I have seen this long while."[123] Later, in April 1854, Coleridge would, in a public review, find Matt's poems guilty of having "no relevancy to actual life," of "passing by God's truth and the facts of man's nature as if they had no existence," of failing "to ennoble and purify, and help us in our life-long struggle with sin and evil." The judge pronounced his verdict: such poetry, "however beautiful, however outwardly serene and majestic, is false and poor and contemptible."[124] What really stung Arnold, though, was the charge of plagiarism, of failing to acknowledge his indebtedness to narrative sources. In reply, Arnold wrote to a common friend, "My love to J. D. C., and tell him that the limited circulation of the *Christian Remembrancer* makes the unquestionable viciousness of his article of little importance. I am sure he will be gratified to think that it is so."[125] Stanley interceded, and after the friends were reconciled, he wrote to Coleridge, reminding him that Dr. Arnold "laid it down as a rule never to review the writings of a friend." This was a policy that Matt himself had learned to follow only after, in private letters, having been harshly critical of Clough's poems.[126]

Through Coleridge, Arnold was introduced into the social beehive of the Inns of Court and soon developed friendships with Wyndham Slade and Walter Bagehot. On one fateful evening, Slade and Coleridge brought Arnold as their guest to a party hosted by Sir William Wightman. Judge Wightman was—beside being a High Churchman, a Tory, and a close friend of John Wilson Croker (the brutal antagonist of lyric poets and Christian Socialists)—the father of the lovely Frances Lucy. Arnold, unaware of the "consequence yet hanging in the stars," was a Montague in the palace of the Capulets. Other parties followed, and by the end of July 1850, Clough was, with evident amusement, writing to Tom of Matt's deep "flirtation" with Miss Wightman: "It is thought it will come to something, for he has actually been to Church to meet her."[127] The "thought" to which Clough refers was certainly not Judge Wightman's, for Arnold was—besides being an Arnold—a poet with little means and less promise. As soon as the judge became aware of the dangerous flirtation, he forbade the two to meet.

Arnold was forced by love to make a life-changing decision. His Oriel fellowship, along with his salary as Lord Lansdowne's secretary, provided him with not only the means to live a bachelor's life, but—what was of greater value—the leisure to live a poet's life. It was a life with advantages. Yet, if he were to have the slightest chance of winning the hand of Miss Wightman, he would have to surrender his fellowship and secure gainful employment. Near the end of the year, he writes to Frances Lucy ("Flu") from Fox How, "Lingen, who is Education Secretary, and was once my tutor at Oxford, and a genius of good counsel to me ever since, says he means to write me a letter of advice about inspectorships."[128] While Lingen and Lansdowne worked to find a place for Arnold in the ranks of Her Majesty's inspectors of schools, the poet adopted an Empedoclean air, as he gazed downward, into the dark crevice of fate: "The aimless and unsettled, but also open and liberal state of our youth we must perhaps all leave and take refuge in our morality and character; but with most of us it is a melancholy passage from which we emerge shorn of so many beams that we are almost tempted to quarrel with the law of nature which imposes it on us."[129] On 23 March 1851 Arnold was appointed inspector, and then successfully made arrangements with the Judge for a June wedding.

Marriage, children, and an extremely time-consuming and wearisome job did not shear off *all* of Arnold's beams or put an end to his career as a poet, but it—along with his own high standards—did severely curtail his production. According to one popular myth, as Arnold became more of his father's son, more of a champion of the Church and State, the poet in him suffocated. Those who adopt this view almost invariably call forth as their witness "Sohrab and Rustum," Arnold's 1853 "plagiarized" poem, taken from a story of Firdousi's, which had been reproduced in Sainte-Beuve's *Causeries du Lundi*. The story tells of a father, Rustum, who comes to embrace his son only after having first fatally wounded him. Despite the fact that Arnold's declared intent is to translate the narrative into Homeric verse, the psychological critics maintain that what the poet composes is, in fact, unconscious autobiography.[130] The weakness in this hypothesis is that it submits a cause (unconscious and suppressed feeling) when there is already sufficient cause to account for the end result. There is no need for psychological hypotheses to explain either Arnold's interest in this story or his transition from poetry to prose. In regard to the latter, Professor Super observes that any teacher "brought up in the rigorous discipline of reading student papers until it seems that every spark of vital energy has been drained from him" should know "what happened to Arnold's muse."[131]

Upon his return from a honeymoon in Italy, Switzerland, and France, Arnold was immediately assigned and sent out to a district of 104 nonconformist schools. Away from home for lengthy periods, traveling by train and carriage, and dining on "greasy and ill-served" food at roadside taverns, he made the circuit among the Methodists, Presbyterians, Baptists, Quakers, and Unitarians. The government would provide a grant to nonconformist schools only if three-fourths of their pupils passed an examination. If the school itself was approved, then a certain percentage of its pupils could apply for funding as pupil-teachers. Arnold's job consisted, therefore, of making factual reports of conditions and standards and of testing the knowledge of the students and the abilities of the pupil-teachers. This involved the inspector in the never-ending tasks of correcting papers and filling out forms, and it demanded that he orally examine an average of 18,000 to 19,000 children a year. What is difficult to understand is not why Arnold wrote less poetry, but rather how he could have managed to write more prose—for, as Park Honan notes, "The system almost broke Arnold."[132]

Arnold and Stanley before 1857

In the years following 1849 a number of shared events and circumstances would draw the sympathies of Arnold and Stanley closer. First, in September of '49, just after visiting with Jowett and the Arnolds in the Lake District, Stanley received word that his father, the bishop of Norwich, had fallen ill. Stanley arrived at his bedside only hours before death. In the next year, sisters of both Stanley and Arnold would marry. Catherine Stanley married her brother's friend of Rugby days, C. J. Vaughan, and Jane Arnold married the Quaker apologist and liberal reformer William E. Forster. Brothers of both Stanley and Arnold would die abroad, Charles Stanley at Van Diemen's Land in 1850 and William Delafield Arnold at Gibralter in 1859. Both also had siblings who, in 1856, converted to Roman Catholicism. Moreover, during the '50s, as Arnold's thoughts on Church and State were drawn into increasing conformity with his father's ideas, they would also bring him into unison with Stanley.

But first, their paths had to separate. While Arnold pursued his "Flu" and read Spinoza, Stanley followed the Gorham case and penned his protest against the bishop of Exeter.[133] While Arnold was on his honeymoon, Stanley worked as secretary for the University Commission, attended the opening, on 1 May 1851, of the Great Exhibition in the Crystal Palace, and accepted, in July, a canonry at Canterbury. In November, just as Arnold was getting started in his inspectorship, Stanley writes from the cathedral to Jowett, "Two advantages this place certainly has over both Oxford and London, and those are, rest and seclusion; and in my present condition both are greatly to be prized." With amusement, he observes that Dr. Arnold's "much abused theory of having different sects worship in the same church is here fulfilled even to exaggeration, inasmuch as a Presbyterian service is carried on in the Crypt at the same hour as the Cathedral service above."[134] While Arnold was sounding the depths of his pupils in Birmingham, Stanley was searching for history in the crevices and corners of his new home. He writes excitedly, "On December 29th, the day of the murder [of Abp. Becket], I went to the spot at 5 p.m.— the fatal hour—with what results you shall hear. The place absolutely teems with history and ghosts, ancient and modern."[135] Of course, not all of Stanley's work was play, and his historical researches and ecclesiastical responsibilities would result in the *Memorials of Canterbury* (1854) and a volume of *Canterbury Sermons* (1859).

Arnold's and Stanley's crowded schedules and peripatetic routines steadily kept them apart. In the spring of 1852, while Stanley was involved in the final preparations for the Report of the University Commission and Arnold was inspecting, Mary Arnold, Clough, Jowett, Conington, and Shairp, along with his sister "Binny," met at Rugby and from there set off to explore the countryside of nearby Naseby. In August, while Stanley was in Italy, Arnold and Clough met in Wales. Clough had been dismissed from his post at University Hall and had just received an invitation from Emerson to join him in Massachusetts. At the end of the year, while Arnold was looking over a stack of papers, Stanley and Walrond were sailing up the Nile, and Clough was reading lectures *gratis* to undergraduates at Harvard. In the following March, when Stanley was somewhere between Mt. Sinai and Jerusalem, Arnold was eating bread pudding in the home of a Quaker and feeling that life was "positive purgatory."[136] And so it continued—Arnold laboring to do his duty, with occasional and fragmented escapes into literature and criticism, and Stanley, with book in hand, rediscovering the world. Each, from within his own sphere, appreciated the work of the other, but neither could imagine that their interests and abilities would, one day soon, benefit from collaboration.

Stanley had no aversion against collaboration, but the person toward whom he felt the greatest affinity and admiration was Jowett, with whom he had worked in preparing the *Sermons and Essays on the Apostolical Age* (1847). It was then that the two men conspired together to demonstrate, by means of a two-part work on the

New Testament, what English scholarship trained in German methods of biblical criticism could produce. Part I was to be on the Gospels, Part II on the Acts and Epistles. Neither part could be produced, however, until the authors had journeyed through Palestine and the Mediterranean. The beginning was postponed, and then, with the death of Stanley's father, their plans began to go astray, and the first volumes in the projected series were not released until June 1855. Their publication, according to Lake, "may be described as marking the beginning of the period of religious doubt."[137]

Jowett's translation and commentary, the *Epistles of St. Paul to the Thessalonians, Galatians and Romans*, was released first. In this work, the author's endeavor, his biographer tells us, "had been nothing less than to penetrate the clouds of tradition, and apprehend the original meaning of the Apostle."[138] Outside of theological circles, the excellences of the book, in scholarship and literary style, were immediately recognized; however, religious prejudice was aroused by the bold manner in which its author questioned received dogmas, explained the apocalyptic language of St. Paul by reference to "the divine sense of good and evil" rather than to any definite historical events, suggested that "the doctrine of Sacrifice or Satisfaction is not a central truth of Christianity," condemned on moral grounds the Evangelical conception of the Atonement, and recommended for his readers' edification a vision of "the great theological teachers of past ages, who have anathematized each other in their lives, resting together in the communion of the same Lord."[139] Stanley thought the reaction of the religious press an illustration of the fact that a layman might say with impunity, if not with praise, what a clergyman dare not, for Coleridge's *Aids to Reflection* "is a book beloved by the most orthodox of men. And yet his chapter on the Atonement is identically the same as Jowett's."[140] In the next year Jowett's fourteen pages on the Atonement would be completely overshadowed by John McLeod Campbell's widely influential treatise, *The Nature of the Atonement and Its Relation to Remission of Sins and Eternal Life*. Following its publication Jowett and Stanley began their visits, often with Shairp, to Thomas Erskine, a friend of Campbell's, at Linlathen.

Stanley's *Epistles of St. Paul to the Corinthians* immediately followed its companion volume. These two Epistles to the Church at Corinth are, in Stanley's estimation, "the *historical* Epistles," the first presenting "the earliest chapter of the history of the Christian Church," and the second providing "the history of the Apostle himself."[141] Rowland Prothero provides a terse comparative analysis of Stanley's and Jowett's works:

The one [Stanley's] is essentially historical, the other metaphysical; the one is 'external, positive, definite to the verge of superficiality,' the other 'subjective, negative, profound at the risk of obscurity'; the one multiplies, the other avoids, illustrations; the one delights in detecting unobtrusive resemblances, the other in unmasking false analogies. . . . In all that relates to the form and colour of St. Paul's thought, . . . Stanley's

edition of the Epistles is of lasting value. But in other respects the
Commentary proved to be full of faults. It was deficient in scholarship
and accuracy.[142]

The result is that, while Jowett's work evoked theological censure, Stanley's
evoked academic censure. J. B. Lightfoot—a fellow of Trinity, Cambridge, and
later, bishop of Durham—put his fingers in all the holes of Stanley's work and,
motivated by no malevolent spirit, pulled it apart.[143] The public reception affected
both authors, and while Jowett turned to revision, thinking that the offense of his
work resulted from the difficulty of the language and an inadequate substantiation of
premises, Stanley decidedly turned away from any further contribution to biblical
criticism, realizing that his talents found their proper object in historical research and
writing. His *Sinai and Palestine* (1856) was immensely successful, and its reception
confirmed the author in the direction of his labors.

Arnold read the reviews with interest. He knew that it had been the ambition of
his father to devote his energies to a critical explication of St. Paul, and he recognized in Stanley the continuation of the Arnoldian tradition. But, at the same time,
he felt that his own sphere of labor lay elsewhere—and so it did, for the moment. At
the beginning of 1855 he released *Poems, Second Series*, which included a selection
from his first two volumes and one new poem, "Balder Dead," based on the Teutonic
story in the *Prose Edda*. Stanley liked it better than "Sohrab and Rustum" and
thought that Arnold, by applying his talents to similar narratives, might eventually
produce a book of verse that would be of interest to historians.[144]

Modern Oxford

When, on 10 December 1856, Stanley received from Palmerston the offer of the
professorship of ecclesiastical history, it was a modern Oxford that beckoned, and
Stanley himself had been partly responsible for the change. He, along with Jowett,
Mark Pattison, Richard Congreve, John Conington, and Goldwin Smith, had, in
1848, become the leaders of a reform movement, and their agitations succeeded, in
April 1850, in eliciting from John Russell the promise of a Royal Commission of
Inquiry. From the perspective of Oxford's High Church Tories—such men as E. B.
Pusey, John Keble, and William Sewell—it was awful enough that Parliament
should dare to intervene in the affairs of the university, but when, four months later,
the University Commission was established, they were outraged. The president of
this new commission was Samuel Hinds, Archbishop Whately's old friend and
former assistant who was now bishop of Norwich. The six commissioners appointed
under Hinds included Tait, Baden Powell, and Stanley as secretary. Although Jowett
and Pattison were not on the commission, they nevertheless assisted in its work and
provided important testimony on its behalf. Former Rugbeian H. Halford Vaughan,
professor of modern history, also took a prominent role before the commission.
These men were known liberals in politics and religion, and though state-appointed,

they were as welcome among the Hebdomadal Board as Herodians among the Sanhedrin.

Reform, however, was inevitable, and Gladstone, only days before the declaration of war against Russia in March of 1854, introduced the Oxford University Bill. After considerable debate and conciliation in the Houses of Parliament, the University Reform Bill received royal assent on 7 August. Among the changes, the most significant were the following: subscription, oaths, and declarations upon matriculation and for the Bachelor's degree were abolished, the constituency of the Hebdomadal Board (now Hebdomadal Council) and Congregation was revised and English was introduced into their discussions, residence requirements that appeared especially prohibitory to poorer students were annulled or revised, and college revenues could be apportioned with a view to enlarging and endowing the professoriate. Further ordinances in 1857 and '58 aimed at establishing uniform college statutes and opening scholarships and fellowships within the entire university for free competition. As a result, "The old oligarchical monopolies in the University and in the Colleges began to disappear. . . . The happy days of privilege and nomination ceased."[145]

To Pusey the University Bill was the abomination of desolation, and the appointment of Stanley to the chair of ecclesiastical history was a certain sign that the end of Oxford was nigh. Even Lake, in a letter to Tait, expressed himself against Stanley's appointment:

> I do not *wish* him to come here, I confess; for I know that his very amicability will make him as mere wax in the hands of Jowett, and I shall deeply regret his lending his religious influence to the Triumvirate or Quatuorvirate, whose policy is to secularize the University, and who are really opposed, not to one form or the other, but to all *active religion* under *any* form.[146]

The reception awaiting Stanley was, by all accounts, cold. "How many letters of congratulations," he asks a friend, "do you suppose I have received from residents in Oxford? One from Jowett, and—*not one besides*." Those at Oxford who shared Stanley's values and *could* have sincerely congratulated him refrained from doing so, for they knew too well what the transition meant—the removal from a position of quiet contentment and dignified leisure to a post on the front lines of battle. To Kingsley, Stanley writes, "To-morrow I leave a home which I have enjoyed increasingly for seven years, to enter on a life of turmoil and confinement, which derives its only charm from the hope, at times very faint, of being more useful than I have been here."[147] Stanley's friends, knowing that he had accepted the professorship through a sense of duty rather than in the pursuit of happiness, naturally gave him their respect and honor, and as naturally felt their congratulations contrived and awkward.

The Oxford of the Decade days was no more, and in returning to a place of beloved memories, Stanley felt that which the first parents of the human race sensed after their loss of innocence—that "a flaming Sword, / In signal of remove, waves fiercely round" and that Paradise is no more.[148] Though the "Oxford sentiment," as understood by Arnold, is an eternal ideal, the atmosphere of Oxford had ceased to be religious and had become, instead, merely political. Mark Pattison observed the dramatic contrast: "If any Oxford man had gone to sleep in 1846 and had woke up again in 1850 he would have found himself in a totally new world. . . . Theology was totally banished from the Common Room, and even from private conversation. Very free opinion on all subjects was rife."[149] If Pattison could see only amelioration, there were plenty of others who took a different view. For Lake, the decline of the "religious movement," beginning with the loss of Dr. Arnold and Newman, resulted in "the withdrawal of any great religious power and of nearly all religious interest from the University for something like a quarter of a century." In October of 1854, Arnold, after meeting with Lake and Walrond at Balliol, notes that "the place, in losing Newman and his followers, has lost its religious movement, which after all kept it from stagnating, and has not yet, so far as I see, got anything better." Yet, Arnold is optimistic, and looks forward to the University Tests Act of 1871, saying, "We must hope that the coming changes, and perhaps the infusion of Dissenters' sons of that muscular, hard-working, *unblasé* middle class . . . may brace the flaccid sinews of Oxford a little."[150]

Under the existing conditions, a professor of ecclesiastical history was not likely to attract a large audience, and Stanley soon found cause for complaint. To Shairp he writes, "The dusty, secular dried-up aspect of the place is very unpleasing. The stiffness of the undergraduates in social intercourse is only surpassed by their marvelous lack of interest (as far as appears in my lectures) in anything like theological study."[151] On the other hand, the 1850s were a turning point in the study of English literature. As an academic discipline it was still accorded second- or even third-class status, deemed appropriate for working-men's and women's colleges, where the students could not be expected to have knowledge of classical languages. In 1873 Oxford would grudgingly acknowledge English literature in its pass examination. Not until 1885 would the Merton Professorship of English Language and Literature be founded.[152] So, as interest in theology waned, interest in literature, whether classical, foreign, religious, *or not*, waxed strong. Under the existing conditions, a professor of poetry might expect a larger audience, especially if he lectured in English.

On 5 May 1857 Arnold was elected professor of poetry. "It was an immense victory," he tells his mother, "some 200 more voted than have ever, it is said, voted in a Professorship election before." Thinking of how his father "would have rejoiced in his son's thus obtaining a share in the permanence and grandeur of that *august* place," Arnold felt doubly the worth of his victory.[153] Historically, Arnold's election may indicate a number of things, and certainly the public recognition of his talent as a poet is not least, but it signified also the triumph of liberalism and the recognition among the liberals of Dr. Arnold's contribution to Oxford's progress. Perhaps, too, it signified the longing of Oxford for the return of its scholar-gipsy.

The Making of a Critic

Had Keble known that Arnold would, "with somewhat of a hereditary boldness, cast off the yoke of a foreign language,"[154] perhaps he would not have cast a vote in his favor. Arnold, having noted that "there is no direction whatever in the Statute as to the language in which the lectures shall be" and that "only the most intelligent and cultivated" students had been able to attend the lectures of Copleston and Keble, made it his first matter of business to inquire of the Hebdomadal Council whether the lectures might be given in English instead of the old and universal language of scholarship. The council, in keeping with the spirit of reform, gave its unanimous consent.[155]

Even Stanley had difficulty in following Keble's terminal lecture, but afterwards was certain that he had heard, "in words as plain as Latin can express it," a curious argument that aimed "to show that Homer was a Tory—not a poetical Tory, but a thoroughly downright political Tory."[156] Arnold would have conceded the point, for both Keble and Homer were, like Latin itself, of a bygone age. In fact, the new professor of poetry, in his inaugural lecture "On the Modern Element in Literature," given on 14 November, observes that, whereas Æschylus and Sophocles were "modern"—in the sense of representing the intellectual maturity of humanity by possessing a critical and tolerant spirit—Homer was decidedly not modern. By applying the circular theory of history (advanced by Vico and propagated by Niebuhr) to a criticism of literature, Arnold concludes that modern England has most to gain through the "instructive fulness of experience" found in the poetry of an age and nation that is also modern.[157] Only by means of a comparative study of literature, Arnold urges, can students hope to attain to a true estimation of the development and merits of the literature of any age and nation.

Oxford would have been more impressed had Arnold lectured in Latin, for the language would, then, have been commensurate with the rhetorical style. What the Oxford tutors could hardly tolerate was being lectured to in a rather pompous, dogmatic fashion by a thirty-four-year-old poet, who dared to make generalizations about the literatures of all ages and nations. If Arnold knew what "the grand style" was, he had not yet adapted it for oratorical performance. Not until the lectures "On Translating Homer," begun three years later, in November 1860, does Arnold find his natural voice, which is not that of a *professor*—whatever that may be—but is, rather, that of a critic. Without in the least sacrificing his scholarship, Arnold falls back upon his natural aptitude of fault-finding, and by first demonstrating the bad, is then able to explicate the good. The good, in fact, can never be adequately demonstrated, as it is an ideal, but the principles by which perfection is to be pursued can be explicated. In "On Translating Homer," the effect produced by the absence of correct principles is repeatedly demonstrated by reference to an unfortunate translation of Francis Newman's.

Although this chapter can only refer to these first Oxford lectures in passing, they mark an important transition in Arnold's life. Having for years agonized over the circumstances preventing him from writing poetry, he now becomes aware of another calling, that he has gifts by which he can reach a larger audience, and though he contribute less of beauty to the world, he may, by bringing light, hasten the advent of a poetical age.

The Decade in 1860

The previous chapter marked how the publication of *Essays and Reviews* in March 1860 affected the signification of the phrase "Broad Church movement" and what Maurice and Kingsley understood to be the theological value of that controversial volume, but it did not provide any discussion of the essays or of their influence. Such discussion has been reserved for this chapter, yet only insofar as it is necessary for an appreciation of the development of Arnold as a religious writer.

First, it may prove helpful to establish where the diaspora of the Decade had situated its members at the time of the book's appearance. The period of *Essays and Reviews*—beginning with H. B. Wilson's first efforts, in January 1858, to enlist the assistance of other writers in putting together the volume, and ending with the responsive Episcopal Manifesto of February 1861—very nearly marks the period of the Newcastle Commission—beginning with the initial resolution in the House of Commons in February 1858 for an inquiry into measures for "the Extension of sound and cheap elementary instruction to all classes of the People," to the issuance of the *Report* of the commission in March 1861.

Those of the Decade involved in the work of the Newcastle Commission included Lake, Matthew Arnold, and Temple. Lake—who was among the seven commissioners, along with J. T. Coleridge, Nassau Senior, Goldwin Smith, William Rogers, and Edward Miall—had already, in 1856, served on the military education board, investigating the training provided in military academies on the Continent. Clough, as an examiner in the Education Office, had given valuable assistance to Lake in France, Prussia, and Austria, but Clough was now putting the final touches to his five-volume edition of Plutarch and was happily confined to London. On this occasion, Lake procured the appointment of Mark Pattison as foreign assistant-commissioner to Germany.[158] Fitzjames Stephen, the secretary of the education commission, asked Arnold, near the end of January 1859—just four months after he had returned from climbing the Alps with Walrond—to go to France and the French speaking cantons of Switzerland and Holland as the second foreign assistant-commissioner. His assignment, "to report on the systems of elementary education there," would provide the raw data for *The Popular Education of France* and *A French Eton*.[159] Temple, who had contributed an article on "National Education" for the 1856 edition of *Oxford Essays*, was called upon to offer evidence for the commissioners.

Early in 1858 Temple was persuaded by Jowett to contribute to a volume of essays in liberal theology. He would use the opportunity to revise into essay form a sermon on "The Fullness of Time" that he had prepared for an Oxford audience.[160] In November 1857 Temple had been elected as the headmaster of Rugby and had moved into the position vacated by Goulburn. Goulburn, who had been made Doctor of Divinity in the previous year, had accepted the ministry of Quebec Chapel, St. Marylebone.

In August of '58, Jowett, having met with success in the enlistment of Temple, sent a similar entreaty to Stanley:

> Wilson wishes me to write to you respecting a volume of Theological Essays. . . . The persons who have already joined in the plan are Wilson, R. Williams of King's, Pattison, [Alexander] Grant, Temple, [Max] Müller, if he has time, and myself. The object is to say what we think freely within the limits of the Church of England. A notice will be prefixed that no one is responsible for any notions but his own. . . . We do not wish to do anything rash or irritating to the public or the University, but we are determined not to submit to this abominable system of terrorism, which prevents the statements of the plainest facts, and makes true theology or theological education impossible. . . . We shall talk A. D. 1868. I want to point out that the object is not to be attained by any anonymous writing.[161]

If Jowett was becoming reckless, Oxford had driven him to it. After being passed by for the mastership of Balliol, he was, in 1855, elected professor of Greek, a chair with an annual salary of 40£. As a result of the University Commission, the Hebdomadal Council had agreed to endow the professorship, but upon Jowett's election, the plan was dropped. Moreover, the vice-chancellor of Oxford—acting upon vague charges of heresy brought against Jowett by Evangelical and High Church leaders C. P. Golightly and E. B. Pusey—had humiliated the new professor by making him re-sign the Thirty-nine Articles. Oxford had, thus, been of material assistance in making Jowett a free man, as it had failed to give him anything to lose. Besides, when Wilson contacted him, he was already at work on an essay "On the Interpretation of Scripture" that had been originally intended for the second edition of *St. Paul's Epistles*, but which had not been completed on time for inclusion.[162]

Stanley, however, thought the project unwise and counseled Jowett to withdraw. After the volume's publication, Stanley explained his own position in an article sent to the editor of the *Edinburgh Review*:

> The project of such a composite work was, as we have thought from the very first, a decided blunder. It was a combination almost sure to produce an illusion of a kind most fatal to a just and calm consideration of the

subjects discussed. The joint appearance of the "Essays" was certain to excite the suspicion of an identity of sentiment, where no such identity really existed.[163]

The conception and plan of the book was foolish in that it brought together on an equal platform writers of unequal abilities, encouraged the illusion of a conspiracy, suggested agreement between authors regarding matters upon which there was, in fact, none, and brought to public discussion issues for which the public could not be prepared.

Shairp—who in October of 1857 had returned to Scotland to work at St. Andrews, first as an assistant to the professor of Latin, and, beginning in 1861, as the professor—agreed with Stanley in regard to the unequal abilities of the contributors. Upon the publication of *Essays and Reviews*, he writes to his old Rugby friend Edward Scott, "I have only read Temple's, which I greatly like. It had been better elsewhere. . . . Jowett's is probably the only other I shall care to read. Williams's seems feather-headed. Of B. Powell we know what he has to say already. . . . However, it is a great thing, the free ventilation of opinion. No honest belief without it."[164]

Not all of the Decade members were as moderate as Stanley and Shairp in their criticism. Lake, although disliking the "narrowness" of the Orthodox party, was in agreement with the Episcopal Manifesto and thought, "It is a good thing in our shifting days that both clergy and laity should have shown a zeal even, if not quite, 'according to knowledge,' in defence of Scriptural truth."[165] R. W. Church complained of "the guerilla way in which these men write, each man fighting for his own hand, though with a common purpose . . . so as to exclude the Divine, almost entirely."[166]

Clough, having already freed himself from all religious formularies, stood, by 1860, at a position farthest away from Lake and Church. Yet, we might compare Clough to John Sterling, in that neither could ultimately sympathize with what is sometimes called "the Broad Church compromise"—that is, any intellectual effort with pretensions to freedom of inquiry that, at the same time, circumscribed itself "within the limits of the Church of England."[167] In his "Notes on the Religious Tradition," he argues, "It is impossible for any scholar to have read, and studied, and reflected without forming a strong impression of the entire uncertainty of history in general, and of the history of Christianity in particular. . . . Manuscripts are doubtful, records may be unauthentic, criticism is feeble, historical facts must be left uncertain." For Clough, the "Religious Tradition" was to be sought not in the Bible alone, but in every aspect of life, and in every example provided by those "who have really tried to order their lives by the highest action of the reasonable and spiritual will."[168] Not surprisingly, we find that *Essays and Reviews* occupies very little of Clough's time or concern. Yet, he would not live to witness the ensuing acts of the ecclesiastical drama. By the autumn of 1860 Clough had lost his health, and, despite all of his efforts to regain it in warmer climes, he died on 13 November 1861.

Arnold habitually destroyed the letters that he received, unless they had, from his perspective, some obvious value or the signature was collectible. After Clough's death he regretted having saved not a single letter. Not only was Arnold without correspondence for his friend's memoirs, but when Clough's widow solicited a memorial verse, Arnold took four years to write an elegy that was, in the end, so little about Clough that he refused to send it to her. Finally, the poor woman—convinced that the poet would dig up his hidden treasures if only she pointed to the right spot—told Arnold that she would settle for a brief sketch or reminiscence. Still, he replied, "I am quite sure I should neither satisfy you nor myself if I tried to throw into form for publication my recollections of your husband."[169] She wisely abandoned her effort. For Arnold, emotion, if merely personal, was too personal for public expression. Only those feelings the expression of which were natural to intense situations and noble personages were properly raw material for poetry. The poet-philosopher looks not deep but wide, little reflecting that it is only when a man is most intensely personal that he strikes the deepest chords of fellow-feeling, reveals the human heart to itself, and affects on the unconscious level what beauty and truth too often aims at only by way of metaphor and argument. After Arnold published his quiet elegy, "Thyrsis," Shairp—who *had* contributed reminiscences to the memoir[170]—remonstrated with the poet that he had slighted his subject and his own heart in order to gratify an aesthetic sensibility. Shairp's indignant response deserves to be heard:[171]

> No Thyrsis thou, for old idyllic lays,
>   But a broad-browed, deep-souled, much suffering man,
> Within whose veins, thrilled by these latter days,
>   The ruddy lifeblood ran.
>   . . . .
> Too soon, too soon, the place of early trust
>   Constrained to leave, down Thought's strong current whirled,
> And face to face alone too rudely thrust
>   With problem of the world.
>
> And Voices then the loudest England knew
>   In his distracted ear were thundering. Some
> "Push boldly forward"; some—"lo! here the haven true,
>   Here rest, or be undone."
>   . . . .
> These things he saw, and felt, as few can feel,
>   Nor wotting God's long patience with His world,
> Too deeply questioned, till faith 'gan to reel,
>   From its old centre hurled.
>
> Soul-sick, he cried, "how long"! "O heaven, how long,
>   Shall rich men surfeit—the poor die for need?"
> Still unabashed the kingdom stands for wrong.
>   Is then Christ risen indeed?

New Wine for Old Bottles

At Oxford *Essays and Reviews* aroused no immediate opposition. H. L. Mansel, Oxford's select preacher, did not have the leisure of selecting his battles. As a result of his controversial lectures, he was now constantly having to defend himself. Hardly would he have a moment to recover from Maurice's attack when the pugnacious Goldwin Smith would enter the ring. Eventually, Mansel would write a reply to Powell's essay, but for the moment, he was content to wait and watch.[172] When Frederick Harrison visited the university at the end of term, he met with "one of Mr. Jowett's friends and colleagues," who told him that "it was Jowett's desire to have the real character and aim of the book made evident." Harrison interpreted this aim as "an effort to claim for clergymen of the Established Church a thorough liberty of Free Thought both in respect to the Scriptures and to the Creeds," and he spent the long vacation writing what would be his first published article, "Neo-Christianity," the article that woke the watchdogs of orthodoxy.[173] Aroused by the fearsome apparition of a free-thinking clergy, Pusey alerted Wilberforce, and the dogs began their maddening bark. Archbishop Tait signed his name on 12 February 1861 to an Episcopal Manifesto—subsequently published in the *Times*—expressing doubt whether certain opinions expressed in the controversial volume "can be held consistently with an honest subscription to the formularies of our Church, with many of the fundamental doctrines of which they appear to us essentially at variance."[174]

The real doubt at Oxford was whether the dogs could bite or whether, as Harrison had suggested, they were, in fact, "toothless." Arnold fully entered into the discussion, and it is not an exaggeration to say that the controversy surrounding *Essays and Reviews* was the impetus that launched Arnold's career as a social and religious critic. A month after the publication of the Episcopal Manifesto, a letter to his mother reveals that Arnold was still thinking his way through the moral, legal, ecclesiastical, and cultural perplexities brought to the fore by the volume:

> It seems to come out clearer and clearer that, however doubtful may be the position of the Essayists, there is no ecclesiastical authority which public opinion is willing to entrust with the power of censuring or punishing in these matters, and I think public opinion is right. As to the Essays, one has the word of Scripture for it that "new wine should be put into new bottles," and certainly the wine of the Essays is rather new and fermenting for the old bottles of Anglicanism.[175]

Arnold spoke too soon. One of his father's earliest pupils, W. K. Hamilton, now bishop of Salisbury, would soon initiate legal proceedings against Rowland Williams, the author of the review of "Bunsen's Biblical Researches," and J. D. Coleridge would provide legal representation for Hamilton. In addition, Samuel Wilberforce—having been blocked by Archbishop Tait from pushing for an episcopal condemnation of Bishop John Colenso's *Commentary on St. Paul's Epistle to the Romans* (1861)—would, instead, help finance the prosecution of H. B. Wilson, the author of an essay on the "multitudinist" principle of the National Church. Both authors would be brought to trial in the Court of Arches, the ecclesiastical court of the archbishop of Canterbury, beginning in December 1861. Stephen Lushington pronounced his final judgment on 15 December 1862, at which time Williams— having been convicted of heresy in regard to the doctrines of inspiration, propitiation, and justification—and Wilson—having been found guilty of heretical views on inspiration and on the everlasting punishment of the wicked—were suspended from their clerical offices for one year. They would both appeal to the higher court of the Privy Council, and thus, in June 1863, the issues of the drama would again be brought before the public. Nor should it be supposed that the dust settled with the final judgment of acquittal, pronounced on 8 February 1864. For a period of not less than three and a half years the civil liberty of an English clergyman to engage in biblical criticism was a subject of no little debate, and Arnold would take a leading role in the public discussion.

Temple did not escape the general censure placed upon *Essays and Reviews*. The attention that this book and its authors was receiving in the press aroused the curiosity of the older boys at Rugby, and the headmaster was called upon to answer for the unwanted influence he had brought into the school. His own essay on "The Education of the World" was recognized by most as, if not quite orthodox, at least not heretical, and Temple argued convincingly that, although he could not condone the episcopal action taken against the book, he had "taken considerable pains to counteract" what he considered erroneous in the book. Moreover, he assured the trustees that, had he been asked for his contribution *after* his appointment as headmaster, he would never have consented.[176] The scandal abated, and in the long run, the offending essay did not prove terribly injurious to Temple's ecclesiastical career.

Matthew Arnold, as we have seen, was at work "On Translating Homer" when *Essays and Reviews* made its appearance in the world. He immediately recognized the value of Jowett's essay "On the Interpretation of Scripture," and one can find striking similarities and instances of agreement in Arnold's lectures. In fact, the passage from the Synoptic Gospels to which Arnold refers in the letter quoted above also appears in Jowett's essay: "A tendency may be observed within the last century to clothe systems of philosophy in the phraseology of Scripture. But new wine cannot thus be put 'into old bottles.'"[177] The fact appears to be that, by the time Arnold wrote of *Essays and Reviews* to his mother, after he had delivered his third lecture on Homer, he had already thoroughly digested "On the Interpretation of Scripture." Whereas Jowett tells us that the interpretation of Scripture requires neither the rhetorical effulgence of the preacher nor the philological pedantry of the scholar, but "an effort of thought and imagination, requiring the sense of a poet as well as a critic," Arnold assures us that the translation of Homer requires neither the literary and rhetorical crucible of Pope nor the philological correctness of Francis Newman, but both poetical feeling and scholarship.[178] Whereas Jowett's plea is for the meaning of Scripture to be placed on the same scientific basis as that which is given to classical authors, Arnold's plea is that Homer be translated with that same simplicity and nobility given by the translators of the authorized version of Scripture.

Jowett recognizes that the object of the interpreter is "to open his eyes and see or imagine things as they truly are," and Arnold recognizes a similar object for the translator—"to press to the sense of the thing itself with which one is dealing, not to go off on some collateral issue about the thing." That "thing" is, for Arnold's immediate purpose, "the critical perception of poetic truth," although he would later, in "The Function of Criticism at the Present Time" (1864), remark that the business of the critical power is, "in all branches of knowledge, . . . to see the object as in itself it really is."[179] Of course, there must be some method by which, if pursued, the critical faculty might attain its lofty goal, and both authors, in different terms, direct their audience to the same means. According to Jowett, the interpreter must pursue a course of *disengagement*. He must transport himself into the time and place of the author and intended audience and "disengage himself from all that follows," so that "all the after-thoughts of theology are nothing to him" and his reading may be kept "absolutely pure from the refinements or distinctions of later times." According to Arnold, the critic must embrace "the Indian virtue of *detachment*": "I say, the critic must keep out of the region of immediate practice in the political, social, humanitarian sphere, if he wants to make a beginning for that more free speculative treatment of things."[180] However naïve their talk of perceiving "the thing itself" may appear, neither author is suggesting an ante-Kantian epistemology, but only that the critic's primary obligation to scholarship is to remain aloof, uninfluenced by practical concerns or bound by the intellectual straitjacket of a single paradigm, philosophy, or religion.

We might well suppose, based on their agreements, that Jowett and Arnold both believed that new wine must, somehow, be placed in the old bottles of Anglicanism, or—as H. B. Wilson argued—that a method must be found "of adjusting old things to new conditions."[181] We shall see, nevertheless, just how widely they disagreed.

Spinoza and Colenso

Students of Arnold soon come to realize that, in direct proportion as he is condescending toward or dismissive of an author with slight or qualified praise, they should suspect that Arnold has, at some time, sat at that author's feet. As this is true in regard to Carlyle and Coleridge, this also proves to be the case with reference to Jowett. In evaluating the contents of *Essays and Reviews*, Arnold says of this professor's contribution, that it "contains nothing which is not given, with greater convincingness of statement and far greater fulness of consequence in Spinoza's seventh chapter [of the *Theological-Political Treatise*], which treats of the Interpretation of Scripture." Even so, as Stanley, in his brief notice of Jowett's essay, had already expressed contempt for any reader "unimpressed by the lofty tone which breathes through its exposition of the power of our Lord's words," Arnold was unwilling to go so far as to deny that the essay had one redeeming quality, unction, "which, at the tribunal of literary criticism, is sufficient to justify it."[182] The truth of the matter is that Jowett's essay was no more a *réchauffé* of Spinoza's chapter than Temple's essay was of Lessing's "Education of the Human Race." Arnold was not only sufficiently astute to discern the sources to which the essayists were most indebted; he also knew very well that the two essayists had recast their material, bringing fresh light upon old ideas and making them their own.[183] Unfortunately, Arnold—like many other critics—was sensitive to the fact that, if he praised too highly, he risked being thought of as indiscriminating, but if he judged too harshly, he would be respected as one having exceptionally high standards.

Jowett's essay served a double purpose for Arnold. It not only gave him confidence in his criticism of Homer and assisted him in his expression, but—more important—it led him to think of what he had learned from Spinoza, and to think of these things in connection with the current controversy over *Essays and Reviews*. Ten years had passed since Arnold's reading of Goethe had led him to Spinoza, and his absorption in this philosopher had further led him to the literature of the Pantheist Controversy, including works by Lessing, Jacobi, Herder, and Schleiermacher. But it was Spinoza, more than any other thinker, who furnished Arnold with the principles he needed to interpret Scripture and identify, on the one hand, the necessity of Christianity for the perfection of culture and, on the other, the limitations of reason in its relation to religion. As Lowry observes, one half of Arnold's religious teaching is to be found in Spinoza, the other half in Jesus Christ.[184] According to William Robbins, "What most impresses Arnold in Spinoza is the combination of critical honesty and acumen with a moral earnestness which insists that so sturdy a support for frail humanity as the Christian religion should be preserved, even if it means placing ethical values above intellectual rigour."[185]

From Arnold's point of view, Jowett had made the very highest claims on behalf of the Bible when he distinguished it from all classical literature as alone providing the "contemplation of man" *sub specie æternitatis*—under the aspect of eternity or from the viewpoint of God—and by further identifying this "sense of things" as essential for the human pursuit of perfection.[186] Such a merging of Spinozan and Protestant sensibilities impressed Arnold, and it is not surprising that he would subsequently grasp an opportunity to bring Spinoza to bear more directly upon the issues facing contemporary culture. Even so, without the inspiration provided by Stanley, Arnold would not have written "The Bishop and the Philosopher." To understand how this essay came about, we need to momentarily back up in order to get a larger view of the context and sequence of events.

While a fellow of St. John's, Cambridge, in the early 1840s, John Colenso became a devoted admirer of Maurice. Understandably, Colenso was outraged by the treatment his revered teacher received at the hands of the High Church *Quarterly*, the fiercely Evangelical *Record*, and the trustees of King's College, and so—a few weeks before his consecration as bishop of Natal, in 1853—Colenso courageously dedicated a volume of *Village Sermons* to Maurice. Although deeply touched by this gesture, Maurice knew that it would result in Colenso's name being placed foremost on the Evangelical party's list of suspected heretics. "I could have wished that you had stifled all your regard for me rather than run this risk," replied Maurice. "Nevertheless, I do so thoroughly and inwardly believe that courage is the quality most needed in a bishop, and especially a missionary bishop, that I did at the same time give hearty thanks to God that He had bestowed such a measure of it upon you."[187]

Maurice had not yet witnessed the full measure of Colenso's courage. As we saw in the previous chapter, Maurice had been dismissed from King's College on account of his peculiar understanding of "Eternity" and inspiration, but President Jelf had refused to jeopardize the decision of the trustees by placing Maurice's *Essays* before a tribunal competent to weigh theological statements. Maurice sought a theological judgment, but it was denied him. Although in 1853 Colenso had not yet arrived at Maurice's conclusion regarding the notion of endless punishment, he did ultimately arrive there, and in 1861, in a *Commentary on St. Paul's Epistle to the Romans*, he clearly stated his entire agreement with Maurice. By this time, the queen and Lord Palmerston had publicly expressed their confidence in Maurice by bestowing upon him, in July of 1860, the incumbency of the Chapel of St. Peter's in Vere Street. Archbishop Tait required no prophetic vision to see that, if Colenso succeeded in forcing his teaching before an ecclesiastical court, Maurice—to the embarrassment of the crown—would have been necessarily implicated in the hearing. Therefore, Colenso's *Commentary* was allowed to slide into the obscuring shadow cast by *Essays and Reviews*.

Meanwhile, Colenso had been busy in the mission work of translating into Zula, with the help of natives, first the New Testament, and then parts of the Old. In a letter to Harold Browne, soon to be bishop of Ely, Colenso tells of his experience:

> While translating the story of the Flood, I have had a simple-minded, but intelligent, native,—one with the docility of a child, but the reasoning powers of mature age,—look up and ask, "Is all that true? Do you really believe that all this happened thus,—that all the beasts, and birds, and creeping things, upon the earth, large and small, from hot countries and cold, came thus by pairs, and entered into the ark with Noah?" . . . My heart answered in the words of the Prophet, "Shall a man speak lies in the name of the Lord?" Zech. xiii.3. I dared not do so. . . . I gave him, however, such a reply as satisfied him for the time, without throwing any discredit upon the general veracity of the Bible history.
>
> But I was thus driven,—against my will at first, I may truly say,— to search more deeply into these questions. . . . And now I tremble at the result of my enquiries. . . . Should my difficulties not be removed, I shall, if God will, come to England, and there again consult some of my friends.[188]

Unable to rid himself of these distressing doubts regarding the historical veracity of the Old Testament narratives, Colenso appealed to Hebrew scholars, Davidson, Kurtz, Hengstenberg, Ewald, and others. In the end, the inquirer was made so thoroughly convinced of "the unhistorical character of very considerable portions of the Mosaic narrative" that he no longer stood in need of counsel: "I had no longer any doubts; my former misgivings had been changed to certainties. The matter was become more serious. I saw that it concerned the whole Church." In the Preface to *The Pentateuch and Book of Joshua Critically Examined*, Part I (1862), the author explains that the difficulties felt by himself "would be felt, and realised in their full force, by most intelligent Englishmen, whether of the Clergy or Laity." This being the case, it seemed necessary to the bishop that the clergy should not wait for the enlightenment of the laity, who—"if they have any reason to suppose that we are willing to keep back any part of the truth, and are afraid to state the plain facts of the case, as we know them"—would lose confidence in the honesty and good faith of the clergy.[189]

While preparing his exposé of the historical, geographical, and mathematical errors and absurdities of the Pentateuch, the bishop sent one of the privately printed copies of his current work to Maurice, who in reply expressed no little concern and asked if they could meet. Accordingly, in early September 1862, the two men met in Bayswater. To the theologian it appeared that Colenso's views had stretched beyond the latitude that the people of England allowed their clergy: "Well," he said, "I think the consciences of Englishmen will be very strongly impressed with the feeling that you ought to resign your bishopric." Colenso responded, "Oh, you know, if it comes to that, there are plenty of people who say that you have no business to hold your living." Anyone else might have recognized that the bishop's response was merely intended to throw into question the legitimacy of an appeal to "the consciences of Englishmen" as an arbiter in theological disputation, but Maurice, feeling that his own integrity had been called into question, hastily replied, "Very well, if that is so—if there are those who conscientiously believe that I am holding my belief in the Church's Creeds and in the Bible for the sake of money I get for my chapel—I think that that is so great a scandal that I shall at once resign my living."[190]

Colenso had distributed additional copies of his work to Stanley, Jowett, and J. Llewelyn Davies, among others. Stanley—who had recently returned from a second journey through the Holy Land, this time acting, on the queen's request, as guide to the prince of Wales—met with the bishop in August. Afterwards, he wrote to Jowett, "An excellent man, and an able book; but it is so written as to vex me a good deal. I have urged him, if possible, to write it more like a defence, and less like an attack." Davies concurred, saying of the book, "It is the most purely negative criticism I ever read."[191] In replying to Stanley, Jowett took a different view: "I think the tone is a good deal mistaken. But don't be hurt or pained by it. You work in one way, he in another, I perhaps in a third way. All good persons should agree in heartily sympathizing with the effort to state the facts of Scripture exactly as they are."[192]

Once the precipitating cause behind Maurice's decision to resign his living was known, Stanley warned Maurice that the public would not understand his motives and would think that he was trying to influence the hearing of the case against Wilson in the Court of Arches—as if to say that, should it be determined that Wilson, by having expressed his views against the notion of the everlasting punishment of the wicked, must forfeit his position in the Church, then Wilson will not be the only minister forced out. Maurice admitted that he would be "exceedingly grieved" if such an interpretation were placed upon his actions, but remained unswayed by Stanley's argument. Finally, at the end of October, just before the publication of *The Pentateuch*, Colenso's brother-in-law wrote Maurice, expressing concern that, should he resign out of protest against the book, he would be taking unfair advantage of the trust that had been placed in him when the bishop gave him the draft: "You are prepared to betray him," wrote Mr. Bunyon, "by having an engine of attack to be issued simultaneously with the book. . . . *I think this involves a question of honour.*" Maurice retracted his resignation, which Archbishop Tait had, in the meantime, refused to sign. To Stanley, Maurice wrote, "I soon perceived that I had been about to injure Colenso, when I fancied I was only injuring myself. Then it became clear to me that people did—as you said they would—utterly mistake my meaning and suppose me to be leaving the Church."[193]

Before another two weeks had elapsed Arnold met with Stanley and Jowett for a lively discussion at Oxford. During the summer the university commissioners had relaxed the stipulations forbidding the marriage of fellows, allowing *professorial* fellows *in certain cases* to marry. Jowett, thereupon, submitted a motion to allow *all* fellows to marry, but his motion was ignored. In addition, Stanley was still laboring without success to secure an endowment for the professor of Greek. At about the time that Arnold met with Jowett, the professor wrote to a friend, "My College wants to get rid of me, which is rather hard." Something like this must have been said at their meeting, but Arnold, rather comically, misunderstood and wrote to his mother, "There is a move to turn [Jowett] out of his Fellowship for his heresies, and Stanley chooses this moment to revive in Congregation the question of his salary."[194]

The main subject of the day was, of course, Colenso's book. Stanley talked about his protracted exchange with the author, in which he "had urged again and again, both in conversations and letters," that, as in the case of *Essays and Reviews*, "the whole plan" of the book was a mistake. Stanley compared his own current work on *The Jewish Church* with the work of Colenso: "My object for twenty years, and my object in my forthcoming book, is to draw forth the inestimable treasures of the Old Testament, both historically, geographically, morally, and spiritually. To fix the public attention on the mere defects of structure and detail is, to my mind, to lead off the public mind on a false scent and to a false issue."[195] Jowett talked about the two-fold responsibility, insisting that "there is a duty to speak the truth as well as a duty to withhold it," and that, whereas the majority of the clergy and laity may urge the latter course, "a higher expediency pleads that 'honesty is the best policy,' and that truth alone 'makes free.'" Nevertheless, Jowett concluded, "In this conflict of reasons, individual judgment must at last decide."[196]

Arnold spent the next day or two reflecting on this discussion. He thought that the essayist who had looked to Spinoza for his material had, in the matter of practical application, failed to follow the philosopher's wisdom. To his mother Arnold writes,

> I think, *apropos* of Colenso, of doing what will be rather an interesting thing—I am going to write an article called "The Bishop and the Philosopher," contrasting Colenso and Co.'s jejune and technical manner of dealing with Biblical controversy with that of Spinoza in his famous treatise on the *Interpretation of Scripture*, with a view of showing how, the heresy on both sides being equal, Spinoza broaches his in that edifying and pious spirit by which alone the treatment of such matters can be made fruitful, while Colenso and the English Essayists, from their narrowness and want of power, more than from any other cause, do not.[197]

The Few and the Many

Thus begins Arnold's foray into social and religious criticism. Little could he have imagined that the current of the stream into which he so confidently stepped would cut the ground from under his legs and threaten to drown him "like some boy, some pig-boy / swept away, trying to ford a winter torrent in a storm."[198] A dozen years would pass before Arnold would again step upon the smooth plain of literary criticism, but even there the current would pursue him. Against its angry swirl he would strengthen his limbs and earn his humble place among the immortal names of religious and theological criticism.

Arnold's promised article appeared in the January 1863 issue of *Macmillan's Magazine*. It begins badly. Colenso's book, we are told, "has to justify itself before another tribunal besides an ecclesiastical one; it is liable to be called up for judgment, not only before a Court of Arches, but before the Republic of Letters." This is a claim that, by its unmitigated arrogance, stunned Maurice, who responded in a public letter, "If I am appealed to as a clergyman, I must speak as one. I must say distinctly I think there *is* a higher judge than the Critic."[199] As a clergyman, even as a human being, Colenso labored as one in the sight of God, but as a bishop he labored as a shepherd over the people of God. There were, thus, two seats of judgment—a higher and a lower court, so to speak—before which Colenso had to stand. In light of this, Arnold's bold proclamation that Colenso had also to recognize and heed the authority of a third tribunal, a Republic of Letters—over which, presumably, Arnold himself presided—was regrettably audacious.

Having, thus, succeeded in alienating himself from the greater part of the clergy—whom, one might have supposed, he had intended to persuade—Arnold proceeds to make his argument. For the sake of simplicity, we might divide it into two parts, each of which is based upon a governing principle: (1) on reserve; (2) on the State. Under these two headings we discover thoughts fundamental to the development of Arnold as a religious thinker.

The principle of *reserve* is given by Isaac Williams in Tract LXXXVII (1840):

> Religious doctrines and articles of faith can only be received according to certain dispositions of the heart; these dispositions can only be formed by a repetition of certain actions. And therefore a certain course of action can alone dispose us to receive certain doctrines; and hence it is evident that these doctrines are in vain preached unless these actions are at the same time practised and insisted on as most essential.[200]

J. H. Newman speaks of the same principle under the name of *economy*, observing that "this cautious dispensation of the truth, after the manner of a discreet and vigilant steward, is denoted by the word 'economy.' It is a mode of acting which comes under the head of Prudence, one of the four Cardinal Virtues."[201] This principle of reserve or economy is sometimes confused with two other related but distinct ideas. The first of these is the principle of *accommodation*, which Dr. Arnold—following Semler and Lessing—had propounded in his 1834 *Essay on the Right Interpretation and Understanding of the Scriptures*. Accommodation is, essentially, God's practice of reserve. It is the idea that God does not reveal his will for the human race all at once, but gradually, according to the preparedness of the human heart and mind. The second doctrine with which both reserve and accommodation are, occasionally, confounded is the anterior concept of *development*, from which the other ideas logically derive. According to "development," the human race grows up unto maturity, much in the same way as an individual, so that—as Temple states the case—"We may expect to find, in the history of man, each successive age incorporating into itself the substance of the preceding."[202] Both reserve and accommodation presuppose development and are the practical application of the larger principle.

Although divine accommodation and human reserve are not, in themselves, incompatible, theologians who emphasize one or the other are generally found to have opposing notions of how God operates upon and through humanity in history. On the one hand, those who perceive revelation as a gradual and continuous process operating upon the world tend to regard the practice of reserve as a usurpation of the divine office and an instance of priestcraft. When the "fullness of time" has come for a new message to enter the world, who is to say that this message is not to be sent to the furthest corners? On the other hand, there are those who perceive revelation as a sudden outpouring upon a select few who are, even themselves, unable to fully apprehend what has been committed to their care. Through prayer and holy living they are slowly—perhaps, even over generations or centuries—led to discern the hidden spiritual truths. Are these few to "cast their pearls" before those who have done nothing to prepare the ears of the soul to hear and the eyes of the soul to see?

We find this opposition of ideas most fully developed by the two greatest English theologians of the nineteenth century, Maurice and Newman. Arnold decidedly cast his lot with Newman. Thus, from Newman's *Essay on the Development of Christian Doctrine* (1845), Arnold presents this passage in support of one of the author's "profound and valuable ideas":

> From the nature of the human mind, time is necessary for the full comprehension and perfection of great ideas. The highest and most wonderful truths, though communicated to the world once for all by inspired teachers, could not be comprehended all at once by the recipients; but, as admitted and transmitted by minds not inspired, and through media which were human, have required only the longer time and deeper thought for their full elucidation.[203]

In support of the principle of reserve Arnold appeals to Matt. 13:11, "It is given unto you to know the mysteries of the kingdom of heaven, but to them it is not given," but he appears to ignore the larger context of the passage. Maurice, in *What Is Revelation?* (1859), looking at the question that the disciples had asked Jesus, and the *entire* answer that they received, persuasively argues that Jesus—far from acting upon any principle of reserve—used the sensual imagery of parables to teach the masses that which they were unprepared to receive through their spiritual senses. Arnold had probably not known of this explication, for, by his own admission, he did not have ears to hear Maurice.[204]

It is from Newman's exposition of "development" that Arnold adopts and makes use of the notion of a *disciplina arcani*, not as something that any longer exists in criticism, but which once did, and which Spinoza had the wisdom to take advantage of when he published his *Theological-Political Treatise* in Latin. For Spinoza understood that which Colenso apparently overlooked—that "The great mass of the human race have to be softened and humanised through their heart and imagination, before any soil can be found in them where knowledge may strike living roots." The cultural transition from the condition of the many to the condition of the few is fraught with peril, and demonstrations that appeal only to the intellect before the soil of the heart and imagination is thoroughly prepared may be worse than premature and futile; they may, in fact, impede this softening and humanising process, in which case "they are even noxious; they retard their development, they impair the culture of the world."[205]

Arnold had already, in 1857, pointed out a fact that was immediately obvious to anyone who considered it: few were the scholars proficient in Latin. If Colenso wrote to English clerics, he had no choice but to publish in a language accessible to all literate Englishmen. Arnold knew this, and he should have used it as the beginning point of his argument. He might, then, have observed that, were an English writer to publish, he would publish to all—to both the "higher culture of Europe" *and* to "the little instructed" masses. An author writing on religion would have to assume a general readership and, in so doing, aim to instruct and edify. However, Arnold blundered. Falling back upon the principle of reserve and the ideal of a *disciplina arcani*, he argues, instead, that literary criticism has the right to impose two conditions upon all religious books: "*edify the uninstructed*, it has a right to say to them, *or inform the instructed*." Spinoza's *Treatise* satisfies both demands: "In Spinoza there is not a trace either of Voltaire's passion for mockery or of Strauss's passion for demolition. His whole soul was filled with desire of the love and knowledge of God." Part I of Stanley's *Lectures on the History of the Jewish Church* (1863), also meets both demands, for its author, "treating Scripture history with a perfectly free spirit,—falsifying nothing, sophisticating nothing—treats it so that his freedom leaves the sacred power of that history inviolate." However, because the "ruthlessly negative" criticism of Colenso's book could not possibly fulfill the former condition, and because a simple *reductio ad absurdum* does not fulfill the latter, "the Bishop of Natal's book cannot justify itself for existing." Arnold then proceeds to pass the same judgment upon *Essays and Reviews*, sparing only Pattison's instructive "Tendencies of Religious Thought in England, 1688-1750" and Jowett's edifying contribution on the subject of interpretation.[206]

There is only one reply to Arnold's application of "reserve" that we need to note, that by W. R. Greg, "Truth *Versus* Edification." None other was so well argued. With notable civility Greg begins by confessing his surprise that Arnold, "so practiced a disputant," would venture to take up "a position so unsafe." He then concedes to the "general principle, that in all cases, mental as well as material, the soil must be prepared before the seed is sown." However, that being said, Greg proceeds to make his case that Arnold's application of the principle is "slippery and unfair." Given that the deplorable education of the English clergy is such as to justify their being classified among the uninstructed, Colenso's book will undoubtedly prove as instructive to them as Lessing, Eichhorn, DeWette, Ewald, and Strauss have been to the clergy of Europe. Moreover, to the extent that the doctrine of plenary verbal inspiration has obstructed religious devotion, Colenso's book will prove edifying, for it is singularly successful in removing this obstruction. "The plain truth," concludes Greg, "is, that the assumption of an instructed clergy and an unin-structed laity is a purely imaginary one; and in the fact that this line of demarcation *is* imaginary lies the substantial justification of all works like Dr. Colenso's."[207]

When Arnold insists that a religious book should have as its object to edify *and* instruct, he is building his house on a rock. Bishop Thomas Wilson (1663-1755) had laid down as a maxim that which became Arnold's theme: "That knowledge, which helps to reform the heart, is of much more use to us than that which only enlightens the understanding."[208] Even poetry, said Arnold, must not only provide an accurate and interesting representation of its subject; it must also "inspirit and rejoice the reader."[209] But, when he ventures to argue that there are two separate audiences, a large one that requires *only* to be edified and a small one that needs *only* to be instructed, he is building upon the sand. Jowett was undoubtedly correct when he suggested that such difficulties as pointed out by Colenso "are found to affect the half-educated, rather than either the poor, or those who are educated in a higher sense." The happiest are those who either do not perceive the difficulties or have learned to reconcile the difficulties that they perceive.[210] The third audience, however, the half-educated, is ignored by Arnold, even though *this* audience is, in fact, the most appropriate audience for a *religious* book. H. B. Wilson, too, appears to have noted this, for he speaks of the recoil "on the part of large numbers of the more acute of our population, from some of the doctrines which are to be heard at church and chapel."[211]

Arnold could not but feel the weight of the objections made against his argument, and he retreated. First, he abandons the proposition that there is a readership that requires *only* to be edified. Those who need so little do not read. Second, in agreement with Jowett, he redefines the largest audience as "the half-educated," and—picking up a term with which he had become acquainted while reading Goethe, Schleiermacher, Heine, Coleridge, and Carlyle—he begins, in August of 1863, to speak of the "strong, dogged, unenlightened" body of *Philistines*,[212] a word that is roughly equivalent to a contemporary English slang term, "Stumpfs." Third, he dispenses with the notion that there is a readership of religious books that requires *only* to be instructed: "The world of the few—the world of speculative life—is not the world of the many, the world of religious life."[213] Between the writing of "The Bishop and the Philosopher" and "Marcus Aurelius" (November 1863), Arnold's position had entirely changed. In Bishop Wilson, Arnold read, "There is a great deal of difference betwixt knowing God as a philosopher, and as a Christian. The first has little or no effect upon the heart. . . . To a man, for instance, in affliction, in disgrace, etc., say all the fine things that Marcus Aurelius, Seneca, etc., ever said, and see if his mind will rest satisfied with them."[214] For Bishop Wilson, as for Arnold, moral rules that act only upon the understanding are "for the sage only," whereas "the paramount virtue of religion is, that it has *lighted up* morality; that it has supplied the emotion and inspiration needful for carrying the sage along the narrow way perfectly."[215] Thus, for all practical purposes, Arnold gave up the distinction between the few and the many, but he would, instead—as we shall see—insist all the more strongly upon the great divide separating clergy and laity.

The Clergy and the Laity

Colenso, in the Preface to Part I of *The Pentateuch and Book of Joshua Critically Examined*, states, "I cannot but believe that our Church, representing, as it is supposed to do, the religious feeling of a free, Protestant, nation, requires us now, as in the days of the Reformation, to protest against all perversion of the Truth, and all suppression of it, for the sake of Peace, or by mere Authority."[216] In response, Arnold protests that Colenso was merely crying out for a different Church, having forgotten "that the clergy of a Church with formularies like those of the Church of England, exist in virtue of their relinquishing in religious matters full liberty of speculation." For Arnold, the point at issue is not whether Colenso is right in claiming that it is time for the Church to change, but rather, whether that change is to be precipitated by the hired servants of the Church. "It may be time," he argues, "for the State to institute, as its national clergy, a corporation enjoying the most absolute freedom of speculation; but that corporation will not be the present clergy of the Church of England."[217]

Arnold, like Clough, had arrived at a twofold conclusion that is directly pertinent to the idea of a Broad Church movement. On the one hand, the man who became a minister of the Church under the conditions of subscription to the Thirty-nine Articles, morally obligated himself either to abide under the intellectual restrictions thus imposed upon him or to relinquish his orders. On the other hand, the intellectual progress through which Arnold's generation had passed, particularly during the years 1843-1853, had effected so great a disparity between modern thought and the ideas expressed within the formularies of the Church that it was no longer possible for a clergyman to engage in criticism and still maintain a "sound position." The clergyman who does attempt criticism inevitably either fails at his object or ends up in a false position in relation to the Church. That is to say, he either consciously *feels*—regardless of what he professes to *think*—that he is transgressing the dogma of the Thirty-nine Articles, or he professes "to see Christianity through the spectacles of a number of second or third-rate men who lived in Queen Elizabeth's time," which latter position is "an intolerable absurdity." To his mother, Arnold suggested that "papa . . . is the last free speaker of the Church of England clergy who speaks without being shackled, and without being obviously aware that he is so."

This being the case, we might ask, what is a clergyman to do? Arnold answers, "He is to abstain from dealing with speculative matters at all: he may confine himself to such matters as Stanley does, or to pure edification. . . . But the moment he begins to write for or against Colenso, he is inevitably in a false position."[218] The proper object of the clergyman who would deal with new ideas is not to propagate them, but rather to reconcile them with the religious life. Arnold esteems Stanley as a clergyman who has gone, perhaps, as far as any clergyman can go in integrating the fruits of modern scholarship with the purposes of the Church: "Everywhere he keeps in mind the purpose for which the religious life seeks the Bible—to be enlarged and strengthened, not to be straightened and perplexed."[219] In this respect, Stanley is working in the tradition of Dr. Arnold, whose greatness "consists in his bringing such a torrent of freshness into English religion by placing history and politics in connexion with it," by bringing into religion "a number of other things which the old narrow religionists thought had nothing to do with it."[220]

It should be noted that Arnold is protesting against the essayists' position, but the essayists insist that they are *not* propagating new ideas, but are, in fact, reconciling them with the Articles. Wilson reminds his readers, "It is more difficult than might be expected, to define what is the extent of the legal obligation of those who sign them; and in this case the strictly legal obligation is the measure of the moral one. Subscription may be thought even to be inoperative upon the conscience by reason of its vagueness." It is because of this very vagueness in the Articles that Stanley consistently defended Tract XC, Ward's *Ideal*, the essayists, and Colenso, and laid down as a rule of thumb, "No man ought ever to write himself down as a heretic."[221] Even Maurice and Kingsley took the position that the Articles should be read as a lawyer might read them, regardless of what might be the popular or dominant interpretation of them. The Maurician viewpoint is that the compilers of the Articles "rose much above their ordinary level, when they met as in the presence of God," that they received a gift of wisdom and "of necessity spoke words beyond their own comprehension," and that—this being the case—the notion that the Articles must be interpreted "by the words and acts of the Reformers, when they were fulfilling a less high vocation, and endued with a lower inspiration," is repugnant to a proper respect for the Articles.[222] For Maurice, the Providence of God not only allowed for, but intended, that the Articles be interpreted as a legal document, *not*—as Arnold would appear to demand—according to the probable intent of the compilers.

To most, if not all, of the Broad Churchmen—regardless of their agreement with Maurice—the liberty of a clergyman to interpret the Articles was presumed to be a *civil* right, secured as one of the privileges of Establishment. In one sense, this position was nothing new within Anglicanism, and Arnold's position, as Hastings Rashdall suggests in *Anglican Liberalism* (1908), is radically opposed to the historical practice of the clergy:

> The claim of the clergy to interpret very freely—often in a sense notoriously opposed to the meaning of their framers—large portions of the Church's formulæ can only be refused on a principle which involves the imputation of "dishonesty" to, it may be almost said, a majority among the clergy from the days of the Reformation down to the present, including the most famous and revered leaders of every school of thought.[223]

The principle difference between the liberal churchmen of the nineteenth century and of former times is that, whereas the Latitudinarians sought to reconcile the formularies to suit their interpretation of Scripture, the Broad Churchmen were faced with the double task, first, of reconciling Scripture to new discoveries in history and science and, then, of reconciling the formularies so as to allow for this new understanding of Scripture.

From Arnold's perspective, however, the very idea of the State appears contrary to the notion that each and every clergyman should interpret the Articles as he likes. Although it is true that the law may allow a clergyman the freedom to express extreme views, the cost of exercising this freedom is bitterness and party feeling. "By our everyday selves," Arnold argues in *Culture and Anarchy*, "we are separate, personal, at war. . . . But by our *best self* we are united, impersonal, at harmony," and it is this "best self, or right reason" that suggests the idea of *"the State*, or organ of our collective best self, or our national right reason."[224] This notion of "the State," as well as of "the best self," was Dr. Arnold's. After attending a sermon of Stanley's "on the benefits Christianity had derived from the just and intelligent administrative system of the Roman Empire," Arnold was reminded, he tells his mother, of "papa's influence." And, indeed, Arnold never dealt with considerations about the State without feeling himself on his father's ground.[225] But we might doubt whether Dr. Arnold would have fully agreed with his son in this matter respecting the Articles, for the father, too, struggled with the formularies of the Church, and although—as Keble expresses the fact—it was "a defect of his mind" that he could not "get rid of a certain feeling of objections,"[226] Thomas Arnold, nevertheless, took orders.

Leslie Stephen, on the other hand, who resigned his orders when he could not get rid of objections, is quick to point out what he perceives as the logical inconsistencies of Arnold's position. If Arnold objects to clerical nonconformity within the Church, logic itself should lead him to recognize the reasonableness of clerical dissent: "Mr. Arnold seems to look too exclusively to one side of the mischief, and to attribute to the gratuitous perversity of Dissenters what is the natural consequence of trying to construct or to maintain a State Church when it no longer corresponds to the wants of society."[227] Stephen's argument is not difficult for Arnold to rebut. It is not logic, but rather "doing as one likes," that leads men to becomes dissenting clerics in opposition to the Established Church.

Arnold was not greatly concerned about the clergy who either resigned or were removed from the Church of England. His concern was, rather, with the many who chose to remain within it, and he could not forever withstand the force of their outcry. Slowly, but significantly, his position relaxed. By 1876 he felt free to tell ministers not "to disquiet themselves about having given a consent to the Articles formerly, when things had not moved to the point where they appear now, and did not appear to men's minds as they now appear." He suggests to a clergyman that, if there are parts of the Prayer Book that "he cannot accept as literal," he may regard such parts "as language *thrown out* by other men, in other times, at immense objects ... concerning which, moreover, adequate statement is impossible."[228] Of course, by this time Arnold himself—through the publication of his trilogy, *St. Paul and Protestantism* (1869), *Literature and Dogma* (1873), and *God and the Bible* (1875)—had already taken a very public role in effecting a change in the interpretation of Scripture. It would have appeared rudely inconsistent in him had he not allowed for a clergyman's liberty of *private* interpretation.

There were, however, other factors that had precipitated a reconsideration. The acquittal of Williams and Wilson by the Privy Council in 1864 had, in the words of Stanley, "declared to be no doctrine of the Church of England that 'every part of the Bible is inspired, or is the Word of God.'" Moreover, it had been the judgment of the council that the Church could not pledge itself to "any popular theory of the future punishment of the wicked or of the mode of justification."[229] Thus, the State, while endorsing no particular interpretation of the Articles, had sanctioned the essayists' interpretation. In 1865 Convocation passed, as a logical development upon the judgment of the Privy Council, a less stringent form of clerical subscription—one that replaced the "unfeigned assent and consent" to the proposition that everything within the Thirty-nine Articles and Book of Common Prayer is "agreeable to the Word of God," substituting it with a twofold declaration, first, of assent to the Articles and Prayer Book, and second, of belief that "the doctrine of the Church of England as therein set forth" is "agreeable to the Word of God."[230] H. R. Haweis, speaking to fellow clergymen in *The Broad Church, or What is Coming* (1891), observes, "The relaxed subscription of 1865 is, as the late Dean [Stanley] of Westminster pointed out, a mere 'rag and tatter of Subscription.' It simply binds us to an administrative Assent, and to belief in a Fact which . . . is of no doctrinal importance whatever." That which is of "no doctrinal importance" is the agreement of the formularies to "the Word of God," for—as Haweis explains—even if "the Word of God" is understood as synonymous with the canonical writings, "it is difficult to conceive of any theological proposition that could not be proved to be *agreeable to the Word of God*, with a little 'vigour and rigour.'"[231]

In consideration of these reforms, we must ask, what is the practical significance of the relaxation of conscience claimed by Arnold on the behalf of the clergy? It is this: the authorized interpretation of the formularies was no longer to be restricted by authorial intent. But Arnold does not say with Maurice and Stanley that clergy are at liberty to interpret the Creeds and Articles *as a lawyer might*; rather he says that clergy are free to interpret the formularies *as a poet might*—that is, "as approximative language, and as poetry." It is the clergyman's role to keep the old and cherished images, but "as far as possible," to instill them with "the soul of the new Christian ideal." This is the manner, says Arnold, that Jesus used the religious language of his day, and although such a way of using language must lead to misapprehension, it is, nevertheless, "the best way and the only one."[232] As far as the moral obligations of clergymen are concerned, this appears to be the full extent of Arnold's change in policy.

Arnold never altered his position that the formularies of the Church can only be changed through the executive office of the State and that a man, having accepted as binding the Articles and Canons of the Church upon ordination, Church and State rightfully demand of him a conforming submission. In a period of concentration, the Church does not need revolutionary reformers like Luther; it needs constitutional reformers like Erasmus. In fact, "two powers must concur, the power of the man and the power of the moment, and the man is not enough without the moment." From Joubert, Arnold derives his maxim, "*Force till right is ready*." Until the moment is ripe and the progress of ideas certifies that the fulness of time has come, "force, the existing order of things, is justified."[233] When right is ready, then someone will arise, who, in the spirit of Spinoza, will make "a fervent appeal to the State, to save us from the untoward generation of metaphysical Articlemakers."[234] The great error of men like Luther is that, by attempting to effect a premature change, they arouse a party of opposition and, thus, set back the progress of culture. Arnold explains this position well in "Puritanism and the Church of England" (1870):

> Philosophy and criticism have become a great power in the world, and inevitably tend to alter and develop Church doctrine, so far as this doctrine is, as to a great extent it is, philosophical and critical. Yet the seat of the developing force is not in the Church itself, but elsewhere; its influences filter strugglingly into the Church, and the Church slowly absorbs and incorporates them. And whatever hinders their filtering in and becoming incorporated, hinders truth and the natural progress of things.[235]

In acknowledging the shaping influence of the Time-Spirit upon Christian thought, Arnold says no more than that which had already been said as clearly by the essayists: Temple observes that "physical science, researches into history, a more thorough knowledge of the world . . . have an influence, whether we will or no, on our determinations of religious truth"; Baden Powell notes, "Paley caught the prevalent tone of thought in his day," and that "new modes of speculation—new forms of scepticism" have now rendered Paley obsolete; and Mark Pattison—whose entire essay is a delineation of the movements of the eighteenth-century zeitgeist in relation to the Church of England—states, "Rationalism was not an anti-Christian sect outside the Church making war against religion. It was a habit of thought ruling all minds, under the conditions of which all alike tried to make good the peculiar opinions they might happen to cherish."[236] These are thoughts with which Arnold could not but agree. In fact, Pattison's essay would provide the inspiration for Arnold's "Bishop Butler and the Zeit-Geist" (1876). Where Arnold parts company with the essayists is in his insistence that—although the Time-Spirit affects all of culture, making no distinction between clergy and laity—the wheel of reformation is, nevertheless, to be turned only by laity.

Greg, in his response to Arnold, appealed to "a great analogy between the only effectual course of proceeding available to reformers in theological and in political matters." According to Greg, Church and State are immovable until the pressure of public opinion necessitates a response: "Does anyone believe that, till the people *are* thus enlightened, there is any prospect of this discreditable and injurious state of things being amended?"[237] Of course, the problem with Greg's analogy is that, whereas a disgruntled citizen may petition, hold a public demonstration, or withhold a vote, a parishioner is more likely to join a nonconformist body or stop attending services and, thus, subvert the natural progress of reform by removing the tension that is needed to instigate it. Arnold is aware of this problem, and in "Modern Dissent" (1870) he observes that, just as the participation of the ritualists has brought much of value to the Church, so too would the reintegration of the Dissenters: "There could come nothing but health and strength from blending this body with the Establishment, of which the very weakness and danger is that it tends

. . . to be an appendage to the upper-class Barbarians."[238] What, therefore, the Church needs is an apologist, someone who can appeal to the Dissenters on the behalf of the Establishment and can, at the same time, appeal to the Establishment to meet the Dissenters half way.

We can safely say that, by the time Arnold completed *Culture and Anarchy* (1869), he had arrived at two conclusions regarding the Broad Church movement. First, the idea of the Broad Church was, in the main, a gift of the Time-Spirit and, thus, quite right and necessary for the advancement of culture in England. Second, the Broad Church clergy were, to the extent that they attempted to change the accepted teaching of the Church, in a false position. W. J. Conybeare had, in 1853, divided Broad Churchmen into two groups, the theoretical and the nontheoretical. The latter "neither stultify the Articles, nor mutilate the Liturgy; but heartily embrace the truths presented to them in each under a different aspect."[239] For both Conybeare and Arnold, Stanley is a representative of the nontheoretical school, and in Arnold's estimation, this is the only legitimate Broad Church school for clergymen. After the death of Stanley in July of 1881, Arnold would write, "What is clear is that the Broad Church *among the clergy* may be almost said to have perished with Stanley—for the moment, at any rate; there is plenty of it in the nation, but Stanley's signal merit was that in his person it became a power *among the clergy* likewise." He observes, "The great centre-current of our time is a *lay* current."[240] The laity is, as Dr. Arnold had defined it, "the Church, *minus* the clergy." To appreciate the full force of this definition, we need only remember that, from the Erastian perspective of Dr. and Matthew Arnold, the English Church is the State of England. As Stanley argues, in a Christian nation "the lay element" is "the motive guiding force that rules the intelligence and the conscience of the whole country," and this, "in its highest form, is what we call the Government or the State."[241] The final thought of Arnold in regard to the Broad Church movement appears to be that, during the years between the death of his father and the death of Stanley, it had become—if we may borrow a useful term from S. T. Coleridge—a lay movement of the *clerisy*. As such, it had become all the more powerful in bringing about cultural change within the nation.

Christianity and Culture

At the end of 1863, following the death of Richard Whately, R. C. Trench, dean of Westminster, was elevated to the archbishopric of Dublin and Stanley was offered the deanery in his stead. To the dismay of Jowett, Stanley accepted the offer, and in almost the same breath announced his engagement to Lady Augusta Bruce, the sister of Lord Elgin, governor-general of India. When the Privy Council, in February 1864, passed its judgment in the case of Williams and Wilson, Stanley had been dean of Westminster for nearly a month. Although the transition was a loss to Oxford, Stanley now began to take a prominent role in Convocation, and the issues about which he argued in the Lower House he would also discuss with Arnold.

It must not be supposed that Arnold, in any sense, *followed* Stanley. We must not imagine any implicit trust, such as that between Kingsley and Maurice, binding the one to the other in mutual agreement. But, that there was a chord of sympathy between the two is undeniable. Upon first viewing the corpse of his father, Arnold was struck with the thought—as he afterwards told Stanley—that his "sole source of *information* was gone."[242] When Stanley became dean of Westminster, *he* became Arnold's inside source of information in regard to the politics and personali-ties of the Church of England, and—insofar as the subsequent writings of Arnold deal with ecclesiastical matters, Stanley was his muse. Even so, when the issue was one that pertained to religious feeling, Arnold went his own way. This is especially clear in regard to the ritualist movement, the controversies of which in the 1860s and '70s led to the Worship Regulation Act of 1874. Addressing Convocation, in 1866, Stanley defines the ritualist practices as insignificant trifles to be tolerated, for—as his biographer tells us—"Fastening upon the paramount importance of the moral and spiritual aspects of religion, he depreciated the value of the ceremonial obser-vances in which they were enshrined"[243] Arnold, however, valued the aesthetic contributions of ritualism for the feelings of devotion that they helped to evoke. As early as 1863 he argues, "The signal want of grace and charm in English Protes-tantism's setting of its religious life is not an indifferent matter; it is a real weakness."[244] These High Church sentiments of Arnold's were much appreciated by his Roman Catholic brother, Tom, who—having accepted J. H. Newman's invitation—was now teaching English literature at the Catholic University of Dublin. We can hardly doubt that these sentiments would have been appreciated by Dr. Arnold as well.[245]

The culture of Protestantism and its effects upon the worship of the Church, although a subject of concern in itself, was only one example of the impact of middle-class Philistinism upon the quality and aspirations of English life—and this, of course, was the graver concern not only for Arnold, but for nearly everyone with whom he came into contact at his favorite London club, where he regularly went to correct papers, the Athenæum. With the passing in 1867 of the Second Reform Bill, which extended the franchise to most male workers, *culture*—as an ideal—became a staple of conversation, but few had given *paideia*, *humanitas*, and *bildung* as much thought as had Arnold. Finding himself peculiarly trained by the habits of his mind to address this topic, now of general concern, he decided to deliver, as his final lecture as professor of poetry, an encomium on the culture of Oxford, as he had come to know and love it during his Decade years:

> We in Oxford, brought up amidst the beauty and sweetness of that
> beautiful place, have not failed to seize one truth,—the truth that beauty
> and sweetness are essential characters of a complete human perfection.
> When I insist on this, I am all in the faith and tradition of Oxford. I say
> boldly that this our sentiment for beauty and sweetness, our sentiment

against hideousness and rawness, has been at the bottom of our attachment to so many beaten causes, of our opposition to so many triumphant
movements.[246]

Arnold afterwards explained to his mother, "I tried to make this last lecture one in
which I could keep to ground where I am in sympathy with Oxford, having often
enough startled them with heresies and novelties."[247] Oxford received this gesture
with generous applause.

In his speech on "Culture and Its Enemies," the professor does not set out to
defend the idea of culture, but rather, he occupies the common ground of his
audience and argues from the presupposition that culture is something good and
desirable. He, then, both in this lecture and in "Anarchy and Authority"—afterwards
published together with a Preface as *Culture and Anarchy*—proceeds to delineate
what makes culture good, which necessarily revolves upon what, in fact, culture *is*.
As it turns out, culture is to the State what religion is to the Church, and in a Christian
nation the two are the same thing—the pursuit of "perfection" or the "partaking of
the divine nature"—merely seen from divergent perspectives. The method of Arnold
and Spinoza is comparable in that they each posit a dual paradigm, secular and
religious (i.e., Nature/God, culture/religion) whereby a single reality may be comprehended. But, the argument of *Culture and Anarchy* is comparable to
Schleiermacher's *Speeches* in that, while both arguments address an audience that
has an imperfect notion of religion, placing culture either above it or below it, the
authors propose a broader concept of religion—one that is contemplative, consists
in emotions and dispositions, and realizes human perfection in a synthesis of dual
impulses. Ironically, although the work of Arnold and Schleiermacher is apologetic,
their strongest opposition originally came from the religious despisers of culture.

As a corrective response to Arnold's "aesthetic culture" and T. H. Huxley's
"scientific culture," Shairp—upon his promotion to principal of the United College
of St. Andrews—delivered a series of lectures, subsequently published as *Culture
and Religion in Some of Their Relations* (1870). Our concern here, of course,
cannot extend beyond Principal Shairp's evaluation of Arnold's teaching. Shairp
observes that, for Arnold, the aim of culture coincides with the aim of religion in
three considerations:

> *First*, in that it places perfection not in any external good, but in an
> internal condition of the soul. . . . *Secondly*, in that it sets before men a
> condition not of having and resting, but of growing and becoming as the
> true aim. . . . *Thirdly*, in that it holds that a man's perfection cannot be
> self-contained, but must embrace the good of others equally with his own,
> and as the very condition of his own.

Thus far, Shairp professes complete agreement with Arnold; however, "There is a
fourth note of perfection as conceived by culture, in which, as Mr. Arnold thinks, it

transcends the aim of religion. . . . For religion, Mr. Arnold thinks, aims at the cultivation of some, and these, no doubt, the highest powers of the soul, at the expense,
even at the sacrifice, of other powers, which it regards as lower."[248] The passage
against which Shairp expresses his dissents is, quite possibly, the most misunderstood passage in all of *Culture and Anarchy*:

> But, finally, perfection—as culture from a thorough disinterested study
> of human nature and human experience learns to conceive it,—is a
> harmonious expansion of *all* the powers which make the beauty and
> worth of human nature, and is not consistent with the over-development
> of any one power at the expense of the rest. Here culture goes beyond
> religion, as religion is generally conceived by us.[249]

The professor of Latin misinterprets the qualifying passage with which this quotation ends, as though it says, "as I, along with most people, conceive religion." Shairp
misses the fact that Arnold is clarifying the greatness of culture only to conclude by
demonstrating that culture and religion *properly conceived* (*not* "as religion is
generally conceived by us") are identical. However, to say that they are identical, in
the sense that they have the same objective, is not to say that they are alternatives
independent of each other. Thus, when Shairp declares, in objection to Arnold's
position, "They who seek religion for culture-sake are aesthetic, not religious, and
will never gain that grace which religion adds to culture," he is not saying anything
with which Arnold would disagree. Truly, "Before it can educe the highest capacities of which human nature is susceptible, culture must cease to be merely culture,
and pass over into religion."[250] Culture and religion must both be sought for the sake
of human perfection, but it is as vain to suppose that perfection can be attained
without culture as it is to suppose that it can be attained without religion. The
disagreement between Arnold and Shairp is, in fact, strikingly analogous to the
Erasmus/Luther debate in regard to the relationship between will and grace, and just
as, in Erasmus, will is placed in a subordinate position to grace, "in Arnold's mature
writings on religion"—as James Livingston notes—"culture clearly becomes
ancillary to religion."[251] Even though this subordination may not be as obvious in
Culture and Anarchy as in subsequent writings, we might discern that, for Arnold,
as early as 1868, culture without Christianity is an impossible dream.

   Culture is *a study of perfection* that "moves by the force, not merely or primarily
of the scientific passion for pure knowledge, but also of the moral and social passion
for doing good." As such it has for its object—in the words of Bishop Wilson—"To
make reason and the will of God prevail," and Arnold explains, we are "to come at
reason and the will of God by means of reading, observing, and thinking."[252] There
are, thus, two "great spiritual disciplines" that impel us forward toward perfection,
and whereas "the governing idea of Hellenism is *spontaneity of consciousness*; that
of Hebraism [is], *strictness of conscience*," but at the bottom of each "is the desire,
native in man, for reason and the will of God, the feeling after the universal order,—

in a word, the love of God."[253] Hellenism is ineffectual without the help of Hebraism, for "there is something which thwarts and spoils all our efforts" as we strive to move toward light and beauty, and "this something is *sin*." Therefore, in looking over the history of civilization, we find, "Through age after age and generation after generation, our race, or all that part of our race which was most living and progressive, was *baptized into a death*." Likewise, Hebraism is stunted in its growth if not nourished by Hellenism, so that "the Puritan's great danger" is that he remains satisfied with the Bible and the Bible alone, when in fact, "even the most precious writings and the most fruitful, must inevitably, from the very nature of things, be but contributions to human thought and human development."[254] The Protestant conception of revelation, limited to the writers of the Bible, discounts the inspiration of other writers and thwarts the godly desire to fill one's consciousness with the best that is thought and said in the world. So extensive is this Bibliolatry, this false conception of an *unum necessarium* (or one thing needful), that it has determined the way in which religion "is generally conceived by us."

Temple, in *Essays and Reviews*, had noted the tension between the Hebrew "supremacy of conscience" and the Greek "cultivation of the reason and the taste." He observed an intermittent Greek effort, through "moments of generous emotion," to reach the level of Hebrew religion. However, even the merging of Hebraism and Hellenism was incomplete without the Roman contribution of a "spirit of order and organization" and the Asiatic contribution of an inspiration in rest, from which has come the doctrine of the soul's immortality. Temple observes, "the Hebrews may be said to have disciplined the human conscience, Rome the human will, Greece the reason and taste, Asia the spiritual imagination." Only then, after this education, was the world prepared for the example of Jesus Christ.[255] Perhaps, Temple and Arnold discussed these ideas when they met for dinner, together with Stanley and Walrond, in August 1867, for in the February 1868 installments of "Anarchy and Authority" we find that Arnold, too, is aware that "to the whole development of man Hebraism itself is, like Hellenism, but a contribution."[256] David DeLaura suggests, "The central intention of *Culture and Anarchy* is surely the definition of an ideal which will cancel the historical oscillation of Hebraism and Hellenism, the extremes of moralism and intellectualism, by somehow combining them in a higher synthesis."[257] For Arnold, the pathway toward attaining this higher synthesis leads to right reason and harmony with the will of God, which Christianity, when it is seen as in itself it really is, makes possible. Among the English, however, Christianity has been hindered in its working, obstructed by a misunderstanding of St. Paul.

It is often and rightly noted that *Culture and Anarchy* is a pivotal work for Arnold, in the sense that it leads him seamlessly from social to religious criticism. Having pointed out that English culture is flawed by a misunderstanding of revelation and a misinterpretation of St. Paul, Arnold now turns his talents to an exegesis of this Apostle in *St. Paul and Protestantism*. What is not often enough noted is that Arnold laid the foundation of *Culture and Anarchy* with the death of his last-born son, Basil, and set up its gate with the death of his first-born son, Thomas. In the background to Arnold's most well-known work is this less-known family tragedy. In March, two months after the death of their infant, Basil, the Arnolds moved into Byron House at Harrow, where one of the masters, F. W. Farrar— Cambridge Apostle and, afterwards, dean of Canterbury—asked Arnold "as a favour to let him have the three boys [Thomas (Tommy), Trevenen (Budge), and Richard Penrose (Dicky)] in his pupil-room without fee." Although Arnold was opposed to accepting this gift, he did allow his boys to be admitted as "foundation" scholars, and Tommy and Dicky subsequently were taught by Farrar.[258] Toward the end of the first summer break, before returning from Fox How to Harrow, Tommy fell from a pony. His weak heart struggled to recover, and for the next eleven weeks the Arnolds watched his health ebb and flow. Arnold would sit by his son's bedside, and from an old leatherbound edition of Bishop Wilson's *Maxims* that he had removed from his father's library, he would read, "Afflictions bring us the nearest way to God" and "We are purified by afflictions, and made fit for heaven."[259] On 22 November, while watching over his son, Arnold began to write the Preface to *Culture and Anarchy* but, finding the effort too strenuous, laid down his pen. On the following morning, Tommy died. A month later, on his forty-sixth birthday, Arnold writes this most significant letter to his mother:

> Everything has seemed to come together to make this year the beginning of a new time to me: the gradual settlement of my own thought, little Basil's death, and then my dear, dear Tommy's. And Tommy's death in particular was associated with several awakening and epoch-marking things. The chapter for the day of his death was that great chapter, the 1st of Isaiah; the first Sunday after his death was Advent Sunday, with its glorious collect, and in the Epistle the passage [Rom. xiii.13] which converted St. Augustine. All these things point to a new beginning, yet it may well be that I am near my end, as papa was at my age, but without papa's ripeness, and that there will be little time to carry far the new beginning. But that is all the more reason for carrying it as far as one can, and as earnestly as one can, while one lives.[260]

Because, in his public writings, Arnold converts his feelings into ideas, and shapes his ideas according to the dictates of the understanding, it is not in his public works that we find—as we do find so clearly here—the essentially religious nature of Arnold. His sense and taste for the Infinite, his inner awareness of a holy presence and calling, his joyful submission or resignation to the will and workings of God— it is in these unspeakable things that we find Arnold's *personal* religion, regardless of how, upon reflection, his intellect leads him to define and explain. Although, as Dean Farrar observes, "some of his views . . . were startling to orthodox Churchmen," his general expression is "serious, sincere, and deeply reverent."[261] The logical flow of his thought leads him from literary to social to religious criticism, but it is Arnold's religion, the buried stream, that guides the flow of his life's work.

Concurrent Endowment

Before leaving the Preface of *Culture and Anarchy*, we might note that Arnold is indebted to two lectures that Stanley presented at Sion College, London. In the first of these, "The Connection of Church and State," delivered on 15 February 1868, Stanley argues that the "lay element" of the Church operates through the State in the decisions of Parliament and the Courts of Law. He points to the Proconsul Gallio as "the chief example of a Judge on religious matters whom St. Paul and St. Luke hold up to us as a model of impartial justice.... 'He cared for none of these things,' says the author of the Acts, with a genuine burst of admiration, as he records his noble indifference to the popular clamour of the Jews at his judgment-seat." The judgments of the State in matters of religion "are far more likely to be in conformity with the feelings of the whole community, and of the most intelligent part of it, than those which are proposed and carried by majorities in excited clerical or quasi-clerical meetings." It is from the intelligence and calm indifference of the laity, in its highest forms of expression, that the Church derives some of its greatest blessings. Stanley then proceeds to suggest a "practical and efficient" remedy that the State might apply to heal the exclusiveness of the Established Church—"the permission of our Nonconforming brethren of England, and our Presbyterian brethren of the Scottish Church, to preach in our pulpits."[262]

Arnold, as we have seen, is in agreement with Stanley in regard to the high calling of the laity, and in his Preface observes that "culture makes us fond sticklers to no machinery," and is "disposed to be rather indifferent" about all such matters as are not fatal to the objects of culture. Therefore, culture is not inclined to insist upon any one system of church government. What is fatal to culture, however, is provincialism, and as this is the result of separation from the mainstream of national life, the concern of the laity should be in finding a remedy for separatism or Nonconformity. The problem with Stanley's approach, says Arnold, is that it fails "to take sufficient account of the course of history, or of the strength of men's feelings in what concerns religion, or of the gravity which may have come to attach to points of religious order and discipline merely."[263] In making this objection against Stanley, Arnold is, of course, being equally critical of his father's *Principles of Church Reform*. The problem with latitudinarian blueprints for the construction of a single, comprehensive temple is that they are drawn up long after the synagogues have all been built and their traditions established. Before looking at Arnold's alternative remedy to the problem, we need to turn our attention to the second of Stanley's Sion College lectures.

Gladstone, on 23 March 1868, submitted to the House of Commons his resolution in favor of the disestablishment of the Irish Church, and in subsequent meetings he obtained a majority against the position of the government, represented by Disraeli. A dissolution of Parliament was inevitable, and Stanley, aware of the gravity of the issue, left for Ireland in August in order to commit himself to an uninterrupted study of the religious situation of the country and to arrive at his own proposal. In "The Three Irish Churches," presented on 28 January 1869, Stanley lays on the table the fruit of his patient thought and study. The position he takes is neatly summarized in a letter to the master of Balliol, H. G. Liddell: "On the whole, . . . I adhere to my view—(1) a triple endowment; (2) a legal recognition of the Roman Catholics in the South and West, and of the Presbyterians in the North; (3) a reduction of the Church of England staff where it is not needed, and, if necessary, a series of Acts placing it on the same legal basis as the Church of England in India."[264] In his lecture, Stanley observes that, "whereas the Church of England may, in a certain sense, be called the national Church of England" because the Noncon-formist bodies do not represent a different nationality, the case is altogether different in Ireland: "In Ireland, on the contrary, there is not only a difference of religious belief and of race, but the religious divisions derived most of their force from the divisions of race; and thus, in point of fact, there are three Churches."[265]

Arnold, although impressed with Stanley's proposal for Ireland, apparently found unconvincing Stanley's rationale in arguing a different policy for England. "Why should not a Presbyterian Church," he asks, "be established,—with equal rank for its chiefs with the chiefs of Episcopacy, and with admissibility of its ministers, under a revised system of patronage and preferments, to benefices—side by side with the Episcopal Church?"[266] If concurrent endowment is culture's answer to the religious divisions of Ireland, then it is also culture's answer to the besetting problem of religious life in England. H. B. Wilson, in *Essays and Reviews*, in arguing on behalf of the multitudinist principle inaugurated by Constantine, observed that a national and multitudinist Church is not necessarily Episcopal or hierarchical; rather, "it can well admit if not pure Congregationalism, a large admixture of the congrega-tional spirit." Moreover, "a combination of the two principles will alone keep any Church in health and vigour."[267] Arnold agrees. Although Presbyterianism "has that warrant given to it by Scripture and by the proceedings of the early Christian churches," at a critical moment in the history of the Church, Constantine "placed Christianity . . . in contact with the main current of human life. And his work was justified by its fruits." Had Constantine not placed the Church in vital connection with the State, "Christianity might have lost itself in a multitude of hole-and-corner churches like the churches of English Nonconformity after its founders departed."[268] On the other hand, Episcopalianism, isolated from Congregationalism, has fostered sacerdotalism. Only by bringing both systems of government within the establish-ment is the isolation destroyed that is fatal to culture and conducive to excesses and exaggerations.

Three weeks after the publication of *Culture and Anarchy*, Arnold, at the invitation of Huxley, the president of the Geological Society, attended the society's annual dinner, at which both Huxley and Stanley made speeches. In a letter following this event, Arnold tells his mother, "Arthur Stanley moved his chair round to me after dinner, and told me of his delight with my Preface, and how entirely the ideas of it—particularly those of a passage about Constantine—were exactly what papa would have approved."[269] Afterwards, in a letter to J. D. Coleridge, Stanley wrote of this Preface, "I think that it contains some of the wisest matter, and 'most necessary for these times' that I have read for many a long day." He then offers to send a copy of his own lecture on the Irish Churches.[270]

Rescuing St. Paul from the Philistines

As we noted earlier, Jowett and Stanley had, in 1855, contributed to modern biblical scholarship with their commentaries on St. Paul. A few years earlier, Baron Bunsen, in *Hippolytus and His Age* (1852), had set out to elucidate the rational or philosophical sense of the Pauline Epistles, and Rowland Williams, in his review of Bunsen, states, "Our author believes St. Paul, because he understands him reasonably," not reading him "with that dullness which turns symbol and poetry into materialism."[271] No doubt, Arnold had read these volumes with interest, but he appears to have been especially engaged by a book of Richard Whately's. Whately, we should recall, is the Oxford Noetic who became archbishop of Dublin, with whom Dr. Arnold enjoyed the closest friendship. Although Whately's manner was, likely enough, too rough for young Matt's taste, the mature Arnold could speak, in *Literature and Dogma*, of "that Oriel group, whose reputation, I, above most people, am bound to cherish."[272] Over half a century ago, William Blackburn observed that Arnold read Whately's *Essays on Some of the Difficulties in the Writings of the Apostle Paul and in Other Parts of the New Testament* (1828) "to good purpose, for Arnold's mode of criticism is exactly that of Whately's: the effort, that is, to release St. Paul's literary expressions from the metaphysical sophistications which encumber them."[273]

It is remarkable that the resemblances between Whately's *Essays* and Arnold's two *Cornhill Magazine* articles on *St. Paul and Protestantism* were not noted by any of Arnold's contemporary reviewers. Even James Spedding, a Cambridge Apostle of the late 1820s and early '30s, expressed his attraction to "the higher & rarer interest of your two papers on S. Paul—a penetrating piece of Biblical Criticism to me both new & true."[274] But much had been written on the Apostle to the Gentiles during the intervening forty years, and a new generation of thinkers had placed Whately's *Essays* on a dusty shelf, next to Paley's *Horæ Paulinæ* (1790).[275] Moreover, it was Arnold's method to reincarnate an old idea, once it had, in the public mind, passed through the river of Lethe. He would embody the idea in new forms of expression and, in the process, make it his own.

In *Culture and Anarchy*, Arnold borrowed Goethe's observation on comparative philology, "He who knows one language, knows none," and declared, "No man, who knows nothing else, knows even his Bible."[276] The "heavy-handed Protestant Philistine," deficient in wide and critical reading, lacks familiarity with language and the sense of proportion necessary to interpretation. Conflating the figurative with the literal, he arrives at a materialistic, thaumaturgic, and legalistic conception of Christianity. Arnold, recognizing that this misconception is at the root of separatist sentiment and disdain for culture, proposes—with great boldness and, perhaps, a touch of arrogance—"to rescue St. Paul and the Bible from the perversions of them by mistaken men."[277] Whately, likewise, begins by noting the interdependence of knowledge, that whereas the Apostolic Epistles cannot be fully understood without a prior knowledge of other books, these other books cannot be fully understood without a prior knowledge of the Epistles. Therefore, "if we are to begin at all," says Whately, "we must, of course, begin in imperfection." He proceeds to suggest some principles of interpretation, "the neglect of which has given occasion to most of the errors into which 'the unlearned and unstable' have fallen."[278] The declared object of the authors appears to be identical, but their *ethos* makes all the difference. Arnold is the fault-finding critic, whose purpose is to correct. His cure is as the sting of a ruler across the back of the hand. Whately is the tutor, whose instruction is not curative, but preventative. While Arnold is fighting Goliath, Whately is shepherding young Oxford scholars.

The Oriel tutor carefully weighs the Calvinist doctrines of election, predestination, perseverance, assurance, and imputed righteousness, and while doing so, he sifts the wheat from the chaff. Christians are, indeed, elected; however, their election is "not to blessing, absolutely, but to a *privilege* and *advantage*;—to the *offer* and *opportunity* of obtaining a peculiar blessing." The Bible leaves abstract metaphysical questions "exactly where it finds them, undecided and untouched," for revealed doctrines are "not matters of speculative curiosity but of *practical* importance." Although "the doctrines of Perseverance in godliness and of Assurance of salvation, in *some* sense or other, have received the full sanction of the Apostle Paul," he never approached anything like Antinomianism. Rather, it was the Apostle's experience that, the greater the confidence in final victory, "the more will the sinner be encouraged to begin in earnest, and pursue with vigour, the great work of reformation." In regard to the notion of imputed sin and imputed righteousness, Whately concludes that it is "altogether fanciful and groundless." And, having dispensed with the cardinal doctrines of Calvinism, the Noetic asks, "Is there not ground to suspect that many divines have been unconsciously involved in embarrassing disputes about words, from expecting in the Sacred Writers a more scientific accuracy and uniformity of language than they ever aimed at?"[279]

Arnold too discovers that, if the Apostle ever appears to endorse Calvinism, it is only because he Judaizes—that is, he uses the Jewish Scriptures "in a Jew's arbitrary and uncritical fashion, as if they had a talismanic character." Even so, St. Paul, "whom Calvin and Luther and their followers have shut up into the two scholastic doctrines of election and justification, would have said, could we hear him, just what he said about circumcision and uncircumcision in his own day: 'Election is nothing, and justification is nothing, but the keeping of the commandments of God.'" St. Paul, with his practical religious sense and profound awareness of "the moral law in human nature," would be repelled by a scholastic theology and the conception of God as "a magnified and non-natural man." He would have us replace, says Arnold, "the three essential terms" of Calvinist doctrine, *calling, justification*, and *sanctification*, with these three: "*dying with Christ, resurrection from the dead*, and *growing into Christ*."[280]

It is at this point that Arnold, dispensing with Whately, picks up a leading idea from a professor of Latin at University College, London. Macmillan & Co. had, in 1865, published, among other significant titles, Arnold's *Essays in Criticism* and the anonymous *Ecce Homo*, and truly was, in a sense, becoming "the intellectual centre" of the Broad Church movement.[281] *Ecce Homo*, despite its subtitle, is not, strictly speaking, a *Life* of Christ, but is rather a thoughtful study about Christ's message and method. Appearing two years after Ernest Renan's *Vie de Jésus*, *Ecce Homo* appealed to the general interest that Renan had aroused, but while making use of modern scholarship, sought—with what R. W. Church called its "deep tone of religious seriousness"—to edify as well as instruct. Stanley thought that, unlike Renan, the English author had "struck with marvellous tact and feeling the true historical chord, without losing a sense of the infinite possibilities and capacities wrapped up in the character."[282] Because the book demonstrates a power of observation, originality, literary ability, and sensitivity toward religious issues, and at the same time raises crucial questions in regard to the relation between historical criticism and theology, there was soon a widespread interest in its authorship. Macmillan & Co. had received the manuscript through a third party, "and they had come at length to guess that Mr. Shairp might be the man." Shairp, however, had only his admiration and ignorance to confess. Meanwhile, at Oxford, fingers were pointing toward Goldwin Smith; at the Athenæum, the word was out that George Eliot was the author, although James Martineau confided to Arnold "he was quite positive it was not by her."[283] In the spring of 1866, Arnold was still attempting to solve the mystery, and while discussing clues with Alexander Macmillan, settled upon W. H. Thompson, the master of Trinity, Cambridge. He was mistaken. Finally, on 19 December 1866—as Arnold was more than a little pleased to tell Maurice, Stanley, and J. D. Coleridge at the Athenæum on the following Saturday—he met the author of *Ecce Homo*—the "*very* young and intelligent" John Robert Seeley.[284]

According to Seeley, the success of Christianity cannot be accounted for on the basis of originality in doctrine, nor on the grounds of its subsequent creeds, but only by the personal attraction of its founder, Jesus Christ. "It was neither for his miracles nor for the beauty of his doctrine that Christ was worshipped," says Seeley. Rather, "it was the combination of greatness and self-sacrifice which won their hearts, the mighty powers held under a mighty control, the unspeakable condescension, the *Cross of Christ*." The quality in a person that creates this attraction and results in discipleship is *faith*—that is, moral worth or goodness: "He who, when goodness is impressively put before him, exhibits an instinctive loyalty to it, starts forward to take its side, trusts himself to it, such a man has faith." Approached from an intellectual viewpoint, his disciples were "a society of doubters," but from a moral viewpoint, they comprised a society developed for the cultivation and diffusion of goodness, motivated from within by principles of philanthropy, edification, and forgiveness. Whereas Socrates exercises his influence through the intellect, Christ exercises "a personal influence upon feeling." The religion of Christ is based upon an *attachment* or identification that the disciple has with his Master, and—inspired by the Master's example—it is a self-sacrificial *enthusiasm of Humanity*, "a love for the race, or for the ideal of man, in each individual." This enthusiasm or inspiration that looks for Christ in every person is "the distinctive and essential mark of a Christian," and it is this, rather than any intellectual idea, that makes every Christian a moral law unto himself.[285]

Arnold recognized in Seeley's representation of Christianity the key to the conversion and subsequent teaching of St. Paul.[286] Paul's own unsatisfiable longing for righteousness could not forever withstand Jesus's "ineffable force of attraction" —defined, in *Literature and Dogma*, as his *epiekeia* or "sweet reasonableness." In agreement with Seeley, Arnold observes that the moral motive force, "a holding fast to an unseen power of goodness," is faith in a general sense, whereas Christian faith, the *faith* of which St. Paul speaks, is "a holding fast . . . *through identification with Christ*." Arnold notes how "a powerful attachment will give a man spirits and confidence which he could by no means call up or command of himself," and that "Paul felt this power penetrate him; and he felt, also, how by perfectly identifying himself through it with Jesus, by appropriating Jesus, and in no other way, could he ever get the confidence and the force to do as Jesus did." This experience, says Arnold, is what St. Paul means by "faith that worketh through love," but what makes the Apostle original is that he clarifies the means by which one appropriates or becomes identified with Christ. To "the elemental power of sympathy and emotion in us," Paul assigns one unalterable object— "*to die with Christ to the law of the flesh, to live with Christ to the law of the mind*." This doctrine of the *necrosis*, in conjunction with a spiritual principle of resurrection, is St. Paul's contribution to Christianity, that "which makes his profoundness and originality."[287]

Arnold's articles on St. Paul, though indebted to Whately and Seeley, are by no means merely derivative. Arnold, bringing all of his critical and rhetorical power to bear upon his subject, produced a book that continues to be, long after the downfall of Calvinism, both edifying and instructive. It is hard to imagine anyone, even today, passing that judgment against Arnold's "careful exhibition and criticism" which the author himself was prone to pass, when—sixteen years after the two articles were first published—he fancied them "almost a waste of labour."[288] Shairp was so taken with the articles that he brought them to the attention of his friend and mentor, Erskine of Linlathen, whose life was now ebbing away:

> To me it has been a great pleasure to find an old friend, generally believed
> to be more Hellenic than Christian, and to care for none of these things,
> yet a man of evident "culture," and looked up to by all the young men of
> so-called culture, at last recognising, and stating in his own eloquent way,
> that St. Paul saw further into, and spoke more to the Reality, than any one
> of all the poets and philosophers.[289]

Natural Religion

Arnold agrees with Whately that the Biblical authors "were popular, not scientific," that they expressed themselves using such terms and images most suitable for their audience; however, Arnold would hasten to add that what gives a religious teacher "his permanent worth and vitality, is, after all, just the scientific value of his teaching." What Whately refers to as the "popular sense," Arnold calls the "poetic sense"; what both terms signify is the approximative, sensual, concrete, or anthropomorphic characteristic of religious language, as opposed to the language of criticism, which "must stand the test of scientific examination."[290] Although the religious world, for the most part, mistakes the language it uses for the language of science, it is, in fact, "materialised poetry."[291] What Arnold refers to as "the scientific value" of religious teaching is that which is validated by "internal evidence" or religious experience. For example, "the moral law in human nature," though unprovable to the understanding, "is in our actual experience among the greatest of facts."[292]

When a poem is reduced to a prose synopsis, it ceases to have poetic value and loses much, if not all, of its aesthetic and emotional appeal. Likewise, when the popular language of religion is translated into scientific statement, it ceases to function as the language of worship. Nevertheless, the truth value of poetic language—or that which makes its appeal not to the aesthetic and emotional sense, but to the reason—is neither more nor less than its scientific value. For Arnold, as for Schleiermacher, this is Natural Religion or that which, according to the German theologian, "never appears as the basis of a religious communion, but is simply what can be abstracted uniformly from the doctrines of all religious communions of the highest grade, as being present in all but differently determined in each."[293] Arnold merely takes Schleiermacher one step further in insisting that Natural Religion can even be abstracted from the teaching of the communion of scientists. Accordingly, Arnold insists, that which the Hebrew prophet felt as "the *Eternal not ourselves that makes for righteousness,*" a man of science might render as "that *stream of tendency by which all things seek to fulfil the law of their being.*" Since both phrases have a common referent, the practical lesson is that the citizen of Jerusalem and the citizen of Athens should not feel anxious if, in casual speech, they share the same term, *God.*[294]

Neither Arnold nor Schleiermacher denies the existence of a "supra-rational" dimension in religion, but only Schleiermacher consistently assigns religious experience to this category. Because dogma has its origin in such experience, and because "everything experiential is supra-rational," there is a sense, says Schleiermacher, in which "all Christian dogmas are supra-rational." He insists that whatever is suprarational cannot be conveyed in terms amenable to the scientific reason, and thus is properly only the subject of religious language—whether poetical, rhetorical, or didactic. Arnold, on the other hand, recognizes "internal evidence" as a criteria whereby scientific validity can be measured.[295] Thus, while endeavoring to place the religion of the Bible on a *scientific* foundation, Arnold extends the width of that foundation into the region that Schleiermacher identifies as properly belonging to *dogma*. For example, Arnold defends the proposition "Jesus is the Son of God because he gives the method and secret by which alone righteousness is possible" by appealing to experience: "It *is* so! try, and you will find it to be so! Try all the ways to righteousness you can think of, and you will find that no way brings you to it except the way of Jesus, but that this way does bring you to it!"[296]

To Arnold's discredit, Sense overrules Sensibility in this passage. His deeply ingrained sense of the reasonableness of morality momentarily distracts him from his deeper intuitions and mystical sensibilities, leaving him justly vulnerable to criticism. For, if the experience of Jesus's method and secret can be tested *scientifically*, then it would follow that Christianity, insofar as it is a moral force, can be reducible to a nonreligious formula. However, such a translation would be impossible without first removing altogether the *attachment to* or *identification with Christ*, without which the formula is impotent. In other words, Arnold's appeal to place Christian morality on the rational basis of experimentation is, in essence, an appeal to taste of the fruit of conversion before any planting and nourishing of that precious seed out of which the fruit germinates. Even if such an experiment *could* work, it would only serve to undermine religion by proving it superfluous. It would, then, appear that Schleiermacher is right. If religious conversion is suprarational, then *all* religious experience resulting from conversion must also be regarded as suprarational and irreducible to scientific language.

Although Arnold and Schleiermacher differ in regard to the verification of religious experience, they remain fundamentally agreed upon much that, to each of them, is essential. As Ruth apRoberts observes, "Schleiermacher's insistence on the validity of experience, his understanding of religion as the 'most highly and fully developed form of self-consciousness,' and of the word *God* not as a concept of perfect being but 'the felt relationship of absolute dependence' are all concepts clearly contributory to those of Matthew Arnold."[297] This striking accord between the two thinkers can, in part, be accounted for on the basis of their prior agreement with Spinoza. Nowhere is this more evident than in their treatment of supernatural religion.

The seventeenth-century Dutch philosopher, in his *Theological-Political Treatise*, argues against the existence of the miraculous on the grounds of principle and reason. Assuming that such a phenomena as a miracle does exist, Spinoza defines it as "an event that cannot be explained through a cause, that is, an event that surpasses human understanding. But from such an event, and from anything at all that surpasses our understanding, we can understand nothing." The belief in miracle per se, thus, has no religious value. Only the belief in God's omnipotence—or that "whatever occurs does so through God's will and eternal decree"—is capable of inspiring trust.[298] If the occurrence of events that surpass human understanding were, at one time, an aid to religious feeling, they are so no longer. On this basis established by Spinoza, Schleiermacher concludes, "As regards the miraculous, the general interests of science, more particularly of natural science, and the interests of religion seem to meet at the same point, *i.e.* that we should abandon the idea of the absolutely supernatural because no single instance of it can be known by us, and we are nowhere required to recognize it."[299]

Underlying the arguments of both Spinoza and Schleiermacher, there is the realization that miracle is, to any religion, a vestige of its creation. As Western consciousness slowly awakens to the fact of its independence from the supernatural, the traditional apology for supernatural religion gradually transforms from a *building*-block (*edifice*-making or *edifi*cation device) of faith into a stumbling-block. Baden Powell, in his contribution to *Essays and Reviews*, emphasizes this very point: "In whatever light we regard the 'evidences' of religion, to be of any effect, whether external or internal, they must always have a special reference to the *peculiar capacity and apprehension of the party addressed*." Powell, carefully avoiding the theological question of miracles and strictly confining his attention to the mental condition of modern humanity, concludes that the elements of modernity "tend powerfully to evince the inconceivableness of imagined interruptions of natural order, or supposed suspensions of the laws of matter."[300] Jowett also, "without entering on the vexed question of miracles," seeks to dispense with them, believing that "the time has come when we must no longer allow them to be stumbling-blocks in the way of those who desire to be the followers of Christ."[301]

Arnold, having previously embraced the position of Spinoza and Schleiermacher in regard to the relation of miracles and religion, now takes up the rhetorical method of Powell and Jowett. Having first defined his audience as "those who are incredulous about the Bible and inclined to throw it aside," Arnold refuses to take a stand upon either affirmative or negative demonstrations of the historical veracity of Scripture-miracles: "For it is what we call the *Time-Spirit* which is sapping the proof from miracles,—it is the 'Zeit-Geist' itself. Whether we attack them, or whether we defend them, does not much matter. The human mind, as its experience widens, is turning away from them."[302] Robert Shafer, impatient in his explication, remarks, "This, of course, was simply to say that the real objection to miracles is that they do not occur."[303] Such a retort, of course, misses the point. The objection is *not* that miracles do not occur, but that, even if they were to happen right before our eyes, we lack that peculiar mental condition that apprehends them.[304] Perhaps, the modern mind most nearly approaches that condition when it is overwhelmed with awe and wonder at the grandeur of nature and the universe.

For Arnold, the *only* issue in regard to miracles that the Church has any urgent need to consider is whether Christianity can survive without them. In reply to the criticism of his sister Fan, Arnold writes, "To treat miracles and the common anthropomorphic ideas of God as what one may lose and yet keep one's hope, courage, and joy, as what are not really matters of life and death in the keeping or losing of them, this is desirable and necessary, if one holds, as I do, that [they] . . . must and will inevitably pass away."[305] For this reason, when F. W. Farrar—now headmaster of

Marlborough—released his immensely popular *Life of Christ* (1874), Arnold complained to its author, "I regard the belief in miracles on a par, in respect of its inevitable disappearance from the minds of reasonable men, with the belief in witches and hobgoblins. . . . Therefore I see with regret, and almost impatience, attempts on the part of a man whom I like and esteem to defend them."[306]

Stanley and Arnold differed in regard to the future development of Christianity. Whereas Arnold held that "Christianity will survive because of its natural truth," the dean took the side of Farrar. Although, in his preaching and correspondence, Stanley emphasizes the "natural" aspect of religion, recognizing this as Christianity's firm foundation in a skeptical age, in his private religion he maintains a relationship with a God he conceives as over Nature, and thus, Stanley argues that the progress of the Church depends upon "an increasing recognition of the fact that the essentially supernatural elements of religion are those which are moral and spiritual."[307]

Clearly, the nature/supernature antithesis that accommodates the traditional definition of "miracle" is not one to which Arnold could assent. Even before he had drunk from Spinoza, he had devoured Carlyle. In *Sartor Resartus* (1833), the Sage of Chelsea had proclaimed the advent of a transformed faith, in which "Natural Supernaturalism" breaks down the old antitheses fostered by the illusions of Time and Space. How could humanity, when its myopic vision drew unreal distinctions between humanity and nature, not conceive of its anthropomorphic deity as also, in some sense, opposed to nature? Carlyle and Coleridge both had called upon their readers to recognize a truth beyond "clothes" and "symbols," beyond the limitations of our senses and our language. But, once the antithesis of nature and supernature dissolves, not only is the conventional concept of miracle lost, but so too is all theistic anthropomorphism. The same illusions by which we imagine God as a magician also allow us to conceive God as a person (or vice versa). Indeed, we can hardly begin to anthropomorphize deity without placing a magic wand in his hand.

Nevertheless, if religion is a matter of feeling, and if we say what we feel, without taking care to modify our expression so as to maintain consistency with our philosophical conceptions, we will always speak of God as a person. This is the poetic license of religion, the language that we throw out in order to speak of that which transcends verbal expression. Were this not the case, were we not hopelessly anthropomorphic, we might, even to our injury, lose the capacity of finding grace and truth in Christ. Paul Tillich resolves the apparent contradiction between the heart and head by concluding, "'Personal God' does not mean that God is *a* person. It means that God is the ground of everything personal and that he carries within himself the ontological power of personality."[308] Because Stanley, in his religious experience, could only feel a personal God, he could not bring himself to acknowledge a God who is not a person; because Arnold could only conceive God as nonperson, he could not bring himself to speak of a personal God. "I am afraid on the question of 'a personal God,'" Arnold wrote, in 1873, "I am an incurable heretic!" Still, as Livingston notes, "the evidence is abundantly clear" that Arnold did not "think of God as less than personal."[309]

Mr. Smith and the Broad Church

On 7 January 1872, Stanley preached before a Presbyterian congregation at Edinburgh. That same week he delivered his "Lectures on the History of the Church of Scotland," tracing the moderate movement back to the original constitution and character of the National Church. In this year John Tulloch (1823-1886), principal and professor of theology at St. Mary's College, St. Andrews, became—after the death of Norman Macleod—the most eminent member of the Church of Scotland. And, before the close of the year, he completed the great work upon which his literary reputation now chiefly rests, *Rational Theology and Christian Philosophy in England in the Seventeenth Century.* Jowett and Stanley visited with Tulloch as the final pages were being prepared, and they read "with interest" the Preface, along with the final chapter of the second volume, the author's "General Estimate."[310] Stanley's friendship with Shairp and autumnal visits to St. Andrews had brought the dean into association with Tulloch, so that St. Andrews became "a primary locale for the recognition and celebration of all that the English and Scottish sections of the Broad Church had to offer."[311] Both men sought to bring the national cultures of their two nations closer, and while Charles Wordsworth, bishop of St. Andrews, invited Stanley to preach in the churches of his diocese, the dean of Westminster, in his turn, offered the Abbey pulpit to both Tulloch and *this* Bishop Wordsworth (*not* the bishop of Lincoln, who, in 1868, had published a pamphlet in protest against Stanley's preferment).[312]

When Stanley returned home, he found himself nominated as a university preacher at Oxford. In December, when Convocation ruled in favor of his nomination, the Evangelical Goulburn, in protest, resigned his post as select preacher. Replying to a letter that Goulburn sent him, Stanley reveals his immersion in Tulloch's two-volume work:

> When I remember the same kind of opposition, with the same epithets of "Rationalist," "Latitudinarian," "Socinian," "Heretic," "Erastian," were lavished on men of whom the world was not worthy, and with whom I am not worthy to place myself, except in the humble endeavour to walk in their footsteps—Tillotson, Chillingworth, Jeremy Taylor, Cudworth, Locke, Arnold—I know not whether I should not rather rejoice to share their obloquy.[313]

Arnold, at this time, was reviewing the proofs for his book *Literature and Dogma,* which was published at the end of January 1873. Afterwards, his "Review of Objections"—first serialized in *The Contemporary Review* and, then, published as *God and the Bible*—would occupy his thoughts until the very end of 1875. Not until 1876 would Arnold read Tulloch's *Rational Theology.* In the meanwhile, Tulloch not only read Arnold, but at the beginning of 1873, published a rather biting review in the pages of *Blackwood's Magazine.* By his own admission, Tulloch wrote while suffering from a recurring brain fever, later diagnosed as a symptom of "gout-poisoning." The principal began his review "in rather a defiant, bumptious way," and "finished the paper in depression and misery."[314] A year later, when Tulloch and Shairp journeyed into London on university business, they stopped by the Athenæum and had an awkward encounter with Arnold. Before leaving the club, Tulloch wrote this letter:

> Matthew Arnold has just come in, and we have had a talk. I thought at first he looked a little as if he did not approve of my pitching into him, but then he said very nicely that he had seen a speech of mine, which he liked very much. I told him Shairp was here and wished to see him. "Ah!" he said, "Shairp and you must diverge a good deal." I told him Shairp was not so narrow as he used to be. "Ah!" he said again, "he has so much feeling. He moves hither and thither under the impulse of his enthusiasm." Arnold's manner is very ha-ha; but I have no doubt he is a very good fellow.[315]

The speech to which Tulloch refers is his "Dogmatic Extremes," published in *The Contemporary Review* (January 1874). From this speech, Arnold had jotted the following lines in his notebook: "True religious thought is always and necessarily indefinite—Haze is of its very nature. . . . Imperfection or partial error is of the very essence of Christian dogma."[316] These were words with which Arnold could fully agree. Even so, neither Arnold nor Tulloch appear to have thought much of each other during the next two years.

Stanley, however, continued to work closely with the two principals of St. Andrews for the advancement of religious moderation and unity in the cultural exchanges of England and Scotland. In November 1874 he was elected lord rector of St. Andrews, and four months later, Shairp was present when the dean delivered his inaugural address on "The Study of Greatness" to an "intent, eager, and responsive" student body. Later, Stanley, in an effort to assist Tulloch and Shairp in the establishment of a college at Dundee, volunteered to address the town. In the spring of 1876, the two principals each presented a series of lectures at Dundee, Shairp's subject being "The Poetic Interpretation of Nature," Tulloch's being "Comparative Religion and Religious Thought."[317]

In the summer of 1876, after completing his essay on Bishop Butler, Arnold picked up Tulloch's *Rational Theology*, second edition (1874). In August, he writes to Stanley, "I have a last article coming in the *Contemporary* for November, partly on the subject of the natural truth of Christianity in spite of errors in its records and reporters. . . ; and then I shall quit the subject of theology—at any rate the direct treatment of the subject."[318] This essay, "A Psychological Parallel," is certainly not Arnold's last word on theology, although it will serve as his final word in this chapter.

The "psychological parallel" to which Arnold's title refers is that similar appre-hension and treatment of a subject that we find when looking at both St. Paul on the resurrection and John Smith on witchcraft. Smith is one of a small and moderately influential body of scholars, the Cambridge Platonists, a "noble but neglected group" Arnold calls them. Smith, as a significant contributor to this group, had been considered in some detail by Tulloch in the second volume of *Rational Theology*. The so-called Platonist school (essentially Platonism as interpreted by Plotinus as interpreted by Ficino and, then, Anglicized) arose at Cambridge under the leading influence of Benjamin Whichcote (1609-1683)—who was, incidentally, an Aristotelian in the tradition of Hooker. In early modern England, poets and philosophers like Henry More and Ralph Cudworth, who were most eager to brush off the old Aristotelian cobwebs from their outer garments, were generally oblivious to the fact that the more energetically they shook themselves, the more their feet stuck fast upon the web on which they stood. We might, therefore, agree with Arnold, that "Principal Tulloch has given . . . somewhat too much space to their Platonic philosophy"; however, it is that very infusion of Renaissance Platonism that facilitates "their extraordinarily simple, profound, and just conception of religion" and makes this school so very refreshing and interesting to us.[319]

John Smith (1618-1652) entered the Puritan college of Emmanuel at the age of eighteen and was, apparently, tutored by both Whichcote and Cudworth during his undergraduate years.[320] After obtaining his M.A. in 1644, he was elected fellow of Queen's. He was a better writer than both of his mentors, but he died young, in 1652, and his remains are collected into a single volume, the *Select Discourses*, compiled by John Worthington in 1660. Tulloch suggests that the ten discourses are the highest literary accomplishment of the Cambridge School. "They carry us," he writes, "so directly into an atmosphere of divine philosophy, luminous with the richest lights of meditative genius."[321] Indeed, the quality of the discourses mark Smith's work as pre-eminently *literary*—Arnold's verdict to the contrary notwithstanding[322]—so that we have cause to believe that his early death deprived the English literature of religion in the same way, and very nearly to the same extent, that the early death of Keats abridged the canon of English poetry.

In Arnold's estimation, the "grand merit" of Smith's discourses "is that they insist on the profound *natural truth* of Christianity, and thus base it upon a ground which will not crumble under our feet." Arnold recognizes that although Smith, like St. Paul, shared the peculiar supernaturalism of his contemporaries, both men showed themselves superior to their age by emphasizing the natural, experiential truth upon which the supernatural belief was constructed. In other words, both the Platonist and the Apostle betray an awareness, however vague, that—as Rudolf Bultmann states the case—the "real intention" of the objectifying character of myth is "to talk about a transcendent power to which both we and the world are subject."[323] For example, although Smith was no different from his contemporaries in his belief in witchcraft, in his sermon "A Christian's Conflicts and Conquests" he adds an important qualifier: "When we say the devil is continually busy with us, I mean not only some apostate spirit as one particular being, but the spirit of apostacy which is lodged in all men's natures." In this latter phrase, "the spirit of apostacy which is lodged in all men's natures," Arnold sees that "Smith had what was at bottom experimental and real. And the whole effort of the sermon is to substitute this for what men call the devil, hell, fiends, and witches, as an object for their serious thought and strenuous resistance."[324]

Thus, Arnold finds in Smith that very quality that he has been praising in St. Paul for the past decade. As early as *Culture and Anarchy*, Arnold had noted the Apostle's critical sense pertaining to supernatural religion:

> The whole religious world, one may say, use now the word *resurrection* ... in one sense only. They use it to mean a rising again after the physical death of the body. Now it is quite true that St. Paul speaks of resurrection in this sense. . . . But it is true, also, that in nine cases out of ten when St. Paul thinks and speaks of resurrection, he thinks and speaks of it in a sense different from this;—in a sense of a rising to a new life before the physical death of the body, and not after it.[325]

When Thoas, in the *Iliad*, calls out to his men, "Look—a genuine miracle right before my eyes! / Hector's escaped again, he's risen from the dead!," the idea of a bodily resurrection from the dead appears as hyperbole; when Paul says, "If ye then be risen with Christ, seek those things which are above," resurrection is metaphor and poetry.[326] Whereas Homer cannot conceive of resurrection as anything other than material fact, the Apostle not only apprehends the fact as spiritual event, but recognizes that it is both independent of and of greater religious import than the material event.

St. Paul and John Smith have, therefore, already resolved the problem that plagues the enlightened Churchman. The Apostle was not troubled by the realization that the Pharisees and Sadducees would not understand his faith when, standing before the High Priest, he cried out, "Of the hope and resurrection of the dead, I am called in question."[327] Paul knew very well that they could only suppose that he spoke of a material resurrection of the body, and yet he had no qualms of conscience in using the accepted religious language of the day. As long as the clergy can *feel* the appropriateness of the traditional terms, even when they can no longer be taken literally, but "as approximations to a profound truth," then, says Arnold, the clergy can *use* them.[328]

In "A Psychological Parallel," Arnold, in briefly reviewing Tulloch's work on the Cambridge Platonists, suggests, "It is not so much a history of this group which is wanted, as a republication of such of their utterances as show us their real spirit and power." He then provides a few authors and titles that would be fitting for such a work, and concludes, "It were well if Principal Tulloch would lay us under fresh obligations by himself extracting this and giving it to us; but given some day, and by some hand, it will surely be."[329]

Two months hardly passed before Arnold was at work on "Falkland," his essay on Lucius Cary, inspired by the lengthy section on Lord Falkland in the first volume of Tulloch's *Rational Theology*. In addition, he was in contact with Macmillan, proposing a book to be titled *Broad Church in the Seventeenth Century*. It was to include "the best of [John] Hales and Whichcote, and Cudworth's two sermons."[330] The title was suggested by Tulloch, who had noted that the philosophical and theological questions with which the Cambridge group were concerned are "very much the questions still discussed under the name of Broad-Churchism."[331] Macmillan was interested, and when Arnold, in the summer of 1877—just after Shairp's election as professor of poetry at Oxford—met with Tulloch at the Athenæum, he still had every intent to push the project forward. Tulloch, however, was less than pleased:

> I have seen a great deal of Matthew Arnold lately. He referred me to the last volume of essays, where he has spoken still more highly of my book than in his sketch on Falkland; and he is going to publish with Macmillan a selection from Whichcote, J. Smith, Cudworth, &c., under the title of "The Broad Church in the Seventeenth Century." He invited me to do this in his essay, and it seems rather cool his undertaking the task himself, without waiting to see whether I would do it. The selections, I have no doubt, will be taken chiefly from my volumes, which are too large, he says, for the general reader. Quite true, and I am not sorry he should do the thing.[332]

Tulloch need not have been anxious, for—although Arnold did, in 1882, furnish an introductory essay to W. M. Metcalfe's *The Natural Truth of Christianity: Selections from the "Select Discourses" of John Smith*—Arnold never went ahead with his *Broad Church* book. Moreover, as late as 1932, Ernst Cassirer could confidently state, "Not even the most recent English publications have superseded Tulloch's results either in content or in principle."[333]

The Abbey and the Churchyard

England lost two of its greatest voices in 1881. When Thomas Carlyle died in February, Stanley preached a "discriminating" sermon in his honor. A few months later Stanley himself fell ill. On Saturday, 9 July, he went to the Athenæum to prepare his evening sermon. After walking home, he felt faint and sick, but insisted on attending the Abbey service. It was his last. As his condition gradually worsened, he took to his bed. Finally, on Monday morning, the 18th, Canon Farrar administered the Sacrament. Arnold, who had been out of town on business, returned to London to hear from James Fraser, bishop of Manchester, that "the Dean's life had been despaired of, but that there was a slight rally at present." That evening Archbishop Tait and C. J. Vaughan prayed with Stanley, and just before midnight, he died. One week later, Arnold and nine others, including Temple and Jowett, served as pall-bearers, and the funeral service was read in Westminster Abbey by Vaughan, as Stanley had requested.[334]

In November Arnold wrote his elegy on Stanley, "Westminster Abbey," which, like "Thyrsis," is not really about the person memorialized, but only half-inspired by him. As Arnold explained to J. D. Coleridge, "The great thing is to produce, as Gray did, what will wear, and will not come to look ridiculous as time goes on."[335] Two stanzas may, perhaps, be all that we here need.

> What! for a term so scant
> Our shining visitant
> Cheered us, and now is passed into the night?
> Couldst thou no better keep, O Abbey old,
> The boon thy dedication-sign foretold,
> The presence of that gracious inmate, light?
> A child of light appeared;
> Hither he came, late-born and long-desired,
> And to men's hearts this ancient place endeared;
> What, is the happy glow so soon expired?
>
> . . . .
> Ay me! 'Tis deaf, that ear
> Which joyed my voice to hear;
> Yet would I not disturb thee from thy tomb,
> Thus sleeping in thine Abbey's friendly shade,
> And the rough waves of life for ever laid!
> I would not break thy rest, nor change thy doom.
> Even as my father, thou—
> Even as that loved, that well-recorded friend—
> Hast thy commission done; ye both may now
> Wait for the leaven to work, the let to end.[336]

There is a significance to that phrase "child of light" which we cannot ignore. It calls to our mind a passage of St. Paul's in his Epistle to the Ephesians, "Ye were sometimes darkness, but now are ye light in the Lord: walk as children of light," which was the text from which J. C. Hare preached his 1828 Cambridge sermon, "The Children of Light." The delivery of that sermon, we may recall from the previous chapter, has been heralded as the advent of the Broad Church movement. Certainly, its description of children of light as those who do not despise the past as darkness, nor "exult and boast that the veil has now at once been completely withdrawn," but rather to their love of truth add a reverence for the past and a wholesome distrust of their present selves,[337] seems to perfectly describe A. P. Stanley, the greatest spokesman the Broad Church has ever had among the clergy.

Matthew Arnold survived Stanley by seven years. He lived long enough to be honored with doctorate degrees from three universities—Edinburgh, Oxford, and Cambridge—and to be received in the United States as warmly as his best-selling books. He also lived to see his daughter Lucy, who traveled with him to America in 1883, in the following year marry a New Yorker, Frederick Whitridge. In April of 1888, the Arnolds journeyed to Liverpool to welcome their pregnant daughter off a trans-Atlantic steamer. Arnold brought with him a novel that he had begun to read, the author of which had presented him with an inscribed copy: "To my dear Uncle Matthew Arnold—a small acknowledgement of all I owe to his books & his influence."[338] In one of his last letters, five days before his death, he writes with obvious excitement of the sensation that his niece's latest work, *Robert Elsmere*, was making in the literary world: "George Russell was here a day or two ago; he was staying at Aston Clinton with Gladstone, and says it is all true about his interest in the book: he talked of it incessantly."[339]

The seed of the novel had been planted only a few months before Stanley's death. In the spring of 1881 Thomas Arnold's daughter Mary, in the company of her husband, Humphry Ward, went to hear the first of John Wordworth's Bampton Lectures, *The One Religion*. Wordsworth, later bishop of Salisbury,[340] was at this time a tutor and fellow of Brasenose and, therefore, a colleague of Ward's. The first lecture was called "The Present Unsettlement in Religion," and by directly connecting that unsettlement with sin, both as cause and consequence, it gave Mary "the shock of indignation" that ultimately developed into *Robert Elsmere*. The author recalls the moment:

> The sermon expounded and developed this outline with great vigour, and every skeptical head received its due buffeting in a tone and fashion that now scarcely survive. . . . My heart was hot within me. How could one show England what was really going on in her midst? Surely the only way was through imagination; through a picture of actual life and conduct; through something as "simple, sensuous, passionate" as one could make it.[341]

According to Mary, her uncle did not live to read the final chapter of her best-selling novel.[342] Likely enough, even if Arnold had so lived, he would have made no public comment regarding the author's unsympathetic representation of the Broad Church. In any event, that task was left for Broad Church apologist Hugh Reginald Haweis.[343] On 15 April, just hours before Lucy's arrival, Arnold—now weighing almost 240 lbs.[344]—had a heart attack. Four days later, Jowett and J. D. Coleridge, among other clerics and literati, accompanied the remains of Arnold to the churchyard of his birthplace, Laleham.

Notes

1. Ernest Hartley Coleridge, *Life and Correspondence of John Duke Lord Coleridge, Lord Chief Justice of England*, 2 vols. (New York: D. Appleton and Company, 1904), 1:78.

2. Randall Thomas Davidson and William Benham, *Life of Archibald Campbell Tait, Archbishop of Canterbury*, 3rd ed., 2 vols. (London: Macmillan and Co., 1891), 1:80-97.

3. Issac Williams, *Autobiography*, ed. George Prevost (London: Longmans, Green, and Co., 1892), 137-48; E. H. Coleridge, 1:90-94; G. D. Boyle, *Recollections* (London: Edward Arnold, 1895), 123.

4. John Henry Newman, *Apologia Pro Vita Sua*, ed. David J. DeLaura (New York: W. W. Norton and Co., 1968), 120.

5. Memorial Inscription (Edward C. Alden, *Alden's Oxford Guide* [Oxford: Alden and Co., Ltd., 1921], 111).

6. Christopher Hollis, *The Oxford Union* (London: Evans Brothers Ltd., 1965), 62.

7. W. C. Lake to the editor of the *Pall Mall Gazette*, 12 June 1897, in Katherine Lake, ed., *Memorials of William Charles Lake* (London: Edward Arnold, 1901), 38.

8. William Knight, *Principal Shairp and His Friends* (London: John Murray, 1888), 411-12.

9. Although J. D. Coleridge, in his memorial sketch of Shairp, had suggested that Ralph R. W. Lingen may have been a member, this suggestion was afterwards recognized as "a mistake" (E. H. Coleridge, 77). David Williams has placed A. C. Tait among its members (*Too Quick Despairer: The Life and Work of Arthur Hugh Clough* [London: Rupert Hart-Davis, 1969], 53-54), but I have seen no documentation to corroborate this inclusion.

10. Lake, 38.

11. George Butler, 1841, in Evelyn Abbott and Lewis Campbell, *Life and Letters of Benjamin Jowett, M.A., Master of Balliol College, Oxford*, 2 vols. (London: John Murray, 1897), 1:81.

12. E. G. Sandford, ed., *Memoirs of Archbishop Temple, by Seven Friends*, 2 vols. (London: Macmillan and Co., 1906), 2:453.

13. Sandford, 1:54.

14. Mary C. Church, ed., *Life and Letters of Dean Church* (London: Macmillan and Co., 1895), 17.

15. *Concise Dictionary of National Biography*, 2nd Supplement (London: Oxford University Press, 1920), 49. The Oxford "Rugby Club" was not founded until 1871.

16. Arnold to J. C. Shairp, 12 April 1866, in Cecil Y. Lang, ed., *The Letters of Matthew Arnold*, 5 vols. (Charlottesville: University Press of Virginia, 1996-2001), 3:34-35.

17. Arnold to his mother, 18 February 1871, in Lang, 4:13.

18. Lake, 7-8.

19. Lake, vi.

20. Clough to J. N. Simpkinson, 31 December 1839, in Frederick L. Mulhauser, ed., *The Correspondence of Arthur Hugh Clough*, 2 vols. (Oxford: Clarendon Press, 1957), 1:98.

21. William Tuckwell, *Reminiscences of Oxford* (London: Cassell and Co., 1900), 207.

22. M. Arnold to Jane Arnold, qtd. in a letter of J.A. to T. Arnold, in Lang 1:161.

23. George Rawlinson, Preface, in Lake, x.

24. Tuckwell, 208-09. Lake refers to his years as Rector as having given him "for over ten years an experience . . . of the actual work of a parish" (Lake, 92 n.).

25. A. P. Stanley, "Archdeacon Hare," *Quarterly Review* (July 1855), in *Essays Chiefly on Questions of Church and State, from 1850 to 1870* by A. P. Stanley (London: John Murray, 1870), 536-71, 554.

26. Lake, 31; Abbott and Campbell, 1:231; *Concise D.N.B.*, 148.

27. Rowland E. Prothero, *The Life and Correspondence of Arthur Penrhyn Stanley, Late Dean of Westminster*, 2 vols. (New York: Charles Scribner's Sons, 1894), 1:168-69. R. W. Church would have us believe that Ward, "under the influence of Arthur Stanley, . . .

learned to admire Dr. Arnold" (*The Oxford Movement: Twelve Years, 1833-45*, 3rd ed. [1892; New York: Archon Books, 1992], chap. 12, 237).

28. Lake, 31.

29. Prothero, 1:112, 134.

30. Cardinal Newman to Lake, Birmingham, 18 August 1882, in Lake, 259.

31. Mary Church, 14.

32. Mark Pattison observes, "I presume that Church was Newman's candidate, though so accomplished a scholar as the Dean need not have required any party push." With hopes of better success, Pattison next competed for a fellowship at University College, but—to his amazement and grief—found himself competing against Stanley. After another unsuccessful attempt, this time for Balliol, Pattison finally succeeded in competition for Lincoln (*Memoirs* [London: Macmillan and Co., 1885], 162-63, 174-84).

33. Lang, 1:211.

34. Jane Arnold to T. Arnold, Fox How, 30 November 1849, in Lang, 1:161; Lake, 172-75.

35. J. B. Hope Simpson, *Rugby since Arnold: A History of the School from 1842* (London: Macmillan, 1967), 22.

36. Knight, 33, 49.

37. M. Arnold to the University of Glasgow, ca. 14 April 1866, in Lang, 3:38.

38. John Campbell Shairp, *Studies in Poetry and Philosophy* (1868; New York: Houghton Mifflin Co., n.d.), 212-13.

39. Boyle, 80.

40. Peter Hinchliff, *Benjamin Jowett and the Christian Religion* (Oxford: Clarendon Press, 1987), 48.

41. Abbott and Campbell, 1:81.

42. Abbott and Campbell, 1:88-89.

43. Abbott and Campbell, 1:229.

44. E. H. Coleridge, 1:73-76.

45. E. H. Coleridge, 1:59.

46. M. Arnold to J. D. Coleridge, 8 January 1843, in E. H. Coleridge, 1:122-23.

47. Sandford, 1:48, 89.

48. Sandford, 1:91.

49. Sandford, 1:55 n., 2:10-11. Desmond Bowen observes that Temple is, in his acceptance of the idea of apostolical succession, representative of a growing number of Anglican clergymen upon whom the Tractarian movement exerted a seminal influence (*The Idea of the Victorian Church: A Study of the Church of England, 1833-1889* [Montreal: McGill University Press, 1968], 87-88).

50. Sandford, 1:153.

51. Thomas Arnold, 58.

52. Howard Foster Lowry, ed., *The Letters of Matthew Arnold to Arthur Hugh Clough* (Oxford: Clarendon Press, 1932), 2.

53. Clough to J. P. Gell, 15 January 1838, in Blanche Clough, ed., *The Poems and Prose Remains of Arthur Hugh Clough*, 2 vols. (London: Macmillan and Co., 1869), 1:76.

54. Clough to J. P. Gell, September 1838, in Clough, 1:79.

55. Clough, 1:14.

56. Clough to J. N. Simpkinson, 27 August 1840, in Clough, 1:86.

57. Lowry, 22-23.

58. Knight, 75.

59. Tom Arnold, 59.

60. Clough, 1:30-32.

61. Robert Morier, Balliol, 9 May 1847, in *Memoirs and Letters of the Right Hon. Sir Robert Morier, G. C. B., from 1826 to 1876, by His Daughter Mrs. Rosslyn Wemyss*, 2 vols. (London: E. Arnold, 1911), 1:37, 75-76, 82.

62. Boyle, 124.

63. Park Honan, *Matthew Arnold: A Life* (London: Weidenfeld and Nicolson), 64.

64. Knight, 103-06; Tom Arnold, 61-62.

65. Abbott and Campbell, 1:126.

66. Knight, 98. Arnold, in a letter to T. Arnold, refers to a Rugby mastership as "the most hideous and squalid of occupations" (Lang, 1:211).

67. Lang, 3:373.

68. Simpson, chap. 3, "Calamity," 67-100.

69. Lang 1:168-69; see also Kathleen Tillotson, "Rugby 1850: Arnold, Clough, Walrond, and *In Memoriam*," in *Mid-Victorian Studies*, ed. Geoffrey and Kathleen Tillotson (London: Athlone Press, 1965), 180-203, esp. 184-89.

70. Lang, 1:359.

71. Tom Arnold, 57-58, 64-65, 150-53.

72. Tom Arnold, 84-92.

73. Tom Arnold, 112-14.

74. Tom Arnold, 122-55.

75. Honan, 441 n.

76. M. Arnold to his mother, 19 February 1862, in George W. E. Russell, ed., *Letters of Matthew Arnold*, 2 vols. (New York: Macmillan and Co., 1895), 1:183.

77. Clough to J. N. Simpinson; 16 July 1836, in Blanche Clough, 1:72.

78. Friedrich D. E. Schleiermacher, *Soliloquies: A New Year's Gift*, trans. Horace Leland Friess (Chicago: The Open Court Publishing Co., 1926), 36, 43.

79. Eph. 4:14.

80. "Stanzas in Memory of the Author of 'Obermann,'" lines 143-44, in *The Poems of Matthew Arnold*, ed. Kenneth Allott (London: Longmans, Green, and Co., 1965), 136.

81. Arthur Edward Waite, Introduction to *Obermann* by Etienne Pivert de Senancour (London: William Rider and Son, 1919), 2-7.

82. "Stanzas in Memory of the Author of 'Obermann,'" line 103, in Allott, 134.

83. Joseph Glanvill presents his story of the scholar-gipsy as an example of "the power of advanc'd *Imagination*" or hypnotic suggestion. In the revised edition, titled *Scepsis Scientifica* (1665), which Glanvill dedicated to the Royal Society, he omits the account altogether, replacing it with a passage illustrating the more moderate power of "*secret influence*"—attested by the emotional reactions that people sometimes have when in close proximity with other persons. In both editions, Glanvill is concerned with an ability "to bind the thoughts of another, and determine them to their particular objects" (*The Vanity of Dogmatizing: Or, Confidence in Opinions: Manifested in a Discourse of the Shortness and Uncertainty of our Knowledge, and Its Causes* (London: B. C., 1661), Ch. XX, 195; *Scepsis Scientifica: Or, Confest Ignorance, the Way to Science; In an Essay of the Vanity of Dogmatizing, and Confident Opinion* (London: E. Cotes, 1665), Ch. XXIV, 146. Glanvill's tale is of an Oxford lad who, forced by poverty to leave the university, joins a company of gypsies: "Among these extravagant people, by the insinuating subtilty of his carriage, he quickly got so much of their lore, and esteem; as that they discover'd to him their *Mystery*: in the practice

of which, by the pregnancy of his wit and parts he soon grew so good a proficient, as to be able to out-do his Instructors." Coming, once, upon some Oxford friends, he gives them an account of his experience and of the strange art he had learned, "And to evince the truth of what he told them, he said, he'd remove into another room, leaving them to discourse together; and upon his return tell them the sum of what they had talked of: which accordingly he perform'd, giving them a full account of what had pass'd between them in his absence." The scholar-gipsy then explains that "what he did was by the power of *Imagination*, his Phancy *binding* theirs; and that himself had dictated to them the discourse." Finally, he assures his old friends that, once he has mastered the whole secret art, he will return to publish his account (*Vanity*, 196-98).

84. "The Scholar-Gipsy," lines 203, 221-26, in Allott, 342-43.

85. "The Scholar-Gipsy," lines 171-73, in Allott, 340.

86. "Stanzas from the Grande Chartreuse," line 188, in Allott, 293.

87. "Empedocles on Etna," lines 323b-34a, in Allot, 185.

88. "Stanzas from the Grande Chartreuse," lines 97-98, "Resignation," lines 192, 198, in Allott, 289, 91-92.

89. Arthur Edward Waite, Introduction to *Obermann* by Senancour, xxxv.

90. M. Arnold to his mother, 16 November 1867, in Russell, 1:436-37; cf. Lang 3:189.

91. Russell, 1:208.

92. M. Arnold to J. H. Newman, 29 November 1871 and 28 May 1872, in Arnold Whitridge, ed., *Unpublished Letters of Matthew Arnold* (New Haven: Yale University Press, 1923), 56, 65-6.

93. Sandford, 1:81 n.

94. Clough, 1:94; Honan, 78-80.

95. Russell, 1:161, 257.

96. M. Arnold to his mother, Balliol, ca. June 1844, in Lang, 1:59.

97. Arthur Penrhyn Stanley, *Sermons and Essays on the Apostolical Age*, 2nd ed. (Oxford: John Henry Parker, 1852), 17.

98. Stanley, *Sermons and Essays*, 18.

99. Stanley, *Sermons and Essays*, 26.

100. Stanley, *Sermons and Essays*, 8. Eugene L. Williamson notes "the opposed ideas but closely parallel diction" between this passage in Stanley's sermon and Arnold's "Dover Beach," lines 21-28 ("Words from Westminster Abbey: Matthew Arnold and Arthur Stanley," *Studies in English Literature* 11 [1971]: 749-61, 759-60).

101. Prothero, 1:368-70.

102. Prothero, 1:391; Lang, 1:99.

103. Honan, 85.

104. Lang 3:330; Russell, 2:28.

105. Clough, 1:90-92, 95.

106. Clough, 1:97.

107. Clough, 1:101-02.

108. Francis W. Newman, *What Is Christianity without Christ?* (London: Trübner and Co., 1881), 4-5.

109. Clough to his sister, Oriel, May 1847, in Clough, 1:110-11.

110. A. H. Clough, "Easter Day. II," lines 18-25, in Clough, 2:107.

111. A. H. Clough, "Review of Mr. Newman's *The Soul*," in Clough., 1:299. Clough's criticism is, in this edition, published under the wrong title (*vide* Richard M. Gollin, Walter E. Houghton, and Michael Timko, eds. *Arthur Hugh Clough: A Descriptive Catalogue: Poetry, Prose, Biography, and Criticism* [New York: Astor, Lenox, and Tilden Foundations, 1966].)

112. J. Estlin Carpenter, *James Martineau, Theologian and Teacher* (Boston: American Unitarian Association, 1906), 349.

113. M. Arnold to Clough, May 1850, in Lang 1:172, and Lowry, 115. Benjamin Jowett said of *Phases of Faith*, "The first impression given by the book is, How good and simple this man was! and yet how easily affected by all the influences of the age in which he lived!" (*College Sermons*, ed. W. H. Freemantle, 3rd ed. [London: John Murray, 1896], 310).

114. M. Arnold to his mother, 24 December 1863, in Russell 1:248. In *Literature and Dogma*, Arnold distinguishes the "personal religion" of Christianity, "consisting in the inward feeling and disposition of the individual himself," from the Old Testament tendency "to make religion social rather than personal, an affair of outward duties" (R. H. Super, ed., *The Complete Prose Works of Matthew Arnold*, 11 vols. [Ann Arbor: University of Michigan Press, 1960-77], 6:217).

115. Edward Hawkins would later write in regard to subscription, "What difficulties or scruples may be felt by individuals we can only know indeed, when they are confided to us by those who feel them; but I cannot but suspect that their real difficulties . . . grow not out of the Articles, or out of any human expressions or statements, but out of the very *doctrines* to which the Articles refer, and which lie at the foundation of the Faith. . . . They would not be removed by the removal of Subscription: rather, they would be increased by it" (*Notes upon Subscription, Academical and Clerical* [Oxford: John Henry and James Parker, 1864], 28-29).

116. Clough to T. Arnold, Oriel, 31 January 1848, in Clough, 1:117; T. Arnold to Clough, Wellington, 26 June 1848, in James Bertram, ed., *New Zealand Letters of Thomas Arnold the Younger* (London: Oxford University Press, 1966), 57-58.

117. Clough, 1:117.

118. Clough, 1: 96; Lowry, 95. In later correspondence, Arnold referred to this letter and assured Clough, "Your company and mode of being always had a charm and a salutary effect for me, and I could not have foregone these on a mere theory of intellectual dietetics" (12 February 1853, in Lang, 1:253).

119. M. Arnold to Clough, Thun, Sunday, 23 September 1849, in Lowry, 111.

120. *V.* Honan, Ch. 7. More recently, Nicholas Murray dismisses Honan's identification as unsubstantiated, on the grounds that "there is no evidence whatsoever to place [Mary Claude] in Switzerland that year (although it is true that she had relatives in Geneva)." Murray, however, fails to provide any positive evidence to preclude this identification (*A Life of Matthew Arnold* [New York: St. Martin's Press, 1996], Ch. 3, esp. 81-82).

121. J. A. Froude to Charles Kingsley, 27 February 1849, in Waldo Hilary Dunn, *James Anthony Froude: A Biography, 1818-1856* (Oxford: Clarendon Press, 1961), 134; Froude to Clough, 6 March 1849, in Mulhauser, 1:251.

122. M. Arnold to his sister Jane, London, May 1849, in Whitridge, 15. Arnold later (5 June 1869) expressed his belief that his poems were ahead of their time, that they represent "the main movement of mind of the last quarter of a century, and thus they will probably have their day as people become conscious to themselves of what that movement of mind is" (Russell, 2:10).

123. E. H. Coleridge, 1:190.

124. E. H. Coleridge, 1:208-09.

125. M. Arnold to Wyndham Slade, Dover, 3 August 1854, in Russell, 1:40.

126. E. H. Coleridge, 1:211; Lang, 3:406.

127. Mulhauser, 1:286.

128. Russell, 1:16.

129. M. Arnold to his sister Jane, Mrs. W. E. Forster, London, 25 January 1851, in Russell, 1:17.

130. David Edwards, for example, suggests that the psychological and biographical interpretation is the *only* reading of the poem (*Leaders of the Church of England, 1829-1944* [London: Oxford University Press, 1971], 29-34).

131. R. H. Super, *The Time-Spirit of Matthew Arnold* (Ann Arbor: University of Michigan Press, 1970), 4.

132. Honan, 260-62; John William Adamson, *English Education, 1789-1902* (Cambridge: Cambridge University Press, 1964), 206-08; Russell, 1:61-62.

133. Arthur Penryhn Stanley, "The Gorham Controversy," *Edinburgh Review* (July 1850), in *Essays Chiefly on Questions of Church and State, from 1850 to 1870* by A. P. Stanley (London: John Murray, 1870), 2-45.

134. Prothero, 1:428.

135. Prothero, 1:431.

136. Prothero, 1:447-65; Russell, 1:32.

137. Lake, 83.

138. Lewis Campbell, Preface to *The Epistles of St. Paul to the Thessalonians, Galatians and Romans* by Benjamin Jowett, 3rd ed. (London: John Murray, 1894), vi-vii.

139. Benjamin Jowett, "Essay on the Man of Sin," in *Epistles of St. Paul*, 86-103; Jowett, *The Interpretation of Scripture and Other Essays* (London: George Routledge and Sons, n.d. [ca. 1907], 476, 504); Abbott and Campbell, 1:233-34.

140. Prothero, 1:478. The Evangelical critic James H. Rigg states, "Mr. Jowett's objections against the orthodox doctrine of the Atonement are substantially the same as those urged by Coleridge, Maurice, and the whole semi-Socinian school" (*Modern Anglican Theology*, 2nd ed. [London: Alexander Heylin, 1859], 336).

141. A. P. Stanley, *The Epistles of St. Paul to the Corinthians*, 2nd ed. (reprint, Minneapolis: Klock and Klock Christian Publishers, n.d.), Preface, xi.

142. Prothero, 1:473-75.

143. Lightfoot's review was published in *The Journal of Classical and Sacred Philology* 3 (March 1856): 81-121.

144. Russell, 1:54-55; Allott, 351. Samuel Wilberforce, bishop of Oxford, thought "Balder Dead" was the best poem Arnold had written (Lang, 1:321).

145. Charles Edward Mallet, *A History of the University of Oxford: Modern Oxford* (London: Methuen and Co., 1927), 325-28.

146. W. C. Lake to A. C. Tait, 4 December 1856, in Lake, 195-96. Thirteen years after Stanley's death, Lake would still complain of "how much harm such work as [Stanley's] and Jowett's is doing among young men of talent, especially at Oxford," and would even suggest that a "crushing review of Stanley might do a great deal of good, in showing how really anti-Christian his pseudo-liberality was" (Lake, 315-16).

147. Prothero, 2:1.

148. John Milton, *Paradise Lost*, 12.592b-93.

149. Mark Pattison, *Memoirs*, 244.

150. Lake, 83; Russell, 1:45. Connop Thirlwall, in his *Letter to the Rev. Thomas Turton, D.D.* (1834), had suggested that, if the University authorities wanted to awaken religious feeling among students, they could best do this by admitting Dissenters.

151. Prothero, 2:2-3.

152. Mallet, 453-54.

153. M. Arnold to his mother, Sunday, 10 May 1857, in Lang, 1:357-58.

154. John Taylor Coleridge, *A Memoir of the Rev. John Keble*, 3rd ed. (Oxford: James Parker and Co., 1870), 211.

155. M. Arnold to Robert Scott, Hampton, 18 and 22 May 1857, in Lang, 1:360, 363.

156. Prothero, 1:130.

157. Matthew Arnold, "On the Modern Element in Literature," in R. H. Super, ed., *The Complete Prose Works of Matthew Arnold*, 11 vols. (Ann Arbor: University of Michigan Press, 1970-72), 1:18-37, 22, 31.

158. Lake, 58.

159. M. Arnold to his mother, 2 Chester Square, 28 January 1859, in Lang, 1:413; Honan, 297.

160. John Richard Green, the Oxford historian, was an undergraduate of Magdalen when he heard Temple's sermon. Years later, he spoke of the event to Haweis: "Why, old boy! it was splendid; it was throwing down the gauntlet before Pusey, Burgon, and all the other stick-in-the-muds. Think what it was to preach such a sermon then!" (H. R. Haweis, *The Dead Pulpit* [London: Bliss, Sands, and Co., 1896], xxx).

161. Jowett to Stanley, Keswick, 15 August 1858, in Abbott and Campbell, 1:275; cf. Rowland Williams to his sister-in-law, H. M. P., 8 January 1870, in Ellen Williams, ed., *The Life and Letters of Rowland Williams*, 2 vols. (London: Henry S. King and Co., 1874), 2:366.

162. Abbott and Campbell, 1:236-39, 273.

163. A. P. Stanley, "Essays and Reviews," *Edinburgh Review*, April 1861, in *Essays*, 46-96, 59.

164. Knight, 201.

165. Lake to Tait, Huntspill, 9 July 1864, in Lake, 206-07.

166. R. W. Church to George Moberly, Whatley, 14 September 1860, in Mary Church, 155.

167. See "The Broad Church Compromise" in *Essays and Reviews: The 1860 Text and Its Readings*, ed. Victor Shea and William Whitla (Charlottesville: University Press of Virginia, 2000), 123-26.

168. A. H. Clough, "Notes on the Religious Tradition," in Clough, 1:421, 424.

169. M. Arnold to Blanche Clough, 22 January 1862 and 14 October 1868, in Lowry, 160-62.

170. Nearly all of J. C. Shairp's brief reminiscence of Clough appears in *The Poems and Prose Remains of Arthur Hugh Clough* (1869), and the entire piece was published in *Portraits of Friends* (1889).

171. M. Arnold to J. C. Shairp, 12 April 1866, in Russell 1:380; Knight, 88-90.

172. John William Burgon, *Lives of Twelve Good Men*, 2 vols. (London: John Murray, 1888), 2:149-237, esp. 189-99; H. L. Mansel, "On Miracles as Evidences of Christianity," *Aids to Faith: A Series of Theological Essays*, ed. William Thomson (New York: D. Appleton and Co., 1862), 9-52.

173. Frederick Harrison, *The Creed of a Layman: Apologia Pro Fide Mea* (London: Macmillan and Co., 1907), 28-29. "Neo-Christianity" (*Westminster Review* 146 [October 1860]: 293-332), is herein reprinted, 95-157.

174. Shea and Whitla, 649.

175. M. Arnold to his mother, 14 March 1861, in Russell, 1:151-52.

176. Sandford, 1:220-25. Temple seems to have forgotten the true sequence of events.

177. Benjamin Jowett, "On the Interpretation of Scripture," in Shea and Whitla, 477-536, 478.

178. Shea and Whitla, 478-79, 508; Matthew Arnold, *On Translating Homer*, in Super, 1:111-12, 117-18.

179. Shea and Whitla, 482; Super, 1:174, 3: 261. In *The Epistles of St. Paul* (2:408-09), Jowett says, "The great lesson, which Christians have to learn in the present day, is to know the world as it is; that is to say, to know themselves as they are; human life as it is; nature as it is; history as it is. Such knowledge is also a power, to fulfill the will of God and to contribute to the happiness of man" (*Select Passages from the Theological Writings of Benjamin Jowett*, ed. Lewis Campbell [London: John Murray, 1902], 102).

180. Shea and Whitla, 481-82; Super, 3:274-75.

181. Henry Bristow Wilson, "Séances historiques de Genève–the National Church," in Shea and Whitla, 275-309, 277.

182. Matthew Arnold, "The Bishop and the Philosopher," in Super, 3:40-55, 54; Stanley, "Essays and Reviews," in *Essays*, 69.

183. E. M. Goulburn, in his 1861 review, "The Education of the World," observed the close similarity between Temple's and Lessing's essay and chastised Temple for "confusing the progress of the species by civilization with the progress of the Church in divine knowledge" (*Replies to "Essays and Reviews,"* 2nd ed. [Oxford and London: John Henry and James Parker, 1862], 1-54, 21).

184. Lowry, 51.

185. William Robbins, *The Ethical Idealism of Matthew Arnold* (Toronto: University of Toronto Press, 1959), 66-67.

186. Shea and Whitla, 533-34.

187. F. D. Maurice to Colenso, 7 October 1853, in Frederick Maurice, ed., *The Life of Frederick Denison Maurice, Chiefly Told in His Own Letters*, 2 vols. (New York: Charles Scribner's Sons, 1884), 2:185, and in George W. Cox, *The Life of John William Colenso, D.D., Bishop of Natal*, 2 vols. (London: W. Ridgway, 1888), 1:48.

188. John William Colenso, *The Pentateuch and Book of Joshua Critically Examined*, People's Edition (London: Longman, Green, Longman, Roberts, and Green, 1865), pt 1, Preface, 8-12.

189. Colenso, *The Pentateuch*, 15, 19.

190. Maurice, 2:421-23.

191. Prothero, 2:100; Maurice, 2:423.

192. Abbott and Campbell, 1:301.

193. Maurice, 2:432-34.

194. Abbott and Campbell, 1:308 and n.; Russell 1:203.

195. Prothero, 2:104.

196. Shea and Whitla, 501.

197. M. Arnold to his mother, 14 November 1862, in Russell 1:204.

198. Homer, *Iliad* 21.319b-20, trans. Robert Fagles (New York: Viking, 1990), 529.

199. Super, 3:40; *Spectator* 36 (7 February 1863): 1608, qtd. in Sidney Coulling, *Matthew Arnold and His Critics: A Study of Arnold's Controversies* (Athens: Ohio University Press, 1974), 125.

200. Isaac Williams, "On Reserve in Communicating Religious Knowledge (Conclusion)," *Tracts for the Times*, No. LXXXVII (1840), selections reprinted in Eugene R. Fairweather, ed., *The Oxford Movement* (New York: Oxford University Press, 1964), 260-70, 263-64.

201. John Henry Newman, *Apologia pro Vita Sua*, ed. Charles F. Harrold (London: Longmans, Green, and Co., 1947), Note F, 311.

202. Frederick Temple, "The Education of the World," in Shea and Whitla, 137-64, 138.

203. Matthew Arnold, "Puritanism and the Church of England," in Super 6:72-107, 86. R. H. Super notes that Newman wrote "as received and transmitted," not "as admitted and transmitted," 437.

204. Super 3:44; F. D. Maurice, *What Is Revelation?: A Series of Sermons on the Epiphany* (Cambridge: Macmillan and Co., 1859), 90-97; Lang 5:423. Arnold did, however, have ears to hear J. R. Seeley, who presented some of the same ideas "more directly, more straightforwardly, than Maurice" (Sheldon Rothblatt, *The Revolution of the Dons* [New York: Basic Books, 1968], 165).

205. Super, 3:44.

206. Super, 3:44-53; "Spinoza and the Bible," 3:158-82, 179; "Dr. Stanley's Lectures on the Jewish Church," 3:65-82, 65.

207. William Rathbone Greg, "Truth *Versus* Edification," *Westminster Review* 23 (April 1863), reprinted in *Literary and Social Judgments* (Boston: James R. Osgood and Co., 1873), 309-27, 311-19.

208. Thomas Wilson, *Maxims of Piety and of Christianity*, ed. Frederic Relton (London: Macmillan and Co., 1898), 81.

209. Matthew Arnold, "Preface to *Poems*. 1853," in Super, 1:2.

210. Shea and Whitla, 527.

211. Shea and Whitla, 278.

212. Matthew Arnold, "Heinrich Heine," in Super 3:107-32, 111-12. I have seen no usage of the term "Philistine" or description of its referent that approaches so closely to Arnold's as in Schleiermacher's *Soliloquies*, esp. pt. 3, "The World."

213. Super, 3:66-67.

214. Thomas Wilson, 82, 99.

215. Matthew Arnold, "Marcus Aurelius," in Super 3:133-57, 134-35.

216. Colenso, *The Pentateuch*, 23.

217. Super, 3:51.

218. M. Arnold to his mother, 17 December 1862, in Russell, 1:206-07.

219. Super, 3:69.

220. M. Arnold to his mother, 18 November 1865, in Russell, 1:362, and 1 August 1867, in Lang 3:166.

221. Shea and Whitla, 295; Prothero, 2:100, 102. Leslie Stephen appears to have taken Wilson's dictum as normative: "The theory of the Broad Church party is that the legal restrictions upon the clergy are the measure of the moral restrictions" ("The Broad Church," *Fraser's Magazine* 81 (March 1870), in *Essays on Freethinking and Plain-speaking* [London: Longmans, Green, and Co., 1873], 1-40, 4). Edward Copleston, bishop of Llandaff and former provost of Oriel College, argued in his 1848 charge that, because the law recognizes "a latitude or comprehensiveness of meaning in words," clerical subscription "is an engagement of *conscience*, equally binding indeed, or even more binding on the individual than submission to the law" (*Charge Delivered to the Clergy of the Diocese of Llandaff* [London: Francis and John Rivington, 1848], 16).

222. Frederick D. Maurice, *Thoughts on the Rule of Conscientious Subscription, on the Purpose of the Thirty-nine Articles, and on Our Present Perils from the Romish System: in a Second Letter to a Non-Resident Member of Convocation* (Oxford: John Henry Parker, 1845), 18-19.

223. Rashdall Hastings, "Clerical Liberalism," in *Anglican Liberalism, by Twelve Churchmen* (London: Williams and Norgate, 1908), 77-134, 81.

224. Matthew Arnold, *Culture and Anarchy: An Essay in Political and Social Criticism*, in Super 5: 87-256, 134-36. In 1865 Arnold read in J. R. Seeley's *Ecce Homo*, "A member of a state is one who has ceased to have a personal object. . . . He sacrifices himself to the body of which he has become a member" (Eversley ed. [London: Macmillan and Co., 1895], 136).

225. Russell, 1:263, 442-43. In a letter to C. J. Vaughan, Dr. Arnold wrote that a man's "desire to preserve his best self" is "the true fulfillment of the law" (A. P. Stanley, *The Life and Correspondence of Thomas Arnold, D.D.*, 2 vols., 12th ed. [London: John Murray, 1881], 2:200).

226. John Keble to J. T. Coleridge, 14 February 1819, in Stanley, *Life and Correspondence*, 1:19-20.

227. Leslie Stephen, "Mr. Matthew Arnold and the Church of England," *Fraser's Magazine* 82 (October 1870): 414-28, 420-21.

228. Matthew Arnold, "A Psychological Parallel," in Super, 8:111-47, 132; cf. Super, 7: 396.

229. A. P. Stanley, "The Three Pastorals," *Edinburgh Review* (July 1864), reprinted as "Judgment on Essays and Reviews," in *Essays*, 97-147, 121, 127.

230. Davidson and Benham, 1:494-95.

231. Hugh R. Haweis, *The Broad Church, or What is Coming* (New York: John W. Lovell Co., n.d.), 37-38.

232. Super, 8:136-37.

233. Super, 3:261, 265-66.

234. Super, 3:171.

235. Super, 6:91-92.

236. Shea and Whitla, 161, 253, 389.

237. Greg, 316-17.

238. Matthew Arnold, "Modern Dissent," in Super 6:108-27, 120-21.

239. W. J. Conybeare, "Church Parties," *Edinburgh Review* 98, no. 200 (October 1853): 273-342, 333.

240. M. Arnold to M. Fontanès, July and March 1881, in Russell, 2:224, 221.

241. A. P. Stanley, "The Connection of Church and State," in *Essays*, 344-72, 349-51.

242. A. P. Stanley to Mary Stanley, 15 June 1842, in *Letters and Verses of Arthur Penrhyn Stanley, D.D., between the Years 1829 and 1881*, ed. Rowland E. Prothero (London: John Murray, 1895), 74.

243. Prothero, 2:184, 208-12.

244. Matthew Arnold, "Eugénie de Guérin," in Super, 3:83-106, 97-98; Russell, 1:226-27.

245. W. C. Lake draws attention to an "elaborate defence . . . of the use of the crucifix" in one of Dr. Arnold's sermons, and quotes a lengthy passage in which the Rugby Headmaster speaks of the "many good institutions and practices and feelings" that, although associated with the Roman Catholic Church, "would be most desirable to restore among ourselves" (Lake, 15). Blanco White complains about this passage in Arnold's *Sermons* (John Hamilton Thom, *Life of the Rev. Joseph Blanco White*, 3 vols. [London: John Chapman, 1845], 2:154). See Thomas Arnold, *Sermons*, 4 vols. (London: B. Fellowes, 1845), 3:40, 4:56). Park Honan's suggestion that Dr. Arnold "opposed the Anglican Ritualists" (352) is not only anachronistic; it misses the point of contention between the headmaster and the Tractarians.

246. Super, 5:106. Arnold, in his 1865 Preface to *Essays in Criticism*, refers to Oxford as a "home of *lost causes*, and *forsaken beliefs*" (Super, 3:290). Goldwin Smith, in his 1859 *Inaugural Lecture* as professor of modern history, suggests that Oxford Conservatism should be "an enlightened Conservatism, not a Conservatism of *desperate positions* and *ruinous defeats*" (*Inaugural Lecture* [Oxford: J. H. and Jas. Parker, 1859], 19; italics mine).

247. M. Arnold to his mother, 4 June 1867, in Russell, 1:422-23.

248. J. C. Shairp, *Culture and Religion in Some of Their Relations*, 3rd ed. (Boston: Houghton, Mifflin, and Co., 1884), 78-79; cf. Super, 5: 93-94.

249. Super, 5:94.

250. Shairp, *Culture and Religion*, 90-91.

251. James C. Livingston, *Matthew Arnold and Christianity: His Religious Prose Writings* (Columbia: University of South Carolina Press, 1986), 66; Erasmus, *On Free Will*, §57, in *Erasmus-Luther: Discourse on Free Will*, trans. and ed. Ernst F. Winter (1961; New York: Continuum, 1997), 85-86.

252. Super, 5:91, 129.

253. Super, 5:163-65.

254. Super, 5:168-70, 180-81.

255. Shea and Whitla, 142-47.

256. Lang, 3:168; Super, 5:171.

257. David DeLaura, *Hebrew and Hellene in Victorian England: Newman, Arnold, and Pater* (Austin: University of Texas Press, 1969), 37.

258. M. Arnold to his mother, 9 April 1868, in Lang, 3:243; Frederick W. Farrar, *Men I Have Known* (New York: Thomas Y. Crowell and Co., 1897), 77.

259. Thomas Wilson, 2, 31. Arnold does not so much as mention, in the Preface to *Culture and Anarchy*, the existence of John Keble's 1863 edition of Bishop Wilson's *Maxims*. In a footnote, Arnold says that the S.P.C.K., in 1870, republished their 1812 edition (Super, 5:231), but this is an error. It was Parker and Co. that, in 1870, republished Keble's edition. Arnold also fails to note J. H. Newman's 1838 edition of Wilson's *Sacra Privata*.

260. Russell, 1:466.

261. Farrar, 85. Similarly, M. Creighton, comparing Arnold with Ruskin, says, "Both are one-sided, both omit much, but the spirit, the tone of M. Arnold is fruitful, while that of Ruskin (save in art) is not" (Mrs. Creighton, ed., *Life and Letters of Mandell Creighton, D.D.*, 2 vols. [London: Longmans, Green, and Co., 1906], 1:325).

262. Stanley, *Essays*, 357-58, 369.

263. Super, 5:253-54, 245.

264. Prothero, 2:265.

265. A. P. Stanley, "The Three Irish Churches," in *Essays*, 378-429, 409.

266. Super, 5:249-50.

267. Shea and Whitla, 287.

268. Super, 5:249-51.

269. Russell, 2:3-4.

270. Stanley to J. D. Coleridge, 1 March 1869, in E. H. Coleridge, 2:163.

271. Shea and Whitla, 195-97.

272. Super, 6:386.

273. William Blackburn, "Matthew Arnold and the Oriel Noetics," *Philological Quarterly* 25 (January 1946): 70-78, 73.

274. James Spedding to M. Arnold, November 1869, in Lang, 3:386.

275. Mark Pattison, for example, speaks of "the school of Lardner, Paley, and Whately" as characteristic of the latter half of the age of rationalism (Shea and Whitla, 391). On the other hand, according to W. J. Fitzpatrick, Whately's *Essays on the Difficulties in the Writings of the Apostle Paul*, "perhaps the ablest of his theological lucubrations—was one of the sins which his Evangelical flock in Dublin never forgot or forgave." Fitzpatrick notes an acrimonious reply to it published as late as 1862 (*Memoirs of Archbishop Whately, Archbishop of Dublin*, 2 vols. [London: Richard Bentley], 1:353-6).

276. Super, 5:184; cf. Max Müller: "The same applies to religion. *He who knows one, knows none*" (*Introduction to the Science of Religion, Four Lectures Delivered at the Royal Institution* [London: Longmans, Green, and Co., 1873], First Lecture [19 February 1870], 16).

277. Super, 6:7-8, 70.

278. Richard Whately, *Essays on Some of the Difficulties in the Writings of the Apostle Paul and in Other Parts of the New Testament*, 6th ed. (London: John W. Parker, 1849), 57, 63-64.

279. Whately, *Essays*, 72-77, 85, 89, 99-101, 147-49.

280. Super, 6:50, 60-63, 22, 27-29.

281. Charles L. Graves, *Life and Letters of Alexander Macmillan* (London: Macmillan and Co., 1910), 103.

282. R. W. Church, *Guardian*, 7 February 1866; qtd. in Daniel L. Pays, *The Victorian "Lives" of Jesus* (San Antonio: Trinity University Press, 1982), 44-45; Prothero, 2:254-55.

283. Knight, 291-92; Graves, 243; Russell, 1:369.

284. Lang, 3:39, 96, 98.

285. J. R. Seeley, *Ecce Homo: A Survey of the Life and Work of Jesus Christ*, Eversley ed. (London: Macmillan and Co., 1895), 55, 75-76, 91, 103, 109, 162-66, 182-86, 202.

286. It is significant that W. R. Greg thinks it worthwhile to point out the *differences* between Seeley's *Ecce Homo* and Arnold's *Literature and Dogma* (*The Creed of Christendom: Its Foundations Contrasted with Its Superstructure*, Introduction to the Third Edition, 8th ed., 2 vols. [London: Trübner and Co., 1883], xviii-xx).

287. Super, 6:43-44, 219, 38-39, 46-47.

288. Super, 6:3.

289. Knight, 214-15.

290. Whately, 81; Super, 6:8.

291. Super, 7:396.

292. Super, 6:19, 29-30.

293. F. D. E. Schleiermacher, *The Christian Faith*, §10.3, trans. from the 2nd German ed., ed. H. R. Mackintosh and J. S. Stewart, 2 vols. (New York: Harper and Row, 1963), 1:48.

294. Super, 6: 182-88, 9-10. Rowland Williams observes that Bunsen, in his *Bible for the People*, had used "the Eternal" as a translation for "Yahweh" or "Jehovah" (Shea and Whitla, 187).

295. Schleiermacher, *The Christian Faith*, §13.Postscript, 1:67.

296. Super, 6:375.

297. Ruth apRoberts, *Arnold and God* (Berkeley: University of California Press, 1983), 69.

298. Baruch Spinoza, *Theological-Political Treatise*, trans. Samuel Shirley, ed. Seymour Feldman (Indianapolis: Hackett Publishing Co., 1998), chap. 6, 74-76.

299. Schleiermacher, *The Christian Faith*, §47.3, 1:183-84.

300. Baden Powell, "On the Study of the Evidences of Christianity," in Shea and Whitla, pp. 233-61, 250, 242. According to Alfred W. Benn, "If a clergyman may now openly express his disbelief in miracles, and yet remain in the Church, he owes that liberty very largely to Baden Powell" (*The History of English Rationalism in the Nineteenth Century*, 2 vols. [1906; New York: Russell and Russell, 1962], 2:98).

301. Jowett, *Select Passages*, 171.

302. Super, 6:245-46.

303. Robert Shafer, *Christianity and Naturalism* (New Haven: Yale University Press, 1926), 170.

304. See, for example, the Gospel of St. Luke 16:31.

305. M. Arnold to Frances Arnold, November 1874, in Russell, 2:138-39.

306. M. Arnold to Frederic William Farrar, 19 October 1874, in Lang, 4:224.

307. Super, 8:161; Prothero, 2:463.

308. Paul Tillich, *Systematic Theology*, 3 vols. (Chicago: University of Chicago Press, 1951), 1:245.

309. M. Arnold to C. E. Appleton, 12 September 1873, in Lang, 4:174; Livingston, 155.

310. Prothero, 2:271-74; M. O. W. Oliphant, *A Memoir of the Life of John Tulloch, D.D., LL.D.*, 3rd ed. (Edinburgh: William Blackwood and Sons, 1889), 275.

311. David Randell Boone, *An Inclusive Compact: The Broad Church Program of Arthur Stanley, John Tulloch, and A. K. H. Boyd* (Dissertation: Vanderbilt University, 1987), 334.

312. Prothero, 2: 393-94; John Henry Overton and Elizabeth Wordsworth, *Christopher Wordsworth, Bishop of Lincoln, 1807-85* (London: Rivingtons, 1888), 152-53.

313. Prothero, 2:226-28.

314. Oliphant, 282, 284.

315. Oliphant, 386-87.

316. H. F. Lowry, Karl Young, and W. H. Dunn, eds., *The Note-Books of Matthew Arnold* (London: Oxford University Press, 1952), 209.

317. Prothero, 2:459-61; Knight, 319-22, Oliphant, 315-16.

318. Lang, 4:337.

319. Super, 8:121-22.

320. John Tulloch, *Rational Theology and Christian Philosophy in England in the Seventeenth Century*, 2nd ed., 2 vols. (Edinburgh: William Blackwood and Sons, 1874), 2:123; J. A. Passmore, *Ralph Cudworth: An Interpretation* (London: Cambridge University Press, 1951), 39 n.

321. Tulloch, 2:186.

322. Super, 8:123.

323. Rudolf Bultmann, "New Testament and Mythology: The Problem of Demythologizing the New Testament Proclamation" (1841), in *New Testament and Mythology, and Other Basic Writings*, ed. and trans. Schubert M. Ogden (Philadelphia: Fortress Press, 1984), 1-43, 10.

324. John Smith, *Select Discourses* (London: F. Fletcher, 1660), 463; Super, 8:126.

325. Super, 5:182-83.

326. Homer, *Iliad* 15.339-40, trans. Robert Fagles, 397; Col. 3:1a.

327. Acts of the Apostles, 23:6.

328. Super, 8:136.

329. Super, 8:122-23.

330. Lang, 4:353-54, 359-60; Russell, 2:158.

331. Tulloch, 1:x.

332. Oliphant, 321.

333. Ernst Cassirer, *The Platonic Renaissance in England*, trans. James P. Pettegrove (Austin: University of Texas Press, 1953), 4-5. Ruth apRoberts, placing Tulloch's work beside Cassirer's and others, states that it "is still one of our best authorities on the subject" ("Arnold and the Cambridge Platonists," *CLIO* 17 [1988]: 139-50, 146). An excellent selection of readings is provided in C. A. Patrides's *The Cambridge Platonists* (Cambridge: Harvard University Press, 1970).

334. Prothero, 2:564, 566-72; Russell, 2:223-24.

335. Letter of M. Arnold to J. D. Coleridge; 10 January 1882, in Lang, 5:185.

336. Matthew Arnold, "Westminster Abbey," lines 1-10, 161-70, in Allott, 549-56.

337. Julius Charles Hare, "Children of Light," in *The Victory of Faith and Other Sermons* (London: Griffith, Farran, Okeden and Welsh, n.d.), 146-72, 151.

338. William S. Peterson, *Victorian Heretic: Mrs. Humphry Ward's Robert Elsmere* (Leicester: Leicester University Press, 1976), 31.

339. Russell, 2:441.

340. John Wordsworth (1843-1911) was the eldest son of Christopher Wordsworth (1807-1885), bishop of Lincoln, who was the youngest son of Christopher Wordsworth (1774-1846), master of Trinity College, Cambridge, who was the youngest brother of William Wordsworth, the poet.

341. Mrs. Humphry [Mary Augusta] Ward, *A Writer's Recollections*, 2 vols. (New York: Harper and Brothers, 1918), 1:223-25; E. W. Watson, *Life of Bishop John Wordsworth* (London: Longmans, Green, and Co., 1915), 117-20.

342. Ward, 2:73.

343. Haweis, 13-15. See the Introduction, 5-6.

344. Honan, 418.

Conclusion

An Evaluation

During the final quarter of the nineteenth century, the popularity of the Broad Church reached its peak and, then, by an ingenious trick of the Time-Spirit, the movement appeared slowly to vanish, while its distinctive shades gradually blended into a more critical, mystical, and at the same time, more tolerant and less partisan, Anglicanism. The Coleridgean-Mauricean and Tractarian traditions had partly overlapped, and whereas, on the one hand, a Broad Churchman might now uphold the high dignity of the episcopal office and even believe in apostolical succession, on the other hand, a High Churchman might—as demonstrated by the publication of *Lux Mundi* (1889)—recognize the need "'to succour a distressed faith' by endeavouring to bring the Christian Creed into its right relation to the modern growth of knowledge, scientific, historical, critical; and to the modern problems of politics and ethics."[1] Meanwhile, the Low Churchman, after the first Keswick Convention in 1875, shifted his emphasis from the dogmatic to the practical, devotional, and evangelistic aspects of Christianity. Although the Church of England would never be without its liberal or latitudinarian element, that specific movement known as the Broad Church had served its purpose.

Hugh R. Haweis, writing at the close of 1896, observes, "The future historian of the English Church will mark the translation of Dr. Temple to Canterbury and Dr. Creighton to London as a turning-point in the destinies of Broad Church Theology." Haweis, who had begun his ecclesiastical career in 1861 as a curate under Maurice at St. Peter's, and had gone on to become a popular expositor of Mauricean theology, interpreted the elevations of Frederick Temple and Mandell Creighton as signal events, betokening the transition "between the simple historico-ethical Broad Church school and the semi-scientific, semi-mystic, Liberal theology of the near future."[2] During the first decades of the twentieth century, the clergy who had been last to identify with the Broad Church protest against partisanship and provincialism would merge into the current of a diffusive modernism and mysticism.

The popular tradition of assigning precise dates to mark the commencement and closure of historical movements is, no doubt, a useful pedagogical tool. As is evident in St. Matthew's convenient succession of "fourteen generations,"[3] the markers serve as heuristics in the teaching of chronology; however, more often than not, they are hindrances to the understanding of history. They are like training wheels on a bicycle that, having served their purpose, can only with great difficulty be removed; although, at first, they may provide a sense of security and balance, they inevitably stunt development and inhibit the acquiring of independence. *"Did the Broad Church movement end?"* is, at the very least, as good a question as *"When did it end?*," and though I cannot answer the first, except to say that the Broad Church *qua* movement has long been indistinct, I also recognize, as Matthew Arnold states the case, "The expression to speak *ex cathedra* in itself implies what is expected in one who speaks from a Professor's chair."[4] Therefore, assuming both vanity and dogmatism, I offer this answer to the second question (to be received *cum grano salis*): 1897. The movement that began in November 1828, with J. C. Hare's sermon "The Children of Light," ended in January 1897, with the archiepiscopal enthrone-ment and installation of one of the seven contributors to *Essays and Reviews*.

Perhaps, a more profitable inquiry in concluding this study would be to ask, *What were the most prominent objections raised against the movement?* The answer to this question comes with neither chair nor salt, and thus needs no apology. The literature speaks for itself. First, we hear the outcry from within the Church that the movement was entirely negative. J. H. Blunt, in his *Dictionary of Sects, Here-sies, Ecclesiastical Parties, and Schools of Religious Thought* (1874), presents this point of view as an established fact:

> The designation "Broad" has been assumed as expressive of the compre-hensiveness which the theology of this school offers to men of various opinions; but it is scarcely a fitting designation, as well defined opinions of a positive kind are not included. The most distinctive characteristic of the Broad Church School is, in reality, its rejection of traditional beliefs, and the substitution in their place of what has been aptly called a "Negative Theology," in which much is doubted and rejected, and very little believed.[5]

Bluntly stated, the Broad Church was nothing less than the tares among the wheat, and nothing more than a wolf in sheep's clothing; it was the expression of sectarian unbelief from within the community of faith. Were this point of criticism merely the expression of a few bitter attitudinarians, we should do well to overlook it, but it is— at the time it was written—a perspective representative of both High and Low Church. Moreover, it cannot be dismissed as having no basis in fact.

All movements originating in high ideals have a tendency toward degeneration, and the Broad Church was an exception to the rule only so long as it avoided popularity and combination. As we have seen, the first generation of Broad Churchmen did not call themselves by that name or gather together under any partisan banner. They were simply clergy who recognized that the Christian belief held in common by both High and Low Churchmen was not merely a *sufficient* basis of unity, but the *only* basis recognized by the Established Church. If they were antagonistic to any notions peculiar to a party, it was only because that extra-belief had been set up by the party as an additional criteria for fellowship. It was never in the nature of the Broad Church to cling to any positive beliefs which would distinguish it as a partisan movement, other than the recognition that the notions distinctively Low or High are essential neither to Christianity nor to fellowship within the Church of England. Thus, from the very beginning, although the central idea of the movement was a *Broad* Church, it was vulnerable to the charge of making itself realized by means of a negative theology.

The actual deterioration of the movement can be dated from the moment when the negations themselves began to usurp the place of the idea, and fellowship on the basis of unbelief and denial became a practical possibility. Although the decay of the Broad Church was gradual and never thorough, the process was appreciably hastened, first, by the notoriety of *Essays and Reviews* as a "Broad Church" publication and, second, by the ultimate acquittal by the Privy Council of essayists Wilson and Williams. Suddenly, the prospect of being at once socially respectable and scandalous, conjoined with the freedom of speaking one's mind with impunity, endowed the liberal school of theology with a sort of sensational grandeur that was to attract not only honest doubters, but a growing number of irreverent deniers. The subsequent change in the tenor of the Broad Church movement can be inferred from Stopford Brooke's reply, in 1867, to a request for his participation in producing a quarterly review of liberal theology:

> The very first principle of such a paper should be reverence for all that men truly hold sacred. . . . Let them be opposed if necessary, fairly, decidedly, but with the reverence due to things held dear, and sacred by the heart. . . . I fairly own I am sometimes sick of the intolerant bigotry I hear talked by our liberals and of the growing cant of the Broad Church school.[6]

Brooke, himself, was at this time a leading figure in the school. Not only had he recently published the *Life and Letters of Fredk. W. Robertson* (1865), but he was now a chaplain to the queen and an immensely popular preacher, delivering sermons to packed audiences at St. James's Chapel and Westminster Abbey. In addition, he was lecturing three times a week at Queen's College on English history and literature. Yet, the irreverence, cant, and intolerance of so many young men affiliating themselves with a *party* called the Broad Church alienated Brooke from identifying with it, and as his own thoughts led him away from dogmatic rationalism into deeper channels of a pantheism tinged with mysticism, he came to regard subscription an intolerable bondage and, in 1880, resigned his orders. Brooke's secession from the Broad Church and the death of Dean Stanley in the following year depleted the movement of half its vitality—in fact, some critics have identified Stanley's death with the demise of the movement.[7]

Haweis, who had, in 1880, just published *Poets in the Pulpit*, was critical of Brooke's decision and, in a letter to the *Daily News*, referred to his secession as "an anachronism"—meaning, of course, that it was the sort of decision of conscience that one might expect a man to make at the beginning rather than near the end of his career.[8] Haweis, too, regretted the prominence of a negative theology in the movement and was prepared to handle all dogmas, "even the Dogma of the Infallibility of the Pope," with sympathy and tenderness. His message in *The Broad Church* (1891) was that the time had come for the movement to move beyond negation toward positive restatement, to turn "dead Dogma into living Doctrine."[9]

Haweis's remark concerning papal infallibility (a doctrine declared by the First Vatical Council, 1870) might, indeed, evoke the very argument that is next to be considered: that—whether for cowardice, sloth, greed, pride, or mere lack of self-knowledge—the Broad Churchman was less than honest in subscribing to the formularies of the English Church. Charles N. Wodehouse, canon of Norwich under Bishop Stanley, observed, in 1843, that, although language is imperfect, "truth is a real thing, and every honest man knows that it is so; for whoever speaks that to another which he knows is not understood in his own sense by the hearer; whoever twists written language from the plain purpose of the writer; whoever, by a studied obscurity, veils his real opinions in order to mislead others, is a liar."[10] Wodehouse, doubting that the sense in which he subscribed to the Articles was their legitimate sense, offered, as early as 1841, to resign his post. The offer was not accepted, and he spent the next nineteen years wrestling with his conscience and pleading for an authoritative explication of the Articles. Finally, in 1860, when asked to officiate at an ordination, he resigned his orders, unable—as he says—"to approve of a Form, to which, in its literal sense, I had always objected, and which I could not now look upon as in any sense consistent with Scriptural truth."[11] Thus, Wodehouse ultimately rejected the idea of clerical restatement on the grounds that it is inconsistent with an honest subscription.

Two years later, in 1862, another clergyman, Leslie Stephen, came to the same conclusion and also withdrew from the ministry. Stephen, the brother of James Fitzjames Stephen (the diligent junior counsel who had so ably defended Rowland Williams before the Court of Arches in 1861-1862), soon found a public platform and, taking Wodehouse's arguments in hand, made himself public prosecutor of the Broad Church movement. In "The Broad Church," published in *Fraser's Magazine*, Stephen neatly distinguishes four classes of Broad Churchmen. First, there are those—like himself, Wodehouse, and William G. Clark, the "distinguished resident at Cambridge"—who have the honesty to admit to themselves that they are in a false position and the integrity to surrender their livings, regardless of the personal costs. Second, there are those (like Stanley and Haweis) who abide by their theory "that the legal restrictions upon the clergy are the measure of the moral restrictions," and thus, neither transgress the law, nor trouble their consciences in regard to where they may stand in relation to the intent of the framers of the Church formularies. Third, there are those (like Colenso and Charles Voysey—"the *enfant terrible* of the Broad Church party") who knowingly push the limits of their lawful liberties with the intent of forcing a relaxation of the terms of subscription. Fourth, there are those (like Maurice) who, by ostensibly unconscious bias, arrive at the conclusion that the Articles express their deepest convictions.

Although Stephen concedes that the leaders of the Broad Church are, for the most part, "honest and able men" and that "the allegiance of thinking men" to the Church of England is "due to the Broad Church element amongst the clergy," he doubts that any but the first class of clergymen have adequately grasped the paramount importance and duty of "perfect intellectual sincerity." He urges, "It does not follow that because the law allows a certain liberty, it is right or wise to take advantage of it." Regardless of personal or social consequences, everyone should speak plainly what he or she believes; only in this way will the noxious advance of utter scepticism be curtailed.[12]

John Morley, impressed by Stephen's essay, attempted to take the argument further, to locate "the most general principles which ought to regulate the practice of compliance" and to identify "the boundary that divides wise suspense in forming opinions, wise reserve in expressing them, and wise tardiness in trying to realise them, from unavowed disingenuousness and self-illusion, from voluntary dissimulation, and from indolence and pusillanimity."[13] His essay *On Compromise* (1874) identifies the historical and economic influences that had detracted from the Englishman's pursuit of intellectual integrity, and locates the consequence in an effeminate latitudinarianism. Convinced of "the essential and profound immorality of the priestly profession . . . which makes a man's living depend on his abstaining from using his mind, or concealing the conclusions to which use of his mind has brought him," Morley tells the clergy that "the new faith when it comes will be of little worth, unless it has been shaped by generations of honest and fearless men."[14] Lest there be any doubt as to his book's intended audience, the author prefixes a motto from Archbishop Whately: "It makes all the difference in the world whether we put Truth in the first or in the second place." This is a sentiment that brings to our minds that oft-quoted warning of Coleridge's: "He, who begins by loving Christianity better than Truth, will proceed by loving his own Sect or Church better than Christianity, and end in loving himself better than all."[15]

The combined efforts of the *Cornhill Magazine*, edited by Stephen from 1871 to '82, and the *Fortnightly Review*, edited by Morley from 1867 to '82, rear-ended the Broad Church movement, dinted it, and, at the same time, pushed it forward. Stephen and Morley inadvertently reinforced the truth which their clerical readers already suspected: it was inconceivable that any clergyman could sincerely uphold a strict interpretation of the Thirty-nine Articles; *therefore, if the Established Church was to survive, its clergy had to be progressive.* From the Broad Church-man's perspective, to argue that the process of doctrinal restatement necessarily involves intellectual dishonesty, is to make a case for the immorality of every establishment of religion, for no statement of faith, however brief, can mean the same thing from one person to another and one generation to another. Benjamin Jowett, in a memorial sermon for Stanley, made this observation to his audience in Balliol Chapel:

> To the question . . . whether a person of what are termed liberal opinions can subscribe the Thirty-nine Articles, I think that the best answer is given in the striking words of the Dean of Westminster himself, "that if subscription is strictly enforced, then every one, from the Archbishop of Canterbury to the humblest clergyman in the wilds of Cumberland, must leave the Church. For the difficulty is not one which presses upon one party only, but almost equally upon all."[16]

The same course of time that hallows, by our frequent use, the words by which we express our faith, also creates a tension between the alleged intent of the framers of those words and our interpretations of them. Eventually, the words may have to be discarded; but, in the meantime, the gains of doing so must be measured against the losses, and if the gains are ours and the losses are our neighbors', then we might do well to look to the example of the founder of the Church and head of the human race:

> The policy of the Broad Church, the policy of reform from within, is called dishonest, but it was nevertheless the policy of Jesus. He was the greatest spiritual Reformer whom the world had ever seen: but He used the synagogue—it was "His custom" to go there on the Sabbath. He did not approve of everything there, but He used what He found. He said: Moses says this, but I tell you something different, yet I come not to destroy but to fulfill.[17]

Contrary to the Pharisees and Essenes, Jewish sects that sought holiness through either a rigid interpretation and application of scripture or isolation from the world, Jesus taught that the way of righteousness was to change the condition of the "heart," so that the law written on the heart could be discerned and understood. In Coleridgean-Mauricean terms, Jesus taught the priority of the Reason or appre-hending faculty over, but not against, Scripture. He fully endorsed the policy of restatement. In fact, it might be fairly argued that Jesus's mission was to inaugurate a Broad Synagogue movement, although—as Matthew Arnold would have pointed out—it was the mission of a layman.

Finally, we might consider the viewpoint from which the Broad Church is dismissed as having no intellectual foundation and having provided nothing of lasting value, but instead, of "being the transition form between the new and the old orthodoxy"—that is, the sea of doubt between the two shores of Science and Theology. Such was Julia Wedgwood's verdict, with which Dean Lake expressed complete agreement.[18] According to this view, the Broad Churchman, having freed himself from the traditional moorings, scripture and ecclesiastical authority, was like a boat tossed by the waves. To illustrate this point, Wedgwood identifies Kingsley as the most "prominent and characteristic specimen," a man afloat on an ideal called "Religion, modified by Science."[19]

Have not the four chapters of this book been sufficient to answer such a charge? Is it not rather the case that religion begins in the involuntary response of the human spirit to that eternal Spirit from which it comes and in which it lives? Religion, thus, cannot be "modified by science." Theology, on the other hand, consists in propositional statements, which are at best approximations to the facts of which religion is the inarticulate response—or, as St. Paul prefers, the "groanings, which cannot be uttered."[20] Broad Churchmen like Kingsley simply recognized the fact that, when the language of approximation conflicts with the language of precision, it is not the latter that, for the sake of harmony and truth, must be modified.

Retired Episcopal Bishop John Shelby Spong appears to agree with Wedgwood's criticism, identifying the Broad Church as the establishment's rearguard operating from within the school of progressive thought. *Essays and Reviews*, he says, is a "a 19th century liberal attempt to make theistic Christianity believable."[21] If this assessment is true of so progressive a book as *Essays and Reviews*, we may accept it as generally true of clerical liberalism in Victorian England. According to Haweis—who had publicly declared his entire agreement with the nontheistic language of Matthew Arnold[22]—Temple's contribution to *Essays and Reviews* "is the strongest in the book, and, I might almost say, the most revolutionary. It foreshadows boldly the direction in which all thoughtful theology has been traveling ever since 1860."[23] In order to address Spong's assessment, we need only ascertain whether Temple's essay anticipates the development of nontheistic Christianity or, conversely, aims to preclude its development. If Temple's thesis is correct, if each generation does, in fact, "receive the benefit of the cultivation of that which preceded it,"[24] then we should expect to find therein *not* a conservative effort to withstand the inevitable decline of theism, but rather indications of a movement away from the mythic and anthropomorphic aspects of prescientific religion. And, of course, this is exactly what we do find. Temple, having observed that the human race is moving forward to a condition of freedom from legal restraint, notes that religion itself is slowly throwing off the impediments of an external law, a coercive church, and a threatening God, and is assuming a form more in agreement with the power of independent thought, the form of "an internal law, a voice which speaks within the conscience, and carries the understanding along with it."[25] According to Temple, the conservative habit that Christians evince by perpetually returning to the Bible for their dogmas and traditions is a tendency obscurantist and retarding, and "he is guilty of high treason against the faith who fears the result of any investigation, whether philosophical, or scientific, or historical."[26] Surely, Spong himself is a spiritual heir of Broad Churchmen like Temple.

Theology changes with the advance of knowledge, and to no single idea, however precious to one generation, can we confidently ascribe lasting value. Even so, as long as there are people with genuine religious feeling who find themselves unable, for intellectual reasons, to fully subscribe to the creed of their community, the *example*—if not the positive ideas—of the Broad Churchmen will have value. By faith, Coleridge, through long wanderings, kept alive the heart in the head and was granted a wisdom vindicated by its children. By faith Thomas Arnold placed principles before preferment, for which service God translated his life into a sermon. By faith Maurice and Kingsley fought for a kingdom in which life is eternal; therefore, they drew the sword and threw away the scabbard. By faith Stanley, having traced the development of the revelation of God within the Jewish Church, redefined what it means to have an *historical* faith. He listened for the still, small voice, and God was pleased to make him a peacemaker among his brethren. "And what shall I more say?"[27]

Notes

1. *Lux Mundi: A Series of Studies in the Religion of the Incarnation*, ed. Charles Gore, 14th ed. (London: John Murray, 1895), Preface to the Tenth Edition, x.

2. Hugh R. Haweis, *The Dead Pulpit* (London: Bliss, Sands, & Co., 1896), xli, 58.

3. Matt. 1:17.

4. Matthew Arnold to Mrs. W. E. Forster, 8 February 1861, in *Unpublished Letters of Matthew Arnold* (New Haven: Yale University Press, 1923), 52.

5. John Henry Blunt, ed., *Dictionary of Sects, Heresies, Ecclesiastical Parties, and Schools of Religious Thought* (London: Rivingtons, 1874), 85.

6. Letter of Stopford Brooke to J. R. Green; in Lawrence Pearsall Jacks, *Life and Letters of Stopford Brooke*, 2 vols. (New York: Charles Scribner's Sons, 1917), 1:224-25.

7. Julia Wedgwood, *Nineteenth Century Teachers and Other Essays* (London: Hodder and Stoughton, 1909), 100.

8. Jacks, 1:327 n.

9. Hugh R. Haweis, *The Broad Church; or, What is Coming* (London: Sampson, Low, Marston, Searle, and Rivington, 1891), 40-41.

10. C. N. Wodehouse, *Subscription the Disgrace of the English Church* (London: Longman, Brown, Green, and Longmans, 1843), 5-6.

11. C. N. Wodehouse, *The Claims of Truth* (London: Jarrold and Sons, 1861), 28-29.

12. Leslie Stephen, "The Broad Church," *Fraser's Magazine* 81 (March 1870), reprinted in *Essays on Freethinking and Plainspeaking* (London: Longmans, Green, and Co., 1873), 5-9, 32-36.

13. John Morley, *On Compromise* (1874; London: Macmillan and Co., 1886), 2-4.

14. Morley, 194, 200.

15. S. T. Coleridge, *Aids to Reflection*, ed. John Beer, *The Collected Works of Samuel Taylor Coleridge* 9 (Princeton: Princeton University Press, 1993), M & R Aph XXV, 107; quoted by J. S. Mill in "Coleridge," *London and Westminster Review*, March 1840; reprinted in *Mill on Bentham and Coleridge*, ed. F. R. Leavis (London: Chatto and Windus, 1950), 99-168, 113.

16. Benjamin Jowett, "Arthur Penrhyn Stanley," *Sermons Biographical & Miscellaneous*, ed. W. H. Fremantle (London: John Murray, 1899), 130-51, 145. William G. Ward had, for other reasons, come to the same conclusion: "I am firmly convinced that no one clergyman of our Church, who will look honestly in the face the formularies which he is called on to subscribe, will be able to subscribe them *all* in a *natural* and *straightforward* sense. I attribute this fact to the utter want of fixed religious principles displayed by the leading Reformers" (*The Ideal of a Christian Church Considered*, 2nd ed. [London: James Toovey, 1844], 481).

17. Haweis, *The Broad Church*, 29.

18. Wedgwood, 48-49; Letter of W. C. Lake to the editor of the *Spectator*, 5 October 1897, in *Memorials of William Charles Lake*, ed. Katherine Lake (London: Edward Arnold, 1901), 325.

19. Wedgwood, 89-90.

20. Rom. 8:26.

21. John Shelby Spong to the author, 20 June 2002. Spong traces the intellectual and moral error of the Christian Church to the anthropomorphic language of Scripture, and like Moses on Mount Pisgah, beckons all nontheistic believers to a "Church beyond the exile" in which "Christ... is not the arbiter at the gate determining who is worthy of entering but rather an inviting presence who says to all, 'Come unto me and discover the infinite dimension of transcendent wonder'"(*Why Christianity Must Change or Die* [New York: HarperCollins, 1998], 189). Adopting Leslie Stephens's phrase, we might dub Spong the *enfant terrible* of the postmodern Church.

22. On 16 July 1871, H. R. Haweis preached, "I can say to you I do not know what the whole of God is, but I will tell you what He is thus much accurately. God is the stream of tendency by which all things fulfil the law of their being. . . . Something not himself has impressed upon [man] a physical law. Science may call it a stream of tendency—we will call it God" (*Thoughts for the Times: Sermons* [New York: Holt & Williams, 1872], 54-55).

23. Haweis, *The Dead Pulpit*, xxix.

24. Frederick Temple, "The Education of the World," in Victor Shea and William Whitla, eds., *Essays and Reviews: The 1860 Text and Its Reading* (Charlottesville: University Press of Virginia, 2000), 138.

25. Temple, 156-57.

Bibliography

Abbott, Evelyn, and Lewis Campbell. *The Life and Letters of Benjamin Jowett, M.A.* 2 vols. London: John Murray, 1897.

Adamson, John William. *English Education: 1789-1902.* Cambridge: Cambridge University Press, 1930.

Akenson, Donald Harman. *A Protestant in Purgatory: Richard Whately, Archbishop of Dublin.* Hamden, Conn.: Archon Books, 1981.

Alden, Edward C. *Alden's Oxford Guide.* Oxford: Alden and Co., 1921.

Allen, Peter. *The Cambridge Apostles: The Early Years.* New York: Cambridge University Press, 1978.

apRoberts, Ruth. *Arnold and God.* Berkeley: University of California Press, 1983.

Arnold, Matthew. *The Complete Prose Works of Matthew Arnold.* Ed. R. H. Super. 11 vols. Ann Arbor: University of Michigan Press, 1960-77.

———. *The Letters of Matthew Arnold.* Ed. Cecil Y. Lang. 5 vols. Charlottesville: University Press of Virginia, 1996-2001.

———. *The Letters of Matthew Arnold: 1848-1888.* Ed. George W. E. Russell. New York: Macmillan and Co., 1895.

———. *The Letters of Matthew Arnold to Arthur Hugh Clough.* Ed. Howard Foster Lowry. Oxford: Clarendon Press, 1932.

———. *The Note-Books of Matthew Arnold.* Ed. H. F. Lowry, Karl Young, and W. H. Dunn. London: Oxford University Press, 1952.

———. *The Poems of Matthew Arnold.* Ed. Kenneth Allott. London: Longmans, Green, and Co., 1965.

———. *Unpublished Letters of Matthew Arnold.* Ed. Arnold Whitridge. New Haven: Yale University Press, 1923.

Arnold, Thomas. *The Miscellaneous Works of Thomas Arnold, D.D.* Ed. A. P. Stanley. London: B. Fellowes, 1845.

———. *The Miscellaneous Works of Thomas Arnold, D.D.* 1st American ed. New York: D. Appleton and Co., 1845.

———. *Sermons.* 2 vols. 2nd ed. London: B. Fellowes, 1834.

————. *Sermons*. 4 vols. London: B. Fellowes, 1845.

Arnold, Thomas (the younger). *New Zealand Letters of Thomas Arnold the Younger*. Ed. James Bertram. London: Oxford University Press, 1966.

————. *Passages in a Wandering Life*. London: Edward Arnold, 1900.

B., R. E. "The Broad Church Movement." *Fraser's Magazine* 17 (March 1878): 353-64.

Badger, Kingsbury. "Christianity and Victorian Religious Confessions." *Modern Language Quarterly* 25 (1964): 86-109.

Balleine, G. R. *A History of the Evangelical Party in the Church of England*. Revised ed. London: Church Book Room Press, 1951.

Barth, Robert J. *Coleridge and Christian Doctrine*. New York: Fordham University Press, 1987.

————. *Coleridge and the Power of Love*. Columbia: University of Missouri Press, 1988.

Benn, Alfred W. *The History of English Rationalism in the Nineteenth Century*. 2 vols. London: Longmans, Green, and Co., 1906.

Bentham, Jeremy. *"Swear not at all": Containing an Exposure of the Needlessness and Mischievousness, as well as Antichristianity, of the Ceremony of an Oath*. London: R. Hunter, 1817.

Bigg, Charles. *The Christian Platonists of Alexandria*. Oxford: Clarendon Press, 1886.

Bill, E. G. W. *University Reform in Nineteenth-Century Oxford: A Study of Henry Halford Vaughan, 1811-1885*. Oxford: Clarendon Press, 1973.

Blackburn, William. "Matthew Arnold and the Oriel Noetics." *Philological Quarterly* 25 (January 1946): 70-78.

Blanco White, Joseph. *Practical and Internal Evidence against Catholicism*. London: John Murray, 1826.

Blunt, John Henry. *Dictionary of Sects, Heresies, Ecclesiastical Parties, and Schools of Religious Thought*. London: Rivingtons, 1874.

Boethius. *The Consolations of Philosophy*. Trans. W. V. Cooper. New York: Modern Library, 1943.

Boone, David Randell. *An Inclusive Compact: The Broad Church Program of Arthur Stanley, John Tulloch, and A. K. H. Boyd*. Dissertation: Vanderbilt University, 1987.

Bowen, Desmond. *The Idea of the Victorian Church: A Study of the Church of England, 1833-1889*. Montreal: McGill University Press, 1968.

Brock, M. G., and M. C. Curthoys, eds. *The History of the University of Oxford, Vol. VI: Nineteenth-Century Oxford, Part I*. Oxford: Clarendon Press, 1997.

Brooke, Stopford A., ed. *Life and Letters of Fredk. W. Robertson, M.A.* 1865. 4th ed. New York: Harper and Brothers, n.d.

Brookfield, Frances M. *The Cambridge "Apostles."* New York: Charles Scribner's Sons, 1907.

Bultmann, Rudolf. *New Testament and Mythology, and Other Basic Writings*. Ed. Schubert M. Ogden. Philadelphia: Fortress Press, 1984.

Bunsen, Christian Karl Josias. *Hippolytus and His Age: Or, The Beginnings and Prospects of Christianity*. 2 vols. London: Longman, Brown, Green, and Longmans, 1854.

Bunsen, Frances Baroness. *A Memoir of Baron Bunsen*. 2 vols. London: Longmans, Green, and Co., 1868.

Burgon, John William. *Lives of Twelve Good Men*. 2 vols. London: John Murray, 1888.

Burnet, Gibert. *An Exposition of the Thirty-nine Articles of the Church of England*. 1699. London: William Tegg and Co., 1850.

Bush, L. Russ, ed. *Classical Readings in Christian Apologetics*. Grand Rapids: Academie Books, 1983.

Carlyle, Thomas. *Chartism*. Pp. 149-232 in *Selected Writings*, ed. Alan Shelston. New York: Penguin Classics, 1971.

———. *The Life of John Sterling*. 1851. New York: P. F. Collier and Son, 1901.

Carpenter, J. Estlin. *James Martineau, Theologian and Teacher*. Boston: American Unitarian Association, 1906.

Cassirer, Ernst. *The Platonic Renaissance in England*. Trans. James P. Pettegrove. 1953. New York: Gordion Press, 1970.

Cecil, David. *Melbourne: "The Young Melbourne" and "Lord M" in One Volume*. London: Reprint Society, 1955.

Chadwick, Owen. *The Spirit of the Oxford Movement: Tractarian Essays*. New York: Cambridge University Press, 1990.

———. *The Victorian Church: Part I*. New York: Oxford University Press, 1966.

———. *The Victorian Church: Part II*. New York: Oxford University Press, 1970.

Chandos, John. *Boys Together: English Public Schools, 1800-1864*. New Haven: Yale University Press, 1984.

Cheyne, T. K. *The Divine Call in the History of a College: A Commemoration Sermon, Preached in Oriel Chapel, October 20th, 1889*. Oxford: Horace Hart, 1889.

Chretien, Charles Peter. *A Letter to the Reverend F. D. Maurice, on Some Points Suggested by His Recent Criticism of Mr. Mansel's Bampton Lectures*. London: John W. Parker, 1859.

Christenson, Merton A. "Thomas Arnold's Debt to German Theologians: A Prelude to Matthew Arnold's *Literature and Dogma*." *Modern Philology* 55 (1957): 14-20.

Church, Mary, ed. *Life and Letters of Dean Church*. London: Macmillan and Co., 1895.

Church, Richard William. *The Oxford Movement: Twelve Years, 1833-1845*. 3rd ed., 1892. Reprinted, New York: Archon Books, 1966.

Churton, Edward. *A Letter to an Edinburgh Reviewer, on the Case of the Oxford Malignants and Dr. Hampden*. London: J. G. and F. Rivington, 1836.

Clark, John Willis. *Old Friends at Cambridge and Elsewhere*. London: Macmillan and Co., 1900.

———, and Thomas McKenny Hughes. *The Life and Letters of the Reverend Adam Sedgwick*. 2 vols. Cambridge: Cambridge University Press, 1890.

Clough, Arthur Hugh. *The Correspondence of Arthur Hugh Clough*. Ed. Frederick L. Mulhauser. 2 vols. Oxford: Clarendon Press, 1957.

Clough, Blanche, ed. *The Poems and Prose Remains of Arthur Hugh Clough*. 2 vols. London: Macmillan and Co., 1869.

Clubbe, John, ed. *Froude's Life of Carlyle*. London: John Murray, 1979.

Colenso, John William. *The Pentateuch and Book of Joshua Critically Examined*. People's Edition. London: Longman, Green, Longman, Roberts, and Green, 1865.

Coleridge, Ernest Hartley. *Life and Correspondence of John Duke Lord Coleridge, Lord Chief Justice of England*. 2 vols. New York: D. Appleton and Co., 1904.

Coleridge, John Taylor. *A Memoir of the Rev. John Keble, M.A., Late Vicar of Hursley*. Oxford: James Parker and Co., 1870.

Coleridge, Samuel Taylor. *Aids to Reflection*. Ed. John Beer. *The Collected Works of Samuel Taylor Coleridge*, vol. 9. Princeton: Princeton University Press, 1993.

————. *Biographia Literaria: Or, Biographical Sketches of My Literary Life and Opinions.* Ed. James Engell and W. Jackson Bate. 2 vols. *The Collected Works of Samuel Taylor Coleridge*, vol. 7. Princeton: Princeton University Press, 1983.

————. *Collected Letters of Samuel Taylor Coleridge.* Ed. Earl Leslie Griggs. 6 vols. Oxford: Clarendon Press, 1956-1959.

————. *Confessions of an Inquiring Spirit.* Ed. H. J. Jackson and J. R. de J. Jackson. *The Collected Works of Samuel Taylor Coleridge*, vol. 2. Princeton: Princeton University Press, 1995.

————. *The Friend.* Ed. Barbara Rooke. 2 vols. *The Collected Works of Samuel Taylor Coleridge*, vol. 4. Princeton: Princeton University Press, 1969.

————. *Lay Sermons.* Ed. R. J. White. *The Collected Works of Samuel Taylor Coleridge*, vol. 6. Princeton: Princeton University Press, 1972.

————. *The Literary Remain of Samuel Taylor Coleridge.* Ed. Henry Nelson Coleridge. 4 vols. London: Pickering, 1839.

————. *The Notebooks of Samuel Taylor Coleridge.* Ed. Kathleen Coburn and Merton Christensen. 4 vols. Princeton: Princeton University Press, 1990.

————. *On the Constitution of the Church and State.* Ed. Henry Nelson Coleridge. London: William Pickering, 1839.

————. *Poetical Works.* Ed. Ernest Hartley Coleridge. New York: Oxford University Press, 1912.

————. *The Statesman's Manual.* Ed. J. R. White. *The Collected Works of Samuel Taylor Coleridge*, vol. 6. Princeton: Princeton University Press, 1972.

Colloms, Brenda. *Charles Kingsley: The Lion of Eversley.* London: Constable, 1975.

The Constitutions and Canons Ecclesiastical. London: Prayer-Book and Homily Society, 1852.

Conway, Moncure D. *The Parting of the Ways: A Study on the Lives of Sterling and Maurice.* Finsbury: Printed for the Author, 1872.

Conybeare, John Josias. *An Attempt To Trace the History and To Ascertain the Limits of the Secondary and Spiritual Interpretation of Scripture.* Oxford: Oxford University Press, 1824.

Conybeare, William John. "Church Parties." *Edinburgh Review* 98, no. 200 (October 1853): 273-342.

Copleston, Edward. *Charge Delivered to the Clergy of the Diocese of Llandaff.* London: Francis and John Rivington, 1848.

Cornish, Francis Warre. *The English Church in the Nineteenth Century.* 2 vols. London: Macmillan and Co., 1933.

Correspondence of John Henry Newman with John Keble and Others, 1839-1845. Ed. Birmingham Oratory. London: Longmans, Green, and Co., 1917.

Corsi, Pietro. *Science and Religion: Baden Powell and the Anglican Debate, 1800-1860.* New York: Cambridge University Press, 1988.

Coulling, Sidney. *Matthew Arnold and His Critics: A Study of Arnold's Controversies.* Athens: Ohio University Press, 1974.

Cox, George W. *The Life of John William Colenso, D.D., Bishop of Natal.* 2 vols. London: W. Ridgway, 1888.

Creighton, Louise. *Life and Letters of Mandell Creighton, D.D.* 2 vols. London: Longmans, Green, and Co., 1906.

Croker, John W. "Revolutionary Literature." *Quarterly Review* 178 (September 1851): 491-543.

Crowther, Margaret A. *Church Embattled: Religious Controversy in Mid-Victorian England.* Hamden, Conn.: Archon Books, 1970.

Cudworth, Ralph. *The True Intellectual System of the Universe.* 2 vols. London: Printed for Richard Royston, 1678. Facsimile reprint, New York: Garland, 1978.

Culverwell, Nathaniel. *An Elegant and Learned Discourse of the Light of Nature.* Ed. Robert Greene and Hugh MacCallum. Toronto: University of Toronto Press, 1971.

Darwin, Charles. *Autobiography.* Ed. Nora Barlow. New York: W. W. Norton, 1958.

Davidson, Randall Thomas, and William Benham. *Life of Archibald Campbell Tait, Archbishop of Canterbury.* 2 vols. 3rd ed. London: Macmillan and Co., 1891.

Davies, Walter Merlin. *An Introduction to F. D. Maurice's Theology.* London: S.P.C.K., 1964.

DeLaura, David. *Hebrew and Hellene in Victorian England: Newman, Arnold, and Pater.* Austin: University of Texas Press, 1969.

De Quincey, Thomas. *Confessions of an English Opium-Eater and Other Writings.* New York: Oxford University Press, 1996.

Denison, George Anthony. *Notes of My Life, 1805-1878.* Oxford: James Parker, 1878.

Distad, N. Merrill. *Guessing at Truth: The Life of Julius Charles Hare.* Shepherdstown, W.Va.: The Patmos Press, 1979.

Dunn, Waldo Hilary. *James Anthony Froude: A Biography.* 2 vols. Oxford: Clarendon Press, 1961.

Edwards, David. *Leaders of the Church of England, 1829-1944.* London: Oxford University Press, 1971.

Erskine, Thomas. *The Brazen Serpent: Or, Life Coming through Death.* 3rd ed. Edinburgh: David Douglas, 1879

———. *Letters of Thomas Erskine of Linlathen.* Ed. William Hanna. Edinburgh: David Douglas, 1878.

Emerson, Edward Waldo. *A Correspondence between John Sterling and Ralph Waldo Emerson, with a Sketch of Sterling's Life.* Boston: Houghton, Mifflin, and Co., 1897.

The Extraordinary Black Book: An Exposition of Abuses in Church and State, Courts of Law, Municipal Corporations, and Public Companies. London: Effingham Wilson, 1835.

Farrar, Adam S. *A Critical History of Free Thought in Reference to the Christian Religion.* London: John Murray, 1862.

Farrar, Frederick W. *The History of Interpretation.* 1885. Grand Rapids: Baker Book House, 1961.

———. *Men I Have Known.* New York: Thomas V. Crowell and Co., 1897.

Fitzpatrick, John William. *Memoirs of Richard Whately, Archbishop of Dublin: With a Glance at His Cotemporaries & Times.* 2 vols. London: Richard Bentley, 1864.

Fuller, Thomas. *The History of the University of Cambridge, from the Conquest to the Year 1634.* Ed. Marmaduke Prickett and Thomas Wright. Cambridge: Cambridge University Press, 1840.

Froude, James Anthony. *The Nemesis of Faith.* 1849. New York: Garland Press, 1975.

———. "The Oxford Counter-Reformation." Pp. 151-235 in *Short Studies on Great Subjects* by J. A. Froude, 4th series. New York: Charles Scribner's Sons, 1883.

Gladstone, William E. *Correspondence on Church and Religion of William Ewart Gladstone.* Ed. D. C. Lathbury. 2 vols. London: John Murray, 1910.

Glanvill, Joseph. *Scepsis Scientifica: Or, Confest Ignorance the Way to Science; In an Essay of the Vanity of Dogmatizing, and Confident Opinion; with a Reply to the Exceptions of the Learned Thomas Albius.* London: E. Cotes, 1665. Facsimile reprint, New York: Garland Publishing, 1978.

———. *The Vanity of Dogmatizing: Or, Confidence in Opinions; Manifested in a Discourse of the Shortness and Uncertainty of Our Knowledge, and Its Causes, with Some Reflexions on Peripateticism; and an Apology for Philosophy.* London: B. C., 1661. Facsimile reprint, New York: Columbia University Press, 1931.

Gooch, G. P. *History and Historians in the Nineteenth Century.* 2nd ed. London: Longmans, Green, and Co., 1952.

Gore, Charles, ed. *Lux Mundi: A Series of Studies in the Religion of the Incarnation.* 14th ed. London: John Murray, 1895.

Graves, Charles L. *Life and Letters of Alexander Macmillan.* London: Macmillan and Co., 1910.

Gregg, William Rathbone. *The Creed of Christendom: Its Foundation Contrasted with Its Superstructure.* 8th ed. 2 vols. London: Trübner and Co., 1883.

———. *Literary and Social Judgments.* Boston: James R. Osgood and Co., 1873.

Gross, John. *The Rise and Fall of the Man of Letters: English Literary Life since 1800.* 1969. Reprint, Chicago: Ivan R. Dee, 1991.

Hampden, Henrietta, ed. *Some Memorials of Renn Dickson Hampden, Bishop of Hereford.* London: Longmans, Green, and Co., 1871.

Hampden, Renn Dickson. *Inaugural Lecture, Read before the University of Oxford in the Divinity School on Thursday, March 17th, 1836.* 3rd ed. London: B. Fellowes, 1836.

———. *A Lecture on Tradition, Read before the University, in the Divinity School, Oxford, on Thursday, March 7th, 1839.* London: B. Fellowes, 1839.

———. *Observations on Religious Dissent.* Oxford: J. H. Parker, 1834.

———. *The Scholastic Philosophy Considered in Its Relation to Christian Theology.* Oxford: J. H. Parker, 1833.

Hardwick, Charles. *A History of the Articles of Religion.* Cambridge: John Deighton, 1851.

Hare, Augustus J. C. *The Life and Letters of Frances Baroness Bunsen.* 2 vols. New York: George Routledge and Sons, 1879.

———. *Memorials of a Quiet Life.* 9th ed. 2 vols. London: A. Strahan & Co., 1873.

Hare, Julius Charles. *The Mission of the Comforter, with Notes.* Ed. E. H. Plumptre. 4th ed. London: Macmillan and Co., 1877.

———. "Samuel Taylor Coleridge and the English Opium-Eater." *The British Magazine and Monthly Repository* 7 (1835): 15-27.

———. "Sketch of the Author's Life." Vol. 1, pp. 1-232 of *Essays and Tales, by John Sterling,* ed. J. C. Hare, 2 vols. London: John W. Parker, 1848.

———. *Thou Shalt Not Bear False Witness against Thy Neighbour: A Letter to the Editor of the English Review, with a Letter from Professor Maurice to the Author.* London: John W. Parker, 1849.

———. *The Victory of Faith.* Ed. E. H. Plumptre. 3rd ed. London: Macmillan and Co., 1874.

———. *The Victory of Faith and Other Sermons.* London: Griffith, Farran, Okedon and Welsh, n.d.

Harrison, Frederick. *The Creed of a Layman: Apologia pro Fide Mea.* London: Macmillan and Co., 1907.

Haweis, Hugh R. "The Broad Church: Or, What is Coming?" *The Contemporary Review* 57 (June 1890): 900-10.

————. *The Broad Church, or What is Coming.* London: Sampson, Low, Marston, Searle, and Rivington, 1891.

————. *The Dead Pulpit.* London: Bliss, Sands, and Co., 1896.

————. *Thoughts for the Times: Sermons.* New York: Holt and Williams, 1872.

Hawkins, Edward. *Notes upon Subscription, Academical and Clerical.* Oxford: John Henry and James Parker, 1864.

————. *An Inquiry into the Connected Uses of the Principle Means of Attaining Christian Truth.* Oxford: John Henry Parker, 1841.

Hazlitt, William. *Selected Writings.* Ed. Ronald Blythe. New York: Penguin Classics, 1982.

Hinchliff, Peter. *Benjamin Jowett and the Christian Religion.* Oxford: Clarendon Press, 1987.

Hollis, Christopher. *The Oxford Union.* London: Evans Brothers, 1965.

Holmes, Richard. *Coleridge: Darker Reflections, 1804-1834.* New York: Pantheon, 1998.

————. *Coleridge: Early Visions, 1772-1804.* New York: Pantheon, 1989.

Holroyd, Michael. *Lytton Strachey: A Biography.* New York: Penguin, 1971.

Homer. *Iliad.* Trans. Robert Fagles. New York: Viking, 1990.

Honan, Park. *Matthew Arnold: A Life.* London: Weidenfeld and Nicolson, 1981.

Hook, Walter Farquhar. *A Church Dictionary.* London: Houlston and Stoneman, 1842.

Hooker, Richard. *Of the Laws of Ecclesiastical Polity.* Ed. A. S. McGrade and Brian Vickers. New York: St. Martin's Press, 1975.

Hughes, Thomas. *James Fraser, Second Bishop of Manchester: A Memoir, 1818-1885.* London: Macmillan and Co., 1887.

————. *The Manliness of Christ.* Boston: Houghton, Mifflin, and Co., 1881.

————. *Memoir of Daniel Macmillan.* London: Macmillan and Co., 1883.

Hunt, John. *Religious Thought in England in the Nineteenth Century.* London: Gibbings and Co., 1896.

Hutton, Richard Holt. *Aspects of Religious and Scientific Thought.* London: Macmillan and Co., 1899.

————. *Essays on Some of the Modern Guides to English Thought in Matters of Faith.* 1887. Freeport, N.Y.: Books for Libraries Press, 1972.

Hutton, William Holden. *William Stubbs, Bishop of Oxford: 1825-1901.* London: Archibald Constable and Co., 1906.

Huxley, Thomas Henry. *Agnosticism and Christianity and Other Essays.* Buffalo: Prometheus Books, 1992.

Jacks, Lawrence Pearsall. *Life and Letters of Stopford Brooke.* 2 vols. New York: Charles Scribner's Sons, 1917.

Jackson, J. R. de J., ed. *Samuel Taylor Coleridge: The Critical Heritage.* 2nd ed. 2 vols. New York: Routledge, 1995.

Jenkins, Roy. *Gladstone: A Biography.* New York: Random House, 1997.

Jowett, Benjamin. *College Sermons.* Ed. W. H. Fremantle. London: John Murray, 1896.

————. *The Epistles of St. Paul to the Thessalonians, Galatians, and Romans.* 3rd ed. London: John Murray, 1894.

————. *The Interpretation of Scripture and Other Essays.* London: George Routledge and Sons, n.d.

————. *Select Passages from the Theological Writings of Benjamin Jowett.* Ed. Lewis Campbell. London: John Murray, 1902.

————. *Sermons Biographical and Miscellaneous.* Ed. W. H. Fremantle. London: John Murray, 1899.

————. *Sermons on Faith and Doctrine.* Ed. W. H. Fremantle. New York: E. P. Dutton and Co., 1901.

Kierkegaard, Søren. *The Sickness unto Death.* Trans. Alastair Hannay. New York: Penguin Classics, 1989.

Kingsley, Charles. Preface to *Theologia Germanica*, trans. Susanna Winkworth, ed. Dr. Pfeiffer. 2nd ed. London: Longman, Brown, Green, and Longmans, 1854.

————. *The Water Babies.* 1863. New York: Oxford University Press, 1995.

————."Why Should We Fear the Romish Priests?" *Fraser's Magazine* 37 (April 1848): 467-74.

————. *The Works of Charles Kingsley.* 28 vols. London: Macmillan and Co., 1880-85.

Kingsley, Francis, ed. *Charles Kingsley: Letters & Memories.* Bideford Edition. 2 vols. London: The Co-operative Publication Society, 1899.

Knight, William. *Principal Shairp and His Friends.* London: John Murray, 1885.

Lake, Katherine, ed. *Memorials of William Charles Lake, Dean of Durham, 1869-1894.* London: Edward Arnold, 1901.

A Letter to His Grace the Archbishop of Canterbury; Explanatory of the Proceedings at Oxford, on the Appointment of the Present Regius Professor of Divinity. London: B. Fellowes, 1836.

Letters on the Church, by an Episcopalian. Reprinted as *Christianity Independent of the Civil Government.* New York: Harper and Brothers, 1837.

Levi, Peter. *Tennyson.* New York: Charles Scribner's Sons, 1993.

Lewis, C. S. *Surprised by Joy: The Shape of My Early Life.* New York: Harcourt Brace & Co., 1956.

Liddon, Henry Parry. *Life of Edward Bouverie Pusey.* Ed. J. O. Johnston and Robert J. Wilson. 4 vols. London: Longmans, Green, and Co., 1893.

Livingston, James C. *Matthew Arnold and Christianity: His Religious Prose Writings.* Columbia: University of South Carolina Press, 1986.

Lessing, Gotthold. *Lessings Theological Writings.* Ed. Henry Chadwick. Stanford: Stanford University Press, 1957.

Loades, Ann. "Coleridge as Theologian: Some Comments on His Reading of Kant." *The Journal of Theological Studies* 29 (1978): 410-26.

McFarland, Thomas. *Coleridge and the Pantheist Tradition.* New York: Oxford University Press, 1969.

Mack, Edward C., and W. H. G. Armytage. *Thomas Hughes: The Life of the Author of "Tom Brown's Schooldays."* London: Ernest Benn, 1952.

Mallet, Charles Edward. *A History of the University of Oxford.* 2 vols. New York: Longmans, Green, and Co., 1924.

————. *A History of the University of Oxford: Modern Oxford.* London: Methuen and Co., 1927.

Mansel, Henry Longueville. *An Examination of the Rev. F. D. Maurice's Strictures on the Bampton Lectures of 1858.* London: John Murray, 1859.

————. *Letters, Lectures, and Reviews.* Ed. Henry W. Chandler. London: John Murray, 1873.

———. *The Limits of Religious Thought Examined*. 1st American ed. Boston: Gould and Lincoln, 1860.

Martineau, Harriet. *Biographical Sketches*. New York: Hurst and Co., n.d.

Martineau, James. *Essays, Reviews, and Addresses*. 4 vols. London: Longmans, Green, and Co., 1890.

Masterman, C. F. G. *Frederick Denison Maurice*. London: A. R. Mowbray and Co., 1907.

Masterman, N. C. *John Malcolm Ludlow: The Builder of Christian Socialism*. Cambridge: Cambridge University Press, 1963.

Maurice, Frederick, ed. *The Life of Frederick Denison Maurice, Chiefly Told in His Own Letters*. 2 vols. New York: Charles Scribner's Sons, 1884.

Maurice, Frederick Denison. *Eustace Conway: Or, the Brother and Sister*. Ed. Elmer Cleveland Want. 2 vols. Dissertation: Vanderbilt University, 1968.

———. "The French Stage and Mr. Croker of the Quarterly Review." *The Athenæum*, no. 25 (18 April 1828): 391-92.

———. *The Kingdom of Christ: Or, Hints to a Quaker Respecting the Principles, Constitution, & Ordinances of the Catholic Church*. Ed. Alec R. Vidler. London: SCM Press, 1958.

———. *A Letter to the Right Hon. & Right Rev., the Lord Bishop of London, in Reply to the Article in No. CLXXII of the Quarterly Review, Entitled "Queen's College, London."* London: John W. Parker, 1850.

———. "Mr. De Quincey and the London University." *The Athenæum*, no. 61 (24 December 1828): 969.

———. *The New Statute and Mr. Ward*. Oxford: J. H. Parker, 1845.

———. *Reasons for Not Joining a Party in the Church: A Letter to the Ven. Samuel Wilberforce, Archdeacon of Surrey: Suggested by the Rev. Dr. Hook's Letter to the Bishop of Ripon, on the State of Parties in the Church of England*. London: J. G. and F. Rivington, 1841.

———. Review of "The Children of Light" by J. C. Hare. *The Athenæum*, no. 62 (31 December 1828):977.

———. Review of *Guesses at Truth, by Two Brothers*. *The Athenæum*, no. 42 (13 August 1828): 656.

———. *Sequel to the Inquiry, What Is Revelation?* Cambridge: Macmillan and Co., 1860.

———. *Subscription No Bondage; Or, the Practical Advantages Afforded by the Thirty-nine Articles as Guides in All the Branches of Academical Education, by Rusticus*. Oxford: J. H. Parker, 1835.

———. *Theological Essays*. 1853. New York: Harper and Brothers, 1957.

———. *Thoughts on the Rule of Conscientious Subscription, on the Purpose of the Thirty-nine Articles, and on Our Present Perils from the Romish System: in a Second Letter to a Non-Resident Member of Convocation*. Oxford: John Henry Parker, 1845.

———. *Three Letters to the Rev. W. Palmer, Fellow and Tutor of Magdalen College, Oxford, On the Name "Protestant"; On the Seemingly Ambiguous Character of the English Church; and on the Bishopric at Jerusalem*. London: J. G. and F. Rivington, 1842.

———. *What Is Revelation?: A Series of Sermons on the Epiphany*. Cambridge: Macmillan and Co., 1859.

———. *The Word "Eternal," and the Punishment of the Wicked: A Letter to the Rev. Dr. Jelf, Canon of Christ Church, and Principal of King's College*. 2nd ed. New York: C. S. Francis and Co., 1854.

Max Müller, Friedrich. *Introduction to the Science of Religion: Four Lectures Delivered at the Royal Institution.* London: Longmans, Green, and Co., 1873.

Mill, John Stuart. *Autobiography.* 1873. New York: Columbia University Press, 1924.

————. *Mill on Bentham and Coleridge.* Ed. F. R. Leavis. London: Chatto and Windus, 1950.

Morley, Edith J., ed. *Blake, Coleridge, Wordsworth, Lamb, Etc.: Selections from the Remains of Henry Crabb Robinson.* New York: AMS Press, 1967.

————, ed. *Crabb Robinson in Germany, 1800-1805.* London: Oxford University Press, 1929.

Morley, John. *On Compromise.* 1874. London: Macmillan and Co., 1886.

Mozley, James. *Essays Historical and Theological.* 2 vols. Oxford: Rivington, 1878.

Mozley, Thomas. *Reminiscences Chiefly of Oriel College and the Oxford Movement.* 2 vols. London: Longmans, Green, and Co., 1882.

Muirhead, John H. *Coleridge as Philosopher.* 1930. New York: Humanities Press, 1970.

Murphy, Martin. *Blanco White: Self-banished Spaniard.* New Haven: Yale University Press, 1989.

"The New Oxford School, or Broad Church Liberalism." *The Biblical Repository and Princeton Review* 33 (January 1861): 59-84.

Newman, Francis William. *Phases of Faith; Or, Passages from the History of My Creed.* 1850. New York: Humanities Press, 1970.

————. *What Is Christianity without Christ?* London: Trübner and Co., 1881.

Newman, John Henry. *Apologia pro Vita Sua.* Ed. David J. DeLaura. New York: W. W. Norton: 1868.

————. *Essays and Sketches.* 3 vols. New York: Longmans, Green, and Co., 1948.

————. *The Letters and Diaries of John Henry Newman.* Ed. Charles Stephen Dessain. 31 vols. Oxford: Oxford University Press, 1961-1984.

Norton, Charles, ed. *Correspondence of Thomas Carlyle and Ralph Waldo Emerson, 1834-1872.* 2 vols. Boston: James R. Osgood and Co., 1883.

O'Rorke, L. E. *The Life and Friendships of Catherine Marsh.* London: Longmans, Green, and Co., 1918.

Oliphant, Margaret O. W. *A Memoir of the Life of John Tulloch, D.D., LL.D.* 3rd ed. Edinburgh: William Blackwood and Sons, 1889.

Overton, John Henry, and Elizabeth Wordsworth. *Christopher Wordsworth, Bishop of Lincoln, 1807-85.* London: Rivingtons, 1888.

Packe, Michael St. John. *The Life of John Stuart Mill.* New York: Macmillan, 1954.

Palmer, William. *Narrative of Events connected with the Publication of the Tracts for the Times, with an Introduction and Supplement extending to the Present Time.* London: Rivingtons, 1883.

Parker, Charles Stuart, ed. *Sir Robert Peel: From His Private Papers.* 3 vols. London: John Murray, 1899.

Passmore, J. A. *Ralph Cudworth: An Interpretation.* London: Cambridge University Press, 1951.

Patrides, C. A., ed. *The Cambridge Platonists.* The Stratford-upon-Avon Library, vol. 5. London: Edward Arnold, 1969.

Pattison, Mark. *Essays by the Late Mark Pattison, Sometime Rector of Lincoln College.* 2 vols. Ed. Henry Nettleship. Oxford: Clarendon Press, 1889.

————. *Memoirs.* London: Macmillan and Co., 1885.

Pattison, Robert. *The Great Dissent: John Henry Newman and the Liberal Heresy.* New York: Oxford University Press, 1991.

Pays, Daniel L. *The Victorian "Lives" of Jesus.* San Antonio: Trinity University Press, 1982.

Peterson, William S. *Victorian Heretic: Mrs. Humphry Ward's "Robert Elsmere."* Leicester: Leicester University Press, 1976.

Politics for the People. London: John W. Parker, 1848.

Powell, Baden. *The State Church: A Sermon Preached before the University of Oxford at St. Mary's on the 5th of November, 1850.* Oxford: T. Combe, 1850.

————. *Tradition Unveiled: Or, An Exposition of the Pretensions and Tendency of Authoritative Teaching in the Church.* London: B. Fellowes, 1839.

Prothero, Rowland E. *The Life and Correspondence of Arthur Penrhyn Stanley, Late Dean of Westminster.* 2 vols. New York: Charles Scribner's Sons, 1894.

Purcell, Edmund Sheridan. *The Life of Cardinal Manning, Archbishop of Westminster.* 2 vols. London: Macmillan and Co., 1896.

Puseyism: The School of the Infidels; or "Broad Church" the Offspring of "High Church": With a Few Words to the Evangelicals, by A Layman of the Established Church. London: Arthur Miall, 1865.

Pym, David. *The Religious Thought of Samuel Taylor Coleridge.* New York: Barnes and Noble, 1979.

"Queen's College—London." *Quarterly Review* 172 (March 1850): 364-83.

Rannie, David Watson. *Oriel College.* London: F. E. Robinson & Co., 1900.

Rashdall, Hastings. "Clerical Liberalism." Pp. 77-134 in *Anglican Liberalism; by Twelve Churchmen.* London: Williams and Norgate, 1908.

Raven, Charles E. *Christian Socialism: 1848-1854.* London: Macmillan and Co., 1920.

Replies to "Essays and Reviews." 2nd ed. Oxford: John Henry and James Parker, 1862.

Rigg, James H. *Modern Anglican Theology: Chapters on Coleridge, Hare, Maurice, Kingsley, and Jowett, and on the Doctrine of Sacrifice and Atonement.* London: Alexander Heylin, 1857.

Robbins, William. *The Ethical Idealism of Matthew Arnold.* Toronto: University of Toronto Press, 1959.

Robertson, F. W. *Analysis of Mr. Tennyson's "In Memoriam."* 15th ed. London: Kegan Paul, Trench, Trubner, and Co., 1901.

Robson, Robert. "Trinity College in the Age of Peel." Pp. 312-35 in *Ideas and Institutions of Victorian Britain*, ed. R. Robson. London: G. Bell and Sons, 1967.

Rogers, Thomas. *The Catholic Doctrine of the Church of England: An Exposition of the Thirty-nine Articles.* Ed. J. J. S. Perowne. Cambridge: Cambridge University Press, 1854.

Root, Howard Eugene. "Beginning All Over Again." Pp. 3-19 in *Soundings: Essays Concerning Christian Understanding*, ed. A. R. Vidler. Cambridge: Cambridge University Press, 1962.

Rose, Hugh James. *The State of Protestantism in Germany, Described.* 2nd ed. London: C. J. G. and F. Rivington, 1829.

Rothblatt, Sheldon. *The Revolution of the Dons: Cambridge and Society in Victorian England.* New York: Basic Books, 1968.

Rowan, Frederica, ed. *The Life of Schleiermacher: As Unfolded in His Autobiography and Letters.* London: Smith, Elder, and Co., 1860.

Rule, Philip C. "Coleridge's Reputation as a Religious Thinker: 1816-1972." *Harvard Theological Review* 67 (1974): 289-320.

Sanders, Charles R. *Carlyle's Friendships and Other Studies.* Durham, N.C.: Duke University Press, 1977.

———. *Coleridge and the Broad Church Movement.* Durham, N.C.: Duke University Press, 1942.

———. *Was Frederick Denison Maurice a Broad-Churchman?: A Part of a Dissertation Submitted to the Faculty of the Division of the Humanities in Candidacy for the Degree of Doctor of Philosophy.* Chicago: University of Chicago Libraries, 1934.

Sandford, E. G., ed. *Memoirs of Archbishop Temple, by Seven Friends.* 2 vols. London: Macmillan and Co., 1906.

Schlegel, Friedrich. *Philosophical Fragments.* Trans. Peter Firchow. Minneapolis: University of Minnesota Press, 1991.

Schleiermacher, Friedrich D. E. *The Christian Faith.* Ed. H. R. Mackintosh and J. S. Stewart. 1928. New York: Harper and Row, 1963.

———. *On Religion: Speeches to Its Cultured Despisers.* Trans. John Oman. Louisville: Westminster/John Knox Press, 1994.

———. *Soliloquies: A New Year's Gift.* Trans. Horace Leland Friess. Chicago: Open Court Publishing Co., 1926.

Seeley, J. R. *Ecce Homo: A Survey of the Life and Work of Jesus Christ.* Eversley Edition. London: Macmillan and Co., 1895.

Shafer, Robert. *Christianity and Naturalism.* New Haven: Yale University Press, 1926.

Shairp, John Campbell. *Culture and Religion in Some of Their Relations.* 3rd ed. Boston: Houghton, Mifflin, and Co., 1884.

———. *Portraits of Friends.* Boston: Houghton, Mifflin, and Co., 1889.

———. *Studies in Poetry and Philosophy.* 1868. New York: Houghton, Mifflin, and Co., n.d.

Shea, Victor, and William Whitla, eds. *Essays and Reviews: The 1860 Text and Its Readings.* Charlottesville: University Press of Virginia, 2000.

Simpson, J. B. Hope. *Rugby since Arnold: A History of the School from 1842.* London: Macmillan, 1967.

Smith, Goldwin. *Inaugural Lecture.* Oxford: J. H. and Jas. Parker, 1859.

Smith, John. *Select Discourses.* London: F. Fletcher, 1660. Facsimile reprint, Delmar, N.Y.: Scholars' Facsimiles and Reprints, 1979.

Smith, Warren Sylvester. *The London Heretics: 1870-1914.* London: Constable and Co., 1967.

Spinoza, Baruch. *Ethics.* Trans. Samuel Shirley. Ed. Seymour Feldman. Indianapolis: Hackett Publishing Co.,1992.

———. *Theological-Political Treatise.* Trans. Samuel Shirley. Ed. Seymour Feldman. Indianapolis: Hackett Publishing Co., 1998.

Spong, John Shelby. *Why Christianity Must Change or Die.* New York: HarperCollins, 1998.

Stanley, Arthur Penrhyn. *The Epistles of St. Paul to the Corinthians: With Critical Notes and Dissertations.* 2nd ed. London: John Murray, 1858.

———. *Essays Chiefly on Questions of Church and State, from 1850 to 1870.* London: John Murray, 1870.

———. *Letters and Verses of Arthur Penrhyn Stanley, D.D., between the years 1829 and 1881.* Ed. Rowland E. Prothero. London: John Murray, 1895.

———. *The Life and Correspondence of Thomas Arnold, D.D.* 12th ed. 2 vols. London: John Murray, 1881.

———. *Sermons and Essays on the Apostolical Age.* 2nd ed. Oxford: John Henry Parker, 1852.

Stephen, James. *Essays in Ecclesiastical Biography.* 2 vols. London: Longman, Brown, Green, and Longmans, 1849.

Stephen, Leslie. *An Agnostic's Apology and Other Essays.* London: Smith, Elder, and Co., 1893.

———. *Essays on Freethinking and Plainspeaking.* London: Longmans, Green, and Co., 1873.

———. *Hours in a Library.* 3 vols. 1874. London: Folio Society, 1991.

———. "Mr. Matthew Arnold and the Church of England." *Fraser's Magazine* 82 (October 1870): 414-28.

Stephens, W. R. W., ed. *Life and Letters of Walter Farquhar Hook.* 2 vols. London: Richard Bentley and Son, 1880.

———. *A Memoir of Richard Durnford, D.D.* London: John Murray, 1899.

Sterling, John. "Characteristics of German Genius." Vol. 1, pp. 382-421, in *Tales and Sketches, by John Sterling,* ed. J. C. Hare. London: John W. Parker, 1848.

———. "Letter to the Bishop of Chester: III." *The Athenæum,* no. 26 (14 May 1828): 460.

———. "The Lord Bishop of Chester and the London University: Letter I." *The Athenæum,* no. 26 (23 April 1828): 412.

———. "The Lord Bishop of Chester and the London University: Letter II." *The Athenæum,* no. 27 (30 April 1828): 426-27.

Storr, Vernon F. *The Development of English Theology in the Nineteenth Century, 1800-1860.* London: Longmans, Green, and Co., 1913.

Strachey, Lytton. *Eminent Victorians.* 1918. New York: Penguin, 1986.

Stuart, J. A. "The Augustinian 'Cause of Action' in Coleridge's *Rime of the Ancient Mariner.*" *Harvard Theological Review* 60, no. 2 (1967): 177-211.

Super, R. H. *The Time-Spirit of Matthew Arnold.* Ann Arbor: University of Michigan Press, 1970.

Symes, J. E. *Broad Church.* London: Methuen and Co., 1913.

Taylor, Jeremy. *A Discourse of the Liberty of Prophesying, 1647.* Menston, Yorkshire: Scolar Press, 1971.

Tennyson, Alfred. *In Memoriam.* London: Edward Moxon, 1850.

———. *Maud, and Other Poems.* London: Edward Moxon, 1855.

Thirlwall, Connop. "Dr. Littlefield's Article on 'Church Parties." *Contemporary Review* 26 (October 1875): 703-05.

———. *A Letter to the Rev. Thomas Turton, D.D., on the Admission of Dissenters to Academical Degrees.* Cambridge: Pitt Press, 1834.

———. *Letters Literary and Theological of Connop Thirlwall.* Ed. J. J. Stewart Perowne and Louis Stokes. London: Richard Bentley and Sons, 1881.

———. *Letters to a Friend.* Ed. A. P. Stanley. London: Richard Bentley and Son, 1882.

Thirlwall, John Connop. *Connop Thirlwall: Historian and Theologian.* London: S.P.C.K., 1936.

Thom, John Hamilton, ed. *The Life of the Rev. Joseph Blanco White.* 3 vols. London: John Chapman, 1845.

Thomson, William, ed. *Aids to Faith: A Series of Theological Essays; by Several Writers; Being a Reply to "Essays and Reviews."* New York: D. Appleton and Co., 1862.

Tillich, Paul. *Systematic Theology.* 3 vols. Chicago: University of Chicago Press, 1951-1963.

Tillotson, Kathleen. "Rugby 1850: Arnold, Clough, Walrond, and *In Memoriam.*" Pp. 180-203 in *Mid-Victorian Studies*, ed. Geoffrey and Kathleen Tillotson. London: Athlone Press, 1965.

Tollemache, Lionel A. *Benjamin Jowett: Master of Balliol.* London: Edwin Arnold, n.d.

Trench, Mary, ed. *Richard Chenevix Trench, Archbishop: Letters and Memorials.* 2 vols. London: Kegan Paul, Trench, and Co., 1888.

Trollope, Anthony. *Clergymen of the Church of England.* 1886. London: The Trollope Society, n.d.

Tuckwell, William. *Pre-Tractarian Oxford: A Reminiscence of the Oriel "Noetics."* London: Smith, Elder, and Co., 1909.

———. *Reminiscences of Oxford.* London: Cassell and Co., 1900.

Tulloch, John. *Movements of Religious Thought in Britain during the Nineteenth Century.* New York: Charles Scribner's Sons, 1885.

———. *Rational Theology and Christian Philosophy in England in the Seventeenth Century.* 2nd ed. 2 vols. Edinburgh: William Blackwood and Sons, 1874.

Valee, G., J. B. Lawson, and C. G. Chapple, eds. *The Spinoza Conversations between Lessing and Jacobi.* New York: University Press of America, 1988.

Vidler, Alec R. *F. D. Maurice and Company: Nineteenth-Century Studies.* London: SCM, 1966.

———. *Witness to the Light: F. D. Maurice's Message for Today.* New York: Charles Scribner's Sons, 1948.

Walton, John K. *Chartism.* New York: Routledge, 1999.

Ward, Mary Augusta. *Robert Elsmere.* London: Smith, Elder, and Co., 1888.

———. *A Writer's Recollections.* 2 vols. New York: Harper and Brothers, 1918.

Ward, William George. *The Ideal of a Christian Church Considered.* 2nd ed. London: James Toovey, 1844.

Watson, E. W. *Life of Bishop John Wordsworth.* London: Longmans, Green, and Co. 1915.

Wedgwood, Julia. *Nineteenth Century Teachers, and Other Essays.* London: Hodder and Stoughton, 1909.

Wemyss, Rosslyn. *Robert Morier, G. C. B., from 1826 to 1876, by His Daughter.* 2 vols. London: Edwin Arnold, 1911.

Wendling, Ronald C. *Coleridge's Progress to Christianity: Experience and Authority in Religious Faith.* London: Associated University Presses, 1995.

Whately, Elizabeth Jane, ed. *The Life and Correspondence of Richard Whately, D.D., Late Archbishop of Dublin.* 3rd ed. London: Longmans, Green, and Co., 1875.

Whately, Richard. *Cautions for the Times: Addressed to the Parishioners of a Parish in England, by Their Former Rector.* London: John W. Parker and Son, 1853.

———. *Essays on Some of the Difficulties in the Writings of the Apostle Paul and in Other Parts of the New Testament.* 6th ed. London: John W. Parker, 1849.

———. *Essays on Some of the Peculiarities of the Christian Religion.* 6th ed. London: John W. Parker, 1850.

———. *Historic Doubts relative to Napoleon Buonaparte.* 6th ed, 1837. Reprinted in *Richard Whately: A Man for All Seasons*, ed. Craig Parton. Edmonton, Alberta: Canadian Institute for Law, 1997.

―――. *The Kingdom of Christ Delineated, in Two Essays on Our Lord's Own Account of His Person and of the Nature of His Kingdom, and on the Constitution, Powers, and Ministry of a Christian Church, as Appointed by Himself.* New York: Wiley and Putnam, 1842.

Whitridge, Arnold. *Dr. Arnold of Rugby.* London: Constable and Co., 1928.

Wigmore-Beddoes, Dennis G. *Yesterday's Radicals: A Study of the Affinity between Unitarianism and Broad Church Anglicanism in the Nineteenth Century.* Cambridge: James Clarke and Co., 1971.

Wilberforce, Reginald G. *The Life of the Right Reverend Samuel Wilberforce, D.D.* 3 vols. London: John Murray, 1881.

Willey, Basil. *More Nineteenth Century Studies: A Group of Honest Doubters.* New York: Columbia University Press, 1956.

―――. *Nineteenth Century Studies.* New York: Columbia University Press, 1949.

Williams, David. *Too Quick Despairer: The Life and Work of Arthur Hugh Clough.* London: Rupert Hart-Davis, 1969.

Williams, Ellen, ed. *The Life and Letters of Rowland Williams, D.D.* 2 vols. London: Henry S. King and Co., 1874.

Williams, Isaac. *Autobiography.* Ed. George Prevost. London: Longmans, Green, and Co., 1892.

―――. "On Reserve in Communicating Religious Knowledge." *Tracts for the Times,* no. 87 (1840). Selections reprinted in *The Oxford Movement,* ed. Eugene R. Fairweather. New York: Oxford University Press, 1964.

Williamson, Eugene L., Jr. *The Liberalism of Thomas Arnold: A Study of His Religious and Political Writings.* University: University of Alabama Press, 1964.

―――. "Words from Westminster Abbey: Matthew Arnold and Arthur Stanley." *Studies in English Literature* 11 (1971): 749-61.

Wilson, Thomas. *Maxims of Piety and of Christianity.* Ed. Frederic Relton. London: Macmillan and Co., 1898.

Winstanley, D. A. *Early Victorian Cambridge.* Cambridge: Cambridge University Press, 1940.

―――. *Later Victorian Cambridge.* Cambridge: Cambridge University Press, 1947.

Wodehouse, Charles N. *The Claims of Truth.* London: Jarrold and Sons, 1861.

―――. *Subscription the Disgrace of the English Church.* London: Longman, Brown, Green, and Longmans, 1843.

Woodward, Llewellyn. *The Age of Reform: 1815-1870.* 2nd ed. Oxford: Oxford University Press, 1962.

Young, G. M., and W. D. Handcock, eds. *English Historical Documents 1833-1874.* New York: Oxford University Press, 1956.

Young, John. *The Province of Reason: A Criticism of the Bampton Lecture on "The Limits of Religious Thought."* New York: Robert Carter and Brothers, 1860.

Index

339

About the Author

Tod E. Jones teaches at the University of Maryland, College Park (UMCP), where he is appointed as adjunct faculty in the Department of English and as a special lecturer for User Education Services in the university library. His academic background and interests are in Victorian literature and culture. He has articles published in *The Victorian Newsletter* and intermittently chairs the Literature and Religion forum at the Annual Central New York Conference for Language and Literature. He holds a Ph.D. in English from UMCP, an M.A. in English from San Diego State University, and a B.A. in Biblical Studies from Harding University, Arkansas.